Counselor Supervision

FOURTH EDITION

Counselor Supervision

Nicholas Ladany and Loretta J. Bradley

EDITORS

FOURTH EDITION

Routledge
Taylor & Francis Group
New York   London

Portions of this book are drawn from chapters previously published in L. Bradley & N. Ladany (Eds.). (2001). *Counselor supervision: Principles, process, and practice* (3rd ed.). Philadelphia, PA: Brunner-Routledge (Authors to be recognized from this previous edition, some of whom are represented in the current edition, include Julie Ancis, Lorie Blackman, Carolyn Brennan, M. Kristine Bronson, Loretta Bradley, James Cheek, Mary Deck, L. J. Gould, Richard Hayes, C. Bret Hendricks, Marcia Kaufman, Jeffrey Kottler, Nicholas Ladany, Deborah Lehrman-Waterman, Judith Lewis, Sandy Magnuson, Keith Morgan, Janet Muse-Burke, Ken Norem, Kristen Planny, Gerald Parr, and Peggy Whiting).

Routledge
Taylor & Francis Group
270 Madison Avenue
New York, NY 10016

Routledge
Taylor & Francis Group
27 Church Road
Hove, East Sussex BN3 2FA

© 2010 by Taylor and Francis Group, LLC
Routledge is an imprint of Taylor & Francis Group, an Informa business

Printed in the United States of America on acid-free paper
10 9 8 7 6 5 4 3 2 1

International Standard Book Number: 978-0-415-80149-2 (Hardback)

Library of Congress Cataloging-in-Publication Data

Counselor supervision / [edited by] Nicholas Ladany & Loretta J. Bradley. -- 4th ed.
    p. cm.
    Includes bibliographical references and index.
    ISBN 978-0-415-80149-2 (hardback : alk. paper)
    1. Counselors--Supervision of. I. Ladany, Nicholas. II. Bradley, Loretta J. III. Title.

BF636.6.C677 2010
361'.060683--dc22   2009045354

Visit the Taylor & Francis Web site at
http://www.taylorandfrancis.com

and the Routledge Web site at
http://www.routledgementalhealth.com

To all those who aspire to help others

Contents

Part III Specialized Models of Counselor Supervision

Part IV Professional Issues in Counselor Supervision

List of Figures

List of Tables

Preface

Counselor Supervision, (4th ed.) is a theoretically guided, empirically based, and practically meaningful text that is intended for counselor educators and counselor supervisor practitioners who work in a variety of educational and mental health settings. Primary supervision theories are reviewed and critiqued with the intent of informing supervisor practitioners, counselor educators, and supervisor trainees. Additionally, cutting edge topic areas are covered that include (1) multicultural issues in counselor supervision (e.g., how to balance and manage multiple identities such as gender, racial, sexual orientation, age, and disability in the context of influencing trainee multicultural competence); (2) the supervisory relationship (an essential but sometimes forgotten component of supervision) and its influence on supervision process and outcome; (3) supervision of career counselor trainees (e.g., supervision challenges unique to career counseling trainees such as integrating personal and career development); (4) supervision of school counselors (e.g., supervision challenges unique to school counselors such as confidentiality and balancing multiple roles); (5) supervision of family and group counselors; (6) group supervision; (7) understanding and conducting research in counselor supervision and training; (8) ethical and advocacy issues in supervision; and (9) supervisor training. Case examples are used throughout the book to illustrate the application of theory to practical issues that counselor supervisors encounter.

Overview of the Book

The book is divided into four major parts consisting of Part I: Counselor Supervision: Essentials for Training; Part II: Theoretical Approaches to Counselor Supervision; Part III: Specialized Models of Counselor Supervision; and Part IV: Professional Issues in Counselor Supervision. Each of these major areas are composed of several chapters.

Part I begins with a chapter that offers an overview of the basic principles, roles, and functions involved in effective supervisory practice. Chapter 2 describes how the supervisory relationship provides a foundation for the implementation of supervisory interventions, and is also the key to understanding effective and ineffective supervision. Although we infuse multicultural issues throughout the book, Chapter 3 provides a framework for understanding supervision from a multicultural perspective. It is hoped that this multicultural framework will provide the reader with a template for appraising supervision models and interventions. Chapter 4 attends to the various techniques that supervisors can implement to enhance their supervision.

Part II provides an overview of the primary theoretical models of supervision. We divide the types of supervision models into those that were derived specifically for the supervision context that we refer to as supervision-based integrative models (Chapters 5 and 6 address interpersonal and developmental models, respectively) and supervision models that were derived from, or are extensions of, psychotherapy models (i.e., Chapter 7). The reviewed models are presented in a similar format to assist the reader with understanding and evaluating the salient tenets of the models. The format in which the models are reviewed consists of the following sections: overall framework, primary concepts and theoretical assumptions, integration of the supervisory relationship, focus and goals, methodology and techniques, a case example, and critique of strengths and weaknesses.

Part III contains seven chapters devoted to specialized models of counselor supervision. As the field of supervision has embraced expanded general models of supervision, there has come the recognition that certain settings and supervision enterprises would benefit from supervision models geared toward these settings and enterprises. To this end, Part III attends to specialized supervision models that include group supervision of individual counseling (Chapter 8), group work supervision, a new chapter (Chapter 9), supervising pre-degreed and professional school counselors (Chapter 10), supervision of career counselors (Chapter 11), supervision of family counselors (Chapter 12), and supervision of assessment, a new chapter (Chapter 13).

Part IV consists of four chapters pertaining to professional issues in counselor supervision. In particular, the necessary process of trainee evaluation is reviewed in Chapter 14. Professional counselors interested in supervision research, as well as students conducting supervision research as part of a thesis or dissertation, are presented with Chapter 15 as a way to help them understand and conduct supervision research. The most recent and primary ethical principles and guidelines for supervisors are presented in Chapter 16, and Chapter 17 provides a practical model of training supervisors.

What's New in this Edition?

Portions of many of the chapters were originally included in *Counselor Supervision* (Boyd, 1978) and later in *Counselor Supervision: Principles, Process, and Practice* (Bradley, 1989; Bradley & Ladany, 2001). However, all of these chapters have been modified to bring them up-to-date with current information and references. In particular, the chapters were completely updated to reflect current theory, research, and practice in counselor supervision. Furthermore, we added chapters to reflect innovations in counselor supervision theory, research, and practice that include chapters on supervisor techniques, supervision of group work, supervision of pre-degree school counselors, and supervision of assessment.

Audience

This book is intended for both clinical and administrative supervisors. This book should be beneficial to supervisors-in-training, whether enrolled in university graduate training programs or seeking professional development or licensure as a counselor supervisor, as well as to supervisors seeking additional supervisory information. For clinical supervisors enrolled in graduate supervision classes, this book is intended as a primary text. For the clinical and administrative supervisor employed in an agency, the book is intended as a primary tool for in-service training and professional development. For the practicing supervisor, regardless of setting, the book is envisioned as a guide for implementing the supervisory process. Finally, the professional counselor seeking licensure as a licensed professional counselor or licensed supervisor should find this book to be a useful and relevant resource.

Although the title *Counselor Supervision* might suggest the book is only intended for counselors, in reality the book is written to serve a variety of human service providers. In addition to counselors and counseling psychologists, the book should prove beneficial to clinical psychologists, directors of human resource providers in business and industry, employee assistance coordinators, directors of pupil personnel services, career and vocational counselors and supervisors, family therapy supervisors, psychiatrists, and social workers.

Ultimately, it is our hope that you will find this book useful and relevant to your supervisory purposes.

References

Boyd, J. D. (1978). *Counselor supervision: Approaches, preparation and practices.* Muncie, IN: Accelerated Development.

Bradley, L. J. (1988). *Counselor supervision: Principles, process, and practice.* Muncie, IN: Accelerated Development.

Bradley, L. J., & Ladany, N. (2001). *Counselor supervision: Principles, process, and practice.* Philadelphia, PA: Brunner-Routledge.

Acknowledgments

We are extremely grateful to Candice Presseau for her citation assistance and proofing of the book. We also extend our appreciation to Dana Bliss for his laudable editorial assistance throughout the process of putting this book together.

I (Nicholas Ladany) want to offer my heartfelt appreciation to people who have enhanced my personal and professional life. To Randa El Jurdi, for her unending love, support, kindness, and joy. To Farah, Mona, and Nisrine, who have immeasurably enriched my life. I am also personally indebted to my colleagues and mentors who have fostered the development of my abilities, provided the foundation for my ideas, and inspired me. Thank you Julie R. Ancis, Sandy Banks, Susan Drumheller, Mike Ellis, Micki Friedlander, Charlie Gelso, Dick Haase, Clara Hill, Arpana G. Inman, Bob Kaufman, Maxine Krengel, Debbie Schult, Bruce Sharkin, Barbara Vivino, Barbara Thompson, Jay Walker, and William West. Last, but certainly not least, I am truly grateful to the students with whom I have worked, and from whom I have learned a great deal about supervision.

I (Loretta J. Bradley) want to express my sincere appreciation to my family, friends, and colleagues for their encouragement and support in my professional career. To the students that I have supervised, I express my thanks to you, for you have played an important role in helping me to formulate and implement my beliefs about supervision theory, practice, and process. To my husband, Charles, and sons, Brian and Brett, a special thanks for your kindness and encouragement.

Editors

Nicholas Ladany, PhD, is Professor of Counseling Psychology, Program Coordinator and Director of Doctoral Training at Lehigh University in Bethlehem, Pennsylvania. He also has served as Chair of the Department of Education and Human Services at Lehigh University. Before his affiliation with Lehigh University, he was an Assistant Professor of Counseling Psychology at Temple University and a Visiting Faculty in Counseling Psychology at the University of Maryland. He received his PhD at the University at Albany, State University of New York, in 1992. He has published numerous articles and presented nationally and internationally in the area of counseling and psychotherapy supervision and training. His primary research interests and activities include the interrelationships between supervision process and outcome, and counseling and psychotherapy process and outcome, including such issues as the working alliance, self-disclosures and nondisclosures, multicultural training, ethics, and social justice. He has served on the editorial board of the *Journal of Counseling Psychology* and *Counselor Education and Supervision* and currently is the Associate Editor of *Psychotherapy: Theory, Research, Practice, and Training*. He is the author of three books: *Practicing Counseling and Psychotherapy: Insights from Trainees, Clients, and Supervisors* (Routledge, 2008); *Critical Events*

in Psychotherapy Supervision: An Interpersonal Approach (American Phychological Association, 2005); and *Counselor Supervision: Principles, Process, and Practice* (3rd ed.) (Brunner-Routledge, 2001). He is a Licensed Psychologist in Pennsylvania.

Loretta J. Bradley, PhD, holds a Paul Whitfield Horn Professorship in Counselor Education at Texas Tech University. Prior to her affiliation with Texas Tech University, Dr. Bradley was Associate Professor of Human Development Counseling at Peabody College of Vanderbilt University and an Assistant Dean, College of Education at Temple University. She earned her PhD at Purdue University. Dr. Bradley is former President of the American Counseling Association, the Association for Counselor Education and Supervision, and the Texas Association for Adult Development and Aging. She has also served as Treasurer of the American Counseling Association and a member of their Governing Council. Dr. Bradley is a Fellow of the American Counseling Association and the Salzburg Institute in Austria. She is the co-recipient of the Outstanding Research Award from the British Association for Counselling and Psychotherapy, American Counseling Association, and the Association for Counselor Education and Supervision. Her book *Counselor Supervision: Principles, Process, and Practice* (2nd ed.) received the 1990 ACES Best Publication Award. Dr. Bradley is a Licensed Professional Counselor in Texas, Licensed Professional Counselor—Supervisor, Licensed Marriage and Family Therapist and Supervisor in Texas. Dr. Bradley is a National Certified Counselor, a National Certified Career Counselor, and a National Certified Supervisor. In addition, Dr. Bradley holds certification as school counselor and teacher.

Contributors

Julie R. Ancis, PhD, is a professor in the Department of Counseling and Psychological Services at Georgia State University. She has published and presented in the area of multicultural competence, race and gender, university climate, and women's legal experiences. She is the author of several books including *The Complete Women's Psychotherapy Treatment Planner* (Wiley, 2007), and *Culturally Responsive Interventions: Innovative Approaches to Working with Diverse Populations* (Taylor & Francis, 2004). Dr. Ancis's professional activities include serving on the editorial boards of the *Journal of Counseling and Development* and other counseling and psychology journals, legal and legislative representative of the Georgia Psychological Association's Division F, and committee for the development of the APA Guidelines for Psychological Practice with Girls and Women. She is currently writing a book on women's legal experiences in the area of divorce and custody disputes.

Clyde Beverly, MS, is a doctoral candidate in counseling psychology at Lehigh University and a pre-doctoral intern at the Girard Medical Center-Outpatient Psychiatric Clinic in Philadelphia, Pennsylvania. He received his degree in counseling psychology from the University of Kentucky. His research interests include multicultural counseling competence, supervision, college student issues, racial identity development, and ethnic minority academic achievement/attainment.

M. Kristine Bronson, PhD, is a licensed psychologist in private practice in Wilmington, Delaware. She provides individual and group career counseling, psychotherapy, and counseling to adults and adolescents.

She teaches as an adjunct instructor and provides supervision and training to counselors and mental health professionals. Dr. Bronson also consults with businesses, colleges, universities, and organizations on career development, workplace change, diversity issues, and stress reduction.

Catherine Y. Chang, PhD, is an associate professor in the Department of Counseling and Psychological Services at Georgia State University and coordinator of the counselor education and practice doctoral program. Her areas of interest include multicultural counseling and supervision, Asian and Korean concerns, and social justice issues in counselor education.

Jennifer Crall, MEd, is a doctoral candidate in the counseling psychology program at Lehigh University in Bethlehem, Pennsylvania. She is a frequent presenter at international, national, and local conferences. Her research and practice interests include child and adolescent psychotherapy, family therapy, crisis management, the provision of therapy in educational settings, faith-based practices, ethics, and supervision.

Rachel E. Crook Lyon, PhD, is a faculty member in the counseling psychology doctoral program at Brigham Young University in Provo, Utah. Her research interests include the use of dream work in psychotherapy and the preparation and training of supervisors.

Richard L. Hayes, EdD, is dean of the College of Education and professor of clinical and counseling psychology at the University of South Alabama. His research applies a democratic philosophy of education to group work using a constructivist developmental psychology. Currently, this work is addressed to educational interventions across cultures internationally.

Bret Hendricks, EdD, is an associate professor of counselor education at Texas Tech. He is a licensed professional counselor and licensed professional counselor—supervisor. Dr. Hendricks has numerous research publications and is a frequent speaker at professional conferences. Dr. Hendricks is the past-president of the International Association of Marriage and Family Counselors.

Pilar Hernández-Wolfe, PhD, LMFT, LCPC, is an associate professor and director of the clinical community counseling program at Johns Hopkins University, president of the Maryland Association for Counseling and Development and board member of the American Family Therapy Academy. Her research examines applications of systemic and contextually responsive models to clinical practice and clinical supervision, vicarious resilience, and traumatic stress.

Shirley A. Hess, PhD, LPC, ACS, is an associate professor of counseling at Shippensburg University of Pennsylvania. Her professional interests include dream work, the training and supervisory processes, grief and loss, and qualitative research. Shirley has practiced in college counseling centers, outpatient, and in college student personnel settings. She enjoys the outdoors, especially hiking on the Appalachian Trail.

Arpana G. Inman, PhD, received her degree in counseling psychology from Temple University in Pennsylvania. Currently, she is an associate professor in counseling psychology at Lehigh University in Bethlehem, Pennsylvania. Her areas of research include South Asian identity, Asian American coping and mental health, international counseling and psychology, and multicultural competencies in supervision and training.

Anju Kaduvettoor, MEd, is currently a pre-doctoral intern at the Center for Counseling and Student Development at the University of Delaware and a doctoral candidate in counseling psychology at Lehigh University in Bethlehem, Pennsylvania. She completed her dissertation on the impact of discrimination on South Asians and is interested in Asian American mental health, supervision and training, and multicultural competence.

Kurt L. Kraus, EdD, is professor of counseling and student college personnel at Shippensburg University of Pennsylvania. His professional interests include life span development, group work, and counseling children and adolescents.

Matthew A. Malouf, MEd, is a counseling psychology doctoral student at Lehigh University in Bethlehem, Pennsylvania. His scholarly interests include multicultural competence as applied to clinical practice, supervision, and research methodologies. More specifically, his expertise lies in qualitative research around marginalized populations and on issues relevant to social justice.

Rayna D. Markin, PhD, is an assistant professor at Villanova University in the Department of Education and Human Services in Pennsylvania. Her research focuses on psychotherapy process and outcome in individual and group psychotherapies and clinical training. She is a member of the Society for Psychotherapy Research and Divisions 29 and 39 of the American Psychological Association.

Yoko Mori, MS, is a pre-doctoral intern at the counseling center at the University of Illinois at Chicago and is a doctoral candidate in counseling psychology at Lehigh University in Pennsylvania. She completed her dissertation on international trainees' supervision experiences. Her research interests include international and immigrant students, social justice, training and supervision, and multicultural, and feminist approaches to therapy and training.

Caroline O'Hara, MS, is a graduate student at Georgia State University. She received her degree in professional counseling in 2009 and is currently completing a specialist in education degree in professional counseling. Her areas of interest include sexual and gender diversity, counseling theory, multicultural counseling, and social justice counseling.

Tiffany O'Shaughnessy, PhD, is a postdoctoral fellow at Counseling and Psychological Services, University of California, Berkeley. She obtained her doctorate in counseling psychology from Lehigh University in Pennsylvania. Her research interests include lesbian, gay, bisexual, transgender, and queer issues in counseling and training, feminist therapy, supervision and counseling process and outcome, and multicultural competency. She was the 2009 recipient of the Association of Psychology Postdoctoral and Internship Centers Student Research Award.

Gerald Parr, PhD, is a professor in the counselor education program in the college of education at Texas Tech University. His recent publications and presentations have focused on ethics, creativity, and group work. He has held positions as a counselor educator, a department chair, and an associate dean.

Kirti A. Potkar, MS, is a doctoral student in the counseling psychology doctoral program at Brigham Young University in Utah.

Katie M. Rhode, MA, BA, is a doctoral student in counselor education at Texas Tech University. She is a graduate of Duke University and Texas Tech University's Honors College with her degrees, respectively. During her graduate studies, she has served as a research assistant and as a counselor for juvenile offenders in a substance abuse facility. Her research focus is largely with gifted and at-risk populations.

P. Clay Rowell, PhD, NCC, LPC, is an assistant professor of counseling at North Georgia College and State University. He is a recipient of the Courtland C. Lee Multicultural Excellence Award. His specialty areas include clinical supervision, group counseling, and diversity issues in career/work development. He is the father of two young daughters.

Sepideh S. Soheilian, MEd, BA, is a doctoral student in counseling psychology at Lehigh University. She received her MEd in counseling and human services from Lehigh University, Pennsylvania and BA in psychology from Georgetown University, Washington, DC. Her research interests include Middle Eastern American population, stigma, help-seeking attitudes, and multicultural competencies in counseling and clinical supervision.

James Tres Stefurak, PhD, is an assistant professor of clinical and counseling psychology in the College of Education at the University of South Alabama. His research interests are in the areas of juvenile delinquency, group work/consultation in juvenile court systems, psychology of religion/ spirituality, and integrative approaches to clinical training.

Jessica A. Walker, PhD, is a staff psychologist at the W.G. (Bill) Hefner Department of Veterans Affairs Medical Center in Salisbury, North Carolina. She graduated with her degree in counseling psychology from Lehigh University, Pennsylvania. Prior to her affiliation at the Veterans Affairs Medical Center, she served as a psychotherapist and instructor at University of North Carolina, Charlotte and University of North Carolina, Wilmington.

Ryan D. Weatherford, MEd, is a doctoral candidate in counseling psychology at Lehigh University, Pennsylvania and a pre-doctoral intern at The Center for Counseling & Psychological Services at Penn State University. He received his degree in counseling and human services at Lehigh University. His research interests include college student issues, multicultural counseling competence, supervision/counseling outcome and process, and college student alcohol and drug use.

Laura E. Welfare, PhD, is an assistant professor of counselor education at Virginia Tech in Blacksburg. Prior to her academic appointment, she was a licensed professional counselor and worked with children, adolescents, and adults.

Peggy P. Whiting, PhD, is a professor of counselor education at North Carolina Central University and has served on the faculty of both Vanderbilt and Winthrop Universities. She is a K–12 licensed school counselor, a licensed professional counselor, a national certified counselor, and a certified grief educator and therapist.

PART I

Counselor Supervision
Essentials for Training

CHAPTER 1

Overview of Counseling Supervision

LORETTA J. BRADLEY, NICHOLAS LADANY,
BRET HENDRICKS, PEGGY P. WHITING, and KATIE M. RHODE

Counselor supervision is arguably the primary way in which educators facilitate or inhibit counselor competence (Ladany & Inman, in press). Supervision comes in many shapes and sizes and reflects many of the chapters in this book (e.g., individual supervision, group supervision, supervision of family counseling, etc.). The most common form of supervision is individual supervision and it is here where we start with a definition. Ladany and Inman broadly define individual supervision as a

> dyadic activity whereby the supervisor facilitates the provision of feedback to the supervisee, which is based on the interpersonal communication between both members of the dyad and can pertain to the work in supervision, the supervisee, the supervisee's clients, or the supervisor. (Ladany & Inman, in press)

We can expand this definition to encompass all types of supervision in the following manner: Counselor supervision is a didactic and interpersonal activity whereby the supervisor facilitates the provision of feedback to one or more supervisees. This feedback can pertain to the work in supervision, the supervisee(s), the supervisees' clients, or the supervisor, and can positively or negatively influence supervisee counselor competence and client outcome.

This definition obviates the problems with other definitions of supervision that typically only address individual supervision of individual counseling, leaving other valuable forms of supervision such as peer and group supervision unaddressed. Moreover, it addresses the interrelated types of supervision traditionally referred to as administrative supervision (e.g., supervisor helps the supervisee function effectively as a part of the organization with the overall intent to help the organization run smoothly and efficiently) and clinical supervision (e.g., supervisor assists with supervisee-related and client-related issues).

With this definition in hand, we spend the remaining part of this chapter attending to aspects of *being a supervisor* that sets the stage for the book. These aspects include: a brief history of counselor supervision, supervisor qualifications, supervisor skills and attributes, and purposes of counselor supervision.

A Brief History of Counselor Supervision

Supervision can be traced back to the field of social work in the late 1800s (Munson, 2002). Charity Organization Societies, as it was called, retained staff members who supervised apprentice workers. The format typically consisted of supervisors, each of whom supervised multiple supervisees occasionally through individual, and later group, conferences. Freud, in 1902, set the stage for supervision, whereby the analyst was analyzed (Goodyear & Guzzardo, 2000) and in 1925, supervision first became a required aspect of training (Kugler, 1995). In the middle of the twentieth century, theories of supervision were largely modeled after theories of psychotherapy (e.g., Ekstein & Wallerstein, 1958) and it wasn't until the 1980s when supervision-based models emerged and supervision was seen as a distinct subfield within counseling (Bernard, 2005). It was also during the 1980s when research on supervision process and outcome began to burgeon (Ladany & Inman, in press). Since that time, empirical studies have been published at a moderate rate of about 12 per year, and the fields most linked with the theoretical and empirical work in supervision have been counselor education, counseling psychology, and social work.

Supervisor Qualifications

The necessary academic preparation and background experiences of counselor supervisors have been investigated by Borders (2005); Eriksen, Ellison, and Throckmorton (2008); McAdams and Foster (2007); Richardson and Bradley (1986); Thompson (2004); and previously by Riccio (1961, 1966), and the Association for Counselor Education and Supervision (ACES) survey (1969). Additionally, ACES has developed standards for supervisors (1993). Results from these studies indicate that the majority of supervisors in field settings (i.e., agencies, state departments, and schools) have gained a significant level of education beyond the master's degree. Despite these high levels of educational attainment, the alarming fact remains that only a token number of supervisors, regardless of work setting, have received specific preparation for supervision.

A reasonable assumption is that many counselor supervisors achieved their supervisory positions on the basis of educational level, tenure, and successful counseling experiences. It would also be realistic to expect that such professionals are well connected politically within their organizations to attain positions of authority and power. However, counseling experience and an accumulation of academic credits must be viewed as insufficient qualifications, by themselves, for supervisors of counselors. This is especially the case with supervisors who attained their positions because they were well connected with dominant power structure within the organization. Preparation in supervision methodology must become an entrance criterion if supervision practice is to be validated (Barnes, 2004; Hazler & Kottler, 2005; Holloway & Neufeldt, 1995; McWhirter & McWhirter, 2007; Neufeldt, 1999, 2007).

Skills and Attributes

The literature on supervisory job functions generates some information about the necessary personality attributes of a supervisor. The supervisor must be a serious, committed professional who has chosen counseling and supervision as a long-term career (Bernard & Goodyear, 2009). This assumption implies that the supervisor is energetic and ambitious, but not in an egotistical or opportunistic manner. Instead, the supervisor is committed to and ambitious about developing and maintaining accountable helping services.

The supervisor must possess the skills of empathy, respect, genuineness, supportive-confrontation, and immediacy (Blocher, 1983; Juhnke, Kelly, & Cooper, 2008). In addition, other descriptions of the good supervisor included concern for the growth and well-being of the supervisee (Bernard, 1992; Estrada, 2005; Mueller & Kell, 1972; Norcross & Beutler, 2008), as well as the welfare of the client (Bernard, 2005; McWhirter & McWhirter, 2007). Other positive supervisor characteristics included integrity, courage, sense of humor, capacity for intimacy, sense of time, openness to self-inspection (Ellis & Robbins, 1993), responsibleness (Borders & Brown, 2005; Holloway & Neufeldt, 1995) and a nonthreatening, nonauthoritarian approach to supervision (Geldard & Geldard, 2008; Pearson, 2006). Supervisors should also possess the capacity to be flexible, tolerant, and open to various styles and levels of learning (Borders, 2005).

In short, supervisors should themselves be able to demonstrate the conditions and characteristics they expect of their supervisees. This means that they become living examples of all those qualities, skills, and behaviors that they consider important for others (Bradley, Lewis, Hendricks,& Crews, 2008).

The essential criteria for selection of supervisors include an expectation of competence and success in a broad range of helping activities. In addition to such professionally demonstrable qualities, a supervisor should possess confidence and professional assurance. A hesitant, unsure supervisor cannot offer the kind of leadership that is needed in supervisory positions. This is particularly true in agencies and schools where counselors are subordinate to other administrators. The supervisor needs to be confident and strong when working with those who have administrative power over counselors, as well as when grappling with the difficult decisions that arise in supervision.

A supervisor should command both the professional and the personal respect of colleagues and associates in the work environment. Professional respect is, in part, founded on competence and ability, first as a good counselor and then as a capable supervisor. Personal respect relates to whether the supervisor is accepted as a person by her or his associates based upon integrity and ethical indices that are reflected through professional behavior.

Finally, the supervisor must be highly committed to protecting the welfare of others, including the ability and willingness to serve as an advocate for counselors and their clients. All individuals need support, and counselors as a group suffer from a lack of professional affirmation. A supervisee needs to feel that the supervisor believes in her or his potential to become a more effective practitioner.

To summarize, the supervisor is a well-prepared individual who has entered the supervisory position after attaining a high degree of training, experience, and wisdom as a practitioner with specialized knowledge of supervision in counseling. The supervisor is respected as a person of exemplary character and is regarded as a mentor from whom other counselors can learn. The supervisor is an advocate for counselors and is dedicated to her or his personal and professional development.

Purposes of Counselor Supervision

What are the purposes of supervision? There are obvious functions, to be sure, but also subtle ones as well. Statements of purpose are often overlapping, but they are extremely important because they register intent and set direction.

Counselor supervision has three main purposes:

1. Facilitation of counselor professional and personal development
2. Promotion of counselor competencies
3. Promotion of accountable counseling services and programs

Singularly and collectively, these purposes provide a rationale for the work of supervisors (Borders, 2005; Bradley, 1989; Bradley & Ladany, 2001).

Facilitation of Counselor Personal and Professional Development

The first purpose of supervision is a dual one: to facilitate the personal and professional development of counselors. The supervisor acts in the role of mentor and advocate, as well as teacher and consultant. Concurrently, supervisors must pursue professional and personal continuing education on a regular and on-going basis (*Ethical Guidelines for Counseling Supervisors*; ACES, 2003) to insure that they have the necessary resources and skills to provide supervisees with relevant training. In order for supervisors to monitor the counseling performance of supervisees, supervisors must themselves be aware of current trends and techniques of counseling.

Assuming agreement that facilitation of counselors' personal development should be a purpose of supervision, the next questions we need to ask are how much and what kind of emphasis should be placed on personal development. Answers to these questions are a matter for debate, but the following guidelines may be helpful in arriving at a partial resolution.

1. The foremost purposes of counselor supervision are facilitating professional development, increasing competencies, and promoting accountability in counseling.
2. Supervision should offer the supervisee an optimal opportunity for self-initiated personal development and encourage the supervisee to take advantage of the opportunity.
3. Supervisory interventions into the counselor's personal development should be undertaken typically when psychological distress is obviously and deleteriously affecting the counselor's performance. "Facilitation" of personal development is, however, a continuing supervisory effort.
4. The counselor's personal and professional development is interrelated. Damage to, or facilitation of, one of these concepts has a reciprocal effect on the other. Furthermore, facilitating personal development can be construed as contributing indirectly to all purposes of supervision.

Professional development, an interrelated part of the dual purpose of supervision, is a concept that must be clearly defined if the supervisor is to functionalize its intent. In a broad sense, professional development encompasses all that makes the counselor a professional, including increasing and improving competencies. In the context of this presentation, however, a more narrow definition is used, since competency improvement is designated as a separate supervisory purpose. Professional development, as defined here, refers to four tasks that have been adapted from concepts of Becker and Carper (1956); Bernard (2005); Green, Shilts, and Bacigalupe (2001); Hart and Prince (1970); and Ellis (2006).

1. The counselor must accept the name and image of the profession as part of her or his self-concept. This task causes problems for counselors because their preparation may lead to a wide variety of positions, each with a different job or professional title (e.g., child/adult development specialist, counseling psychologist, group facilitator, human development counselor, mental health counselor, family therapist, human resource specialist, or school counselor).

2. One must have a commitment to, and a clear perception of, the professional role and function. Counselors do not typically enter positions where their role and function have already been established. In fact, establishing this operational base is one of the most important and difficult tasks of the newly employed counselor. Occasionally, situational conditions can be so restrictive that the environment is unfit for good professional practice. A frequently slighted facet of the counselor's role and function is support of the profession and contribution to its growth and strength. Counselors are in dire need of professional affirmation however; ironically, the only way to receive this affirmation is to produce it! Participation in local, state, and national professional associations is a start.

3. The counselor must be committed to the goals of the institution in which counseling services are performed while ensuring that the goals do not contradict effective counseling practice. This commitment additionally includes the counselor's influence on establishment or alteration of institutional goals.

4. The counselor will recognize and appreciate the significance of the profession for individuals, groups, institutions, and society as a whole. A true profession exists to meet the needs of society, and professional accountability begins with recognition of these needs, an understanding of how the profession meets them, and an assessment of the profession's impact.

Promote Counselor Competence

The second purpose of supervision, to increase counselor competencies, incorporates helping the counselor acquire, improve, and refine the skills required by the counselor's role and function. Counselor competence has been defined as consisting of three subconstructs: knowledge, self-awareness, and skills (Ladany & Inman, in press). Knowledge pertains to an understanding of the theoretical and empirical work related to counseling clients. Of course knowledge alone is insufficient to work effectively with clients. Self-awareness refers to the ability to self-reflect on how the counselor is influencing counseling process and outcome, as well as a self-examination of how one's biases may be influencing counseling process and outcome. For example, counselors must work toward overcoming oppressive beliefs they possess based on their societal and cultural indoctrination. Finally, with greater knowledge, and enhanced self-awareness, counselors must be able to demonstrate skills in working with clients. Skills can be framed along four levels: (1) nonverbal behaviors; (2) response modes (e.g., helping skills); (3) covert processes (e.g., internal thoughts and feelings); and (4) therapeutic strategies and techniques (Ladany, Walker, Pate-Carolan, & Gray Evans, 2008). In all, the supervisor's role is to facilitate the development of counselor competence attending—often simultaneously—to all the aforementioned areas. No easy task!

Promotion of Accountability

To say that the helping professions, and particularly counseling, are presently in an "age of accountability" would be an understatement. Accountability is, and should be, demanded by the public. The consequences of not being able to satisfy public expectations could be disastrous for helping professionals. To ignore the public's need would be irresponsible, but these forces should not be the motivation for helping services and programs to respond to the need of demonstrating accountability. Such forces from outside the profession may serve as a cue to raise serious questions about effectiveness, but the motivation for demonstrating accountability must come from within. A profession emerges in response to the needs of a society and exists for the purpose of meeting those needs. Accountability is the profession's index of validity and evidence that the profession is meeting society's needs. The profession's obligation, not society's, is to establish accountability.

As a term, *accountability* has been given many definitions (Corey, Corey, & Callanan, 2007; Gysbers, 2008; Jenkins, 2006; Koerin & Miller, 1995; Sanchez-Hucles & Jones, 2005; Sexton, 1998). The core concept relates to accomplishment of the purposes and goals a person or institution has contracted or promised to accomplish. Glass (1972) compared this core element of meaning to "the simple economic relationship of vendor and buyer" (p. 636). The public is the buyer of helping services and counselors are the vendors. An accountable relationship between these two parties would involve:

1. Complete disclosure concerning the service being sold.
2. Testing of the effectiveness of the service.
3. Redress if the service is found by the public to be ineffective or falsely advertised.

According to this vendor–buyer paradigm, counselors are accountable to their employers: the public. Counselors must openly and honestly explain their functions and what their services can do. Counselors must test and evaluate their services and share the findings with the public. Lastly, counselors must be responsible for the consequences (good and bad) of their work and make adjustments when their work is ineffective.

Counselor supervision is a means for promoting accountability in services, programs, and relationships between helping services and the public. Supervised assistance to an individual counselor improves that person's accountability, while supervision applied to a staff of counselors involved in program development, management, and evaluation is a route to program accountability. In both cases, a special set of skills—a technical expertise—is needed by the supervisor if accountability is to be achieved.

Conclusion

Counselor supervision has been presented as a professional specialty with a methodology requiring highly developed skills. Successful counseling experience is a necessary but insufficient prerequisite for supervision and should be supplemented with advanced preparation in supervisory methods. The importance of supervision to the future of help-giving services should again be stressed. Counselor supervision is an indispensable component of counselor preparation programs. Coupled with the supervisee's self-developmental process, counselor supervision is a key to accountable helping services and attainment of the supervisee's professional potential. It is not an exaggeration to say that counselor supervision can be one of the most instrumental factors affecting future development of the helping professions. The remainder of this book will attempt to show you how all of this can be done!

References

Association for Counselor Education and Supervision. (1993, August 3). *Ethical guidelines for counselor supervisors.* Retrieved from acesonline.net/ethical_guidelines.asp

Association for Counselor Education and Supervision, Committee on Counselor Effectiveness. (1969). *Commitment to action in supervision: Report of a national survey of counselor supervision.* Alexandria, VA: Author.

Barnes, K. L. (2004). Applying self-efficacy theory to counselor training and supervision: A comparison of two approaches. *Counselor Education and Supervision, 44,* 56–69.

Becker, H. S., & Carper, J. W. (1956). Development of identification with an occupation. *American Journal of Sociology, 41,* 289–298.

Bernard, J. M. (1992). The challenge of psychotherapy-based supervision: Making the pieces fit. *Counselor Education and Supervision, 31,* 232–237.

Bernard, J. M. (2005). Tracing the development of clinical supervision. *Clinical Supervisor, 24,* 3–21.

Bernard, J. M., & Goodyear, R. K. (2009). *Fundamentals of clinical supervision* (4th ed.). Boston, MA: Allyn & Bacon.

Blocher, D. H. (1983). Toward a cognitive developmental approach to counseling supervision. *The Counseling Psychologist, 11,* 16–24.

Borders, L. D. (2005). Snapshot of clinical supervision in counseling and counselor education: A five-year review. *Clinical Supervisor, 24,* 69–113.

Borders, L. D., & Brown, L. L. (2005). *The new handbook for counseling supervision* (3rd ed.). Mahwah, NJ: Lahaska Press.

Bradley, L. J. (1989). *Counselor supervision: Principles, process and practice.* Muncie, IN: Accelerated Development.

Bradley, L. J., & Ladany, N. (2001). *Counselor supervision: Principles, process, and practice* (3rd ed.). New York: Brunner-Routledge.

Bradley, L. J., Lewis, J., Hendricks, B., & Crews, C. (2008). *Advocacy implications for supervision training.* (ACAPCD-13). Alexandria, VA: American Counseling Association.

Corey, G., Corey, M., & Callanan, P. (2007). *Issues and ethics in the helping professions* (7th ed.). Pacific Grove, CA: Brooks/Cole.

Ekstein, R., & Wallerstein, R. S. (1958). *The teaching and learning of psychotherapy.* New York: Basic.

Ellis, M. (2006). Critical incidents in clinical supervision and in supervisor supervision: Assessing supervisory issues. *Training and Education in Professional Psychology, 5,* 122–132.

Ellis, M. V., & Robbins, E. S. (1993). Voices of care and justice in clinical supervision: Issues and interventions. *Counselor Education and Supervision, 32,* 203–212.

Eriksen, K., Ellison, L., & Throckmorton, W. (2008). Competence, clinical oversight, and clarification of roles: Whose job is it, anyway? In L. Tyson, J. Culbreth, & J. Harrington (Eds.), *Critical incidents in clinical supervision: Addictions, community, and school counseling* (pp. 101–108). Alexandria, VA: American Counseling Association.

Estrada, D. (2005). Multicultural conversations in supervision: The impact of the supervisor's racial/ethnic background. *Guidance & Counseling, 21,* 14–20.

Geldard, K., & Geldard, D. (2008). *Personal counseling skills: An integrative approach.* Springfield, IL: Charles C. Thomas Publisher.

Glass, G. V. (1972). The many faces of educational accountability. *Phi Delta Kappan, 10,* 636–639.

Goodyear, R. K., & Guzzardo, C. R. (2000). Psychotherapy supervision and training. In S. Brown & R. W. Lent (Eds.), *Handbook of counseling psychology* (3rd ed., pp. 83–108). New York: Wiley.

Green, S., Shilts, L., & Bacigalupe, G. (2001). When approval is not enough: Development of a supervision consultation model. *Journal of Marital and Family Therapy, 27,* 515–525.

Gysbers, N. (2008). Improving school guidance and counseling practices through effective and sustained state leadership. *Professional School Counseling, 9,* 245–247.

Hart, D. H., & Prince, D. J. (1970). Role conflict for school counselors: Training versus job demands. *Personnel and Guidance Journal, 48,* 374–380.

Hazler, R. H., & Kottler, J. A. (2005). *The emerging professional counselor* (2nd ed.). Alexandria, VA: American Counseling Association.

Holloway, E. L., & Neufeldt, S. A. (1995). Supervision: Its contributions to treatment efficacy. *Journal of Consulting & Clinical Psychology, 63,* 207–213.

Jenkins, P. (2006). Supervisor accountability and risk management in healthcare settings. *Healthcare Counselling and Psychotherapy Journal, 6,* 6–8.

Juhnke, G. A., Kelly, V. A., & Cooper, J. B. (2008). Mandated supervision: Trouble for an external consulting clinical supervisor. In L. E. Tyson, J. R. Culbreth, & J. A. Harrington (Eds.), *Critical incidents in clinical supervision: Addictions, community, and school counseling* (pp. 25–32). Alexandria, VA: American Counseling Association.

Koerin, B., & Miller, J. (1995). Gate-keeping policies: Terminating students for non-academic reasons. *Journal of Social Work Education, 31,* 247–260.

Kugler, P. (1995). *Jungian Perspectives on Clinical Supervision.* Einsiedeln, Switzerland: Daimon Publishers.

Ladany, N., & Inman, A. G. (in press). Training and supervision. In E. A. Altmaier & J. I. Hansen (Eds.), *Oxford handbook of counseling psychology.* New York: Oxford University Press.

Ladany, N., Walker, J., Pate-Carolan, L., & Gray Evans, L. (2008). *Experiencing counseling and psychotherapy: Insights from psychotherapy trainees, their clients, and their supervisors.* New York: Taylor & Francis.

McAdams, C. R., & Foster, V. A. (2007). A guide to just and fair remediation of counseling students with professional performance deficiencies. *Counselor Education and Supervision, 47,* 2–13.

McWhirter, E. H., & McWhirter, B. T. (2007). Grounding clinical training and supervision in an empowerment model. In *Advancing social justice through clinical practice* (pp. 417–442). Mahwah, NJ: Lawrence Erlbaum Associates Publishers.

Mueller, W. J., & Kell, B. L. (1972). *Coping with conflict: Supervising counselors and psychotherapists.* New York: Appleton-Century-Crofts.

Munson, C. E. (2002). *Handbook of clinical social work supervision.* New York, London, Oxford: Haworth Press.

Neufeldt, M. L. (2007). *Supervision strategies for the first practicum* (3rd ed.). Alexandria, VA: American Counseling Association.

Neufeldt, S. A. (1999). *Supervision strategies for the first practicum* (2nd ed.). Alexandria, VA: American Counseling Association.

Norcross, J. C., & Beutler, L. E. (2008). Integrative psychotherapies. In R. J. Corsini & D. Wedding, *Current psychotherapies* (8th ed.) (pp. 481–510). Belmont, CA: Brooks/Cole.

Pearson, Q. (2006). Psychotherapy-driven supervision: Integrating counseling theories into role-based supervision. *Journal of Mental Health Counseling, 28,* 241–252.

Riccio, A. C. (1961). The counselor educator and the guidance supervisor: Graduate training and occupational mobility. *Counselor Education and Supervision, 1,* 10–17.

Riccio, A. C. (1966). Counselor educators and guidance supervisors: A second look at graduate training. *Counselor Education and Supervision, 5,* 73–79.

Richardson, B. K., & Bradley, L. J. (1986). *Community agency counseling: An emerging specialty within counselor preparation programs.* Washington, DC: American Association for Counseling and Development.

Sanchez-Hucles, J., & Jones, N. (2005). Breaking the silence around race in training, practice, and research. *Counseling Psychologist, 33,* 547–558.

Sexton, T. L. (1998). Reconstructing counselor education: Supervision, teaching, and clinical training revisited. *Counselor Education and Supervision, 38,* 2–5.

Thompson, J. (2004). A readiness hierarchy theory of counselor-in-training. *Journal of Instructional Psychology, 31,* 135–142.

CHAPTER 2

The Supervisory Relationship

RACHEL E. CROOK LYON and KIRTI A. POTKAR

Tell me and I will forget. Show me and I will remember. Involve me and I will understand.

—Confucius

The supervisory relationship has long been hailed by theorists as the central means by which supervisors facilitate the development of trainees (Ekstein & Wallerstein, 1972; Holloway, 1987; Loganbill, Hardy, & Delworth, 1982). Research has consistently supported the view that the quality of the supervisory relationship is vital to positive outcomes in supervision (Gray, Ladany, Walker, & Ancis, 2001; Nelson & Friedlander, 2001; Patton & Kivlighan, 1997; Stoltenberg, McNeill, & Delworth, 1998; Worthen & McNeill, 1996; Worthington & Roehlke, 1979). Furthermore, trainees report that the supervisory relationship is the key element in supervision (Ellis, 1991; Ramos-Sanchez et al., 2002). Finally, research shows that the relationship between supervisors and trainees is a critical factor in the professional development of supervisees (Ronnestad & Skovholt, 1993).

The purpose of this chapter is to explore and discuss the supervisory relationship. First, we define the supervisory relationship based on Bordin's (1983) conceptualization of the supervisory working alliance and enhanced by Holloway's (1997) notions of power and involvement. We then focus on the beginning, mature, and terminating stages of the supervisory relationship (Holloway, 1995) as well as transformational aspects of supervision when supervisors serve as mentors to trainees (Johnson, 2007). The third section discusses the formation, maintenance, and measurement of supervisor relationships. We then turn to positive and negative factors that impact the supervisory relationship. Such factors include contributions of supervisees, contributions of supervisors, and interactions within the supervisory relationship. Finally, we consider how the supervisory relationship influences supervision outcomes. Before proceeding, we feel it is important to identify that this chapter will focus on individual supervision between a supervisor and a single supervisee. Hence, the unique features of the supervisory relationship in other modalities of supervision, such as dyadic or group supervision, are left to the other chapters in this book.

The Supervisory Relationship Defined

We have chosen to use Bordin's (1983) conceptualization of the supervisory working alliance as foundational to our definition of the supervisory relationship. Numerous theorists and researchers assert that an understanding of the supervisory working alliance is fundamental to the process of supervision (Ladany & Inman, in press; Patton & Kivlighan, 1997; Ramos-Sanchez et al., 2002; Wood, 2005). The *supervisory working alliance* is defined as an association for change that involves three elements: (1) mutual agreement and understanding between the supervisor and supervisee on the goals of supervision; (2) mutual agreement and understanding of the tasks of each partner to accomplish those goals; and (3) the emotional bonds between the supervisor and supervisee necessary to sustain the endeavor (Bordin, 1983). A unique facet of the supervisory working alliance is the notion of mutuality or mutual connections between supervisors and supervisees. In other words, instead of a unidirectional concept of trust within the supervisory relationship, for example, the supervisor trusts the trainee, the supervisor perceives that mutual trust exists with the trainee (Ladany, Walker, & Melincoff, 2001).

Goals

Bordin (1983) described the principal goals of the supervisee within the supervisory relationship: (a) mastering specific skills; (b) enlarging one's understanding of clients; (c) expanding one's awareness of process issues; (d) increasing awareness of one's self and one's impact on the counseling process; (e) overcoming personal and intellectual obstacles toward learning and mastery; (f) deepening one's understanding of concepts and theory; (g) providing a stimulus to research; and (h) maintaining standards of service. An example of a goal may be the supervisor and supervisee mutually agreeing to work on increasing the supervisee's awareness of client nonverbal cues during the counseling session. Depending on the developmental level of the trainee, certain goals may take precedence over other goals. Thus, a neophyte supervisee may focus on mastering specific counseling skills, for example, how to begin and end sessions, the use of silence, how to lessen the uncertainty created by a specific client. Bordin stressed the importance of first establishing a goal orientation in supervision before turning to the tasks by which the supervisory dyad will achieve the goals.

Tasks

The supervisor seeks mutual agreement and understanding with the supervisee on the tasks, each of them must complete to attain supervisory goals. The strength of the working alliance depends not only on the mutual understanding of the supervisee and supervisor of the supervisory tasks but also on the extent to which the supervisee recognizes the connection between the goals and tasks of supervision. In other words, a supervisee might not comprehend that a discussion of the supervisee's thoughts and feelings about nonverbal behaviors is related to the supervisory goal of improving the supervisee's awareness of such behaviors in counseling. Bordin (1983) identified several tasks that may be of use in supervision. One task is for supervisees to prepare a written or oral report of the counseling hours under review. Then, depending on the supervisory goals, the supervisor can provide feedback on specific skills, focus attention on the supervisee's feelings and awareness, or expanding the supervisee's repertoire of responses. A second task is for the supervisor to observe the supervisee's counseling session through audiotape, videotape, or direct observation. Bordin argues that without such observation, the supervisor relies only on the selectivity of the trainee in reporting events and issues for supervision. Indeed, he stated, "The therapist's report has the virtue of dramatically illustrating the selectivity in his or her self-observation. It is important that the supervisor not be a prisoner of that selectivity" (Bordin, 1983, p. 38). A third task is for the supervisee to select problems and issues for presentation in supervision. In other words, rather than a routine presentation of clients in the past week, the supervisee is asked to direct the focus of the supervision session, for example, "What would you like to work on today?"

Bond

The emotional bond is the third component of the supervisory working alliance. Bordin (1983) described the bonds necessary in the supervisory alliance "to fall somewhere between those of teacher to class members and therapist to patient" (p. 38). The bonds are described as feelings of liking, caring, and trusting the supervisee and supervisor share. As the supervisor and supervisee spend time together and work on the goals and tasks of supervision, an emotional bond arises. Bordin identified the inescapable evaluation element in supervision as potentially problematic to the formation and maintenance of the supervisory bond. In fact, he recommended relying on the process of building a strong working alliance to counteract the tension associated with status differences between supervisor and supervisee.

Although similarities between counseling and supervision exist, supervisors should be careful in equating the counseling and supervisory working alliances (Borders & Leddick, 1987; Leddick & Bernard, 1980; Ladany, Ellis, & Friedlander, 1999) given that supervision, unlike counseling, is involuntary, mandatory, and evaluative. Holloway (1997) extended this discussion of evaluation and emphasized the significance of power and involvement within the supervisory relationship. As an expert and evaluator, the supervisor holds formal power within the hierarchical relationship, but power may be shared through the ongoing interactions between the supervisor and supervisee. In addition, the supervisor's power may be moderated by the trainee's perceptions of the supervisor's expertness and competence as well as the trainee's age, level of experience, and support base (Skovholt & Ronnestad, 1992). The involvement of supervisor and supervisee within the supervisory relationship also influences the utilization and impact of power in the relationship (Holloway, 1997). For instance, a supervisor may have substantial power in a relationship with a supervisee who perceives the supervisor as being extremely skilled clinically, and has limited counseling experience, and few peer supports. Both the supervisor and supervisee, then, shape the distribution of power and involvement in the supervisory relationship (Holloway, 1997).

Phases of the Supervisory Relationship

As with a counseling (or indeed any other) relationship, the supervisory relationship begins tentatively with a certain testing of the grounds and building and strengthening of the relationship allows for the work of the supervision process to proceed. Holloway (1995) suggests three stages through which every supervisory relationship may be expected to pass: the beginning phase, the mature phase, and the terminating phase. She suggests that the development of a supervisory relationship is a progression from a noninterpersonal to an interpersonal relationship. As the participants get better acquainted, they rely less on social and cultural cues or group stereotypes in predicting the other person's behaviors and reactions. This ability to predict means that there is less uncertainty in the relationship allowing for better use of control strategies and communicative modes that reduce possible conflicts. Further, there is greater likelihood of self-disclosure due to increased feeling of safety. In Holloway's terms, this is a transition from the beginning to the mature phase.

Holloway (1995) suggests that the beginning phase involves a clarification of the relationship with the supervisors and the establishment of a supervisory contract. The supervisory contract involves a discussion of the evaluative nature of the relationship, the evaluation criteria, the expectations and goals of supervision, and the ethical aspects like the limits of confidentiality and boundary issues (Ekstein & Wallerstein, 1972; Holloway, 1995; Shohet & Wilmot, 1991). It is here that the supervisor and supervisee make the commitment to engage meaningfully in the relationship (Shulman, 2005). The supervisor "teaches" the supervisee various appropriate techniques to use and helps in developing competencies and treatment plans.

In the mature phase, the relationship becomes increasingly individual and collegial with less importance given to the role of each individual. There is increasing social bonding allowing for mutual influence. The relationship allows for a confrontation of personal issues as they impact the professional performance of the supervisee. Feelings of trust and sensitivity engendered through these discussions make for a better relationship. The supervisee is focused on developing case conceptualization skills and experiences increasing self-confidence and self-efficacy in counseling (Holloway, 1995). Ekstein and Wallerstein (1972) highlight the educational nature of this phase by calling it the *learning phase,* suggesting that the supervisee is involved in increasing professional skill, therapeutic sensitivity, and competence.

The terminating phase coincides with an increased ability in the supervisee to understand the connections between theory and practice in relation to specific clients. The supervisee experiences a decreased need for direction from the supervisor (Holloway, 1995). In addition, Hoffman (1994) suggests that the goals of supervision as well as the progress made needs to be reviewed at this point. The fact that the end of the supervisory relationship typically coincides with the end of the therapeutic relationship with clients and the evaluation of both supervisor and supervisee (Ekstein & Wallerstein, 1972) makes the termination process more complex. Special attention is required to ensure a smooth negotiation through this process.

Worthen and McNeill (1996) in their qualitative investigation of good supervisory events highlight a similar process. They suggest that initially the supervisee experiences fluctuating levels of confidence and displays an aversion to overt evaluation. They desire a rewarding supervision experience but may have reservations due to past unrewarding supervision. This is the existential baseline. Next, they experience a sense of inadequacy through a disruption in the usual processes of counseling with some anxiety-induced emotional arousal. This sets the stage for good supervision experiences. Here the supervisee experiences the supervisory relationship as empathic, nonjudgmental, and validating. The supervisee feels encouraged to explore and experiment due to a normalization of his or her struggles. Further, there is a reduced need to protect themselves, which leads to a greater receptivity of supervisory input as well as more willingness to indulge in nondefensive analysis and reexamination of own assumptions as well as the acquisition of a metaperspective.

An aspect of the supervisory relationship that deserves mention here is its similarity to the mentoring relationship. A mentoring relationship is a dynamic, emotionally connected, and reciprocal relationship where the supervisor shows deliberate and generative concern for the trainee beyond mere skill acquisition (Johnson, 2003). Contrasting this definition with the supervisory relationship, it is apparent that supervision and mentorship tend to be complementary in many respects (Johnson, 2007), like the focus on the interpersonal relationship to assist in the development of the trainee. Johnson (2007) further suggests that as the supervisee matures and develops professionally, every supervisory relationship typically progresses from the exclusively transactional form to a collaborative or transformational form. The supervisory relationship can become more beneficial and personally meaningful for the supervisee through an incorporation of a number of mentoring functions.

It must be noted that Worthen and McNeill (1996) highlight two aspects of good or positive supervision experiences. The first aspect is a good supervisory relationship consisting of warmth, acceptance, respect, understanding, and trust (citing Hutt, Scott, & King, 1983; Martin, Goodyear, & Newton, 1987) especially for beginning trainees (citing Heppner & Roehlke, 1984). The second aspect involves attending to the task of developing counseling skills that good supervisors model through self-disclosure (Black, 1988) thus creating an atmosphere of experimentation, which allows for mistakes (Allen, Szollos, & Williams, 1986; Hutt et al., 1983). The level of experience of the trainees may well moderate the type of input they require during supervision.

Forming Strong Supervisory Relationships

Identified as one of the four pillars of effective supervision, the development of a strong working alliance between supervisor and supervisee is essential for supervision (Overholser, 2004). Likewise, the primary task in early supervisory sessions, according to Patton and Kivlighan (1997) is for a supervisor to form a strong working alliance with the supervisee. In this section, we review the theoretical and empirical literature around the formation, maintenance, and measurement of supervisory relationships.

One aspect for supervisors to consider when beginning a new supervisory relationship is the developmental level of the trainee. Research has shown that trainees at advanced developmental levels were more likely to report a stronger supervisory alliance than were trainees at beginning developmental levels (Ramos-Sanchez et al., 2002). Hence, supervisors working with novice counselors should focus on establishing a strong supervisory relationship by building trust, actively supporting trainees, advocating for supervisees, and processing the supervisory relationship

(Ramos-Sanchez et al., 2002). Similarly, Efstation, Patton, and Kardash (1990) suggested that the development of rapport in supervision might be more important to beginning supervisees than to more experienced ones.

Another aspect that has been shown to facilitate alliance formation is effective evaluation practices. Lehrman-Waterman and Ladany (2001) found strong working alliance ratings among trainees who perceived their supervisors as effectively managing evaluation practices such as goal setting and feedback in supervision. The authors suggest that supervisors incorporate goal setting at the beginning of supervision so as to facilitate supervisory alliance formation. Likewise, if supervisors sense a problematic relationship with trainees, focus on goal setting and feedback may serve a reparative function.

A third factor that aids the development of supervisory alliances is discussions of cultural variables like race/ethnicity, gender, and sexual orientation. Research and theory in this area highlights the importance of paying attention to these issues in order to form and maintain strong supervisory alliance and enhance the learning process of the supervisee (see for example, Burkard et al., 2006; Doughty & Leddick, 2007; Gatmon et al., 2001; Halpert & Pfaller, 2001; Halpert, Reinhardt, & Toohey, 2007; Ladany, Friedlander, & Nelson, 2005; Nelson & Friedlander, 2001; Russell & Greenhouse, 1997; Tummala-Narra, 2004; Walker, Ladany, & Pate-Carolan, 2003). These issues have been discussed in detail in other chapters of this book.

With respect to maintaining a strong supervisory alliance, there is theoretical and empirical support for the notion of the counseling working alliance as a dynamic rather than static interaction (Bordin, 1983; Safran & Muran, 1998; Sommerfield, Orbach, Zim, & Mikulincer, 2008). In this view, the constant rupturing and subsequent repairing of the alliance is the process by which change occurs. In a similar fashion, the supervisory alliance can be seen as a series of ruptures and repairs as the supervisor and supervisee work together on the goals and tasks of supervision. Factors that relate to the process of supervisory working alliance ruptures and repairs include the experience level of the supervisee, differences in theoretical orientation, supervisee presentation style, and issues surrounding evaluation (Burke, Goodyear, & Guzzard, 1998). Specifically, the authors found that when ruptures in the supervisory alliance focused on evaluation issues, such issues often remained unresolved. An interesting finding was that supervisory dyads with a relatively high number of unresolved ruptures still viewed the process and outcome of supervision sessions positively. It seems as though there may be aspects of supervision, such as the supervisor's expertise, which might override unresolved ruptures.

There are several different measures of the supervisory working alliance. Three instruments (e.g., Bahrick, 1990; Baker, 1990, Smith, Younes,

& Lichtenberg, 2002) are based on modifications of the widely used measure of the counseling alliance, the Working Alliance Inventory (Horvath & Greenberg, 1989). These instruments are based on Bordin's (1983) conceptualization of the supervisory working alliance and hence include Goals, Tasks, and Bond subscales. The Bahrick (e.g., Ladany, Brittan-Powell, & Pannu, 1997; Ladany, Ellis, & Friedlander, 1999; Ladany & Friedlander, 1995; Lehrman-Waterman & Ladany, 2001) and Baker measures of supervisory working alliance have been used in several studies (e.g., Ramos-Sanchez et al., 2002). Another measure is that of Efstation and colleagues (1990) who developed their widely used alliance measure, the Supervisory Working Alliance Inventory scale (SWAI) particular to supervision. The SWAI supervisor scale includes three subscales: Client Focus, Rapport, and Identification, whereas the trainee scale includes Client Focus and Rapport subscales.

Factors That Influence the Supervisory Relationship

The review of literature on the formation and maintenance of the supervisory working alliance highlights the fact that both the supervisor and supervisee have to work in order to make the relationship work. The supervisor needs to be open to the supervisee's input and the supervisor needs to foster a trusting and safe atmosphere in which the supervisee is able to learn. A positive supervisory relationship is one where both supervisor and supervisee work in concert to create a safe place of learning within the relationship. Given the centrality of the supervisory alliance, it seems valuable to consider the factors that facilitate the development of a strong working alliance. Bordin (1983) suggested that individual characteristics of supervisors and trainees play an essential role in the formation of the supervisory working alliance. Here we discuss some of the supervisee and supervisor contributions that relate to the development of the supervisory relationship.

Supervisee Contributions

Supervisee Resistance

As with therapy, Liddle (1986) suggests that resistance may serve a self-protective function in supervision being employed in the face of some threat. However, Bernard and Goodyear (2009) point out that some instances of resistance may reflect the supervisee's need to individuate from the supervisor (developmental need) as well as supervisee–supervisor conflict in terms of tasks and goals. Some of the manifestations of resistance they highlight include: (a) resistance to the supervisor's influence through non-disclosure, deflecting the focus of discussion away from certain topics, and so on; (b) resistance of the supervisory experience itself by being late for supervision or missing the session completely; (c) being noncompliant with the tasks of supervision like taping the sessions; and (d) being noncompliant in terms of the implementation of mutually agreed upon plans for the client. Ekstein and Wallerstein (1972) suggested that supervisee resistance may be a reflection of the client's resistance through the parallel processes of supervision where the client–counselor dyad interactions may be replayed in the supervisor–supervisee dyad (discussed in more detail later). Resistance may arise due to factors like a lack of trust or safety within the supervisory relationship, disagreement about goals and tasks, high level of supervisor directiveness especially when the supervisee does not understand the rationale of the supervisor's instructions, and developmental level of the supervisee (e.g., Ronnestad & Skovholt, 1993; Stoltenberg et al., 1998). Further, Dowd (1989) suggested that resistance is not merely situation specific (as suggested by Brehm & Brehm, 1981) but is a reflection of the resistance trait of the person. Hence, a high reactive individual is likely to show higher vigilance and hence higher resistance. Interestingly, Kennard, Stewart, and Gluck (1987) found that when supervisors perceived the trainee as being interested in the supervisor's feedback and suggestions regarding professional development, the trainees themselves were likely to rate their supervisory experience more positively. In other words, openness to the supervisor (as opposed to resistance) leads to positive supervisory experiences. Kauderer and Herron (1990) found similar results with supervisors rating supervisees' participation and increased assertiveness as significant positive elements within the supervisory relationship.

Supervisee Anxiety

A supervisee may experience anxiety on many fronts: due to the ambiguity and the expectations within supervision as well as within the counseling relationship. This anxiety may be moderated by factors like the experience or developmental level of the supervisee (Ekstein & Wallerstein, 1972; Shohet & Wilmot, 1991; Skovholt & Ronnestad, 1992), personality variables, and the nature of their supervisory as well as therapeutic relationship. The supervisee's anxiety is likely to impact their ability to learn, perform, and respond within the relationship (see for example, Dombeck & Brody, 1995; Friedlander, Keller, Peca-Baker, & Olk, 1986; Schauer, Seymour, & Geen, 1985), as well as the extent of supervisee disclosure (see for example, Ladany, Hill, Corbett, & Nutt, 1996; Ronnestad & Skovholt, 1993). It must be noted that the evaluative nature of the supervisory relationship brings with it a pressure to perform and a need to feel and appear competent. This need may be moderated by the developmental level of the supervisee: (a) the more advanced the level of the supervisee, the more confident they are likely to be in themselves (along with the reduced dependence and defensiveness noted above; see also, Loganbill, Hardy, & Delworth, 1982; Rabinowitz, Heppner,

& Roehlke, 1986); (b) midlevel trainees are likely to experience the depen-
dency-autonomy conflict—oscillating between a feeling of overconfidence
and being overwhelmed (Stoltenberg, 1981). Harvey and Katz (1985) further
suggest that when the "felt adequacy" (perceptions of own competence) is
lower than actual competence the trainee may end up feeling like an imposter or a fraud. Despite this limiting impact of anxiety, a certain amount of
anxiety as well as the ability to "sit with it" may well serve to enhance the
learning process (see for example, Rioch, Coulter, & Weimberger, 1976).

Research has shown that role induction (education about roles and expectations in supervision) was helpful in reducing supervisee anxiety (see for
example, Bahrick, Russell, & Salmi, 1991). There is a need to optimize the
level of supervisor challenge and support (see, for example, Blocher, 1983;
Worthington & Roehlke, 1979). Beginning level trainees may benefit from
a high level of structure (see also Freeman, 1993; Friedlander & Ward, 1984;
Sansbury, 1982; Usher & Borders, 1993), prompt and clear feedback about
progress and challenges, and a directive instructional approach that makes a
wider repertoire of skills available to the supervisee (Ronnestad & Skovholt,
1993). Encouraging self-disclosure and reflection (see Baird, 1999; Ronnestad
& Skovholt, 1993), normalizing fears (Costa, 1994; Grater, 1985; Ronnestad &
Skovholt, 1993), and humor have been found to be useful in reducing anxiety
also. Additionally, when dealing with defensive reactions it is helpful to tune
in and respond to the underlying anxiety or concern of the supervisee rather
than the overt words or behavior (Shulman, 2005).

Supervisee Disclosures and Nondisclosures

Exploration and reflection are two of the basic ways in which trainees
learn the art of counseling, and a good supervisory relationship provides
ample opportunities for the same. Disclosure regarding one's clients, the
counseling as well as the supervisory relationships, and about themselves
is considered essential for the supervisee to gain the maximum benefits
from the supervision process (e.g., Blocher, 1983; Bordin, 1983; Loganbill
et al., 1982; Stoltenberg, 1981; Stoltenberg & Delworth, 1987) as supervisors cannot help the trainees with problems that they are not aware of.
Failure to disclose is closely linked with the perceived quality of the supervisory relationship as well as the outcomes of supervision (see for example,
Ladany et al., 1996; Murphy & Wright, 2005). Webb and Wheeler (1998)
found that the supervisees' willingness to disclose was associated with the
perceived rapport with their supervisor. Further, they were more willing to
self-disclose if they had chosen their supervisor rather than being assigned
to them. Ladany et al. (1996) highlighted some of the reasons for nondisclosure given by supervisees: the information is viewed as too personal
or unimportant; negative feelings such as shame, embarrassment, or discomfort; feelings of deference toward the needs of the supervisor; poor

alliance with the supervisor; or a fear of being perceived negatively. Other reasons for supervisee nondisclosure include: feeling of shame (Yourman, 2003), the evaluative nature of the supervisory relationship (Kaplan, 1977), a desire to create a positive impression (e.g., Ward, Friedlander, Schoen, & Klein, 1985). Interestingly, Murphy and Wright (2005) found that supervisees may withhold information within supervision as power against the supervisor, which again speaks to poor alliance. As many scholars have noted, supervision is an involuntary process where the supervisee has very little power (Holloway, 1992; Holloway, Freund, Gardner, Nelson, & Walker, 1989) and withholding information may be used as a way of gaining some control within the relationship.

Implications for Supervisors Regarding Supervisees' Contributions

- Pay attention to the development of a safe, trusting, and caring environment where the supervisee can self-disclose and develop.
- Set clear guidelines about the roles of both the supervisor and supervisee and what is allowed and expected from each (e.g., it is allowable for the supervisee to disagree with or do something different from the supervisor).
- Clarify goals and expectations as well as the evaluation criteria being used at the outset (see for example, Baird, 1999; Costa, 1994; McCarthy, Sugden, Koker, & Lamendole, 1995).
- Take the differing needs of the supervisee (in terms of developmental level, personal variables, and so on) into account when drawing up the supervision contract.
- Examine supervisee's skills with care: any appearance of attacking the person's learning and skills may create vulnerability and resistance.
- Increase the supervisee's perceived level of control in order to reduce vulnerability.
- Attend to the supervisee's level of anxiety and its impact on performance.
- Model self-disclosing in order to reassure and encourage supervisee self-disclosure.
- Elicit feedback about what is helping or hindering the supervisee within the supervisory relationship.
- Remember: The supervisor carries the legal and ethical responsibility of the supervisee's actions within the counseling relationship.

Case Example

Susan, a 31-year-old fourth-year doctoral student, has been supervised by Dr. P at a university counseling center for three months. Dr. P has worked hard to establish a good rapport with Susan, and Susan has appeared to enjoy meeting for supervision. Over the past two weeks, however, Susan has been a few minutes late for sessions, and has appeared anxious, disorganized, and unprepared for supervision. She mentioned offhand that she has been very stressed out as she prepares her predoctoral internship application. Concerned by this change in Susan's behavior, Dr. P wonders what may be behind Susan's apparent anxiety and resistance. Dr. P gently probes for what may be troubling Susan, but Susan quickly replies that everything will settle down once she completes the application.

Supervisor Contributions

Supervisory Style

Supervisory style is defined as different approaches to supervision and responses to supervisees. Friedlander and Ward (1984) identified three supervisory styles: attractive, interpersonally sensitive, and task-oriented, which coincide with Bernard's (1997) three basic supervisory roles: consultant, counselor, and teacher. Supervisors who utilize an attractive style tend to be warm, open, and supportive toward their supervisees much like the consultant role. Supervisors who adopt an interpersonally sensitive style are likely to be perceptive and therapeutic with their supervisees as in the counselor role in supervision. Finally, supervisors who adopt a task-oriented style tend to be goal oriented and structured in supervision much like the teacher role. Although developmental theorists (e.g., Stoltenberg & McNeill, 1997) have proposed utilizing certain styles or engaging in particular roles depending on the trainees' developmental level (e.g., that supervisors should be more task-oriented and adopt a teacher role with beginning trainees), the empirical support is mixed (Ellis & Ladany, 1997; Holloway, 1995). Fundamentally, supervisors should have the flexibility to engage in a variety of supervisory styles and roles with supervisees at any level (Bernard, 1997). Research shows that supervisory style is related to a variety of supervisory process and outcome variables including supervisor's theoretical orientation (Friedlander & Ward, 1984), content and frequency of supervisor self-disclosure (Ladany et al., 2001; Ladany & Lehrman-Waterman, 1999), and supervisory working alliance (Efstation et al., 1990; Ladany et al., 2001). Specifically, supervisors adopting a more attractive style made more frequent self-disclosures than those utilizing interpersonally sensitive or task-oriented styles (Ladany & Lehrman-Waterman, 1999). With respect to supervisory style and content of supervisor self-disclosure, the more supervisors engaged in an attractive style, the more likely they were to disclose neutral counseling experiences; the converse was true of interpersonally sensitive supervisors who were less likely to reveal neutral counseling experiences. Finally, those supervisors who adopted a task-oriented style in supervision were less likely to disclose personal issues or successes in counseling (Ladany & Lehrman-Waterman,

1999). Supervisory style is also related to nondisclosures by supervisees such that supervisees reported more nondisclosures when they perceived their supervisors as unattractive, interpersonally insensitive, and less task-oriented (Ladany et al., 1996). In particular, trainees indicated withholding valuable information during supervision when they viewed their supervisors as adopting an unattractive style.

Interpersonal Power

Due to the hierarchical nature of supervisory relationships and differences in roles, training, and level of experience and expertise between supervisors and supervisees, power is a recurring subject in the literature on supervisory relationships (Holloway et al., 1989; Murphy & Wright, 2005). Research shows that power differences can have a marked effect on supervisees' development and even on counseling outcomes (Jacobs, 1991; Nelson & Friedlander, 2001). Supervisors may manage the power that is inherently theirs in the supervisory relationship in a variety of ways including empowering the supervisee (Nelson, 1997). As Nelson describes it:

> The supervisor is in a powerful position regarding monitoring and guiding the trainee's learning, yet must still find a way to allow the trainee to professionally emerge with his or her own sense of power. In other words, the supervisor must use his or her expert power to assist the trainee in assuming power. (1997, p. 125)

In a qualitative study investigating the use of power in the supervisory relationship from the trainee's perspective, Murphy and Wright (2005) found that supervisors' positive power uses included empowering supervisees, discussing power, cultivating a safe atmosphere, collaborating with supervisees, providing opinions, giving feedback, and making evaluations. Negative uses of supervisors' power included favoritism and imposing therapeutic style/orientation, whereas supervisors' misuses of power included violation of confidentiality. The authors noted that supervisees expected their supervisors to have power and to use it appropriately.

Similarly, in a related study on control within supervision, Quarto (2002) showed that both supervisees and supervisors acknowledge that there are times when supervisors control the supervisory process. However, only supervisees perceived aspects of the supervisory relationship in which the supervisee had control. In other words, supervisors had a narrower perception of control than supervisees who perceived themselves to play an active role in controlling supervisory interactions. Beginning supervisees viewed themselves as assuming less control in supervision than advanced students. Furthermore, there was a positive relationship between supervisory control and the supervisory working alliance such that when supervisees contributed to the discussion and process of supervision sessions they perceived a stronger rapport with the supervisor.

It is important to remember that although supervisors are generally considered to have most of the power in the supervisory relationship given their role as evaluator, supervisees also have a degree of power that they can abuse by withholding valuable information from the supervisor and making unfair evaluations of the supervisor (Ladany, 2004).

Supervisor Disclosures and Nondisclosures

Supervisor self-disclosure is defined by Ladany and Lehrman-Waterman (1999) as personal statements a supervisor shares with the trainee that could:

> Reflect favorable or unfavorable aspects of the supervisor, for example, counseling successes or failures; mirror similar or dissimilar concerns the trainee brings to supervision; pertain to the supervisor's past or present experiences; be highly intimate or nonintimate; or be self-involving statements, which can be seen as in-the-moment process comments reflecting the supervisor's experience of the trainee in supervision. (p. 144)

Ladany and Walker (2003) have described five categories of disclosures: personal material, therapy experiences, professional experiences, reactions to the trainee's clients, and supervision experiences. Case examples of the harmful self-disclosures include the uncontrollable narcissist in which the supervisor discloses extensive and inappropriate personal information and the indomitable altruist when the supervisor bombards the trainee with therapy experience self-disclosures in an attempt to facilitate insight on the part of the trainee.

As with supervisee disclosure, higher frequency of supervisor self-disclosure was related to trainees' perceptions of a stronger working alliance (Ladany & Lehrman-Waterman, 1999). More specifically, trainees viewed a stronger emotional bond with those supervisors who more frequently disclosed counseling struggles. Supervisor self-disclosure has also been found to relate to supervisory style. For instance, the more supervisors adopted the attractive role in supervision, the more likely supervisors perceived themselves to self-disclose (Ladany et al., 2001). Similarly, the more supervisors engaged in an interpersonally sensitive role, the more they perceived themselves to self-disclose in supervision. There was no relationship, however, between the more task-oriented supervisors and perceived supervisor self-disclosure. In other research, supervisors used self-disclosure to enhance the development of supervisees and to normalize supervisees' experiences (Knox, Burkard, Edwards, Smith, & Schlosser, 2008). Typically, supervisory self-disclosures occurred in good supervisory relationships, focused on supervisors' reactions to clients, and were instigated by supervisees' struggling. The authors suggest that supervisor self-disclosure may be a way to strengthen or repair the supervisory working alliance.

Supervisors may also choose not to disclose information in supervision. Ladany and Melincoff (1999) found that most supervisors (98%) in their sample withheld some information in supervision, for example, personal issues, positive reactions to trainee's counseling, and professional performance. This latter finding seemed problematic to the authors who suggested that disclosing positive feedback to the trainees would likely strengthen the supervisory relationship. Reasons supervisors reported for nondisclosures focused on concerns that such disclosures would harm the supervisory relationship or that the supervisory relationship was not sufficiently developed to handle the disclosure.

Implications for Supervisors Regarding Their Own Contribution

- Supervisors should be flexible in their supervisory style, recognizing that an attractive style contributes to all three supervisory alliance components.
- Supervisors must be aware of and attend to the power they hold in supervision by using it appropriately.
- Supervisors should be aware of and manage countertransference reactions within the supervisory relationship.
- Supervisors using self-disclosures appropriately can enhance the supervisory relationship.

Case Example (continued)

After the supervision session, Dr. P reflects on the rupture in the supervisory relationship. She examines her own contributions to the supervisory relationship; with respect to supervisory style, Dr. P self-identifies as having an attractive style and is comfortable in a warm and supportive role. She feels that this style will help her explore what may be troubling Susan. At the next supervision session, Dr. P discloses her perception that the past two sessions have felt different from their previous sessions and in an attempt to share power she would like to collaborate with Susan in developing ways to enhance their work in supervision. Susan remains silent for a moment and then reveals that she is not clear about Dr. P's perception of Susan's clinical skills. Susan expresses anxiety over her upcoming application for internship and who to ask for a recommendation. She had automatically thought of Dr. P., but then realized that although they have had meaningful discussions about clients and enjoy a comfortable working relationship, Susan feels as though she is not clear what Dr. P expects of her clinically or with respect to supervision; furthermore, Susan has not received clear feedback on her counseling skills. Dr. P realizes although she established a good rapport with Susan and a nurturing and supportive environment in supervision, she failed to clearly identify the evaluation criteria for Susan or to offer specific feedback on her counseling skills. Dr. P acknowledges her error to Susan, and suggests that they spend time that session discussing their respective expectations of supervision. In a further effort to empower Susan, Dr. P and Susan agree to each review the same client tape for the next supervision session and to discuss their perceptions of Susan's clinical strengths and growth edges:

In this supervisory case example, Susan's resistance, anxiety, and nondisclosure contributed to a ruptured supervisory alliance. Similarly, Dr. P's failure to clearly identify expectations and provide feedback played a part in the strained supervisory relationship. Dr. P then utilized a warm supervisory style in disclosing her perception of the relationship rupture and worked on sharing power with Susan to strengthen the supervisory alliance.

Supervisory Process and The Supervisory Relationship

Parallel Process

Friedlander, Siegel, and Brenock (1989) defined the parallel process as "a phenomena whereby trainees unconsciously present themselves to their supervisor as their clients have presented to them. The process reverses when the trainee adopts attitudes and behaviors of the supervisor in relating to the client" (p. 149). It may be noted that when the concept of parallel process was first introduced it was believed to be unidirectional with the supervisee–client relationship being mirrored in the supervisor–supervisee relationship. Later Doehrman's (1976) dissertation research findings highlighted the bidirectionality of this process. Mothersole (1999) has suggested a possible third aspect of this process whereby the supervisee may be broadcasting problematic issues in both directions and impacting both the supervisory as well as the counseling relationship. Additionally, Jacobsen (2007) based on his case study also highlights the inadequacy of a bidirectional description of the parallel process. Rather, he suggests that these processes are kaleidoscopic as "one figure is mirrored and rotated along many axes" (p. 32). Various research studies have been carried out to confirm or refute the existence of the parallel process as well as to understand its implications.

In a case study investigation of this parallel process, Friedlander et al. (1989) found interconnections between the counseling and supervisory processes: the supervisee held similar evaluations of both the supervision and counseling processes, clients rated the counseling session more favorably than the counselor trainee and the supervisee rated the supervision session more favorably than the supervisor, and the supervisor lead and the supervisee cooperated in the supervision session and the counselor trainee lead and the client cooperated in the counseling session. Further, both relationships were characterized as friendly and supportive with little conflict and were considered relatively successful in terms of outcome.

More recently, Raichelson, Herron, Primavera, and Ramirez (1997) found empirical validation of the theoretical literature about the existence of the parallel process, its utilization in supervision, its applicability to a variety of theoretical orientations, and its impact on supervisor and supervisee. Specifically, they found that supervisors with a psychodynamic orientation were more likely to attend to the parallel process than supervisors from other orientations. Similarly, Jacobsen (2007) in a case study of supervision regarding a client with schizophrenia found evidence for the existence of parallel processes and highlighted its potential use in fostering insight and understanding of the therapeutic relationship. Additionally, Morrissey and Tribe (2001) not only convey the usefulness of the parallel process in the growth and development of the supervisee, but also suggest that it enhances the teaching and learning of the supervisor by helping them monitor their own relationships with their supervisees. Ladany, Constantine, Miller, Erickson, and Muse-Burke (2000) found that the parallel process was relevant in the understanding and possibly the resolution of countertransference reactions. Patton and Kivlighan (1997) found the week-to-week fluctuations in the quality of the supervisory relationship predictive of the fluctuations in the therapeutic alliance of the supervisee and client. Williams (2000) has found a link between the interpersonal styles of the supervisor and supervisee with a greater affiliative interpersonal style of the supervisor being associated with less controlling or dominant style of the supervisee. As Shulman (2005) points out in his discussion of empirical and clinical evidence regarding supervision, there is a parallel process involved in most supervisory relationships and effective supervision can help increase the possibility of effective practice.

Ellis and Douce (1994) suggested that the resolution of various issues raised in the supervisory relationship through the parallel process may well lead to the resolution of similar issues in the counseling relationship. Attending to the parallel processes occurring in supervision, understanding the interpersonal dynamics that are giving rise to the problem issues, and responding to them within supervision in a manner that is different from the trainee's response in the counseling session will ultimately help the trainee's learning (Ellis & Douce, 1994). Similarly, Neufeldt, Iverson, and Juntunen (1995) suggest that supervisors may model how to respond to the client issues within the supervisory relationship. Jacobsen (2007) suggests the primacy of containing the anxiety of the supervisee and then interpreting the parallel process and negotiate it within the supervisory relationship. He stresses the importance of concordance in the way the supervisor models responses: "the supervisor's *way* of intervening is in accord with the verbal *content* of his interventions and the *spirit* of what he wants to convey" (p. 32, italics in the original). Additionally, Shohet and Wilmot (1991) suggest that the supervisee may resolve the parallel process by noticing and addressing atypical reactions in the supervisory relationship. They further highlight the importance of the supervisory relationship (its openness as well as a focus on the here and now of supervision and interpersonal interactions) in allowing for a resolution of the parallel processes. Morrissey and Tribe (2001) in their overview also highlight the importance of the supervisees' readiness and understanding of the concept of parallel process. They suggest that a lack of understanding may in fact make the use of parallel processes counterproductive to the supervisees' learning. Interestingly, some researchers, while acknowledging the value of the parallel process, express caution against its overuse or irresponsible invocation within the supervisory relationship (see for example, Feiner, 1994; Feltham & Dryden, 1994; Schimel, 1984).

Issues of Ethnic and Racial Identity

With an increasing awareness of how different racial and ethnic identities differentially influence human interactions (especially the research regarding the counseling relationship) comes the realization that these issues may well impact the supervisory relationship as well (see for example, Helms & Cook, 1999). Race and ethnicity has become the central defining feature of individual differences and may be important in multiple areas from case conceptualization to assessment.

Fong and Lease (1997) highlight the typical challenges a White counselor is likely to face in providing culturally sensitive supervision: unintentional racism, power dynamics, issues of trust, and communication issues. Further, they suggest that it is considered the supervisor's privilege to initiate a discussion of racial and ethnic issues (see for example, Kleintjes & Swartz, 1996). This becomes relevant in the light of Duan and Roehlke's (2001) findings that supervisors reported having initiated more discussion on racial and cultural issues than supervisees perceived. In contrast, when a Black supervisor works with a White supervisee, issues of trust and communication become predominant (see Priest, 1994; Williams & Halgin, 1995). Priest (1994) highlighted the possible negative expectations that White supervisee's may carry as well as the potential for harmful miscommunication due to ignorance of differential communication styles. Remington and DaCosta (1989) highlight the need to address such multicultural issues right from the beginning rather than waiting for any problems or conflict to arise (see also Estrada, Frame, & Williams, 2004).

Cook (1994) suggested that power dynamics play out in two ways within the supervisory relationship for a White supervisor and a supervisee from a minority group: (a) the supervisor has more power than the supervisee, and

(b) the supervisor also wields greater power as a dominant group member. This negotiation of power is further complicated by the unintentional racism of supervisors who are unaware of their own racial identity development (see Cook, 1994; Fong & Lease, 1997). Cook (1994) suggests that when a supervisor's racial identity is less well-developed than the supervisee's, the result will be regressive supervision, whereas when the supervisor's identity is better developed than the supervisee's, progressive supervision will occur. Similarly, Ladany, Brittan-Powell, and Pannu (1997) found that a matched high racial identity development was predictive of the supervisory alliance, was associated with positive feelings of liking and trust for each other, and influential in multicultural competence development. Progressive interaction was the next best, while regressive interactions and matched low racial identity development were the least influential in terms of multicultural competence development. Ladany, Inman, Constantine, and Hofheinz (1997) have also highlighted the association between racial identity development and the self-perceptions of multicultural competence, though not necessarily with multicultural case conceptualization ability.

Interestingly, Inman (2006) found that supervisor multicultural competence was positively associated with supervisory working alliance and perceived supervision satisfaction and had a negative effect on trainee etiology conceptualization abilities. Gatmon et al. (2001) conducted a study on the impact of discussion of cultural variables within the supervisory relationship. They found that only limited discussions occurred but when these discussions did occur, supervisees reported enhanced supervisory working alliance and increased satisfaction with supervision. Burkard et al. (2006) also found that culturally responsive supervision (where supervisees felt supported for exploring cultural issues) positively affected the supervisee, the supervision relationship, and client outcomes. In contrast, culturally unresponsive supervision (where cultural issues were ignored, actively discounted, or dismissed by supervisors) negatively impacted these variables. On a disturbing note, they also found that supervisees of color experienced more unresponsive supervision with greater negative effects than European American supervisees. Similarly, Constantine and Sue (2007) have also found that Black supervisees working with White supervisors are likely to experience microaggressions through invalidation of racial–cultural issues, stereotypic assumptions about Black clients as well as Black supervisees, interactions (like evaluative feedback) being impacted by the supervisor's fear of being viewed as racist, primary focus on clinical weaknesses, blaming clients of color for problems stemming from oppression, and offering culturally insensitive treatment recommendations. Not unnaturally, such microaggressions had a detrimental impact on the Black trainees, the supervisory relationship, as well as an indirect negative impact on clients of color. These findings highlight the pressing need for culturally sensitive supervision practices. Tummala-Narra (2004) further proposes that the integration of issues of racial and cultural diversity in clinical supervision is an essential component of clinical competence with important implications for provision of services to ethnic minorities and better understanding of the clients' intrapsychic and interpersonal worlds.

Some of the other factors found to be important in cross-cultural supervision include: perceived conditional interest expressed in an atmosphere of caring and perception that the supervisor liked them (Cook & Helms, 1988); perception of the relationship and perception of positive attitudes toward each other (Duan & Roehlke, 2001); perceptions of openness and support, culturally relevant counseling, opportunities to work in multicultural activities, lack of supervisor cultural awareness, and questioning supervisee abilities due to cultural factors (Fukuyama, 1994). Interestingly, McRoy, Freeman, Logan, and Blackmon (1986) found that both supervisees and supervisors expected more problems than benefits from a cross-cultural supervisory relationship.

Another important factor in the discussion of multicultural issues is the impact of other diversity factors like nationality, gender, sexuality, religious/spiritual orientation, and so on. Gubi (2007), for instance, found that many trainees do not report on their use of prayer in counseling to their supervisors because they do not perceive a culture of openness toward the use of prayer in counseling. Killian (2001) has highlighted the complexities of supervision of international students, where certain aspects of cultural and value differences may get overlooked because of a lack of awareness or uncertainty about how to respond to them.

Issues of Gender

As with many issues, it is important for supervisors to consider the ways that gender impact their behavior in interpersonal relationships (Doughty & Leddick, 2007; Ladany et al., 2005; Nelson, 1991). The literature has provided some evidence that gender influences supervisors' behavior. Female supervisors tend to display a greater relational focus and spend more time in supervision sessions on the trainee than did male supervisors. Male supervisors tend to devote more attention and time to male trainee's clients (Sells, Goodyear, Lichtenberg, & Polkinghorne, 1997). Likewise, supervisees may expect a female supervisor to be more nurturing than a male supervisor, whereas a male supervisor may be expected to focus more on the appropriateness of the supervisee's action than a female supervisor (Borders & Leddick, 1987). In this section, we will focus on issues surrounding empowerment for female supervisees and gender role conflict for male supervisees.

A discouraging find from a series of studies has shown that both male and female supervisors are less likely to empower female trainees (Chung,

Marshall, & Gordon, 2001; Granello, 2003; Granello, Beamish, & Davis, 1997; Nelson & Holloway, 1990). Specifically, Nelson and Friedlander (2001) showed that supervisors, regardless of gender, were less likely to promote the assumption of power by female supervisees compared to male supervisees. Furthermore, female supervisees more often displayed a deferential interaction pattern with the supervisor. The authors expressed their concern:

> It appears that individuals in the expert role, regardless of gender, may assume more power in interaction with their female subordinates than with their male subordinates, either by withholding support for the female subordinates' attempts at exerting power or by simply exerting stronger influence with female subordinates. In the supervisory relationship the female trainee may respond to this stance on the part of her supervisor by declining opportunities to assert herself as an expert. It appears that equal power for trainees may not be engendered across supervision contexts. This lack of parity in the process may result in the disempowerment of women in supervision and may influence the development of a female counselor's professional identity (p. 479).

Likewise, other research shows that female and male supervisors asked female supervisees for their opinion in supervision half as often as male supervisees (Granello et al., 1997). These authors concluded that type of supervision provided to male supervisees reflects developmental models of supervision, whereas that for females did not. In an analogue study, findings suggest that male supervisors were more likely than female supervisors to evaluate a female negatively (Chung et al., 2001). Given the overrepresentation of male supervisors and female supervisees, the authors urge supervisors to consider the impact of gender issues on evaluation. Biased evaluations, Chung et al. (2001) caution, could adversely impact female trainees' self-efficacy, self-esteem, and damage the supervisory relationship.

An interesting finding in a follow-up study was that although male trainees offered more suggestions and were asked their opinion more in supervision by supervisors, the ideas of female supervisees were more often accepted and followed by supervisors, regardless of the supervisor's gender (Granello, 2003). Further research shows that trainees who discussed gender similarities and differences with their supervisors also reported greater satisfaction with supervision (Gatmon et al., 2001). In contrast, some trainees who perceived that their supervisor was unwilling to discuss gender differences in supervision felt unsupported and discounted (Nelson & Friedlander, 2001; Walker et al., 2003).

Ladany and colleagues (2005) suggest that supervisors should initiate discussions about gender as well as other multicultural variables early on in the supervisory relationship so as to open a door for future discussions as the need arises. The authors further describe ways to repair misunderstandings between supervisor and supervisee that originate from gender role expectations. They define *misunderstanding* as either a stalemate in the supervisory relationship due to different behavioral expectations of gender roles or as *missed understandings* about how gender dynamics impact relationships. Ladany and colleagues recommend that in the process of empowering female supervisees, supervisors who identify that the supervisory relationship is the basis for gender misunderstandings should focus on the supervisory alliance and evaluation.

Gender role conflict for men refers to a sense of anxiety men feel regarding the discrepancy between traditional male role expectations, including restricted emotionality, and the intimacy demands of interpersonal relationships, specifically those of counseling and supervision (Levant, 1995; O'Neill, 1981). Indeed, men are often socialized to present an image of competence and that discussing feelings and displaying vulnerability are undesirable. Counseling and supervision, then, may produce a challenge for male supervisees as they are simultaneously required to identify and express emotions and engage in a training process in which they feel incompetent (Ladany et al., 2005). An informed supervisor can strengthen the supervisory relationship by being aware of male supervisee's potential vulnerability around competency and by being patient with their expressions of emotions. Attempting to facilitate emotional expression too early in supervision can weaken the supervisory alliance (Wester & Vogel, 2002). Instead, Ladany and colleagues recommend that supervisors allow male supervisees a grace period to develop comfort around the discussion of emotions. Also, the authors offer some cautions to both male and female supervisors in working with male supervisees—female supervisors may need to remind themselves to allow more time for male supervisees' emotionality to emerge whereas male supervisors may need to push back against the societal expectation that two men rarely discuss sensitive issues and feelings.

Sexual Orientation Issues

Issues surrounding sexual orientation of the client, counselor, and supervisor also influence the supervisory relationship (Halpert et al., 2007; Halpert & Pfaller, 2001; Russell & Greenhouse, 1997). Just as with other multicultural issues, a supervisor should be aware of his or her biases and values surrounding sexual orientation in order to facilitate a strong supervisory relationship. Furthermore, an understanding of homophobia and heterosexism is critical to facilitating professional development on the part of sexual minority trainees (Pfohl, 2004). Although the empirical research on the impact of sexual orientation issues on the supervisory relationship is scant, some studies suggest that sexual minority trainees have experienced discrimination or negative reactions (Gatmon et al., 2001; Murphy, Rawlings, & Howe, 2002; Pilkington & Cantor, 1996). Supervisees who discussed sexual orientation similarities and differences with their supervisors were satisfied with supervision and perceived the supervisor as being competent at providing good supervision (Gatmon et al., 2001). The ability of the supervisor to cultivate a safe atmosphere for discussing sexual orientation issues seems vital.

Theoretically, Halpert and colleagues (2007) advocate for the use of affirmative supervision to be used concurrently with the supervisor's existing theoretical model. The foundation of affirmative supervision is the notion that all sexual orientations and gender identities are equally valid. Two models of affirmation will be briefly described. First, Pett's Gay-Affirmative model of supervision (2000) includes several elements for an affirmative supervisor: (1) respect for gay, lesbian, bisexual, and heterosexual orientations as equally valid; (2) responsibility to engage in self-exploration regarding beliefs, attitudes, and feelings that could impede work with a sexual minority supervisee; (3) respect for supervisees' sexuality and choices; (4) understanding of the impact of homophobia and other biases on the lives of sexual minority individuals. Buhrke's (1989) conflictual situation model focuses on situations in working with homophobia in supervision. The four possibilities are divided into nonconflictual and conflictual. The most productive situation, according to Buhrke, is when neither the supervisor nor the supervisee is homophobic. Ironically, the most damaging situation, for a sexual minority client, is also nonconflictual in that both the supervisor and supervisee are homophobic. In this case, the supervisor and supervisee will reinforce each others' biases and fail to attend to the needs of the client. In the first of the two conflictual situations, when the supervisor is not homophobic but the supervisee is, Buhrke identifies that there is the possibility of discussion of sexual orientation issues and increased awareness on the part of the supervisee. A more challenging pairing happens when the supervisee is not homophobic but the supervisor expresses homophobic sentiments.

Supervisory Conflicts

Borders et al. (1991) contend that supervisors hold responsibility for developing, maintaining, and terminating the supervisory relationship. Hence, when struggles or conflicts arise within the supervisory relationship, the supervisor should consider such questions as: What part am I contributing to the problem? How is the supervisee contributing to the problem? What is the dynamic between us that is contributing to the problem? What are we doing that is working in supervision? How can I contribute a solution to the problem? In what ways could I utilize this problem to strengthen the supervisory relationship or facilitate growth on the part of my supervisee?

(Pearson, 2000). Conflicts in the supervisory relationship can arise from a variety of sources. In this section, conflicts arising from differences in expectations of and roles within supervision will be outlined. Olk and Friedlander (1992) defined role conflict in supervision as occurring when a supervisee is required by the supervisor to engage in behaviors that conflict with the supervisee's views or to engage in multiple roles that entail conflicting behaviors. For example, the expectations of the trainee's role as student may conflict with the expectations of the trainee's role as counselor. Role ambiguity results when supervisees are uncertain about their expected roles in supervision. Olk and Friedlander found that role ambiguity was more relevant for the novice as opposed to advanced trainees, whereas role conflict was more salient for advanced supervisees.

There is empirical support for the relationship of supervisory conflicts to the strength of the supervisory relationship (Gray et al., 2001; Ladany & Friedlander, 1995; Nelson & Friedlander, 2001). For instance, a strong supervisory bond, irrespective of agreement on tasks and goals, was related to less role conflict perceived by trainees (Ladany & Friedlander, 1995). Trainees who perceived more role conflict in supervision also reported less agreement with the supervisor on the goals and tasks of supervision, regardless of the strength of the bond (Ladany & Friedlander, 1995). Likewise, the goal–task component, but not the bond component, of the supervisory working alliance uniquely predicted trainee's role ambiguity. Trainees experienced less role ambiguity when the supervisor was explicit about expectations in supervision, irrespective of the strength of the perceived bond between the supervisor and supervisee. In other words, a trainee may like and trust a supervisor and still experience uncertainty about their roles in supervision (Ladany & Friedlander, 1995).

Literature on ineffective or lousy supervision also highlights the importance of managing conflicts within supervision (Magnuson, Wilcoxon, & Norem, 2000; Watkins, 1997). In a qualitative study of supervisees, Magnuson and colleagues found principles and spheres of lousy supervision. The overarching principles were: supervision was unbalanced with too much focus on some elements and not enough on others, supervision was developmentally inappropriate, supervisor was intolerant of differences, supervisor portrayed a poor model of professional/personal attributes, the supervisor was untrained in supervision, and supervisor was professionally apathetic. The three spheres included organizational/administrative; technical/cognitive; and relational/affective. In the latter sphere, supervisees reported that the supervisor failed to provide a safe environment, gave too much or too little corrective feedback, was insensitive to the supervisee's professional needs and avoided issues between supervisor and supervisee. One former supervisee related an experience when "… the relationship was not important. You were … told what to do and if you disagreed, God help you. …When you're called names, browbeaten, and told you're stupid, dumb, worthless, inferior … it's very difficult to hear anything else the person is saying." Likewise, Watkins suggested that ineffective supervisors manifest lower skill levels, display higher levels of intolerance, fail to establish a strong supervisory working alliance, and ignore issues of parallel process and countertransference within supervision. By identifying potentially damaging supervisor behaviors and practices, it is hoped that supervisors will increase their awareness of such possibilities as they work on building a supervisory relationship.

Ethical Issues

It is expected that supervisors will adhere to the ethical guidelines of their respective professions and to assist their supervisees in developing strong ethical understanding (Borders, 2005; Gottlieb, Robinson, & Younggren, 2007). However, supervision requires additional roles and expertise; hence, supervisors need to review ethical standards, such as "Ethical Guidelines for Counseling Supervisors" (Association for Counselor Education and Supervision [ACES], 1995) specific to supervision in directing their work with supervisees. Research on supervisor's ethical practices shows that in general, most supervisors engage in ethical practices in counseling and supervision (e.g., Erwin, 2000; Ladany, Lehrman-Waterman, Molinaro, & Wolgast, 1999). There are situations, however, when supervisors did not exclusively adhere appropriately. Supervisees in one study, for example, reported that more than half of their supervisors did not follow at least one ethical guidelines (Ladany et al., 1999). Ethical violations reported by supervisees were in the following domains: (a) performance evaluation and monitoring of supervisee activities (33%); (b) confidentiality issues in supervision (18%); (c) ability to work with alternative perspectives (18%); (d) session boundaries and respectful treatment (13%); (e) orientation to professional roles and monitoring of site standards (9%); (f) expertise/competency issues (9%); (g) disclosure to clients (8%); (h) crisis coverage and intervention (7%); (i) multicultural sensitivity to clients (7%); (j) multicultural sensitivity to trainees (7%); (k) dual roles (6%); (l) termination and follow-up issues (5%); and (m) sexual issues (1%). The researchers also investigated the impact of supervisors' adherence to ethical guidelines on the supervisory relationship. Results showed that supervisees who indicated that their supervisors adhered to ethical guidelines also reported strong supervisory working alliances. Conversely, supervisees whose supervisors demonstrated less adherence to ethical guidelines reported a weaker supervisory alliance. Indeed Ladany et al. showed that more than 47% of the variance in the supervisory working alliance was attributable to the supervisors' ethical practices.

Games Supervisees and Supervisors Play

Berne (1961) suggests that games are a goal-directed set of actions with concealed motivations behind the individual's actions. Within the supervisory relationship, games may emerge in order to deal with the anxiety, shame, discomfort, and interpersonal conflict between the supervisor and supervisee. Kadushin (1968) defined supervisory games as "recurrent interactional incidents between supervisor and supervisee that have a payoff for one of the parties" (p. 23). Typically, games within the supervisory relationship accrue gains like increased power and control, reduction in anxiety and distress, or a reprieve from conflictual interactions. The excessive use of games will serve to block the supervisory process and inhibit trainee's learning and growth. Kadushin (1968) suggests that supervisee's may initiate games due to feelings of inadequacy about their work or their self. He has highlighted four possible series of games that supervisees may play. These games are highlighted in Table 2.1. Additionally, supervisors may initiate games (Hawthorne, 1975; Kadushin, 1968) when they feel threatened, feel uncertain and uncomfortable in their role, are hesitant to use their authority, or feel hostility toward their supervisee. Hawthorne (1975) has highlighted two categories of supervisor initiated games: (1) abdication, which involves giving up responsibility, and (2) power, which keeps the relationship closed and fosters a feeling of helplessness in the supervisee. Examples of supervisor games are highlighted in Table 2.2.

Given the detrimental impact of supervisory games (whether initiated by the supervisee or supervisor) it becomes imperative that supervisors remain alert to their existence within the supervisory relationship and take appropriate steps to reduce their incidence. Kadushin (1968) has forwarded many suggestions regarding the identification and reduction of game playing within the supervisory relationship. As feelings of inadequacy may trigger game playing by the supervisee, he suggests that supervisors provide positive feedback and encourage the development of healthy self-efficacy in the supervisees. Highlighting the (largely threatening) changes in thinking and believing entailed in learning the art of counseling, he suggests the use of empathy with regard to the ambiguity and confusion that the trainee is experiencing. Further, he suggests that supervisor self-awareness and willingness to risk anger, hostility, and rejection are key to avoiding both supervisee and supervisor games. Open relationships allowing for direct communication and utilizing anxiety and conflict as tools for learning will reduce the possibility of playing games.

Kadushin (1968) also suggests steps to take once games are initiated such that the problems can be dealt with and the supervisory relationship can be strengthened. He suggests that the supervisor may utterly refuse to

Table 2.1 Games Supervisees Play

Series 1: Manipulating Demand Levels

Two Against the Agency or Seducing the Subversive. An attempt to reduce supervisor's enforcement of agency rules and regulations through a focus on the needs of the client population.

Be Nice to Me Because I Am Nice to You. Use of flattery to soften the evaluative focus of the supervisee's client contacts.

Series 2: Redefining the Relationship

Protect the Sick and Infirm; OR Treat Me, Don't Beat Me. An appeal to the counselor in the supervisor through a revelation of personal concerns.

Evaluation Is Not for Friends. Redefining the relationship on more social, informal terms with the expectation that friends are less accountable.

Maximum Feasible Participation. A stress on the peer–peer relationship such that the supervisee gains extensive decision-making power regarding what he or she needs to know.

Series 3: Reducing Power Disparity

If You Knew Dostoyevsky Like I Know Dostoyevsky. Highlights the intellectual power of the supervisee and his/her ability to educate the supervisor.

So What Do You Know About It? Alluding to own knowledge about an area where the supervisor has little expertise or experience.

All or Nothing at All. The supervisee seeks broader visions and the greater meaning of life, suggesting that the supervisor has abandoned his/her idealism.

Series 4: Controlling the Situation

I Have a Little List. Utilizing a list of work-related concerns to control and direct the supervisor's attention away from the supervisee.

Heading Them Off at the Pass. Indulging in self-flagellation in order to elicit reassurance from the supervisor.

Little Old Me. Feigning weakness in order to seek "prescriptions" of what to do from the supervisor.

I Did It Like You Told Me. Hostile interactions involving "spiteful obedience" that aims at putting the supervisor on the defensive.

It's All So Confusing. Seeking suggestions and guidance from multiple sources in an attempt to erode the supervisor's authority.

What You Don't Know Won't Hurt Me. Employing selective sharing in order to present a favorable picture and maintain distance between the supervisee and supervisor.

Source: Adapted from J. L. Muse-Burke, N. Ladany, & M. D. Deck, 2001, The supervisory relationship, In L. Bradley & N. Ladany (Eds.), *Counselor supervision: Principles, process, and practice* (3rd ed., pp. 28–62), Philadelphia, PA: Brunner-Routledge.

Table 2.2 Games Supervisors Play

Games of Abdication

They Won't Let Me. Avoidance of decision making through a projection of responsibility onto the agency or institutional rules or authorities.

Poor Me. Using excessive demands of other tasks as an excuse to avoid supervision commitments with the implication that the supervisee should not make additional demands.

I'm Really One of You OR I'm Really a Nice Guy. Approval seeking, either through siding with the supervisee's point of view or based on personal qualities.

One Good Question Deserves Another. Responding to a question with another question in order to stall for time or to avoid answering, deciding, or disclosing information to the supervisee.

Games of Power

Remember Who's Boss. Explicit reminders of power and authority (through memos, evaluations, and manner of address), with the aim of blocking contradictions and assuming an omnipotent position.

I'll Tell on You. Threatening disciplinary action by a higher power that allows for both retention of power and abdication of responsibility.

Parent (Father or Mother) Knows Best. Invoking own experience and wisdom with the aim of preserving and guiding the helpless, dependent supervisee.

I'm Only Trying to Help, OR I Know You Can't Really Do It Without Me. Lowered expectations with assumptions of supervisee incompetence or failure disguised in a cloak of help and caring.

I Wonder Why You Really Asked That Question. Retaining control through the implication that supervisee's question denotes psychological resistance; the supervisor remains in power while avoiding validation of the supervisee's viewpoint or hypothesis.

Source: Adapted from J. L. Muse-Burke, N. Ladany, & M. D. Deck, 2001, The supervisory relationship, In L. Bradley & N. Ladany (Eds.), *Counselor supervision: Principles, process, and practice* (3rd ed., pp. 28–62), Philadelphia, PA: Brunner-Routledge.

play the supervisee's game or use gradual interpretation and confrontation to manage game playing. However, he cautions that the timing and dosage of the confrontation should be carefully monitored and the supervisor needs to remain compassionate about the supervisee concerns that triggered the games in the first place. It should be noted that many games carry benefits for both the supervisee *and* the supervisor and hence the supervisor may find it difficult to resist game playing. It is very important that the supervisor remain aware of his or her own roles and needs as well as be attentive to the needs of the supervisee.

Concluding Thoughts

We have asserted throughout this chapter that the supervisory relationship is essential to effective supervision. We conclude this chapter by briefly describing research supporting the relationship between the supervisory alliance and supervisory outcomes. For instance, a trainee's self-efficacy has been shown to significantly relate to supervisory alliance (Efstation et al., 1990). Furthermore, the supervisee's perception of the supervisory alliance was significantly related to the client's perception of the counseling alliance as well as to a trainee's treatment adherence (Patton & Kivlighan, 1997). Finally, trainees perceived negative events within supervision to have a detrimental impact on their current training experience, general training experience, and counseling alliance with clients (Ramos-Sanchez et al., 2002). These findings underscore the centrality of the supervisory relationship to effective supervision.

In this chapter, several elements of the supervisory relationship were presented. Bordin's (1983) supervisory working alliance was conceptualized as a definition of the supervisory relationship containing three components: (1) mutual agreement and understanding between the supervisor and supervisee of the goals of supervision; (2) mutual agreement and understanding of the tasks of the supervisee and supervisor; and (3) the emotional bond between the supervisee and supervisor. We also discussed the phases of supervision with the beginning, mature, and terminating stage as well as the possibility of supervision to transform into a mentoring relationship. Factors that contribute to the development and maintenance of strong supervisory relationships were presented including supervisors' effective evaluation practices and the ability of the supervisor and supervisee to repair ruptures in the supervisory alliance. In addition, supervisees' resistance, anxiety, disclosures, and nondisclosures within the supervisory relationship can impact the supervisory working alliance. Likewise, supervisors' supervisory style, interpersonal power, disclosures, and nondisclosures were shown to influence the supervisory relationship. The impact of supervisory interaction variables such as parallel process, race/ethnic identity, gender identity, and issues surrounding sexual orientation on the supervisory relationship was discussed. Finally, we noted the games supervisors and supervisees may play in supervision.

Although there is a considerable body of literature on the supervisory relationship, we caution the reader in assuming that she or he now has a comprehensive understanding of the supervisory relationship. Rather we hope that theorists and researchers alike will be stimulated to further investigate this vital topic in contributing to the foundation on which supervisees and supervisors can form effective supervisory relationships.

References

Allen, G. J., Szollos, S. J., & Williams, B. E. (1986). Doctoral students' comparative evaluations of best and worst psychotherapy supervision. *Professional Psychology: Research and Practice, 17*(2), 91–99.

Association for Counselor Education and Supervision. (1995). Ethical guidelines for counseling supervisors. *Counselor Education and Supervision, 34*(3), 270–276.

Bahrick, A. S. (1990). Role induction for counselor trainees: Effects on the supervisory working alliance. *Dissertation Abstracts International, 51*(3-B), 1484–1484 (Abstract No. 1991-51645).

Bahrick, A. S., Russell, R. K., & Salmi, S. W. (1991). The effects of role induction on trainees' perceptions of supervision. *Journal of Counseling and Development, 69*, 434–438.

Baird, B. N. (1999). *The internship, practicum, and field placement handbook: A guide for the helping professions* (2nd ed.). Upper Saddle River, NJ: Prentice-Hall.

Baker, D. E. (1990). The relationship of the supervisory working alliance to supervisor and supervisee narcissism, gender, and theoretical orientation. *Dissertation Abstracts International, 51*(7-B), 3602–3603. (Abstract No. 1991-54991).

Bernard, J. M. (1997). The discrimination model. In C. E. J. Watkins (Eds.), *Handbook of psychotherapy supervision* (pp. 310–327). Hoboken, NJ: John Wiley & Sons.

Bernard, J. M., & Goodyear, R. K. (2009). *Fundamentals of Clinical Supervision* (4th ed.). Upper Saddle River, NJ: Pearson.

Berne, E. (1961). *Transactional analysis in psychotherapy: A systematic individual and social psychiatry*. New York, NY: Grove Press.

Black, B. (1988). Components of effective and ineffective psychotherapy supervision as perceived by supervisees with different levels of clinical experience (Doctoral dissertation, Columbia University, 1987). *Dissertation Abstracts International, 48*, 3105B.

Blocher, D. H. (1983). Toward a cognitive-developmental approach to counseling supervision. *The Counseling Psychologist, 11*, 27–34.

Borders, L. D. (2005). Snapshot of clinical supervision in counseling and counselor education: A five-year review. *Clinical Supervision, 24*(1–2), 69–113.

Borders, L. D., Bernard, J. M., Dye, H. A., Fong, M. L., Henderson, P., & Nance, D. W. (1991). Curriculum guide for training counseling supervisors: Rationale, development, and implementation. *Counselor Education and Supervision, 31*, 58–82.

Borders, L. D., & Leddick, G. R. (1987). *Handbook of Counseling Supervision*. Alexandria, VA: Association for Counselor Education and Supervision.

Bordin, E. S. (1983). A working alliance based model of supervision. *The Counseling Psychologist, 11*, 35–41.

Brehm, S. S., & Brehm, J. W. (1981). *Psychological reactance: A theory of freedom and control*. New York, NY: John Wiley & Sons.

Buhrke, (1989). Incorporating lesbian and gay issues into counselor training: A resource guide. *Journal of Counseling and Development, 68*, 77–80.

Burkard, A. W., Johnson, A. J., Madson, M. B., Pruitt, N. T., Contreras-Tadych, D. A., Kozlowski, J. M., . . . Knox, S. (2006). Supervisor cultural responsiveness and unresponsiveness in cross-cultural supervision. *Journal of Counseling Psychology, 53*(3), 288–301.

Burke, W. R., Goodyear, R. K., & Guzzard, C. R. (1998). Weakenings and repairs in supervisory alliances: A multiple-case study. *American Journal of Psychotherapy, 52*(4), 450–462.

Chung, Y. B., Marshall, J. A., & Gordon, L. L. (2001). Racial and gender biases in supervisory evaluation and feedback. *Clinical Supervisor, 20*(1), 99–111.

Constantine, M. G., & Sue, D. W. (2007). Perceptions of racial microaggressions among black supervisees in cross-racial dyads. *Journal of Counseling Psychology, 54*(2), 142–153.

Cook, D. A. (1994). Racial identity in supervision. *Counselor Education and Supervision, 34*(2), 132–141.

Cook, D. A., & Helms, J. E. (1988). Visible racial/ethnic group supervisees' satisfaction with cross-cultural supervision as predicted by relationship characteristics. *Journal of Counseling Psychology, 35*(3), 268–274.

Costa, L. (1994). Reducing anxiety in live supervision. *Counselor Education and Supervision, 34,* 30–40.

Doehrman, M. (1976). Parallel processes in supervision and psychotherapy. *Bulletin of the Menninger Clinic, 40,* 3–104.

Dombeck, M. T., & Brody, S. L. (1995). Clinical supervision: A three-way mirror. *Archives of Psychiatric Nursing, 9,* 3–10.

Doughty, E. A., & Leddick, G. R. (2007). Gender differences in the supervisory relationship. *Journal of Professional Counseling: Practice, Theory, & Research, 35,* 17–30.

Dowd, E. T. (1989). Stasis and change in cognitive psychotherapy: Client resistance and reactance as mediating variables. In W. Dryden & P. Trower (Eds.), *Cognitive psychotherapy: Stasis and change* (pp. 139–158). New York, NY: Springer-Verlag.

Duan, C., & Roehlke, H. (2001). A descriptive 'snapshot' of cross-racial supervision in university counseling center internships. *Journal of Multicultural Counseling and Development, 29*(2), 131–146.

Efstation, J. F., Patton, M. J., & Kardash, C. M. (1990). Measuring the working alliance in counselor supervision. *Journal of Counseling Psychology, 37*(3), 322–329.

Ekstein, R., & Wallerstein, R. S. (1972). *The teaching and learning of psychotherapy* (2nd ed.). New York, NY: Basic Books.

Ellis, M. V. (1991). Critical incidents in clinical supervision and in supervisor supervision: Assessing supervisory issues. *Journal of Counseling Psychology, 38,* 342–349.

Ellis, M. V., & Douce, L. A. (1994). Group supervision of novice clinical supervisors: Eight recurring issues. *Journal of Counseling and Development, 72,* 520–525.

Ellis, M. V., & Ladany, N. (1997). Inferences concerning supervisees and clients in clinical supervision: An integrative review. In C. E. J. Watkins (Eds.), *Handbook of psychotherapy supervision* (pp. 447–507). Hoboken, NJ: John Wiley & Sons.

Erwin, W. J. (2000). Supervisory moral sensitivity. *Counselor Education and Supervision, 40*(2), 115–127.

Estrada, D., Frame, M. W., & Williams, C. B. (2004). Cross-cultural supervision: Guiding the conversation toward race and ethnicity. *Journal of Multicultural Counseling and Development, 32,* 307–319.

Feiner, A. H. (1994). She wuz framed. *Contemporary Psychoanalysis, 30*(1), 48–56.

Feltham, C., & Dryden, W. (1994). *Developing Counsellor Supervision.* London, United Kingdom: Sage Publications.

Fong, M. L., & Lease, S. H. (1997). Cross-cultural supervision: Issues for the white supervisor. In D. B. Pope-Davis & H. L. K. Coleman (Eds.), *Multicultural counseling competencies: Assessment, education and training, and supervision.* (pp. 387–405). Thousand Oaks, CA: Sage Publications.

Freeman, S. C. (1993). Structure in counseling supervision. *Clinical Supervisor, 11*(1), 245–252.

Friedlander, M. L., Keller, K. E., Peca-Baker, T. A., & Olk, M. E. (1986). Effects of role conflict on counselor trainees' self-statements, anxiety level, and performance. *Journal of Counseling Psychology, 33*, 73–77.

Friedlander, M. L., Siegel, S. M., & Brenock, K. (1989). Parallel process in counseling and supervision: A case study. *Journal of Counseling Psychology, 36*, 149–157.

Friedlander, M. L., & Ward, L. G. (1984). Development and validation of the supervisory styles inventory. *Journal of Counseling Psychology, 4*, 541–557.

Fukuyama, M. A. (1994). Critical incidents in multicultural counseling supervision: A phenomenological approach to supervision research. *Counselor Education and Supervision, 34*(2), 142–151.

Gatmon, D., Jackson, D., Koshkarian, L., Martos-Perry, N., Molina, A., Patel, N., & Rodolfa, E. (2001). Exploring ethnic, gender, and sexual orientation variables in supervision: Do they really matter? *Journal of Multicultural Counseling and Development, 29*(2), 102–113.

Gottlieb, M. C., Robinson, K., & Younggren, J. N. (2007). Multiple relations in supervision: Guidance for administrators, supervisors, and students. *Professional Psychology: Research and Practice, 38*(3), 241–247.

Granello, D. H. (2003). Influence strategies in the supervisory dyad: An investigation into the effects of gender and age. *Counselor Education and Supervision, 42*(3), 189–202.

Granello, D. H., Beamish, P. M., & Davis, T. E. (1997). Supervisee empowerment: Does gender make a difference? *Counselor Education and Supervision, 36*(4), 305–317.

Grater, H. A. (1985). Stages in psychotherapy supervision: From therapy skills to skilled therapist. *Professional Psychology: Research and Practice, 16*, 605–610.

Gray, L. A., Ladany, N., Walker, J. A., & Ancis, J. R. (2001). Psychotherapy trainees' experience of counterproductive events in supervision. *Journal of Counseling Psychology, 48*(4), 371–383.

Gubi, P. (2007). Exploring the supervision experience of some mainstream counsellors who integrate prayer in counseling. *Counselling and Psychotherapy Research, 7*, 114–121.

Halpert, S. C., & Pfaller, J. (2001). Sexual orientation and supervision: Theory and practice. *Journal of Gay and Lesbian Social Services: Issues in Practice, Policy and Research, 13*(3), 23–40.

Halpert, S. C., Reinhardt, B., & Toohey, M. J. (2007). Affirmative clinical supervision. In K. J. Bieschke, R. M. Perez, K. A. DeBord, K. J. Bieschke, R. M. Perez & K. A. DeBord (Eds.), *Handbook of counseling and psychotherapy with lesbian, gay, bisexual, and transgender clients* (2nd ed., pp. 341–358). Washington, DC: American Psychological Association.

Harvey, C., & Katz, C. (1985). *If I'm so successful, why do I feel like a fake? The imposter phenomenon*. New York, NY: St. Martin's Press.

Hawthorne, L. (1975). Games supervisors play. *Social Work, 20*, 179–183.

Helms, J. E., & Cook, D. A. (1999). *Using race and culture in counseling and psychotherapy: Theory and process*. Boston, MA: Allyn & Bacon.

Heppner, P. P., & Roehlke, H. J. (1984). Differences among supervisees at different levels of training: Implications for a developmental model for supervision. *Journal of Counseling Psychology, 31*, 76–90.

Hoffman, L. W. (1994). The training of psychotherapy supervisors: A barren scape. *Psychotherapy in Private Practice, 13*, 23–42.

Holloway, E. L. (1987). Developmental models of supervision: Is it development? *Professional Psychology: Research and Practice, 18*, 209–216.

Holloway, E. L. (1992). Supervision: A way of teaching and learning. In S. D. Brown & R. W. Lent (Eds.), *Handbook of counseling psychology* (pp. 177–214). New York, NY: John Wiley & Sons.

Holloway, E. L. (1995). *Clinical supervision: A systems approach*. Thousand Oaks, CA: Sage Publications.

Holloway, E. L. (1997). Structures for the analysis and teaching of supervision. In C. E. J. Watkins (Eds.), *Handbook of psychotherapy supervision* (pp. 249–276). Hoboken, NJ: John Wiley & Sons.

Holloway, E. L., Freund, R. D., Gardner, S. L., Nelson, M. L., & Walker, B. E. (1989). Relation of power and involvement to theoretical orientation in supervision: An analysis of discourse. *Journal of Counseling Psychology, 36*, 88–102.

Hutt, C. H., Scott, J., & King, M. (1983). A phenomenological study of supervisees' positive and negative experiences in supervision. *Psychotherapy: Theory, Research & Practice, 20*(1), 118–123.

Horvath, A. O., & Greenberg, L. S. (1989). Development and validation of the working alliance inventory. *Journal of Counseling Psychology, 36*(2), 223–233.

Inman, A. G. (2006). Supervisor multicultural competence and its relation to supervisory process and outcome. *Journal of Marital and Family Therapy, 32*(1), 73–85.

Jacobs, C. (1991). Violations of the supervisory relationship: An ethical and educational blind spot. *Social Work, 36*, 130–135.

Jacobsen, C. H. (2007). A qualitative single case study of parallel processes. *Counseling and Psychotherapy Research, 7*(1), 26–33.

Johnson, W. B. (2003). A framework for conceptualizing competence to mentor. *Ethics and Behavior, 13*, 127–151.

Johnson, W. B. (2007). Transformational supervision: When supervisors mentor. *Professional Psychology: Research and Practice, 38*(3), 259–267.

Kadushin, A. (1968). Games people play in supervision. *Social Work, 13*(3), 23–32.

Kaplan, H. S. (1977). Training of sex therapists. In W. H. Masters, V. E. Johnson, & R. D. Kolodny (Eds.), *Ethical issues in sex therapy and research* (pp. 182–189). Boston, MA: Little, Brown.

Kauderer, S., & Herron, W. G. (1990). The supervisory relationship in psychotherapy over time. *Psychological Reports, 67*, 471–480.

Kennard, B. D., Stewart, S. M., & Gluck, M. R. (1987). The supervision relationship: Variables contributing to positive versus negative experiences. *Professional Psychology: Research and Practice, 18*, 172–175.

Killian, K. D. (2001). Differences making a difference: Cross-cultural interactions in supervisory relationships. *Journal of Feminist Family Therapy, 12*(2–3), 61–103.

Kleintjes, S., & Swartz, L. (1996). Black clinical psychology trainees at a 'White' South African university: Issues for clinical supervision. *Clinical Supervisor, 14*(1), 87–109.

Knox, S., Burkard, A. W., Edwards, L. M., Smith, J. J., & Schlosser, L. Z. (2008). Supervisors' reports of the effects of supervisor self disclosure on supervisees. *Psychotherapy Research, 18*(5), 543–559.

Ladany, N. (2004). Psychotherapy supervision: What lies beneath. *Psychotherapy Research, 14*, 19.

Ladany, N., Brittan-Powell, C. S., & Pannu, R. K. (1997). The influence of supervisory racial identity interaction and racial matching on the supervisory working alliance and supervisee multicultural competence. *Counselor Education and Supervision, 36*, 284–304.

Ladany, N., Constantine, M. G., Miller, K., Erickson, C. D., & Muse-Burke, J. L. (2000). Supervisor countertransference: A qualitative investigation into its identification and description. *Journal of Counseling Psychology, 47*, 102–115.

Ladany, N., Ellis, M. V., & Friedlander, M. L. (1999). The supervisory working, trainee self-efficacy, and satisfaction. *Journal of Counseling and Development, 77*, 447–455.

Ladany, N., & Friedlander, M. L. (1995). The relationship between the supervisory working alliance and trainee's experience of role conflict and role ambiguity. *Counselor Education and Supervision, 34*, 220–231.

Ladany, N., Friedlander, M. L., & Nelson, M. L. (2005). Repairing gender-related misunderstandings and missed understandings: It's not just "he said, she said." *Critical events in psychotherapy supervision: An interpersonal approach* (pp. 155–182). Washington, DC: American Psychological Association.

Ladany, N., Hill, C. E., Corbett, M. M., & Nutt, E. A. (1996). Nature, extent, and importance of what psychotherapy trainees do not disclose to their supervisors. *Journal of Counseling Psychology, 43*, 10–24.

Ladany, N., & Inman, A. G. (in press). Training and supervision. In E. A. Altmaier & J. I. Hansen (Eds.), *Oxford handbook of counseling psychology.* New York, NY: Oxford University Press.

Ladany, N., Inman, A. G., Constantine, M. G., & Hofheinz, E. W. (1997). Supervisee multicultural case conceptualization ability and self-reported multicultural competence as functions of supervisee racial identity and supervisor focus. *Journal of Counseling Psychology, 44*(3), 284–293.

Ladany, N., & Lehrman-Waterman, D. E. (1999). The content and frequency of supervisor self-disclosures and their relationship to supervisory style and the supervisor working alliance. *Counselor Education and Supervision, 38*, 143–160.

Ladany, N., Lehrman-Waterman, D., Molinaro, M., & Wolgast, B. (1999). Psychotherapy supervisor ethical practices: Adherence to guidelines, the supervisory working alliance, and supervisee satisfaction. *Counseling Psychologist, 27*(3), 443–475.

Ladany, N., & Melincoff, D. S. (1999). The nature of counselor supervisor nondisclosure. *Counselor Education and Supervision, 38*, 161–176.

Ladany, N., & Walker, J. A. (2003). Supervision self-disclosure: Balancing the uncontrollable narcissist with the indomitable altruist. *Journal of Clinical Psychology, 59*(5), 611–621.

Ladany, N., Walker, J. A., & Melincoff, D. S. (2001). Supervisory style: Its relation to the supervisory working alliance and supervisor self-disclosure. *Counselor Education and Supervision, 40*, 263–275.

Leddick, G. R., & Bernard, J. M. (1980). The history of supervision: A critical review. *Counselor Education and Supervision, 19*(3), 186–196.

Lehrman-Waterman, D., & Ladany, N. (2001). Development and validation of the evaluation process within supervision inventory. *Journal of Counseling Psychology, 48*(2), 168–177.

Levant, R. F. (1995). Toward the reconstruction of masculinity. In R. F. Levant & W. S. Pollack (Eds.), *A new psychology of men* (pp. 229–251). New York, NY: Basic Books.

Liddle, B. J. (1986). Resistance in supervision: A response to perceived threat. *Counselor Education and Supervision, 26*(2), 117–127.

Loganbill, C., Hardy, E., & Delworth, U. (1982). Supervision: A conceptual model. *The Counseling Psychologist, 10*(1), 3–42.

Magnuson, S., Wilcoxon, S. A., & Norem, K. (2000). A profile of lousy supervision: Experienced counselors' perspectives. *Counselor Education and Supervision, 39*, 189–202.

Martin, J. S., Goodyear, R. K., & Newton, F. B. (1987). Clinical supervision: An intensive case study. *Professional Psychology: Research and Practice, 18*, 225–235.

McCarthy, P., Sugden, S., Koker, M., & Lamendole, F. (1995). A practical guide to informed consent in clinical supervision. *Counselor Education and Supervision, 35*(2), 130–138.

McRoy, R. G., Freeman, E. M., Logan, S. L., & Blackmon, B. (1986). Cross-cultural field supervision: Implications for social work education. *Journal of Social Work Education, 22*, 50–56.

Morrissey, J., & Tribe, R. (2001). Parallel process in supervision. *Counseling Psychology Quarterly, 14*(2), 103–110.

Mothersole, G. (1999). Parallel process: A review. *Clinical Supervisor, 18*(2), 107–121.

Murphy, J. A., Rawlings, E. I., & Howe, S. R. (2002). A survey of clinical psychologists on treating lesbian, gay, and bisexual clients. *Professional Psychology: Research and Practice, 33*(2), 183–189.

Murphy, M. J., & Wright, D. W. (2005). Supervisees' perspectives of power use in supervision. *Journal of Marital and Family Therapy, 31*(3), 283–295.

Muse-Burke, J. L., Ladany, N., & Deck, M. D. (2001). The supervisory relationship. In L. Bradley & N. Ladany (Eds.), *Counselor supervision: Principles, process, and practice* (3rd ed., pp. 28–62). Philadelphia, PA: Brunner-Routledge.

Nelson, M. L. (1997). An interactional model for empowering women in supervision. *Counselor Education and Supervision, 37*, 125–139.

Nelson, M. L., & Friedlander, M. L. (2001). A close look at conflictual supervisory relationships: The trainee's perspective. *Journal of Counseling Psychology, 48*, 384–395.

Nelson, M. L., & Holloway, E. L. (1990). Relation of gender to power and involvement in supervision. *Journal of Counseling Psychology, 37*(4), 473–481.

Nelson, T. S. (1991). Gender in family therapy supervision. *Contemporary Family Therapy: An International Journal, 13*(4), 357–369.

Neufeldt, S. A., Iverson, J. N., & Juntunen, C. L. (1995). *Supervision strategies for the first practicum.* Alexandria, VA: American Counseling Association.

Olk, M. E., & Friedlander, M. L. (1992). Trainees' experiences of role conflict and role ambiguity in supervisory relationships. *Journal of Counseling Psychology, 39*(3), 389–397.

O'Neill, J. M. (1981). Male sex-role conflicts, sexism, and masculinity: Implications for men, women, and the counseling psychologist. *The Counseling Psychologist, 9,* 61–80.

Overholser, J. C. (2004). The four pillars of psychotherapy supervision. *The Clinical Supervisor, 23,* 1–13.

Patton, M. J., & Kivlighan, D. M., Jr. (1997). Relevance of the supervisory alliance to the counseling alliance and to treatment adherence in counselor training. *Journal of Counseling Psychology, 44*(1), 108–115.

Pearson, Q. M. (2000). Opportunities and challenges in the supervisory relationship: Implications for counselor supervision. *Journal of Mental Health Counseling, 22,* 283–294.

Pett, J. (2000). Gay, lesbian and bisexual therapy and its supervision. In D. Davies & C. Neal (Eds.), *Therapeutic perspectives on working with lesbian, gay and bisexual clients* (pp. 54–72). Maidenhead, Berkshire England: Open University Press.

Pfohl, A. H. (2004). The intersection of personal and professional identity: The heterosexual supervisor's role in fostering the development of sexual minority supervisees. *Clinical Supervisor, 23*(1), 139–164.

Pilkington, N. W., & Cantor, J. M. (1996). Perceptions of heterosexual bias in professional psychology programs: A survey of graduate students. *Professional Psychology: Research and Practice, 27*(6), 604–612.

Priest, R. (1994). Minority supervisor and majority supervisee: Another perspective of clinical reality. *Counselor Education and Supervision, 34*(2), 152–158.

Quarto, C. J. (2002). Supervisors' and supervisees' perceptions of control and conflict in counseling supervision. *The Clinical Supervisor, 21,* 21–37.

Rabinowitz, F. E., Heppner, P. P., & Roehlke, H. J. (1986). Descriptive study of process and outcome variables of supervision over time. *Journal of Counseling Psychology, 33*(3), 292–300.

Raichelson, S. H., Herron, W. G., Primavera, L. H., & Ramirez, S. M. (1997). Incidence and effects of parallel process in psychotherapy supervision. *The Clinical Supervisor, 15*(2), 37–48.

Ramos-Sanchez, L., Esnil, E., Goodwin, A., Riggs, S., Touster, L. O., Wright, L. K., . . . Rodolfa, E. (2002). Negative supervisory events: Effects on supervision satisfaction and supervisory alliance. *Professional Psychology: Research and Practice, 33,* 197–202.

Remington, G., & DaCosta, G. (1989). Ethnocultural factors in resident supervision: Black supervisor and white supervisees. *American Journal of Psychotherapy, 43*(3), 398–404.

Rioch, M. J., Coulter, W. R., & Weinberger, D. M. (1976). *Dialogues for therapists: Dynamics of learning and supervision.* San Francisco, CA: Jossey-Bass.

Ronnestad, M. H., & Skovholt, T. M. (1993). Supervision of beginning and advanced graduate students of counseling and psychotherapy. *Journal of Counseling Development, 71*, 396–405.

Russell, G. M., & Greenhouse, E. M. (1997). Homophobia I the supervisory relationship: A invisible intruder. *Psychoanalytic Review, 84*, 27–42.

Safran, J. D., & Muran, J. C. (1998). *The Therapeutic Alliance in Brief Psychotherapy.* Washington, DC: American Psychological Association.

Sansbury, D. L. (1982). Developmental supervision from a skills perspective. *Counseling Psychologist, 10*(1), 53–57.

Schauer, A. H., Seymour, W. R., & Geen, R. G. (1985). Effects of observation and evaluation on anxiety in beginning counselors: A social facilitation analysis. *Journal of Counseling and Development, 63*(5), 279–285.

Schimel, J. L. (1984). In pursuit of truth: An essay on an epistemological approach to psychoanalytic supervision. In L. Caligor, P. M. Bromberg, & J. D. Meltzer (Eds.). *Clinical perspectives on the supervision of psychoanalysis and psychotherapy* (pp. 231–241). New York, NY: Plenum Press.

Sells, J. N., Goodyear, R. K., Lichtenberg, J. W., & Polkinghorne, D. E. (1997). Relationship of supervisor and trainee gender to in-session verbal behavior and ratings of trainee skills. *Journal of Counseling Psychology, 44*(4), 406–412.

Shohet. R., & Wilmot, J. (1991). The key issue in the supervision of counsellors: The supervisory relationship. In W. Dryden & B. Thorne (Eds.), *Training and supervision for counselling in action* (pp. 87–98). London, UK: Sage Publication.

Shulman, L. (2005). The clinical supervisor-practitioner working alliance: A parallel process. *Clinical Supervisor, 24*(1–2), 23–47.

Skovholt, T. M., & Ronnestad, M. H. (1992). *The evolving professional self: Stages and themes in therapist and counselor development.* Chichester, England: Wiley.

Smith, T. R., Younes, L. K., & Lichtenberg, J. W. (2002). *Examining the working alliance in supervisory relationships: The development of the working alliance inventory of supervisory relationships.* (ERIC Document Reproduction Service No. ED471440)

Sommerfield, E., Orbach, I., Zim, S., & Mikulincer, M. (2008). An in-session exploration of ruptures in working alliance and their associations with clients' core conflictual relationship themes, alliance-related discourse, and clients' post-session evaluations. *Psychotherapy Research, 18*, 377–388.

Stoltenberg, C. (1981). Approaching supervision from a developmental perspective: The counselor complexity model. *Journal of Counseling Psychology, 28*, 59–65.

Stoltenberg, C. D., & Delworth, U. (1987). *Supervising counselors and therapists.* San Francisco. CA: Jossey-Bass.

Stoltenberg, C. D., & McNeill, B. W. (1997). Clinical supervision from a developmental perspective: Research and practice. In C. E. J. Watkins (Eds.), *Handbook of psychotherapy supervision* (pp. 184–202). Hoboken, NJ: John Wiley & Sons.

Stoltenberg, C. D., McNeill, B., & Delworth, U. (1998). *IDM supervision: An integrated developmental model for supervising counselors and therapists.* San Francisco, CA: Jossey-Bass.

Tummala-Narra, P. (2004). Dynamics of race and culture in the supervisory encounter. *Psychoanalytic Psychology, 21*(2), 300–311.

Usher, C. H., & Borders, L. D. (1993). Practicing counselors' preferences for supervisory style and supervisory emphasis. *Counselor Education and Supervision, 33*(2), 66–79.

Walker, J. A., Ladany, N., & Pate-Carolan, L. M. (2003). Gender-related events in psychotherapy supervision: Female trainee perspectives. *Counseling and Psychotherapy Research, 7*(1), 12–18.

Ward, L. G., Friedlander, M. L., Schoen, L. G., & Klein, J. C. (1985). Strategic self-presentation in supervision. *Journal of Counseling Psychology, 32,* 111–118.

Watkins, C. E., Jr. (1997). The ineffective psychotherapy supervisor: Some reflections about bad behaviors, poor process, and offensive outcomes. *Clinical Supervisor, 16*(1), 163–180.

Webb, A., & Wheeler, S. (1998). How honest do counsellors dare to be in the supervisory relationship? An exploratory study. *British Journal of Guidance and Counselling, 26*(4), 509–524.

Wester, S. R., & Vogel, D. L. (2002). Working with the masculine mystique: Male gender role conflict, counseling self-efficacy, and the training of male psychologists. *Professional Psychology: Research and Practice, 33*(4), 370–376.

Williams, A. B. (2000). Contribution of supervisors' covert communication to the parallel process (Doctoral dissertation, University of Houston, 2000). *Dissertation Abstracts International Section A: Humanities and Social Sciences, 61*(3-A), 1165.

Williams, S., & Halgin, R. P. (1995). Issues in psychotherapy supervision between the white supervisor and the black supervisee. *Clinical Supervisor, 13*(1), 39–61.

Wood, C. (2005). Supervisory working alliance: A model providing direction for college counseling supervision. *Journal of College Counseling, 8*(2), 127–137.

Worthen, V., & McNeill, B. W. (1996). A phenomenological investigation of "good" supervision events. *Journal of Counseling Psychology, 43*(1), 25–34.

Worthington, E. L., & Roehlke, H. J. (1979). Effective supervision as perceived by beginning counselors-in-training. *Journal of Counseling Psychology, 26,* 64–73.

Yourman, D. B. (2003). Trainee disclosure in psychotherapy supervision: The impact of shame. *Journal of Clinical Psychology, 59*(5), 601–609.

CHAPTER 3

A Multicultural Framework for Counselor Supervision

JULIE R. ANCIS and NICHOLAS LADANY

The demographic composition of the United States has become increasingly diverse. It is estimated that visible racial/ethnic minority groups will constitute a numerical majority between the years 2030 and 2050 (Sue & Sue, 1999; U.S. Census Bureau, 1996, 2001). Also, there have been significant demographic shifts in professional roles and positions, including a greater number of women entering the workforce and in supervisory positions (Gilbert & Rossman, 1992; Munson, 1997). Moreover, people who are lesbian, gay, bisexual, and transgendered have been increasingly recognized as deserving of human rights such as those in the workplace (e.g., in 2009 the U.S. President Obama authorized same-sex partner benefits for federal employees). All of these transformations have implications for both counseling and supervision, as the potential for multicultural interactions among supervisors, supervisees, and clients increase.

Attention to multicultural issues within supervision is essential to training counselors who are able to conduct ethical and effective practice with diverse clientele, as well as ensuring that supervisors are attending to the needs of diverse supervisees and clients. Research suggests that counselor trainees often possess racial, gender, and sexual orientation biases, limited self-awareness, and a lack of knowledge regarding multicultural counseling (Ancis & Sanchez-Hucles, 2000; Ancis & Szymanski, 2008; Johnson, Searight, Handal, & Gibbons, 1993; Ponterotto, 1988). Moreover, research has demonstrated that supervisees may perceive their supervisors as lacking in multicultural sensitivity toward clients, as well as toward supervisees (Fukuyama, 1994; Ladany, Lehrman-Waterman,

Molinaro, & Wolgast, 1999). Perhaps not coincidentally, many current supervisors likely did not receive multicultural counseling train- ing (or even training in supervision). Thus, supervisees may be more knowledgeable about multicultural counseling than their supervisors (Constantine, 1997; D'Andrea & Daniels, 1997). Overall, although the relevance of multicultural issues within supervision is rather clear, these issues have generally not been addressed in the supervision literature (Brown & Landrum-Brown, 1995; Kaduvettoor et al., 2009; Leong & Wagner, 1994).

Our chapter presents a comprehensive model of multicultural super- vision competence. This framework delineates the multiple dimensions within the context of supervision, thereby offering a definition of multicul- turally competent supervision. This comprehensive framework of multicul- tural competent supervision is intended to describe the salient dimensions of supervisor multicultural competence, thereby rectifying a diffuse and fragmented approach that has been the hallmark of the literature to date. Finally, we will present a case study that highlights the manner in which supervisor multicultural competence presents itself in supervision.

Counselor/Supervisee Multicultural Competence

In order to understand how supervision can enhance multicultural com- petence, we must first offer a conceptualization about how multicultural competence is exhibited, or not exhibited, by both the supervisee and supervisor. First, we believe it's important to clarify what is meant by mul- ticultural. In the literature, the term has tended to refer to race, and at times gender, perhaps at least in part, because the bulk of the literature has focused on these areas. We clarify from the outset that multicultural refers to multiple cultures and identities; including gender, race, ethnicity, sexual orientation, disability, socioeconomic status, age, and religion, as well as their intersections. We believe that counselor multicultural competence is an essential component of general counselor competence and as such, a definition of the latter is the first step to defining the former. We conceptu- alize and define general counselor competence (including supervisee com- petence that reflects competence displayed in supervision) in the context of education and training, based in part on general definitions of compe- tence (e.g., Ladany & Inman, in press; Ladany, Walker, Pate-Carolan, & Gray Evans, 2008; Rodolfa et al., 2005). Specifically, general counselor competence consists of three interrelated subconstructs: knowledge (e.g., foundations of counseling, research methods, theoretical approaches), self- awareness (e.g., self-reflective ability), and skills (e.g., nonverbals, helping skills, techniques).

With this scheme of general counselor competence in mind, and based on previous conceptualizations of counselor multicultural competence (e.g., Ancis, 2004; Ancis, & Ladany, 2001; Ancis, Szymanski, & Ladany, 2008; Arredondo et al., 1996; Atkinson, Morten, & Sue, 1993; Constantine & Ladany, 2000; Ridley, Mendoza, Kanitz, Angermeier, & Zenk, 1994; Sue, Arredondo, & McDavis, 1992; Sue et al., 1982; Sue & Sue, 1999), we similarly, and in a more circumscribed manner, define counselor multicultural competence as consisting of three interrelated subconstructs: multicultural knowledge, multicultural self-awareness, and multicultural skills. Multicultural knowledge is comprised of general knowledge about multicultural issues such as an academic or intellectual understanding of how factors such as gender, race, sexual orientation, disability, nationality, religion, and so forth, may influence a clients life; and multicultural knowledge unique to the specific clients seen for counseling (e.g., culture as expressed in one's family, specific religious beliefs, etc.).

Multicultural self-awareness refers to the ability to reflect upon and understand one's own multiple multicultural identities (e.g., gender identity), and how these identities are expressed in a counseling relationship (e.g., biases and personal values derived from one's multiple multicultural group memberships). The third subconstruct, multicultural skills, are reflected in multicultural counseling self-efficacy (i.e., confidence to perform particular multicultural skills) along with the adeptness to carry out these multicultural skills (e.g., multiculturally sensitive nonverbal displays, the ability to develop a multicultural counseling working alliance, and techniques and interventions that are culturally relevant to the work in counseling such as the discussion of racial similarities and differences between the counselor and client). There have been a variety of measures that have been created and to varying extents have been validated that supervisors can use to assess multicultural counselor competence. Such measures include: (a) Multicultural Awareness/Knowledge/Skills Survey (MAKSS; D'Andrea, Daniels, & Heck, 1991), Multicultural Awareness Knowledge Skills Survey-Counselor Edition, rev. (Kim, Cartwright, Asay, & D'Andrea, 2003); (b) Multicultural Counseling Inventory (MCI; Sodowsky, Taffe, Gutkin, & Wise, 1994); (c) Multicultural Counseling Knowledge and Awareness Scale (MCKAS; Ponterotto, Rieger, Gretchen, Utsey, & Austin, 1999); (d) The California Brief Cultural Competence Scale (Gamst et al., 2004); (e) the Sexual Orientation Counselor Competency Scale (Bidell, 2005); and (f) Counseling Women Competencies Scale (Ancis et al., 2008). A supervisor's first task is to understand and be able to assess counselor multicultural competence. However, in order to assess multicultural counselor competence, supervisors must have a level of multicultural competence themselves.

Supervisor Multicultural Competence

Supervisor multicultural competence, similar to counselor multicultural competence, can be defined as consisting of three interrelated subconstructs: multicultural knowledge, multicultural self-awareness, and multicultural skills. Next, these three subconstructs are defined and discussed.

Supervisor Multicultural Knowledge

Supervisor multicultural knowledge can be roughly divided into three areas: (1) knowledge about multicultural counseling competence; (2) supervision theory that attends to multicultural issues; and (3) ethics related to multicultural supervision. Knowledge about multicultural counselor competence has been addressed in the previous section and the later two areas will now be discussed in more detail.

Supervision Theory and Multiculturalism

Traditional models of supervision include psychotherapy theory-based supervision (e.g., Ekstein & Wallerstein, 1972; Rice, 1980; Watkins, 1997), interpersonal supervision models (e.g., Bernard, 1997; Holloway, 1992; Ladany, Friedlander, & Nelson, 2005), and developmental approaches to supervision (e.g., Chagon & Russell, 1995; Skovholt & Rønnestad, 1992; Stoltenberg, McNeill, & Delworth, 1998). Psychotherapy theory-based supervision includes approaches from many theoretical perspectives, such as psychodynamic, person-centered, cognitive-behavioral, and systemic, among others. The particular theoretical perspective influences the approach to supervision. For example, consistent with behavioral theory, behavioral supervision focuses on teaching appropriate therapist behaviors and extinguishing inappropriate behaviors (Boyd, 1978; Levine & Tilker, 1974). Psychotherapy theory-based supervision, like contemporary models of counseling and psychotherapy, has paid little or no attention to multicultural factors in supervision.

Interpersonal supervision models focus on the interaction between the supervisee and supervisor as well as the supervisor's role as related to the supervisee's professional development (e.g., Bernard, 1997; Holloway, 1992, 1997; Ladany et al., 2005). Bernard's discrimination model focuses on encouraging the supervisor to consider a range of responses and to discriminate among them for the trainee's maximum development. Bernard (1997) admits that the discrimination model is largely inattentive to cultural variables within supervision. In Holloway's (1992; 1995) Systems Approach to Supervision (SAS), she describes seven interrelated dimensions/factors: four contextual factors (the institution, the supervisor, the client, and the trainee), supervision functions, supervision tasks, and the supervision relationship (the core factor). Multicultural factors are mentioned within the descriptions of two contextual factors—that is, supervisor factors and trainee factors. However, this is done in a cursory fashion and with no specificity with regard to handling multicultural issues within a supervisory framework. Rather, cultural characteristics are generally noted as relevant to the supervisor's performance and to the trainees' attitudes and actions toward their clients and supervisors.

Ladany et al.'s (2005) Critical Events in Supervision (CES) model directly attends to multicultural issues, both as a process or intervention (focus on multicultural awareness), as well as in two of the nine types of major critical events (i.e., heightening multicultural awareness and repairing gender misunderstandings and missed understandings). Every critical event consists of four basic elements: the supervisory working alliance, a marker, the task environment, and the resolution (see Chapter 6 for more details of the model). The task environment consists of interaction sequences, or interventions, which the supervisor implements for a particular event. For a "heightening of multicultural awareness" event, where the multicultural concern can be a single or multiple multicultural issues (e.g., disability and race), the interaction sequences consist of an exploration of feelings, an assessment of multicultural knowledge, a focus on multicultural awareness, a focus on skill (conceptual), normalizing the supervisee's experience, and a focus on the supervisory alliance. For a "repairing gender misunderstandings and missed understandings" event, the interaction sequences consist of exploration of feelings, focus on the therapeutic relationship, assess multicultural knowledge (gender role socialization), and focus on self-efficacy. In both types of multicultural events described, the purpose is to assist the supervisee to become more knowledgeable, self-aware, and skilled in relation to multicultural issues. In sum, the CES model offers supervisors a conceptual framework for integrating multicultural issues in supervision. That said, additional empirical work is needed to support the hypothesized connections.

Developmental approaches to supervision focus on how supervisees change as they gain training and supervised experience (Bernard & Goodyear, 2009). Several developmental models of supervision exist (e.g., Hogan, 1964; Littrell, Lee-Borden, & Lorenz, 1979; Loganbill, Hardy, & Delworth, 1982; Skovholt & Rønnestad, 1992; Stoltenberg, McNeill, & Delworth, 1998). The trainee is typically conceptualized as moving from a level of dependency and limited personal and professional awareness to increased autonomy, awareness, and skill. Developmental models attempt to match supervisor behavior to the trainees' developmental needs. Several authors (e.g., Loganbill et al., 1982; Stoltenberg et al., 1998) attend to individual differences as one domain of clinical training and practice. These authors describe the trainee as progressing from stereo-typic thinking and a limited awareness of personal prejudices to increased awareness, a view of the client as an individual and a person-in-context, and ongoing self-examination as he or she moves through the various lev-els of development. While these authors describe appropriate supervisory approaches for trainees at various stages of development, specific strategies for increasing trainees' cultural counseling competence are not addressed.

Several authors have described developmental approaches to train-ing that specifically attend to multicultural counseling competence (e.g., Carney & Kahn, 1984; Sabnani, Ponterotto, & Borodovsky, 1991). Carney and Kahn's (1984) counselor development model, influenced by the work of several authors including Stoltenberg (1981), consists of five stages of trainee development related to the acquisition of cross-cultural counsel-ing competencies and appropriate learning environments. Each stage attends to the trainees' knowledge of cultural groups, attitudinal aware-ness and cross-cultural sensitivity, and specific cross-cultural counseling skills. Sabnani and colleagues (1991) model of multicultural training inte-grates work in cross-cultural training development, racial identity, and cross-cultural competency. Their multicultural training model for White, middle-class counselors focuses on White racial identity development. However, the above mentioned models do not address the implications of each developmental stage in terms of the trainee's clinical interventions. Additionally, these models focus exclusively on the trainee's development of multicultural counseling competence and do not address the supervisor's identity, the supervisor's multicultural competence, or the supervision relationship.

Research on counselor supervision in several different countries (e.g., Cheng, 1993; Richards, 2000) highlights the effects of the supervi-sor, supervisee, and client's culture on the supervision process. Several supervision models directly address the supervisor, supervisee, and cli-ent triad. One such model, influenced by the work of several researchers (Myers, 1991; Nichols, 1976; Nobles, 1972), is the worldview congruence model (Brown & Landrum-Brown, 1995). Brown and Landrum-Brown describe eight worldview dimensions: (1) psychobehavioral modality; (2) axiology (values); (3) ethos (guiding beliefs); (4) epistemology (how one knows); (5) logic (reasoning process); (6) ontology (nature of reality); (7) concept of time; and (8) concept of self. In addition, they present five pat-terns of conflict and/or complements relevant to the supervisory triad and assert that worldview conflicts may result in distrust and hostility within the triadic relationship. The authors do not describe specific issues that may arise within the triadic relationship for each of the eight worldview dimensions in each potential situation or related supervisor interven-tions. Nonetheless, Brown and Landrum-Brown (1995) provide a useful framework that begins to address the multicultural complexities within the supervision relationship.

A postmodern approach to multicultural clinical supervision developed by González (1997) integrates Interpersonal Process Recall (Kagan, 1976), Bernard's (1979) discrimination model, and live supervision. Attention to power differentials in supervision is acknowledged. Supervisors, supervisees, and clients are all encouraged to share their perspectives and mutual expertise. In addition to the supervisor's roles as teacher, counselor, and consultant, González proposes a fourth role; that is, supervisor as partial learner. This approach describes cultural and linguistic nuances of clients' constructions, as well as the potential for misses by monolingual service providers. Supervisors are advised to attend to language usage, supervisee's expression of strong affect in supervision, and client verbal and nonverbal behavior as influenced by gender role socialization and cultural background.

Another model of multicultural supervision that stresses supervisor's awareness of their own culture and how this affects the supervisee and the process of supervision is the VISION model (Garrett et al., 2001). The model includes attention to the values and belief systems of the supervisor and supervisee, the supervisee's interpretation of experiences in counseling and supervision, the way that the supervisor structures the supervisory relationship and models structuring the counseling relationship, preferred communication style between the supervisor and supervisee, intentionality of the supervisor and supervisee in using culturally based strategies of achieving desired goals, and perceived needs of the supervisor and supervisee within supervision. The VISION model is presented as a guide for increasing supervisor's effectiveness when working with culturally diverse supervisees and for training effective counselors.

Several authors have discussed various approaches to multicultural counseling supervision, including encouraging the supervisee to examine her or his own sociocultural background, beliefs, and biases (Morgan, 1984; Remington & DaCosta, 1989), recruiting diverse faculty and students (Morgan, 1984), and providing cultural training and courses throughout the curriculum (Remington & DaCosta, 1989). In addition, several authors (e.g., Ault-Riche, 1988; Brodsky, 1980; Cook, 1994; Fong & Lease, 1996; Gardner, 1980; Lopez, 1997; Priest, 1994; Remington & DaCosta, 1989; Vargas, 1989) have written about problems in cross-cultural supervision, including unintentional racism, supervisor gender bias, miscommunication, undiscussed racial–ethnic issues that distort the supervisory relationship, overemphasis on cultural explanations for psychological difficulties, and overdependence on supervisor's knowledge.

Despite advances in the area, overall, the literature focusing on multicultural supervision can be characterized as both general and fragmented, but occasionally hitting the mark. Presently, the extant models of multicultural supervision warrant at least one of the following critiques: they (a) tend to focus on the supervisee's multicultural competence without attending to the supervisor's competence; (b) tend to focus exclusively on race–ethnicity while disregarding other aspects of identity (e.g., gender, sexual orientation); (c) do not provide a comprehensive framework for approaching multicultural issues within a supervisory context (Leong & Wagner, 1994); and (d) lack empirical research support. Moreover, the multicultural supervision literature tends to present global issues and difficulties that may arise and relatively global suggestions for overcoming such difficulties. A model that describes the multiplicity of supervisor and supervisee identities, the relationship between supervisor and supervisee when both possess varied perspectives, and the relationship's influence on supervision and client outcome would contribute to the literature (Brown & Landrum-Brown, 1995). In sum, this model can help to provide supervisors with knowledge about multiple aspects of multicultural supervision and provide suggestions for fostering multicultural counseling practice.

Multicultural Supervision Competencies as Ethical Practice

Supervisors play a significant role in developing trainees' conceptual, diagnostic, and intervention skills. If the counseling profession is truly committed to the promotion of culturally competent practice, supervisors must possess the competencies necessary to foster culturally competent trainees. We propose that competent multicultural supervision is an ethical imperative given the demographic diversity of clients, supervisees, and supervisors. As such, we next review and discuss the American Counseling Association (ACA) and American Psychological Association (APA) documents pertaining to ethical principles and standards to examine the extent to which attention is paid to multicultural issues within supervision.

Traditionally, ethical guidelines for counseling supervisors were embedded within, or deemed translatable from guidelines for practitioners. The APA developed Guidelines on Multicultural Education, Training, Research, Practice, and Organizational Change (American Psychological Association [APA], 2003). Recent demographic data on racial and ethnic diversity in the United States is presented as the primary rationale for the guidelines. The application of multiculturalism in education and training is discussed; however, the focus is curriculum and classroom interactions versus supervision. Other APA guidelines have focused on psychotherapy practice, such as the Guidelines for Psychotherapy with Lesbian, Gay, and Bisexual Clients (APA, 2000). Supervision and training is often indicated in these guidelines, although in a relatively minor way. For example, Guideline 20 of the Guidelines for Psychological Practice with Older

Adults (APA, 2004) describes using supervision to increase knowledge, understanding, and skills in working with older adults. The Guidelines for Psychological Practice for Girls and Women (APA, 2007) makes mention of the importance of teaching and supervision in it's description of guideline applications. This includes being knowledgeable about theoretical and empirical support for supervision practices used with women and girls, gaining specialized education and training relevant to the experiences and problems of girls and women, and being aware of both challenges and strengths of women and girls within supervision. It is important to note that these guidelines are aspirational in nature and not mandatory as is the case for standards of practice.

The ACA's *Code of Ethics and Standards of Practice* (1995) included a section on "Teaching, Training, and Supervision" (Section F). The only areas within Section F that directly attended to diversity were subsections F.1.a: "Counselor educators should make an effort to infuse material related to human diversity into all courses and/or workshops that are designed to promote the development of professional counselors" and F.2.i: "Counselors are responsive to their institution's and program's recruitment and retention needs for training program administrators, faculty, and students with diverse backgrounds and special needs." Relative to the 1995 Code of Ethics and Standards of Practice, ACA's more recent (2005) Code of Ethics seems even more limited with respect to attending to diversity in supervision and training. The section on Supervision, Training, and Teaching (Section F) of the 2005 version contains two areas specific to diversity. Subsection F.2.b of Counselor Supervision Competence indicates, "Counseling supervisors are aware of and address the role of multiculturalism/diversity in the supervisory relationship." Under F.4.d. Termination of the Supervisory Relationship, the following relatively ambiguous sentence is included, "When cultural, clinical, or professional issues are crucial to the viability of the supervisory relationship, both parties make efforts to resolve differences." Similar to the 1995 Code, no mention is made of exploring trainees' personal and professional biases or ensuring that trainees are culturally competent. While issues of counselor nondiscrimination and cultural sensitivity are mentioned in other sections of the ACA *Code of Ethics and Standards of Practice*, multicultural issues are given only limited attention in the section on teaching, training, and supervision.

Only recently did the Association for Counselor Education and Supervision (ACES), a division of ACA, develop and publish ethical guidelines specifically for supervisors (ACES, 1990, 1995). Two documents are directly relevant to ethical principles and guidelines for counseling supervision: (1) the "Standards for Counseling Supervisors" developed by the Supervision Interest Network of ACES (1990), and (2) "Ethical Guidelines for Counseling Supervisors" that were adopted in 1993 (ACES, 1995).

The "Standards for Counseling Supervisors" (ACES, 1990), adopted by the American Association for Counseling and Development (AACD) Governing Council in 1989, consists of 11 core areas of knowledge, competencies, and personal traits characterizing effective supervisors. The standards do acknowledge that effective counseling supervisors are sensitive and knowledgeable about individual differences and understand the impact of these differences in supervisory relationships. However, the standards provide only a superficial acknowledgment of multicultural issues, and thus supervisors lack a guiding framework from which to provide culturally competent supervision. Interestingly, the ACES's (1995) "Ethical Guidelines for Counseling Supervisors" provides no mention of multicultural competence. Even though this document was first published three years after the "Standards for Counseling Supervisors" (see Hart, Borders, Nance, & Paradise, 1993), standards related to multicultural issues were not transferred into the ethical guidelines. The lack of significant attention to multicultural supervision and training in documents that serve as guiding principles of the counseling profession is a major limitation within a diverse society. This shortcoming notwithstanding, we believe that supervisors must presume an ethical stance in relation to multicultural supervision in order to perform their roles effectively and ethically.

Multicultural Self-Awareness

Many educators mistakenly believe that a course in multicultural issues is adequate to provide the necessary information to become a multicultural counselor or supervisor. However, a general course, at best, typically offers the bulk of the learning in the realm of multicultural knowledge, with some minimal attention to multicultural self-awareness and skills. In this section, we first offer a model, the Heuristic Model of Nonoppressive Interpersonal Development (HMNID) that addresses the self-awareness aspect of supervisor multicultural competence. The HMNID attends to the multiple and interrelated dimensions of supervisor's and supervisee's identity. It is designed to offer supervisors a heuristic framework for understanding patterns of thoughts, feelings, and behaviors about themselves, their trainees, and clients across specific demographic variables (i.e., race, ethnicity, gender, sexual orientation, disability, socioeconomic status).

Heuristic Model of Nonoppressive Interpersonal Development (HMNID)

Over the past three decades, it has been recognized that one's identity can play a key role in understanding clients' as well as counselors' psychological makeup. Moreover, it is presumed that general models of identity development (e.g., Marcia, 1966), as well as the simple knowledge of a particular nominal or demographic variable (e.g., biological sex), insufficiently predicts a person's beliefs and behaviors. Identity models have been created to reflect a variety of specific personal demographic variables, including race (Cross, 1971, 1995; Hardiman, 1982; Helms, 1990, 1995; Helms & Cook, 1999; Sue & Sue, 1999), ethnicity (Phinney, 1989; Sodowsky, Kwan, & Pannu, 1995), gender (Downing & Roush, 1985; McNamara & Rickard, 1989; Ossana, Helms, & Leonard, 1992), and sexual orientation (Cass, 1979; Chan, 1989; Fassinger, 1991; Rust, 1993; Troiden, 1989). To some extent, these models, specifically racial identity and gender identity, have been applied to the supervision context (Carney & Kahn, 1984; Cook, 1994; Helms & Cook, 1999; Ladany, Brittan-Powell, & Pannu, 1997; Porter, 1995; Rarick, 2000; Vasquez & McKinley, 1982). However, levels of identity with respect to multiple demographic characteristics have not been considered within the supervision context. Furthermore, these models have primarily focused on psychological identity, with limited attention being paid to behavioral manifestations of identity. To this end, the purpose of our model of nonoppressive interpersonal development is to offer supervisors a heuristic model for understanding patterns of thoughts, feelings, and behaviors about themselves, their trainees, and clients across specific demographic variables (i.e., race, ethnicity, sexual orientation, gender, disability, socioeconomic status). It is important to begin this discourse by noting that this model is not intended to wholly replace the specific identity models. Instead our intention is to offer supervisors a way of managing the multiple models without diluting their value. In fact, it is our contention that supervisors should learn about the specific identity models across demographic variables as a way of supplementing the tenets of our model. With this caveat in mind, we present an updated version of our model from 2001 (Ancis & Ladany, 2001).

We believe that for any given demographic variable, people can belong to one of two societally based groups: (1) a socially oppressed group (SOG; female, person of color, gay/lesbian/bisexual, disabled, working class), or (2) a socially privileged group (SPG; male, White, heterosexual, European American, physically abled, middle to upper class). For example, in terms of the demographic variable sex, women belong to the SOG and men belong to the SPG. Furthermore, based on this conceptualization, people could simultaneously belong to both a SOG and a SPG when considering their multiple personal demographic variables (e.g., female, White).

We also believe that for each demographic variable, people progress through phases of what we call Means of Interpersonal Functioning (MIF): thoughts and feelings about oneself, as well as behaviors based on one's identification with a particular demographic variable (e.g., the psychological and behavioral manifestations of being a person who is disabled). Our position, similar to that of the identity theorists, is that the demographic variable itself does not account for one's thoughts, feelings, and behaviors. Rather, how one perceives oneself and interacts with others is largely due to an environmental press that exerts its influence on individuals based on their demographic characteristics. We also argue that regardless of the group to which one belongs, people progress through similar phases of MIF with respect to each identified group, albeit there are common and unique features depending upon the identified group. As an example, both women and men are capable of progress in terms of their MIF. The developmental stages of MIF for both women and men will have common features (e.g., both will exhibit complacency regarding societal change in the less advanced stages) as well as unique features (e.g., generally, women will feel less empowered and men will perceive greater entitlement). Similar schemes can be produced for gender, race, sexual orientation, ethnicity, disability, nationality, and socioeconomic status.

We should note three additional assumptions to our model. First, we believe that people can be more advanced in terms of their MIF for one demographic variable (e.g., gender) than for another (e.g., race). For example, a White woman may have an understanding of sexism and the limiting effects of sex role socialization, but lack an awareness of White privilege. Second, this model restrictively applies to people who live in the United States, the country from which the social context of the model is derived. Third, processes and outcomes in supervision and counseling can be characterized and predicted by the knowledge of each dyadic member's MIF for each demographic variable.

It is believed that people have the ability to developmentally progress through four phases or stages of MIF (i.e., adaptation, incongruence, exploration, and integration). These stages represent a progression from complacency and limited awareness regarding cultural differences and oppression to increased awareness of multicultural issues, cognitive complexity, and commitment to cultural competence. We will define each stage and include examples of feelings, thoughts, and behaviors that are characteristic of people for each stage across different demographic variables. Further examples of thoughts, feelings, and behaviors as they occur across stages, for three of the multicultural variables (i.e., gender, race, sexual orientation) can be found in Table 3.1.

Adaptation

The first stage of MIF is adaptation. Adaptation features that are common to both SOG and SPG members involve complacency and apathy regarding, and conformity to, the socially oppressive environment (e.g., "there will always be poor people"), a superficial understanding of differences among people (e.g., "we all are from the same melting pot"), stereotypic

Table 3.1 Examples of Multicultural Identity Development for a Sample of Multicultural Variables

Multicultural Variable	Means of Interpersonal Functioning	Examples of Thoughts, Feelings, and Behaviors
Gender: Female	Adaptation	Equality exists between the sexes in all parts of our culture. Salary discrepancies based on gender are "made-up." Staying at home to raise children is completely my choice. Primary defense is denial. Unable to easily identify feelings associated with cultural issues.
	Incongruence	I just learned that women make less than men, even in the counseling profession where we are supposed to be more advanced. My supervisor makes disparaging comments about women, but he probably does not believe them and I should just blow it off. Primary defense is minimization and rationalization.
	Exploration	I think Gloria Steinem was correct, "Either you're a feminist or a masochist." Looking back on my life, I see how I was often the target of lewd comments and behavior because I am a woman. Primary feelings are anger and frustration.
	Integration	It is my responsibility to modify my own and others gender stereotypic understanding and behavior. Understands and advocates for human rights, particularly in relation to gender equality. Engages in multiple forms of advocacy. Primary feelings are sadness about existing inequality and hope/optimism that change can occur.
Gender: Male	Adaptation	The basic fact is men and women are different genetically and that explains their psychological differences. Primary defense is denial. Unable to easily identify feelings associated with cultural issues.
	Incongruence	I'm okay with having women in the workplace, but I think it is best if they stay at home with the children. Primary defense is minimization and rationalization.
	Exploration	I'm becoming very aware of the advantages of what it means to be a man in my culture. Primary feeling is guilt.

(Continued)

Table 3.1 Examples of Multicultural Identity Development for a Sample of Multicultural Variables (*Continued*)

Multicultural Variable	Means of Interpersonal Functioning	Examples of Thoughts, Feelings, and Behaviors
	Integration	I strive to challenge learned behaviors that serve to disparage women. Understands and advocates for human rights, particularly in relation to gender equality. Engages in multiple forms of advocacy. Primary feelings are sadness about existing inequality and hope/optimism that change can occur.
Race: Person of Color	Adaptation	African Americans are poor because they don't try hard enough. I was able to pull myself up by my bootstraps, so should others. Primary defense is denial. Unable to easily identify feelings associated with cultural issues.
	Incongruence	I am uncomfortable that my white friend told me that she never thought of me as African American. I am unsure if I should take that as a compliment. Primary defense is minimization and rationalization.
	Exploration	I need to primarily associate with other people of color if I am ever going to be understood. Associates with groups or organizations that strongly identify with People of Color (e.g., Black Student Union). Primary feelings are anger and frustration.
	Integration	I support the struggles and empowerment of people from all backgrounds. Understands and advocates for human rights, particularly in relation to racial equality. Engages in multiple forms of advocacy. Primary feelings are sadness about existing inequality and hope/optimism that change can occur.
Race: White	Adaptation	I am colorblind. We all belong to the human race. Primary defense is denial. Unable to easily identify feelings associated with cultural issues.
	Incongruence	Sure there is racism, but I wasn't responsible for it and I don't have any privilege because of it. Focusing on race just creates bad feelings and perpetuates racism. Primary defense is minimization and rationalization.

	Exploration	Ever since I witnessed my African American friends being followed in department stores, I have really begun to think about how my being White has impacted my experiences in the world. Actively explores what it means to be White and the privileges that come from being White. Primary feeling is guilt.
	Integration	I believe that for change to occur, we all need to support each other's struggles and actively engage in dismantling racism. Understands and advocates for human rights, particularly in relation to racial equality. Engages in multiple forms of advocacy. Adept at interacting with People of Color and White people who are at various stages of means of interpersonal functioning. Primary feelings are sadness about existing inequality and hope/optimism that change can occur.
Sexual Orientation: LGBT	Adaptation	I can force myself to be heterosexual. A heterosexual life is an ideal I strive for. Identifies with heterosexual norms in the U.S. culture. Primary defense is denial. Unable to easily identify feelings associated with cultural issues.
	Incongruence	Hiding my sexual feelings toward same-sex individuals may be starting to take its toll on my mental and physical health. I should put more effort into not paying attention to these feelings. Feelings are becoming more difficult to ignore and there's a tension between being out versus closeted. Primary defense is minimization and rationalization.
	Exploration	A lot of straight people can never understand what it means to be gay. I realize how I have adopted a lot of negative stereotypes of gay men and would like to work on reversing that. Associates with groups or organizations that strongly identify with people who are LGBT (e.g., attend a gay pride parade). Primary feelings are anger and frustration.
	Integration	I support gay rights so that all people can benefit and live more productive lives. Understands and advocates for human rights, particularly in relation to sexual orientation equality. Engages in multiple forms of advocacy. Primary feelings are sadness about existing inequality and hope/optimism that change can occur.

(*Continued*)

Table 3.1 Examples of Multicultural Identity Development for a Sample of Multicultural Variables (*Continued*)

Multicultural Variable	Means of Interpersonal Functioning	Examples of Thoughts, Feelings, and Behaviors
Sexual orientation: Heterosexual	Adaptation	Homosexuality is immoral and a sin. A person can change their sexual orientation if they really put their mind to it. I am fine with it as long as they don't bother or come on to me; then there is a problem. Comfortable with hearing and telling jokes about people who are LGBT. May engage in occasional gay-bashing, verbally and perhaps physically. Against gay marriage. Primary defense is denial. Unable to easily identify feelings associated with cultural issues.
	Incongruence	I feel uncomfortable hearing other people make fun of or put down gay people. I find myself trying to ignore such comments. Begins to question unhealthy heterosexist stance based on contact experiences. Primary defense is minimization and rationalization.
	Exploration	I have come to realize that the freedom I experience to show affection to my partner is not one experienced by gay and lesbian people. Actively explores and examines the privileges associated with being heterosexual. Primary feeling is guilt.
	Integration	I believe that as a heterosexual ally, I can contribute to the rights of all people regardless of their sexual orientation. Understands and advocates for human rights, particularly in relation to sexual orientation equality. Engages in multiple forms of advocacy. Primary feelings are sadness about existing inequality and hope/optimism that change can occur.

attitudes toward particular cultural groups (e.g., "Hispanics are lazy and unmotivated"), minimal conscious awareness of oppressive state of affairs (e.g., unaware of public transportation that is inaccessible to persons who are disabled), and limited emotional awareness (e.g., anger without insight). Although people in this stage are adaptive in the social context in which they live, their intrapersonal and interpersonal functioning is maladaptive and results in the perpetuation of the oppressive status quo (Thompson & Neville, 1999). The primary defense mechanisms include denial and resistance. Behaviors range on a continuum from passive acceptance of oppression of others (e.g., looking the other way) to active endorsement of oppressive contingencies (e.g., endorsement of political figures who advocate oppression of SOGs) to active participation in oppressing members of SOGs (e.g., directed violence against members of SOGs). Unique features of people in a SOG is an idealization of and identification with people in the SPG (e.g., to be healthy is to be wealthy) limited awareness of oppressive events that they personally experience (e.g., a woman who believes she has never been the recipient of an oppressive act), limited motivation to change one's own circumstance, and abandonment of SOG features (e.g., active efforts to hide or deny one's Jewish ethnicity). Unique to SPG members is an obliviousness to differences (e.g., a color-blind perspective on race, such as "we all belong to the human race"), a belief that all people are the same and have similar interpersonal experiences (e.g., women have no obstacles to career advancement), denigration of members of SOGs (e.g., gays and lesbians are immoral; gay people deserve the diseases that afflict them), and unawareness of privilege associated with being a member of a SPG (e.g., any poor person who works as hard as me has the same opportunities).

Based on an understanding of one's MIF stage, predictions about supervisors' and trainees' thoughts, feelings, and behaviors relevant to supervision and counseling can be made. For a given demographic variable, both SOG and SPG supervisors in the adaptation stage are more likely to (a) minimize and dismiss trainees' expression of multicultural interest and competence; (b) refer to clients based on inaccurate stereotypes; (c) become anxious if oppression issues emerge in supervision; (d) inaccurately perceive oneself as quite multiculturally competent; (e) exhibit oppressive beliefs in the presence of SPG trainees; and (f) demonstrate limited integrative complexity when it comes to conceptualizing trainees and clients within a multicultural framework. Integrative complexity is defined as the ability to differentiate (identify multiple multicultural factors) and integrate (link these factors) when conceptualizing clients (Constantine & Ladany, 2000; Ladany, Inman, Constantine, & Hofheinz, 1997) and can also be extended to conceptualizing trainees. Supervisors in the adaptation stage are less likely to (a) address multicultural issues between the supervisor and trainee (i.e., negative parallel process) and between the trainee and her or his clients; (b) accurately empathize with SOG trainees who are at a higher MIF; (c) facilitate MIF development in SPG trainees; and (d) admit to a lack of comfort with multicultural issues (less likely to attend to areas of less expertise). Adaptation-stage supervisors will not explore either their own or supervisees' biases, background, and world-view and how these are related to supervision. They will be unaware of the limitations of traditional counseling approaches with diverse clients and will foster a restricted range of interventions with their trainees. Moreover, they will be unable to identify trainees' personal and professional strengths and weaknesses in the area of multicultural counseling. Supervisors who find themselves in the adaptation stage should ethically seek supervision of supervision or personal counseling to assist them in working through their oppressive beliefs; however, they are unlikely to do so unless they encounter an experience that facilitates their development to the next stage of MIF.

For a given demographic variable, both SOG and SPG trainees in the adaptation stage are less likely to (a) attend to multicultural issues in super-vision or with their clients (e.g., not likely to address multicultural issues in case conceptualization reports and presentations, not likely to address multicultural issues with clients), or to (b) consider demographic vari-ables beyond the mere mention of them in case conceptualizations (verbal and written). Trainees are also more likely to (a) blame clients and ignore environmental influences on clients' functioning, and (b) miss salient multicultural issues that emerge for the client and between themselves and their clients (e.g., may mistake a client's culturally consistent deference as dependence).

Incongruence

The second stage of MIF is incongruence. People from both SOGs and SPGs in this stage are likely to experience conscious incongruence, whereby their previous beliefs about oppression and privilege seem incongruent, disso-nant, or inconsistent with events of which they become aware. For example, a widely publicized news event that describes a violent attack on a person of color due solely to the person's race may conflict with one's beliefs that the world is just and people are treated equally. Additional common fea-tures include conflict, confusion, dissonance, and some awareness, yet no real commitment to advocacy. During incongruence, denial is no longer as effective a defense mechanism as it was during adaptation. Rather, mini-mization and rationalization are the more predominant defense mecha-nisms. Even though awareness is raised, behaviors are still often congruent with the more passive oppressive interactions (e.g., passive acceptance of gender stereotypes).

Although members of both SOGs and SPGs may experience an event that leads them to question their previously held beliefs, the event itself may be different or will likely involve different personal consequences. For people in SOGs, the event may be a personal discrimination experience that leads to an awareness of oppression (e.g., a White friend tells an African American person that she never thought of her as African American since she is so articulate). A SPG member may experience indirect discrimination through association with a member of a SOG or may witness a discriminatory event (Ancis & Szymanski, 2001). Also, this transition from the adaptation to incongruence stage could be the result of one significant event or the culmination of a series of events such that the person can no longer ignore the reality of oppression. People in SOGs may have some awareness of oppression but are conflicted about their identification with either the SOG or the SPG. For people in SPGs, an event may help them recognize that oppression exists (e.g., salary differences between women and men) but change is still believed to be the responsibility of members of SOGs, and there is little recognition of SPG privilege (e.g., "Affirmative action is not fair!").

Supervisors in the incongruence stage are unlikely to attend to multicultural issues in supervision, or at best, they give it minimal attention. They may attempt to have the trainee collude with their rationalizations regarding SOG members. For example, knowing that trainees will likely feel compelled to agree with them, supervisors may actively try to dismiss multicultural issues as being irrelevant (e.g., supervisor may say to the trainee "I think women deserve equal rights but these feminists take it too far sometimes"), rather than ignore multicultural issues completely, as they did in the adaptation stage. Supervisors may begin to explore their own background and worldview but find an examination of personal biases too threatening.

Trainees in the incongruence stage are likely to be somewhat aware of multicultural issues but are unlikely to bring them up in supervision, particularly if they believe the supervisor does not consider multicultural issues important and if they are influenced by the supervisory power differential. They may bring it up during supervision in an indirect fashion (e.g., note a particular demographic) but they are likely to take the supervisors' lead on whether to explore the multicultural issue further. They are likely to include demographic information in case conceptualizations, but the information is not well differentiated or integrated. Furthermore, trainees are likely to approach multicultural issues during supervision in an approach/avoidance fashion.

Exploration

The third stage of MIF is exploration. Common features for both SOG and SPG members include active exploration of what it means to be a member of their respective SOG or SPG. Additionally, anger may be a prominent emotion, some of which is founded on current recognition of oppressive situations, but also fueled by guilt or shame for not having recognized the oppressive state of affairs previously. Unlike the anger when one is in the adaptation stage, anger in the exploration stage is insightful (i.e., linked to the recognition of the oppressive status quo). Individuals may consider their own role in perpetuating oppressive environments and will likely seek out "encounter-like events" (e.g., reach out to the gay and lesbian community). Furthermore, individuals in the exploration stage are more likely to seek counseling to help them understand and process these experiences. SOG members are likely to immerse themselves in the particular culture (e.g., may wear Asian American influenced clothing, participate in a gay pride event) and affiliate with other members of their SOG (e.g., associate with other people who are disabled). SPG members are likely to explore what it means to be a member of a SPG and consider the resulting privileges (e.g., advantages associated with White privilege; Ancis & Szymanski, 1999; Bulhan, 1985; Fine, Weis, Powell, & Mun Wong, 1997). Finally, what begins as an awareness of oppressive events may lead to a hypervigilance or hyperawareness.

For a particular demographic variable, both SOG and SPG supervisors will likely attend to multicultural issues in supervision and actively engage trainees to facilitate their multicultural awareness. However, their eagerness and enthusiasm to create insight may paradoxically result in greater resistance on the part of the trainee, especially if the trainee is in the adaptation or incongruence stage. Supervisors will likely initiate self-exploration among themselves and their trainees. They will be relatively open to exploring alternative conceptualizations and interventions with trainees (e.g., feminist theoretical approaches). A potential danger in terms of process and outcome of supervision is an overemphasis on multicultural issues to explain concerns or difficulties that are not well connected with additional and related unresolved conflicts. Furthermore, supervisors may begin to initiate trainees' personal exploration of biases, but then be at a loss as to how to follow through or intervene.

Both SOG and SPG trainees will likely look to their supervisors for guidance and be open to exploring multicultural issues. However, they may overemphasize multicultural issues at the expense of other relevant counseling issues and may have difficulty integrating both personal and multicultural issues in conceptualizing clients. Also, trainees will begin to generalize their exploration stage beliefs for a given demographic characteristic to another demographic characteristic in which they are in the adaptation or incongruence stage. For example, a White trainee who was raised in an upper socioeconomic class home and who is exploring what it means to have White privilege may begin to become aware of socioeconomic advantages as well. They may thus begin to make parallels between various social identities.

Integration

The fourth stage of MIF is integration. Common features for both SOGs and SPGs include multicultural integrity, integrative awareness, proficiency in associating with multiple SOG groups, recognition of oppressive occurrences, insight into oppressive interactions, and accurate feelings. Behaviorally, there is a committed pursuit of nonoppression in the environment (e.g., engage in advocacy for oppressed groups) and an ability to accurately empathize with members of multiple groups (SPG and SOG). Defense mechanisms are primarily fantasy, imagining what things could be like rather than become overwhelmed from focusing on the multiple components of everyday oppression. The SOG members are likely to reach out to members of their own SOG in order to offer mentoring. Members of SPGs will capitalize on opportunities to counter misguided reasoning presented to them by fellow SPG members who are at less advanced MIF stages (e.g., present counterarguments to misinformed stereotyping). They will likely utilize their privileges toward promoting equality and will work toward changing infrastructures within which they work.

For a given demographic variable, supervisors who are members of either a SOG or a SPG are likely to be adept at facilitating trainee development in their MIF. Supervisors are also able to discuss and process differences and similarities between themselves and their trainees, which in turn models for trainees how to interact with their clients (i.e., positive parallel process). Supervisors can also address multicultural issues in supervision effectively and competently. Supervisors have spent time on their own MIF and strive toward changing the training environment in which they work. Supervisors are able to assist trainees in developing client advocacy skills, use power constructively in supervision, and facilitate discussions of diversity with trainees at different MIF stages.

Trainees in the integration stage are likely to be able to conceptualize clients in an integratively complex fashion across multiple demographic variables. They are also able to (a) accurately empathize with SOG and SPG clients across clients' MIF for a given demographic variable; (b) continue to challenge their own socialized biases in supervision and understand how their internalized biases may influence their work with clients; and (c) be able to distinguish between countertransference-based biases and client transference. Furthermore, trainees in this stage become more adept at generalizing their integrative beliefs across other demographic characteristics and use supervision as one method of accomplishing this process.

Supervision Relationship Types

How can knowledge about stages of interpersonal functioning be used to understand the supervision relationship? Depending on the stage in which the supervisor and trainee belong, relationship dynamics could be hypothesized. These stages are similar to the interpersonal interactions proposed by Helms (1990), Cook (1994), and Helms and Cook (1999) for racial identity interactions. There are two primary extensions: (1) we have extended the conceptualization to multiple demographic groups, and (2) we offer specific supervisory interventions across developmental stages.

In regard to the HMNID, there are four possible supervisor–trainee interpersonal interaction dynamics that could be exhibited, depending on the respective stages of the supervisor and trainee. For the purposes of this model, supervisors and trainees are considered in a delayed phase of MIF if they are in the adaptation or incongruence stage and are considered in an advanced phase of MIF if they are in the exploration or integration stage. The four supervisor–trainee interpersonal interaction dynamics are (1) progressive, where the supervisor is at a more advanced stage than the trainee (e.g., supervisor, integration; trainee, adaptation); (2) parallel-advanced, where the supervisor and trainee are at comparable advanced MIF stages (i.e., supervisor, exploration or integration; trainee, exploration or integration); (3) parallel-delayed, where the supervisor and trainee are at comparable delayed MIF stages (i.e., supervisor, adaptation or incongruence; trainee, adaptation or incongruence); and (4) regressive, where the trainee is at a more advanced stage than the supervisor (e.g., trainee, integration; supervisor, adaptation). Types of interpersonal interactions have implications for trainee outcome and client outcome. Specifically, it can be predicted that a variety of supervision processes (e.g., the supervisory working alliance) and outcomes (e.g., trainee multicultural competence) would be enhanced from most to least in the following types of interactions: parallel-advanced, progressive, parallel-delayed, and regressive.

Parallel-advanced interactions would likely involve a mutual collaboration between the supervisor and trainee regarding the importance of facilitating multicultural competence in the trainee. Hence, the supervisory alliance would be enhanced, as would trainee multicultural competence. Progressive interactions would also likely enhance trainee multicultural competence, but there would likely be some resistance on the part of the trainee that would result in a less-than-optimal working alliance. Parallel-delayed and regressive relationships would likely result in weak supervisory alliances and possibly negatively influence trainee multicultural competence. In these instances, both the supervisor's and trainee's less-than-functional defense mechanisms (e.g., resistance

and denial) would likely interfere with healthy relationship development. Moreover, because multicultural client issues are not likely to be
discussed, or, when discussed, likely to be done in a negative fashion,
the trainee's multicultural competence will be stilted and negatively
influenced.

In terms of client outcome, a different pattern would likely emerge.
Specifically, as with trainee outcome, parallel-advanced supervisory
interactions would result in the greatest client outcome (e.g., counseling
alliance, client engagement, client satisfaction, and participation in counseling). Contrary to trainee outcome, regressive relationships would likely
result in the next greatest client outcome. This prediction is due to the
supposed buffering effect that a more advanced trainee would provide
between the client and the supervisor. However, the trainee risks negative
consequences such as receiving a negative supervisor evaluation because
the supervisor doesn't believe the trainee is conducting the type of counseling the supervisor wants. Clearly, this is not an ideal supervisory situation,
but it will likely offer better client outcomes than in the case of progressive and parallel-delayed interactions, where the trainee is less adept at
handling multicultural issues. In these instances either the supervisor is
attempting to facilitate the trainee to become more multiculturally adept
or the supervisor is doing nothing in terms of working with the trainee
on multicultural issues, respectively. A regressive supervisory relationship
may also be quite common given that current supervisors in the field were
unlikely to have received multicultural training whereas current trainees
are very likely to have received multicultural training (Constantine, 1997;
Priest, 1994).

Supervisor Interventions

As can be seen in the possible outcomes based on the interaction types,
supervisors can play a crucial role in facilitating trainee development. In
fact, it is argued that it is the supervisor's ethical and professional responsibility to facilitate trainee nonoppressive interpersonal development
(Ladany et al., 1999). Hence, specific supervisor interventions could be
effective in moving trainees to an advanced stage of nonoppressive development. It should be noted that movement through stages is not an easy
process and will likely involve some resistance from trainees. The supervisor will also likely have to fight an environmental press that tends to push
people toward less advanced stages of development. Most importantly,
there must be a reasonably strong supervisory working alliance between
the trainee and supervisor for interventions to be effective. The primary
means by which such a relationship is founded is through empathic
understanding of the trainee and her or his level of development.

Across developmental stages, there are a number of effective and appropriate supervisory interventions. Many of these interventions have been identified in the preceding section on behaviors of supervisors in the integration stage (e.g., discussion of multicultural issues between the supervisor and trainee). First, for trainees in the adaptation stage, the supervisor's task is to create dissonance and move the trainee to the incongruence stage (e.g., offer readings, focus on the knowledge dimension of multicultural competency, challenge the trainee's oppressive belief system). For trainees in the incongruence stage, supervisors can intervene by facilitating multiple encounter-like events in order to move the trainee to the exploration stage (e.g., give homework to attend a social function of an oppressed group, focus on the knowledge dimension of multicultural competency, challenge the trainee's oppressive belief system). For trainees in the exploration stage, supervisors can intervene by providing emotional support and teach strategies to move beyond guilt (e.g., facilitate trainee movement to integration stage, focus on skills and self-awareness dimensions of multicultural competency). Supervisors can also teach trainees to understand both intrapsychic and environmental explanations of events. Furthermore, with the emergence of intense emotions, supervisors could recommend that trainees seek personal counseling to process their intense emotional experiences and help uncover additional unconscious oppressive beliefs. Finally, for trainees in the integration stage, supervisor interventions can include helping trainees integrate multiple experiences (e.g., process trainee experiences in supervision, focus on skills and self-awareness dimensions of competency, use a trainee's integrative status for one demographic variable to help her or him develop along another demographic variable on which she or he is less developed). Also, supervisors can help trainees deal with clients who are at various stages of MIF. Overall, while the optimal effectiveness of these supervisor interventions are presumed to be stage specific, in all likelihood they can be used effectively across all stages.

We also believe it is important to expand upon one assumption that underlies our proposed model. Specifically, we believe that moving through the MIF stages is an ethical imperative for supervisors and trainees. Furthermore, we do not ascribe to the belief that counselors must recognize their multicultural limitations and, as a result, believe they can choose not to work with certain groups of clients who fall outside their desired expertise (e.g., gay or women clients). In most settings in which counselors work (e.g., community mental health centers or schools), they will not be able to decide whether to work with someone who is a member of one of the demographic groups we identified. They will also not have the option of referring clients with whom they would prefer not to work (e.g., gay or women clients). As such, supervisors and counselors must consider whether they can work through their oppressive beliefs so that they are not only not harmful, but also effective, and supervisors should recognize that they are accountable for ensuring that counselors adhere to this responsibility. Moreover, supervisors should assist counselors in recognizing from where oppressive beliefs are derived and should not be distracted by cultural overtones of some oppressive beliefs (e.g., homosexuality is immoral, women should be subservient to men). In the end, supervisors should assist counselors in evaluating the extent to which oppressive beliefs can be remediated and whether the counseling profession is an appropriate choice for them.

Research into this model is clearly warranted. For example, additional research is needed to determine if the interventions are indeed optimized in a stage-specific fashion. Furthermore, scales need to be developed that operationalize the stage constructs. Moreover, specific issues across stages for each demographic variable could be further delineated and examined. It is through these investigations and refined conceptualizations that this model can be refined and retested.

The HMNID highlights the multiple and interrelated identities of both supervisors and supervisees. We propose that this model has significant implications for the affect, cognitions, and behaviors of supervisors and supervisees; the supervisory relationship; the supervisee's professional development; and client outcome. The multiple and interrelated dimensions of identity within the supervisor–supervisee–client triad related to multiple demographic variables present challenges to providing culturally competent supervision. In the next section, we provide a framework of multicultural supervision competencies that attends to the supervisory triad.

Supervisor Multicultural Skills

Grounded in supervisory multicultural knowledge in relation to theory and ethics, along with a motivation to strive for multicultural self-awareness, supervisors can acquire and become adept at supervisor multicultural skills. As with counselor multicultural skills, supervisor multicultural skills are reflected in multicultural supervision self-efficacy (i.e., confidence to perform particular supervisor multicultural skills) along with the adeptness to carry out these multicultural skills (e.g., multiculturally sensitive nonverbal displays, the ability to develop a multicultural supervisory working alliance, and techniques and interventions that are culturally relevant to the work in counseling and supervision such as the discussion of racial similarities and differences among the supervisor, counselor, and client). It is important to recognize that self-efficacy in one's skills does not necessarily translate into demonstrated adeptness. Drawing from the counseling literature (e.g., Ladany, Inman, et al., 1997), it is likely that supervisors believe that they are more multiculturally competent than they actually are. In essence, confidence does not translate directly into competence. Specific supervisor multicultural skills are presented in the next section.

A Framework for Supervisor Multicultural Competence

A comprehensive framework of supervisor multicultural competence would provide supervisors with a more complete definition of multicultural supervision and would serve as a guide in the education and training of counselors. First, this framework would delineate how multicultural competencies are manifested in supervision. Second, a comprehensive framework would go beyond an exclusive focus on race and ethnicity and attend to the multiple and interrelated dimensions of identity. Third, a comprehensive framework of multicultural supervision competencies would hold supervisors accountable in providing effective, ethical, and appropriate supervision. Fourth, such a framework would facilitate systematic empirical research by providing specific and relevant dimensions of multicultural supervision. To that end, the purpose of this section is to provide a multicultural framework for supervisor multicultural competence.

Background of Multicultural Supervision Competencies

The present competencies for multicultural supervision were influenced by several documents in the fields of counseling and psychology: the "Guidelines for Culturally Competent Practice, and Education and Training" endorsed by Divisions 17, 35, and 45 of the APA (Ivey, Fouad, Arredondo, & D'Andrea, 1999); Porter's (1995) description of integrating antiracist, feminist, and multicultural perspectives in supervision, ACA and APA codes of ethics for supervision and training; Sue et al.'s (1992) cross-cultural counseling competencies; and the extant multicultural supervision literature described above (e.g., Lopez, 1997).

Our multicultural supervision guidelines for developing competence are divided into six domains: supervisor-focused personal development; supervisee-focused personal development; conceptualization; interventions; process; and evaluation. These areas have been most consistently identified in the literature as relevant to supervisor's and supervisee's personal and professional development, as well as activities most frequently related to counseling/clinical situations. The guidelines also include supervisor activities that are consistent with the role of social activist. The role of the counselor as social activist is becomingly increasingly recognized as essential to eradicating oppression and promoting psychological, physical, and spiritual growth. In fact, the organizational affiliate of ACA, Counselors for Social Justice, endorses confronting societal oppression and privilege as part of its mission (Guerra, 1999).

The domain of personal development has two components, supervisor focused and trainee focused. Supervisor-focused personal development refers to supervisor's self-exploration regarding their own values, biases, and personal limitations. This dimension also refers to being knowledgeable about cultural differences. Moreover, personal development refers to participation in educational, consultative, and training experiences that promote one's self-exploration and knowledge. For example, a White supervisor in the exploration stage recognizes and actively challenges her tendency to evaluate African American supervisees as less competent than White supervisees by attending antiracism training. Supervisee-focused personal development refers to fostering the self-exploration, awareness, and knowledge of supervisees. For example, an integration-stage supervisor might engage an incongruence-stage supervisee who is counseling a gay couple considering adopting a child to explore the supervisee's attitudes toward gay parenting.

The conceptualization dimension refers to promoting an understanding of the impact of individual and contextual factors on clients' lives, an understanding of the impact of stereotyping and oppression on presenting concerns, and an encouragement of alternative explanations for events. For example, an integration-stage supervisor might assist an integration-stage supervisee who is counseling a recently laid-off and depressed Asian American client to identify the potential relationships among the client's situational stressors, experiences of racism and ethnic identity development, and psychological difficulties.

The skills dimension refers to encouraging flexibility with regard to counseling interventions and practicing relevant and sensitive interventions when working with diverse clientele. For example, the integration-stage supervisor and exploration-stage supervisee could role-play a gender role analysis for use with a female client who has expressed feeling restricted by sex-role stereotypic behaviors.

The process dimension refers to a relationship between the supervisor and the supervisee characterized by respect and open communication. This dimension attends to the use of power in supervision and the development of a supervisory climate where diversity issues can be addressed. For example, the exploration-stage supervisor might openly process an incongruence-stage Asian supervisee's expressions of anxiety with regard to feeling misunderstood by White clients. This dimension also refers to demonstrating flexible approaches to supervision when working with diverse supervisees.

The outcome/evaluation dimension is consistent with the notion that the primary goal of supervision is helping the client of the counselor (ACES, 1990). Moreover, the evaluation dimension is consistent with Guideline 2.12 of the ACES's (1995) "Ethical Guidelines for Counseling Supervisors":

> Supervisors, through ongoing supervisee assessment and evaluation, should be aware of any personal or professional limitations of supervisees which are likely to impede future professional performance. Supervisors have the responsibility of recommending remedial assistance to the supervisee and of screening from the training program, applied counseling setting, or state licensure those supervisors who are unable to provide competent professional services.

Section F (Supervision, Teaching, and Training) of The ACA's (2005) *Code of Ethics* reiterates these responsibilities. An example of this dimension is an integration-stage supervisor who diligently listens to the audiotapes of a supervisee's counseling sessions with diverse clients and evaluates the supervisee's multicultural competence. It should be noted that, given the multiple and interrelated nature of supervisors' roles and responsibilities, there is some overlap among the multicultural supervision competencies across the dimensions identified in the subsequent sections.

Domains of Supervisor Multicultural Competence

Domain A: Supervisor-Focused Personal Development

- Supervisors actively explore and challenge their own biases, values, and worldview and how these relate to conducting supervision (e.g., multicultural identity development).
- Supervisors actively explore and challenge their attitudes and biases toward diverse supervisees.
- Supervisors are knowledgeable about their own cultural background and its influence on their attitudes, values, and behaviors.
- Supervisors possess knowledge about the background, experiences, worldview, and history of culturally diverse groups.
- Supervisors are knowledgeable about alternative helping approaches other than those based in a North American and Northern European context.
- Supervisors possess knowledge and keep informed of the theoretical and empirical literature on multicultural counseling

and multicultural supervision (e.g., impact of race on trainees' expectations of supervisor).

- Supervisors are knowledgeable about the limitations of traditional therapies with diverse clientele, such as women, racial/ethnic minorities, and gay and lesbian clients. Supervisors are aware of the cultural values inherent in traditional counseling theories and how these values may be inconsistent with the worldview of culturally different clients (e.g., focus on individualism, emotional/behavioral expressiveness, mind/body dichotomy, self-disclosure, intrapsychic causes).
- Supervisors maintain an ongoing network of feedback regarding personal and professional cultural competence (e.g., a diverse group of supervisors meet regularly to discuss issues related to supervision and diversity).

Domain B: Supervisee-Focused Personal Development

- Supervisors facilitate the exploration of supervisees' identity development (e.g., race, ethnicity, gender, sexual orientation).
- Supervisors facilitate supervisees' exploration of their values, attitudes, and behaviors and their relationship to working with diverse clients.
- Supervisors facilitate supervisees' exploration of biases that may impede effective and competent practice.
- Supervisors help supervisees understand the impact of social structures on supervisee and client behavior, including how class, gender, and racial privilege may have benefited the counselor.
- Supervisors encourage supervisees' participation in professional groups that attend to multicultural counseling (e.g., ACA's Association of Multicultural Counseling and Development).
- Supervisors encourage supervisees to participate in activities that foster multicultural competence (e.g., support groups, reading groups, attendance at conferences).
- Supervisors emphasize that counselor self-exploration is an ongoing process.

Domain C: Conceptualization

- Supervisors facilitate supervisees' understanding of the impact of oppression, racism, and discrimination on client's lives and presenting concerns to minimize victim blaming and pathologizing.
- Supervisors facilitate supervisees' understanding of both individual and contextual factors in clients' lives.
- Supervisors facilitate supervisees' understanding of culture-specific norms, as well as heterogeneity within groups.

- Supervisors facilitate supervisees' understanding of the intersections of multiple dimensions of diversity, or socioidentities, in clients' lives.
- Supervisors encourage supervisees to examine clients' individual, group, and universal identities in case conceptualization.
- Supervisor promotes supervisees' understanding of how stereotyping influences case conceptualizations, treatment objectives, and choice of interventions.
- Supervisors discuss with supervisees the implications of an overreliance or underreliance on cultural explanations for psychological difficulties.
- Supervisors helps supervisees explore alternative explanations to traditional theoretical perspectives.
- Supervisors explore with supervisees the limitations and cultural biases of traditional psychological assessment and testing.

Domain D: Skills/Interventions

- Supervisors model and train supervisees in a variety of verbal and nonverbal helping responses.
- Supervisors encourage supervisee flexibility with regard to traditional interventions and the use of alternative therapeutic interventions, such as those emphasizing group participation and collective action.
- Supervisors encourage supervisees to gain knowledge of community resources that may benefit clients.
- Supervisors encourage an appreciation of multiple sources of support, including indigenous helping networks.
- Supervisors encourage supervisees to collaborate with the client in the development of goals and objectives.
- Supervisors assist supervisees in developing client advocacy and social justice skills.
- Supervisors encourage supervisees to interact in the language requested by the client. Referral to an outside resource may be necessary.
- Supervisors train supervisees in multiple methods of assessment and evaluation.
- Supervisors ensure that supervisees do not enter into counseling situations where their biases or prejudices would adversely impact the supervisees' ability to effectively work with clients.

Domain E: Process

- Supervisors are honest about their biases and struggles to achieve cultural competence.

- Supervisors are able to competently and effectively work with diverse supervisees.
- Supervisors foster a climate that will facilitate discussion of diversity issues.
- Supervisors model respect for diversity and equality with supervisees and clients.
- Supervisors use power constructively in supervision, including jointly establishing objectives and criteria for performance, developing mechanisms for feedback pertaining to both the performance of supervisees and the supervisor, and handling supervisees' self-disclosures with respect and sensitivity.
- Supervisors attend to and process issues related to power dynamics between supervisor and supervisee and supervisee and client.
- Supervisors facilitate discussions of diversity, including the supervisees' diversity attitudes and their relationship to counseling clients.

Domain F: Outcome/Evaluation

- Supervisors are able to identify supervisees' personal and professional strengths and weaknesses in the area of multicultural counseling.
- Supervisors provide ongoing evaluation of supervisees to ensure multicultural competence.
- Supervisors are familiar with instruments that assess multicultural competence (e.g., Ancis et al., 2008; D'Andrea et al., 1991; Ponterotto et al., 1996; Sodowsky et al., 1994).
- Supervisors are able to recommend appropriate remedial training to supervisees who do not demonstrate multicultural competence.
- Supervisors recognize their responsibility to recommend remedial assistance and screen from the training program, applied counseling setting, or state licensure those supervisees who do not demonstrate multicultural competence.
- Supervisors recognize their responsibility for ensuring that their supervisees provide multiculturally competent counseling.

It follows that supervisors who are in the integration stage in terms of their MIF are most likely to demonstrate multicultural supervision competencies. Similarly, integration-stage supervisees are most likely to demonstrate multicultural counseling competencies with clients, as well as in supervision. Such supervisees will exhibit openness to (a) exploring their attitudes, worldview, and biases; (b) alternative conceptualizations of client concerns; (c) engaging in varied counseling approaches; and (d) processing multicultural issues within supervision.

Testing the Supervisor Multicultural Competence Framework

The Ancis and Ladany (2001) model has been empirically tested using both qualitative and quantitative methodologies. In one study, doctoral level psychology supervisees were interviewed about their supervisor's multicultural competence in supervision (Ancis & Marshall, in press) using the Ancis and Ladany framework. The study sought to explore how supervisees who perceive their supervisors as culturally competent describe the process of supervision, and whether multicultural competence is demonstrated according to the domains identified by Ancis and Ladany (2001).

Data analysis resulted in a classification scheme of two to four themes for each of the five domains of the model. Results were consistent with the proposed framework. Supervisees described their supervisors as actively engaged in multicultural dialogue and genuinely invested in developing a greater understanding of clients and of themselves. Similarly, supervisors were described as interested in the supervisees' and clients' perspectives on multicultural issues. Supervisors also openly disclosed the limits of their multicultural knowledge and were honest about their own cultural background and biases. Supervisors were described as encouraging supervisee self-awareness by highlighting the importance of exploring one's own background, including biases, in their work with clients.

Overall, supervisors were described as open, accepting, and flexible throughout the supervision experience. Supervisors facilitated a collaborative relationship between the counselor and client as supervisees were encouraged to explore the client's perspectives and discuss their understanding with the client. Supervisors facilitated a safe supervisory climate whereby supervisees felt that they could be vulnerable and take risks. Moreover, supervisees believed that their supervisors helped them to facilitate client awareness about social issues and problems. Such a stance appeared to positively impact both the supervisory relationship and the clinical relationship. Supervisees described their supervisors as not only comfortable with cultural differences existent in the supervisory relationship, but also encouraging of discussions related to the impact of the counselor's cultural differences on client conceptualization.

Similarly, other studies have demonstrated the positive impact of supervisee's perceptions of supervisor's multicultural competence on the supervisory working alliance, supervisee's satisfaction, and supervisor credibility (Inman, 2006; Silvestri, 2003; Tsong, 2005; Yang, 2005).

Interestingly and perhaps most importantly, Ancis and Marshall (in press) found that supervisees described multiculturally competent supervision as positively impacting their clinical work, particularly in terms of increasing their own and client's self-awareness and consciousness. For example, they described a relationship between supervisor's open and genuine disclosure and their own comfort with increased self-disclosure. Supervisees reported that the process of discussing multicultural issues in supervision positively affected client outcomes.

These results highlight the complex impact that supervision has on client outcomes, and generally suggests that culturally competent supervision is one way to increase the quality of the therapy that trainees provide with diverse clients.

Two additional studies explored Ancis and Ladany's (2001) model via a quantitative approach (Inman, 2006; Mori, Inman, & Caskie, 2009). Both studies used a measure of supervisor multicultural competence that was based directly on the competencies provided in the Ancis and Ladany (2001) model. Initial validity and reliability estimates of the Supervisor Multicultural Competence Inventory (SMCI; Inman, 2006) indicated positive psychometric properties. An exploratory factor analysis indicated that the measure works best as a single score or one-factor solution, and the internal consistency estimates when used in both studies was alpha = 0.97.

Results from both studies indicate that supervisor multicultural competence was positively associated with the supervisory working alliance and perceived satisfaction by marriage and family therapy trainees (Inman, 2006) and supervisor multicultural competence was positively related to international trainee's experience with supervision, both in a direct and indirect fashion (Mori et al., 2009). In sum, the SMCI holds promise to serve as a measure to assess supervisor multicultural competence. Additional work is needed to determine its continued efficacy. Moreover, similar to the counselor multicultural competence scales, the field would be served well if additional conceptualizations and measures are created to describe and assess supervisor multicultural competence.

Case Example

Mary, the supervisee, is a 22-year-old Chinese American female completing her doctoral practicum in a Veteran Administration (VA) hospital. For the past five months, Mary has been assigned to the rehabilitation medicine division of the hospital. Mary has developed positive professional relationships with both patients and staff and has consistently received favorable evaluations from her two supervisors. One of Mary's supervisors, Tom, is a 45-year-old White male psychologist who has worked in the VA hospital for the past 12 years, having completed his doctoral internship at the same site. One of Mary's patients, Juan, is a 42-year-old Nicaraguan male who has been working in construction for most of his life. He injured his back after falling off a ladder two months ago and is receiving disability payments. In order to supplement the family income, Juan's wife has pursued several part-time jobs cleaning houses. During the first several sessions, Juan indicated that he was having a difficult time adjusting to his physical condition and related financial burdens. He indicated that he felt as though he was not really contributing to the family and that he felt worthless. At the fourth session, Juan began to sexually harass Mary. He described explicit fantasies involving Mary and stated that since she was so cute he could not control himself. For the next several sessions, Mary waivered between ignoring these comments and asking Juan to explain why he verbalized these fantasies to her. Although Mary was feeling very anxious and uncomfortable with Juan, she was reluctant to discuss this situation with her supervisor. Despite receiving consistently positive evaluations, she felt as though this experience was somehow reflective of her counseling abilities. However, to some extent Mary also understood that she was not to blame for the sexual harassment. Moreover, Mary empathized with Juan's economic, physical, and vocational stressors and wanted to be of assistance to him. After much thought and feeling at a loss as to how to handle the situation, Mary discussed the situation with her supervisor, Tom. Initially, Tom expressed empathy and stated that this must be an uncomfortable experience. However, Tom indicated that since this was a VA hospital with primarily male patients, Mary needed to become accustomed to this sort of thing. He did not discuss any strategies for handling the situation and indicated that continuing to counsel Juan would be good practice; that is, it would help her to tolerate this behavior in the future. In addition, Tom suggested that Juan's behavior as a Hispanic male was culturally consistent and to be expected, and that Mary should become more aware of any seductive behavior on her part.

Mary left supervision feeling confused and frustrated. She respected her supervisor and had heard many glowing comments about his abilities from her professors. Nonetheless, Mary did not agree with her supervisor's assessment of Juan's behavior as culturally consistent and continued to doubt that she was somehow responsible for Juan's behavior. She began to feel angry at her supervisor's statements and lack of help, Mary had heard prejudicial and stereotypic statements about Asians throughout her life and understood their irrational basis. Moreover, Mary was currently enrolled in a multicultural counseling course that explored issues of gender, and she was knowledgeable about the prevalence of sexual harassment. Mary began to feel uncomfortable in her supervision sessions and became increasingly reluctant to discuss any personal issues with her supervisor. Feeling increasingly anxious with Juan's behavior, Mary decided to discuss the situation with one of her female professors. The professor validated

Mary's anxiety and frustration and offered her suggestions for confronting the situation.

For purposes of this example, the supervisor, Tom, may be characterized as a SPG member in terms of his gender and race. The supervisee may be characterized as a SOG member in terms of her gender and ethnicity. In regards to MIF, Tom is in the adaptation stage in the area of ethnicity and gender issues. He demonstrates stereotypic attitudes toward Hispanics and a lack of awareness with regard to gender issues. Mary is in the exploration stage in the area of gender issues and in the integration stage in the area of ethnic issues. With regard to gender issues, Mary has begun to develop an understanding of the significance of being female and related power dynamics in counseling. She is struggling with issues of self-blame and feelings of powerlessness. She has sought guidance from her supervisor and professor. Mary empathizes with the ethnic stereotypes and social stressors experienced by Juan, but does not overidentify to the point of dismissing the sexual harassment. In the area of ethnic and gender issues, the supervisee–trainee interpersonal interaction may be characterized as regressive. The supervisor's MIF have significant implications for the degree to which he engages in multiculturally competent supervision. For example, in the area of personal development, it is clear that Tom has neither explored nor challenged his own biases and values and how these relate to conducting supervision. Moreover, as a function of his lack of awareness and understanding of gender issues, he is unable to facilitate an exploration of Mary's ethnic or gender identity. It is quite likely that Tom would not appreciate the benefit of such an exploration. Since Tom possesses ethnic stereotypes, he promotes a stereotyped understanding of Juan's behavior. He does not provide Mary with training in ways of approaching and/or confronting Juan's inappropriate behavior. Issues related to power imbalances between Mary and Juan and between Mary and Tom are unattended to and, in fact, encouraged. As such, there is a poor supervisory working alliance characterized by supervisee anxiety and limited communication. However, Mary's advanced MIF in the areas of ethnicity and gender may still result in a meaningful counseling relationship. Mary may choose to demonstrate empathy with Juan's condition and foster his coping skills. In addition, she may confront Juan's inappropriate behavior, assert her rights to be treated fairly and with respect within the counseling relationship, and continue to counsel Juan under the conditions that the sexual harassment ceases. If Juan decides to continue in counseling within the established boundaries, counselor and client may develop a relationship based on mutual respect and open communication. Discussions of how power dynamics within the larger society have impacted Juan's life and that of his family may ensue.

Summary

The potential for diversity within the supervisor–supervisee–client triad is enormous. Models for both a better understanding of the complexity of multicultural supervision and to effective intervention are needed. In the present chapter, we have presented both a model to aid supervisors in understanding the multicultural supervision process and a framework to provide multiculturally competent supervision. Further theoretical and empirically based work in this area is imperative to furthering an understanding of the personal and professional development of supervisors and supervisees and, in a related fashion, facilitating clients' psychological health and well-being.

References

American Counseling Association (ACA). (1995). *Code of ethics and standards of practice.* Alexandria. VA: Author.

American Counseling Association (ACA). (2005). *Code of ethics.* Alexandria. VA: Author.

American Psychological Association (APA). (2000). Guidelines for psychotherapy with lesbian, gay, and bisexual clients. *American Psychologist, 55,* 1440–1451.

American Psychological Association (APA). (2003). Guidelines on multicultural education, training, research, practice, and organizational change. *American Psychologist, 58,* 377–402.

American Psychological Association (APA). (2004). Guidelines for psychological practice with older adults. *American Psychologist, 59,* 236–260.

American Psychological Association (APA). (2007). Guidelines for psychological practice with girls and women. *American Psychologist, 62,* 949–979.

Ancis, J. R. (Ed.). (2004). *Culturally responsive interventions: Innovative approaches to working with diverse populations.* New York, NY: Brunner-Routledge.

Ancis, J. R., & Ladany, N. (2001). A multicultural framework for counselor supervision. In L. J. Bradley & N. Ladany (Eds.), *Counselor supervision: Principles, process,and practice* (3rd ed., pp. 63–90). Philadelphia: Brunner-Routledge.

Ancis, J. R., & Marshall, D. (in press). Supervisee's perceptions of culturally competent supervision. *Journal of Counseling and Development.*

Ancis, J. R., & Sanchez-Hucles, J. V. (2000). A preliminary analysis of counseling students' attitudes toward counseling women and women of color: Implications for cultural competency training. *Journal of Multicultural Counseling and Development, 28,* 16–31.

Ancis, J. R., & Szymanski, D. M. (2001). Awareness of white privilege among white counseling trainees. *The Counseling Psychologist, 29,* 548–569.

Ancis, J. R., Szymanski, D. M., & Ladany, N. (2008). Development and psychometric evaluation of the counseling women competencies scale (CWCS). *The Counseling Psychologist, 36,* 719–724.

Arredondo, P., Toporek, R., Brown, S. P., Jones, J., Locke, D. C., Sanchez, J., & Stadler, H. (1996). Operationalization of the multicultural counseling competencies. *Journal of Multicultural Counseling and Development, 24,* 42–78.

Association for Counselor Education and Supervision (ACES). (1990). Standards for counseling supervisors. *Journal of Counseling and Development, 69,* 30–32.

Association for Counselor Education and Supervision. (1995). Ethical guidelines for counseling supervisors. *Counselor Education and Supervision, 34,* 270–276.

Atkinson, D. R., Morten, G., & Sue, D. W. (1993). *Counseling American minorities: A cross-cultural perspective* (3rd ed.). Madison, WI: Brown & Benchmark.

Ault-Riche, M. (1988). Teaching an integrated model of family therapy: Women as students, women as supervisors. *Journal of Psychotherapy and the Family, 3,* 175–192.

Bernard, J. M. (1979). Supervisory training: A discrimination model. *Counselor Education and Supervision, 19,* 60–68.

Bernard, J. M. (1997). The discrimination model. In C. E. Watkins (Ed.), *Handbook of psychotherapy supervision* (pp. 310–327). New York, NY: Wiley.

Bernard, J. M., & Goodyear, R. K. (1998). *Fundamentals of clinical supervision* (2nd ed.). Needham Heights, MA: Allyn & Bacon.

Bernard, J. M., & Goodyear, R. L. (2009). *Fundamentals of clinical supervision* (4th ed.). Boston, MA: Allyn and Bacon.

Bidell, M. P. (2005). The sexual orientation counselor competency scale: Assessing attitudes, skills, and knowledge of counselors working with lesbian, gay, and bisexual clients. *Counselor Education and Supervision, 44,* 267–279.

Boyd, J. (1978). *Counselor supervision: Approaches, preparation, practices.* Muncie, IN: Accelerated Development.

Brodsky, A. M. (1980). Sex role issues in the supervision of therapy. In A. K. Hess (Ed.), *Psychotherapy supervision: Theory, research, and practice* (pp. 474–508). New York, NY: Wiley.

Brown, M. T., & Landrum-Brown, J. (1995). Counselor supervision: Cross-cultural perspectives. In J. G. Ponterotto, J. M. Casas, L. A. Suzuki, & C. M. Alexander (Eds.), *Handbook of multicultural counseling* (pp. 263–286). Thousand Oaks, CA: Sage.

Bulhan, H. A. (1985). *Frantz Fanon and the psychology of oppression.* New York, NY: Plenum.

Carney, C. G., & Kahn, K. B. (1984). Building competencies for effective cross-cultural counseling: A developmental view. *The Counseling Psychologist, 12,* 111–119.

Cass, V. C. (1979). Homosexual identity formation: A theoretical model. *Journal of Homosexuality, 4,* 219–235.

Chagon, J., & Russell, R. K. (1995). Assessment of supervisee developmental level and supervision environment across supervisor experience. *Journal of Counseling and Development, 73,* 553–558.

Chan, C. S. (1989). Issues of identity development among Asian-American lesbians and gay men. *Journal of Counseling & Development, 68,* 16–20.

Cheng, L. Y. (1993). Psychotherapy supervision in Hong Kong: A meeting of two cultures. *Australian and New Zealand Journal of Psychiatry, 27,* 127–132.

Constantine, M. G. (1997). Facilitating multicultural competency in counseling supervision. In D. B. Pope-Davis & H. L. K. Coleman (Eds.), *Multicultural counseling competencies: Assessment, education and training, and supervision* (pp. 310–324). Thousand Oaks, CA: Sage.

Constantine, M. G., & Ladany, N. (2000). Self-report multicultural counseling competence instruments and their relation to multicultural case conceptualization ability and social desirability. *Journal of Counseling Psychology, 46,* 155–164.

Cook, D. A. (1994). Racial identity in supervision. *Counselor Education and Supervision, 34,* 132–141.

Cross, W. E., Jr. (1971). The negro-to-black conversion experience. *Black World, 20,* 13–27.

Cross, W. E., Jr. (1995). The psychology of nigrescence: Revising the Cross model. In J. G. Ponterotto, J. M. Casas, L. A. Suzuki, & C. M. Alexander (Eds.), *Handbook of multicultural counseling* (pp. 93–122). Thousand Oaks, CA: Sage.

D'Andrea, M., & Daniels, J. (1997). Multicultural counseling supervision: Central issues, theoretical considerations, and practical strategies. In D. B. Pope-Davis & H. L. K. Coleman (Eds.), *Multicultural counseling competencies: Assessment, education and training, and supervision* (pp. 290–309). Thousand Oaks, CA: Sage.

D'Andrea, M., Daniels, J., & Heck, R. (1991). Evaluating the impact of multicultural counseling training. *Journal of Counseling and Development, 70,* 143–150.

Downing, N. E., & Roush, K. L. (1985). From passive-acceptance to active commitment: A model of feminist identity development for women. *The Counseling Psychologist, 13*(4), 695–709.

Ekstein, R., & Wallerstein, R. S. (1972). *The teaching and learning of psychotherapy* (2nd ed.). New York, NY: International Universities Press.

Fassinger, R. E. (1991). The hidden minority: Issues and challenges in working with lesbian women and gay men. *The Counseling Psychologist, 19,* 157–176.

Fine, M., Weis, L., Powell, L. C., & Mun Wong, L. (Eds.). (1997). *Off-white: Readings on race, power, and society.* London, UK: Routledge.

Fong, M. L., & Lease, S. H. (1996). *Cross-cultural supervision: Issues for the white supervisor.* Newbury Park, CA: Sage.

Fukuyama, M. A. (1994). Critical incidents in multicultural counseling supervision: A phenomenological approach to supervision research. *Counselor Education and Supervision, 34,* 142–151.

Gamst, G., Dana, R. H., Der-Karabetian, A., Aragon, M., Arellano, L., Morrow, G., & Martenson, L. (2004). Cultural competency revised: The California brief multicultural competence scale. *Measurement and Evaluation in Counseling and Development, 37,* 163–184.

Gardner, L. M. H. (1980). Racial, ethnic, and social class considerations in psychotherapy supervision. In A. K. Hess (Ed.), *Psychotherapy supervision: Theory, research, and practice* (pp. 474–508), New York, NY: Wiley.

Garrett, M. T., Borders, L. D., Crutchfield, L. B., Torres-Rivera, E., Brotherton, D., & Curtis, R. (2001). Multicultural superVISION: A paradigm of cultural responsiveness for supervisors. *Journal of Multicultural Counseling and Development, 29,* 147–158.

Gilbert, L. A., & Rossman, K. M. (1992). Gender and the mentoring process for women: Implications for professional development. *Professional Psychology: Research and Practice, 23,* 233–238.

González, R. C. (1997). Postmodern supervision: A multicultural perspective. In D. B. Pope-Davis & H. L. K. Coleman (Eds.), *Multicultural counseling competencies: Assessment, education and training, and supervision* (pp. 350–386). Thousand Oaks, CA: Sage.

Guerra, P. (1999, May). Counselors for social justice becomes organizational affiliate. *Counseling Today*, pp. 1, 25.

Hardiman, R. (1982). White identity development: A process-oriented model for describing the racial consciousness of white Americans. *Dissertation Abstracts International, 43*, 104A. (University Microfilms No. 82–10330)

Hart, G., Borders, L. D., Nance, D., & Paradise, L. (1993). Ethical guidelines for counseling supervisors. *ACES Spectrum, 53*, 5–8.

Helms, J. E. (1990). *Black and white racial identity: Theory, research, and practice.* New York, NY: Greenwood.

Helms, J. E. (1995). An update of Helms' white and people of color racial identity models. In J. G. Ponterotto, J. M. Casas, L. A. Suzuki, & C. M. Alexander (Eds.), *Handbook of multicultural counseling* (pp. 181–198). Thousand Oaks, CA: Sage.

Helms, J. E., & Cook, D. A. (1999). *Using race and culture in counseling and psychotherapy: Theory and process.* Boston, MA: Allyn & Bacon.

Hogan, R. A. (1964). Issues and approaches in supervision. *Psychotherapy: Theory, Research, and Practice, 1,* 1739–1741.

Holloway, E. (1992). Supervision: A way of teaching and learning. In S. D. Brown & R. W. Lent (Eds.), *Handbook of counseling psychology* (pp. 177–214). New York, NY: Wiley.

Holloway, E. L. (1995). *Clinical supervision: A systems approach.* Thousand Oaks, CA: Sage.

Holloway, E. L. (1997). Structures for the analysis and teaching of supervision. In C. E. Watkins (Ed.), *Handbook of psychotherapy supervision* (pp. 249–276). New York, NY: Wiley.

Inman, A. G. (2006). Supervisor multicultural competence and its relation to supervisory process and outcome. *Journal of Marital and Family Therapy, 32,* 73–85.

Ivey, A. E., Fouad. N. A., Arredondo, P., & D'Andrea, M. (1999). *Guidelines for multicultural counseling competencies: Implications for practice, training, and research.* Unpublished manuscript.

Johnson, M. K., Searight, H. R., Handal, P. J., & Gibbons, J. L. (1993). Survey of clinical psychology graduate students' gender attitudes and knowledge: Toward gender-sensitive psychotherapy training. *Journal of Contemporary Psychotherapy, 23,* 233–249.

Kaduvettoor, A., O'Shaughnessy, T., Mori, Y., Beverly, C., Weatherford, R. D., & Ladany, N. (2009). Helpful and hindering multicultural events in group supervision: Climate and multicultural competence. *The Counseling Psychologist, 37*(6), 786–820.

Kagan, N. (1976). *Influencing human interaction.* Washington, DC: American Association for Counseling and Development.

Kim, B. S. K., Cartwright, B. Y., Asay, P. A., & D'Andrea, M. J. (2003). A revision of the multicultural awareness, knowledge, and skills survey—Counselor edition. *Measurement and Evaluation in Counseling and Development, 36,* 161–180.

Ladany, N., Brittan-Powell, C. S., & Pannu, R. K. (1997). The influence of supervisory racial identity interaction and racial matching on the supervisory working alliance and supervisee multicultural competence. *Counselor Education and Supervision, 36,* 284–304.

Ladany, N., Friedlander, M. L., & Nelson, M. L. (2005). *Critical events in psychotherapy supervision: An interpersonal approach.* Washington, DC: American Psychological Association.

Ladany, N., & Inman, A. G. (in press). Training and supervision. In E. M. Altmaier and Hansen, J. (Eds.). *The Oxford Handbook of Counseling Psychology.* New York: Oxford University Press.

Ladany, N., Inman, A. G., Constantine, M. G., & Hofheinz, E. (1997). Supervisee multicultural case conceptualization ability and self-reported multicultural competence as functions of supervisee racial identity and supervisor focus. *Journal of Counseling Psychology, 44,* 284–293.

Ladany, N., Lehrman-Waterman, D., Molinaro, M., & Wolgast, B. (1999). Psychotherapy supervisor ethical practices: Adherence to guidelines, the supervisory working alliance, and supervisee satisfaction. *The Counseling Psychologist, 27,* 443–475.

Ladany, N., Walker, J. A., Pate-Carolan, L., & Gray Evans, L. (2008). *Practicing Counseling and Psychotherapy: Insights from trainees, clients, and supervisors.* New York, NY: Routledge.

Leong, F. T. L., & Wagner, N. S. (1994). Cross-cultural counseling supervision: What do we know? What do we need to know? *Counselor Education and Supervision, 34,* 117–131.

Levine, F. M., & Tilker, A., II. (1974). A behavior modification approach to supervision and psychotherapy. *Psychotherapy: Theory, Research, and Practice, 11,* 182–188.

Littrell, J. M., Lee-Borden, N., & Lorenz, J. A. (1979). A developmental framework for counseling supervision. *Counselor Education and Supervision, 19,* 119–136.

Loganbill, C., Hardy, E., & Delworth, U. (1982). Supervision: A conceptual model. *Counseling Psychologist, 10,* 3–42.

Lopez, S. R. (1997). Cultural competence in psychotherapy: A guide for clinicians and their supervisors. In C. E. Watkins, Jr. (Ed.), *Handbook of psychotherapy supervision* (pp. 570–588). New York, NY: Wiley.

Marcia, J. E. (1966). Development and validation of ego identity status. *Journal of Personality and Social Psychology, 3,* 551–558.

McNamara, K., & Rickard, K. M. (1989). Feminist identity development: Implications for feminist therapy with women. *Journal of Counseling and Development, 68,* 184–189.

Morgan, D. W. (1984). Cross-cultural factors in the supervision of psychotherapy. *The Psychiatric Forum, 12*(2), 61–64.

Mori, Y., Inman, A. G., & Caskie, G. I. L. (2009). Supervising international students: Relationship between acculturation, supervisor multicultural competence, cultural discussions, and supervision satisfaction. *Training and Education in Professional Psychology, 3,* 10–18.

Munson, C. E. (1997). Gender and psychotherapy supervision: The partnership model. In C. E. Watkins, Jr. (Ed.), *Handbook of psychotherapy supervision* (pp. 549–569). New York, NY: Wiley.

Myers. L. J. (1991). Expanding the psychology of knowledge optimally: The importance of worldview revisited. In R. L. Jones (Ed.), *Black psychology* (3rd ed., pp. 15–28). Berkeley, CA: Cobb & Henry.

Nichols, B. (1976, November). *The philosophical aspects of cultural differences.* Paper presented at the conference of the World Psychiatric Association, Ibadan, Nigeria.

Nobles, W. (1972). African philosophy: Foundation for black psychology. In R. L. Jones (Ed.), *Black psychology* (1st ed., pp. 18–32). New York, NY: Harper & Row.

Ossana, S. M., Helms, J. E., & Leonard, M. M. (1992). Do "womanist" identity attitudes influence college women's self-esteem and perceptions of environmental bias? *Journal of Counseling & Development, 70,* 402–408.

Phinney, J. S. (1989). Stages of ethnic identity development in minority group adolescents. *Journal of Early Adolescence, 6,* 34–49.

Ponterotto, J. G. (1988). Racial consciousness development among white counselor trainees: A stage model. *Journal of Multicultural Counseling and Development, 16,* 146–156.

Ponterotto, J. G.; Gretchen, D., Utsey, S. O., Rieger, B. P., Austin, R. (2002). A revision of the Multicultural Counseling Awareness Scale. *Journal of Multicultural Counseling and Development, 30*(3), 153–180.

Ponterotto, J. G., Rieger, B. P., Barrett, A., Sparks, R., Sanchez, C. M., & Magids, D. (1996). Development and initial validation of the multicultural counseling awareness scale. In G. R. Sodowsky & J. C. Impara (Eds.), *Multicultural assessment in counseling and clinical psychology* (pp. 247–282). Lincoln, NE: Buros Institute of Mental Measurements.

Porter, N. (1995). Supervision of psychotherapists: Integrating anti-racist, feminist, and multicultural perspectives. In H. Landrine (Ed.), *Bringing cultural diversity to feminist psychology* (pp. 163–175). Washington, DC: American Psychological Association.

Priest, R. (1994). Minority supervisor and majority supervisor: Another perspective on clinical reality. *Counselor Education and Supervision, 34,* 152–158.

Rarick, S. (2000). The relationship of supervisor and trainee gender match and gender attitude match to supervisory style and the supervisory working alliance. *Dissertation Abstracts International,* DAI-A 61/11, p. 4299.

Remington, G., & DaCosta, G. (1989). Ethnocultural factors in resident supervision: Black supervisor and white supervisees. *American Journal of Psychotherapy, 43*(3), 398–404.

Rice, L. N. (1980). A client-centered approach to the supervision of psychotherapy. In A. K. Hess (Ed.), *Psychotherapy supervision: Theory, research, and practice* (pp. 136–147). New York, NY: Wiley.

Richards, K. (2000). Counsellor supervision in Zimbabwe: A new direction. *International Journal for the Advancement of Counselling, 22,* 143–155.

Ridley, C. R., Mendoza, D. W., Kanitz, B. E., Angermeier, L., & Zenk, R. (1994). Cultural sensitivity in multicultural counseling: A perceptual schema model. *Journal of Counseling Psychology, 41,* 125–136.

Rodolfa, E., Bent, R., Eisman, E., Nelson, P., Rehm, L., & Ritchie, P. (2005). A Cube model for competency development: Implications for psychology educators and regulators. *Professional Psychology: Research and Practice, 36*(4), 347–354.

Rust, P. C. (1993). "Coming out" in the age of social constructionism: Sexual identity formation among lesbian and bisexual women. *Gender & Society, 7,* 50–77.

Sabnani, H. B., Ponterotto, J. G., & Borodovsky, L. G. (1991). White racial identity development and cross-cultural counselor training: A stage model. *The Counseling Psychologist, 19,* 76–102.

Silvestri, T. J. (2003). The temporal effect of supervisor focus, the supervisory working alliance, and the graduate training environment upon supervisee multicultural competence (Doctoral dissertation, Lehigh University, 2003). *Dissertation Abstracts International, 63,* 6108.F

Skovholt, T. M., & Rønnestad, M., II. (1992). Themes in therapist and counselor development. *Journal of Counseling and Development, 70,* 505–515.

Sodowsky, G. R., Kwan, K. L. K., & Pannu, R. (1995). Ethnic identity of Asians in the United States: Conceptualization and illustrations. In J. G. Ponterotto, J. M. Casas, L. A. Suzuki, & C. M. Alexander (Eds.), *Handbook of multicultural counseling* (pp. 123–154). Newbury Park, CA: Sage.

Sodowsky, G. R., Taffe, R. C., Gutkin, T. B., & Wise, S. L. (1994). Development of the multicultural counseling inventory: A self-report measure of multicultural competencies. *Journal of Counseling Psychology, 41,* 137–148.

Stoltenberg, C. (1981). Approaching supervision from a developmental perspective: The counselor-complexity model. *Journal of Counseling Psychologists, 28,* 59–65.

Stoltenberg, C. D., McNeill, B. W., & Delworth, W. (1998). *IDM: An integrated developmental model for supervising counselors and therapists.* San Francisco, CA: Jossey-Bass Publishers.

Sue, D. W., Arredondo, P., & McDavis, R. J. (1992). Multicultural counseling competencies and standards: A call to the profession. *Journal of Counseling and Development, 70,* 477–486.

Sue, D. W., Bernier, J. B., Durran, M., Feinberg, L., Pedersen, P., Smith, E., & Vasquez-Nuttal, E. (1982). Position paper: Cross-cultural counseling competencies. *The Counseling Psychologist, 10,* 45–52.

Sue, D. W., & Sue, D. (1999). *Counseling the culturally different: Theory and practice* (3rd ed.). New York, NY: Wiley.

Thompson, C. E., & Neville, H. A. (1999). Racism, mental health, and mental health practice. *The Counseling Psychologist, 27,* 155–223.

Troiden, R. R. (1989). The formation of homosexual identities. *Journal of Homosexuality, 17,* 43–73.

Tsong, Y. V. (2005). The role of supervisee attachment styles and perception of supervisors' general and multicultural supervision in supervisory working alliance, supervisee omissions in supervision, and supervision outcome (Doctoral dissertation. University of Southern California, Los Angeles, 2005). *Dissertation Abstracts International, 65,* 3291.

U.S. Census Bureau. (1996). *Population projections of the United States by age, sex, race, and Hispanic origin: 1995–2000.* United States Department of Commerce. Washington, DC: U.S. Government Printing Office.

U.S. Census Bureau (2008). US Population Projections. 2008 National Population Projections. Retreived from http://www.census.gov/Press-Release/www/releases/archives/population/012496.html. Retrieved January 29, 2010.

Vargas, L. A. (1989, August). *Training psychologists to be culturally responsive: Issues in supervision.* Paper presented at a symposium at the 97th Annual Convention of the American Psychological Association, New Orleans.

Vasquez, M. J., & McKinley, D. L. (1982). Supervision: A conceptual model: Reactions and an extension. *The Counseling Psychologist, 10,* 59–63.

Watkins, C. E., Jr. (Ed.). (1997). *Handbook of psychotherapy supervision.* New York, NY: Wiley.

Yang, P. H. (2005). The effects of supervisor cultural responsiveness and ethnic group similarity on Asian American supervisee's perception of supervisor credibility and multicultural competence (Doctoral dissertation, University of California, Santa Barbara, 2004). Dissertation Abstracts International, 65, 6681.

CHAPTER 4

Supervision Techniques

JESSICA A. WALKER

As other chapters in this book will attest, supervision theory, research, process/outcome variables, and assessment are all important factors to consider when conducting supervision. Strong supervisory relationships, like positive therapeutic relationships, will be grounded in theory, charted by models, driven by empiricism, and fueled by the factors of a supportive and challenging working alliance. However, in between the complexities of supervision philosophy, are the standard weekly supervision sessions where supervisors practice techniques. Supervision techniques play one of four parts in a larger scheme of supervision process skills (Ladany, Walker, Pate-Carolan, & Gray Evans, 2008). Supervisors may use (1) nonverbal behaviors (e.g., eye contact, proximity, head nodding); (2) response modes (e.g., what is actually said and how it is said); (3) covert processes (internal thoughts and feelings); and (4) theoretically based therapeutic strategies and techniques for change. These strategies may include dialog, silence, role-plays, interpretation, praise, critique, disclosure, projection, comfort, empowerment, instruction, or emotional expression. Although there are countless paths of supervision process skills to choose in any given scenario, this chapter is meant to highlight a few suggested supervision techniques, including interpersonal process recall (IPR), the supervision genogram, processing issues of culture, helping a supervisee understand and manage countertransference, the reflective process, supervisor self-disclosure, and using structured peer group format techniques in individual supervision. We will also take a look at the role of technology and posit techniques of the future. The following is a how-to look at what goes on in a supervision session.

Interpersonal Process Recall

IPR is undoubtedly one of the most well-known supervision techniques. The IPR was developed by N. I. Kagan, Krathwohl, and Miller at Michigan State University in the early 1960s. The IPR involves stimulating recall of the counseling session from a supervisee or client with the power of videotape playback. During these recall sessions, the supervisee or client is given control of the remote control with the power to stop and start the recording. When the recording is stopped, a supervisor trained in IPR asks questions meant to identify feelings. The main goal is to address underlying thoughts and feelings more so than to critique the work. Questions such as "What do you think he or she was trying to say? What were you thinking when he or she said that? Did anything prevent you from sharing your feelings at that time? What do you think her or his perceptions of you are? Can you tell me what you felt at that point? Can you recall more of the details of your feelings?"

Kagan and colleagues observed that counselors and clients were able to recall and evaluate their thoughts and feelings of a counseling session in meaningful depth after watching the session played back via a video recording. Additionally, it was noted that a third party (supervisor/inquirer) positively contributed to the playback exposure by using a series of inductive questions during the recall session. In fact, it is the inquirer role and function that serve as the "heart and soul" of the IPR, making it a "powerful tool for discovery and training" (Kagan & Kagan, 1991, p. 222).

Practical Implication

When using this technique, Kagan and colleagues discovered two interesting practical implications. First, although beginning counselors initially acted as if they took their client's words for face value, during recall sessions, these trainees realized that they did indeed notice and understand a deeper meaning behind their clients' statements (but were unable to act on their understanding in session). This is called "feigning of clinical naïveté." Note the following examples from Kagan (1980):

> I knew she [the client] was very unhappy underneath that put-on smile, but—and I know this is stupid—I was afraid she might cry if I told her I knew she was "hurting," and then I would feel that I had made her cry or I knew[the client] was lying but I didn't call him on it. ... I was afraid he wouldn't come back for a next session if I was honest with him ... he might even get up and walk right out of the room. ... I guess I would feel hurt if he did these things, and yet I know he probably wouldn't, but I couldn't risk it, I guess. (p. 264)

The second dynamic that IPR can highlight is when trainees exhibit "tuning out" behavior. Some trainees are worried about what to say and wanting to make a good impression. It is during these times that counselors in training may actually stop hearing or seeing the client for a period of time. However, during recall sessions with a supervisor, trainees have been able to see and hear what they were tuning out. Relatedly, Kagen and colleagues (1980) observed that after trainees are exposed to IPR as a supervision technique, they engage in tuning out less often. Thus, the idea is that improvement of trainee communication skills may positively contribute to overall counseling skills. Relatedly, the trainee may use recall strategies to help clients in their interpersonal relationships.

Future Research Directions

IPR has been used in a variety of work settings for a diverse range of people in training including medical students, counseling students, military personnel, Australian cockpit crews, newly brain injured patients, lupus patients, and emergency medical staff in a fire department (Kagan & Kagan, 1997). Empirically, a cost/benefit analysis of the IPR technique compared to traditional supervision was examined by Kingdon (1975). The IPR did not demonstrate significantly different effects in the areas of counselor empathy, client satisfaction, supervisor rating, or client self-reported inhibition. However, there were significant results related to self-exploration (i.e., after initial exposure to IPR, the IPR group's level of self-exploration fell below that of the comparison group. However, the IPR self-exploration levels recovered by the third session.).

Current research is warranted looking specifically at long-term comparative effects of IPR, specifically for training in the mental health field. It would inform the literature to revisit Kingdon's variables of IPR's effect on counselor empathy and client satisfaction, but it would also be beneficial to examine supervision process and outcome variables. Of particular interest, future research could focus on how using the IPR supervision technique affects the supervisory working alliance.

The Supervision Genogram

Aten, Madson, and Kruse (2008) introduced the supervision genogram primarily as a tool for preparing supervisors-in-training. For this chapter, I would like to highlight how the supervision genogram can also be used as a technique between a supervisor and advanced trainee (e.g., predoctoral intern). The supervision genogram asks a trainee to outline his or her history of psychotherapy supervisors. Using a code system similar to a family genogram, the trainee identifies his or her supervisors' demographics, the nature of the supervisory alliances, the professional contexts where supervision occurred, and the modes of supervision utilized. Other features that can be added are the theoretical orientations of supervisors, descriptors of supervisory styles, evaluation processes, and positive and negative critical events. At the end of the exercise, the trainee possesses a visual representation and time line of his or her supervisory experiences (see Figure 4.1).

Practical Implication

The supervisor can use this genogram exercise to prompt a series of reflective questions to help ascribe meaning and interpretations from the genogram (e.g., What personal/professional characteristics of your supervisors do you admire? How was conflict handled? How did culture impact your supervisory relationships?). Again, these questions were originally intended to increase the awareness of a supervisor-in-training (e.g., how do these personal supervisory experiences affect your new role as a supervisor?). However, the genogram technique also can be used to educate a supervisor about his or her counseling trainee's expectations for supervision, previous supervisory connections and conflicts, preferred supervisory modalities, and working alliance factors. Note the clinical case example from Aten et al. (2008):

> As he described his previous supervision relationships I was able to gain insight into his prior experience and understanding of supervision. For instance, he brought attention to the fact that most of his supervisors were "cognitive therapists," but did so with some hesitancy in his voice. I found that his primary therapeutic theoretical orientation was psychodynamic and he was concerned that I may discourage him from sharing his psychodynamic conceptualizations with supervisees. At this point, I was able to discuss my therapeutic theoretical orientation (reality therapy) and to assure him that both perspectives would be respected ... the supervision genogram provided William and I with a strong foundation for our supervisory relationship and helped us begin to navigate the nuances of supervision. (p. 114)

When using the supervision genogram with a supervisee who is late in their training, there will likely be several supervision experiences on which to reflect. One area that may be helpful for this population in particular is to look for gaps in their supervision genogram. For instance, what do they *not* see? What *isn't* there? Perhaps the intern has never had a supervisor who communicates directly, or a supervisor that self-discloses. Maybe the intern has never experienced a supervisory alliance that is task-focused, or one that is emotionally bonding. Is there a particular theoretical orientation by which the trainee has never been influenced? These gaps can be a helpful guide. Supervisors may choose to use the genogram technique to ask trainees what they hope to get out of supervision that they have never received in the past.

Finally, as a supervisory evaluation tool, a supervisor can ask their trainee to revisit the genogram halfway through their internship year and

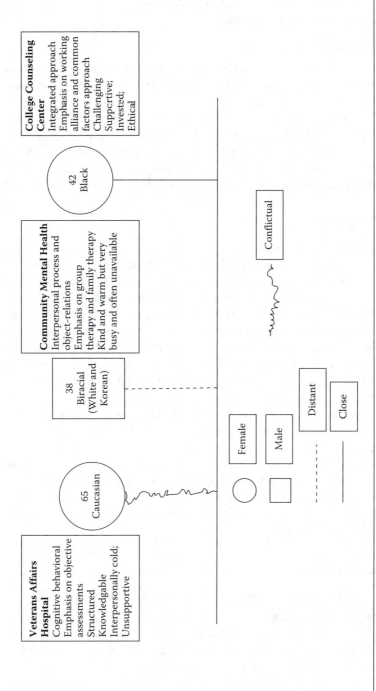

Figure 4.1   Supervision Genogram.

add their current supervision relationship. Then, both the trainee and supervisor can use the visual representation to observe what factors are similar, different, positive, or negative.

Future Research Directions

Research on the supervision genogram may be an exciting next empirical step. Potential research questions may include: (1) How does using the supervision genogram contribute to the factors of the supervisory working alliance? (2) How does using the supervision genogram shape the supervisory style? (3) How do supervisees experience the supervision genogram as a tool for their own self discovery? (4) In what ways does creating the supervision genogram affect supervisors in training? (5) How does using the genogram in supervision parallel the supervisee's use of family genograms in counseling?

Processing Issues of Culture

The literature has demonstrated that supervisors can strengthen supervisory relationships and positively affect the trainee experiences if they constructively respond to issues of culture (Burkard et al., 2006). Similarly to how training programs encourage therapists to process issues of culture with their clients, so too do supervision training programs instruct supervisors to engage in such genuine and multiculturally competent discussions with their trainees. However, many supervisors still may feel unprepared or uncomfortable with this task. In Chapter 3 of this volume, Ancis and Ladany outlined several areas of exploration: personal development (supervisor-focused and supervisee-focused), conceptualization, skills, process, and evaluation. This next section will build upon the framework of these domains, and provide three how-to techniques to process issues of culture in supervision. First, an outline will be provided to encourage supervisees to concretely consider steps of personal development. Second, examples will be given that address integrating and documenting supervisees' conceptualization skills. Third, a template will be provided to prompt cultural dialog within the supervision relationship (addressing the domains of both process and evaluation).

Practical Implication

Fostering Supervisee-Focused Personal Development

Encouraging a supervisee to increase her or his personal multicultural development may seem like an abstract concept, but there are several structured strategies that may be appropriate. In Chapter 3 of this volume, Ancis and Ladany outlined several areas of exploration to facilitate (e.g., identity development, values, and attitudes) as well as areas of activities in which to encourage participation (e.g., conferences, professional groups). Below please note three structured techniques that may supplement the domain of fostering supervisee personal development.

Bibliosupervision and Multicultural Reading Worksheet

First, consider the importance of bibliosupervision. Outside readings are not just for the classroom, but rather can be an integral part of the supervision process. Initial suggestions for supervisee personal multicultural development include:

- *A Race is a Nice Thing to Have* (Helms, 1992)
- *Overcoming Our Racism* (Sue, 2003)
- White Privilege: Unpacking the Invisible Knapsack (McIntosh, 2003)
- Racial Microaggression in Everyday Life: Implications for Clinical Practice (Sue et al., 2007)
- Treating the Purple Menace: Ethical Considerations of Conversion Therapy and Affirmative Alternatives (Tozer & McClanahan, 1999)
- APA Guidelines for psychotherapy with lesbian gay and bisexual clients (2000)
- *Race, Class and Gender* (Andersen & Collins, 1995)
- *Diagnosis in a Multicultural Context* (Paniagua, 2001)
- *Bringing Cultural Diversity to Feminist Psychology: Theory Research and Practice* (Landrine, 1995)
- *A Framework for Understanding Poverty* (Payne, 2001)

Bibliosupervision does not end with a library check-out. Instead, it requires referencing the readings and challenging supervisees to consider how these cultural factors apply to their *own* lives. Consider the following worksheet to supplement a reading assignment:

Multicultural Reading: _____ Date: _____

- The part of the reading that I identified with the most:
- The part of the reading that I identified with the least:
- One way the reading influenced the way I think:
- One way the reading affected the way I feel:
- One way the reading may shape my future behavior:
- I have become more aware of:
- I have learned more about:
- Questions I have about the reading:
- Questions I have in general, as generated from this reading:
- Ways in which my reaction to this reading material may affect my clinical work:

Another suggestion is to encourage your supervisee to conduct his or her own specific literature review for a unique area of appropriate personal development. This literature review in and of itself can be a project of personal growth (e.g., experientially participating in the pursuit of knowledge). The review can also serve as a means to increase knowledge about the variety of perspectives on a population.

Journaling

Another recommendation is to have your supervisee engage in a journal exercise recording observations related to a specific and unique personal development goal. For instance, after reading "Racial Microaggressions in Everyday Life" (Sue et al., 2007), the supervisee could keep a daily or weekly log of the microaggressions he or she notices from the self and/or others. Observations can even include microaggressions that occur in supervision (Constantine & Sue, 2007). The point of this exercise is to increase the supervisee's awareness of a multicultural interpersonal dynamic or pattern. Another example may be daily or weekly journaling about the supervisees awareness of internalized isms. A female supervisee may wish to expand her insight related to internalized sexism. A bisexual supervisee may not be aware of his or her own internalized homophobia. A journaling activity can assist with this.

Personal Development Goal Contract

For some supervisees, it may be helpful to have personal development goals in writing. A final recommendation for this domain is to utilize a written goal created and maintained by the supervisee for her or his own self-evaluation. Key elements are (1) the overarching goal; (2) challenging but attainable steps to achieve within a specific time frame; (3) a way to measure success; and (4) what the supervisee sees as the supervisor's role in the process. See below for an example:

Personal Development Goal Contract:

- Increase knowledge of Cherokee populations of Western North Carolina region
- Increase comfort and therapeutic skills with clients who identify as transgendered or gender variant
- Increase awareness of ageism

Steps I will take in the next month:

- Conduct a literature review of Cherokee populations
- Read APA guidelines for working with LGBT populations
- Attend community PRIDE event
- Maintain a daily assumption/bias journal for my observations of ageism

How I will assess progress toward this goal:

- Create one page summary of bulleted information learned re: Cherokee
- Decrease in anxiety when sitting with clients who identify as transgendered
- Increase in observations of ageism in journal entries

Role of my supervisor in this process:

- Review a multicultural reading worksheet every two weeks
- Review tapes of my work with clients who identify as transgendered and look for any interfering anxiety
- Allow time in supervision to process observations of ageism

Using one or all three of these techniques can aid in fostering your supervisee's self-awareness: (1) a multicultural reading worksheet based on bibliosupervision assignment; (2) journaling exercise; and (3) a personal development goal contract. Next we turn to ways the supervision structure can be adapted to increase supervisee cultural conceptualization skills.

Conceptualization Skills

Many supervisors find themselves valuing cultural factors and being well intentioned to integrate culture into supervisory conversations, but prioritize other ethical and therapeutic components ahead of multiculturalism. These supervisors often find themselves at the end of the supervision period without having much to measure or evaluate in terms of their supervisee's multicultural competence. The following are some concrete procedural steps to put in place at the beginning of the supervision period (and to use throughout) that will routinely integrate issues of culture in your supervision work.

First, add a section for cultural considerations into the formal template for case conceptualizations and treatment plans. Whenever your supervisee is required to present a formal write-up or document a diagnostic change, be certain to include this portion in the written template of the conceptualization. This will serve as a routine reminder for your supervisee to consider and articulate cultural components. It will also allow you as a supervisor to routinely review your supervisee's multicultural conceptualizations.

Of note, remember to ask about cultural considerations for *every* client, not just those that appear to be ethnically different from your supervisee. For example, there are cultural factors to consider between a Latina Catholic able-bodied heterosexual therapist who counsels a Latina Catholic able-bodied heterosexual client. Additionally, these issues can be processed with her Latina Catholic able-bodied heterosexual supervisor. One of the most important messages to teach our supervisees is that multiculturalism is vast, complicated, and anything but obvious.

Second, add cultural considerations into the written template of your supervision notes. When documenting weekly supervisee progress, add awareness and skills related to multiculturalism just as you would have a heading for skills related to theory, interventions, or diagnosis. This will serve as a weekly reminder to assess cultural factors in your supervisee's therapeutic work.

Third, a critical piece of conceptualization is not only to articulate our assumptions, biases, and considerations toward our clients, but also to comprehend how our clients may hold assumptions about us. Remember to discuss with your supervisee any thoughts or feelings about how the counselor may be perceived by the client. To assist with this discussion, see below for a list of considerations:

- What are the assumptions others may make about me based on my ethnicity/race?
- What are some assumptions others may make about me based on my gender expression?
- What are some assumptions others may make about me based on what is visible in my office? (e.g., having a Christian cross on wall, hanging a PRIDE flag, the content of books on the shelves, pictures of children on desk, degrees, etc.)
- What are some assumptions others may make about me based on my visible tattoos?
- What are some assumptions others may make about me wearing a wedding band/ not wearing a wedding band?

More specifically, it is important for our White supervisees to be aware of their power and privilege in the room (Hays, Dean, & Chang, 2007), explore their racial identity development as part of the majority culture (Hays & Chang, 2003), and understand how they may be perceived by their clients from racial or ethnic oppressed groups. Hays and Chang (2003) provide a list of questions that are important for White supervisees to consider when conceptualizing a client (e.g., How might racial heritage influence your relationship with minority clients?). A supervisee of mine said it best when she noted, "Multicultural competence is not just about how I see my clients, but about how *they* see *me*."

Cultural Dialog in the Supervision Relationship

Based on the VISION model of culture (Baber, Garrett, & Holcomb-McCoy, 1997), in psychotherapy supervision, the superVISION model describes an interactional process of culture between the trainee and supervisor (Garrett et al., 2001). Each letter in VISION represents an element of this cultural relational process (i.e., Values, Interpreting, Structure, Interactional style, Operational strategies, and Needs). By using the superVISION paradigm, supervisors are guided by a model of six factors to consider. Practically, these factors can be addressed with open-ended questioning and a willingness for supervisors to disclose their own answers. This next section is meant to outline some of the questions and topics of discussion proposed by Garett and colleagues to process culture in supervision. By following the superVISION model, supervisors can create a foundation that allows for further discussions about cultural variables. The questions do not make assumptions based on stereotypes. Rather, they are open-ended in nature and inquire about the uniqueness of one's expectations, beliefs, interpersonal preferences, and perceptions. These questions can serve as a guide for supervisors when they begin working with a new supervisee, or if they would like to deepen their relationship with their current supervisee. The following are some examples taken from the superVISION model:

Values and belief system:
- What is important to you and why?

Interpretation of experiences:
- What assumption do you make about me in this moment? What perceptions do you have about me in this relationship?

Structuring/Interactional style:
- How should we structure our relationship and supervision process? For example, thoughts about personal space, eye contact, touching, displays of affection, attitudes about gender roles, nonverbal cues, and so forth. What are your preferences for communication style?

Operational strategies:
- How do you select and work toward goals? Where do you find motivation to work toward goals? What are your top goals for this supervision relationship or this semester?

Needs (perceived):
- What do you want or need in terms of outcome for this relationship/this semester? What are your assumptions about how I define/communicate outcome?

Ultimately, the idea is for supervisees to not only dialog about their values and beliefs in supervision, but also model for their clients, in a parallel process that it is safe and helpful to discuss cultural similarities and differences.

Future Research Directions

Hays and colleagues (2007) used a qualitative analysis to explore issues of privilege and oppression in counseling and counselor training. The majority of informants (practicing counselors) felt underprepared from their academic and clinical training to address issues of privilege and oppression in counseling; further, informants advocated for a paradigm shift to promote growth in both the classroom and supervision. Positive training experiences included when supervisors "focused didactic work and case presentations to highlight multicultural issues, particularly privilege and oppression" (p. 322).

Future empirical directions could continue to analyze specific relationships between supervisory interventions and supervisee multicultural competencies. It would seem important to evaluate if levels of awareness, knowledge and skills increase with the implementation of these supervisory techniques. Relatedly, client outcome as a result of multicultural techniques in the supervision relationship could be explored.

Helping a Trainee Understand and Manage Countertransference

Countertransference has recently been defined as exaggerated interfering or exaggerated facilitating thoughts, feelings, or behaviors a therapist has toward a client (Ladany et al., 2008). At best, awareness of countertransference can serve as a gateway to effective, dynamic, and curative interventions. At worst, countertransference can prevent therapists from helping their clients, or even cause harm. Thus, perhaps one of the most important techniques we can learn as supervisors is to help our trainees better understand and manage their countertransference.

Previous authors have noted the importance of managing countertransference. For instance, Hayes and colleagues (1998) qualitatively examined the experiences of eight psychologists as reported through origins, triggers, and manifestations of countertransference. Their findings supported a framework for both therapists and supervisors to consider the utility of (1) examining manifestations of countertransference by scrutinizing trainee feelings toward the client; (2) exploring triggers of countertransference by identifying events that provoked trainee reactions; and (3) looking within the trainee for origins of countertransference from unresolved conflicts. Additionally, Gelso and Hayes (2001) outlined five factors central to therapist's countertransference management (self-insight, self-integration, anxiety management, empathy, and conceptualizing ability). Finally, Ladany et al. (2008) followed the experience of four therapists-in-training over the course of a two year study, asking about countertransferential thoughts, feelings, and behaviors after every weekly counseling session. From these data, the authors developed a five step model countertransference management advising trainees to (1) become familiar with personal issues/triggers; (2) identify emotional reactions or behavioral changes; (3) examine therapeutic impact; (4) explore the origins of countertransference using personal therapy if necessary; and (5) utilize supervision.

The purpose of this next section is to draw from the literature mentioned above, as well as integrate the critical events in supervision (CES) model, into a tangible four step how-to approach, specifically for supervisors, when addressing countertransference with trainees.

Practical Implication

Prepare for Countertransference By Exploring Potential Triggers In Advance

In the beginning of a supervision relationship, the supervisor and trainee should familiarize themselves with potential countertransferential triggers. To the extent that it is relevant to the trainee's clinical work, it may be helpful to explore a number of contextual issues (e.g., family of origin dynamics, relationship models, interpersonal pet peeves, critical life events, hot buttons, moral values). These contextual issues may serve as a foundation of unique emotional arousal points, or triggers for countertransference. For example, a trainee may harbor resentment toward his father who suffered from alcoholism and relatedly finds it challenging to work with clients who suffer from addiction. Perhaps a trainee finds herself repulsed by older men, and thus exhibits disconnection with older male clients. A trainee could have trouble dealing with individuals he considers lazy, rude, tardy, self-absorbed, and so forth. These perfectly normal feelings make for a rich supervision topic, as surely the trainee will encounter clients that he perceives to be lazy, rude, tardy or self-absorbed! Also, a recent negative life event (e.g., miscarriage, death of a parent, financial trouble, fight with significant other) or positive transition (e.g., falling in love, getting a raise, moving into a new home) could serve as a prompt to affect one's clinical work.

Questions to explore triggers with your trainee might include: What factors do you value in a relationship? How do you define intimacy? How do you define trust? Talk about your perception of healthy boundaries in a relationship. What personality characteristics do you most appreciate in others? What personality characteristics do you find difficult to tolerate? What current life events could serve as distractions during the counseling session? What acts, if any, do you consider so immoral that if your client confessed them to you, you would experience difficulty continuing to work with him or her? It is important during this step to be clear with the trainee that such exploration is not a form of providing personal therapy.

Rather, it is a mutual investigation of how the trainee's cultural context may influence his or her clinical work.

Identify Flags By Looking for Cues During the Counseling Sessions

The supervisor and trainee should identify emotional reactions or behavioral changes that may serve as cues that the trainee is experiencing countertransference *during the counseling session*. In other words, "how will we know if you're having an exaggerated response to a client?" What will it look like in the counseling session? What will it look like in the supervision session? Some trainees may note that when they are angry they withdraw, or when they are anxious they tend to ask a lot of questions. Ladany et al. (2008) mentioned several potential cues. Supervisors are advised to notice any of the following trainee behaviors during their counseling work:

Apparent daydreaming
Appearing agitated or frustrated
Fidgeting
Looking bored
Habitual late arrival to the counseling session
Habitually extending the session over time
Overly self-disclosing
Engaging in jovial exchanges instead of therapeutic interaction
Prohibiting any periods of silence in session by prompting constant dialog

In addition, supervisors would also be advised to notice the following behaviors during supervision sessions:

Utilizing every supervision hour focused exclusively on one certain client
Frequently avoiding discussing a certain client
Displaying a significant shift in mood when discussing a client
Describing the client's symptoms with a more pathological bent than appropriate

Once the supervisor and trainee have mutually identified these flags, then both parties can be responsible for examining recordings of counseling sessions for such indicators.

Using the CES model, identifying a flag would be considered a marker. Remember that a marker can be expressed verbally or behaviorally and is the first of three phases embedded within a supervision context (The Marker, the Task Environment, and the Resolution; Ladany, Friedlander, & Nelson, 2005). According to the CES model of supervision, once a marker is established, the supervisor and supervisee can move through to the next phase of the Task Environment.

Investigate Further By Questioning How the Therapeutic Work May Be Affected

Once the supervisor and trainee have familiarized themselves with potential personal triggers, and identified the cues that serve to signify when countertransference may be playing out in session, the next step is to examine how countertransference has affected or can affect the therapeutic work. For instance, often countertransference outside of one's awareness can serve as a barrier to empathy. The supervision technique at this point becomes challenging for your trainee to find a way to connect with the client. Questions include: With what part of this client's experience can you relate? When was the last time you felt the way your client is feeling? What was helpful or unhelpful from others during that time?

Most importantly during this step, supervisors are advised to normalize and validate trainee feelings. If a therapist is aware of her or his countertransference, this disclosure should be encouraged and not pathologized. Remember, "the carpenter has the hammer, the surgeon has the scalpel, the therapist has the self" (Hayes & Gelso, 2001, p. 1041). Perhaps a trainee's feelings of confusion or boredom will serve as the launching pad for an appropriate interpersonal process intervention for the future. Maybe the trainee's impatience and anxiety can be the portal to empathize and relate to the client's similar feelings. Questioning, exploring, and discovering how the therapeutic work can be affected by countertransference may be the most important part of the technique.

Using the CES model, this step of investigation might be considered one of the common interactional sequences in the Task Environments of critical events. Ladany et al. (2005) explained that the Task Environment phase is comprised of various supervision strategies including exploration of feelings, focusing on the supervisory alliance, normalizing experience and exploration of the countertransference. Asking a supervisee to reflect on how their behaviors affect clinical work, while normalizing and validating his or her experience, address both the explanation and clarification pieces of the Task Environment model. According to CES, the next phase is resolution.

Implement a Plan With Your Trainee

For supervisors of a more cognitive-behavioral persuasion, a supervision technique to manage trainee countertransference can be creating a behavioral plan with your trainee. This can involve (1) increasing awareness by self-monitoring countertransferential feelings (e.g., keeping a session log of exaggerated feelings); (2) brainstorming alternative behaviors to perform when the countertransference is evoked and agreeing to goals of behavior change (e.g., decrease the duration of closed body posture); or (3) using the following template of countertransference management: When I notice myself _____, I will be more mindful of _____. I will try instead to think about _____ and behaviorally _____.

Examples include:

- When I notice myself fidgeting, I will be more mindful of my anxiety. I will try instead to remind myself that I have strong clinical skills and fold my hands on my lap.
- When I notice myself yawning, I will be more mindful that both my client and I are not using this time therapeutically. I will try instead to empathize with the valid reasons why a client would avoid discussing painful material, and compassionately challenge or redirect the session if appropriate.
- When I notice myself extending the session time limit, I will be more mindful of the importance of maintaining consistent boundaries. I will try instead to think about the advantages for the client if we end on time, and say "we have to stop for today."
- When I notice tension in my jaw, I will be more mindful that I'm feeling frustrated with my client for rebelling against her mother. I will try instead to tap into my personal experience of expressing autonomy and ask my client to share more about her strengths of independence.

Model Countertransference Awareness and Management

As a final note, perhaps one of the best ways to educate trainees about countertransferential management is by modeling. Awareness, acknowledgment, discussion, and management of one's own personal reactions as a supervisor can serve as an inspiring technique to model for counselors-in-training how to work through their interfering thoughts and feelings in therapy.

Future Research Directions

Future research might benefit by intersecting investigations of countertransference with the analysis of multicultural dynamics in counseling and supervision. It is somewhat unclear where an unconscious countertransferential moment ends and an unconscious racial bias begins, but perhaps future models could focus on dividing or integrating the two concepts. Empirically, it would be interesting to uncover how countertransferential triggers may change as multicultural awareness increases.

Reflective Process

Reflectivity refers to an internal process of attention and thought—a focused contemplation. In the context of supervision, reflective thinking has been defined as the "active ongoing examination of the theories, beliefs, and assumptions that contribute to counselors' understanding of client issues and guide their choices for clinical interventions" (Griffith & Frieden, 2000, p. 82). To gather a consensus about the process of reflectivity in psychotherapy supervision, Neufeldt, Karno, and Nelson (1996) interviewed five experts (Copeland, Holloway, Rønnestad, Skovholt, and Schön) in the subject area and qualitatively explored reflectivity attributes to form an integrated theory. Findings indicated the following sequence of events define reflectivity:

> An initial problem, a point at which a therapist is puzzled or stuck and unsure how to proceed, begins the sequence. The therapist's own qualities of personality and cognitive capacity influence ensuing reflectivity in supervision, along with the institutional and supervisory environment. The reflective process itself is a search for understanding of the phenomena of the counseling session, with attention to therapist actions, emotions, and thoughts, as well as to the interaction between the therapist and client. The intent to understand what has occurred, active inquiry, openness to that understanding, and vulnerability and risk taking, rather than defensive self-protection, characterize that stance of the reflective supervisee. (p. 8)

Practical Implication

Several authors have summarized and outlined the steps to facilitating supervisee reflective thinking (Bernard & Goodyear, 2004; Griffith & Frieden, 2000; Neufeldt, 2007). Bernard and Goodyear (2004) and Neufeldt (2007) remind us that the first step to facilitating reflectivity is creating an environment in supervision that includes a supportive working alliance and the space and time to reflect. Next, a dilemma or problem is presented by the supervisee. This is a clinical example of feeling stuck or confused about how to move forward in therapy. Griffith and Frieden (2000) suggest teaching strategies to stimulate critical thinking during these stuck moments including Socratic questioning, journal writing, IPR, and the use of reflecting teams. The common goal among these techniques is to foster a deeper understanding by using thoughtful questions. To facilitate a meaningful reflective event, the supervisee must demonstrate a change in some way (Neufelt, 2007). This change may be illustrated in a different behavior toward their client in the next therapy session, or a change in their level of awareness or insight related to themselves or the therapy process.

Case Example

Manuel, a counselor-in-training, has been working with Andrea for five sessions in a counseling center at a midsized state university. Andrea originally presented with symptoms of adjustment disorder with depressed mood after the break up with her boyfriend, but at her most recent session she met the criteria for a major depressive episode. Manuel learns that

Andrea is considering returning to her previous relationship, with a man that has been emotionally and physically abusive to her in the past. Manuel feels protective of Andrea and angry at her former boyfriend.

Manuel feels somewhat confused by this shift in Andrea's mood, thought process, and case complexity. He remembers that Andrea reported that she was unhappy in the relationship with her ex-boyfriend. Manuel predicted that over time her symptoms would alleviate, given the nature of her dissatisfying relationship. Manuel presents in supervision with a list of reasons why Andrea should not return to the relationship, which he plans to spell out for Andrea during their next therapy session.

The point of fostering reflectivity through Socratic questioning would be to expand and deepen Manuel's thinking process and understanding for Andrea and the therapy process. Questions a supervisor could ask might include:

- What are the costs and benefits of telling Andrea what to do?
- What are the pros and cons of supporting her decision?
- When is the last time you felt like others did not support your decision? What was helpful about it? What was unhelpful?
- How would your interventions be different if you had a different value system?
- What theory are you coming from and how does it support your intervention strategy?
- How will Andrea's reactions inform your next steps?

The idea is for Manuel to be mindful of his interventions and aware of his theoretical underpinnings, his values related to decision making, and the possible outcomes of his interventions.

Future Research Directions

Empirical directions might include comparing the different kinds of effectiveness between Griffith and Frieden's (2000) four specific reflectivity-fostering suggestions (i.e., Socratic questioning, journaling, IPR, and reflective teams). It would be interesting to investigate how these different techniques uniquely foster the supervisee thinking process. Further, it seems important to understand what factors of the supervisory working alliance contribute to the most effective facilitation of reflectivity in the relationship. For example, is it most important to have a strong emotional bond or a solid mutual agreement on the tasks of supervision for the reflective process to be fostered? Additionally, what kind of supervisor is most likely to effectively engage in reflectivity in supervision? Future research could examine supervisory personal characteristics, style, and theoretical orientation to analyze what supervisors are most effective with this technique.

Supervisor Self-Disclosure

Supervisors self-disclose about a number of topics, from personal counseling strengths and weaknesses to professional advice or opinions about the field (Ladany & Lehrman-Waterman, 1999). For some, personal disclosures may be spontaneous irrelevant and unscripted narratives, without thoughtful intention. However, mindful purposeful disclosures can be a powerful supervision technique. For guidance, supervisors may find it helpful to follow a model offered by Ladany and Walker (2003) that considers how the disclosure may address three general personalization dimensions (1) discordant versus congruence; (2) intimate versus nonintimate; and (3) in the service of the supervisor versus the trainee.

Discordant versus congruence: first, supervisors should ask themselves if their disclosures are congruent with their trainee's presenting material, needs, and concerns. For example, although there is evidence to suggest that sharing personal counseling struggles builds the supervisory relationship, supervisors need to appreciate that exposing their flaws without specific trainee congruence will not be helpful. For instance, if a highly anxious trainee is plagued by worry about client safety, the trainee's needs and concerns during that session may include both a review of ethical duties and anxiety reduction through normalization and encouragement. A supervisor who shares a personal story about losing a client to suicide would be using a disclosure that was discordant with the needs of the trainee. However, if a trainee is having difficulty grasping the concept of therapeutic limitations and exercising unrealistic expectations of their work, the same disclosure about a supervisor's counseling struggles may be extremely congruent with a trainee's presenting material. Indeed, such a disclosure could provide a much needed perspective.

Intimate versus nonintimate: second, using self-disclosure as a positive technique requires asking the question, "Is this disclosure relatively intimate without being inappropriately personal?" Sharing narratives that are too professional can be perceived as cold, distancing, and emotionally removed. Sharing narratives that are too personal can blur boundaries and make a trainee feel emotionally responsible for their supervisor. Remember, it is not solely your decision as a supervisor to monitor where appropriate boundaries are created and maintained. The cultural context, identity factors, and previous experiences of your trainee are paramount to consider when acknowledging appropriate intimacy.

In the service of the supervisor versus the trainee: third, the most important question, and the one hardest to answer, is the third personalization dimension: "Is this disclosure more in the service of my trainee, or is this disclosure serving my needs as a supervisor?" If we give supervisors the benefit of the doubt, we can assume that most disclosures originate from altruistic intentions (e.g., I'm showing that I can relate to my trainee by sharing this personal story about myself; I'm providing expertise by describing my successes; I'm providing perspective by explaining how the politics at this agency work). However, some evidence has been found that supervisors may at times behaviorally manage their supervisory countertransference by talking more, a potentially vulnerable opportunity for unhelpful disclosure serving the needs of the supervisor (Ladany et al., 2008). Thus, unconsciously or consciously, it is possible that supervisors use self-disclosure to serve their own needs at times (e.g., to receive support, validation or sympathy from the trainee when venting about their own frustrations, resentment or anxieties about their professional responsibilities).

The overarching message about supervisory self-disclosures is that when used appropriately, they can be a positive supervision technique. When making a disclosure, remember the three personalization dimensions: considering congruence with trainee issues, appropriate intimacy, and operating in the service of the trainee.

Future Research Directions

Future research could benefit from examining disclosures across these specific personalization dimensions. For instance, what supervisor personality characteristics share a relationship with more intimate disclosures? What kinds of supervisor engage in more disclosures that are in the service of the supervisor? It would be important to collect data from supervisees concerning their reactions to supervisor disclosures across these dimensions. Specifically, what combination of dimensions lead to the most helpful and effective disclosure according to supervisees?

Using Structured Peer Group Format Techniques in Individual Supervision

Borders (1991) provided a systematic approach to peer group supervision. The structured peer group supervision (SPGS) is intended for small groups of three to six counselors in training and includes the following steps: (1) the counselor identifies a question and requests feedback; (2) peers in the group are assigned different roles while reviewing the recorded segment of the counseling session (e.g., the observer of nonverbals, the role of the counselor, client, parent, spouse, friend, or other significant other, the lens of a particular theoretical orientation, the creator of a metaphor describing the counseling process, etc.); (3) the counselor shows a preselected recorded segment of the counseling session; (4) peers give feedback from their different roles being mindful of the questions specified by the counselor; (5) the supervisor facilitates the discussion, functioning as moderator and process observer; and (6) the supervisor summarizes the feedback and the counselor indicates if the goals were met. In essence, the listening and responding to the videotape segment from the perspectives of different roles is meant to increase conceptualization skills in each of the members in the group.

Practical Implication

For the purposes of this chapter, I would like to highlight and elaborate Border's recommendation of how the structured peer group format can be extended and adapted for individual supervision. Namely, three techniques will be suggested: (1) mute observations; (2) "As the _____ I'm feeling...;" and (3) playing the theoretical devil's advocate.

First, as a means to help your trainee assume the role of "the observer of nonverbals," try watching the preselected recorded segment of the counseling session on mute. Ask the trainee to speak out loud while watching the silent segment, identifying what messages are being nonverbally communicated between parties. It may be helpful to do the mute observations first, before watching the segment with sound, so that the trainee and supervisor are not hearing the audio version in their minds while watching. Trainees may exclaim unexpected observations such as "I look really bored!" or "The client seems angry." This serves as a gateway to deeper exploration of transference, countertransference, or greater nonverbal awareness.

Second, supervisors or trainees themselves can take on several different roles while watching a recorded segment of session (e.g., the counselor, client, parent, friend, coworker, child, etc). Borders (1991) suggests having the supervisor or trainee verbalize feedback using the structure "As the _____ I'm feeling..." I would suggest that the supervisor preview the segment in advance and screen for the most important roles for the trainee to play. For instance, if the supervisor feels as though a trainee is experiencing overidentification with the client's boyfriend, then it may be most helpful for the trainee to articulate "As the boyfriend, I'm feeling ..." to generate awareness of the emotion. If the supervisor perceives the counselor is experiencing negative countertransference (e.g., resentment toward the client), then it may be most helpful for the trainee to verbalize "As the client, I'm feeling..." to expose this countertransferential dynamic.

A third supervision technique we can adapt from Border's (1991) peer group format encourages the trainee to consider their therapeutic work from a different theoretical perspective. A beginning trainee may have a goal to learn more about a different theoretical orientation (e.g., a first year practicum student who is trained in cognitive-behavioral therapy might request exposure to Gestalt perspectives). Also, an advanced trainee may have more comfort and familiarity with a range of orientations, but may be looking to better infuse different orientations into a more integrated approach. Therefore, this technique can be useful at any level of trainee development. First, a trainee can show a prerecorded segment of a counseling session and articulate the orientation from where he or she is most comfortable (e.g., explain the etiology of the problem, the goal of treatment, and the interventions that lead toward change from his or her theoretical perspective). Next, a supervisor can challenge the trainee to play his or her own "theoretical devil's advocate." Imagine the following examples:

- The cognitive-behavioral perspective is a symptom-reduction approach. What would a pro-symptom approach look like (e.g., coherence therapy)?
- The psychodynamic perspective pathologizes resistance, talk about this client from an orientation that honors and legitimizes resistance (e.g., feminist therapy).
- Behavioral interventions address progress toward operationalized goals. Explain this client's movement using the stages of change model. Explain the client's underlying dynamics related to change from an object-relations standpoint.
- Critique your cognitive therapy expertise from a motivational interviewing bent.
- What are the limitations to the interventions promoted by the positive psychology movement?

Depending on the trainee, I would argue that these questions can be spontaneous during the supervision session, or premeditated answers (e.g., "In preparation for supervision next week, I'd like you to review this session and consider it from an interpersonal process approach. Here are some readings from Teyber for your consideration"). In either case, the hope of this supervision technique is to supportively challenge the trainee to take on a different role and to see their work from multiple perspectives. Ultimately, "the articulation of a theoretical perspective gives life to philosophy and ideas, help counselors become aware of the rationale and intentions for their actions, and significantly contributes to the development of a consistent, integrated professional identity" (Borders, 1991, p. 250).

Future Research Directions

Although one research project has compared the SPGS model to another peer supervision model (Crutchfield & Borders, 1997), none of the analyses examining treatment effects were significant. However, a more long-term or longitudinal study would likely yield different results. In terms of individual supervision, future research could examine the effects of using techniques from the SPGS model between a supervisor and supervisee. Specifically, supervisees could be asked after every supervision session what role was the most helpful to play. These data could be compared to what roles the supervisors thought were most helpful to examine in supervision. It also may help to investigate the unique differences in learning when a supervisee plays the role versus watching another person play out that role.

A Word About Technology

Supervision methods are incorporating technological advances. Tiny webcams and digital recordings have replaced the old fashioned VHS video recording equipment and the even older audiotape methods of the past. Other examples of advancing technology used in supervision are the Bug in the Eye (BITE) approach (Klitzke & Lombardo, 1991; Miller, Miller, & Evans, 2002), using e-mail as a vehicle for supervision (Graf & Stebnicki, 2002) or as a supplement to clinical supervision (Clingerman & Bernard, 2004; Stebnicki & Glover, 2001), utilizing web-based peer supervision groups (Butler & Constantine, 2006; Gainor & Constantine, 2002), and using on-line services for individual supervision (Kanz, 2001).

The empirical research on technological advances remains scarce. Clingerman and Bernard (2004) found that using e-mail as a supplemental modality for clinical supervision may encourage greater intimacy, Graf and Stebnicki (2002) found that conceptual messages via e-mail followed a developmental path, and Butler and Constantine (2006) found that web-based supervision groups effectively increased collective self-esteem and case conceptualization ability in school counselor trainees. However, none of these studies utilized a control group or comparison group, so the findings are somewhat limited. Gainor and Constantine (2002) compared web-based to face-to-face multicultural peer group supervision cohorts. They found that although both groups increased in multicultural case conceptualization abilities, the in-person peer group counselor trainees demonstrated greater multicultural case conceptualization abilities when compared to the web-based peer group. Possible explanations for this result include the lack of perceptual relationship cues in the web-based group.

Future directions for research on technological advances in supervision are endless. A large scale quantitative project would nicely complement the preliminary qualitative findings and general discussions about the pros and cons to technological advances. Interestingly, e-mail has already become an outdated medium in comparison to instant messaging (IM) and texting modalities. Future directions of research could focus on the utility of using IM capabilities in comparison to e-mail and face-to-face supervision.

On a parallel level, it would be important to look at the utility of having the supervision method match the counseling method (i.e., is web-based supervision more effective when working with supervisees conducting web-based therapy in comparison to supervisees conducting face-to-face therapy?). Investigations in the future would also benefit from acknowledging age and familiarity with technology as a powerful variable. For example, current college students (the next generation of supervisees) often describe some of their most intimate connections as having been established and/or maintained on-line. This new generation of supervisees and clients will add a rich perspective to the use of technology in mental health.

Conclusion

The purpose of this chapter was to highlight some supervision techniques, the how-tos look at what goes on in a supervision session. Although techniques play only one of four parts in a larger scheme of supervision process skills (nonverbals, response modes, covert processes; techniques; Ladany et al., 2008), techniques are an integral part of supervision. This chapter meant to highlight strategies such as IPR, the supervision genogram, processing issues of culture, helping a supervisee understand and manage countertransference, the reflective process, supervisor self-disclosure, and using structured peer group format techniques in individual supervision. Considerations of technological advances were also presented.

The dynamics that occur in supervision can be spontaneous and mindless or intentional and purposeful. The hope is that supervisors use this chapter and others as a guide to practice implementing more purpose and intention behind the questions they ask and the support they provide.

References

American Psychological Association (2000). APA Guidelines for psychotherapy with lesbian gay and bisexual clients, *American Psychologist, 55*(12), 1440–1451.

Andersen, M. L., & Collins, P. H. (1995). *Race, class and gender: An anthology* (2nd ed.). Belmont, CA: Wadsworth Publishing Company.

Aten, J. D., Madson, M. B., & Kruse, S. J. (2008). The supervision genogram: A tool for preparing supervisors-in-training. *Psychotherapy: Theory, Research, Practice, Training, 45*, 111–116.

Baber, W. L., Garrett, M. T., & Holcomb-McCoy, C. (1997). VISION: A model of culture for counselors. *Counseling and Values, 41*, 184–193.

Bernard, J. M., & Goodyear, R. L. (2004). *Fundamentals of clinical supervision* (3rd ed.). Boston, MA: Allyn and Bacon.

Borders, L. D. (1991). A systematic approach to peer group supervision. *Journal of Counseling & Development, 69*, 248–252.

Burkard, A. W., Johnson, A. J., Madison, M. B., Pruitt, N. T., Contreras-Tadych, D. A., Kozlowski, . . . Knox, S. (2006). Supervisory cultural responsiveness and unresponsiveness in cross-cultural supervision. *Journal of Counseling Psychology, 53*, 288–301.

Butler, S. K., & Constantine, M. G. (2006). Web-based peer supervision, collective self-esteem, and case conceptualization ability in school counselor trainees. *Professional School Counseling, 10*, 146–152.

Clingerman, T. L., & Bernard, J. M. (2004). An investigation of the use of e-mail as a supplemental modality for clinical supervision. *Counselor Education & Supervision, 44*, 82–95.

Constantine, M. G., & Sue, D. W. (2007). Perceptions of racial microaggressions among black supervisees in cross-racial dyads. *Journal of Counseling Psychology, 54*, 142–153.

Crutchfield, L. B., & Borders, L. D. (1997). Impact of two clinical peer supervision models on practicing school counselors. *Journal of Counseling & Development, 75*, 219–230.

Gainor, K. A., & Constantine, M. G. (2002). Multicultural group supervision: A comparison of in-person versus web-based formats. *Professional School Counseling, 6*, 104–111.

Garrett, M. T., Borders, L. D., Crutchfield, L. B., Torres-Rivera, E., Brotherton, D., & Curtis, R. (2001). Multicultural superVISION: A paradigm of cultural responsiveness for supervisors. *Journal of Multicultural Counseling and Development, 29*, 147–158.

Gelso, C. J., & Hayes, J. A. (2001). Countertransference management. *Psychotherapy: Theory, Research, Practice, Training, 38*, 418–422.

Graf, M. N., & Stebnicki, M. A. (2002). Using email for clinical supervision in practicum: A qualitative analysis. *The Journal of Rehabilitation, 68*(3), 41–49.

Griffith, B. A., & Frieden, G. (2000). Facilitating reflective thinking in counselor education. *Counselor Education and Supervision, 40*, 82–93.

Hayes, J. A., & Gelso, C. J. (2001). Clinical implications of research on countertransference: Science informing practice. *Journal of Clinical Psychology, 57*, 1041–1051.

Hayes, J. A., McCracken, J. E., McClanahan, M. K., Hill, C. E., Harp, J. S., & Carozzoni, P. (1998). Therapist perspectives on countertransference: Qualitative data in search of a theory. *Journal of Counseling Psychology, 45*, 468–482.

Hays, D. G., & Chang, C. Y. (2003). White privilege, oppression, and racial identity development: Implications for supervision. *Counselor Education and Supervision, 43*, 134–145.

Hays, D. G., Dean, J. K., & Chang, C. Y (2007). Addressing privilege and oppression in counselor training and practice: A qualitative analysis. *Journal of Counseling & Development, 85*, 317–324.

Helms, J. E. (1992). *A race is a nice thing to have: A guide to being a white person or understanding the white persons in your life.* Topeka, KS: Content Communications.

Kagan, H., & Kagan, N. I. (1997). Interpersonal process recall: Influencing human interaction. In C. E. Watkins, Jr. (Ed.), *Handbook of psychotherapy supervision* (pp. 296–309). New York, NY: Wiley.

Kagan, N. I. (1980). Influencing human interaction: Eighteen years with IPR. In A. K. Hess (Ed.), *Psychotherapy supervision: Theory, research, and practice* (pp. 262–283). New York, NY: Wiley.

Kagan, N. I., & Kagan, H. (1991). Interpersonal process recall. In D. W. Dowrick (Ed.), *Practical guide to using video in the behavioral sciences* (pp. 221–230). New York, NY: Wiley.

Kanz, J. E. (2001). Clinical-supervision.com: Issues in the provision of online supervision. *Professional Psychology, Research and Practice, 32,* 415–420.

Kingdon, M. A. (1975). A cost/benefit analysis of the interpersonal process recall technique. *Journal of Counseling Psychology, 22,* 353–357.

Klitzke, M. J., & Lombardo, T. W. (1991). A 'bug-in-the-eye' can be better than a 'bug-in-the-ear': A teleprompter technique for on-line therapy skills training. *Behavior Modification, 15,* 113–117.

Ladany, N., Friedlander, M. L., & Nelson, M. L. (2005). *Critical events in psychotherapy supervision: An interpersonal approach.* Washington, DC: American Psychological Association.

Ladany, N., & Lehrman-Waterman, D. E. (1999). The content and frequency of supervisor self-disclosures and their relationship to supervisor style and the supervisory working alliance. *Counselor Education and Supervision, 38,* 143–160.

Ladany, N., & Walker, J. A. (2003). Supervisor self-disclosure: Balancing the uncontrollable narcissist with the indomitable altruist. *In Session: Journal of Clinical Psychology, 59,* 611–621.

Ladany, N., Walker, J. A., Pate-Carolan, L. M., & Gray Evans, L. (2008). *Practicing counseling and psychotherapy: Insights from trainees, supervisors and clients.* New York, NY: Routledge.

Landrine, H. (1995). *Bringing cultural diversity to feminist psychology: Theory research and practice.* Washington DC: American Psychological Association.

McIntosh, P. (2003). White privilege: Unpacking the invisible knapsack. In S. Plous (Ed.), *Understanding prejudice and discrimination* (pp. 191–196). New York, NY: McGraw-Hill.

Miller, K. L., Miller, S. M., & Evans, W. J. (2002). Computer-assisted live supervision in college counseling centers. *Journal of College Counseling, 5,* 187–192.

Neufeldt, S. A. (2007). *Supervision strategies for the first practicum.* Alexandria, VA: American Counseling Association.

Neufeldt, S. A., Karno, M. P., & Nelson, M. L. (1996). A qualitative study of experts' conceptualization of supervisee reflectivity. *Journal of Counseling Psychology, 43,* 3–9.

Paniagua, F. A. (2001). *Diagnosis in a multicultural context: A casebook for mental health professionals.* London, UK: Sage Publications.

Payne, R. K. (2001). *A framework for understanding poverty.* Highlands, TX: Aha! Process, Inc.

Stebnicki, M. A., & Glover, N. M. (2001). E-supervision as a complementary approach to traditional face-to-face clinical supervision in rehabilitation counseling: Problems and solutions. *Rehabilitation Counseling, 15,* 283–293.

Sue, D. W. (2003). *Overcoming our racism: The journey to liberation.* San Francisco, CA: Jossey-Bass.

Sue, D. W., Capodilupo, C. M., Torino, G. C., Bucceri, J. M., Holder, A. M. B., Nadal, K. L., & Esquilin, M. (2007). Racial microaggressions in everyday life: Implications for clinical practice. *American Psychologist, 62,* 271–286.

Tozer, E. E., & McClanahan, M. K. (1999). Treating the purple menace: Ethical considerations of conversation therapy and affirmative alternative. *The Counseling Psychologist, 27*(5), 722–742.

PART II

Theoretical Approaches to
Counselor Supervision

CHAPTER 5

Supervision-Based Integrative Models of Counselor Supervision
Interpersonal Models

SHIRLEY A. HESS and KURT L. KRAUS

> If the only tool you have is a hammer, everything begins to look like a nail.
>
> **—Anonymous**

It is likely most of us have heard clinicians or supervisors utter statements such as, "I conceptualize from an existential philosophy but my practice is technically eclectic," "I use a variety of theoretical perspectives and techniques when I counsel and supervise," or "It really doesn't matter what theoretical model I follow, because one model is as effective as the next, and my approach is based on the needs of my supervisees." These statements reflect the evolution of supervision practice's movement beyond the adherence to a particular theory and its corresponding techniques to the mixing and blending of existing theories and techniques that may well result in the creation of new theoretical models. The construction and use of such integrative supervision methods may allow supervisors flexibility and more options for addressing multiple supervision situations than does one approach with a more narrow range of techniques and interventions (Bradley, Gould, & Parr, 2000).

Bradley et al. (2000) identify two types of integrative approaches to counselor supervision: integration of supervision theory and technical eclecticism described as a combination of techniques or methodology from at least two approaches. Often the terms *technical eclecticism* and *integrationism* are used interchangeably; however Norcross and Napolitano (1986) use a metaphor to explicate the subtle differences between the two: "the eclectic selects among several dishes to constitute a meal [but] the integrationist creates new dishes by combining different ingredients" (p. 253). Despite the nuanced language, Bernard and Goodyear (2009) believe that most supervisors borrow from a range of theories, techniques, and philosophies to create their own integrative perspective.

Our position is that integration does *not* afford a muddling of theoretical ideologies. In other words, we believe that an integrative approach is best represented metaphorically by a grocery store rather than a buffet (see Kraus & Hulse-Killacky, 1996). Imagine in the grocery store, shoppers (here supervisors and supervisees) wheel their carts purposefully, guided through well-stocked shelves of desired foods, flavors, and tools. Whereas, from the buffet line we are to choose from what others have prepared, perhaps a nibble of this or that to see if we like it. The buffet tempts us to eat too much and to eat without thinking—we leave wishing we had never arrived. In our grocery store the shoppers find that the aisles are well marked; although only some aisles are of interest, often determined by what is on the menu for that evening. It is also imperative to recognize that the ingredients alone do not make a meal. The shopper must take the ingredients back to the kitchen and concoct them according to a desired outcome (maybe a novice chef will follow a written recipe where another more accomplished may seemingly create spontaneously). It is incredible, the shoppers extol, to shop in such a store that holds such culinary possibilities. Now being careful not to over work the metaphor, let us add, shoppers—supervisors and supervisees—must know what to do with the ingredients, they must have the requisite skills, and they must understand the intricate relationship between the chef and whoever may choose to dine. The chef that prepares a spicy meal for a diner who craves only bland food is surely at a culinary (clinical) impasse. In order to apply any of the three integrative models that we explicate in this chapter, emerging supervisors must have a sturdy theoretical foundation from which to practice.

Three prominent integrative models—discrimination, systems approach to supervision (SAS), critical events model—are discussed in this chapter. Each model will be examined according to its primary concepts and theoretical assumptions as well as its methodology and techniques framework. An illustrative case will be provided at the end of each model. Then a case study is presented followed by examples of how the three integrative models discussed earlier could be utilized.

Discrimination Model of Supervision

Bernard's discrimination model was conceived as a teaching model for use with novice supervisors in introducing them to the process of supervision (Bernard, 1997; Bernard & Goodyear, 2009). It is one of the most studied models and has received support from empirical research (e.g., Ellis & Dell, 1986; Ellis, Dell, & Good, 1988; Goodyear, Abadie, & Efros, 1984; Lazovsky & Shimoni, 2007; Putney, Worthington, & McCullough, 1992). The model is designed to reduce counseling supervision to its simplest components by first helping the supervisor determine what to focus on in supervision and then identifying the most functional supervisory role.

Primary Concepts and Theoretical Assumptions

The discrimination model is atheoretical and based on technical eclecticism (Bernard, 1979, 1997). The central assumption of the discrimination model is that supervision should relate directly to the act of counseling. In addressing the supervisee's action, the discrimination model identifies three separate foci of supervisee competence (i.e., intervention skills, conceptualization skills, and personalization skills) and three supervisory roles (i.e., teacher, counselor, and consultant; Bernard, 1979, 1997).

Focus Areas

Intervention (or process) skills are what the supervisor observes the supervisee doing in the session. These skills, ranging from simple to complex, include all the behaviors that distinguish counseling as a purposeful therapeutic interpersonal activity, from greeting the client at the beginning of a session to using empathy, confrontation, interpretation, pacing, salience, or other counseling skills (Bradley et al., 2000). The focus of this area is the supervisee's ability to skillfully deliver interventions. *Conceptualization skills,* the second focus area, requires the supervisor to ascertain supervisees' ability to understand what is occurring in the counseling session, read covert and overt cues, identify client themes and patterns, and appropriately select therapeutic interventions (Bernard & Goodyear, 2009). The final focus, *personalization skills,* addresses the supervisee's personal style and unique individual contribution to counseling, and how these factors (e.g., personality, cultural background, connection with others, personal issues, countertransference) influence the counseling process.

Implicit in the model is the assumption that for every counseling skill, a potential skill deficit exists. Therefore, when a specific deficit is identified, the supervisor must determine if it occurred because the supervisee (a) did not know what to do (conceptualization); (b) did not know how to deliver the skill (intervention); and (c) was uncomfortable with either the client or using the skill (personalization). Identification of the focus area(s) containing the skill deficit allows the supervisor to use an appropriate supervisory intervention to rectify it (Bradley et al., 2000).

Supervisor Roles

When supervisors have determined their supervisee's competence within each focus area, they then choose a supervisory role to facilitate their supervision goals (Bernard & Goodyear, 2009). Bernard (1979, 1997) describes three supervisor roles (i.e., teacher, counselor, consultant). In the *teacher role,* supervisors take the responsibility for determining the action necessary for supervisees' acquisition of counseling competence. The teacher role evaluates supervisees' skill development, deficits, and ability to deliver interventions. The second role, *counselor,* addresses the interpersonal and intrapersonal factors influencing the therapeutic relationship and the counseling process. In the role of counselor, supervisors work to facilitate supervisee reflection, meaning making, and insight about events occurring in counseling sessions. The final supervisory role is *consultant.* As consultant, supervisors and supervisees work collaboratively and share responsibility for supervisees' learning. Although the consultant supervisor remains a stable resource for supervisees, the supervisees are also encouraged to trust their own reactions, thoughts, feelings, and insights about their work with clients.

Methodology and Techniques of the Discrimination Model of Supervision

The discrimination model is situation specific and assumes supervisors will tailor their responses to meet the needs of their individual supervisees (Bernard & Goodyear, 2009). It is not unusual for focus areas to overlap both within a session and across sessions. Therefore, applying the model requires supervisors to be flexible, observant, and able to discern what supervisee needs are most salient at any given time and to avoid choosing a focus area based on the supervisor's personal preference (Bernard & Goodyear, 2009).

Similarly, the discrimination model is an eclectic and flexible model that when applied most effectively asks supervisors to be "prepared to employ all roles and address all foci for supervisees at any level" (Bernard & Goodyear, 2009). Unfortunately many supervisors tend to restrict the model by pairing one supervisor role with one focus area: teacher with intervention, counselor with personalization, and consultant with conceptualization (Bernard, 1997). Likewise, Bernard and Goodyear (2009) report that developmental perspectives lean toward matching a teaching role with beginning supervisees and a consultant role with more advanced supervisees. And, often supervisors focus primarily on intervention skills with novice supervisees compared with the utilization of all three foci with advanced supervisees. Such restriction in application of the model limits the potential breadth and depth of its effectiveness.

Oliver and Ella: Case Examples of the Discrimination Model

Ella agreed to supervise Oliver for post-masters clinical hours leading toward completion of his licensure requirements. Oliver was at the time employed in a community mental health counseling center that granted permission for Ella, an approved clinical supervisor, to supervise center cases at Oliver's expense. Ella did not work for the center; rather she was an independent licensed professional counselor with 12 years of clinical practice and was well respected in the area.

Oliver and Ella worked together on a wide variety of his cases. Because of that variety, Ella was carefully attuned to numerous requests and responses by Oliver that guided her supervision. The following excerpts three high-lighted sessions or multiple sessions that Ella conceived as fitting well into the three distinct foci of supervisee competence and the three unique supervisory roles present in the discrimination model (Bernard, 1979, 1997) she undertook in Oliver's supervision.

1. Oliver was counseling a young woman whose brother had been mortally wounded in Afghanistan. He brought to supervision questions around how he might help his client "make sense" of her unique loss as it raised nearly uncontrollable rage against her own government, her brother's "gullibility at becoming a soldier," and her "guilt" at the very utterance of these terrible words. Ella drew from the discrimination model to focus on Oliver's competence in intervention and conceptualization through her role as teacher and consultant.

2. Ella defined her supervisory role as teacher and counselor when Oliver reluctantly shared with her his strong feelings toward a mother who had sought counseling as part of a court-ordered dis-position of a child neglect charge. She states, "This case seemed to raise many very strong, ingrained values for Oliver that pitted him against his client in many ways! I thought it was best that we first explored the feelings around those values and his reaction toward this young mother before we moved into a phase of his helping her to explore her experiences as a mom who had her child removed from her home because of her behaviors." This case was closely fol-lowed by Ella over a period of several months. Toward the middle session of Oliver's work, he eagerly shared with Ella that he had decided to "get some counseling around these reactions toward clients like.... I don't look forward to bringing my own stuff into future cases like this one for the rest of my career."

3. Oliver commented almost in passing one morning that he would really like to learn more about juvenile fire-setters, as a client had been discussed in a treatment team meeting earlier that day and he realized that he had "precious little to add to the conversation." Although Ella was quite knowledgeable about the literature on the topic, she elected to offer a reading list, asked that Oliver bring questions from further treatment team discussions, and take on a role of her teacher to help him develop confidence and begin to build his desired expertise on the topic. Ella's role periodically throughout the next few weeks changed between consultant and teacher—where her role as "student" taught Oliver valuable skills. Perhaps not surprisingly, Oliver's competence across personalization, conceptualization, and gradual intervention skills burgeoned.

The work Ella and Oliver engaged in illustrates well the utility of the discrimination model. As readers can see, the model inherently lends itself to meeting the ever changing, dynamic work required of supervisors—perhaps especially those whose supervisees' work necessitates the wearing of many hats.

Systems Approach to Supervision

Holloway (1995) developed the SAS to provide a framework for teaching and performing supervision. "Her model is based on empirical, conceptual, and practice knowledge in the field of supervision" (Bradley et al., 2000, p. 104).

Primary Concepts and Theoretical Assumptions

Holloway's (1995) comprehensive model considers seven factors that interact in dynamic relationship to each other: tasks, functions, and four contextual factors (i.e., supervisor, supervisee, client, institution) and the supervisory relationship that serves as the "pillar on which rests the other of the model's components" (Bernard & Goodyear, 2009, p. 107).

Methodology and Techniques of the SAS Model

Central to Holloway's (1995) model is the supervisory relationship. It is the core factor around which all other six components revolve. It is through the supervisory relationship that supervisees are empowered to acquire counseling knowledge and skills. Together the supervision dyad develops a collaborative working alliance that accommodates the needs of supervisees. The supervisory relationship is composed of three elements: supervision contract, interpersonal structure, and relationship phases. The

Supervision Contract is constructed through a collaborative process between supervisor and supervisee based on the individual needs of the supervisee. Included in the contract are factors such as the role expectations of both parties, supervision learning goals, and evaluation criteria and procedures. In constructing a workable contract it is also important for the dyad to be clear about their styles of interacting including the supervisee's learning style and the supervisor's supervision/teaching style. The supervision contract is a working document that is reviewed and adjusted periodically to accommodate the changing needs of the supervisee.

In the SAS model, the *Interpersonal Structure* is characterized by how much interpersonal power each member has in the supervisory dyad as well as the level of involvement they have with each other. The relationship is constantly being created and recreated as they negotiate the distribution of power and their level of involvement. Holloway (1995) proposed three *Phases of the Supervisory Relationship* that parallel developmental models. The beginning phase is characterized by supervisees' need for structure, a reduction in ambiguity, and increased support from supervisors. In the advanced phase, supervisees continue to seek support and guidance; however, they also demonstrate an increase in independence, skill acquisition, and self-confidence. Likewise, more mature supervisees may desire challenges in their work with clients and from their supervisors. In the termination phase, supervisees are adept at conceptualizing client issues and able to appropriately apply theory to practice. Supervisees in the termination phase continue to hone their clinical skills, increase self-efficacy, and thus require minimal direction from supervisors.

Tasks and Functions of Supervision

The *Tasks of Supervision* include the professional skills, behaviors, and roles that are required by counselors. The specific tasks addressed in supervision are based on the learning goals and needs of the supervisee. These five tasks include counseling skills, case conceptualization, professional role (principles and ethics of professional counseling), emotional awareness (supervisee self-awareness and insight and interpersonal dynamics in working with clients and the supervisor), and self-evaluation (supervisee assessment of competence and clinical effectiveness). The *Functions of Supervision* in the SAS method are the dynamic interactions between supervisor and supervisee and relate to how the tasks of supervision are accomplished. Supervisors utilize the monitoring/evaluating function to provide formative or summative feedback to the supervisee. Other functions include instructing/advising, modeling, consulting (problem solving in collaboration with the supervisee), and supervisor supporting/sharing at an interpersonal level.

Bradley et al. (2000) describe the combination of task and function as the action of the supervisory process. "The task is the 'what' of supervision and involves an examination of the objectives and strategies used in teaching and learning and the function is 'how' the task is accomplished" (Bradley et al., p. 108). According to Holloway (1997) any task can be paired with any function; however, in reality there are some task and function combinations that are probably more likely to occur in supervision.

Contextual Factors of Supervision

Holloway stresses the importance of four contextual factors that must be considered in the supervisory process. Contextual factors are conditions related to the choice of task and function and the formation of a relationship, with the supervisor, supervisee, client, and the institution in which supervision is occurring.

In the SAS model the five *Supervisor Factors* that are relevant to supervisor performance include professional experience, roles (how the supervisor behaves with the supervisee), theoretical orientation, self-preservation (the verbal and nonverbal behaviors the supervisor uses to "convey a desired impression to others," Bradley et al., p. 109), and cultural elements (e.g., worldview, belief system, values, attitudes). The SAS model stresses the importance of recognizing and attending to cultural factors in supervision and how they interact with and affect other factors in the model. *Supervisee Factors* that influence the supervisory relationship share similarities with some of the supervisor characteristics and consist of experience in counseling (level of competence and need for support and structure), theoretical orientation, learning style and needs, self-presentation, and cultural characteristics.

Since the purpose of supervision is to ensure that clients are being effectively served by supervisees, it is important to consider *Client Factors* in the supervision model. Three factors are identified for clients: client characteristics, client-identified problem and diagnosis, and counseling relationship. Any systems model would not be complete without considering the role of *Institutional Factors* on the supervisory process. All supervision takes place in the context of institutional organizations, whether university counseling centers, hospitals, community agencies, schools, or other service providers. Just as there are unique characteristics of every supervisor, supervisee, and client, institutions also vary in multiple ways (e.g., mission, goals, expectations, policies). Institutional factors consist of organizational clientele, organizational structure and climate, and professional ethics and standards.

Jeremy and Shana: Case Example of SAS Model

Jeremy is completing his first practicum at an outpatient alcohol and drug treatment facility. The supervisor, Shana, is a licensed psychologist who has worked at the center for 15 years. After viewing a tape of one of Jeremy's sessions with his 21-year-old client, Jackson, Shana determines that Jeremy is responding inappropriately by laughing along with Jackson as Jackson describes the recent drug overdose death of his close friend. Shana realizes that she needs to address Jeremy's inappropriate laughter and discover what is going on for Jeremy at this point in the session. As a beginning counselor, Jeremy is likely to be nervous and wanting support and guidance from the supervisor. Shana focuses on Jeremy's emotional awareness, with the goal of helping Jeremy gain some self-awareness and insight into his reaction to Jackson. Jeremy mentions that he knows that although Jackson is laughing, Jackson is devastated by his friend's death and is probably worried about where his own drug use may lead him. Jeremy is uncomfortable with the content of the session and is nervous about working with his first client who is in treatment for substance abuse. Jeremy has never worked in this type of environment. Shana utilizes the functions of monitoring, followed by instructing/advising and modeling. Noticing the inappropriate laughter and bringing it into focus during supervision provides the supervision dyad an opportunity to explore Jeremy's internal states of fear, nervousness, and lack of confidence, his inexperience, as well as his professional role. After examining and discussing Jeremy's internal reactions, Shana normalizes Jeremy's feelings and discloses how she has managed her own uncomfortable feelings during counseling sessions. This use of modeling and instruction not only provides Jeremy with new ways of thinking about how he will manage difficult emotions when they arise but also strengthens the supervisory relationship and reinforces Jeremy's professional role. Shana also provides Jeremy with relevant reading material on addictions and grief and loss and asks Jeremy to come to the next supervision with questions and observations. By arming Jeremy with concrete information and instruction, Shana hopes Jeremy will develop more confidence and competence and further define his professional role. A final piece to the picture relates to Jeremy's concern about not having previously worked "in this environment." Here, Shana and Jeremy spend time discussing the environmental factors that concern Jeremy.

The SAS model is complex, comprehensive, and offers multiple ways of conceptualizing and intervening with supervisees. Probably most important in this model is the prime position given to the supervisory relationship and the overt recognition of the systemic, cultural, and contextual factors that affect every other aspect of the model.

Critical Events-Based Model of Supervision

Ladany, Friedlander, and Nelson's (2005) critical events-based model of supervision is grounded in the task-analysis counseling and psychotherapy literature (e.g., Greenberg, 1986; Safran, Crocker, McMain, & Murray,

1990) where meaningful therapeutic tasks are identified, explored, and resolved. Additionally, the development of the critical events-based model evolved from the authors own experiences as supervisors. With many parallels to the therapeutic process, the authors liken the supervisory process to a "series of episodes, like chapters in a book with each episode having a specific task to be accomplished" (p. 4). Though theoretically linked to a therapy events-based paradigm, Ladany (2004) described supervision as inherently different from therapy in three distinct ways: supervision is evaluative, typically involuntary, and educative in nature. Given this distinction between therapy and supervision, Ladany et al. (2005) suggest that critical events-based models of supervision should differ from those designed for counseling and therapy.

Theoretical Concepts and Assumptions

The Ladany et al. (2005) critical events-based model of supervision is intended to be an investigative, meaningful, and practical tool for identifying and studying common critical events that occur in supervision. Ladany et al. (2005) note five key assumptions of the model: (1) pantheoretical nature makes it applicable to supervision of counseling and psychotherapy across disciplines; (2) has an interpersonal focus, not merely a developmental approach; (3) goes beyond case management as the main goal of supervision and emphasizes supervisees' education and development; (4) likens the supervisory process to a "series of events or episodes," each with a definable beginning, middle, and end that can be explored in one session or stretched over multiples sessions; and (5) critical events chosen for investigation are "salient for supervision outcomes," in that the mechanism of "working through these events to a successful resolution" is assumed to lead to supervisee growth (p. 10). The authors identify seven critical events based on the literature, the authors' experiences as supervisors, and the importance the events have in supervision outcome: remediating skill difficulties and deficits, heightening multicultural awareness, negotiating role conflicts, working through countertransference, managing sexual attraction, repairing gender-related misunderstandings, and addressing problematic attitudes and behavior. The authors note that the seven events are not exhaustive but represent the most common and challenging incidents that occur in psychotherapy supervision (Ladany et al., 2005, p. 19).

Supervisory Relationship

The phases of the model are embedded within a relational context; hence Bordin's (1983) components of the working alliance between the supervisor and supervisee are viewed as paramount for effective supervision (i.e., agreement on supervision goals, tasks, and a strong emotional bond) in the events-based model. Often critical events are signaled by a breakdown in one or more areas of the working alliance. Disagreements between the supervisor and supervisee about supervision goals or tasks or a problem in the quality of the emotional bond can lead to an event that must be addressed and worked through to resolution. In the model, the working alliance is explained as "figure versus ground" (Bordin, 1983, p. 14). At times the supervisory relationship is the issue at hand or the "figure" that is actively being developed or addressed, whereas at other times the working alliance provides the context or "ground" for the other aspects of supervision. Whether figure or ground, the supervisory relationship is ever-present and plays a significant role in effective supervision and in successfully resolving critical events.

Methodology and Techniques
Three phases compose the critical events-based model of supervision: marker, task environment, and resolution (Ladany et al., 2005). During the *Marker* phase, the supervisee signals the need for help in a particular area by making a statement, series of statements, or exhibiting a behavior. The Marker calls the supervisor to action and indicates the type of intervention that is required. It is not unusual for supervisees to directly ask the supervisor for help with a client issue or a professional concern; however, other indicators may be less overt and unspoken such as a supervisee consistently arriving late or avoiding discussion of a particular client (Ladany et al., 2005). The Marker may also be something the supervisor observes during the supervision session or when reviewing a supervisee's session with a client. Ladany et al. (2005) note that when the supervisee is not forthcoming with a Marker, the supervisor is cautioned to proceed gingerly paying close attention to the marker but also the quality of the working alliance. The Marker phase ends when the supervisor is sure about what issue needs addressing.

The second phase, *Task Environment*, is a series of interaction sequences that occur between the interventions applied by the supervisor and the supervisee consequential reactions (Greenberg, 1986). The Task Environments generally include sequences of exploration, clarification, and working through. Within the general sequences, common interactional sequences described by Ladany et al. (2005) include: focus on the supervisory relationship, focus on the therapeutic process, exploration of feelings, focus on countertransference, attend to parallel processes, focus on self-efficacy, normalizing experience, focus on skill, assess knowledge, focus on multicultural awareness, and focus on evaluation. Task Environments differ depending on the type of event, the supervisee's readiness and developmental level, and the complex interaction of contextual factors (e.g., supervisee, supervisor, client, setting; Ladany et al., 2005).

The final component, *Resolution*, is the successful completion of a supervisory task and can be thought of in four broad categories: an enhancement of or decline in (1) self-awareness (understanding of how the supervisee's feelings, behaviors, and belief system affect the therapeutic work); (2) knowledge (conceptual, theoretical practical); (3) skills (microskills to more complex interventions); or (4) the supervisory alliance (enhancing the emotional bond, coming to agreement on goals and tasks, repairing ruptures or impasses in the supervisory relationship (Ladany et al., 2005, p. 18). The event is resolved when the task is accomplished. As with unresolved counseling and therapy events, supervisory events left unresolved or unfinished can be damaging, negatively affecting the supervisee (personally and professionally), the counseling work, or the supervisory relationship.

Linda and James: Case Example of Critical Events Model

Linda is a first-year doctoral student in her second semester being supervised by a fourth-year doctoral student, James. They have met for eight weeks and have established a good working relationship; however, during the past two sessions Linda has smiled nervously, been reserved, and reluctant to talk about one of her clients, Mike. In fact, James noticed Linda behaving in a similarly passive way during one of her sessions with Mike. James sees Linda's reticence to talk about Mike and her change in behavior during supervision as a "Marker" and a potential critical event. At the beginning of the next session, James tells Linda that he's noticed her reluctance to talk about her work with Mike and wonders what has happened. This discussion takes them to the "Critical Event," which is Linda's sexual attraction to her client Mike. Now being fully aware of the critical event, James executes the following "Interactional Sequence" by first exploring Linda's feelings and bringing their working alliance to the foreground or "figure" ("Exploration"), then focusing on the therapeutic relationship ("Clarification"), and finally, "Working Through" the situation by normalizing her experience and then attending to the parallel process in their relationship. "Resolution" occurs when Linda gains insight and self-awareness about how her feelings and behaviors are affecting her work with Mike and when the supervisory working alliance is repaired.

The critical events model has grounding in the literature and professional practice. Similar to the SAS model, the supervisory relationship plays a central role in the phases of the model. Conceptualizing the supervisory process as a series of episodes related to common events lends itself to use by those who are investigative, task-oriented, and solution-focused.

Case Application

Now that you have walked down three separate grocery aisles, we have prepared a meal for you to digest. As you read through the following case, we ask that you put yourself in the position of the supervisor and supervisee and imagine the approaches and techniques that may work for you in either role. Notice now how any of the three models or their components could be used according to the relationship, the case presentation, and the context.

Sarah and Ann

This case involves a practicum student in a counselor education program whose first internship placement is in an urban nondenominational Christian-based institution. In the supervisee's orientation to the site (college counseling center) it is made clear that the center does not work with clients who are nonheterosexual in orientation. Such clients are referred to community resources. However, after the department chair and the faculty supervisor meet with the site supervisor (director of the counseling center), arrangements are made for the supervisee to work with any client regardless of sexual orientation or relationship status.

The supervisee (will be called Sarah) is a White heterosexual woman in her late twenties, who is married and also identifies herself as a Christian. Sarah also attended a similar Christian-based institution as an undergraduate. The faculty supervisor (will be called Ann) is a White partnered lesbian in her early fifties who has a strong fundamentalist religious background, but currently identifies as spiritual and does not subscribe to any organized religion. Sarah and Ann have had two previous classes together and they have a warm connection and a mutual respect for each other.

The supervisee is informed of the outcome of the meeting between the site supervisor, and the department chair and faculty supervisor. Although there is some uneasiness and doubt about the philosophical differences between the site and the department, she is pleased and relieved that the situation is resolved and looks forward to beginning her practicum at the counseling center. Sarah and Ann meet briefly to talk about the results of the meeting.

Ann: There has been some controversy about your site and doubt about whether you'd be able to do your placement there. Now that the site has agreed for you to see any and all types of clients, how are you feeling about beginning your practicum at this site?

Sarah: Well, my first concern was that I would have to find another site and that added some stress to the situation. So, I am glad it worked out. I am very familiar with the site and know some of the people at the counseling center. Really, I am surprised that Dan (the director) made the exception for me to work with any client because the institution has very strict policies about students, and even faculty and staff who are lesbian and gay. I am not sure what will actually happen if I am assigned to work with a client who is lesbian or gay.

Ann: You're glad to have a placement, but you're not quite sure how the situation will work out if you do get to work with a client who is nonheterosexual—you seem to have some doubt about how it will play out.

Sarah: I know what he agreed to, but I just wonder what it will be like to talk with him about my work with a gay or lesbian client knowing what he really believes. I guess we'll just see what happens. But, for the most part, I'm looking forward to getting started.

What if the supervisor had at this moment moved toward a systems approach? It is interesting that there are at least two systems at work here involving two institutions with very different ideologies. Sarah brings the influence of her system to the situation, one that may put her in conflict due to her affiliation with both institutions. Her ambivalence is evident by her last statement, "For the most part, I'm looking forward to getting started." She seems to also be asking why Dan made an exception for her. From Sarah's knowledge of Dan's institutional system, it may seem like he is disagreeing with and going against the institution's doctrine. Perhaps Dan's act of social justice brings to light another system at play and adds to Sarah's confusion and uncertainty.

During the first individual supervision session, in addition to reviewing the supervision contract and discussing goals and expectations for supervision, the supervisory dyad begins the work of building a solid relationship. The two had been talking about the placement site and Sarah became quiet and thoughtful.

Ann: We've been quiet for a while. (pause)

Sarah: I was just thinking about the meeting you had with Dan. (pause) I can't imagine what it was like for you to sit there and listen to him, to have to listen to him talk about the institution's beliefs about gay and lesbian relationships.

Ann: You said you can't imagine, yet I think you probably have a good idea of what he was saying and can imagine how I may have been feeling. At times I felt angry and wanted to say, "Hey, you are talking about me." But at the same time, I did not want to bias the conversation and make it personal, so I stuck to the department's policy and philosophy. What are you feeling as you think about the situation, about what I just said?

Sarah: It makes me really sad to think about how gay people are alienated and set apart as sinners just because they love someone of the same sex. I just feel bad that you had to go through that.

Ann: I'm hearing concern about me and also perhaps some confusion because I know you attended a similar institution as an undergrad but maybe some of your beliefs differ from the doctrine.

Sarah: Yes, I am a very religious person, maybe spiritual is a better word. But my whole family is definitely religious, especially my Dad; he has very rigid beliefs about what the Bible teaches.

Ann: So your belief system may be different in some ways from your family's religious beliefs; there seems to be some conflict there.

Sarah: Yes, I can see myself moving away from some of those rigid teachings so that makes me not fit in as well. The problem is that I don't feel like I could ever say anything about it to them.

Ann: You feel kind of stuck there. I also wonder if you may be concerned about something you mentioned earlier when you said you were not sure what would happen if you were assigned to work with a gay or lesbian and had to discuss that case in supervision with Dan. What will you say or do if you disagree with your supervisor about some aspect of the case?

At that moment, Sarah seemed to be exploring the system closest to her; she's holding the system Ann represents to her next to the one she knows and trying to see them in some new way. Here is a critical moment in Sarah's development as she works to negotiate multiple perspectives as well as the inherent power dynamics in the supervisory relationship.

We also see the discrimination model in action here as Ann takes on the counselor role in discussing the connection between Sarah's role with her father and her similar role with her site supervisor. Ann also utilizes a consultation approach when she poses a "what if" question to Sarah, indicating a movement toward encouraging Sarah to identify and trust her own thoughts and feelings when pondering how she might respond during a possible scenario. Throughout this process, Ann asks Sarah to address her personalization skills, calling into question how her cultural background, personal issues, and belief system may affect her interactions with Ann and Dan.

The very first client assigned to Sarah is a partnered lesbian, Jane. Both Sarah and Ann are amazed that the universe has provided them with what turns out to be a tremendous growth experience for all involved. Jane has entered counseling to address problems in her relationship with her partner, depression, and issues connected to years of childhood ridicule by her father. A theme that persists in their work is Jane's inability to speak up for herself in most situations in her life, including her relationship with her partner.

During one supervision session, Ann and Sarah do a role-play to help Sarah get a better feel for what her client is experiencing when Jane is unable to give voice to her feelings. Sarah took on the role of Jane, and Ann played the counselor role. Also during this session there was a discussion about the possibility of doing more gestalt work and using the empty chair technique with Jane to help her articulate and work out some of the intense feelings she is having about being stifled in her relationship with her partner and feeling like she never has a say in anything about their relationship. Jane feels like her needs are never considered, though she rarely expresses her needs. Although Sarah has been exposed to the empty chair technique, she is not confident that she could properly use the technique. Ann describes the empty chair process, shows and discusses with Sarah a segment from a video of Greenberg utilizing the empty chair, and provides Sarah with an article about the empty chair and two-chair techniques.

The discrimination model is at the crux of this session as Ann assesses Sarah's need for skill development and confidence. Through modeling, explanation and description, didactic instruction, and assigning outside reading, Ann relies heavily on a teacher role. Similarly, Ann might have used the critical events model to address Sarah's skill deficit. The first Marker in this case is Ann's assessment that Sarah may not fully grasp her client's experience. The Task includes sequences of exploration of feelings (what is it like for Sarah to realize Jane's inability to give voice to her feelings?), clarification (focus on the skill of role-play), and working through (exploration of feelings and assess knowledge—examine Sarah's reactions to taking on her client's emotional experience). Resolution occurs as Sarah increases self-awareness and enhances her appreciation for what her client may be experiencing.

To begin the next session, Sarah asks Ann how things are going with Jane and if she has a section of a session for them to review. Sarah chooses to show the section of the session where she had facilitated the empty chair with Jane. The process moved smoothly and was intensely emotional. After the empty chair, Jane voiced some insights and connected her difficulty expressing her needs back to her childhood and her relationship with her father. Sarah stopped the tape and the supervisory dyad processed how the empty chair segment of the tape went. Ann then asks to see a bit more of the session. In the next segment of the tape, Jane expresses her gratitude to Sarah and tells her that no one has ever listened to her and really heard her the way Sarah has. Jane says she feels totally free to express herself with Sarah and feels totally accepted by Sarah. She says she feels closer to Sarah than anyone in her life. Jane now believes she will be able to tell her partner some of the things she processed in the empty chair activity.

Ann: Jane feels very safe with you and is giving you a lot of praise for being attentive to her and her needs. It looks like something is happening for you as she is telling you this, you appear more distant.

Sarah: I didn't notice that during the session but yes, it almost looks like I'm drifting off or something.

Ann: As you watch yourself in the tape, can you recall what you were thinking or feeling there?

Sarah: I look shut down but I'm not sure what I'm feeling. I know that I felt uneasy when she said she felt closer to me than anyone in her life. I don't want that responsibility.

Ann: Your voice sounds tense as you say that, like there is more there than the responsibility piece.

Sarah: Yeah, I think there is a lot swirling around in my head. It's coming back to me as we talk. I think there is a part of me that's worried that she may be attracted to me. And then, when she was talking about her father, I went back to times when I wanted to say things back to my father but I did not dare. In some ways we are struggling with similar issues, standing up for ourselves. So, yes, a lot was going on there—I was in my head and started to shut down emotionally because it was too much to be with there.

In this section Ann notices a shift in the session, as Sarah seems to emotionally distance herself from Jane. As the "inquirer" in the interpersonal process recall technique (Walker, 2010), Ann asks Sarah what she was thinking or feeling at that moment in the session in an attempt to help Sarah reflect on what is happening for her internally. As the scenario unfolds, Sarah reveals conflicting feelings about the client's feelings toward Sarah and old familiar feelings are resurrected as Sarah flashes to thoughts about her father.

From a systems perspective there is much complexity woven into this scenario. Sarah is thrown by the interpersonal dynamics that put her struggle with her spiritual beliefs front and center and are also intertwined with unfinished business with her father. From a critical events perspective, there are multiple markers that signal to Ann a need for immediate intervention. The event that is most prominent is Sarah's countertransference that prevented her from being present with Jane. Sarah noticed Ann's shutting down during the session as a key marker. An interactional sequence might include Exploration where Sarah and Ann may focus on both the supervisory and counseling relationships. What is happening between Sarah and her client and how safe does Sarah feel in the supervisory relationship now that she has revealed her fears about her client and the insights about her past? Next Ann might focus on the countertransference, the triggers, and the parallels between Sarah and her client (Clarification). The working through phase may include a disclosure from Ann of a similar experience to help normalize Sarah's experience. Ann might also attend to the parallel process noting how Sarah became very quiet during the beginning of this segment of supervision that mimicked the clients actions in counseling. Resolution will occur when Sarah gains an increase in self awareness and insight about how her personal reactions, beliefs, and past experiences affect her work with her clients. For Ann to come to complete resolution on this issue, she may seek personal counseling.

We now ask that you go back through this case and try viewing each segment from a different theoretical perspective. For example, where we used the discrimination model, try conceptualizing the case through the lens of the SAS or the critical events Model. By engaging in this exercise, we think you will see the beauty of integrative models and the value of viewing cases from multiple perspectives.

A Final Thought

One of the great values intrinsic in these integrative models and approaches, from our perspective, is flexibility. A supervisor, or supervisors in peer groups, is frequently asked or compelled to lead a supervisee in one direction or another for an almost endless variety of reasons. As cliché as it may seem, to imagine that one model, or the techniques of one model, can fulfill all supervisory possibilities is ambitious. When supervisors are well trained in a variety of approaches—ensuring that each is congruent with their philosophical and theoretical values—they maximize chances that we can select an approach that best suits the circumstance.

References

Bernard, J. M. (1979). Supervisor training: A discrimination model. *Counselor Education and Supervision, 19,* 60–68.

Bernard, J. M. (1997). The discrimination model. In C. B. Watkins, Jr. (Ed.), *Handbook of psychotherapy supervision* (pp. 310–327). New York, NY: Wiley.

Bernard, J. M., & Goodyear, R. K. (2009). *Fundamentals of clinical supervision* (4th ed.). Upper Saddle River, NJ: Pearson Education.

Bordin, E. S. (1983). A working alliance based model of supervision. *The Counseling Psychologist, 11*(1), 35–41.

Bradley, L. J., Gould, L. J., & Parr, G. D. (2000). Supervision-based integrative models of counselor supervision. In L. J. Bradley & N. Ladany (Eds.), *Counselor supervision: Principles, process, and practice* (pp. 93–124). Philadelphia, PA: Brunner-Routledge.

Ellis, M. V., & Dell, D. M. (1986). Dimensionality of supervisor roles: Supervisors' perceptions of supervision. *Journal of Counseling Psychology, 33,* 282–291.

Ellis, M. V., Dell, D. M., & Good, G. E. (1988). Counselor trainees' perceptions of supervisor roles: Two studies testing the dimensionality of supervision. *Journal of Counseling Psychology, 35,* 315–324.

Goodyear, R. K., Abadie, P. D., & Efros, F. (1984). Supervisory theory into practice: Differential perceptions of supervision by Ekstein, Ellis, Polster, and Rogers. *Journal of Counseling Psychology, 31,* 228–237.

Greenberg, L. S. (1986). Change process research. *Journal of Consulting and Clinical Psychology, 54,* 4–9.

Holloway, E. L. (1995). *Clinical supervision: A systems approach.* Thousand Oaks, CA: Sage.

Holloway, E. L. (1997). Structures for the analysis and teaching of supervision. In C. E. Watkins, Jr. (Ed.), *Handbook of psychotherapy supervision* (pp. 249–276). New York, NY: Wiley.

Kraus, K. L., & Hulse Killacky, D. (1996) Balancing process and content: A metaphor. *Journal for Specialists in Group Work, 21*(2), 90–93.

Ladany, N. (2004). Conducting effective clinical supervision. In G. P. Koocher, J. C. Norcross, & S. S. Hill (Eds.), *Psychologists' desk reference* (2nd ed.). New York, NY: Oxford University Press.

Ladany, N., Friedlander, M. L., & Nelson, M. S. (2005). *Critical events in psychotherapy supervision: An interpersonal approach.* Washington, DC: American Psychological Association.

Lazovsky, R., & Shimoni, A. (2007). The on-site mentor of counseling interns: Perceptions of ideal role and actual role performance. *Journal of Counseling and Development, 85,* 303–314.

Norcross, J. C., & Napolitano, G. (1986). Defining our Journal and ourselves. *International Journal of Eclectic Psychotherapy, 5,* 249–255.

Putney, M. W., Worthington, E. L., Jr., & McCullough, M. E. (1992). Effects of supervisor and supervisee theoretical orientation and supervisor-supervisee matching on interns' perception of supervision. *Journal of Counseling Psychology, 39,* 258–265.

Safran, J. D., Crocker, P., McMain, S., & Murray, P. (1990). Therapeutic alliance rupture as a therapy event for empirical investigation. *Psychotherapy: Theory, Research, Practice, and Training, 27,* 154–165.

Walker, J. A. (2010). Supervision techniques. In N. Ladany & L. Bradley (Eds.), *Counselor Supervision.* New York, NY: Brunner Routledge.

CHAPTER 6

Supervision-Based Integrative Models of Counselor Supervision

Developmental Models

CATHERINE Y. CHANG and CAROLINE O'HARA

Numerous authors (e.g., Loganbill, Hardy, & Delworth, 1982; Skovholt & Ronnestad, 1992) have delineated models of supervision. Some of these models are extensions or adaptations of psychotherapy models (e.g., psychodynamic model of supervision, behavioral model of supervision; see Chapter 7) while others were developed specifically for the supervision context. Models developed expressly for the supervision context can be further categorized into integrative models (e.g., discrimination model, interpersonal process recall; see Chapter 5) and developmental models. Developmental models focusing on multicultural supervision, multicultural counseling competencies, and advocacy competencies also have been developed (see Chapter 3). It is outside the scope of this chapter to discuss and review all developmental models. The purpose of this chapter is to provide a brief overview of the supervision developmental models with specific attention given to the integrated development model (IDM; Stoltenberg, McNeill, & Delworth, 1998).

Developmental Models of Supervision

Developmental models of supervision can be traced back to Fleming (1953) and Hogan (1964). Since then there have been several models of supervision that utilize a developmental framework for understanding supervisee growth and conceptualizing the supervisory process (e.g., Loganbill et al., 1982; Skovholt & Ronnestad, 1992; Stoltenberg et al., 1998). These various

145

developmental models all vary in number of stages and labels for each stage; however, all developmental models are based on the following assertions. They recognize that supervisees develop competencies through a progression of developmental stages that are qualitatively different and the nature of the supervisory relationship changes as the supervisees gain experience and competence. Each stage of supervisee development requires a different supervisory environment (Chagnon & Russell, 1995).

Theoretical Assumptions

As with all models, the purpose of the developmental models of supervision is to provide a framework for organizing and processing the supervisory experience. In developmental models, it is assumed that the supervisees grow and change as a result of the supervisory process. "Since supervision is essentially a developmental process, it follows that developmental theory could offer an appropriate foundation" (Loganbill et al., 1982, p. 20). Although there are several developmental models of supervision with distinct terms and descriptions to describe the growth of the supervisee, Campbell (2000) asserts that the concepts of all developmental models mirror that of human development; thus, supervisees continue to gain additional knowledge and develop increasingly more complex skills as they advance through the developmental stages.

Entry-level supervisees like children begin their experience dependent on their supervisors and exhibit unaware, impulsive, and egocentric behaviors. This early stage of supervisee development is characterized with all or nothing thinking and simplistic categorical understanding of the clients. Supervisees at this level are overly concerned with the rules and the right way to behave (Borders & Brown, 2005). For example, a supervisee at this level may view all women with depression the same way and utilize the same intervention for all women with depression. Borders and Brown recommend that supervisors working with entry-level supervisees provide structure and direction and that the supervisory relationship is mainly instructive and skill focused. Additionally, supervisors provide ample support and encouragement to the novice supervisee.

As the entry-level supervisees develop into advanced students (i.e., adolescence), their desire for autonomy and independence increases and they will begin challenging their supervisors. During this middle stage, it is not unusual for the supervisees to experience conflict and confusion; they may disregard suggestions and directives from their supervisors (Campbell, 2000). Also at this level, supervisees are becoming more aware of their strengths and limitations and begin to personalize their interventions and treatment plans. They are beginning to view clients from a more individualized perspective; thus, not all women with depression are viewed the same anymore. During this middle stage, supervisees are more open to dialogue about their reactions to their clients; thus, supervisors can focus on the relationship between the personal life and the professional work. Supervisors at this stage can be more challenging and provide a learning environment that encourages the supervisees to question their hypotheses and assumptions as well as seek multiple perspectives regarding their clinical work. It is believed that most counselors graduate and enter their first professional counseling position at this middle stage of counselor development (Borders & Brown, 2005).

Developmental models of supervision end with the supervisees gaining self-awareness and confidence in their clinical skills (Campbell, 2000). Case conceptualization and interventions are more complex and sophisticated at this stage taking into account not only theory but accumulated experiences, both personal and professional, of the counselor. Supervisors at this stage view supervision from a more collegial perspective. Supervision is focused on assisting the supervisees to think through their choices as well as helping the supervisees see patterns of behavior and themes across sessions and clients. This later stage of counselor development is achieved when there is an integration of professional and personal identities (Borders & Brown, 2005).

Similar to Campbell's (2000) assertion that supervisee development mirrors human development, Falender et al. (2004) assert that the supervisees develop in a manner similar to Lerner's developmental contextualism (1986). Developmental contextualism focuses on the changing relations between the developing individual (i.e., the supervisee) and the supervisee's context (i.e., supervisory process). The supervisee's change is based upon the interaction between the supervisory environment that is largely provided by the supervisor, the training environment, the therapy experience, and the developmental level of the supervisees. Thus, in order to foster optimal growth and development in the supervisees, the supervisors must first assess the developmental level of their supervisees and then adapt their behaviors to match the developmental needs of the supervisees in order to create the optimal supervisory environment. Developmental models are sequential and hierarchal, describing a supervisory process that requires greater complexity and integration (Borders & Brown, 2005).

Theories of Supervisor Development

In addition to general developmental models of supervision that focus primarily on supervisee development, there have been several developmental models that focus specifically on supervisor development (see Hess, 1986; Littrell, Lee-Borden, & Lorenz, 1979; Rodenhauser, 1994; Stoltenberg et al., 1998; Watkins, 1990, 1993). These supervisor developmental models are similar to the general developmental supervision models in that they are metatheoretical, sequential, hierarchical, and advance through several stages that are progressively more advanced and complex (Falender & Shafranske, 2004).

Hess's (1986) model includes three stages (i.e., beginning, exploration, and confirmation of supervisor identity). The beginner supervisor, who may identify more as a supervisee, may be unaware of supervisory issues including structuring of supervision sessions and techniques of supervision. At this stage, the supervisor is sensitive to feedback and thus focuses more on the concrete. According to this model, beginning supervisors are more client-focused and techniques-oriented in supervision. During the exploration stage, the supervisor begins to recognize their impact on the supervisees and sees supervision as a professional activity. Supervisors in this stage are aware of the supervision literature and are more aware of the needs of the supervisees. This model of supervisor development concludes with confirmation of supervisor identity where the supervisors have a strong sense of supervisor identity and facilitates a level of trust in their supervisees.

Rodenhauser (1994) proposed a four-stage model of supervisor development. These stages are: (1) unconscious identification—where the supervisors unconsciously model their style based on their own supervisory experience; (2) conceptualization—where the supervisors begin developing their own personal concept of supervision; (3) incorporation—which is characterized by an understanding that supervision is a relationship; and (4) consolidation of knowledge into a consistent, workable, instructional model.

Another four-stage model of supervisor development was proposed by Littrell et al. (1979). Stage one of this model includes the supervisor using the supervisory role to facilitate goal setting. In stage two, the supervisor takes a more active role and responsibility in structuring and managing the supervision sessions. In this stage, the supervisor acquires the roles of teacher and counselor. During stage three, the responsibility for structuring the sessions shifts to the supervisee with self-evaluation being encouraged. The supervisor serves more as a consultant in this stage. The final stage (stage four) of this model occurs when the supervisee can perform independently from the supervisor.

Stoltenberg et al. (1998) also includes four developmental stages. The first stage is characterized by the supervisor taking on the expert role and preferring a structured feedback format. During the second stage, the supervisor experiences levels of confusion and struggles between providing supervision and focusing on counseling for the supervisee. The third stage is characterized by increased confidence and stability and continues until the supervisor is able to perform as an integrated supervisor (the fourth stage).

Watkins (1990, 1993) proposed the supervisor complexity model that includes four stages: role shock, role recovery/transition, role consolidation, and role mastery. In addition to these four stages, Watkins (1993) identified four primary issues that supervisors face as they progress through the four stages. The primary issues are: (1) competency versus incompetence; (2) autonomy versus dependence; (3) identity versus identity diffusion; and (4) self-awareness versus unawareness. In the role shock stage, the beginning supervisor is getting acclimated to the idea of being a supervisor and lacks confidence and may feel overwhelmed and unprepared. They have limited awareness of their supervisory strengths, styles, supervision theories, and their impact on the supervisees. During the role recovery/transition stage, the supervisors begin to recognize their strengths and begin developing confidence in their supervisory skills and begin recognizing their impact on their supervisees. The supervisors are beginning to develop their supervisory identity, although it is still very fragile and easily shaken when confronted with supervisory difficulties. The role consolidation stage is characterized by a more realistic and accurate perception of self and the supervisees. There is a growing sense of confidence and supervisory identity that is more stable and consistent. The supervisory identity is not easily shaken with supervision problems. During the role mastery stage, the supervisors are well-integrated and have a theoretically consistent supervisory style. In this stage, the supervisors are able to handle supervision problems effectively and appropriately. Further, there is a strong sense of identity as supervisors that is based on a strong personalized theoretical foundation that consistently guides their supervisory practice.

Although all the supervisor developmental models presented describe a final stage in the developmental process, Falender and Shafranske (2004), in summarizing supervisor development, aptly stated that "we believe that there is no final phase of supervisor development: Even the most senior supervisor, in performing as a mentor and leader, is fostering the innovation and development of others and is continuing to evolve and develop him-or herself" (p. 15).

Strengths and Limitations of Developmental Models

In general, developmental supervision models are helpful because they provide specific expectations and roles in supervision. They are metatheoretical and consequently can be applicable to various theoretical approaches. Developmental models provide guidelines for supervisors to identify both the type of intervention and the kind of supervisory relationship that will promote the supervisees' best growth and development (Borders & Brown, 2005; Falender & Shafranske, 2004).

Despite the intuitive appeal of developmental models, there are several practical considerations that limit the usability of developmental models in clinical settings. Supervisees from various disciplines and training traditions are oftentimes grouped together making it more difficult to apply developmental approaches consistently (Falender & Shafranske, 2004). Additionally, there are several aspects to clinical work such as integration of empirical research in treatment planning, use of metaphors, nonverbal communications, assessment strategies, and the importance of culture in case conceptualization that are missing in developmental models (Falender & Shafranske, 2004).

In addition to these practical considerations, the lack of conclusive empirical support for developmental supervision models is troubling. The limited extant research tends to focus primarily on the early stages of development with few addressing development beyond postdegree supervision and counselor development (Borders, 1989; Borders & Brown, 2005; Falender & Shafranske, 2004). Borders (1989) called for a moratorium on new and improved developmental supervision models, the use of self-report as dependent measures, and research conducted in academic settings. In addition, Borders invited a thorough examination of developmental constructs that will lead to practical suggestions for supervisors. Although there have been additional studies related to developmental supervision models since Border's article, the number is still scarce and the findings remain inconclusive. Below is a summary of the existing studies related to developmental supervision models. Studies that examined the IDM will be discussed later in the chapter.

A Review of the Empirical Studies

In three separate studies spanning a two-year period, Heppner and Roehlke (1984) investigated the differences in supervision across levels of counselors-in-training. The results of their study provide general support for developmental models of supervision. More specifically, they found differences across three trainee levels (beginning practicum, advanced practicum, and interns) in relation to variables related to interpersonal influence process, perceived effectiveness of supervisory behaviors, and reporting of different critical incidents within the supervision process.

Several researchers (Marikis, Russell, & Dell, 1985; Stone, 1980; Worthington, 1984a, 1984b) found differences between experienced supervisors and novice supervisors. Experienced supervisors were more verbal, used more self-disclosure, and provided more direct instruction in counseling skills (Marikis et al., 1985), implemented humor more frequently (Worthington, 1984a) and generated more planning statements regarding their supervisees (Stone, 1980). Additionally, the experienced supervisor was less likely to project negative personal attributes onto supervisees who were experiencing difficulties (Worthington, 1984b). Although these studies reported differences among supervisees across developmental levels, one cannot conclusively argue that individuals change and develop over time since different individuals were being compared. According to Holloway (1987) "the lack of information on intraindividual changes across the course of a training program seriously weakens a developmental explanation of behavioral change" (p. 213); thus, there is a need for longitudinal studies to test the validity of the developmental models of supervision.

Although these studies provide general support for developmental models of supervision, they do not provide conclusive support for any specific developmental models. There is one such developmental model that was developed following a thorough examination of the existing empirical literature (McNeill, 1997; Stoltenberg, 2005) and warrants additional consideration—the IDM (Stoltenberg et al., 1998).

Integrated Developmental Model

The IDM (Stoltenberg et al., 1998) has been described as one of the most comprehensive and heuristic developmental models of supervision (Falender & Shafranske, 2004). Accordingly, this chapter ends with a more thorough investigation of the IDM. More specifically, the following topics will be discussed: primary concepts and theoretical assumptions, focus and goal, supervisory relationships, methodology and techniques, and empirical support. Finally, this chapter ends with case studies to illustrate the core concepts of the IDM and a summary critique of the model.

Primary Concepts and Theoretical Assumptions

Harvey, Hunt, and Schroeder (1961) were one of the first to posit that cognitive abilities of counselors may vary across developmental levels while Hogan (1964) was one of the first authors to describe supervision as a process that should focus on the counselor trainee's developmental level. Hogan outlines four levels of counselor development (i.e., dependence of supervisor, conflict between dependence and autonomy, conditional dependence, and mastery) and contends that ideal supervision environments promote optimal growth at each level. Building on these works, Stoltenberg (1981) developed the counselor complexity model (CCM). According to the CCM, counselor trainees progress through four identifiable stages ranging from beginning trainee to master counselor. As they progress through these stages, the counselor trainees become less dependent and more autonomous (McNeill, Stoltenberg, & Pierce, 1985). The CCM was later expanded by incorporating the concepts of other developmental conceptualizations (e.g., Loganbill et al., 1982) and renamed the IDM (Stoltenberg et al., 1998). According to the IDM, supervisees progress through three developmental levels within three structures (i.e., self–other awareness, motivation, and dependency–autonomy) and across eight domains (i.e., intervention skills, client conceptualization, interpersonal assessment, individual differences, theoretical orientation, assessment approaches and techniques, treatment goals, professional ethics) with the ultimate goal of developing a counselor identity. Stoltenberg's model does not provide a specific timeframe for progression through the three levels; instead, it is assumed that supervisees' development varies from individual to individual. Additionally, the model asserts that individuals progress through the stages for different domains at different times. For example, a counselor may be at level three for client conceptualization and level two for intervention skills. Also, according to the model, some individuals may not reach the final integrated level for all eight domains until they have accumulated many years or professional experience and furthermore, some counselors may never reach the master counselor status (Stoltenberg et al., 1998).

The IDM is founded on the following assumptions: (1) supervisees develop over time; (2) supervisees develop as they progress through the supervisory experience; (3) supervisors can facilitate supervisee development by accurately assessing the supervisee's developmental level and creating the optimal supervisory environment that matches that developmental level; and (4) supervisee development is idiosyncratic.

Focus and Goals

There are three main aspects of the IDM: (1) supervisee developmental levels; (2) structures; and (3) domains that collectively structure the focus and goals of IDM.

Supervisee Developmental Levels

The IDM posits three developmental levels (i.e., Level 1, Level 2, and Level 3) of counselor development that culminate in an integrated level called 3i.

Level 1 Supervisees

Supervisees begin their career highly anxious and dependent on their supervisors. They have a strong motivation to become counselors but lack the in-depth understanding of the complexity of the role and process of counseling. They are focused predominately on self and basic skills development, and tend to engage in categorical thinking and learning the right way to conduct counseling. Beginning supervisees have a difficult time conceptualizing cases and integrating ethics into their cases. Additionally, level 1 supervisees are fearful of evaluations.

Level 2 Supervisees

Supervisees at this level experience the "trial and tribulation" period. At this level, the focus shifts from self to client. The supervisees are developing their empathy skills and gaining a better understanding of the uniqueness of the client's worldview. With greater understanding, the supervisees potentially can become overwhelmed and paralyzed. There is the risk of overempathizing with the clients or oversimplifying the client's needs. Characteristics of this level include: experiencing conflict between dependence and autonomy, fluctuating confidence and motivation, linking own mood to success with the clients, having increased understanding of limitations, demonstrating inconsistent theoretical and conceptual integration. Level 2 supervisees are sensitive and anxious about evaluations.

Level 3 Supervisees

The phrase "calm after the storm" is a good description of the level 3 supervisee. At this level, the supervisee/counselor is beginning to develop a personalized approach to counseling, using therapeutic self as part of the intervention. Supervisees at this level have a high degree of self-awareness and are able to address their areas of weakness with increased confidence and nondefensiveness. Having a firm professional identity, an understanding of client, process, and self, as well as an awareness of their strengths and limitations, supervisees at this level are able to operate independently and responsibly. Supervision with level 3 supervisees becomes more consultative and collaborate while being less didactic.

As the mature supervisees continue to develop proficiencies in multiple domains, a personal style of counseling emerges, and the supervisee demonstrates high levels of professional competence. This level is described as level 3i (integrated). At this level of supervisee development, movement is more horizontal than vertical. This level of development is rarely achieved and those who reach this level are considered "masters" by their colleagues and peers.

Structure

The IDM proposes that as supervisees progress through their developmental levels they change in three overriding structures: (1) self and other awareness; (2) motivation; and (3) autonomy.

Self and Other Awareness

This structure refers to the supervisees' thoughts and feelings about themselves and their clients, and thus this level has both cognitive (thoughts related to counselor self-efficacy of counseling performance) and affective (change in emotions in particularly anxiety) components. More specifically, this structure is concerned with the degree of self-preoccupation, awareness of the client's world, and awareness of personal attributes and limitations. Beginning supervisees are highly focused on both self and their own skill acquisitions. As they progress through level 2, they begin to shift their focus to their clients with increasing empathy. This structure concludes (level 3) with the supervisees focusing on the client, counseling process, and self. Supervisees exhibit high levels of empathy and understanding for their clients and exhibit high levels of insight into personal and professional strengths and limitations.

Motivation

This structure relates to the supervisees' investment in the training and practice as experienced over time. Level 1 supervisees exhibit high motivation; this fluctuates during level 2 and stabilizes in level 3. Although motivation is high during level 1 and level 3, the rationale underlying the motivation shifts focus from the level 1 counselors who are motivated by their desire to be a counselor and get things right to level 3 counselors who are motivated because they understand the complexity of the counseling process.

Autonomy

This structure refers to supervisees' dependence on their supervisors and the degree of independence the supervisees exhibit. Level 1 supervisees begin their career highly dependent on their supervisor needing lots of structure and positive feedback. During level 2, supervisees experience conflict between dependence and autonomy. At level 3, the supervisees have a firm belief in their autonomy; they know when and how to seek additional supervision and consultation.

Domains

The three main structures (i.e., self–other awareness, motivation, and autonomy) provide guidance for assessing developmental level across the eight primary domains of professional functioning. The ultimate goal is for supervisees to obtain proficiency across all eight domains.

1. Intervention skills competence: ability to appropriately and accurately implement therapeutic interventions.
2. Assessment approaches and techniques: having an understanding of the assessment process and administrating psychological assessments.
3. Interpersonal assessment: ability to assess the client's interpersonal dynamics accurately.

4. Client conceptualization: ability to understand how the client's environment, history, and personality influence client functioning.
5. Individual differences: ability to recognize and integrate diversity (racial, ethnic, cultural, and other differences) into understanding and treating the client.
6. Theoretical orientation: having an understanding of different theoretical perspectives and demonstrate the ability to conceptualize and intervene from a theoretical framework.
7. Treatment goals and plans: ability to determine appropriate intervention strategies based upon identifiable goals.
8. Professional ethics: ability to integrate professional and personal ethics.

Supervisory Relationship

According to Stoltenberg et al. (1998), the supervisory relationship provides the optimal supervision environment within which supervisees develop and mature in the three areas of self–other awareness, motivation, and autonomy. "[G]ood supervision relationships encompass warmth, acceptance, respect, understanding, and trust ... and create an atmosphere of experimentation and allowance for mistakes" (p. 111). In order to foster this optimal supervision environment, it is incumbent on the supervisor to assess the developmental level of their supervisees and provide appropriate interventions that provide a balance of support and challenge. The supervisory relationship is a function of the changing role of the supervisor based on the supervisee's developmental level. A description of the role of the supervisor based on the developmental level of the supervisees is provided in the following.

Level 1 Supervisors

Since level 1 supervisees exhibit high levels of anxiety, supervisors need to provide structure while managing anxiety. More specifically, the supervisor will want to be supportive and prescriptive, provide structure and positive feedback, and limit direct confrontation. When possible, the supervisor will want to assign clients with mild presenting problems or maintenance cases.

Level 2 Supervisors

Supervisors for level 2 supervisees will want to balance fostering autonomy with support and structure. The goal for the supervisor is to increase autonomy and confidence while maintaining realistic boundaries of competence. Depending on the progress of their supervisees, level 2 supervisors will want to consider addressing the following issues: transferences and countertransferences within the counseling and supervisory relationships, defensiveness within the supervisory relationship, theory, and conceptual framework, and self-exploration of strengths and limitations.

Level 3 Supervisors

Supervision at this level is directed more by the supervisees, and there is a greater focus on personal and professional integration and career decisions. Autonomy and growth are the hallmark of this level. The supervisor assesses consistency in performance areas across domains with the goal of integration across domains. The level 3 supervisor engages in more in-depth exploration of the parallel process and countertransference within the supervisor–supervisee relationship and continues to create a supportive supervisory environment where supervisees can continue their exploration of the impact of self on the client.

As the needs of the supervisees and the role of the supervisor change across developmental levels, there are some techniques and interventions that are more appropriate depending on the level of the supervisees. In the next section, the authors discuss the various methods and techniques most appropriate for each level of development.

Methodology and Techniques

As stated earlier, it is the responsibility of the supervisor to create the optimal supervisory environment that will encourage maximum supervisee development; therefore, the supervisory interventions need to be implemented with intention and purpose following a thorough assessment of the supervisee development level. Stoltenberg et al. (1998) cautions that exposing a supervisee to an environment that is too advanced runs the risk of increasing anxiety and confusion while exposing the supervisee to an environment that is overly structured can lead to supervisees who become bored, inattentive, and resistant.

There are several assessments that are specific to the IDM and can assist supervisors in determining the goals for supervision. Information related to the supervisees' past experiences, self-perceptions of strengths and weaknesses, and exposure to theoretical orientation can be administered using the Supervisee Information Form (see Stoltenberg et al., 1998, p. 193). The Supervisee Levels Questionnaire-Revised (McNeill, Stoltenberg, & Romans, 1992) can be used to measure the three structures of the IDM: self–other awareness, motivation, and dependence–autonomy. Supervisors can use the information gleaned from these inventories to assess supervisee developmental level and inform their selection of appropriate interventions.

Level 1

Interventions at level 1 should be facilitative (supporting, encouraging), prescriptive (suggested approaches), conceptual (beginning to develop theory), and catalytic. Recommended modes of interventions include: observations via video or live, skills training, role-playing, readings, and group supervision. In order to facilitate transition from level 1 to level 2, the supervisor will want to encourage increased autonomy, begin to reduce the supervisory structure, encourage new techniques, and foster a focus on the client.

Level 2

Interventions that are facilitative, decrease the use of prescriptive interventions and focus more on confrontation and encourage alternate conceptualization of client issues are the focus for level 2 supervisees. Supervisors at this level begin to introduce more catalytic interventions including processing comments, highlighting countertransference, and dealing with affective reactions to the client and the supervisor. Recommended modes of interventions include observations, role-playing, interpreting dynamics and parallel process, and group supervision. To foster a transition from level 2 to level 3, the supervisor will want to encourage the following across domains: stable motivation, fostering flexibility to move autonomously in conceptualization and behavior, the formation of a solid professional identity, development of a personalized understanding, and assessment of the impact of personal events on professional life.

Level 3

Supervisors at this level continue to utilize facilitative and confrontational techniques, conceptualization of the client issue explored more from a personal orientation, and catalytic interventions in response to blocks or stagnation. Recommended modes of interventions include peer supervision and group supervision.

Empirical Support for the IDM

Since the IDM (Stoltenberg et al., 1998) is an extension of the CCM (Stoltenberg, 1981) we are including studies that investigated the CCM as a part of this discussion.

Overall, the researchers investigating the concepts outlined by CCM (Stoltenberg, 1981) reported general support for the model. For example, the developmental levels were consistent with level of experience (McNeill et al., 1985) and experience affected the perception of counselor needs consistent with expectations outlined by the model (Stoltenberg, Pierce, & McNeill, 1987). Supervisees and supervisors matched on their ratings of supervisee development and supervisory environment (Stoltenberg, Solomon, &

Ogden, 1986). An investigation by Krause and Allen (1988) included perceptions from both supervisors and supervisees. In their study, supervisors reported varying their supervisory interventions based on the developmental level of their supervisees, although the supervisees did not perceive this difference. Additionally, in this study the supervisees reported less satisfaction and impact in mismatched supervisory relationships.

Several researchers developed inventories to measure the levels of supervisee development as outlined by the CCM (Stoltenberg, 1981) and IDM (Stoltenberg et al., 1998). McNeill et al. (1985) developed the Supervisory Levels Questionnaire (SLQ) to assess supervisee self-awareness, dependence–autonomy, and theory/skills acquisition. This scale was revised (SLQ-R) by McNeill et al. (1992). Wiley and Ray (1986) developed the Supervision Levels scale (SLS) as an inventory for supervisors to use in order to assess supervisee development and the supervision environment.

Research (Borders, 1990; Tryon, 1996) provided longitudinal investigations of the CCM (Stoltenberg, 1981) and the IDM (Stoltenberg et al., 1998). Borders conducted a short-term longitudinal study with practicum supervisees across one semester. Based on the results of her study, Borders concluded that supervisees changed in relation to self–other awareness, dependence–autonomy, and theory/skills acquisitions, thus providing support for the CCM. Tryon's study monitored supervisee change over one academic year along the three dimensions posited by the IDM (i.e., self-other awareness, motivation, and dependence–autonomy). Overall, the results from this study indicate that supervisees develop over time in the areas of self–other awareness, motivation, and dependence–autonomy thus providing support for the IDM.

Leach and Stoltenberg (1997) investigated the Individual Difference and the Intervention Skills Competence domains of the IDM across level 1 and level 2 trainees. Overall, the results provided support of the two domains of the IDM since level 2 trainees reported greater self-efficacy across five counseling areas (i.e., microskills, process, difficult client behavior, cultural competence, and awareness of values) compared to the level 1 trainees.

Lovell (1999) explored the relationship between scores on the SLQ-R scales (self–other awareness, motivation, dependence–autonomy, and total) and a measure of cognitive complexity. Based on the results of the study, Lovell concluded that overall cognitive complexity is an essential element in counselor development, thus providing support for the IDM. Lovell's conclusion was based on significant results of three of the four scales of the SLQ-R; cognitive complexity was not a significant predictor of the motivational scale. Although this study provides support for the importance of cognitive complexity on counselor development, it does not provide support for all three structures of the IDM.

In addition to empirical studies conducted by Stoltenberg and his colleagues on the CCM (Stoltenberg, 1981) and IDM (Stoltenberg et al., 1998), a literature search utilizing PsycINFO found six dissertations (Ashby, 1999; Berg, 2003; Blaisdell, 2000; Crethar, 1997; Gubrud, 2008; Johnson, 2008) that included the IDM as a part of their study. Of these, one was a theoretical dissertation that expanded the IDM to include psychodynamic and relational concepts (Berg, 2003). Gubrud (2008) developed an instrument to measure one supervision structure, a concept rooted in the IDM. Johnson (2008) compared feedback from novice supervisors and expert supervisors with constructs of the IDM and found statistical and conceptual differences in the groups. Supervisee and supervisor match on theoretical orientation and supervisory style on supervisee development as defined by the IDM was the subject on a fourth dissertation (Blaisdell, 2000). Ashby (1999) and Crethar's (1997) dissertations present the most comprehensive examination of the IDM, both only providing partial support for the IDM. Although interesting in expanding our understanding of the IDM, none of these dissertations provided conclusive and consistent empirical support for the IDM.

Case Examples

Level 1 Case Example   Andre is a new counseling student who is just beginning his practicum. He is highly motivated and clearly anxious about "correctly" performing his skills. The site supervisor has told Andre that he will be working with clients who are somewhat familiar with counseling and who have a lesser degree of intensity with their presenting concerns. At first this served to reassure Andre, but he is currently experiencing some difficulties in counseling three of his clients. This only accelerates his anxiety because he knows he is working with "maintenance" cases. During supervision, Andre consistently seeks direction and wants specific instruction as to how to handle his cases.

Effective supervision with Andre will likely have a high degree of structure and facilitative support. With Level 1 supervisees, interventions are often more prescriptive and directive than with more advanced supervisees. A supervisor will assist Andre in strengthening his skills, building confidence, and managing anxiety. For example, a supervisor may provide positive feedback and focus on Andre's existing strengths as a counseling student and intern. It is likely that Andre will be more focused on himself and on concrete measures of his performance than with the growth and development of his clients. This likely reflects the self-preoccupation that often accompanies Level 1 supervisees. It is suggested that confrontations remain minimal and gentle to avoid increasing the existing anxiety of the supervisee. With time, Andre's supervisor will encourage theory development and more of a focus on client concerns.

Level 2 Case Example

Marisol is a counseling student who is interning at a counseling center for women. She has finally become accustomed to meeting with clients and much of the initial performance anxiety about internship has dissipated. However, Marisol finds one case particularly challenging. She is counseling a woman, one year older than she, who has just received a terminal diagnosis of cancer. In many ways, this client reminds Marisol of her own struggles in living with and overcoming cancer. As a result, Marisol finds herself in a state of confusion, overidentification, and frustration. She fears that by dwelling on this case during supervision that she may be "taking a step back" in her development.

Marisol demonstrates some of the key issues of a level 2 supervisee such as increasing other-awareness, immobility, and uncertainty. For this student, supervision will need to be supportive, but slightly less structured. A supervisor could propose a conceptual intervention and suggest that Marisol focus on how her emerging theoretical orientation could help organize her interactions with her client. This may aid not only Marisol's theory development, but also her feelings of immobility and uncertainty. Another intervention could highlight the process that occurs between Marisol and her client. This focus may assist in directly addressing Marisol's understandable countertransference with her client. In addition, the supervisor may offer to review more audio or videotapes of Marisol's sessions with this particular client. Ultimately, the focus will be to aid Marisol in confronting her own reactions, developing more autonomy, and understanding how the professional and personal aspects of her life interact with one another.

Level 3 Case Example

Camille has recently completed her graduate counseling program and has begun work at a counseling center. During her internship, she was able to gain an understanding of her strengths and growing pains as a counselor. One of Camille's areas of lesser development was her work with couples. Since one of her more recent cases is a couple with some intricate and deeply rooted presenting concerns, Camille believes that further supervision and resource identification is in order.

Camille is a good example of a level 3 supervisee. Counselors at this level are likely to be advanced internship students or employees in counseling settings who exhibit higher degrees of insight, stable motivation, increased autonomy, and lesser degrees of defensiveness about their limitations. Camille's insight and willingness to seek assistance demonstrate not only her maturity as a counselor but also highlight one of her strengths, her ability to seek support and supervision when needed. Supervisors of level 3 supervisees are often more consultative and assist in strengthening underdeveloped domains. It is unlikely that Camille will need a high degree of structure or prescriptive interventions during supervision. Recommended support for her might include individual supervision, peer supervision, or group supervision.

Critique

Stoltenberg et al. (1998) contends that supervision is a complex process and through the development of the IDM, the authors developed a comprehensive developmental supervision model that attempts to assist the conceptualization of the supervisory process. Their model is appealing because it provides a useful framework for understanding how supervisees develop with experience and describes the supervision environments and the supervision interventions that are most appropriate for each developmental level (Stoltenberg, 2005). The IDM considers the supervisee's cognitive and affective awareness of the client and proposes a sequence of development culminating with an advanced supervisee who operates independently and is still receptive to seeking appropriate consultation. As the supervisees change, so must the supervisor. The IDM provides guidelines on how supervisors can adjust their behaviors to match the developmental needs of their supervisees.

Despite the comprehensive nature and intuitive appeal of the IDM, additional empirical studies need to be conducted to provide support for the validity of the developmental stages proposed by the model. Ellis and Ladany (1997) conducted a thorough review of research that tested Stoltenberg's CCM (the predecessor to the IDM) and found seven published studies. Based on their review, they concluded that the IDM had not been adequately tested due to the overall quality of the studies. They cited methodological and conceptual concerns that compromise any conclusions derived from the results. A review of the literature only found four additional studies on the IDM that were not reviewed by Ellis and Ladany (i.e., Leach & Stoltenberg, 1997; Lovell, 1999; McNeill, Stoltenberg, & Romans, 1992; Tryon, 1996) other than the six dissertations mentioned earlier in the chapter. Despite Stoltenberg's (2005) contention that the IDM has stimulated considerable research in the areas of supervisee development and the supervision process, the lack of published research on the model since the 1990s calls into question Stoltenberg's claim (the majority of the studies were investigating the CCM). Clearly, more research that is methodologically sound is needed to validate all aspects of the IDM.

Another limitation of the IDM is its lack of direct attention to multicultural issues related to the supervisee, the supervisor, and the client. Given that "individual differences" is one of the eight domains, it could be argued that cultural issues are considered to be a part of the model and Stoltenberg et al. (1998) does recognize the impact of diversity on the supervisory relationship

Lack of knowledge of individual differences due to culture, gender, and sexual orientation and lack of understanding of multicultural models and interventions and experience with culturally diverse clients negatively affects the credibility or quality of the message of the supervisor from the perspective of diverse supervisees. (p. 125)

However, given the importance of addressing cultural issues in supervision and counseling, the authors believe that attention must be given to addressing cultural issues within this model.

Summary

This chapter aims to introduce major themes associated with developmental models of supervision, particularly the IDM. The first half of the chapter reviews theoretical assumptions, theories of supervisor development, and the strengths and limitations of developmental models. The chapter continues by discussing the IDM in more detail. Three case examples are provided to assist in conceptualizing these ideas. Finally, the chapter concludes with a critique and analysis of the IDM.

Although there are numerous developmental models, a common theoretical foundation of developmental models of supervision is that supervisees grow and develop in autonomy and skill over time. In addition, the relationship between supervisor and supervisee also transforms as the supervisee develops. Supervisees progress through an early entry-level stage, an advanced adolescent stage, and an integrated end stage. Supervisors who are attentive to their supervisees' needs and stage level will have a great chance of promoting optimal growth. This chapter also reviews several theories of supervisor development including models proposed by Hess (1986), Littrell et al. (1979), Rodenhauser (1994), Stoltenberg et al. (1998), and Watkins (1990, 1993). Developmental models have wide appeal, given their metatheoretical nature and their usefulness in providing clear expectations and guidelines. However, the main limitation results from the lack of specific and conclusive empirical support found in the literature.

The IDM, formerly known as the CCM, asserts that supervisees advance through three developmental levels within three structures (i.e., self–other awareness, motivation, and dependency–autonomy) and over eight domains (e.g., interpersonal assessment, theoretical orientation, professional ethics) with the eventual aim of gaining an integrated and functional counselor identity. Supervisors also progress through three levels as they increase in competence and autonomy. Methods and techniques for creating optimal environments for growth during supervision are discussed. Empirical outcomes, in general, support the IDM; however, additional research is needed to support the validity of its stages. Further areas of study could integrate multicultural perspectives and analysis into the model.

References

Ashby, R. H. (1999). Counselor development and supervision: An exploratory study of the integrated developmental model of supervision. *Dissertation Abstracts International: Section B: The Sciences and Engineering, 59,* 6482.

Berg, M. R. (2003). Extending Stoltenberg, McNeil, and Delworth's model of supervision: An expansion of the integrated developmental model to include Sullivan's interpersonal theory constructs. *Dissertation Abstracts International: Section B: The Sciences and Engineering, 63,* 3902.

Blaisdell, K. D. (2000). An investigation of the effects of theoretical orientation, supervisory style, and supervisee preferred supervisory style on supervisee development. *Dissertation Abstracts International: Section B: The Sciences and Engineering, 61,* 1072.

Borders, L. D. (1989). A pragmatic agenda for developmental supervision research. *Counselor Education and Supervision, 29,* 16–24.

Borders, L. D. (1990). Developmental changes during supervisees' first practicum. *The Clinical Supervisor, 8,* 157–167.

Borders, L. D., & Brown, L. L. (2005). *The new handbook of counseling supervision.* Mahwah, NJ: Lahaska/Lawrence Erlbaum.

Campbell, J. M. (2000). *Becoming an effective supervisor: A workbook for counselors and psychotherapists.* Philadelphia, PA: Accelerated Development.

Chagnon, J., & Russell, R. K. (1995). Assessment of supervisee developmental level and supervision environment across supervisor experience. *Journal of Counseling and Development, 73*(5), 553–558.

Crethar, H. C. (1997). Development of counselors across supervision: A study of the integrated developmental model of supervision. *Dissertation Abstracts International: Section A: Humanities and Social Sciences, 58,* 0383.

Ellis, M. W., & Ladany, N. (1997). Inferences concerning supervisees and clients in clinical supervision: An integrative review. In C. E. Watkins, Jr. (Ed.), *Handbook of psychotherapy supervision* (pp. 447–507). New York, NY: Wiley.

Falender, C. A., Erickson Cornish, J. A., Goodyear, R., Hatcher, R., Kaslow, N. J., Leventhal, G., … Grus, C. (2004). Defining competencies in psychology supervision: A consensus statement. *Journal of Clinical Psychology, 60*(7), 771–785.

Falender, C. A., & Shafranske, E. P. (2004). *Clinical supervision: A competency-based approach.* Washington, DC: American Psychological Association.

Fleming, J. (1953). The role of supervision in psychiatric training. *Bulletin of the Menninger Clinic, 15,* 157–159.

Gubrud, R. E. (2008). Measure of supervision structure: Instrument development. *Dissertation Abstracts International. Section A: Humanities and Social Sciences, 68,* 3295.

Harvey, O. J., Hunt, D. E., & Schroeder, H. M. (1961). *Conceptual systems and personality organizational.* New York, NY: Wiley.

Heppner, P. P., & Roehlke, H. J. (1984). Differences among supervisees at different levels of training: Implications for a developmental model of supervision. *Journal of Counseling Psychology, 31*(1), 76–90.

Hess, A. K. (1986). Growth in supervision: Stages of supervisee and supervisor development. *The Clinical Supervisor, 4,* 51–67.

Hogan, R. A. (1964). Issues and approaches in supervision. *Psychotherapy: Theory, Research and Practice, I,* 139–141.

Holloway, E. L. (1987). Developmental models of supervision: Is it development? *Professional Psychology: Research and Practice, 18,* 209–216.

Johnson, D. S. (2008). Concept mapping of supervisor competence: A comparative analysis of expert and novice supervisors. *Dissertation Abstracts International: Section B: The Sciences and Engineering, 68,* 4828.

Krause, A. A., & Allen, G. J. (1988). Perceptions of counselor supervision: An examination of Stoltenberg's model from the perspective of supervisor and supervisee. *Journal of Counseling Psychology, 35,* 77–80.

Leach, M. M., & Stoltenberg, C. D. (1997). Self-efficacy and counselor development: Testing the integrated developmental model. *Counselor Education and Supervision, 37,* 115–125.

Lerner, R. M. (1986). *Concepts and theories of human development* (2nd ed.). New York, NY: Random House.

Littrell, J. M., Lee-Borden, N., & Lorenz, J. (1979). A developmental framework for counseling supervision. *Counselor Education and Supervision, 19,* 129–136.

Loganbill, C., Hardy, E., & Delworth, U. (1982). Supervision: A conceptual model. *The Counseling Psychologist, 10,* 3–42.

Lovell, C. (1999). Supervisee cognitive complexity and the integrated developmental model. *The Clinical Supervisor, 18,* 191–201.

Marikis, D. A., Russell, R. K., & Dell, D. M. (1985). Effects of supervisor experience level on planning and in-session supervisor verbal behavior. *Journal of Counseling Psychology, 32,* 410–416.

McNeill, B. W. (1997). Agendas for developmental supervision research: A response to Borders. *Counselor Education and Supervision, 31,* 179–183.

McNeill, B. W., Stoltenberg, C. D., & Pierce, R. A. (1985). Supervisees' perceptions of their development. A test of the counselor complexity model. *Journal of Counseling Psychology, 32,* 630–633.

McNeill, B. W., Stoltenberg, C. D., & Romans, J. S. C. (1992). The integrated developmental model of supervision: Scale development and validation procedures. *Professional Psychology: Research and Practice, 23,* 504–508.

Rodenhauser, P. (1994). Toward a multidimensional model for psychotherapy supervision based on developmental stages. *Journal of Psychotherapy Practice and Research, 3,* 1–15.

Skovholt, T. M, & Ronnestad, M. H. (1992). Themes in therapist and counselor development. *Journal of Counseling and Development, 70,* 505–515.

Stoltenberg, C. D. (1981). Approaching supervision from a developmental perspective: The counselor complexity model. *Journal of Counseling Psychology, 28,* 59–65.

Stoltenberg, C. D. (2005). Enhancing professional competence through developmental approaches to supervision. *American Psychologist, 60,* 857–864.

Stoltenberg, C. D., McNeill, B. W., & Delworth, W. (1998). *IDM: An integrated developmental model for supervising counselors and therapists.* San Francisco, CA: Jossey-Bass.

Stoltenberg, C. D., Pierce, R. A., & McNeill, R. W. (1987). Effects of experience on counselor trainees' needs. *The Clinical Supervisor, 5,* 23–32.

Stoltenberg, C. D., Solomon, G. S., & Ogden, L. (1986). Comparing supervisee and supervisor initial perceptions of supervision: Do they agree? *The Clinical Supervisor, 4,* 53–62.

Stone, G. L. (1980). Effects of experience on supervisor planning. *Journal of Counseling Psychology, 27,* 84–88.

Tryon, G. S. (1996). Supervisee development during the practicum year. *Counselor Education and Supervision, 35,* 287–295.

Watkins, C. E., Jr. (1990). Development of the psychotherapy supervisor. *Psychotherapy, 27,* 553–560.

Watkins, C. E., Jr. (1993). Development of the psychotherapy supervisor: Concepts, assumptions, and hypotheses of the supervisor complexity model. *American Journal of Psychotherapy, 47,* 58–74.

Wiley, M. O., & Ray, P. B. (1986). Counseling supervision by developmental level. *Journal of Counseling Psychology, 33,* 439–445.

Worthington, E. L. (1984a). Empirical investigation of supervision of counselors as they gain experience. *Journal of Counseling Psychology, 31*(1), 63–75.

Worthington, E. L. (1984b). Use of trait labels in counseling supervision by experienced and inexperienced supervisors. *Professional Psychology: Research and Practice, 15,* 457–461.

CHAPTER 7

Counseling and Psychotherapy-Based Models of Counselor Supervision

TIFFANY O'SHAUGHNESSY, YOKO MORI, ANJU KADUVETTOOR,
CLYDE BEVERLY, and RYAN D. WEATHERFORD

Prior to the development of supervision specific models, supervisors typically relied on their training as clinicians and their primary theoretical orientations to guide their work (White & Russell, 1995). It was through this path that psychotherapy-based models of supervision were articulated, modified, and tested. The purpose of this chapter is to explore the frameworks, foci, and methodologies of four psychotherapy-based supervision models. While there are myriad models of psychotherapy-based supervision (e.g., *Adlerian*, Tobin & McCurdy, 2006; *Behavioral*, Follette & Callaghan, 1995; *Systemic*, McDaniel, Weber, & McKeever, 1983), we have chosen to explore two more prominent models with a more extensive literature base (i.e., psychodynamic and cognitive-behavioral) and two newer models with a burgeoning research base (i.e., feminist and solution-focused). The more prominent models were chosen for their historical and contemporary importance (Bernard & Goodyear, 2009), whereas the newer models were chosen to expose the reader to a sampling of promising new directions. The chapter illustrates the relative strengths and limitations of these four supervision models. Additionally, we will utilize the following case example of a supervisee, Janet, throughout this chapter to demonstrate the differences in the approach of the four models presented:

Janet is a second-year doctoral student completing her first practicum experience at a university counseling center. She expressed to Steve, her supervisor, that she has been feeling a lack of confidence in her skills as she does not feel that any of her clients are making positive progress. She reports being particularly frustrated in her work with Chris, a male client she has met with on three occasions regarding his uncertainty about remaining in a relationship with his partner. She feels that they are not getting closer to his making a decision.

Each model addresses Janet's concerns in a unique fashion, which helps highlight the differences in theory, techniques, and supervision strategy.

Though we work to highlight the unique goals, tasks, and concepts in each approach, the reader will likely notice many similarities among the four models. Many common factors permeate our theories (Morgan & Sprenkle, 2007) such as the importance of the supervisory relationship, the multiple roles of supervision, and the importance of insuring quality client care. Additionally, Bradley and Gould (2001) note that "empathy, genuineness, warmth, trust, and positive regard" (p. 147) are universal concepts that are important for all supervisors. However, each model does have a unique approach to the conceptualization and practice of supervision that will be evident in the descriptions and case examples.

Psychodynamic Model of Supervision

Framework of the Psychodynamic Model of Supervision

The primary framework for psychodynamic supervision is rooted in the traditional psychoanalytic model of supervision dating back to Freud (Frawley-O'Dea & Sarnat, 2001; Freud, 1927). The tripartite "master-apprentice" (Binder & Strupp, 1997, p. 44) model in psychoanalytic supervision emphasizes the passing of knowledge and technique from the master analyst to novice analyst. This approach structures training around three activities: (1) didactic coursework steeped in the analytic institute's approach to psychoanalysis; (2) the supervisee's personal analysis; and (3) supervision of the supervisee's clinical work by a master analyst (Binder & Strupp, 1997). Some (e.g., The Berlin Institute) argue that supervision should focus solely on the work occurring between the supervisee and client, relegating analysis of the supervisee's transference/countertransference reactions to their personal analysis. Others (e.g., The Hungarian Institute) integrate these tasks, focusing both on the supervisee's approach to the client's dynamics and the interpersonal/intrapersonal dynamics that influence their work as a therapist and supervisee (Frawley-O'Dea & Sarnat, 2001). While the "teach–treat" (Frawley-O'Dea & Sarnat, 2001, p. 136) argument still exists with some authors (e.g., Gold, 2004) continuing to warn against addressing supervisee personal dynamics, contemporary psychodynamic supervision explores both the client and supervisee's dynamics.

Primary Concepts and Theoretical Assumptions

The psychodynamic supervisor teaches their supervisee the theoretical and technical foundations unique to psychodynamic therapy, including unconscious mental processes, psychic conflict, transference/countertransference reactions, object relations, resistance, ego defenses, free association, dream analysis, and interpretation (Hayman, 2008; Singer, 1990). The supervisor also assumes that the supervisee possesses a unique set of unconscious mental processes, psychic conflict, transference/countertransference reactions, resistance, and ego defenses. The psychodynamic supervisor believes that the supervisee's transference and countertransference reactions influence their counseling work and that the supervisee will provide the best therapy for their client when they are aware of these dynamic reactions and work through maladaptive relational patterns in a safe environment (Frawley-O'Dea & Sarnat, 2001; Hayman, 2008). Based on these assumptions, the psychodynamic supervisor utilizes the primary concepts of transference and countertransference, parallel process, and internalization in supervision.

Transference and Countertransference Though a supervisee learns, on a didactic level, the core components of psychodynamic therapy in supervision, the transference and countertransference dynamics of the therapy relationship represent the most robust learning tools for the supervisory process (Frawley-O'Dea & Sarnat, 2001; Hayman, 2008). Transference, traditionally defined, is a client's projection of a childhood relational pattern onto their therapist. Contemporary psychodynamic theory views transference as the client's dynamic response to the actual behavior of their therapist as well as the projection of a relational template from relationships outside the therapy context (Frawley-O'Dea & Sarnat, 2001). Countertransference, then, is the therapist's projection of a relational pattern onto their client, either in reaction to the client's transferential behavior or the clinician's own childhood relationship patterns (Gabbard, 2004).

While traditional psychoanalytic/psychodynamic theory views intrapsychic and interpersonal dynamic processes as independent of one's cultural environment, recent psychodynamic theory proposes that one's cultural background greatly influences their intrapsychic and interpersonal dynamics (Tummala-Nara, 2004). For example, if an individual experienced prejudice toward a certain racial group, we would assume a transferential reaction reflecting that prejudice with a therapist from that racial group. Additionally, when the supervisor and supervisee avoid discussing cultural issues, this phenomenon may reflect the supervisor and supervisee's resistance and/or ego defenses against discussing cultural issues (Burkard et al., 2006; Tummala-Nara, 2004). The psychodynamic supervisor has many methods of accessing the transference/countertransference material in the therapy and supervisory dyads. The supervisor's most accessible method of exploring these dynamics is parallel process.

Parallel Process   Parallel process occurs when a particular interpersonal dynamic from either the supervisory or the counseling dyad influences the other dyad (Binder & Strupp, 1997). Early ego psychologists believed that supervisees demonstrate a countertransferential response in supervision when they are anxious about the therapy process or evaluation in supervision. Neo-Sullivanian psychologists added that supervisees can act as a transmitter of their client's transferential interpersonal style (Binder & Strupp, 1997). However, these earlier conceptualizations assumed that the supervisor was not an active participant in the manifestation of parallel process and the resolution of these transference/countertransference reactions should occur in a top-down manner, with the supervisor identifying and interpreting the behavior for the supervisee who interprets this behavior for the client (Frawley-O'Dea & Sarnat, 2001). More recent conceptualizations of parallel process suggest that the transference/countertransference reaction is cocreated by the supervisor, supervisee, and client (Frawley-O'Dea & Sarnat, 2001). From this approach, identification and interpretation of parallel process is a collaborative process where each member openly explores their potential impact on the process.

The emergence of transferential and/or countertransferential material through parallel process creates an excellent teaching opportunity for the psychodynamic supervisor. The process of identifying and interpreting this phenomenon offers both a didactic and experiential exercise for the supervisee. Frawley-O'Dea and Sarnat (2001) offer a relational model of working with parallel process where the supervisor and supervisee explore their own thoughts, feelings, and reactions to material in the supervisory process in a safe and nonjudgmental environment. From this relational exploration of parallel process, the supervisor assists the supervisee in achieving greater empathic ability, reinforces their knowledge of the core concepts that influence parallel process, and models the process of working through transferential material.

Internalization   Internalization is the active process of growth that occurs for the supervisee and the ultimate outcome of psychodynamic supervision (Binder & Strupp, 1997). Binder and Strupp outline the stages of internalization that occur within psychodynamic supervision. Similar to the developmental process conceptualized by object relations theory, a supervisee imitates the supervisor's understanding of psychodynamic theory and their technical approach (i.e., interpretation) in the initial phase of supervision. As supervision progresses, the supervisee obtains a deeper understanding of the theory and process of therapy and becomes more proficient in their interventions. Finally, the supervisee reaches an advanced phase of internalization, where they have developed their own autonomous, spontaneous therapeutic style.

Supervisory Relationship

The initial conceptualization of the psychodynamic supervisory relationship was a master–apprentice approach, where the supervisor conferred his knowledge onto the supervisee during supervision (Binder & Strupp, 1997). In this "one-way" relationship, conceptualization of client concerns and therapeutic interventions were passed unidirectionally from supervisor to supervisee and from supervisee to client (Frawley-O'Dea & Sarnat, 2001). The contemporary psychodynamic view of the supervisory relationship reflects a more collaborative working alliance, with an agreement between supervisor and supervisee on the goals and tasks of supervision and a shared relational bond (Bernard & Goodyear, 2009; Bordin, 1983). Similarly, in the "two-way" supervisory relationship, the supervisor, supervisee, and client cocreate their experiences in supervision and therapy (Frawley-O'Dea & Sarnat, 2001).

Focus and Goals of the Psychodynamic Model of Supervision

The primary concepts of psychodynamic supervision represent the core focus (transference/countertransference) and goals (internalization) of this model. Additionally, psychodynamic supervision seeks to instill or solidify a number of qualities in a psychodynamic therapist. A psychodynamic therapist should achieve an increased ability to empathize with client concerns, improved spontaneity in applying theory and techniques to unique clinical data, enhanced curiosity and patience in their therapeutic approach, and a greater ability to self-monitor and self-reflect (Binder & Strupp, 1997). Furthermore, Thorbeck (1992) noted the importance of supervisees developing a proficiency in describing psychodynamic principles and providing interpretations without using jargon.

An additional goal for the psychodynamic therapist is to understand the unfolding process of therapy (Thorbeck, 1992). In the early stages of training, Thorbeck encourages the psychodynamic supervisor to assist the supervisee in developing skills in assessing a client's suitability for therapy, establishing the client's therapeutic goals, and building a therapeutic relationship. In the intermediate stage, the supervisee recognizes the emergence of transference and countertransference material in therapy. In the final stage, supervisees are encouraged to discuss termination with their clients. Moreover, in contemporary psychodynamic supervision, promoting the development of multicultural counseling competence is an important goal. Psychodynamic theory offers an excellent template to explore a supervisee's conscious and unconscious cultural biases or prejudices using parallel process (Tummala-Narra, 2004). By openly discussing these issues in supervision, the supervisor promotes the supervisee's discussion of cultural issues within the therapeutic relationship.

Methodology and Techniques of the Psychodynamic Model of Supervision

The intentionally unstructured nature of the psychodynamic model of supervision allows important dynamics to rise to the surface within the supervisory relationship by allowing the supervisee to present the important material of a session through self-report (e.g., free association, written recall) of session content (Binder & Strupp, 1997). However, the contemporary psychodynamic supervisor recognizes that the supervisee's account of the therapy session may be laden with countertransferential responses, and may utilize a more objective representation of the therapy session such as audio/video taping and live supervision. Kagan and Kagan's (1997) Interpersonal Process Recall (IPR) approach allows the supervisor and the supervisee to explore countertransferential responses by reviewing a counseling session. The supervisor instructs the supervisee to stop the recording when they recall an affective response to the session material, allowing them to explore whether transferential and/or countertransferential material surfaced in the counseling work.

Psychodynamic supervision can also occur in a group setting. Battegay (1990) states that a group modality is an ideal setting to explore natural biases and character traits that may arise as countertransference reactions in therapy. A supervisee's reaction to the hierarchy in group supervision can reflect tendencies toward narcissism, dependence, or social withdrawal. Battegay suggests supervisees move through stages of exploration, regression, catharsis, insight, and social learning throughout a group supervision experience.

Case Example in Psychodynamic Model of Supervision: Janet

The psychodynamic supervisor interprets Janet's consultation needs (i.e., lack of confidence as a counselor, frustration with a male client) as clear manifestations of transference and countertransference reactions in the supervisee's therapy work. Using the relational model of supervision (Frawley-O'Dea & Sarnat, 2001), the conversation may proceed in this way:

Janet: I felt frustrated with Chris in session again. I don't know why I keep feeling this way toward him.

Steve: Would it be helpful for us to listen to your session with him?

Janet: Yeah. That would be good. Let's see (Steve and Janet listen to her tape. Janet stops the tape after Chris spoke.) See! That's what annoys me ... he talks to me like I'm some kid who doesn't know what she's doing! It's very condescending.

Steve: Yeah. I can see where his tone was condescending. Where does condescension fit into Chris's presenting concerns for therapy?

Janet: Well, his biggest concern is his failing relationship with his partner. Actually, he's talked about how he feels bad for making fun of his partner at times.

Steve: How much insight do you think he has about why he puts her down?

Janet: Honestly, it doesn't seem like he has much insight about it at all.

Steve: That might be a good direction to explore further with him; perhaps you could talk about how this occurs in your therapy relationship. Let me ask you about something else, what does feeling like a kid who doesn't know what she's doing bring up for you?

Janet: It reminds me of grade school. It makes me think about failing tests and feeling like the stupid kid in class. This actually keeps coming up for me.

Steve: That sounds painful. We've talked before about how our own personal issues can affect our therapy work. When I have a personal issue that keeps popping up in my clinical work I explore it with my therapist and it helps me understand that it's not a personal attack but more a function of the presenting concern.

Steve and Janet utilized IPR to explore potential transference/countertransference material from the supervisee's perspective. This exploration helped to illuminate potential clinical directions and highlighted areas for Janet to explore in her own therapy. In future sessions, a psychodynamic supervisor may consider exploring whether Janet feels self-conscious in the supervisory relationship to assess parallel process.

Critique of the Psychodynamic Model of Supervision

Strengths Psychodynamic supervision has introduced many concepts common to any supervisory relationship such as parallel process and the supervisory working alliance (Bernard & Goodyear, 2004; Binder & Strupp, 1997). Additionally, the understanding of interpersonal dynamics in counseling and supervision were derived from dynamic concepts. Psychodynamic supervision also provided the first systemic model of the counseling process, highlighting the interplay between the therapy and supervisory dyads as well as the organization structure in which the therapy occurs. Furthermore, a more recent psychodynamic model of supervision (e.g., Tummala-Narra, 2004) integrates psychodynamic principles and cultural context to support the development of a supervisee's multicultural counseling competence.

Limitations Psychodynamic theory utilizes many concepts that are difficult to operationalize in quantitative research. Therefore, little empirical evidence exists for the process and outcome of psychodynamic super-vision. Case studies and anecdotal evidence often are used to support dynamic constructs (Bernard & Goodyear, 2004). However, some initial empirical evidence reflects future directions for the utility of parallel pro-cess in supervision (Patton & Kivlighan, 1997; Williams, 2000). Finally, psychodynamic supervision generally lacks a focus on cultural issues and utilizes constructs encapsulated in a Eurocentric viewpoint (Cushman, 1990). Fortunately, recent contributions to the literature (e.g., Tummala-Narra, 2004) have spurred a reconceptualization of dynamic constructs within a multicultural framework.

Cognitive-Behavioral Models of Supervision

Bernard and Goodyear (2004) note that over time, cognitive and behavioral therapies have merged to form cognitive-behavioral therapy. Similarly, the integration of the two approaches is applicable to supervision. In gen-eral, behavioral theories focus on learning while cognitive theories focus more on thoughts and the consequences of these cognitions (Corey, 2005). The integration of these two models includes a cognitive component that addresses thoughts and a behavioral component that focuses on skills and actual clinical interventions.

Framework of the Cognitive-Behavioral Model of Supervision

Bradley and Gould (2001) note that a cognitive-behavioral supervisory frame-work is one that is flexible and able to meet the needs of a diverse number of supervisees. Many supervisees may use cognitive-behavioral therapy as cli-nicians, thus cognitive-behavioral supervision can serve as a model for these supervisees. This approach to supervision may be helpful in multiple ways (e.g., used to model the approach, influence cognitions, and teach skills).

Primary Concepts and Theoretical Assumptions

The foundational assumption of a cognitive-behavioral approach to super-vision is that supervisees' behavior and affect is controlled or caused by their cognitions (Bradley & Gould, 2001). Another assumption of this approach is that people learn and maintain behaviors through consequences. Thus, the purpose of supervision is to enhance appropriate counseling behaviors while extinguishing maladaptive cognitions and behaviors. Additionally, another primary element of supervision is to teach and assess supervisee's counseling behaviors.

Supervisory Relationship

The cognitive-behavioral supervisor explores cognitions and behaviors within the supervisory relationship. According to Bradley and Gould

(2001), the cognitive-behavioral supervisory relationship is genuine, warm, and empathic. Researchers (e.g., Bernard & Goodyear, 2004; Bradley & Gould, 2001) note that the development of a trusting supervisory relationship, skill assessment, and mutual goal setting are important elements of cognitive-behavioral supervision. The supervisor who follows a cognitive-behavioral perspective will agree to an agenda with a supervisee as well as monitor the progression of skills throughout the supervisory relationship (Bernard & Goodyear, 2004). In a qualitative study, Townend (2008) found that cognitive-behavioral supervisors viewed the supervisory relationship as the agent for skill development and noted collaboration, flexibility, and interpersonal processes as important factors for supervisory relationship. Additionally, supervisors in this study were conscious of the developmental stage of their supervisee and how that might influence their supervisory relationships. For example, supervisors may have been more conscious of discussing supervisee anxiety and related cognitions for beginning supervisees when compared to more advanced supervisees.

Focus and Goals of the Cognitive-Behavioral Model of Supervision

Focus Bradley and Gould (2001) describe the focus of cognitive-behavioral supervision to be educational, interpersonal, and skill based. The focus is on performance and ensuring client care. In general, the focus of cognitive-behavioral supervision is enhancing the supervisee's skills (i.e., counseling behaviors) through instruction and challenging maladaptive cognitions and behaviors (Kindsvatter, Granello, & Duba, 2008).

Goals Researchers (e.g., Bernard & Goodyear, 2004; Bradley & Gould, 2001) have outlined some important goals of cognitive-behavioral supervision. For example, cognitive-behavioral supervision aims to teach appropriate supervisee behaviors while eliminating maladaptive or inappropriate therapeutic behaviors. Furthermore, a cognitive-behavioral supervisor assumes the duties of a therapist are measurable and definable; the goal of supervision is to influence these duties and help ensure progress toward goals. Bradley and Gould (2001) define the goals of cognitive-behavioral supervision as helping supervisees become more knowledgeable about cognitive-behavioral therapy and assisting them to apply this knowledge in counseling. Cognitive-behavioral supervisors can use their supervision as a model for supervisees to use as therapists. Additional goals of cognitive-behavioral supervision include problem identification and correction as well as solution-focused collaboration between supervisor and supervisee.

Cognitive-Behavioral Techniques and Interventions

Kindsvatter et al. (2008) suggest a three-phase approach to applying the cognitive model to supervision. The three phases incorporated in this approach are: (1) *Socialization phase*; (2) *Focus phase*; and (3) *Modification phase*. This approach emphasizes addressing the core beliefs, automatic thoughts, and intermediate beliefs traditionally addressed using the cognitive approach to counseling (Beck, 1995).

Socialization Phase   The socialization phase serves as a clarification and bond-building phase in the approach. Kindsvatter et al. (2008) suggest that supervisees often demonstrate some confusion when supervisors are attempting to implement and discuss the cognitive approach to supervision. To reduce this confusion, cognitive-behavioral supervisors ask their supervisee's permission to focus on her/his thoughts, the fundamentals of the cognitive model, and helping the supervisee understand how this approach to supervision can aid in the supervisee's development.

Focus Phase   In the focus phase, the supervisor works to help the supervisee make sense of the matrix of confusing emotions and experiences often encountered in counseling sessions through discussion in supervision. The supervisor's task is to "slow down" the interpretive process and focus on a *specific manifestation* of the problem in question. After identifying a specific incident to examine, supervisors can use Socratic questioning (Overholser, 1991, 1993a, 1993b) to uncover automatic thoughts and intermediate beliefs associated with the incident. Creating a clear description of the troubling situation along with the supervisee's willingness to discuss specific cognitions sets the stage to begin work on the problem.

Modification Phase   After developing a clear understanding and description of a critical incident (e.g., confusing emotions), it is during the modification phase where the work takes place. Supervisors continue to use Socratic deconstruction to modify and alter troubling cognitive distortions (Kindsvatter et al., 2008). The supervisor and supervisee then work collaboratively to develop a specific plan for putting the new behaviors and thinking strategies into practice. During this phase, supervisors may engage in role-playing and simulation (Bradley & Gould, 2001). Additionally, cognitive restructuring techniques (e.g., disputing irrational thoughts by thinking about the activating event, belief about the event, consequence of belief, disputing belief, and new effect) may be useful to eliminate anxiety related cognitions that supervisees may have (Fitch & Marshall, 2002). It is important for the supervisor to encourage supervisees to actually "do" the new behavior rather than have an agreement to "try" it during supervision (Dinkmeyer & Carlson, 2006). When the supervisee attempts to implement and use the skill in therapy, he or she can use self-appraisal and skill monitoring to affect the outcome of interventions (Bradley & Gould, 2001).

Case Example in Cognitive-Behavioral Model of Supervision: Janet

In the case example, Janet noted that she was feeling frustrated in her work with Chris. The main goal of the cognitive-behavioral supervisor is to challenge the maladaptive cognitions and behaviors that are interfering with Janet's skill development. The supervisor may take this approach to challenging Janet's irrational thoughts regarding her skills:

Janet: I am so frustrated with Chris. I feel like we're getting nowhere and I'm totally incompetent as a therapist when I work with him.

Steve: I understand that you feel frustrated; however, tell me more about your belief of being incompetent as a therapist.

Janet: I just think that has to be the case since we've been meeting for this long and haven't made any progress.

Steve: When we listened to tapes of other clients, we discussed your progress and skill development. Tell me what makes you incompetent in this instance and not in the others.

Janet: I feel like I'm making progress with my other clients, but with Chris I seem to be stuck, so it must mean I'm ineffective in some way.

Steve: So help me understand this, I hear you saying that you feel competent and effective with all your other clients, but because you're stuck with Chris, you believe you must be an incompetent therapist?

Janet: Well, what else can be the reason, I've tried the things that worked with everyone else, but nothing seems to be working.

Steve: After hearing your work with Chris, I agree with your assertion that you are stuck, however I don't believe that you're incompetent at all, just stuck. Would you be open to discussing that stuck feeling more?

Janet: Yeah, If you think that will help, I just want to know why we're stuck!

By challenging Janet's irrational belief that she is an incompetent therapist, Steve is addressing a major obstacle to her continued growth. He highlights her effectiveness with other clients and begins to introduce the idea of further skill development by encouraging dealing with "stuck" feelings. This will provide an opportunity to educate Janet as suggested by Bradley and Gould (2001). Steve will continue to monitor Janet's feelings and thoughts regarding her effectiveness as a therapist and any other maladaptive beliefs and behaviors hindering her skill development.

Critique of the Cognitive-Behavioral Model of Supervision

Strengths There are many strengths of a cognitive-behavioral approach to supervision. Cognitive-behavioral techniques are useful in addressing specific areas of concern in supervision. For example, cognitive-behavioral techniques can reduce supervisee anxiety and increase counseling self-efficacy (Kindsvatter et al., 2008; Urbani et al., 2002). In addition, many cognitive-behavioral supervision techniques have empirical support. For instance, research has shown effectiveness in teaching counseling skills using cognitive techniques such as *The Skilled Counselor Training Model* (Little, Packman, Smaby, & Maddux, 2005). Furthermore, a systematic review of cognitive-behavioral supervision (Milne & James, 2000) noted the positive effects of cognitive-behavioral supervision approaches and techniques (e.g., modeling, providing specific directions and feedback, and close supervisee monitoring).

Limitations   There are also some limitations to a cognitive-behavioral supervision approach. More specifically, cognitive-behavioral supervision does not focus on supervisee contextual factors or client factors (Bradley & Gould, 2001). Multicultural, systemic, and contextual factors may be important for supervisees and their clients (Bernard & Goodyear, 2009); thus, a limitation of this approach is the inadequate focus on these types of factors. Additionally, there is less of a focus on potential underlying issues in cognitive-behavioral supervision. These core or unconscious forces and beliefs may influence a supervisee's counseling work.

Feminist Model of Supervision

The feminist model of supervision effectively trains supervisees to understand the influence of oppression and to develop skills for working within diverse cultural contexts (Douglas & Rave, 1990; Szymanski, 2003). Feminist supervisors follow feminist principles to address issues of sexism and experiences of other oppressed groups by highlighting inequality within our society while acknowledging the knowledge and power that they possess (Hawes, 1998; Szymanski, 2003). Several factors, such as collaborative relationship (CR), power analysis (PA), diversity, and feminist advocacy along with supervisors' attitude toward handling social power differences within the practice of supervision make the model distinct from traditional theories (Szymanski, 2003).

Framework of the Feminist Model of Supervision

The objectives of feminist supervision emerged from the principles of feminist therapy, which address inequality and sociocultural factors and help clients find their voice (Douglas & Rave, 1990; Porter, 1995). Furthermore, feminist supervisors believe supervision is a collaborative process that allows both a supervisor and supervisee to analyze power issues within the supervision relationship (Prouty, 2001; Szymanski, 2003). Thus, feminist supervisors use the supervisory relationship as the framework to train and mentor their supervisees.

Primary Concepts and Theoretical Assumptions of the Feminist Model of Supervision

Szymanski (2003) proposed four dimensions of feminist supervision that represent feminist supervisors approaches and behaviors. These four dimensions of the feminist model of supervision include CR representing nonauthoritarian supervisory relationships, PA addressing inherent power differentials within supervision, diversity and social context (DSC) highlighting the importance of understanding the influence of sociocultural factors on psychological health, and feminist advocacy and activism (FAA) facilitating the feminist perspectives and empowerment of women.

Collaborative Relationship In order to follow feminist principles and to refrain from replicating male privilege in supervision, feminist supervisors commit to creating collaborative supervisory relationships (Barnes & Bernard, 2003; Hawes, 1998). The defining feature of feminist supervision is the supervisors' emphasis on building a CR (Prouty, 2001). Feminist supervisors believe in collaboration and ask questions to stimulate supervisees' creativity and critical thinking instead of focusing on providing an answer (Hawes, 1998). Facilitating a collaborative and mutual supervisory relationship can be challenging especially when the evaluative nature of supervision imposes an inherent power imbalance in the supervisory relationship. However, failure to promote a collaborative supervisory relationship could leave supervisees feeling unsupported or devalued (Martinez, Davis, & Dahl, 1999). In addition to building a collaborative supervisory relationship, supervisors create a safe environment where supervisees exchange new ideas and engage in dialogue with their supervisors (Dankoski, Pais, Zoppi, Kramer, & Lyness, 2003). Furthermore, feminist supervisors' emphasis on promoting a CR helps them focus on enhancing supervisees' competence and empowerment even when they challenge clients (Barnes & Bernard, 2003; Prouty, 2001).

Power Analysis Feminist supervisors practice their conviction in creating a more egalitarian supervisory relationship through addressing the inherent power inequality in supervision. More specifically, feminist supervisors are responsible for engaging supervisees in open dialogues about gender and other factors of oppression (Nelson et al., 2006). When discussing power inequality, feminist supervisors actively reflect on hierarchy and power dynamics within the supervisory relationship (Hawes, 1998; Porter & Vasquez, 1997). Though discussion of power inequality within a supervisory relationship is not easy, the feminist model of supervision strongly encourages supervisors to acknowledge anxiety about discussions of power and avoid intellectualizing it in order to maintain a relationship with their supervisees (Nelson et al., 2006). Furthermore, it is important for feminist supervisors to understand supervisees' vulnerability and the difficulty of providing feedback to a supervisor if the supervisor fails to acknowledge the power inequality or abuses power (Martinez et al., 1999).

Diversity and Social Context   In addition to acknowledging power differences within the supervisory relationship, feminist supervisors address how sociocultural factors contribute to oppression and how oppression influences the well-being of clients, therapeutic work, and the supervisory relationship (Szymanski, 2003). The DSC dimension reflects feminist supervisors' belief that supervision occurs within a social context and these sociocultural factors affect supervision at multiple levels, ranging from supervisees' theoretical assumptions to the supervisory relationship (Porter & Vasquez, 1997; Szymanski, 2003). Supervisees' learning may be stunted when supervisors are unable to address sociocultural factors that contribute to oppression within supervision. For example, supervisees may not develop the ability to conceptualize or identify interventions that work for clients with culturally unique needs if the supervisor fails to explore DSC (Martinez et al., 1999).

Feminist Advocacy and Activism   Feminist supervisors introduce the theory and perspectives of feminist therapy in the supervision context (Szymanski, 2003). This dimension describes feminist supervisors' effort in increasing awareness about feminist issues such as empowerment of women and social change (Szymanski, 2003, 2005). In regards to feminist issues, a qualitative study revealed that feminist supervisors and their supervisees perceived that core ideas for feminist principles, such as socialization, gender, power, diversity, and emotion were integrated in the practice of a feminist model of supervision (Prouty, 2001). In particular, Prouty argues that feminist supervisors and their supervisees experience that socialization, or understanding the influence of larger systems on a person, as the overarching theme of the feminist model of supervision. In the feminist model of supervision, supervisors discuss the issues described above and model feminist attitudes within supervision practice (Porter & Vasquez, 1997; Szymanski, 2003).

Focus and Goals of the Feminist Model of Supervision

Focus   In the feminist model of supervision, supervisees find learning opportunities within the supervision relationship. In other words, the feminist model of supervision is relational, where feminist supervisors model behaviors that facilitate supervisees' growth and increase their awareness about various sociocultural factors. Therefore, the focus of the feminist model of supervision is exploring the influence of sociocultural factors on supervisees' work by building an egalitarian supervisory relationship (Porter & Vasquez, 1997).

Goals Feminist principles emphasize the importance of analyzing power dynamics and inequality (Nelson et al., 2006). Thus, feminist supervisors assist supervisees in identifying clients' issues in relation to various sociocultural factors, building a therapeutic working alliance, and facilitating change by using the supervisory relationship as a tool (Wheeler, Avis, Miller, & Chaney, 1986). Feminist supervisors assume that supervisees develop a realistic understanding of how power and sociocultural factors influence clients' expectations and behaviors when they increase their knowledge of oppression in society. Furthermore, in modeling an egalitarian working relationship, feminist supervisors strive to facilitate a collaborative supervisory relationship by acknowledging inherent power differences in supervision (Douglas & Rave, 1990). For example, a CR with their feminist supervisor helps supervisees understand the importance of the egalitarian approach with their clients while attending to the relationship between sociocultural factors and clients' presenting issues.

Methodology and Techniques

A qualitative study identified three main supervision methods in the feminist model of supervision: (1) supervisor–therapist contracting; (2) collaborative; and (3) hierarchical methods (Prouty, Thomas, Johnson, & Long, 2001). Furthermore, others (e.g., Douglas & Rave, 1990; Nelson et al., 2006) highlight the importance of having open dialogues. These methods in feminist supervision facilitate the egalitarian supervisory relationship (Wheeler et al., 1986).

Contracting Process Feminist supervisors first attend to understanding and agreeing on the supervisees' training goals and evaluation process (Prouty et al., 2001). When contracting the process with supervisees, feminist supervisors engage supervisees in open discussions about supervisees' responsibility to actively participate in supervision and to share what is happening with their clients. Through collaboratively contracting the supervision process with supervisees, supervisors foster an egalitarian supervisory relationship (Barnes & Bernard, 2003).

Collaborative Methods Feminist supervisors often express more enthusiasm with the collaborative approach in supervision. The feminist supervisor works as a consultant when engaging in the collaborative approach (Barnes & Bernard, 2003). In order to collaborate with their supervisees, feminist supervisors use five techniques, including: (1) focusing on fostering supervisees' competence; (2) eliciting multiple perspectives; (3) providing different options; (4) providing alternative approaches through call-ins; and (5) encouraging mutual feedback (Prouty et al., 2001). Feminist supervisors often engage in collaborative methods when their supervisees are experienced and require less direction of what to do during therapy (Prouty et al., 2001). Furthermore, collaborative methods facilitate supervisees' engagement in the supervision process.

Hierarchical Methods While feminist supervisors typically practice a collaborative method in supervision, they also recognize the importance of direct teaching by using their expertise (Prouty et al., 2001). By engaging in a direct teaching role, feminist supervisors provide specific guidelines for how to approach clients in different contexts (Barnes & Bernard, 2003). Use of hierarchical methods, such as direct information giving, modeling, and call-ins are particularly important when the collaborative method is not sufficient such that the client is at risk (e.g., violence), therapy is beyond the supervisees' ability, or unethical behaviors have emerged (Prouty et al., 2001). It is important to note that feminist supervisors apply hierarchical methods to empower their supervisees and stimulate their professional growth. For example, a supervisor engages in a role-play (modeling) with the supervisee to familiarize and increase comfort with the situation.

Open Dialogues Feminist supervisors assume that they are responsible for respecting supervisees' opinions and creativities and inviting them to become a critical part of dialogues in supervision (Wheeler et al., 1986). Thus, supervisors encourage supervisees to discuss both supervision process (e.g., criterion of evaluation, Douglas & Rave, 1990), supervisees' clinical skills (e.g., case conceptualization through different theoretical orientations, Martinez et al., 1999), and factors influencing the therapeutic work (e.g., sociocultural factors and oppression, Wheeler et al., 1986). In particular, feminist supervisors recognize discussing oppression is more important than being politically correct (Nelson et al., 2006). Though discussion about oppression or power differences may provoke emotional reactions in both supervisor and supervisee, the supervisors needs to model desired behaviors in supervision, such as engagement in dialogues and self-analysis about culture and oppression (Nelson et al., 2006). This approach increases supervisees' awareness about themselves and social oppression and strengthens the supervisory relationship.

Case Example in the Feminist Model of Supervision: Janet

A feminist supervisor begins supervision by exploring Janet's goals for the session. Upon stating her goal is to understand her struggles with Chris, the intervention may proceed this way:

Janet: I feel frustrated and anxious working with male clients like Chris, especially when they are unresponsive to therapy.

Steve: Working with clients who are unresponsive to therapy is difficult for many of us. I have seen you being more confident and doing excellent work in helping clients make changes. What makes Chris different from clients with whom you feel comfortable?

Janet: I guess sometimes I feel intimidated by Chris, he can be aggressive at times. At times, I feel like male clients take control of the session and I might censor myself more.

Steve: Hmm ... Seems you associate power with male clients, what is it like to work with me in a supervisory relationship?

Janet: Well ... I understand that we have power difference, but as far as I see our relationship, you are very responsive to my needs and I see your effort in collaboratively working with me, I don't find myself censoring as much with you.

Steve: I truly appreciate your honesty and willingness to share your feelings with me. It can be a very difficult thing to do. So now that we've established a link between power dynamics and you self-censoring, what would be helpful in challenging that?

Steve focused on validating Janet's frustration while encouraging her to explore factors contributing to her struggles in working with the client's unresponsiveness to therapy and gender dynamics. Steve trusted in Janet's ability and empowered her by acknowledging her strengths and what she had done well. Throughout supervision, Steve will invite Janet to open dialogues about her experience with supervision and therapy and to participate collaboratively in evaluation, which in turn, stimulates critical thinking, increases her understanding of the influence of sociocultural factors in therapy, and strengthens the supervisory relationship.

Critique of the Feminist Model of Supervision

Strengths The strong emphasis of the feminist model of supervision is analysis of diversity and oppression. This approach provides opportunities for supervisees to increase their knowledge of how sociocultural factors influence therapy and integrate social contexts in their clinical work (Martinez et al., 1999). Feminist supervisors use their openness to building CRs and open dialogues as tools to teach supervisees how to relate with their clients. Additionally, the supervisors' approach to supervision, particularly their attitude toward valuing collaborative relationship, minimizes the hierarchy within the supervisory relationships (Prouty, 2001; Wheeler et al., 1986). This model can be applied to multiple types of supervision (e.g., medical education; Dankoski et al., 2003).

Limitations While the feminist model of supervision has been practiced, there is still a need for a clearer definition and expanded literature about this model (Prouty, 2001). In particular, guidelines for implementing specific techniques in supervision are not clear in the literature (Hipp & Munson, 1995). Additionally, while the majority of literature on the feminist model of supervision focuses on feminist supervision that utilizes a collaborative method, how feminist supervisors integrate a hierarchical method into their work needs to be discussed in future literature. Lastly, future empirical study on the outcome of feminist approach to supervision would facilitate understanding of the effectiveness of feminist supervision.

Solution-Focused Model of Supervision

The solution-focused model of supervision is born from the constructivist models of therapy, which are postmodern approaches, designed to "construct a sense of competence within clients" (Briggs & Miller, 2005, p. 200). The solution-focused approach is one of the most commonly applied and researched constructivist models of supervision (Bernard & Goodyear, 2009). Constructivist approaches emphasize supervisee strengths and focus on successes instead of problem remediation. The supervisory role tends to be that of consultant rather than teacher (Behan, 2003).

Framework of the Solution-Focused Model of Supervision

The underlying assumptions of solution-focused approaches are that we construct meaning within our contexts and therefore there is no one *right* way to conduct therapy (Bernard & Goodyear, 2009). Furthermore, solution-focused models posit that focusing on the strengths and successes will produce better outcomes than focusing on clinical errors and mistakes (Triantafillou, 1997). As Wetchler (1990) stated, "In an unlimited universe, there are more things clinicians do not know about doing therapy than they can ever possibly know how to do correctly" (p. 129). Therefore, the ultimate goal of this model is to help the supervisee identify what they are doing well and to encourage them to continue with skills that work.

Primary Concepts and Theoretical Assumptions

The solution-focused brief therapy (SFBT) model has many guiding assumptions that have been applied to supervision. Solution-focused therapy (see de Shazer, 1980, 1991) assumes that clients are experts, there is no correct way to view the world, and it is important to focus on exceptions to problems as well as that which is possible and changeable instead of problems. Solution-focused supervision takes these primary guiding assumptions and translates them to work with supervisees (Thomas, 1996).

Reconsidering Insight   One major theme of solution-focused supervision is the premise that it is not important or necessary to understand the cause or function of a behavior or complaint (Wetchler, 1990). While the supervisor should always remain curious about the therapist's perspective, the underlying pathology does not have to be identified in solution-focused supervision. Similar to solution-focused therapy, solution-focused supervisors believe that "The problem is the problem" (Thomas, 1996). Thus, the solution-focused supervisor focuses on examining exceptions to the identified problem and helping the supervisee generate solutions to resolve the problem instead of elucidating the roots of the problem to develop insight.

Shifting Concept of Expertness   The solution-focused supervisor accepts that there truly is no one right way to understand and intervene with clients' problems (Bernard & Goodyear, 2009). Further, the solution-focused supervisor believes that therapists know what will work best for themselves (Thomas, 1996) and therefore the supervisee, not the supervisor, is the expert on what will be most useful for the supervisee. Although this is rare, a supervisee may genuinely lack specific clinical knowledge (Wetchler, 1990). In these situations, the supervisor may also take a clinical education or teacher role; however, the primary focus should be on helping the supervisee recognize the positive work they are doing and encouraging them in this process.

Change   As in SFBT, the solution-focused supervisor assumes that change happens constantly and rapidly (Thomas, 1996). The concept of "flight to health" or that rapid change is superficial and not sustainable does not exist within the SFBT language. Any improvement shown by supervisees is valid and it is not the sign of resistance. If a supervisee appears to be improving in their skills, they are improving, not being resistant to change. Additionally, small changes are valued because they will lead to larger changes. Thus, it is the supervisors' role to notice the changes that are occurring and amplify them for the supervisee (Triantafillou, 1997).

Presuppositional Language   Language is of the utmost importance in the solution-focused model of supervision to expand supervisees' skills (Knight, 2005). Several theorists note the importance of using presuppositional language (e.g., Selekman & Todd, 1995; Thomas, 1996), which is language that assumes a level of competence and elicits responses that affirm the existence of skills and competence. A solution-focused supervisor uses language to reinforce the concept that supervisees already possess skill and strengths (e.g., instead of saying "what would you like to learn about this?" the supervisor might say "how can we continue to develop or enhance your skills in this area?"). These changes in language may seem minor, but when used consistently they begin to paint a picture of success and competence instead of focusing on an absence of skills.

Support and Affirmation Within the Supervisory Relationship   The therapeutic relationship in solution-focused supervision should be constructive and positive (Briggs & Miller, 2005). Again, in taking a consultant role, the supervisor works to sincerely praise successful interventions and to help refine those skills that the supervisee is already demonstrating (Juhnke, 1996). The supervisor focuses on helping the supervisee learn to use their own resources by highlighting their strengths instead of providing direct instruction. Additionally, in being supportive and collaborative, the supervisor helps to reframe or avoid resistance within a supervisory relationship (Bernard & Goodyear, 2009).

Focus and Goals of the Solution-Focused Model of Supervision

Focus   The focus is on assisting the therapist in identifying their strengths and helping them to augment these in their work with clients (Triantafillou, 1997). The supervisor should begin sessions by focusing on what the supervisee has done well (Wetchler, 1990) and understanding what the supervisee would like to enhance or improve upon. The supervisor explores what success would look like for the supervisee and uses the ideas generated to determine the focus of supervision. Juhnke (1996) recommended starting a supervisory relationship with a supervisee preassessment of strengths and skills to clearly articulate the importance of focusing on strengths at the outset.

Goals   The ultimate goal of solution-focused supervision is to facilitate the development of a competent therapist while working to improve client outcomes (Briggs & Miller, 2005). The supervisor accomplishes this through a CR characterized by clear and identifiable goals, a focus on exceptions to problems, and highlighting strengths and successes. Again, the supervisor is a facilitator in this process, and together they cocreate a therapeutic experience that is both positive and conducive to change. Juhnke (1996) noted the importance of having both time-specific long-term goals and session-specific goals in supervision. This approach allows the supervisee to identify the changes they would like to see during the course of supervision with a clear time line, as well as specific changes they want to see within a supervision session. Clear and measurable goals are crucial in solution-focused supervision.

Methodology and Techniques of Solution-Focused Model of Supervision

There are many techniques and methods used to facilitate a focus on successes and facilitating change in the solution-focused model of supervision (Rita, 1998; Selekman & Todd, 1995; Thomas, 1996; Triantafillou, 1997). Several concepts noted earlier such as the use of presuppositional language, setting clear and measureable goals and the importance of focusing on strengths at the onset of supervision are both guiding assumptions as well as techniques within the model. The following represent techniques that are unique for solution-focused supervision.

Languages for Focusing on Goals   Briggs & Miller (2005) offered several suggestions regarding language solution-focused supervisors use to help identify clear goals for sessions. These included: "What would you like to accomplish in supervision today?" "What would you like to have happen during the next hour, so you don't find yourself looking back and saying, 'Wow, that was a waste of time'?" By selecting one's language carefully, the supervisor is able to communicate the supervisees' responsibility for setting the focus (or goals?) and provide hope for meeting supervisees' training needs through supervision.

The Miracle Question (MQ)   The MQ is a unique intervention that helps the supervisees project their problems into the future. It was articulated by de Shazer (1980) for SFBT and it takes many forms but typically looks something like "If a miracle were to happen overnight and you found that this obstacle was no longer in your way, what would be different, how would you know the miracle had taken place?" If this question is asked in response to a clinical concern, the supervisee can then begin to identify how they would be thinking or behaving differently and explore ways to incorporate the behavior or thought change into their work (Thomas, 1996).

Scaling   Scaling is often used in conjunction with the MQ, or simply as a way to clarify goals. Thomas (1996) noted that a major benefit of scaling is that it moves a goal from a dichotomous view of success/failure to a more workable process. Scaling can be used in many forms, but the typical use is to ask a question such as "On a scale from 1 to 10, with 1 being complete failure, and 10 being complete success, how would you rate yourself right now with this problem." After obtaining the number, the supervisor then explores what the supervisee would be doing differently if they increased by two or three points. Alternately, when the supervisee is unable to identify their improved or different performance, supervisor would ask, "well, why not a one, what are you doing now that makes it higher." This helps focus on successful behaviors that the supervisee can continue to integrate into their work.

Exceptions   The solution-focused supervisor focuses on exceptions to problems and making these exceptions meaningful in conjunction with the MQ and scaling (Thomas, 1996). For example, if a supervisee notes anxiety about working with a client, the supervisor might explore when the supervisee did not feel anxious during the last session. By asking questions such as "how were you able to not be anxious in that moment," the supervisor helps the supervisee make those exceptions meaningful. Exceptions always exist, and a skilled solution-focused supervisor can highlight and amplify those exceptions to help the supervisee begin to do more of the behaviors that are already working.

Case Example in Solution-Focused Model of Supervision: Janet

The primary goal of the solution-focused supervisor will be to help Janet begin to identify exceptions and successes. This work may be started using the scaling technique:

Janet: I'm so frustrated in my work with Chris, I really feel like we're making no progress and I am completely ineffective with him.

Steve: I hear you saying you're frustrated with the progress, on a scale of 1 to 10, how effective would you rate your work together?

Janet: I'd say it's about a 3.

Steve: Interesting, why would you say it's a 3 instead of 2?

Janet: Well, I chose a 3 because sometimes Chris seems so relieved to just talk about this situation that it seems a little helpful, and he noted that he's not as frustrated about the need to make a decision.

Steve: It sounds like at times in your session Chris is feeling really listened to and that you are respecting his need to share his story and process the need to make a decision, how might you incorporate more of this into your future sessions?

Using scaling to identify exceptions allowed Steve to compliment actual skills that Janet was demonstrating and reinforce those exceptions to the problem, as well as amplify the small successes. Steve could also explore how Janet would engage in more productive work with her client (e.g., How will your sessions look different when you move from a 3 to a 6 on the scale) and help Janet identify the changes in her behavior and approach that she would like to see. At the following supervision session, Steve will need to check in on improvements since the last session and will continue exploring the skills and strategies that Janet has been using to improve her work with Chris.

Critique of the Solution-Focused Model of Supervision

Strengths   One of the major strengths of this model is that it can help reduce supervisee anxiety by facilitating their sense of competence. Additionally, research has linked supervisor use of solution-focused strategies with increased self-efficacy in supervisees (Koob, 2002). The facilitation of supervisee self-efficacy is crucial in the development of general (Larson & Daniels, 1998) and multicultural counseling competency (Constantine & Ladany, 2001). Additionally, SFBT is a therapy model that works well in brief or time-limited therapy settings and with the current managed care climate, it is important for supervisors to be able to support their supervisees in the development of these skills.

Limitations   While solution-focused therapy has been expanding and successful outcomes have been reported (Kim, 2008), there have been few empirical studies on the benefits of a solution-focused approach to supervision. Koob (2002) represents the strongest example of empirical evidence for the efficacy of solution-focused supervision; however, there are limitations to this study such as not using a standardized form of supervision and therefore more empirically sound research on the efficacy of this supervision model is necessary (Presbury, Echterling, & McKee, 1999). Another challenge of this model lies within the fit between this style and the theoretical orientation of many supervisees. If, for example, a supervisee has a psychodynamic or insight-oriented theoretical orientation, they may feel that a focus on successes instead of examining the origins of their problems (e.g., countertransference) is not what they desire from supervision. Theoretically, this could lead to a struggle in developing a strong working alliance due to a disagreement on the tasks and goals of supervision.

Conclusion and Summary

Counseling and psychotherapy-based theories of supervision provide a framework for handling complex interactions among supervisors', supervisees', and their clients' behaviors, attitudes, and feelings (Bernard & Goodyear, 2009). While these models offer helpful frameworks, it can be complex to utilize them when a supervisor and a supervisee are from different theoretical orientations and cultural backgrounds. This chapter explores two supervision models based on more traditional psychotherapy approaches and two supervision models based on more contemporary psychotherapy approaches and found many commonalities and differences between these models of supervision. In particular, all four models of supervision acknowledge that the supervisory dyad or relationship provides an important learning opportunity for supervisees. The centrality of the relationship in supervision supports the notion that supervisors share similarities, such as the goal to mentor a junior practitioner, regardless of their theoretical backgrounds (Bernard & Goodyear, 2009).

Bernard and Goodyear (2009) anticipate a movement toward a more integrated approach to supervision because supervisors might be able to identify an individualized approach to supervision through integration of various perspectives. However, it is important to acknowledge and appreciate the differences among the various approaches to psychotherapy and supervision (Messer, 2008). Messer argued that there is no right approach to counseling work, thus counseling practitioners must accept the plurality of theory and methodology while continuing dialogues about differences and similarities of theories. It is our hope that this chapter contributes to these dialogues by illustrating multiple approaches to psychotherapy-based models of supervision, thus helping current and future supervisors compare and contrast these models and perhaps deepen their appreciation toward each model for supervision.

References

Barnes, K. L., & Bernard, J. M. (2003). Women in counseling and psychotherapy supervision. In M. Kopala & M. Keitel (Eds.), *Handbook of counseling women* (pp. 535–545). Thousand Oaks, CA: Sage.

Battegay, R. (1990). Complementary individual and group analytic training for future psychotherapists. *Psychotherapy and Psychosomatics, 53*, 130–134.

Beck, J. S. (1995). *Cognitive therapy: Basics and beyond.* New York, NY: Guilford Press.

Behan, C. P. (2003). Some ground to stand on: Narrative supervision. *Journal of Systemic Therapies, 22*, 29–42.

Bernard, J. M., & Goodyear, R. K. (2004). *Fundamentals of clinical supervision* (3rd ed.). Upper Saddle River, NJ: Person Education, Inc.

Bernard, J. M., & Goodyear, R. K. (2009). *Fundamentals of clinical supervision* (4th ed.). Upper Saddle River, NJ: Person Education, Inc.

Binder, J. L., & Strupp, H. H. (1997). Supervision of psychodynamic psychotherapies. In C. R. Watkins, Jr. (Ed.), *Handbook of psychotherapy supervision* (pp. 44–62). New York, NY: Wiley.

Bordin, E. S. (1983). A working alliance model of supervision. *The Counseling Psychologist, 11*, 35–42.

Bradley, L. J., & Gould, L. J. (2001). Psychotherapy-based models of counselor supervision. In L. Bradley & N. Ladany (Eds.), *Counselor supervision: Principles, process, and practice.* (3rd ed., pp. 147–175). Philadelphia, PA: Brunner-Routledge.

Briggs, J. R., & Miller, G. (2005). Success enhancing supervision. *Journal of Family Psychotherapy, 16*, 199–222.

Burkard, A. W., Johnson, A. J., Madson, M. B., Pruitt, N. T., Contreras-Tadych, D. A., Kozlowski, J. M., . . . Knox, S. (2006). Supervisor cultural responsiveness and unresponsiveness in cross-cultural supervision. *Journal of Counseling Psychology, 53*(3), 288–301.

Constantine, M. G., & Ladany, N. (2001). New visions for defining and assessing multicultural counseling competence. In J. G. Ponterotto, J. M. Casas, L. A. Suzuki, & C. M. Alexander (Eds.), *Handbook of multicultural counseling* (2nd ed., pp. 482–498). Thousand Oaks, CA: Sage.

Corey, G. (2005). *Theory and practice of counseling and psychotherapy* (7th ed.). Belmont, CA: Thomson Learning.

Cushman, P. (1990). Why the self is empty: Toward a historically situated psychology. *American Psychologist, 45*, 599–611.

Dankoski, M. E., Pais, S., Zoppi, K. A., Kramer, J. S., & Lyness, A. M. P. (2003). Feminist principles in family medicine education. *Journal of Feminist Family Therapy, 15*, 55–73.

de Shazer, S. (1980). *Clues: Investigating solutions in brief therapy*. New York, NY: Norton.

de Shazer, S. (1991). *Putting difference to work*. New York, NY: Norton.

Dinkmeyer, D. C., Jr., & Carlson, J. (2006). *Consultation: Creating school-based interventions* (3rd ed.). New York, NY: Routledge.

Douglas, M. A. D., & Rave, R. (1990). Ethics of feminist supervision of psychotherapy. In H. Lerman & N. Porter (Eds.), *Feminist ethics in psychotherapy* (pp. 137–46). New York, NY: Springer.

Fitch, T., & Marshall, J. L. (2002). Using cognitive interventions with counseling practicum students during group supervision. *Counselor Education & Supervision, 41*, 335–342.

Follette, W. C., & Callaghan, G. M. (1995). Do as I do, not as I say: A behavior-analytic approach to supervision. *Professional Psychology: Research and Practice, 26*, 413–421.

Frawley-O'Dea, M. G., & Sarnat, J. E. (2001). *The supervisory relationship: A contemporary psychodynamic approach*. New York, NY: Guilford.

Freud, S. (1927). *Essays on psychoanalysis*. Oxford, England, UK: Payot.

Gabbard, G. O. (2004). *Long-term psychodynamic psychotherapy*. Washington, DC: American Psychiatric Publishing.

Gold, J. H. (2004). Reflections on psychodynamic psychotherapy supervision for psychiatrists in clinical practice. *Journal of Psychiatric Practice, 10*, 162–169.

Hawes, S. E. (1998). Positioning a dialogic reflexivity in the practice of feminist supervision. In B. M. Bayer & J. Shotter (Eds.). *Reconstructing the psychological subject: Bodies, practices and technologies* (pp. 94–110). Thousand Oaks, CA: Sage.

Hayman, M. (2008). Psychoanalytic supervision. In A. K. Hess, K. D. Hess, & T. H. Hess, *Psychotherapy supervision: Theory, research, and practice* (pp. 97–113). Hoboken, NJ: Wiley.

Hipp, J. L., & Munson, C. E. (1995). The partnership model: A feminist supervision/consultation perspective. *The Clinical Supervisor, 13*, 23–38.

Juhnke, G. A. (1996). Solution-focused supervision: Promoting supervisee skills and confidence through successful solutions. *Counselor Education and Supervision, 36*, 48–57.

Kagan, H. K., & Kagan, N. I. (1997). Interpersonal process recall: Influencing human interaction. In C. E. Watkins, Jr. (Ed.), *Handbook of psychotherapy supervision* (pp. 296–309). New York, NY: Wiley.

Kim, J. S. (2008). Examining the effectiveness of solution-focused brief therapy: A meta-analysis. *Research on Social Work Practice, 18,* 107–116.

Kindsvatter, A., Granello, D. H., & Duba, J. (2008). Cognitive techniques as means for facilitating supervisee development. *Counselor Education & Supervision, 47,* 179–192.

Knight, C. (2005). Integrating solution-focused principles and techniques into clinical practice and supervision. *The Clinical Supervisor, 23,* 153–173.

Koob, J. J. (2002). The effects of solution-focused supervision on the perceived self-efficacy of therapists in training. *The Clinical Supervisor, 21,* 161–183.

Larson, L. M., & Daniels, J. A. (1998). Review of the counseling self-efficacy literature. *The Counseling Psychologist, 26,* 179–218.

Little, C., Packman, J., Smaby, M., & Maddux, C. (2005). The skilled counselor training model: Skills acquisition, self assessment, and cognitive complexity. *Counselor Education & Supervision, 44,* 189–200.

Martinez, L. J., Davis, K. C., & Dahl, B. (1999). Feminist ethical challenges in supervision: A trainee perspective. *Women and Therapy, 22,* 35–54.

McDaniel, S., Weber, T., & McKeever, J. (1983). Multiple theoretical approaches to supervision: Choices in family therapy training. *Family Process, 22,* 491–500.

Messer, S. B. (2008). Unification in psychotherapy: A commentary. *Journal of Psychotherapy Integration, 18,* 363–366.

Milne, D., & James, I. (2000). A systematic review of effective cognitive-behavioral supervision. *British Journal of Clinical Psychology, 39,* 111–127.

Morgan, M. M., & Sprenkle, D. H. (2007). Toward a common-factors approach to supervision. *Journal of Marital and Family Therapy, 33,* 1–17.

Nelson, M. L., Gizara, S., Hope, A. C., Phelps, R., Steward, R., & Weitzman, L. (2006). A feminist multicultural perspective on supervision. *Journal of Multicultural Counseling and Development, 34,* 105–115.

Overholser, J. C. (1991). The Socratic method as a technique in psychotherapy supervision. *Professional Psychology: Research and Practice, 22,* 68–74.

Overholser, J. C. (1993a). Elements of the Socratic method: I. Systematic questioning. *Psychotherapy, 30,* 67–74.

Overholser, J. C. (1993b). Elements of the Socratic method: II. Inductive reasoning. *Psychotherapy, 30,* 75–85.

Patton, M. J., & Kivlighan, D. M., Jr. (1997). Relevance of the supervisory alliance to the counseling alliance and to treatment adherence in counselor training. *Journal of Counseling Psychology, 44,* 108–115.

Porter, N. (1995). Supervision of psychotherapists: Integrating anti-racist, feminist, and multicultural perspectives. In H. Landrine (Ed.), *Bringing cultural diversity to feminist psychology: Theory, research, and practice* (pp. 163–175). Washington, DC: American Psychological Association.

Porter, N., & Vasquez, M. (1997). Covision: Feminist supervision, process, and collaboration. In J. Worell & N. Johnson (Eds.), *Shaping the future of feminist psychology: Education, research, and practice. Psychology of women book series* (pp. 155–171). Washington, DC: American Psychological Association.

Presbury, J., Echterling, L. G., & McKee, J. E. (1999). Supervision for inner-vision: Solution-focused strategies. *Counselor Education and Supervision, 39,* 146–155.

Prouty, A. M. (2001). Experiencing feminist family therapy supervision. *Journal of Feminist Family Therapy, 12,* 171–203.

Prouty, A. M., Thomas, V., Johnson, S., & Long, J. K. (2001). Methods of feminist family therapy supervision. *Journal of Marital and Family Therapy, 27,* 85–97.

Rita, E. S. (1998). Solution-focused supervision. *Clinical Supervisor, 17,* 127–139.

Selekman, M. D., & Todd, T. C. (1995). Co-creating a context for change in the supervisory system: The solution-focused supervision model. *Journal of Systemic Therapies, 14,* 21–33.

Singer, J. L. (1990). The supervision of graduate students who are conducting psychodynamic psychotherapy. In R. C. Lane (Ed.), *Psychoanalytic approaches to supervision* (pp. 165–175). New York, NY: Brunner/Mazel.

Szymanski, D. M. (2003). The feminist supervision scale: A rational/theoretical approach. *Psychology of Women Quarterly, 27,* 221–232.

Szymanski, D. M. (2005). Feminist identity and theories as correlates of feminist supervision practice. *Counseling Psychologist, 35,* 729–747.

Thomas, F. N. (1996). Solution-focused supervision: The coaxing of expertise. In S. D. Miller, M. A. Hubble, & B. L. Duncan (Eds.), *Handbook of solution-focused therapy* (pp. 128–151). San Francisco, CA: Jossey-Bass.

Thorbeck, J. (1992). The development of the psychodynamic psychotherapist in supervision. *Academic Psychiatry, 16,* 72–82.

Tobin, D. J., & McCurdy, K. G. (2006). Adlerian-Focused supervision for countertransference work with counselors-in-training. *Journal of Individual Psychology, 62*(2), 154–167.

Townend, M. (2008). Clinical supervision in cognitive-behavioral psychotherapy: Development of a model for mental health nursing through grounded theory. *Journal of Psychiatric and Mental Health Nursing, 15,* 328–339.

Triantafillou, N. (1997). A solution-focused approach to mental health supervision. *Journal of Systemic Therapies, 16,* 305–328.

Tummala-Nara, P. (2004). Dynamics of race and culture in the supervisory encounter. *Psychoanalytic Psychology, 21,* 300–311.

Urbani, S., Smith, M. R., Maddux, C., Smaby, M. H., Torres-Rivera, E., & Crews, J. (2002). Skills-based training and counseling self-efficacy. *Counselor Education & Supervision, 42,* 92–106.

Wetchler, J. L. (1990). Solution-focused supervision. *Family Therapy, 17,* 129–138.

Wheeler, D., Avis, J. M., Miller, L. A., & Chaney, S. (1986). Rethinking family therapy education and supervision: A feminist model. *Journal of Family Psychotherapy, 11,* 373–377.

White, M. B., & Russell, C. S. (1995). The essential elements of supervisory systems: A modified Delphi study. *Journal of Marital and Family Therapy, 21,* 33–53.

Williams, A. B. (2000). Contribution of the supervisors' covert communication to the parallel process. *Dissertation Abstracts International Section A: Humanities & Social Sciences, 61*(3-A), 1165–1296.

PART III

Specialized Models of
Counselor Supervision

CHAPTER **8**

Group Supervision of Individual Counseling

P. CLAY ROWELL

Groups are prevalent in society. In fact, we live and work in groups. That is what makes group work in counseling exciting. While many types of groups exist, the counseling profession historically has utilized group work for therapeutic purposes. More recently, counseling group work has been recognized in more far-reaching arenas, such as schools, organizations, and teams. Group supervision of counselors is no exception and poses a viable alternative and/or supplement to individual supervision.

Counseling supervision is a requirement of all counselor education and counseling psychology programs accredited by the Council for Accreditation of Counseling and Related Educational Programs (CACREP, 2009) and the American Psychological Association (APA, 2008), respectively, and of state licensure boards. In fact, group supervision is required by CACREP for counselor education students during their internships. The APA only requires individual supervision for half of the supervision hours that counseling psychology students receive. After graduation, many counselors will experience group supervision either while seeking licensure or during staff meetings at their employment site. Consequently, the vast majority of counselors will experience group supervision at some point in their careers.

Their experiences certainly will differ, however, depending on the type of supervision formats employed. The most common method of group supervision includes a group of supervisees and one supervisor who facilitates the supervision process. Another frequently used approach is peer supervision, in which there is no assigned supervisor and therefore no hierarchical

197

relationships. A hybrid of these two modalities is sometimes incorporated where both supervisor-led and peer formats are infused into the process.

This chapter is intended to describe the scope of group supervision, to help elucidate the usefulness of group supervision, and to offer some guidelines for utilizing group supervision effectively. First, a definition of group supervision will be offered, followed by some discussion of the aforementioned formats and venues of group supervision. Second, some guidelines will be presented as one means of preparing the group to begin its supervisory work. Finally, various strategies for facilitating the process throughout the life of the group will be explored.

The Scope of Group Supervision

Defining group supervision is somewhat challenging because there are a variety of opinions expressed within the literature. Some definitions are as simple as stating that group supervision is supervision with more than one supervisee (Bernard & Goodyear, 2004). Others offer guidelines for the optimal number of supervisees within the group (e.g., Proctor, 2000). The suggestions for the most advantageous number of supervisees range from 4 to 12. One thing is certain, the group must be sufficiently large enough to counteract any disturbances in group dynamics (e.g., absences) while simultaneously being small enough to provide adequate attention to all of the supervisees. If we were to follow the first definition, then we would assume that supervision with a supervisor and just two supervisees would be group supervision. This format, however, has a name of its own: triadic supervision. Triadic supervision has gained attention in the literature and is being examined as a separate modality from individual and group supervision (e.g., Hein & Lawson, 2008). Therefore, we will not include triadic supervision within our working definition.

Furthermore, venues and formats of group supervision play a key role in determining both the size and scope of the group supervision process. The number of supervisees is often dictated by the number of supervisees assigned to, employed by, or chosen by a supervisor. In counselor education programs, CACREP (2009) allows a maximum of 10 supervisees for practicum groups. Riva and Cornish (2008) reported that psychology internship sites typically had three to five supervisees. In the field, the size of the group is usually determined by how many counselors are employed by a particular agency. For example, a college counseling center may have five staff counselors and a director. Therefore, there would be five group members with the director serving as group leader. Additionally, the role of the supervisor is often split between clinical and administrative supervision. Finally, the two primary formats of group supervision (i.e., supervisor-led and peer-led) spark differing group dynamics. Taking all of these factors into consideration, I suggest the following definition of group supervision:

> Group supervision is supervision that (a) includes three or more supervisees; (b) is either supervisor-led or peer-led; (c) attends to both clinical and administrative concerns; and (d) maximizes the potential of supervisees' interpersonal development.

> Group supervision offers a unique opportunity to elicit the maximization of supervisees' interpersonal development, which naturally is an important skill for counselors. I will discuss this later in the chapter.

Venues of Group Supervision

The focus of this section will be on the two most common venues in which group supervision occurs: practicum or internship groups and staff meetings.

The practicum group often is a counselor's first experience with group supervision. In counselor education programs, the practicum usually occurs toward the end of the student's coursework but prior to the internship. Typically, the practicum group is structured like a class that is led by a faculty member or a doctoral student. Students enrolled in the practicum will have clinical field experiences either at a community or university site or within a clinic operated by the program. Students generally meet for group supervision once a week with their university supervisor.

For counselors working in the field, staff meetings occur on a regular basis and serve multiple purposes (i.e., clinical and administrative). The balance between administrative and clinical supervision is often challenging for the supervisor. These meetings often include more administrative foci than clinical, including policies and procedures, productivity and efficiency, and other administrative issues. Sometimes agencies will schedule separate administrative and clinical meetings in order to meet the counseling needs of the clients. Separate clinical meetings typically involve the presentation of difficult cases in an effort to gain help from peers and supervisors. Often, the supervisor experiences conflict between the administrative and clinical needs of the agency and clients, which can pose dilemmas when agency directives are incompatible with ethical codes.

Formats of Group Supervision

Peer supervision involves a group of counselors or counseling students that meet on a regular basis to improve their skills, obtain help with their cases, and/or gain mutual support. Peer supervision is usually less formal than supervisor-led groups because there is not a hierarchical relationship with a supervisor and no formal evaluation. The lack of formal evaluation can lead to more honest disclosures about the counselors' struggles and to more direct critique from peers. Furthermore, this openness may be accepted with less defensiveness because the counselors are not concerned about how a supervisor will evaluate them. This may not always be the case, however, as peer groups also can be unproductive. Peers are sometimes more concerned with their colleagues' feelings and may offer an abundance of support with minimal challenges. Furthermore, the lack of formal leadership may make it difficult for peer groups to stay on task.

The hybrid format infuses both the supervisor-led and peer-led supervision modalities. In fact, this may be ideal for group supervision because the supervisor should invoke the full potential of group work by facilitating affirmation and critique amongst the supervisees, as well as offering her or his own evaluations. Moreover, the supervisor can provide structure when needed and help the group stay on task when it begins to stray. Specific skills about using the hybrid model are found later in this chapter.

Strengths and Growing Edges of Group Supervision

Several authors have described the advantages and limitations to conducting group supervision (e.g., Bernard & Goodyear, 2009; Cohen, 2004). Although I will borrow from their lists, I will add some observations based on my own group supervision experiences. Instead of merely listing and describing the advantages and limitations, I also will offer ways to enhance the positives and manage or reconstruct the negatives. Therefore, I will refrain from using the words "limitations" or "negatives" in favor of the phrase "growing edges" because the former labels seem finite and unmanageable. In fact, the supervisor can use the power of the group to counteract any potential growing edges that the group format might present.

Advantages　There are a number of advantages to using the group format for supervision. The following is not an exhaustive list; although it is a collection of the most frequently observed benefits.

1. *Group supervision offers the opportunity for vicarious learning.* Since the supervisees will be exposed to several counselors, including the supervisor, vicarious learning experiences are inevitable. In my experience, the benefit of vicarious learning most often stated by supervisees is the chance they get to observe and hear about various approaches to counseling. Listening or watching a peer's session with a client, or hearing about a client from a peer, offers supervisees the occasion to learn different ways of doing things and different ways to conceptualize clients.

   The supervisor can enhance this process by prompting the group to ask clarifying questions of how the supervisee worked with the client. The supervisor may also ask the group to share thoughts about other methods from which the supervisee presenting the case could approach the counseling relationship or process. There are a number of other ways the supervisor could enhance vicarious learning, but the important point here is to facilitate the supervisees' dialoguing about various approaches.

2. *Group supervision builds empathy.* The more we are exposed to a variety of people in a variety of contexts, the more empathy will develop. Clearly, when supervisees share their clients' stories, peers are exposed to different human situations they may not have previously experienced. Without question, this exposure helps supervisees develop their empathy.

   The supervisor can intentionally foster empathic development by facilitating dialogue about client conceptualization. In this case, maintaining the discussion specifically about the client (and not about the supervisee's counseling skills) can help the group obtain a better understanding of the client's life-space. Other perspectives can cultivate the building of empathy by providing the group exposure to a range of possibilities that the client may be experiencing.

3. *Group supervision can build multicultural competence.* Connected to building empathy, developing multicultural counseling competence is imperative for counselors. Discussing client conceptualization is not complete without a conversation about multicultural issues. A group of supervisees brings more of a wealth of life experiences, worldviews, values, and other differences (e.g., sexual orientation, religion/philosophy of life, gender, age, ethnicity, etc.) than does one supervisor.

   If the group does not offer multicultural perspectives on its own, the supervisor can specifically direct the supervisees to discuss potential cultural issues that may be affecting the client. Here the goal is to provide the supervisees with the space to think about multiple perspectives and to enhance their awareness, knowledge, and skills that may be needed with current or future clients.

4. *Universality.* Supervisees often struggle with specific problems related to their counseling. These problems may range from particular counseling skills to emotional reactions in their work. Group supervision helps normalize the supervisees' experiences when peers express similar struggles. This can alleviate anxiety and doubt about their abilities, which, subsequently, can boost self-efficacy.

   This type of universality often occurs in group without much aid from the supervisor. Using the group facilitation skill of linking, however, is one way the supervisor can increase universality and encourage mutual support. By focusing on the fact that multiple supervisees seem to be experiencing similar things, the supervisor starts a process that helps supervisees feel that they are not alone in their struggles.

5. *Greater assessment of supervisees.* Groups have been dubbed a microcosm of society (Yalom & Leszcz, 2005). In as much, people tend to relate interpersonally over time in a group setting just as they do in other arenas of their lives. The likelihood that supervisees are relating to others in the group in a similar way that they relate to their clients is extremely high. Therefore, supervisors have an opportunity to observe supervisees in a different context separate from individual supervision.

Furthermore, supervisors also can process the interactions that occur within group supervision sessions in an effort to help illuminate supervisees' interpersonal blind spots. In my own experience, I have used this as an opportunity to help supervisees better understand some of the struggles they have experienced with their clients. If supervisees can understand how parts of their interpersonal styles may be affecting their counseling relationships, they may be able to counsel with their clients in a different (and hopefully more positive) way.

6. *Economy.* Group supervision offers advantages regarding time, costs, effort, and expertise. Of course, this is a similar benefit for group counseling.

Growing Edges   Similar to the section on the benefits of group supervision, the following is not a comprehensive list of growing edges. This list is provided to reflect some of the more common challenges experienced by supervisors.

1. *The group format does not parallel individual counseling.* The process of group supervision is not analogous with the counseling process being supervised (unless the supervisees are conducting group counseling). Therefore, there may be fewer occasions to assess and discuss the parallel process as there might be in individual supervision. Although the interpersonal relationship between the supervisor and supervisee might differ between individual and group counseling, the supervisor still has an opportunity to observe the interactions of the supervisees. Review the fifth advantage of group supervision as a way to attend to the parallel process of individual counseling and supervision.

2. *Confidentiality.* Confidentiality is less secure in groups both for the clients and the supervisees. Typically, supervisees in group

supervision interact with one another outside of the supervision parameters. In counselor education and counseling psychology programs, students often have classes together and socialize with each other. In postgraduation settings, counselors may socialize with one another and they also may work together in various other formats (e.g., coleading groups or serving on committees). It is important for supervisors to discuss the confidentiality of fellow supervisees because the dual relationships may blur the confidentiality lines. They also may consider confidentiality to pertain only to clients.

3. *Individuals may not obtain what they think they need in every group session.* It is highly challenging, if not impossible, in group supervision for supervisees to obtain the amount of attention they would receive in individual supervision. One hour of group supervision does not equate (in terms of personal attention) to one hour of individual supervision. This must be made clear to supervisees at the outset of group supervision so that they will have realistic expectations. Furthermore, it is not the goal of group supervision to provide the same type of guidance and assistance that occurs in individual supervision. Consequently, many counselor education and counseling psychology programs require both individual and group supervision for their students.

    One way the group supervisor can counterbalance this is by asking at the beginning of every group session, "What is one thing you need from the group today?" Although every concern that every group member has may not be addressed, this question encourages the supervisees to prioritize their needs. It also makes the group responsible for addressing what each member wants to work on in that session.

4. *Some group dynamics can hamper development.* Some hindering dynamics may include competition, subgrouping, defensiveness, group-think, and leader challenging. The dynamics that hinder the group's development also may hinder the supervisees' development. Hampering norms that may be established in group supervision include (a) the group does not discuss intrapersonal experiences that arise in the group or in the supervisees' counseling sessions; (b) the group unquestionably agrees with all of the supervisor's ideas and does not generate its own; (c) supervisees do not challenge each other; (d) supervisees are overly supportive and encouraging; and (e) the group always looks to the leader for direction.

The supervisor's role yields power in influencing the dynamics and norms that are established early in the group's life cycle. It is of the utmost importance for group supervisors to attend to the dynamics of the group throughout the group supervision process, but it is particularly essential to understand just how key the supervisor is in developing a productive group from the beginning. Intentional modeling, group-building, and generating supervisee ownership are crucial tasks for the group supervisor. It all begins with creating an environment in the group that capitalizes on the positives of group work and minimizes (or improves) the growing edges. Along with the following sections, I suggest reviewing group counseling texts for a thorough refresher on group leadership skills.

Creating the Environment

One of the main differences between individual and group supervision is that in individual supervision the supervisor and the supervisee are the only agents of professional development. The group supervisor functions more indirectly regarding supervisee development because it is the supervisees' interactions that are the major developmental impetus. Therefore, it is the supervisor's responsibility to create and maintain an environment conducive to effective interaction.

Human behavior is constantly reinforced by the environment. Consequently, the supervisor should encourage the supervisees' behaviors that seem conducive to the group process and discourage those that seem hindering. Remembering the fourth growing edge (i.e., some dynamics hamper development), openness, honesty, and spontaneity of expression should be encouraged within the group. Honesty is not, however, regulated only to the supervisees. A group supervisor who appears picture perfect is an impediment to the group process because this sets an example that the supervisees may think they cannot achieve. Furthermore, it reinforces a hindering group norm that disclosing personal struggles is unwanted. Self-disclosure is important, not only for its potential cathartic release, but because it leads to "deeper, richer, and more complex relationships with others" (Yalom & Leszcz, 2005, p. 134).

Feeling connected to other members of the group is a significant factor in developing group cohesion. Cohesion is one of the most important factors contributing to the effectiveness of a group (Yalom & Leszcz, 2005). Cohesion has been defined as group members' feelings of belonging to the group, having a sense of personal responsibility for the group, and experiencing a "we're in this together" mentality. The more cohesive a group is, the more that supervisees' willingness to influence and be influenced by others will increase, that their willingness to experience frustration will intensify, and that their commitment to each other's professional growth will increase. Additionally, higher levels of cohesion also enhance higher levels of productivity.

The group supervisor has some responsibility in fostering group cohesion. As with any beginning group, supervisees will be looking to the supervisor for guidance on what to do and how to be during the supervision process. The ways in which the supervisor leads and facilitates during the initial stages of the group will have a large impact on how quickly, and to what extent, the group develops. Therefore, it is paramount that group supervisors attend to creating an environment that enables the group to utilize its full potential. Intentionally selecting the methods of achieving connectedness can help propel the group toward cohesiveness. The following sections offer some assistance in this process and serve as examples of ways to facilitate the development of group cohesion.

Modeling How to Be

The first group session is often used to cover many logistical processes (e.g., scheduling, policies and procedures, group rules, etc.). Discussing the policies and procedures is a vital component to any group. In some supervision groups where this process feels mundane, the members have inferred from the supervisor that "we need to get this stuff out of the way." Clearly, many counselors and supervisors did not choose this profession to engage in discussions about rules. Group supervisors should not forget, however, just how much power they have over the group. We often think of modeling in a behavioral context. Certainly, what supervisors do has an impact on the development of group norms, supervisees' comfort levels, group cohesion, and many other dynamics and processes.

One important, but sometimes overlooked, component of modeling is the effect that the supervisor's attitudes have on the group. The above example would have one effect on how supervisees view the importance of policies and procedures. A more positive or enthusiastic attitude might have a different influence. As a discussion of logistics is usually one of the first tasks a group must accomplish, the attitude the supervisor exhibits sets an early tone for the environment. Consequently, that attitude may have an effect on the supervisees' enthusiasm and outlook about the group. In the beginning stages of a group, enthusiasm and outlook are central aspects of building cohesion. Evidence suggests that attitudes displayed by the group leader increases the level of those same attitudes in the group members (Linton & Hedstrom, 2006). Modeling openness, acceptance, enthusiasm, and nondefensiveness will aid in creating a working environment characterized by higher levels of these attitudes displayed by supervisees.

Group Building

The importance of creating group cohesion cannot be overstated. In order to get the group working quickly, the supervisees must feel a sense of belonging and a connection to other members early in the group. Therefore, the group supervisor should attend to enhancing the atmosphere in such a way that supervisees begin to feel comfortable with each other and with the supervisor.

Thinking about how the supervisor wants the group to operate can help determine certain things she or he will do. This is where pregroup planning can make a major difference. If the supervisor can visualize how the group will look during a typical supervision session, he or she can intentionally plan activities that will promote that vision. For example, I once visualized that one component of a supervision group I was to lead would include dialogue about the importance of attending to the counseling relationship. I wanted my supervisees to explore this component of their work to a deeper extent than what I had experienced in previous supervision relationships. My solution was to spend some of our supervision time discussing a book about the counseling relationship in a type of book club format. I introduced this component by explaining that we could use this time to learn together and that each week a different person would lead the discussion. This not only helped facilitate my vision, but it also promoted the idea that I was not the only one who would lead the group. By leading the first book club session, I was able to model how we could work together in the learning process, which in turn enhanced cohesion and helped the group develop toward the working stage.

Examining some of the tasks the group must accomplish in the beginning stages of group supervision, the group supervisor can plan activities specifically designed for group building. Icebreakers are a great way to ease any anxiety and release any tension the supervisees may have about the group supervision process. In the first group session, a discussion about expectations also can help the supervisees explore their excitements, concerns, and goals. This technique begins the process of group building because supervisees can obtain an understanding of what their peers are experiencing and grasp potential commonalities amongst the expectations. Let us not forget modeling here. Supervisors should also share their expectations for the group. Not only will supervisors need to share logistical information, but also they should share their excitements, challenges, and goals. Again, in the earlier stages of group development, the group supervisor is expected to assume most of the leadership roles of the group. Optimally, this will diminish over time as the group develops. Supervisors should think of themselves as part of the group during the group-building process and not just the leader. This can be challenging because most group supervisors will have to evaluate their supervisees, and the supervisees will not easily forget this function of the supervisor's role.

Generating Ownership

An important feature in enhancing the full potential of the group involves getting the supervisees to feel a sense of ownership for the group. When supervisees feel empowered that they bear some responsibility for the success of the group, they will increase their efforts during the group supervision sessions. The more group members accept accountability for the group's work, the more a diversity of resources are available to the group; and consequently, the higher the quantity and quality of feedback that is offered.

At first glance, providing a loose structure for how the group supervision sessions will operate may seem counterintuitive in stimulating supervisee ownership. After all, why would I feel a sense of ownership if I am being told how everything is going to operate? Remember structure is what the group needs in the early stages of group development. I am not suggesting that the supervisor's structure of how the group sessions will run should be staunch and inflexible. I am suggesting, however, that when supervisees know what to expect each week, they will feel more comfortable and will eventually prepare more for group supervision.

Developing group rituals is one method of achieving this. Group rituals are simply activities or processes in which the group engages during every supervision session. If supervisees know that each session will begin with a particular activity or type of discussion (e.g., quick check-in), over time they will more thoroughly prepare for that ritual. Subsequently, the beginning of the sessions may incite more meaningful discussions at a quicker pace. Furthermore, rituals can provide a grounding experience for supervisees who may experience varying levels of anxiety because of the often abstract, complex, and ambiguous nature of counseling work. On many occasions, I have heard supervisees comment how good they feel knowing that when they arrive for a group supervision session they know they will be doing (fill in ritual here) because it is one thing that is concrete in their work. Additionally, rituals that occur at the end of group supervision sessions can be an empowering and/or relaxing way to launch supervisees back into their work roles (e.g., guided imagery).

Another valuable ownership-generating technique is the development of group rules. Supervisors will have their own policies and procedures to follow, and those are often requirements of the graduate program or agency. In terms of group processing, however, there are no mandated requirements of how to interact and how to garner the full potential of the group. The supervisor can ask the supervisees to create of list of conditions they believe are necessary to engage in meaningful, open, and honest dialogue throughout the life of the group. Some common examples of conditions include acceptance, honesty, support, nonjudgmental attitudes, taking risks, and so forth. Regardless of the supervisees' list, it is important that they produce the majority of the rules. Certainly the supervisor will want to make sure that specific conditions are listed (e.g., confidentiality) and may need to state them if the supervisees do not. After the list is completed, the supervisor can ask for discussion or clarification of any of the conditions. Getting the entire group to agree on the list is the final step in this informal contract process. Not only does this begin to foster supervisee ownership, but it fosters accountability for members' behaviors within the group. Many times I have witnessed rich interactions when one supervisee calls out another for not taking risks, for being judgmental, or for violating other group rules.

Using Group Process Skills

Having discussed the value of creating an environment conducive to effective group supervision, this section will focus on using group facilitation skills to enhance the process and outcomes of the supervision work. Group supervisors will utilize many of the same skills used in individual supervision. If the supervisor does not shift from an individual to a group perspective, however, the result could be a continual focus on individuals during group supervision sessions. A kind of "taking turns" may arise during which a series of one-on-one discussions ensue, while the other supervisees remain disengaged.

As mentioned throughout this chapter, the power of group supervision rests within the interactions that occur during the supervision sessions. When all members of the group give and receive, optimal learning can transpire. It is therefore essential that group supervisors view the supervision process from a group-work lens and employ their group facilitation skills to enhance the development of their supervisees. Although a discussion of all group facilitation skills may be prudent, it is beyond the scope of this chapter. However, the following skills (not already discussed in this chapter) seem most relevant to the group supervision process.

Case Presentation Processing

Case presentations are perhaps the most widely used hallmark of group supervision. Most graduate programs and licensing boards require supervisors to evaluate supervisees' work via recorded (audio or video) counseling sessions. Group supervision models are often based on a case presentation approach (Borders & Brown, 2005). These models (e.g., Bernard & Goodyear, 2009) have several things in common, including a structure for how to conduct case presentations. Although each of these models have merit, I will discuss one that is straightforward, both process- and content-oriented, and incorporates the hybrid format of group supervision.

The structured peer group model (SPGM; Borders, 1991) conducts group supervision that intentionally incorporates group process to allow supervisees a constructive, structured way to help each other develop professionally. To prepare for this process, the supervisee records (audio or video) a counseling session and cues the recording to a 5–10-minute segment for which he or she would like feedback. During the group session, the supervisee briefly provides background information of the client and of the counseling work conducted to date. The supervisee then poses several goals of feedback on which to focus while watching or listening to the segment. Before the segment is reviewed, group members are assigned roles (e.g., client, counselor, or significant person in the client's life), specific observations (e.g., nonverbal behavior, counseling relationship, or a counseling skill), or perspectives (e.g., client conceptualization, evaluation of progress, or choice of interventions) on which to concentrate. The assignments can be done by the supervisor, the presenting supervisee, or other group members. Borders suggested that advanced supervisees could be asked to formulate descriptive metaphors for the client, counselor, or counseling relationship.

After the counseling segment is played, group members give feedback based on their assignments, keeping in mind the goals the supervisee wanted addressed. During SPGM, the supervisor facilitates the process using two roles. The first role of *moderator* (a) helps the presenting supervisee convey a specific focus for feedback; (b) keeps the group members on task; (c) ensures that everyone is heard; (d) summarizes feedback and identifies themes; and (e) organizes follow-up exercises (e.g., role-plays). In the *process commentator* role, the supervisor (a) offers feedback on the group dynamics; (b) encourages deeper discussion of roles or perspectives; (c) illuminates ways that group members protect or compete against each other, and (d) discusses any observable parallel processes.

Borders and Brown (2005) stated that they have witnessed the SPGM falter when supervisors were too directive, failed to address hampering group dynamics, or did not challenge the group to delve further into the discussion. They have seen great successes in the process when groups displayed honest, challenging, and supportive comments, when supervisees have experienced "light-bulb" moments, and when supervisees self-confront. Borders and Brown (2005) also stated a comment that parallels a central message I attempt to convey in this chapter. As the group develops,

> The supervisor's role, then, becomes more of a learning facilitator and commentator on the in-moment dynamics that seem to be affecting the learning process. . . . The group supervisor uses the group itself as a tool for learning, intervening, prodding. As a commentator on group process, the supervisor facilitates learning about

clinical dynamics, encourages self-awareness and personal growth, and serves as a role model of a group leader and skilled counselor. (p. 61)

Here-and-Now Processing

I have alluded to the importance of focusing dialogue with in-group dynamics. Focusing on here-and-now interactions, feelings, and thoughts has more power than recalling previous events because the group member is experiencing them in the present moment and can examine them as they are happening. During the life span of any group, members develop thoughts and feelings about other group members, the group leader, and the group as a whole. These thoughts and feelings affect the interactions that occur. These feelings and thoughts also represent important components of the here-and-now focus, but may not enact positive growth if the process is not illuminated for the group. That is where the group supervisor's artistry and skill surface. Focusing on the here-and-now facilitates the development and emergence of feedback, catharsis, and meaningful self-disclosure (Yalom & Leszcz, 2005), which are all important facets of group supervision.

As I stated earlier, even though group supervision of individual counseling does not represent an exact parallel process, the interactions that occur during group sessions embody the overt and subtle nuances of the supervisees' interpersonal styles. With a here-and-now focus, the group supervisor often can make connections between a supervisee's current interactions and her or his struggles with clients. For example, a supervisee shares an instance in her work where she felt stuck with a client. Centering on process, the supervisor not only hears *what* (content) the supervisee said, but also *how* (implicit message) the supervisee said it. The supervisor's response obviously will depend on exactly the nature of the *what* and *how*. For example, if the supervisee sounded frustrated with the client when she presented her case, implementing a group-work lens, the supervisor usually will want to prompt the group to respond before responding herself or himself. The supervisor might say, "How did the group experience what she just said" or "What seemed to be some of her implicit messages" when she talked about the client?" The supervisor may also question the supervisee directly. "Your tone suggests a point of view about the client. I wonder what you really think or feel about him." These types of questions help the group shift from a there-and-then orientation to the here-and-now. They also directly help the supervisee examine intrapersonal experiences and how they affect her counseling relationships.

The here-and-now focus also can be used to enhance awareness of multicultural issues. It likely will be the supervisor's responsibility to help develop a norm of discussing multicultural issues because the supervisees will tend to focus on skill development and case content (Lassiter, Napolitano, Culbreth, & Ng, 2008). If, in the beginning stages of the group, the supervisor continually draws the focus of client discussions toward a multicultural focus, eventually the supervisees will begin to do it on their own. An illustration from my own experience will provide more concrete information.

A female supervisee in one of my groups discussed her issues that she was having with a male client. The client was depressed because he stated that he could not keep a romantic relationship with a woman going for more than a few months. In his descriptions of his previous relationships, he described how much he attended to his girlfriends and self-sacrificed in the spirit of making his girlfriends happy, but they always ended the relationship with him. The supervisee appeared withdrawn when she discussed the client and also stated that she did not look forward to her sessions with him. The group offered support and feedback on various approaches she might take with the client. Then I asked the group if they could identify any multicultural issues that may be causing conflict in the supervisee's relationship with her client. One supervisee asked if gender could be affecting the process. After some meaningful dialogue, the supervisee realized that she was feeling smothered by her client, much in the same way she imagined his previous girlfriends had felt. We were then able to focus the discussion on ways she could manage the relationship and intervene with him appropriately and more effectively.

Multicultural Competence Enhancement

The preceding example is one way that group supervision can enhance multicultural competence. Since groups represent a social microcosm, and supervisees will interact in their natural interpersonal style, group supervision offers a unique setting to develop multicultural counseling competence. Furthermore, multicultural competence is not merely a trend emerging from an age of political correctness. Rather, it is at the very core of who we are as counselors. That is why multicultural competence is paramount in the counseling field and is fully endorsed by helping professions (American Counseling Association [ACA], 2005; APA, 2002; National Association of Social Workers, 2007). Models of training, best practices guidelines, and ethical codes abound in the helping (and other) professions. A salient model is the tripartite model of multicultural counseling competence as outlined by Sue, Arredondo, and McDavis (1992).

The tripartite model of multicultural counseling competence is reviewed extensively in Chapters Three and Four in this volume. In general, the competencies outline distinct attitudes and beliefs, knowledge, and skills deemed necessary for culturally competent counseling. Haynes, Corey, and Moulton (2003) adapted these competencies for supervisors in order to promote three distinct outcomes for supervisees: (1) being aware of your own cultural values and biases; (2) understanding the worldview of clients and supervisees; and (3) developing culturally appropriate intervention strategies and techniques. Regarding the first outcome, certainly the supervisor's own biases and prejudices play a part in the supervision process. The very nature of internalized prejudices suggests that the implicit framework of biases often operate blindly to the individual. Therefore, supervisors are encouraged to engage in continual self-exploration in order to manage their own biases in the supervisory relationship.

Self-exploration is a lifelong commitment, and instilling this commitment in supervisees can be challenging. A lifelong learner and self-explorer mentality is important for counselors, however, simply because of the nature of our work. Counselors' beliefs, values, attitudes, feelings, and thoughts are the tools of our profession. As professionals mature, these characteristics develop. Counselors must continually self-explore to understand how they affect their counseling relationships. Furthermore, the more counselors know about themselves, the more empathic they can be with their clients. The group supervisor can utilize the group toward self-exploration by modeling "how to be" in session. Modeling self-awareness, appropriate challenging and supporting techniques, and here-and-now processing are some important elements affected by biases. The challenge for group supervisors is that the developmental readiness to recognize, discuss, and act on multicultural issues will vary by supervisee (Borders & Brown, 2005).

Whether the group is homogeneous or heterogeneous, the opportunity exists for peers to discuss the multicultural issues with which they are struggling. In general, supervisees in group supervision discuss the counseling skills that they think need developing (e.g., assessment). Effective counseling, cannot operate outside of a multicultural context. Therefore, the group supervisor can help the supervisees deepen the discussions by guiding the group to conceptualize their clients through a multicultural lens.

Using the SPGM is one method supervisors can use to enhance multicultural competence. Lassiter et al. (2008) adapted the SPGM to specifically address multicultural issues in counseling. They suggested that when role or perspective assignments are given prior to session review that one group member could be assigned a "diversity" role. This supervisee would focus on the diversity perspectives of the counseling relationship. In as much, the supervisee would attempt to identify cultural similarities and differences and their effects on the process or relationship. It is believed that this would encourage an ongoing group consciousness about the importance of cultural context in the counseling process. Kaduvettoor et al. (2009) found evidence that promoting multicultural events in group supervision (i.e., multicultural conceptualization, peer vicarious learning, outside-of-group multicultural events, and supervisor direct teaching) enhanced multicultural competence. Therefore, it is crucial that multicultural discussions become a norm of the group supervision process.

Conclusion

Group supervision is an effective method of developing supervisees' awareness, knowledge, and skills. It offers a number of advantages including vicarious learning, peer support, multicultural competence enhancement, and interpersonal growth. Throughout this chapter, I have attempted to convey the importance of using group facilitation skills to enhance supervisee development. Without question, a highly cohesive group of supervisees that appropriately challenges and supports each other, that examines its own process in order to better understand the supervisees' interpersonal styles, and that takes risks with self-disclosure (particularly around multicultural issues) will promote a powerful, meaningful, and rewarding developmental experience.

References

American Counseling Association. (2005). *Code of ethics*. Alexandria, VA: Author.

American Psychological Association. (2002). *Guidelines on multicultural education, training, research, practice, and organizational change for psychologists*. Washington, DC: Author.

American Psychological Association. (2008). *Guidelines and principles for accreditation of programs in professional psychology*. Washington, DC: Author.

Bernard, J. M., & Goodyear, R. K. (2004). *Fundamentals of clinical supervision* (3rd ed.). Needham Heights, MA: Allyn & Bacon.

Bernard, J. M., & Goodyear, R. K. (2009). *Fundamentals of clinical supervision* (4th ed.). Upper Saddle River, NJ: Merrill.

Borders, L. D. (1991). A systematic approach to peer group supervision. *Journal of Counseling and Development, 69,* 248–252.

Borders, L. D., & Brown, L. L. (2005). *The new handbook of counseling supervision*. Mahwah, NJ: Lahaska Press.

Cohen, R. I. (2004). *Clinical supervision: What to do and how to do it*. Belmont, CA: Brooks/Cole.

Council for Accreditation of Counseling and Related Educational Programs. (2009). *CACREP accreditation standards and procedures manual*. Alexandria, VA: Author.

Haynes, R., Corey, G., & Moulton, P. (2003). *Clinical supervision in the helping professions*. Pacific Grove, CA: Brooks/Cole.

Hein, S., & Lawson, G. (2008, September). Triadic supervision and its impact on the role of the supervisor: A qualitative examination of supervisors' perspectives. *Counselor Education & Supervision, 48,* 16–31.

Kaduvettoor, A., O'Shaughnessy, T., Mori, Y., Beverly, C., III, Weatherford, R. D., & Ladany, N. (2009). Helpful and hindering multicultural events in group supervision climate and multicultural competence. *The Counseling Psychologist, 37*(6), 786–820.

Lassiter, P. S., Napolitano, L., Culbreth, J. R., & Ng, K. (2008). Developing multicultural competence using the structured peer group supervision model. *Counselor Education & Supervision, 47,* 164–178.

Linton, J., & Hedstrom, S. (2006). An exploratory qualitative investigation of group processes in group supervision: Perceptions of masters-level practicum students. *Journal for Specialists in Group Work, 31,* 51–72.

National Association of Social Workers. (2007). *NASW standards for cultural competence in social work practice.* Washington, DC: Author.

Proctor, B. (2000). *Group supervision: A guide to creative practice.* London, United Kingdom: Sage.

Riva, M. T., & Cornish, J. A. E. (2008). Group supervision practices at psychology predoctoral internship programs: 15 years later. *Training and Education in Professional Psychology, 2,* 18–25.

Sue, D. W., Arredondo, P., & McDavis, R. J. (1992). Multicultural competencies/ standards: A call to the profession. *Journal of Counseling and Development, 70,* 477–486.

Yalom, I. D., & Leszcz, M. (2005). *The theory and practice of group psychotherapy* (5th ed.). New York, NY: Basic Books.

CHAPTER **9**

Group Work Supervision

RICHARD L. HAYES and JAMES TRES STEFURAK

Many of the skills and methods used within a group setting are no different than those used by all counselors and supervisors in any setting. The same may be said of the general knowledge and skills that any counselor brings to the tasks of helping. Yet being the supervisor of counselors in a group is not the same as supervising them individually, any more than group counseling is merely the counseling of individuals in a group. Moreover, the supervision of counselors who are learning group facilitation skills provides challenges and opportunities that make special use of the parallel process and group dynamics operating in this form of supervision. Adding to these challenges is the dearth of empirical research on the supervision of group work, in general, and the supervision of novice group workers, in particular (Rubel & Okech, 2006).

Whatever the model (e.g., psychoanalytic, humanistic-existential, social learning, TA/Gestalt, rational-emotive, eclectic) or setting (e.g., administrative, clinical) of supervision adopted, the supervisor must also choose a modality by which to apply the model. Different modalities have different effects on supervisees and make different demands on the skills of both the supervisees and the supervisor. In general, supervision should begin at the simplest level (i.e., individual) and move gradually to more complex levels (i.e., group and/or peer supervision). Group supervision represents a median level of supervision that presumes prior experience and demonstrated mastery in individual supervision and that is preparatory to peer supervision. Certainly, any program of supervision might include various patterns of individual, group, and peer supervision that respond to the changing needs of the supervisees and the demand characteristics of the training site (e.g., time, staff, availability of space, etc.). As will be elaborated upon throughout this chapter, group supervision is uniquely well suited to the task of supervising novice group workers.

Dies (1980) found that experienced group psychotherapy supervisors believed that training activities should begin with an academic component and then move progressively through an observational component, an experiential component, and conclude with supervision of actual practice. On the group level, supervisees are not only engaged in a sequence appropriate to their own professional development but are also members of a supervisory group with its own developmental sequence. Attempts to integrate these two dimensions (i.e., individual and group development) within supervision have yet to provide a unified group supervision model (Bernard & Goodyear, 2009; D'Andrea, 1988; Granello & Underfer-Babalis, 2004; Hayes, 1991; Leach, Stoltenberg, McNeill, & Eichenfield, 1997), although the work of Rubel and Okech (2006) is promising in this regard.

The use of a group is widely recognized as offering more to supervision than just an efficient method (Bernard & Goodyear, 2009; Enyedy et al., 2003). In particular, group supervision encompasses the full range of group work, including attention to group dynamics, individual and group development, and the purposes of the supervision, which demands attention to the complex of interactions across these dimensions.

Toward a Definition

In defining group supervision, it is important to distinguish between two potential uses of the term: one in which the supervisees constitute the group and one in which the object of the supervision is the leadership of a group. For the purposes of this chapter, the discussion will be largely confined to group work supervision, that is, *supervision of trainees in a practicum setting focused on learning group facilitation skills by which the supervisor uses the group setting to supervise trainees leading groups themselves.* The critical point to be made here is that true group work supervision takes place in a group and, as such, "the members see themselves and are seen by others as psychologically interdependent and interactive in pursuit of a shared goal" (Dagley, Gazda, & Pistole, 1986, p. 131). The essential task for the group work supervisor, therefore, is to facilitate the development of a productive work group whose goal is to improve the group leadership skills of its members.

Benefits of Group Supervision

Beyond the obvious advantage of reducing supervisory time, the real advantages to be realized in group supervision are from the unique contribution the group can make to the personal and professional development of supervisees. In a theme that will be repeated throughout this chapter, the group work supervisor, who is working with supervisees who are leading their own groups, will necessarily go beyond assuming the benefits to be realized from participation in a supervisory group to making these benefits quite explicit as "grist for the group work mill" in helping group leaders explore the implications for their own group practice.

Drawing upon the work of Bernard and Goodyear (2009), Dagley et al. (1986), and Hillerbrand (1992), the following advantages can be found for group supervision as opposed to individual supervision: (1) Group supervision offers each supervisee the opportunity to reality test self-perceptions; (2) Through group interactions, distorted perceptions and false assumptions of self and others may become more apparent and lose their value; (3) Group supervision may provide a sense of psychological safety to support the elimination of self-defeating behaviors; (4) Group supervision provides an opportunity to interact in real-life situations, thus providing supervisees with chances to try out new behaviors in a safe environment; (5) Responses of others, especially one's peers, can help supervisees to appreciate the universality of some personal concerns; (6) Group supervision enables supervisees to increase their abilities to give and to solicit appropriate self-disclosures and feedback; (7) Interaction with others in a group can enhance one's empathy and social interest; (8) Group supervision exposes supervisees to alternative modes of helping, which can help them to develop deeper understandings of different counseling styles; (9) Consistent feedback from others in group supervision can enhance the supervisee's accuracy of perception and communication; (10) Group supervision provides an arena to learn perspective-taking skills with other group members; (11) Group supervision fosters less dependency on the supervisor than individual supervision; and (12) Novice counselors find it easier to understand each others' cognitive processes rather than an expert's, making the supervision group an excellent place to conceptualize new skills and cases.

Types of Groups

Groups are commonly classified on the basis of such shared properties as the number of members, duration, function, membership characteristics, setting, level of prevention, leadership style, goals, and so forth. These classifications refer to the focus or content of the group and generally describe characteristics of the group that are known prior to its first meeting.

These characteristics describe separate but interacting elements of the group. The number of supervisees anticipated to be in the group, for instance, will affect the formation of the group along other dimensions. The greater the number of members, the greater will be the demands on the setting to provide sufficient seating and privacy for the members. Further, increased numbers will change the nature of the supervision if everyone is to be provided an opportunity to speak and to share his or her concerns. In addition, opportunities for each member to give and receive feedback may demand that the group meets longer or that the interactions are held to certain previously agreed upon limits. How one decides whether and to what extent to involve each member depends in part upon the purposes of supervision and its level of prevention.

Member characteristics such as level of experience and expertise or diversity of work or practicum sites, for example, will affect the level and focus of supervision. Experienced supervisees employed in a community agency are more likely to possess wider variability of experiences and expertise with groups than will be found among pre-practicum students taking their first group course as part of a master's program (Bernard & Goodyear, 2009). Novice group leaders should be encouraged to consider how these characteristics have shaped the supervisory group and to explore how these characteristics interact as they structure their own groups.

Clearly, a host of individual differences aside from their skill levels or professional experiences are likely to influence the dynamic character of any group. Gender, racial, and cultural differences among members can complicate the introduction of potentially divisive topics depending upon how long the group has been together, the relative maturity of group members related to these issues, and the general trust level that has already been established among group members. Recognizing that these same multicultural factors operate within the supervisory group, Okech and Rubel (2007) argue that supervisors "need to have a clear understanding of the impact of diversity upon individuals, groups, supervisees, and themselves" (p. 256). Their SGW model has been used to facilitate the infusion of diversity related content in group work supervision by highlighting the diversity awareness, knowledge, and skills supervisees will need to become competent multicultural group workers.

Supervisory Goals

A review of the group supervision literature yields a general consensus on four components of group supervision and training that meet distinct but overlapping supervisory goals (Bernard & Goodyear, 2009; Rubel & Okech, 2006; Yalom & Leszcz, 2005). These goals may include the mastery of theoretical concepts, skill development, personal growth, self awareness or the integration of the supervisee's skills, knowledge, and attitudes as effective counseling tools. The first of these goals is usually met through some academic component of the supervisee's training and is not a major goal of supervision. Nonetheless, the supervisor may require selected readings on general issues of concern to supervisees or may suggest readings relevant to the concerns of specific students. In addition, group work supervisees should be encouraged to discuss criteria, potential sources, and intended outcomes in selecting readings for the variety of groups they might lead.

The most frequent goal for supervision is skill development. Beyond the development of individual counseling skills, however, group work supervision demands the development of group-specific skills (Association for Specialists in Group Work [ASGW], 2007; Delucia-Waack, 2002) on multiple levels: individual, interpersonal, and group (Hayes, 1990; Kline, 2003; Rubel & Okech, 2006). As Hayes (1990) noted, "at any particular moment, the supervisor must consider the level of cognitive complexity of the supervisee, the developmental level of the group, the level of training of the group members, and the interactive effects of these variables with one another" (p. 225). To these skills, Rubel and Okech (2006) argue that supervisors should target the group work skills of intervention, conceptualization, and personalization (use of self).

As daunting as this situation may appear for the group work supervisor, the group format provides a rich forum for supervisees to develop their group counseling skills through analysis and practice in vivo. Group work supervision should focus upon the identification and intervention in clinical situations that are common among supervisees or common in the clinical milieu, *especially as acted out in the group*. When the supervisees are engaged in group work, skill development should be focused on issues that have a high relevance for the development of group as opposed to individual skills (Wilbur, Roberts-Wilbur, Hart, Morris, & Betz, 1994). Although group supervision can be used to promote personal growth, individual therapeutic change is a secondary consideration to the primary goals of training, which are "the intensive group experience, the expression and integration of affect, and the recognition of here-and-now process" (Yalom, 1995, p. 527). By calling attention to process issues, group work supervisors can not only provide an example of how to move groups into the here-and-now but can lay the foundation for productive exploration of how supervisees can facilitate such movement in their own groups (Rubel & Okech, 2006).

Group supervisors should also consider ethical concerns that are raised when personal growth becomes a goal of group supervision, such as "captive therapy" issues (Prieto, 1996). Ensuring that one has met the goals of mastery, skill development, personal growth, and integration demands that supervisors have an evaluation plan to assess their and the supervisee's performance (ASGW, 2007). Since supervisors often serve as group leader, evaluator, advisor, and teacher at the same time, they are advised to make clear the extent to which self-disclosure will become part of any evaluation and what the penalties are likely to be, if any, for failing to participate (American Counseling Association [ACA], 2005; ASGW, 2007). Due to their multiple relationships, it is important that group supervisors consistently monitor their own objectivity and seek regular consultation from other colleagues (Donigian, 1993; Forester-Miller & Duncan, 1990).

Hayes (1990) has argued that the ethical dilemmas that arise naturally within the context of group supervision can be used by the group work supervisor to structure the group itself. By sharing responsibility for the development of the group supervision, group work supervisors can provide opportunities for challenging students' perceptions about themselves, their relationships with one another, and the implications for their future behavior when leading groups. Addressing issues that are likely to be clinically important and morally relevant for the supervisees (e.g., evaluation, diversity, self-disclosure) grounds them in their own understanding, while building a bridge to a broader understanding of how these issues might play out in their own groups.

Group supervision presents a unique training opportunity by providing a context for integrating basic counseling skills such as reflective listening or reflection of feelings. To these skills, group work supervision adds group conceptualization, and group work-specific intervention skills such as promoting member interaction and interpersonal learning through attending to group process, connecting members across diverse experiences, confronting conflicts among members, facilitating the development of group norms, and using one's own reactions to promote group process and development. Supervisees can promote each other's learning by modeling group behaviors, by offering divergent explanations of information processing, and through trying out different roles as both members and leaders in the group. Group supervision provides an ideal setting for group counselors to develop conceptualization skills at multiple levels by providing recurrent examples of the individual differences among one's peers, interpersonal processing encouraged by the supervisor, and recurrent reflections on the progress of the group as a whole in realizing stated goals.

Sadly, most supervisors do not have any formal training in supervision theory or techniques (Scott, Ingram, Vitanza, & Smith, 2000), let alone training in what to do as part of the supervised group experience (Delucia-Waack, 2002). Although group supervision offers benefits in providing a model in the person of the supervisor and ground for practice in the context of the group, integration of more structured skill development exercises has proven to improve group counseling skills, especially prior to a clinical internship experience (Smaby, Maddux, Torres-Rivera, & Zimmick, 1999). An intriguing innovation in group supervision that may benefit the development of group counseling skills is the use of a reflecting team (Cox, Banez, Hawley, & Mostade, 2003). This procedure involves dividing the supervision group into supervision and reflecting teams that allow for consideration of multiple frames of reference. The method provides a "metaposition" from which supervisees reflect on their work, confront issues in their approach, and receive feedback in a nondefensive manner as an analogue to participation in their own groups.

Group Dynamics

The struggle by group members to balance the forces associated with accomplishing goal-related tasks and building a shared community creates the group's dynamics. Creating an effective group experience depends on the supervisor's ability to provide both high levels of positive interdependence for achieving a common goal and a superordinate group identity that unites the diverse members based on a pluralistic set of values (Johnson & Johnson, 2000).

Group Process

Research has identified a cluster of core group processes that occur in all types of experiential groups regardless of the quality of the members or the leader. Helping supervisees to recognize these processes at work and use them effectively to promote both individual and group development in their own groups is a central concern in group work supervision.

Supervisee Anxiety

Initial anxiety on entering group supervision is a product of both the individual supervisee's personality and the strains associated with having one's counseling skills exposed and evaluated by others. When it is at mild to moderate levels, anxiety can promote growth in supervisees. At higher levels, however, it can serve as a "hindering phenomenon" (Christenson & Kline, 2000; Enyedy et al., 2003). Generally, supervisees perceive the "public exposure" in group supervision as exacerbating their anxiety, although they often are able to benefit from the group as their own self-efficacy and the group's cohesion emerge (Christenson & Kline, 2000; Walter & Young, 1999). Drawing upon their own experience in transcending their initial anxiety helps novice group workers appreciate the significance of creating a welcoming environment early in the group's history as a necessary condition to furthering group development when leading their own groups.

Cohesiveness

The more homogeneous the group, the more likely the group is to experience a sense of "we-ness," yet often at the risk of being more superficial, less creative, and less productive (Merta, 1995). The development of a shared frame of reference helps to bind members to common goals as well as to one another. The more stable structure that results helps members to tolerate greater diversity of opinion within the group and to withstand threats to group solidarity from without. Whatever the goals of the group, therefore, the group supervisor should attempt to establish and maintain group cohesion, especially early in the group's history. Supervisees consistently report that witnessing conflicts in group supervision, between peers and supervisors or between peers, had a negative impact on their learning and growth in supervision (Linton & Hedstrom, 2006). Supervisors must intervene in overt conflicts between supervisees or between supervisees and the supervisor early in the group's life. The supervisor can facilitate group cohesion through structured activities, connecting members, or pointing out similarities among members. The group work supervisor will engage the group in reflecting upon the actions taken by the supervisor to resolve any conflicts and, as the group matures, move toward greater engagement of the supervisees in identifying conflicts *in process* and in proposing alternative interventions.

The level of trust and cohesiveness in the supervision group is also related to the focus or orientation of the group on task versus process/relationship. Ogren, Apelman, and Klawitter (2001) found that group supervisees reported being strongly affected by the overall insecure climate (i.e., low trust and low cohesion) even two years after participating in a supervisory group. They further found that insecure supervisory groups were less able to balance the group's orientation between a focus on task versus a focus on relationship/process. Group work supervisors, therefore, must press supervisees to observe how the climate and orientation are managed in their supervisory group and use these insights when managing the same factors in their own group work.

Norms

Norms refer to behaviors that are "expected" of others and act as guidelines for acceptable behavior in the group. As norms arise within the group as shared expectations, whether implicit or explicit, group members may not be consciously aware of the influence of group norms on their behavior. These "parataxic distortions" (distorted perceptions or beliefs regarding interpersonal relationships; Yalom & Leszcz, 2005) are more likely to arise early rather than later in heterogeneous groups. The task of the supervisor is to help group members to identify norms that may be operating within the group and to help members to examine their relevance for the group's activity.

As norms play such an important role in helping to socialize members into the group (Bernard & Goodyear, 2009), group work supervisors should stress the need to take an active role in modeling appropriate behaviors such as responding empathically, showing genuine concern and respect for others, or confronting out of caring. In addition, the group work supervisor should attend actively to culture building, acknowledging differences, challenging the passive acceptance of stereotypes, and acknowledging conflict while engaging supervisees in examining the efficacy of these interventions and any implications for leading their own groups. Since supervisees are more likely to be committed to norms in which they have had a hand in their development (Hayes & Lunsford, 1994), engaging supervisees in norm-setting, especially early in the group's life, can be an important step toward creating a productive supervisory group.

Supervisees in diverse groups will have the benefit of learning multicultural competencies through interaction with their diverse peer group. However, multicultural issues can also create divisions when neglected, depending upon the norms that are established (Okech & Rubel, 2007). It is common for group members who are different from the majority of group members either in terms of race, ethnicity, or sexual orientation to either isolate themselves from the group or to be isolated by other members. Merta (1995) noted that the optimal amount of group structure, for instance, especially early in the group, is related to one's cultural expectations. Potential positive outcomes are more likely when working with Asian American supervisees, for example, when the group is a highly structured, problem-solving group rather than a free-floating, process-oriented interactional group (Leong, 1992). Ellis and Douce (1994) urge supervisors to ask "how are race, gender, sexual orientation, religion, or other cultural based differences affecting the supervisor and the supervisory relationships?" (p. 523). Through the exploration of these questions in the group, norms can be established that promote the appreciation of diversity among its members while advancing the purposes of the larger group.

The effective group work supervisor must first and foremost be an effective group leader. Beyond possessing the requisite group work knowledge and skills, however, the multiculturally competent group supervisor will also understand the culture of the supervisee, his or her clients, and the potential advantages and disadvantages of using a group format with these supervisees. Moreover, the supervisor must be aware of his or her own cultural identity and be willing to take risks interpersonally to confront racial/ethnic conflict. Critically, the group work supervisor will need to be competent in conceptualizing cultural difference across individual, interpersonal, and group levels. As Okech and Rubel (2007) advise, "supervisors may assist supervisees in developing diversity-competent conceptualizations skills by drawing supervisees' attention to gaps in their knowledge, providing information, encouraging them to research further, and helping them to apply the knowledge they have gained to their groups" (p. 249).

Validation and Feedback

One important outcome of group participation is the opportunity to test perceptions and improve communications with others. Group work supervision provides supervisees the opportunity to receive validation for their own ideas and opportunities to practice their nascent skills while testing emerging theories of group leadership in the company of their peers.

Since the provision of feedback that is both accurate and helpful is especially critical in facilitating group process, group work supervisors will need to help supervisees develop their skill in giving and receiving feedback. Stockton and Morran (1982) have cautioned, however, that positive feedback, whether or not it is followed by negative feedback, is more effective than negative feedback in influencing members to change their behavior, especially in early sessions. Linton (2003) found that even if feedback has a positive/supportive emotional valence, students rated it negatively when it was not perceived as constructive (i.e., positive feedback, which has within it guidance or directives for improvement). Consequently, supervisors are advised to limit feedback in early sessions to behavior description and to emphasize that feedback is only the perception of the giver. Providing opportunities to practice giving and receiving feedback during group supervision helps promote supervisees' skill development, especially when the supervisor can model nondefensive reactions to feedback on the supervisor's leadership. However, supervisees may experience difficulty receiving feedback from peers with whom they had a significant prior relationship (Linton, 2003). Supervisees are more likely to benefit from the collective feedback of a heterogeneous group as well as from the modeling of others when they challenge their biases and stereotypes (Corey, 1995; Linton & Hedstrom, 2006).

Emotional Immediacy

The increased awareness of feelings, especially as generated within the here-and-now context of the group, is an important part of group work. Nonetheless, the expression of all feelings or even of some feelings fully is not necessarily in the best interests of either the group or its members. Although full expression can help in expressing one's feelings, members react with feelings of their own and, if expressed, generate feelings in other members in reaction. Further, the supervisor must be aware of cultural differences in communicating feelings and tolerance for confrontation. For example, Asian Americans are often more uncomfortable with confrontation than their Caucasian American counterparts, who, in turn, are more likely to be uncomfortable with confrontation than their African

American counterparts (Merta, 1995). Sorting through the maze of feelings created in even the briefest exchange can lead to chaos.

To reduce the potential for such breakdowns in communication, the supervisor is advised to limit such exchanges to either the full expression of feelings or to the clarification of ideas. Further, the group work supervisor should be active in acknowledging conflict while also pushing members to make explicit connections to the group's goals for supervision, to norms operating within the group, and to draw implications for their own group leadership.

Problem Solving

If one considers a problem as the difference between how things are and how one thinks they ought to be, then a group provides recurrent opportunities for problem solving as members test their own perceptions and ideals against those of other group members. Group supervision not only provides opportunities for problem solving, but it should require the active participation of all members in assuming responsibility for the productivity of the group. Acting in the context of group-effected, problem-solving processes places responsibility upon supervisees for their own conduct in the group and, in the context of group work supervision, for their conduct in their own groups. The full exploration of alternatives by the group can be particularly effective in building problem-solving skills and is likely to lead to a more effective solution than one offered by single members or even the leader (Johnson & Johnson, 2000). Taking a problem-solving approach to structuring the group can reduce initial anxiety and unnecessary ambiguity, which can increase expressions of personal ownership for the problem while leading to collective responsibility for the outcome.

Leadership

As used here, leadership refers to a dynamic function of the group wherein members' activities are directed to the satisfaction of group goals. Therefore, leadership is viewed as more a function of the group than it is a role occupied by a single member. As the needs of the group change, the demands placed upon its members will change. Although the group work supervisor may begin as the leader of the group, supervisees may be called upon periodically as the group's needs demand. The supervisor acts not so much to direct the group as to create a climate in which the group finds its own direction and supervisees can test emerging skills in group facilitation. Group work supervisors should shift from a more didactic role to a more consultative role as supervisees take on greater leadership as they increase their mastery of group work intervention and conceptualization skills (Rubel & Okech, 2006). Supervisees should be given opportunities to develop skills in leading their supervisory group as preparation for leading other, less receptive groups of their own. Practice in leading their peers will provide supervisees with the opportunity to exert their power and influence under somewhat controlled conditions. The supervisees' efforts should be evaluated in relation to the group's efforts rather than by comparison with the efforts of the supervisor. Accepting that a group presents a microcosm of society, replete with a wide variety of personal and interpersonal problems, group work supervision offers a unique opportunity for integrating theoretical concepts with practical problems likely to arise when leading one's own groups.

Self-Disclosure

The person who enters a group is faced with a dilemma: how to become a part of the group's collective identity and at the same time preserve one's individual identity. Self-disclosure needs come into conflict as members seek affirmation for the resolution of past struggles, on the one hand, while fearing the disapproval that can come with confessing one's weaknesses to others. Many supervisees are unsure about how much to self-disclose, which can lead to role ambiguity and confusion. The anxiety that can result is especially pronounced when the supervisory group is focused on the improvement of group work skills in the context of group work supervision. Ladany and Friedlander (1995) found that the stronger the working alliance between supervisors and supervisees the clearer the roles became to supervisees. Although self-disclosure is the principal vehicle of group interaction, Corey (2004) cautioned that "self-disclosure is foreign to the values of some cultural groups. This premium that is placed on self-disclosure by most therapeutic approaches is often in conflict with the values of some European ethnic groups that stress that problems should be kept 'in the family'" (p. 114). Sensitivity to the cultural norms related to self-disclosure in groups will help to avoid passive acceptance of stereotyping of "strong, silent" males, "shy" women, "stoic" Native Americans, "boisterous" African Americans, and the like.

Researchers disagree about how best to protect the rights of the individual to limit self-disclosure while also creating the proper conditions for realizing the personal benefits from self-disclosing in a group. Although explaining the limits of confidentiality in a group setting is a responsibility of all group leaders, the group work supervisor must also make supervisees aware of the difficulties involved in enforcing and ensuring confidentiality in a group setting and how to handle breaches as they arise.

Complicating the situation for the supervisor is the realization that supervisees not only come to the group with different levels of expertise and experience with groups, but may have different levels of need satisfaction

(Stockton & Morran, 1982). Group supervision offers supervisees a vivid demonstration of the differential needs of persons to self-disclose and can be used effectively by the group work supervisor as an important object lesson in the need to respect clients' rights to self-disclose in their own ways. The group also offers an arena for supervisees to try out perspective-taking skills. Through listening to and understanding the self-disclosures of other members, supervisees can begin to juxtapose several different perspectives and recognize the value in each. Research demonstrates that supervised internship experiences, especially of the kind advocated here for group work supervision, provide the conditions necessary for cognitive growth, which has been linked to many positive counseling characteristics, including improved social perspective taking, client conceptualization, racial tolerance, and cognitive flexibility, among others (Granello & Underfer-Babalis, 2004; Hayes, 1991).

Roles

One of the great benefits to group work supervision is the possibility of testing a variety of roles as both leader and member in practice situations prior to leading one's own group. In a study of group supervision behaviors, Savickas, Marquart, and Supinski (1986) found students judged the following role requirements to be most important for group supervisors: (1) modeling target behaviors; teaching skills, techniques, and strategies; (2) evaluating performance; and (3) facilitating exploration, critical thought, and experimentation (p. 23). Interestingly, Boethius and Ogren (2000) found that group supervisors tend to adopt a more socially dominant/engaged stance and more of a task orientation than supervisees. In light of this finding, supervisors are encouraged to take responsibility for setting the agenda, but should encourage supervisees to take more active roles over the course of supervision. Group work supervisors, in particular, should be quite explicit about the need for supervisees to take an increasingly active role in shaping the group as a laboratory for their own skill development.

Group Development

Research (Kormanski, 1988; Tuckman & Jensen, 1977; Yalom & Leszcz, 2005) has suggested that effective small groups follow a generalizable pattern from initiation to termination. This pattern is formed by a sequence of overlapping stages that are characterized by a set of focal concerns that rise and fall in importance as the group moves toward maturity. Although the particular names and boundaries of these stages vary from description to description, a fair synopsis of this research would provide a sequence of stages that move from: *Forming* (a stage of testing and encounter);

to *Storming* (a stage of intragroup conflict, emotional expression, and role-modeling); to *Norming* (a stage of group cohesion); to *Performing* (a stage of role-relatedness and production); to *Adjourning* (a stage of separation, assessment, and evaluation).

The supervisor who is aware of these different stages recognizes that different tasks must be performed relative to the stage-related needs of the group. During the forming stage, for instance, the supervisor is advised to provide a greater degree of structure and direction in helping supervisees establish personal goals for supervision and in modeling group appropriate behaviors. Supervisees are likely to be fully aware of how they or the group are developing and typically view the supervisor as responsible for managing the group's development (Ogren et al., 2001). To move the group into the storming stage, supervisors need to challenge supervisees to examine their reasons for being in the group and to take greater responsibility for their behavior.

Movement into the norming stage is facilitated by helping the group to identify norms already operating within the group and to encourage an analysis of their effectiveness in reaching individual and group goals. Of course, the general goals for the supervisory group remain, and it is during the performing stage that supervisees are encouraged to get down to the actual work of the group—improving group work skills. Finally, if the group has been at all effective, members will be reluctant to end the experience and/or will attempt to ascribe any success to some uniqueness in the group or its members. During this final stage, the group work supervisor should confront this denial process directly and facilitate the important work of helping supervisees recognize their need to hold on to the group. Developing this understanding will be critical to the ability of supervisees to recognize this same dynamic in their own groups and their potential complicity in undermining termination. The interested reader should consult Bernard and Goodyear (2009), Corey (1995), Gladding (2008), Granello and Underfer-Babalis (2004), and Kormanski (1988) for more detailed descriptions of stage-related group leader behaviors.

Conclusion

Despite its shaky beginnings and the inflated claims of earlier proponents, group work continues to promise unique opportunities for counselor training. Its wide acceptance in counselor supervision is tempered by the recognition that a systematic analysis of the process of group supervision of group work (group work supervision) has yet to be reported. Much of group supervision practice is based upon its client-services analogue—group counseling/therapy, which has a large amount of empirical support for its effectiveness in a variety of settings and from a variety of theoretical approaches. Also, group work as a broad field has a rich tradition of theory building and attention to subtle processes that offer a rich bed upon which more rigorous quantitative and qualitative research can occur. Therefore, group work supervision is in dire need of more focused, theory-driven research that tests specific models that connect supervision and group work practice. Nonetheless, supervisors and counselor educators in search of ways to improve their group work supervision are faced with numerous excellent proposals. Until the necessary program of systematic research reveals the connections between group work, supervision, and counselor effectiveness, supervisors are well advised to take heed of the suggestions for practice offered in the studies cited here.

References

American Counseling Association (2005). *Code of ethics.* Alexandria, VA: Author.

Association for Specialists in Group Work. (2007). *Best practice guidelines.* Alexandria, VA: Author.

Bernard, J. M., & Goodyear, R. K. (2009). *Fundamentals of clinical supervision* (3rd ed.). Upper Saddle River, NJ: Merrill.

Boethius, S. B., & Ogren, M. (2000). Role patterns in group supervision. *The Clinical Supervisor, 19*(2), 45–69.

Christenson, T. M., & Kline, W. B. (2000). A qualitative investigation of the process of group supervision with group counselors. *The Journal for Specialists in Group Work, 25*(4), 376–393.

Corey, G. (1995). *Theory and practice of group counseling* (4th ed.). Pacific Grove, CA: Brooks/Cole.

Corey, G. (2004). *Theory and practice of group counseling* (6th ed.). Pacific Grove, CA: Brooks/Cole.

Cox, J. A., Banez, L., Hawley, L. D., & Mostade, J. (2003). Use of the reflecting team process in the training of group workers. *Journal for Specialists in Group Work, 28*(2), 89–105.

Dagley, J., Gazda. G., & Pistole, C. (1986). Groups. In M. Lewis, R. Hayes, & J. Lewis (Eds.), *An introduction to the counseling profession* (pp. 130–166). Itasca, IL: F. E. Peacock.

D'Andrea, M. (1988). The counselor as pacer: A model for revitalization of the counseling profession. In R. L. Hayes & R. Aubrey (Eds.), *New directions for counseling and human development* (pp. 22–44). Denver, CO: Love Publishing.

Delucia-Waack, J. (2002). A written guide for planning and processing group sessions in anticipation of supervision. *Journal for Specialists in Group Work, 27,* 341–357.

Dies, R. (1980). Group psychotherapy: Training and supervision. In A. K. Hess (Ed.), *Psychotherapy supervision* (pp. 337–366). New York, NY: Wiley.

Donigian, J. (1993). Duality: The issue that won't go away. *Journal for Specialists in Group Work, 18,* 137–140.

Ellis, M., & Douce, L. (1994). Group supervision of novice clinical supervisors: Eight recurring issues. *Journal of Counseling and Development, 72,* 520–525.

Enyedy, K. C., Arcinue, F., Puri, N. N., Carter, J. W., Goodyear, R. K., & Getzelman, M. A. (2003). Hindering phenomenon in group supervision: Implications for practice. *Professional Psychology: Research and Practice, 34*(3), 312–317.

Forester-Miller, H., & Duncan, J. (1990). The ethics of dual relationships in the training of group counselors. *Journal for Specialists in Group Work, 15*, 88–93.

Gladding, S. T. (2008). *Group work: A counseling specialty* (5th ed.). Englewood Cliffs, NJ: Prentice Hall.

Granello, D. H., & Underfer-Babalis, J. (2004). Supervision of group work: A model to increase supervisee cognitive complexity. *Journal for Specialists in Group Work, 29*, 159–173.

Hayes, R. L. (1990). Developmental group supervision. *Journal for Specialists in Group Work, 15*, 225–238.

Hayes, R. L. (1991). Group work and the teaching of ethics. *Journal for Specialists in Group Work, 16*, 24–31.

Hayes, R. L., & Lunsford, B. (1994). Elements of empowerment: Enhancing efforts for school renewal. *People and Education, 2*(1), 83–100.

Hillerbrand, E. T. (1992). Cognitive differences between experts and novices: Implications for group supervision. *Journal of Counseling and Development, 68*, 684–691.

Johnson, D. W., & Johnson, F. P. (2000). *Joining together: Group theory and group skills* (7th ed.). Boston, MA: Allyn and Bacon.

Kline, W. (2003). *Interactive group counseling and therapy.* Upper Saddle River, NJ: Merrill/Prentice Hall.

Kormanski, C. (1988). Using group development theory in business and industry. *Journal for Specialists in Group Work, 13*(1), 30–43.

Ladany, N., & Friedlander, M. L. (1995). Trainees' experience of role conflict and role ambiguity in supervisory relationships. *Journal of Counseling Psychology, 39*, 389–397.

Leach, M. M., Stoltenberg, C. D., McNeill, B. W., & Eichenfield, G. A. (1997). Self-efficacy and counselor development: Testing the integrated developmental model. *Counselor Education and Supervision, 37*, 115–124.

Leong, F. T. (1992). Guidelines for minimizing premature termination among Asian American clients in group counseling. *Journal for Specialists in Group Work, 17*, 218–288.

Linton, J. M. (2003). A preliminary qualitative investigation of group processes in group supervision: Perspectives of master's level practicum students. *Journal for Specialists in Group Work, 28*(3), 215–226.

Linton, J. M., & Hedstrom, S. M. (2006). An exploratory qualitative investigation of group processes in group supervision: Perceptions of masters-level practicum students. *Journal for Specialists in Group Work, 31*(1), 51–72.

Merta, R. J. (1995). Group work: Multicultural perspectives. In J. G. Ponterotto, J. M. Casas, L.A. Suzuki, & C. M. Alexander (Eds.), *Handbook of multicultural counseling* (pp. 567–585). Thousand Oaks, CA: Sage Publications.

Ogren, M. L., Apelman, A., & Klawitter, M. (2001). The group in psychotherapy supervision. *Clinical Supervisor, 20*(2), 147–175.

Okech, J. E. A., & Rubel, D. (2007). Diversity competent group work supervision: An application of the supervision of group work model (SGW). *Journal for Specialists in Group Work, 32*(3), 245–266.

Prieto, L. (1996). Group supervision: Still widely practiced but poorly understood. *Counselor Education and Supervision, 35,* 295–307.

Rubel, D., & Okech, J. E. A. (2006). The supervision of group work model: Adapting the discrimination model for supervision of group workers. *Journal for Specialists in Group Work, 31,* 113–134.

Savickas, M., Marquart, C., & Supinski, C. (1986). Effective supervision in groups. *Counselor Education and Supervision, 26,* 17–25.

Scott, K. J., Ingram, K. M., Vitanza, S. A., & Smith, N. G. (2000). Training in supervision: A survey of current practices. *Counseling Psychologist, 28*(3), 403–422.

Smaby, M. H., Maddux, C. D., Torres-Rivera, E., & Zimmick, R. (1999). A study of the effects of a skills-based versus a conventional group counseling training program. *Journal for Specialists in Group Work, 24,* 152–163.

Stockton, R., & Morran, D. K. (1982). Review and perspective of critical dimensions of therapeutic small group research. In G. Gazda (Ed.), *Basic approaches to group psychotherapy and group counseling* (3rd ed.). Springfield, IL: Charles C. Thomas.

Tuckman, B., & Jensen, M. (1977). Stages of small group development revisited. *Group and Organizational Studies, 2,* 419–427.

Walter, C. A., & Young, T. M. (1999). Combining individual and group supervision in educating for the social work profession. *The Clinical Supervisor, 18*(2), 73–89.

Wilbur, M. P., Roberts-Wilbur, J., Hart, G. M., Morris, J. R., & Betz, R. L. (1994). Structured group supervision (SGS): A pilot study. *Counselor Education and Supervision, 33,* 262–279.

Yalom, I. (1995). *The theory and practice of group psychotherapy* (4th ed.). New York, NY: Basic Books.

Yalom, I., & Leszcz, M. (2005). *The theory and practice of group psychotherapy* (5th ed.). New York, NY: Basic Books.

CHAPTER 10

Supervising Pre-Degreed and Professional School Counselors

PEGGY P. WHITING, GERALD PARR, and LORETTA J. BRADLEY

Professional school counselors are assuming an increasingly important leadership role in education, and school counseling preparation programs are vital to the appropriate development of that role. Professional school counselors significantly contribute to outcomes used to measure the success of students and schools, and students in school counselor preparation programs need direct training and supervision in leadership and the implementation of a comprehensive school counseling program.

—American School Counselor Association

Clarence, a novice school counseling practicum student, requested some time to collaborate with others in his weekly group supervision seminar. He wanted direction in working with a fifth grade student whose father had fatally shot her mother before taking his own life. This particular child was one of five who witnessed this homicide/suicide of both parents. It happened over the weekend and was the unexpected headline at the school on Monday morning when Clarence appeared on-site. The children had been placed in emergency foster care until issues of guardianship could be addressed by relatives coming from out of state. Clarence had immediately discussed the tragedy with his on-site supervisor who felt unprepared to confront this kind of complicated issue. He came next to his practicum faculty supervisor and received suggestions of crisis response, although not guidance for action within the context of a school environment. That faculty supervisor had no background in school counseling.

Clarence talked about viewing his role from the ASCA National Model (American School Counselor Association [ASCA], 2005) that he had learned in his prerequisite school counseling courses. He wondered about delivering appropriate responsive services such as crisis counseling, referral-making, and consultation. Clarence had learned about the school counselor's leadership role in ensuring student success for all students and he was certain such a tragedy would impact the performance of the surviving children. Three of the affected children were to return to school the next day in order to have structure while police and extended family dealt with the immediate implications and needs of the five children.

This event represents a critical moment in the professional development of a school counselor-in-training. It is filled with complexities beyond the developmental scope expected of a practicum student. It is a situation where expert guidance is demanded from a supervisor who can articulate a course of action appropriate to the role of the school counselor. In this case, the on-site supervisor had not dealt with many emotional concerns of the students given her typical day was filled with administrative and testing duties. The supervisor had previously stated to Clarence that school counselors really didn't do any counseling but are, rather, technicians and arms of the administration. The role of the faculty supervisor becomes of paramount importance to the school counseling students-in-training when the long-standing realities of the operational day of a veteran school counselor are inconsistent with newer conceptualizations and standards of professional school counseling as endorsed by ASCA (2005).

Historical Lens of the Need for School Counseling Supervision

The notion that school counselors need supervision has been a dialogue that seems to parallel the profession's development. For example, in the 1920s, Brewer (1924) commended the work of vocational counselors in Boston schools but also expressed concern about the lack of coordination and supervision. A decade later, Fitch (1936) stated that counselors' roles were subject to erosion when supervision was provided exclusively by principals. In the mid-1970s, Boyd and Walter (1975) asserted that the absence of supervision impeded the professional development of counselors, rendering them "stunted specimens" (p. 103). Several years later, Barret and Schmidt (1986) challenged the counseling profession to establish national standards for the supervision of counselors in all settings, thus, emphasizing the need for systematic supervision of school counselors. Borders and Usher (1992) investigated existing postacademic supervision and reported that school counselors represented the largest group of counselors in practice without supervision. Crespi and Fischetti (1998) challenged the professional associations to assume leadership in addressing the void in postacademic supervision. They stated that systematic clinical supervision is a developmental tool that "could serve as a vehicle for emphasizing the unique and vital role counselors make in the schools" (Crespi & Fischetti, 1998, p. 19). The CESNET, a list serve providing a forum for communication among those interested in supervision and training, drew comments affirming the need for clinical supervision in order to address the severity and diversity of contemporary problems with children and youth.

Recent literature reflects continued emphasis on the importance of clinical supervision for school counselors and concern about the current state of this issue (Fischetti & Lines, 2003; Protivnak & Davis, 2008). Dollarhide and Miller (2006) addressed, as the goal of the special section of a recent issue of the *Journal of Counselor Education and Supervision,* "highlighting the crucial connection between supervision, professional identity, and professional viability for school counselors" (p. 243). These authors appealed to renewed commitment to the clinical supervision of practicing school counselors and counselors-in-training in order to "result in a consistent professional identity, improved service delivery consistent with the ASCA National Model, and a transformed profession" (p. 243).

Several salient concerns emerge within the literature. First, prior to the development of the 2003 ASCA National Model, the field of school counseling lacked a cohesive conceptualization of the roles, delivery systems, and standards of practice for school counselors (Hatch, 2008). The adoption of the ASCA model was a critical initial step in articulating a unified identity for this specialized group of counselors and for outlining the resultant educational needs for school counselors-in-training. However, the implementation of the model is time-consuming and incomplete producing a present discrepancy between a transformed and an actual practice of school counseling (Perera-Diltz & Mason, 2008; Rayle & Adams, 2007; Scarborough & Culbreth, 2008). As a new identity for school counseling becomes more fully operationalized, counselor education programs have a corresponding need to transform the preparation of counselors-in-training (Hayes & Paisley, 2002). Studer (2005) reported on the disillusionment of trainees when not provided with performance activities congruent with a comprehensive, developmental school counselor program. The most recent training standards endorsed by the Council for Accreditation of Counseling and Related Educational Programs reflect specialty requirements that school counselors-in-training have knowledge and skill in understanding and implementing the ASCA National Model with its emphasis on counseling, collaboration, consultation, advocacy, and leadership within the school context (Council for Accreditation of Counseling and Related Educational Programs, 2009).

Secondly, there is a lack of coordination between counselor educators and practicing school counselors. Clinical supervision of veteran counselors, many of whom were trained prior to the ASCA National Model, is limited at best (Linton & Deuschle, 2006; Somody, Henderson, Cook, & Zambrano, 2008). The articulation of the model is often left as the responsibility of the district or state within which the counselor practices and is interjected into a harried practice where the ratio of students to counselors is exceedingly high. Even if the model is adequately understood, most practicing school counselors have received no supervision themselves or formal training in clinical supervision (Crespi, 2003; Oberman, 2005). Those practicing school counselors who report a desire for clinical supervision often do not participate (Wilkerson, 2006). The mentoring and acculturation necessary for the identity development and skill acquisition of school counselors-in-training are, more often than not, random and nonsystematic. The faculty supervisor may possess the clinical supervision competence but may not have specialty preparation as a school counselor nor adequate understanding of the supervision needs for those delivering counseling within a school milieu. Davis (2006) discussed the difficulty of staying abreast of changes in the field such as diverse students, technology, and the impact of testing for counselor educators who were trained for school counseling. The profession must meet multifaceted needs to appropriately educate school counselors-in-training, to outreach to practicing school counselors who lack clinical supervision training, to address the lack of specificity of school-based supervision knowledge of faculty supervisors, and to assist school counselor educators in remaining current in the ever-changing practice of school counseling.

Finally, the models and means of supervision specific to school counseling have historically been lacking (Herlihy, Gray, & McCollum, 2002). Akos and Scarborough (2004) reported a wide difference in the clinical training requirements of school counselors-in-training after examining the pedagogical practice for clinical preparation as sampled with 59 school counseling internship syllabi. Murphy and Kaffenberger (2007) stated that the ASCA National Model advanced the structure for school counseling but failed to explicitly address supervision within the components of the model. Magnuson, Norem, and Bradley (2001) presented a table of representative school counselor supervision models from 1975 through 2000. These authors discussed, among others, the following initiatives that have proven instrumental in advancing school specific supervision models: the peer consultation approach (Benshoff & Paisley, 1996); the dyadic supervision model (Henderson & Lampe, 1992); the counselor–mentor program (Peace & Sprinthall, 1998); and peer supervision models (Crutchfield & Borders, 1997).

Promising Current Models of School Supervision

It is clear the profession needs to emphasize the importance of supervision to the school setting, provide a road map for supervising site personnel who may lack clinical supervisory models and skills, and implement school-based models of supervision within counselor education programs that compliment the comprehensive responsibilities inherent in the ASCA National Model and standards of best school counseling practice. The following discussion highlights several best practice methods and models.

Group Supervision Models

Linton and Deushle (2006) discussed four models of group supervision as viable options to address the supervision needs of practicing school counselors. As these authors stated, group supervision is inherently efficient, a considerable factor given the increased demands placed upon counselors in schools. Bernard and Goodyear (2009) differentiated group supervision from other administrative and conference meetings required of school counselors, emphasizing the functions as being identity understanding, role clarity, and service delivery specific to school-aged students. These purposes are met through the context of group process. Linton and Deushle (2006) cautioned about the need for further research on the effects of group supervision on practicing school counselors. There is a need for clarity around how these groups are led, how the group membership occurs relative to amount of experience, how often and for how long the group occurs, and how counselor educators might provide a liaison with the community of practicing school counselors.

Three-Tier School Supervision: Clinical, Developmental, and Administrative

Studer (2005) poignantly described several contemporary issues in school supervision that must be addressed through the supervision developmental stages. Studer discussed the need for identifying role models whose personal perceptions were congruent with the socialization of school counselors for twenty-first century practice. She advocated the use of individual learning contracts as ways to articulate appropriate goals, activities, and evaluations of school counselors-in-training. These written documents can assist in bridging theory and practice when the host site has not fully transformed to the ASCA National Model and in establishing individual needs for students lacking education backgrounds. Furr and Carroll (2003) also endorsed the developmental model and offered many supervisory strategies to enhance the affective and cognitive learning of school counselors at various stages of professional development. As the needs of the trainees change over time, the supervisors' roles alternate from those giving support, direction, consultation, challenge, evaluation, and collaboration (Whiting, Bradley, & Planny, 2001).

Studer (2005) recognized how the supervisor provides three types of supervision to school counselors-in-training: clinical, to improve skill; developmental, to enhance self-efficacy and identity; and administrative, to ensure service delivered to support student success in an accountable and integrated manner to meet the academic, career, and social/personal domains of the ASCA National Model (ASCA, 2005). Page, Pietrzak, and Sutton (2001) reported findings from a random sample of practicing school counselors holding memberships in ASCA that indicated administrative supervision was most often received from school administrators who may not be well versed in contemporary models of counseling delivery in school settings and was more common than clinical supervision. Competence in all these types of supervision is critical to the education and training of competent school counselors.

The School Counseling Supervision Model (SCSM)

Luke and Bernard (2006) proposed the school counseling supervision model, an adaptation of the social role discrimination model (Bernard, 1997), wherein a $3 \times 3 \times 4$ matrix is used to describe the changing roles of *teacher, counselor,* and *consultant* assumed by supervisors as supervisees develop. The focus of supervision is identified as three types of skills: *intervention* (delivery of counseling observable behaviors); *conceptualization* (choice of intervention and organization of goals); and *personalization* (therapeutic use of the self). The four points of entry into supervision included *large group intervention, counseling and consultation, individual and group advisement,* and *planning, coordination, and evaluation.* This model is particularly unique in its correlation with a comprehensive school counseling program and in its utility with both school counselors-in-training and practicing school counselors. As has been previously stated, the supervision issue is twofold, inclusive of student and practitioner needs.

The Goals, Functions, Roles, and Systems Model (GRFS)

Wood and Rayle (2006) detailed a model to prepare school counselors-in-training for the multitude of responsibilities they will perform. Both the direct applicability for school counseling and its emphasis on the interaction of individuals and systems, distinguish this approach from others. The working alliance model of supervision (Bordin, 1983) provided the basis for the *goals* aspect of this approach. Wood and Rayle (2006) expand Bordin's (1983) eight goals of supervision to be school counseling specific and they are as follows: (1) provide a *leadership* role that enhances the school mission; (2) promote *advocacy* through skills to intervene with special populations/students; (3) generate *collaboration* with all stakeholders; (4) engage in data-driven *assessment* and programming in all ASCA domains; (5) provide *system support* for the school's functioning; (6) deliver effective *individual planning* to students, (7) create and implement a successful *guidance curriculum;* and (8) deliver skillful *responsive services*—counseling and crisis management (p. 258). Individual behavioral outcomes are encouraged.

The *functions* aspect of this approach referred to supervisory functions first proposed by Holloway (1995) and included *monitoring/evaluating, instructing, advising, modeling, consulting, supporting,* and *sharing.* The five primary roles for supervisors of school counselors included *evaluator, adviser, coordinator, teacher,* and *mentor.* "The functions of supervision are accomplished when supervisor roles are put into action" (Wood & Rayle, 2006, p. 260). Inherent in this model is the idea that *roles* are enacted within a *system* context that influences those roles.

This approach holds promise for reinforcing the multifaceted aspects of the ASCA National Model (2005) and is especially supportive of the identity and resultant roles and tasks imbedded in the model. For schools where the transformation toward the national model is incomplete, this model may have less utility. It does, however, offer a new vision of school counseling specific supervision.

Initiatives for School Counselors Lacking Educational Backgrounds

Many students enter the school counseling specialty course of study without undergraduate teacher preparation and are, therefore, less identified with the culture of the school environment. Peterson and Deuschle (2006) discussed how "both teachers and nonteachers need and deserve guidance related to entering the school culture as counselors" (p. 268). Several research studies supported the importance of preparation for entry into the climate and context of the school (Littrell & Peterson, 2005). The Peterson-Deuschle model (2006) addressed these five aspects for training and supervision of students with no previous educational experience: *information, immersion, observation, structure,* and *awareness.* The authors of this approach stated that "by the end of an internship, there is little or no difference between teachers and non-teachers in their confidence and competence as school counselors" (p. 270).

The *information* aspect of the model was described as the education given to site supervisors and school administrators about how the professional developmental learning curve for nonteachers will be different from their teacher counterparts and how the sponsoring university will address the issues. School policies and protocols would likely be unfamiliar to nonteachers but could be made explicit for the intern. *Immersion referred* to the need for nonteachers to clock as much school experience as possible, beginning with practicum and moving through internship. *Observation* of classroom teachers, of children and adolescents within the school context, and of the school as a "culture" was recommended as a way to impact credibility and learn cultural norms and expectations (Peterson & Deuschle, 2006, p. 272).

Structure was defined as the establishment of learning goals, expectations, and supervisory methodologies. The authors suggested that faculty supervisors might assist site supervisors in structuring times for meetings with interns and establishing agendas to forward the learning for trainees. Reflective questions were recommended to facilitate professional development. "The meeting can give regular attention to the questions, concerns, pertinent strengths and limitations, insights, and anxieties of the school counselor-in-training" (Peterson & Deuschle, 2006, p. 277). *Awareness* was defined as a component for the supervision of nonteachers who may have gaps in knowledge around classroom management/lesson delivery and developmental understanding pertinent to K–12 students. These skills might be highlighted through initial small group delivery to give a less intimidating experience to the nonteacher. Campus and on-site supervision could be structured to give encouraging but honest feedback to the trainee about their initial work with children and adolescents. Peterson and Dueschle (2006) offered potential indicators of proficiency on the three components of *immersion, awareness, and observation* and encouraged student assessments on a continuum of *emerging, progressing, or proficient* (p. 279).

Case-Based Attempts to Address Challenges in School Counseling Supervision

Several contemporary models of supervision specific to school counseling (Kahn, 1999; Nelson & Johnson, 1999; Peterson & Deuschle, 2006; Studer, 2005; Wood & Rayle, 2006) provide excellent general road maps for supervisors. These models, however, can be abstract and comprehensive, offering few concrete examples that illustrate the challenges that supervisors face when working with supervisees placed in school settings. This section attempts to address supervision challenges using a case-based focus. To provide a bridge from cases to theory, several commentaries about the illustrations will address how practice speaks to theory. Inasmuch as some challenges originate with supervisors while others with supervisees, both sources will be addressed.

Supervisors

A university professor who is unfamiliar of the norms, expectations, and policies of a particular school may fail to take such contextual factors into account when supervising an intern or practicum student's work. This can be especially disconcerting to the supervisee if the university professor and the site-supervising school counselor hold different views about professional behavior and appropriate counseling practices. This problem has been noted by Remley and Herlihy (2007) who observed that supervisors may lack a comprehensive understanding of the school setting, population, needs, context, and tasks of the school counselor. The following case example will illustrate this.

Kyla's first practicum placement was with Ms. Harris at Parker Elementary. Ms. Harris typically allows students to bring a friend or two whenever they request time with her. After several weeks of co-counseling with Ms. Harris, Kyla continues with this practice. She turns in her first transcript that details this practice. The university supervisor asks Kyla if she obtained informed consent from the student who requested to see her. Kyla said no, this was not a customary practice of her supervising school counselor. The university professor pressed her with this question, "Did you obtain any form of consent that accounted for the 'friends' of the counselee?" "No," Kyla replied, "This is not done by the school counselor." The professor asks, "Don't you think having other students present might inhibit the student's self-disclosure, let alone pose serious ethical issues?" At this point, Kyla breaks down and asks if she has ruined her chances of continuing in the program. In addition, Kyla worries that she will be caught in the middle of a conflict between the professor and the school counselor–supervisor.

It is incumbent upon all supervisors to be familiar with the norms, expectations, rules, and policies of their supervisee's placements. Coker (2004) stated, "Collaboration between a university and a school district is the hallmark of a professional development school" (p. 265). Wood and Rayle's (2006) model, which includes goals, functions, roles, and systems (GFRS), explicitly acknowledged the importance of context and roles in supervision. They state, "site supervisors and the university (counselor educator program) must be continually aware of the influence of systems on the supervisory process" (p. 261). Moreover, one of the GFRS suppositions asserted, "shared agreement about the activities, expectations, and optimum outcomes that are negotiated between the university supervisor, site supervisor (school counselor), and school counselor-in-training (SCIT) is the key to successful supervision experience" (p. 256). Thus, at a minimum, a meeting of site and university supervisors should be held at the beginning of each term, followed by regular visits throughout the student's placement. University/college professors should evaluate sites and supervisors to ensure that students will be placed in only those sites that meet professional standards. Similarly, site supervisors and students should have an opportunity to provide summative evaluation of university/college supervisors.

Another potential area that can compromise the effectiveness of supervision is theoretical intolerance by supervisors. This is especially troublesome because the research findings comparing outcomes of different theoretical models have consistently found no significant differences (Miller, Duncan, & Hubble, 1997). In addition, autonomy is a fundamental principle evident in most ethical codes and standards (Cottone & Tarvydas, 2007; Remley & Herlihy, 2007; Sperry, 2007). The following case example illustrates supervisor intolerance.

Mr. Evans, a middle school counselor, observed an intern, Rachelle, work with a student named Janice. Janice was referred because several of her teachers saw her as lonely and somewhat depressed.

Mr. Evans: You seemed somewhat tentative with Janice. I mean you used too many basic listening skills like paraphrases, summaries, reflections of feelings, and the like.

Rachelle: Yes, I suppose so. I have always liked the person-centered approach, which is the model I was using.

Mr. Evans: That won't work in a school setting. You need to learn about how to use a short-term model that goes for behavior change as quick as possible.

Rachelle: I have studied such models in my classes, but for me that just seems so controlling. Besides, I feel I offered high levels of the core conditions to Janice and that this was crucial to gain her trust and to synchronize with her shy disposition.

Mr. Evans: Look, ask her if being a loner is getting her what she wants.

Rachelle: Okay, I am familiar with the model I think you are referring to, and I will address goals, once I am confident she is ready for such a focus.

Counselors should work from a theoretical framework, but as Corey (2005) asserted, the selection of theory is a personal choice, and a choice that can be integrative. Rachelle has made her choice and is not asking for alternatives. With experience, if she is typical of most practitioners (Norcross & Beutler, 2008), she may be integrative in theory and eclectic in the use of techniques. A transtheoretical perspective based on common factors is also a viable alternative to pure models (Hubble, Duncan, & Miller, 1999; Prochaska, & Norcross, 2003) and has been applied to the school setting (Murphy, 1999). If Mr. Evans had suggested that Rachelle get the proper training for school counseling by working under him, for a fee, to secure certification for his model of counseling, an even more egregious violation would have been committed. In that case, not only would autonomy have been disregarded, misuse of power for personal gain would have been at play.

Role-playing is a viable way to model skills, but supervisors should be alert to the possibility that a novice can be overwhelmed by the supervisor's superior skills. A loss of self-efficacy can result. The research on this question has generally confirmed that mastery models are less effective than are coping models (Bandura, 1986). A typical scenario in this case goes something like this. The supervisor listens to the supervisee describe a case and waits for evidence that the neophyte is uncertain how to proceed. Springing into action, the supervisor says, "Let's role-play how you might work with a student with a borderline personality disorder. I will be the therapist, you be your client. Just respond like you think he would." The role-played vignette unfolds, and the counselor displays mature, confident skills. Subsequently, the supervisee applauds the supervisor, declaring, "Gee whiz, you are so good, so smooth. I don't believe I could ever think on my feet like that." There are several problems potentially wrong with this example of supervision. First, was the supervisor or the supervisee's needs met? Did the supervisee acquire new skills? Was the supervisee's level of confidence strengthened or lessened? Perhaps these questions could be answered in a positive way if other aspects of the supervision were included, rehearsal as an example, and if there were a greater focus on the supervisee. As it stands, this is an example of weak, if not harmful, supervision.

Supervisors also face the challenge of walking a fine line between offering too little encouragement and overlooking, or failing to address, critical shortcomings in the supervisee's work. Perhaps the guide here is the behavioral principle of successive approximations (Skinner, 1953), or, more colloquially stated, the use of the sandwich technique. An example of supervision that is too lean with support follows.

Supervisor: I think you used an adult vocabulary with this child—she clearly didn't understand much of what you had to say.
Supervisee: Okay, I will work on that.
Supervisor: And your dress. It is much too informal for our school.
Supervisee: I will remember that in the future. I don't have time to change after work, but I can take my school dress with me next time.

Each of the supervisor's points was relevant, but the weight of so many faultfinding observations, one stacked on top of another, might overwhelm and deflate a fledgling supervisee. An example of supervision to lean on substance, and somewhat patronizing in focus, follows.

Supervisor: Well, what is your take on your session with Alice?
Supervisee: I wasn't sure just how to reach her level, I mean to talk at her level.

Supervisor: You needn't worry about that—these kids know more than we realize.

Supervisee: I feel a bit out of place here ... way younger than most of the teachers.

Supervisor: Not a problem, in fact, I love seeing how the new generation dresses.

Supporting and sharing are integral dimensions in Holloway's (1995) model and the functions dimension of Wood and Rayle (2006) model. Wood and Rayle (2006) wrote, "Sometimes SCITs need caring and encouragement. . . . This is the core of the supporting function in supervision." (p. 260). An equally important facet of supervision, however, is monitoring and evaluation, which is also a dimension of GRFS (Wood & Rayle, 2006). Drawing on Corey's (2008) observations about feedback in group work, effective feedback should be: concise rather than global, timely, nonjudgmental in tone, directed toward those behaviors that can be changed, and reinforcing as well as changing behavior. It is wise to provide positive feedback before giving corrective suggestions (the sandwich approach), and corrective feedback is best received after the supervisor–supervisee bond is strong (Bordin, 1983; Ladany, Friedlander, & Nelson, 2005).

Additional areas where supervisors might create challenges include the following failures: to collaboratively set goals with supervisees; to maintain appropriate role boundaries, (e.g., alternating between a supervisory and therapeutic role; and to act in areas beyond clinical supervision that is, being willing to advise, teach, or mentor as appropriate). Bradley and Ladany's (2001) text on supervision offered an excellent model that differentiated the multiple roles that a supervisor assumes. The following dialogue will illustrate each of these areas:

Supervisee: My professor said you and I should define a plan, a set of goals for my work with you this semester.

Supervisor: Well, you will learn what you need to know by just being here, day by day, and seeing what I do.

Supervisee: Okay, but I wanted you to know that I may be late next week on Tuesday because I am meeting with my attorney regarding my divorce.

Supervisor: I'm sorry to hear about that. Would you like to talk about this?

Supervisee: No, I have a counselor, but I am worried about getting a job once I finish this semester. Could you give me some ideas about how to prepare a portfolio to enter the school counseling job market?

Supervisor: I suggest you go to the placement office of your college. They can help you with that—I haven't been in the job market for ages.

Although this illustration may seem atypical of how site supervisors might function, it dramatizes how supervision missteps might unfold. On the other hand, given how school counseling has struggled to solidify a professional identity (Dollarhide & Miller, 2006), and that many school counselors function in isolation (Matthes, 1992), this illustration may underscore practices that are all too common. Many challenges draw focus on the supervisee. The following section addresses this topic.

Supervisees

Several theorists (Fong, Borders, Ethington, & Pitts, 1998; Granello, 2002; Perry, 1970; Stoltenberg, 1981; Stoltenberg & Delworth, 1987) advocated developmental models that delineate how students learn over time. These models assist supervisors in understanding what supervisees are experiencing and provide clues on how the focus of supervision can synchronize with supervisee readiness. The following dialogue illustrates a student in the dualistic stage (Perry, 1970) and a supervisor who is responsive to that reality.

Supervisee: I didn't know what to say when Raymond mentioned that the teacher was picking on him. What if it is true? What should I say in cases like this? What if I agree with the student and the student tells the teacher? Please, what would you say?

Supervisor: Let's brainstorm your options. What theory comes to mind as you reflect on the process and goals with a student?

Supervisee: I like Adler.

Supervisor: Okay. With that theory in mind, what are your thoughts about how you might intervene with this student at this point?

Supervisee: I guess I would want to focus on behavior and its natural consequences rather than the teacher.

Supervisor: Sounds like a solid idea. So, what might you say at this point?

Supervisee: Something like, "Raymond, let's look at what happens when you act out in class, so we can see the consequences of what you do, okay?" Is that right?

Supervisor: Yes, I think you have found one viable way to work with Raymond. Would you be willing to rewrite the script to hypothetically follow through with this direction?

Supervisee: Sure, I will have it ready next week.

Somewhat unobtrusively, the supervisor avoided reinforcing the student's search for a single, best way to counsel this student. Instead, using Socratic-like questions, the supervisor allowed the student to find their solutions to this case. The next dialogue illustrates a student who exemplifies the multiplistic stage of development (Perry, 1970), which is characterized by a belief that there are no best ways to counsel.

Supervisor: I thought perhaps you used too many questions, back-to-back, on the early part of the tape with the high school senior, Manual.

Supervisee: Yes, but many of the big name theorists use lots of questions. I attended a workshop by Glasser and almost all of his counselor responses were questions.

Supervisor: I see. Yet, could we look at how Manual seems to respond to your questions.

Supervisee: Okay. (Citing the transcript word for word.) Well, I suppose he did seem a bit closed down, but I'm not sure it was because I used too many questions.

Supervisor: Well, perhaps, we could find a segment of your transcript where you didn't use lots of questions, one after another, and see if he is more receptive?

Supervisee: (After reviewing a nonquestioning segment.) Okay. I see your point. I will try to vary my responses more in the future.

Typical of this stage, the supervisee is defensive when the effectiveness of their counseling was in question. The supervisor avoided arguing with the supervisee, and instead, patiently invited the supervisee to engage in collaborative empirical inquiry. A helpful tool when working with a student's transcript is Ivey & Ivey's (2008) microskills template that compares and contrasts skills across 12 theoretical approaches. This tool can help an intern determine if her/his responses are congruent with a theoretical orientation, and thus, keeps the focus of supervision on a professional plane. The third stage of student development in the Perry model (1970) is the relativistic stage wherein students explore how to refine their interventions to be ever more effective given the complete picture of each counselee. The following dialogue illustrates this stage.

Supervisee: I feel that using an imagined dialogue with Ann worked fairly well, but I'm not sure if she didn't see it as too artificial.

Supervisor: Good point. What might you do to bridge the imagined dialogue with another technique that might encourage transfer of training to Ann's life outside the counseling room?

Supervisee: Well, homework comes to mind, of course, but I think having her rehearse how to assert herself would augment the insight we gained by the gestalt, imagined dialogue.

Supervisor: Sounds well conceived. I look forward to reviewing your next tape.

Supervisees who reach the highest level of cognitive development are eager to deepen their understanding of theory and to expand their repertoire of skills. The supervisor's task is to support this motivation in an effort to master the craft of counseling.

Corey (2005) listed several issues beginning counselors typically face. These challenges often are the grist of the supervision mill. Some of the challenges that supervisees must face include the following: coping with high anxiety levels that spring from self-doubt; finding a professional balance that is neither too rigidly role bound nor overly self-disclosing; combating perfectionism; being honest about their limitations; dealing with difficult, demanding, or unmotivated clients; tolerating ambiguity; avoiding overidentification with clients; declining the urge to give advice; avoiding taking too much responsibility for the outcomes of counseling; learning how to select and time techniques effectively; and discovering their own counseling style.

Effective supervision entails a process whereby the supervisee can confront and overcome these challenges. It requires the supervisor to assume multiple roles, including that of mentor, consultant, advisor, role model, and evaluator. This section has illustrated how challenges can be successfully navigated if the supervisor is fully informed about the various facets of the supervisee's context, is tolerant and respectful of the supervisee's right to select the theory of their choice, utilizes coping rather than mastery models, strikes a balance of being supportive and evaluative, and selects appropriate supervision roles. In addition, effective supervision is responsive to the supervisee's stage of development and to the typical challenges of the beginning counselor.

Ethics in School Counseling Supervision

Ethical considerations assume great importance in supervision because of the complexities inherent in this endeavor. Supervisees often answer to multiple supervisors: a university/college professor; a doctoral student who is under the supervision of a professor; a school counselor at the site; and, possibly, an administrator such as a school principal or guidance director. Supervisors must find ways to orchestrate each facet of supervision in ways that protect the interests of students, supervisees, supervisors, organizations, and communities. The developmental levels of supervisees vary (Stoltenberg, McNeill, & Delworth, 1998) as do those of the supervisors (Stoltenberg et al., 1998), thereby creating the possibility of developmental mismatches. Theories of ethics vary (Brincat & Wike, 2000) as do theories of supervision (Sperry, 2007). A supervisor with a relational perspective that is anchored in an ethic of care (Sperry, 2007) approaches supervision quite differently from the supervisor who is guided by a traditional justice model that is grounded in ethical codes and laws.

Fortunately, in spite of the complexities and variable dimensions in supervision, a core body of knowledge regarding ethics in supervision exists to shed light on many of the challenges that arise in clinical supervision. Kitchener's (1984) ethical values, for example, provide a broad-based platform for viewing ethical issues in supervision. These include: autonomy, which fosters a balance of choice and responsibility; nonmaleficence, which serves to avoid and minimize potential harm to students, supervisees, and schools; beneficence, which elevates the process to its highest levels; justice, which leads to fairness and equity; fidelity, which makes the process reliable; integrity, which creates and maintains trust in the process; and respect, which is the cornerstone of professionalism. The publications of several professional organizations address ethics in supervision (American Counseling Association [ACA], 2005; American School Counselor Association [ASCA], 2004; Association for Counselor Education and Supervision [ACES], 1993). Ethical codes and guidelines address core issues in evaluation. These areas include rights and responsibilities of student-clients, supervisees, and supervisors; evaluation of supervisees, plans of remediation, and due process; supervisor competence; and relationship boundaries (ACA, 2005; ACES, 1993; Association for Specialists in Group Work [ASGW], 1998; National Board for Certified Counselors, 1998). The *Ethical Standards for School Counselors* (ASCA, 2004) does not address supervision except for indirect mention of contributions to the profession in Standard F.2. Drawing on the codes and guidelines from these organizations, the next sections will address specific core issues beginning with informed consent.

Informed Consent

Agreements protect students, school-counselor supervisors, supervisees, university/college supervisors and programs, administrative supervisors, and school systems. At the organizational and administrative level, it is common for universities/colleges to have memorandums of agreements with schools to formalize their relationships and expectations. University practica and internships generally include course syllabi detailing expectations and evaluations of students. The school counselor who agrees to supervise an intern should obtain informed consent from the supervisee. Informed consent should be obtained before supervision begins with an agreement that includes the following:

- Supervisor's credentials, relevant experience, supervision theory or style (e.g., relational or traditional);
- General and specific goals and purposes of the supervision;

- Expectations, roles, and responsibilities of the supervisor (e.g., educating, consulting, mentoring, advising, and evaluating), and the supervisee (e.g., individual counseling, testing, large group guidance, small group work, and parent conferences);
- Logistics, that is, frequency of meetings, samples of supervisee's work (audiotapes, videotapes, case notes, and cocounseling), facilities, support material such as DVDs, beginning and ending dates of supervision, and mechanisms for interfacing with college/university supervisor;
- Methods of evaluation, including frequency of formal feedback (summative and formative evaluations), evaluation criteria for purposes of grading or recommendations, and provision for due process and developmental plans should they be needed;
- Risks of counseling under supervision in a new setting, that is, informing supervisees of codes of ethics, legal issues, school and community norms, scheduling challenges with teachers, limits of confidentiality, and so forth;
- Procedures for addressing students in crisis and other emergencies; and
- Procedures to ensure coordination among multiple supervisors.

The following case scenario illustrates the pitfalls of a supervision agreement that was poorly conceived and implemented.

> Enrolling in her first internship, Lupe was assigned to work with Neva, an elementary school counselor at a school having a very diverse student body. Lupe asked her university professor, Dr. Lee, why she was placed at Neva's school. He replied, "You are bilingual and will work well with the student body at that school." Lupe met with Neva the first week of the semester, and Neva oriented her, in general terms, about the school and her typical workday as the school's only counselor. Lupe asked, "I have taken an advanced course in play therapy and would like to use that modality with some of the children I see— would that be okay?" "We don't have time for that kind of counseling, you will see," replied Neva. Neva continued, "We have a pressing deadline to teach all the fourth graders study skills so our school will do well next month when the state mandated exams are taken." "Can we talk about how I can obtain tapes for my internship class?" asked Lupe. Neva retorted, "Don't worry; I will give you a great recommendation. By the way, would you mind dropping off some fifth grade student records to Wilson Middle School on your way home?"

Many questions arise with this scenario: Did the student have a choice about her placement? Was the value of autonomy honored? Did Lupe give informed consent to work with Neva? Did Neva appear to have Lupe's professional development in mind? Would integrity characterize Neva's work with Lupe? This scenario leads to the next topic, boundary issues in supervision.

Boundaries, Multiple Roles, and Conflicts of Interest

Many of the ethical codes regarding supervision parallel those for counseling. Sexual or romantic relationships are prohibited (2005 ACA *Code of Ethics*, Standard F.3.b.) and sexual harassment is neither condoned nor allowed (2005 ACA *Code of Ethics*, Standard F.3.c.). Supervising close relatives and friends of the supervisee is to be avoided (2005 ACA *Code of Ethics*, Standard F.3.d.). The following guidelines for supervisors capture the essential elements of appropriate boundaries:

- Avoid multiple roles with supervisees whenever possible, but if circumstances necessitate that you must assume multiple roles, openly discuss the ramifications of such an arrangement with your supervisee and minimize any actions that would compromise the goals of supervision, for example, if a supervisee pulls the focus of supervision toward counseling, assume that role only briefly and refer the supervisee elsewhere for help.
- Be aware of the power differential inherent in the supervisory relationship and guard against exploitation of that difference for personal gain.
- Be a role model of professionalism by referring to codes of ethics when reviewing cases.
- Be consistent in keeping appointments, anchor knowledge in research, and continually refresh your skills and knowledge.
- Openly address issues of diversity as they might affect the supervisory relationship and the supervisee's work with students.
- Seek out consultation from a professional peer whenever you become aware of thoughts or feelings that might compromise your judgment or responsibilities, for example, having strong feelings of attraction for a supervisee.
- Establish and maintain an open exchange of ideas with supervisees to minimize misunderstandings.

Although boundary violations defy codes of ethics, it is critical that supervisors establish a working alliance with supervisees; otherwise, supervisees may withhold critical information that could prove damaging to student-clients, the supervisee, and the supervisor. Legally, this holds true because of vicarious liability (Disney & Stevens, 1994) wherein supervisors can be held responsible for the actions of their supervisees. In addition,

Sperry (2007) advanced a compelling argument that relational supervision is an enlightening and effective style of supervision. The following scenario addresses boundary and relationship issues in supervision.

> Holt Elementary is a new school staffed by young and social teachers. Jill was very pleased when Tammy, the school counselor, agreed to serve as her supervisor during the fall semester. Jill approached Tammy because she is a close friend of her roommate. After about three weeks into her placement at Holt, Tammy said, "Jill, a counselor works closely with teachers, so it is really important to hang out with them sometimes. Many of us go out for drinks on Fridays after school. I would like to invite you to join us." Somewhat taken off guard, Jill said she would check her schedule and let Tammy know on Thursday. Jill felt conflicted about this invitation. Her course in ethics had made it quite clear that professional boundaries should remain sacrosanct. On the other hand, she really liked Tammy, who was single like herself, and she didn't want to offend her by refusing her offer. Jill agreed and attended the event with Tammy and four of Holt's teachers. Time passed and only Tammy and Jill were left at the establishment. Tammy said, "I'm really hungry, how about the two of us going for dinner at the new steak place down the street." "Fine with me," replied Jill and off they went to dinner. After having another drink at the restaurant, Tammy tired a bit and said, "I want to confide in you about something really troubling me. I am dating a man whose child is a client of mine at Holt. I really love him, but I am racked with guilt and I'm not sure if it's affecting my counseling work. I don't know what to do." Jill attempted to console Tammy and they parted after dinner.

This case is flagrant but perhaps not that uncommon. The following questions come to mind: If Jill were to disclose this occurrence to her university supervisor, what obligations would the professor have? Would disclosure of this by Jill to her professor violate Tammy's rights to confidentiality? How might this boundary violation affect Tammy's willingness to evaluate Jill's work? How difficult might it be for Tammy and Jill to face each other with this disclosure as a backdrop? Would this constitute a clear example of supervisor impairment? This case leads to another core issue in supervision, evaluation of supervisees.

Evaluation and Due Process

One of the ways supervision differs from counseling is that supervision is the inherent evaluative component. In addition to their roles as a teacher, mentor, and role model, supervisors are the gatekeepers for the profession.

Kitchener's (1984) ethical values play a key role in evaluation. The process should be fair and just, should allow for autonomy when feasible, should strive to do no harm, should be sensitive to multicultural issues, and should aspire to high levels of professional development. Informed consent launches the process and heads it in the right direction. The following guidelines help ensure that evaluations in supervision are ethical and legal.

- Informed consent is obtained, the goals of supervision are specified by mutual agreement, and the criteria by which the supervisee will be evaluated are identified.
- The rights and responsibilities of both supervisees and supervisors are clearly defined and consistently followed.
- Feedback regarding the supervisee's performance is frequent and specific and is both formative and summative.
- If the supervisee's performance fails to meet minimal standards as defined by the criteria established, a remedial plan is developed and implemented.
- Due process is afforded to the supervisee if a negative evaluation is received.
- Evaluations take multicultural factors into account such that bias or unexamined assumptions are minimized.
- Supervisees are assigned to approved sites that have adequate facilities.
- Supervisees are supported in their right to select well-established theories, even if choice differs from the supervisor. If incompatibility would impede supervision, an alternative supervisor is selected.

Evaluation is a high stakes process. Career aspirations can be supported or dashed. The profession can be honored or can be compromised. The following scenario highlights how evaluation can pose challenging issues.

Ted is a student in a 48-hour, CACREP-approved master's program. He has passed all of his classes and is currently enrolled in a practicum located at a school site. During his coursework, his professors gave him extra time on exams in a distraction-free environment after the university documented that he had a learning disability. Early in his practicum, however, it became clear to the school-based supervisor and the university supervisor that he could not respond in a timely fashion to the topics and issues brought to him by his counselees. As a consequence of his inability to "think on his feet," his tapes failed to demonstrate that he could establish purposeful direction or substance in his individual or group counseling. He did well in presenting structured guidance lessons. A remedial plan was established and followed, but unfortunately, by the end of the semester, little improvement was evident. His supervisors attempted to explore other career options with him, but to no avail. With the semester coming to a close, a summative evaluation and a final grade were required. With great agony, both supervisors recommended that Ted be given an incomplete grade with the opportunity to continue next semester. Ted objected to this proposal and threatened to file a grievance against both supervisors.

This case illustrates how difficult evaluation can be and how even the coordinated efforts of two supervisors can fail to deter a supervisee from feeling unfairly judged. Many questions arise. Should the coursework leading up to a field placement include performance criteria that identify students who may be ill-suited for the counseling profession? Was the proposal to allow more time for the student to improve too lenient given that a remedial plan has been tried without success? Should more have been done to find ways to accommodate the student's special needs? If the student's grievance was successful and this resulted in a passing grade and graduation, would either supervisor be justified in giving the student a positive recommendation for a counseling position or school counseling certification?

Other Ethical Considerations

Supervisor competence and diversity issues are very relevant to supervision. The Association for Counselor Education and Supervision (1993) identified four functions of supervision: monitoring client welfare, ensuring compliance to ethical, legal, and professional standards in counseling, monitoring performance and development of supervisees, and evaluating supervisees for academic, placement, employment, and credentialing purposes. Sperry (2007) cited several reasons why a supervisor might fail at one or more of these functions. These include inadequate training, lack of experience, and inflexibility. Supervisory impairment denotes a slightly different deficit. Impairment often involves a diminished ability to perform due to a medical condition, substance abuse, personality/emotional problems, legal or ethical violations, or burnout. Supervisor impairment can have deleterious effects on supervisees, including emotional distress and career indecision (Muratori, 2001). Key antidotes to supervisor incompetence or impairment include involvement in professional organizations at the local and national levels, close collaboration with colleagues on a regular basis, a consistent program of personal wellness, and active participation in continuing education.

Supervisors and supervisees bring their contextual histories to their work together. Thus, their dialogue reflects cultural factors such as gender, age, race, class, religion, ethnicity, and sexual orientation. Given the power differential between the supervisor and the supervisee, it is imperative that supervisors guard against imposing their values on supervisees. Rather, issues of diversity should be brought out and explored. Supervisors should encourage supervisees to examine how their backgrounds influence their work with students. The following case scenario will illustrate how diversity plays a major role in counseling.

> Corina, who is in her first semester as a practicum student at a local elementary school, was asked to see a 10-year-old girl, Angie, because the teacher thought Angie had become quite sad and lethargic since the loss of her grandmother. Corina used expressive techniques with Angie and after several sessions, Angie seemed to be more animated and alert in class. When Corina saw Angie for the fourth time, Angie asked if Corina would pray with her. Corina agreed and suggested the prayer be silent. After several minutes of silence, Angie asked, "Do you believe in heaven? Do you think I will see my grandmother ever again when I go to heaven?" Corina was taken aback by this focus as she worried that religious issues fell outside her training and her role as a counselor. Corina evaded Angie's questions and refocused Angie's attention on a book Angie had been assigned to read about grief. In discussing this case with her supervisor, Corina revealed that she was raised as a Catholic but had renounced religion in general because her experiences in a private Catholic school had been traumatically punitive. Corina and her supervisor explored how Corina's history with religion played a role in her indecisiveness with Angie. They discussed how topics such as religion could be addressed in counseling in ways that take into consideration the counselor's beliefs and values.

Summary

Ethics play a major role in the supervision of school counselors. Critical issues include obtaining informed consent, clarifying and honoring appropriate boundaries and roles, and providing ongoing feedback to ensure that evaluations are fair and accurate, allowing for due process as needed. Supervisor competence is assured through training, experience, and professional involvement. Diversity issues are addressed in the supervision process and are featured as an important aspect of the supervisee's training. As explained in the history section, supervision in school settings is often all too infrequent, but when such occasions occur, the challenges and ethical issues inherent in the process provide the profession a rich menu of choices.

Conclusion

Herlihy et al. (2002) poignantly described the current status of school supervision as neglected, unmet, unlikely, and perceived as unnecessary. Supervision to both students in training and practitioners is an opportunity for counselor educators and researchers to envision models and methods specific to a school environment. The emerging transformation of the profession of school counseling must be met with structures of supervision that address the unique aspects of the ASCA National Model (2005) and the parallel specialty requirements of nationally accredited school counseling programs (Council for Accreditation of Counseling and Related Educational Programs, 2009). As Dollarhide and Miller (2006) stated, "renewed awareness of and appreciation for supervision as a means of professional identity development will enhance the clarity of professional roles and functions of school counselors" (p. 250).

Promising models of clinical supervision within the school context are emerging and this chapter examines a few. Group supervision approaches may assist in meeting the supervision needs of veteran school counselors (Linton & Deushle, 2006). Models that account for the clinical, developmental, and administrative aspects of the supervision of school counselors-in-training are critical to building professional competence (Studer, 2005). Existing supervision models might be adapted to specifically correlate with a comprehensive school counseling program with the roles, skills, goals, and functions unique to the educational system (Luke & Bernard, 2006; Wood & Rayle, 2006). Initiatives for responding to school counselors-in-training who lack teaching backgrounds can support the preparation for entry into the unique climate and culture of the school (Peterson & Deuschle, 2006). Finally, case-based scenarios presented in this chapter represent concrete examples of the challenges in school counseling supervision and the ethics and legalities within this area.

The demands of school counseling for the twenty-first century are vast (Baker & Gerler, 2008). School counselors will be challenged to respond to a greater complexity of issues within the K–12 population, to provide culturally sensitive responses to a more diverse clientele, to increase student success in school years and in the transition to the world of work, and to practice a transformed identity for the profession of school counseling. Most assuredly, there is a need for guidance, modeling, and evaluative feedback as the developmental process unfolds from initial graduate education through contribution as a practicing school counselor.

References

Akos, P., & Scarborough, J. L. (2004). An examination of the clinical preparation of school counselors. *Counselor Education & Supervision, 44*(2), 96–107.

American Counseling Association. (2005). The *ACA code of ethics*. Alexandria, VA: Author.

American School Counselor Association. (2004). *Ethical standards for school counselors*. Alexandria, VA: Author.

American School Counselor Association. (2005). *The ASCA national model: A framework for school counseling programs* (2nd ed.). Alexandria, VA: Author.

Association for Counselor Education and Supervision. (1993). ACES ethical guidelines for counseling supervisors. *ACES Spectrum, 53*, 5–8.

Association for Specialists in Group Work. (1998). *Best practices guidelines*. Alexandria, VA: Author.

Baker, S. B., & Gerler, E. R. (2008). *School counseling for the twenty-first century* (5th ed.). Upper Saddle River, NJ: Pearson Education, Inc.

Bandura, A. (1986). *Social foundations of thought and action: A social cognitive theory*. Englewood Cliffs, NJ: Prentice-Hall.

Barret, R. L., & Schmidt, J. J. (1986). School counselor certification and supervision: Overlooked professional issues. *Counselor Education & Supervision, 26*, 50–55.

Benshoff, J. M., & Paisley, P. O. (1996). The structured peer consultation model for school counselors. *Journal of Counseling & Development, 74*, 314–318.

Bernard, J. M. (1997). The discrimination model. In C. E. Watkins, Jr. (Ed.). *Handbook of psychotherapy supervision* (pp. 310–327). New York, NY: Wiley.

Bernard, J. M., & Goodyear, R. K. (2009). *Fundamentals of clinical supervision* (3rd ed.). Boston, MA: Allyn & Bacon.

Borders, L. D., & Usher, C. H. (1992). Post-degree supervision: Existing and preferred practices. *Journal of Counseling & Development, 70*, 594–599.

Bordin, E. S. (1983). A working alliance based model of supervision. *The Counseling Psychologist, 11*, 35–42.

Boyd, J. D., & Walter, P. B. (1975). The school counselor, the cactus, and supervision. *The School Counselor, 23*, 103–107.

Bradley, L., & Ladany, N. (2001). *Counselor supervision: Principles, process, and practice*. Philadelphia, PA: Taylor & Frances.

Brewer, J. M. (1924). *The vocational guidance movement: Its problems and possibilities*. New York, NY: McMillan.

Brincat, C., & Wike, V. (2000). *Morality and the professional life: Values at work*. Upper Saddle River, NJ: Prentice-Hall.

Coker, K. (2004). Conducting a school-based practicum: A collaborative model. *Professional School Counseling, 7*(4), 263–267.

Corey, G. (2005). *Theory and practice of counseling & psychotherapy* (7th ed.). Belmont, CA: Brooks/Cole.

Corey, G. (2008). *Theory and practice of group counseling* (7th ed.). Belmont, CA: Brooks/Cole.

Cottone, R. R., & Tarvydas, V. M. (2007). *Counseling ethics and decision making* (3rd ed.). Upper Saddle River, NJ: Merrill/Prentice-Hall.

Council for Accreditation of Counseling and Related Educational Programs. (2009, January 27). *The 2009 standards.* Retrieved from http://67.199.126.156/doc/2009%20Standards.pdf

Crespi, T. D. (2003). Special section—Clinical supervision in the schools: Challenges, opportunities, and lost horizons. *Clinical Supervisor, 22*(1), 59–73.

Crespi, T. D., & Fischetti, B. A. (1998, September). Clinical supervision in the schools: Forlorn, forgotten, or forsaken? *Counseling Today, 41,* 8, 19.

Crutchfield, L. B., & Borders, L. D. (1997). Impact of two clinical peer supervision models on practicing school counselors. *Journal of Counseling & Development, 75,* 219–230.

Davis, T. E. (2006). Looking forward to going back: A school counselor educator's return to school counseling. *Professional School Counseling, 10*(2), 217–223.

Disney, M., & Stevens, A. (1994). *Legal issues in clinical supervision.* Alexandria, VA: American Counseling Association.

Dollarhide, C. T., & Miller, G. M. (2006). Supervision for preparation and practice of school counselors: Pathways to excellence. *Counselor Education & Supervision, 45*(4), 242–252.

Fitch, J. A. (1936). Professional standards in guidance. *Occupations, 14,* 760–765.

Fischetti, B. A., & Lines, C. L. (2003). Views from the field: Models for school-based clinical supervision. *Clinical Supervisor, 22*(1), 75–86.

Fong, M. L., Borders, L. D., Ethington, C. A., & Pitts, J. H. (1998). Becoming a counselor: A longitudinal study of student cognitive development. *Counselor Education and Supervision, 38,* 100–114.

Furr, S. R., & Carroll, J. J. (2003). Critical incidents in student counselor development. *Journal of Counseling & Development, 81,* 483–489.

Granello, D. H. (2002). Assessing the cognitive development of counseling students: Changes and epistemological assumptions. *Counselor Education and Supervision, 41,* 279–292.

Hatch, T. (2008, September 12). Professional challenges in school counseling: Organizational, institutional and political. *Journal of School Counseling, 6*(22). Retrieved from http://www.jsc.montana.edu/articles/v6n22.pdf

Hayes, R. L., & Paisley, P. O. (2002). Transforming school counselor preparation programs. *Theory into Practice, 41,* 169–176.

Henderson, P., & Lampe, R. E. (1992). Clinical supervision of school counselors. *The School Counselor, 39,* 151–157.

Herlihy, B., Gray, N., & McCollum, V. (2002). Legal and ethical issues in school counselor supervision. *Professional School Counseling, 6*(1), 55–60.

Holloway, E. L. (1995). *Clinical supervision: A systems approach.* Thousand Oaks, CA: Sage.

Hubble, M. A., Duncan, B. L., & Miller, S. D. (1999). *The heart and soul of change: What works in therapy.* Washington, DC: American Psychological Association.

Ivey, A. E., & Ivey, M. B. (2008). *Essentials of intentional interviewing: Counseling in a multicultural world.* Belmont, CA: Thomson Higher Education.

Kahn, B. B. (1999). Priorities and practices in field supervision of school counseling students. *Professional School Counseling, 3,* 128–136.

Kitchener, K. (1984). Intuition, critical evaluation, and ethical principles: The foundation for ethical decisions in counseling psychology. *Counseling Psychologist, 12,* 43–55.

Ladany, N., Friedlander, M. L., & Nelson, M. L. (2005). *Critical events in psychotherapy supervision: An interpersonal approach.* Washington, DC: American Psychological Association.

Linton, J. M., & Deuschle, C. J. (2006, May 2). Meeting school counselors' supervision needs: Four models of group supervision. *Journal of School Counseling, 4*(6). Retrieved from http://www.jsc.montana.edu/articles/v4n6.pdf

Littrell, J. M., & Peterson, J. S. (2005). *Portrait and model of a school counselor.* Boston, MA: Houghton Mifflin/Lahaska Press.

Luke, M., & Bernard, J. M. (2006). The school counseling supervision model: An extension of the discrimination model. *Counselor Education & Supervision, 45*(4), 282–295.

Magnuson, S., Norem, K., & Bradley, L. J. (2001). Supervising school counselors. In L. J. Bradley & N. Ladany (Eds.), *Counselor supervision: Principles, process, and practice* (3rd ed., pp. 207–221). Philadelphia, PA: Brunner-Routledge.

Matthes, W. A. (1992). Induction of counselors into the profession. *The School Counselor, 39,* 245–250.

Miller, S. D., Duncan, B. L., & Hubble, M. A. (1997). *Escape from Babel: Toward a unifying language for psychotherapy practice.* New York, NY: W. W. Norton.

Muratori, M. (2001). Examining supervisor impairment from the counselor trainee's perspective. *Counselor Education and Supervision, 41,* 41–57.

Murphy, J. J. (1999). Common factors of school-based change. In M. A. Hubble, B. L. Duncan, & S. D. Miller, *The heart and soul of change: What works in therapy.* Washington, DC: American Psychological Association.

Murphy, S., & Kaffenberger, C. (2007). ASCA national model [R]: The foundation for supervision of practicum and internship students. *Professional School Counseling, 10*(3), 289–296.

National Board for Certified Counselors. (1998). The *ACS code of ethics.* Greensboro, NC: Author.

Nelson, M. D., & Johnson, P. (1999). School counselors as supervisors: An integrated approach for supervising school counseling interns. *Counselor Education and Supervision, 39,* 80–100.

Norcross, J. C., & Beutler, L. E. (2008). Integrative psychotherapies. In R. J. Corsini & D. Wedding, *Current psychotherapies* (8th ed.). Belmont, CA: Brooks/Cole.

Oberman, A. (2005). Effective clinical supervision for professional school counselors. *Guidance & Counseling, 20*(3/4), 147–151.

Page, B., Pietrzak, D., & Sutton, J., Jr. (2001). National survey of school counselor supervision. *Counselor Education & Supervision, 41,* 142–150.

Peace, S. D., & Sprinthall, N. A. (1998). Training school counselors to supervise beginning counselors: Theory, research, and practice. *Professional School Counseling, 1*(5), 2–8.

Perera-Diltz, D. M., & Mason, K. L. (2008, September 18). Ideal to real: Duties performed by school counselors. *Journal of School Counseling, 6*(26). Retrieved from http://www.jsc.montana.edu/articles/v6n26.pdf

Perry, W. G., Jr. (1970). *Forms of intellectual and ethical development in the college years.* New York, NY: Holt, Rinehart, & Winston.

Peterson, J. S., & Deuschle, C. (2006). A model for supervising school counseling students without teaching experience. *Counselor Education and Supervision, 45,* 267–281.

Prochaska, J. O., & Norcross, J. C. (2003). *Systems of psychotherapy: A transtheoretical analysis* (5th ed.). Belmont, CA: Brooks/Cole.

Protivnak, J. J., & Davis, T. E. (2008, May 7). The impact of the supervision relationship on the behaviors of school counseling interns. *Journal of School Counseling, 6*(19). Retrieved from http://www.jsc.montana.edu/articles/v6n19.pdf

Rayle, A. D., & Adams, J. R. (2007, March 19). An exploration of 21st century school counselors' daily work activities. *Journal of School Counseling, 5*(8). Retrieved from http://www.jsc.montana.edu/articles/v5n8.pdf

Remley, T. P., & Herlihy, B. (2007). *Ethical, legal, and professional issues in counseling.* (2nd ed.). Upper Saddle River, NJ: Merrill and Prentice Hall.

Scarborough, J. L., & Culbreth, J. R. (2008). Examining discrepancies between actual and preferred practice of school counselors. *Journal of Counseling & Development, 86,* 446–459.

Skinner, B. F. (1953). *Science and human behavior.* New York, NY: Macmillan & Co.

Somody, C., Henderson, P., Cook, K., & Zambrano, E. (2008). A working system of school counselor supervision. *Professional School Counseling, 12*(1), 22–33.

Sperry, L. (2007). *The ethical and professional practice of counseling and psychotherapy.* New York, NY: Pearson.

Stoltenberg, C. D. (1981). Approaching supervision from a developmental perspective: The counselor complexity model. *Journal of Counseling Psychology, 28,* 59–65.

Stoltenberg, C. D., & Delworth, U. (1987). *Supervising counselors and therapists.* San Francisco, CA: Jossey-Bass.

Stoltenberg, C. D., McNeill, B., & Delworth, U. (1998). *IDM supervision: An integrated developmental model for supervising counselors and therapists.* San Francisco, CA: Jossey-Bass.

Studer, J. R. (2005). Supervising school counselors-in-training: A guide for field supervisors. *Professional School Counseling, 8*(4), 353–359.

Whiting, P. P., Bradley, L. J., & Planny, K. (2001). Supervision-based developmental models of counselor supervision. In L. Bradley & N. Ladany, *Counselor supervision: Principles, process and practice* (3rd ed., pp. 125–146). Philadelphia, PA: Taylor & Francis.

Wilkerson, K. (2006). Peer supervision for the professional development of school counselors: Toward an understanding of terms and findings. *Counselor Education & Supervision, 46*(1), 59–67.

Wood, C., & Rayle, A. D. (2006). A model of school counseling supervision: The goals, functions, roles, and systems model. *Counselor Education and Supervision, 45,* 253–266.

CHAPTER 11

Supervision of Career Counseling

M. KRISTINE BRONSON

> You will come to a place where the streets are not marked. Some windows are lighted. But mostly they're darked. A place you could sprain both your elbow and chin! Do you dare to stay out? Do you dare to go in? How much can you lose? How much can you win?
>
> **—Seuss, 1990, p. 20**

The above quote, originally from a graduation speech, can also describe the experience of choosing or changing a career. Clients in career counseling are trying to find their way, make sense of their options, and make good choices. They struggle with a lack of direction, uncertainty, and confusion. How can supervision prepare counselors to accompany clients on this journey?

This is a challenging question to answer. While the value of counselor supervision as well as the potential problems associated with supervision have been widely documented (Bernard & Goodyear, 2009; Watkins, 1997), the role of supervision in career counseling has only recently received some attention (O'Brien & Heppner, 1996; Prieto & Betsworth, 1999; Swanson & O'Brien, 2002). Career counseling supervision theory has not been identified or articulated, nor have the unique factors of career counseling supervision been described. Furthermore, few have investigated the role supervision plays in training career counselors (Heppner, O'Brien, Hinkelman, & Flores, 1996; Sumeral & Borders, 1995). The focus of this chapter is to delineate important issues in the supervision and training of counselors providing career counseling in order to stimulate thought, discussion, and research and to offer some guidance for the supervision of career counseling. First, a brief overview of effective supervision will be presented, followed by aspects of effective career counseling. Then, 10 components of effective career counseling supervision will be introduced and described.

What is Effective Supervision?

Supervision is an intervention that extends over time, with the multiple purposes of (a) enhancing the professional functioning of the supervisee; (b) monitoring the quality of professional services offered to clients seen by the supervisee; and (c) serving as a gatekeeper of those who enter the counseling profession. In addition, counselor supervision is the setting in which counselors learn to blend two general realms of clinical knowledge: the "science" of counseling and the "art" of counseling (Bernard & Goodyear, 2009). As has been described in preceding chapters, effective supervision consists of a number of features, including forming a positive supervisory working alliance (Bordin, 1983), flexibility in working from multiple roles (e.g., teacher, counselor, consultant; Bernard, 1997), considering the developmental needs of the supervisee (Stoltenberg & McNeill, 1997), clear communication about the expectancies, supervision goals, and evaluation criteria (Holloway, 1997), and the ability to facilitate learning about and improvements in human interaction (Kagan & Kagan, 1997). These qualities also describe effective career counseling supervision.

What is Effective Career Counseling?

To fully articulate the qualities of effective career counseling supervision, it is necessary to describe the qualities of effective career counseling. The National Career Development Association (NCDA) published a list of career counseling competencies in 1992 (NCDA Professional Standards Committee) and then updated them in 1997 (NCDA Professional Standards Committee). The list published in 1997 states that a professional engaged in career counseling must demonstrate minimum competencies in 11 designated areas including a total of 84 specific competencies. The 11 designated competency areas are: (1) career development theory (i.e., theory and knowledge essential for providing career counseling and development); (2) individual and group counseling skills (i.e., individual and group counseling competencies essential for career counseling); (3) individual/group assessment (i.e., assessment skills essential for providing career counseling); (4) information/resources (i.e., basic information, resources, and knowledge essential for providing career counseling); (5) program promotion, management and implementation (i.e., skills needed to develop, plan, implement, and manage career development programs in various settings); (6) coaching, consultation, and performance improvement (i.e., essential knowledge and skills for assisting organizations and groups to promote individuals' career development); (7) diverse populations (i.e., knowledge and skills essential for providing career counseling and development with diverse client populations); (8) supervision (i.e., knowledge and skills essential for supervising, evaluating, and promoting the professional development of counselors providing career counseling); (9) ethical/legal issues (i.e., knowledge essential for the ethical and legal practice of career counseling); (10) research/evaluation (i.e., knowledge and skills essential for understanding and conducting career counseling research and evaluation); and (11) technology (i.e., knowledge and skills essential for using technology within career counseling). It is argued that these competencies comprise the basis of effective career counseling practice.

Components of Effective Career Counseling Supervision

Given the scant research and theory on how to provide effective supervision of career counseling, the following recommendations extrapolate from the existing supervision and career counseling theory and research. The supervision and career counseling literature is integrated and extended to delineate essential components of career counseling supervision. These recommendations are deemed pantheoretical—that is, applicable across theories of supervision. Furthermore, this model applies to individual, one-on-one supervision of individual career counseling and is not intended to be generalizable to group supervision or to supervising career workshops, supervising psychoeducational career interventions or supervising the creation and management of an entire school guidance program (Gysbers & Henderson, 2006; Henderson & Gysbers, 1998).

Effective career counseling supervision attends to 10 specific components. Briefly defined, these components are: (1) the supervisory relationship (i.e., developing a relationship between the supervisor and supervisee that is characterized by a strong supervisory working alliance); (2) counseling skills (i.e., counseling competencies essential for effective career counseling); (3) case conceptualization (i.e., using career development theory to understand clients' career issues and devise a plan for intervening); (4) assessment skills (i.e., using testing to assess career-related factors such as interests, values, abilities, personality, self-concept, and other issues); (5) resources and information (i.e., possessing knowledge of and the ability to use basic career resources such as books, people, and technology that provide career-related information); (6) the interconnection between personal issues and career issues (i.e., an awareness that career development is impacted by personal characteristics, along with the ability to work with these factors in career counseling); (7) promoting supervisee interest in career counseling (i.e., motivating supervisees to provide quality career counseling by modeling that behavior and by addressing myths about career counseling); (8) addressing career issues in developmentally and age-appropriate ways (i.e., acknowledgment that the development of a career occurs over an entire lifetime and that, as a result, counselors need to be able to intervene in ways that are developmentally and age-appropriate); (9) multicultural issues (i.e., the awareness, knowledge, and skills necessary to provide multiculturally competent career counseling); and (10) ethics (i.e., knowledge of and adherence to the ethical codes appropriate to career counseling). Each of these components will be discussed more thoroughly in subsequent sections.

Effective career counseling supervision is provided via primarily four models of supervision and utilizes a variety of supervision interventions. The four primary models used throughout this chapter are Kagan's interpersonal process recall model (Kagan & Kagan, 1997), the integrated developmental model (Stoltenberg & McNeill, 1997), the discrimination model (Bernard, 1997), and the systems approach to supervision (Holloway, 1997). Suggested supervision interventions include role-plays, case conceptualizations, reading, audiotapes and videotapes of counseling sessions, and interpersonal process recall.

The Supervisory Relationship

The relationship component of effective career counseling supervision is listed first, emphasizing its importance as a foundation upon which effective career counseling supervision is built, grows, and develops. After all, it is within the supervisory relationship that all supervision and supervisory interventions take place (Watkins, 1997) and quite likely this relationship determines the effectiveness of supervision (Hunt, 1986). Attention to the supervisory relationship is recommended throughout the supervision process. Since the supervisory relationship is written about thoroughly in Chapter 2 of this book, this section will highlight only the salient factors in relation to supervising career counseling.

Bordin (1983) proposed that the supervisory working alliance is a collaboration for change that is comprised of three aspects, including mutual agreement and understanding of the goals of supervision, mutual agreement and understanding of the supervision tasks, and an emotional bond between the supervisor and supervisee. Each of these aspects is exemplified below.

The goals in career counseling supervision are likely to be multiple and vary in specificity. For example, the goals could include the supervisee's development of all 11 of the designated career counseling competency areas. Alternatively, a supervisor and supervisee might agree upon a very specific goal for supervision, such as developing proficiency and expertise in career counseling with women returning to work after raising children. The tasks of career counseling supervision should be related to the goals of supervision. For example, supervision tasks could include reviewing audio-tapes of counseling sessions in supervision, discussing career development theory, applying theory to each client seen, and role-playing how to utilize assessment tools. A key feature related to the tasks is that the supervisor and supervisee have come to a mutual agreement regarding when and how these tasks will be utilized in supervision. It is also presumed that as the supervisor and supervisee negotiate a mutual understanding of the goals and tasks of career counseling supervision, a strong emotional bond will develop between them. This emotional connection involves a mutual caring, liking, and trusting between the supervisor and supervisee. The development of a strong supervisory working alliance sets the stage for the implementation of supervisory interventions related to the remaining components.

Counseling Skills

Attention to the supervisee's development of counseling skills is the next component of effective career counseling supervision. Counseling skills include the actions and interventions used with clients such as: attending and listening, restatement, open question, reflection of feeling, challenge, interpretation, self-disclosure, immediacy, information-giving, and direct guidance (Hill, 2004). These are the counseling competencies essential for effective career counseling and they provide the foundation upon which the interactions between counselor and client develop.

Hill (2004) proposes that counseling skills integrating affect, cognition, and behavior are central to effective counseling and are what facilitate clients moving through a three-stage model of change, comprised first of exploration, next insight, and then action. Likewise, it is herein proposed that effective career counseling involves these skills. Correspondingly, effective career counseling supervision helps the supervisee develop these counseling skills while also helping the supervisee employ this three-stage model of helping with clients. For example, supervision can facilitate the development of attending and listening skills through the use of role-playing. The supervisee, role-playing the counselor, practices repeating verbatim what the supervisor, role-playing the client, says. The goal of this type of role-play is to practice listening carefully and hearing exactly what the other is saying.

A variation of the interpersonal process recall (Kagan & Kagan, 1997) is another way of facilitating supervisees' acquisition of counseling skills. The following example illustrates assisting a supervisee in learning the skill of challenge in counseling. The supervisor and supervisee listen to an audio-taped counseling session in which a client is conflicted or confused. They stop the tape after a period of time when the client has clearly disclosed the conflict or confusion. Together the supervisee and supervisor identify as many ways as possible that the supervisee could have challenged the client.

Then, they evaluate the effectiveness of each possible challenge and explore the supervisee's reactions. The following example illustrates this process.

Steve, the client, on audiotape: "I really love art. Ever since I was a child my favorite pastimes have been drawing and painting, music and dance. Art is who I am! But I can't make any money in art. I need to be practical. It's silly to want to spend all my time drawing and dancing. Art really isn't that important to me."

Questions for the supervisor and supervisee to think about:

> Is there a discrepancy present?
> The discrepancy could be between two verbal statements, between words and actions, between two feelings, between values and behaviors, between strengths and weaknesses?
> Is this a defense?
> Is this an irrational belief?

Supervisor and supervisee brainstorm possible ways to challenge the client:

> "I noticed a discrepancy between two things you said, Steve. First you said 'I love art' and then you ended with 'Art really isn't that important to me.'" (This notes a discrepancy between two verbal statements.)
>
> "Steve, you said that art really isn't important to you. Yet, I know that you spend a great deal of your free time involved in artistic activities." (This notes a discrepancy between words and actions.)
>
> "You seem to have some beliefs about careers in art that may or may not be true. You say that you can't make any money in art. You say that you need to be practical, implying that you are not practical if you pursue a career in art. I am not sure that these beliefs are accurate." (This notes irrational beliefs.)

Questions for the supervisor and supervisee to consider, regarding the effectiveness of each possible challenge:

> Is the client ready to hear the challenge?
> Could the challenge be phrased differently so that the client can hear the intervention?
> Is one challenge more important to the client's development at this time?
> Is the counseling relationship well-developed enough for the challenge to be effective?

Questions the supervisor can utilize to explore the supervisee's reactions:

> How do you feel about each of the challenges?
> What, if any, of the challenges would be easiest for you to deliver? Why?

What, if any, of the challenges would be most difficult for you to deliver? Why?

How do you imagine you would feel in a counseling session if you challenged this client?

Clearly, it would be an oversight to disregard the relevance of counseling skills within career counseling. Supervision needs to attend to the development of counseling skills as well as their use specifically with career-related issues if the counselor is to provide true *counseling* and not serve merely as a technician. Attention must be paid to developing counseling skills throughout the supervision process.

Case Conceptualization

Case conceptualization is the use of career development theory (e.g., Holland, 1997; Super, 1990) to understand clients' career issues and devise a plan for intervening and assisting the client in counseling. Conceptualizing cases allows one to use theory to guide both the counseling process as well as the supervisee's interventions so that there is a sound rationale for the goals and tasks of the counseling.

Career counseling supervision can quite naturally facilitate a supervisee's case conceptualization skills. Regularly scheduled case reports can be a part of the supervision process, wherein the supervisee presents a written and verbal presentation of a client. The case report includes information such as: client identifying data, presenting concerns, goals for counseling, theoretical understanding of the client and her or his presenting concerns, proposed course of counseling, assessment data, and current outcomes. The process of writing a case report allows the supervisee to thoroughly think through and write out the why, how, and what of the planned counseling interventions. Formally presenting and discussing the case allows the supervisee to rethink the case, while the supervisor helps the supervisee explore the validity of assertions made about the client, the strength and appropriateness of the theoretical understanding of the client and proposed course of counseling. For this process to be most effective, a collaborative approach between supervisor and supervisee is recommended, the mutual goal is the development of the supervisee's ability to conceptualize. If an antagonistic dynamic develops, then the process will likely feel punishing and belittling to the supervisee.

In the following example, the supervisee has written a case report and is discussing her client, Maria, who is a 30-year-old, married, Latina woman with two children ages six and eight. Maria has a BA in English and has worked part-time writing for a small public relations and marketing company since the birth of her first child. She has sought counseling because she is now interested in returning to work full-time and would like assistance in identifying her options, both within her current industry of public relations/marketing and in other industries and settings as well.

Supervisee: According to Super's Life-Span Theory of Career Development, Maria is recycling through the exploration stage, which is characterized by exploring occupational options, making an occupational choice, becoming more specific about the choice, and then ultimately implementing that choice by finding a job.

Supervisor: Tell me more about the occupational options Maria is exploring.

Supervisee: Well, she is working in PR and marketing now, which she enjoys. So, she is exploring opportunities within PR and marketing, like staying where she is part-time and finding another part-time position, or starting her own PR/marketing company, or working full-time at a company or organization in their PR/marketing department.

Supervisor: What interventions do you think would be helpful to Maria in exploring these options?

Supervisee: Super's theory suggests that knowledge about the world of work is necessary here. So, I think that interventions focused on Maria gathering information about these options would help. I have suggested that Maria read about marketing and PR in the *Occupational Outlook Handbook*. I also think that my suggesting informational interviews would be a good intervention. I don't think that Maria knows about informational interviews.

Supervisor: Yes, those interventions seem timely and very consistent with Super's model. Do you anticipate any barriers to these interventions working with Maria?

Supervisee: Hmmm. I don't know. I really hadn't thought about that. Hmmm ... what do you mean?

Supervisor: Well, sometimes a client could benefit from a particular intervention in counseling and yet, sometimes the intervention is not as successful as we had hoped. I wondered if that might be the case of Maria?

Supervisee: Well, I know that Maria is a bit shy. So the informational interviews might be intimidating for her. That hadn't occurred to me before. Hmmm. I still think they would be helpful to her, though. I wonder how to deal with that?

Supervisor: It seems that you are fine-tuning your conceptualization about Maria.

Supervisee: I guess I am.

The supervisor could also use a text that includes case material to help supervisees reflect on how they apply theory to cases. One such text was recently published by Swanson and Fouad (1999), wherein one primary case example is used throughout the book and is considered from a different theoretical perspective in each chapter. This text includes the use of assessment in the case example, considering assessment from varying theoretical perspectives.

More informally, supervisors can assist counselors' in developing conceptualizing skills by regularly attending to how the supervisee is conceptualizing each client. Examples of thought-provoking questions that facilitate the development of skills in conceptualizing clients include: How do you think the client's age (or gender, race, marital status) impacts the career development process? What led you to choose to use that particular assessment tool with this client? What are its advantages and disadvantages? What theory or theories are you using to understand this client's presenting concerns and developmental process? How does that theory relate to the interventions you are using with this client?

Utilizing case conceptualization in supervision also assists the counselor in developing her or his own theoretical orientation. Stoltenberg and McNeill (1997) posit that supervisees move through three levels of development in supervision. Level 1 is characterized by limited exposure to counseling, assessment, and conceptualizing. Level 2 is characterized by mastery of basic skills and some success experiences with clients, as well as feelings of conflict leading to vacillating between preferring dependency or autonomy within supervision. Level 3 is characterized by a calm focus on growth and is also often characterized by rapid skill development. These three levels can be applied to the development of one's theoretical orientation and conceptualization skills. Supervisees at Level 1 have some idea of their theoretical orientation, but it is based on didactic learning and is largely untested by counseling experience. At Level 2, supervisees' theoretical orientation has been challenged and tested some and is likely in flux and in revision. At Level 3 and beyond, the theoretical orientation has survived many transformations as the result of both counseling experience and the evolution of the counselor as a person.

By always being mindful of its existence, the supervisor assists the supervisee in developing and fine-tuning one's theoretical orientation. Asking the counselor to state her or his theoretical orientation at the beginning of the supervision relationship (and from time to time during the course of supervision) allows both to monitor its development. The supervisor may decide to intervene in a different manner depending on the developmental level of the supervisee. For a supervisee at Level 1, assigning readings consistent with the supervisee's theoretical orientation and then discussing them in supervision may be facilitative. For a Level 2 supervisee, it might be helpful to require the supervisee to conceptualize the same client case from various theoretical orientations. While for a supervisee at Level 3, supervision could focus on helping the supervisee integrate counseling interventions with her or his theoretical orientation.

Assessment Skills

The term *assessment skills* refers to the use of testing (e.g., the Strong Interest Inventory [CPP, Inc., 2004], the Self-Directed Search [PAR, Inc., 1996], the Myers Briggs Type Indicator [CPP, Inc., 1998], SIGI[3] [Valpar International Corp., 2008]) to assess career-related factors such as interests, values, abilities, achievement, personality, decision-making style, self-concept, career maturity, and other related developmental or lifestyle issues to promote clients' career development. Acquiring assessment skills is a complex process, comprised of developing a series of skills, including: (a) the ability to evaluate and select valid and reliable instruments appropriate to the client (given the client's age, gender, sexual orientation, race, ethnicity, and physical and mental abilities); (b) the ability to administer, score, and report assessment findings appropriately; (c) knowledge of and ability to utilize technology, including computer-delivered assessment measures such as SIGI[3] (Valpar International Corp., 2008) and DISCOVER (ACT, Inc., 2008); and (d) the ability to interpret assessment data and present and utilize the data with clients (verbally as well as in written test reports) to facilitate their progress.

Given the complexity of this task, it is no wonder that the field has been critiqued for inattention to how to train counselors to master the array of interlocking skills (Watkins, 1993). While we cannot turn to empirical studies to guide us, some logical suggestions follow. First, within supervision it seems minimally necessary to acknowledge that developing assessment skills is a complex task. Acknowledging that assessment skills are actually a set of skills may demystify the process and allow for the supervisor and supervisee to collaborate on how best to address assessment issues within supervision. This acknowledgment might also lead supervisors and supervisees to devote more time and attention to developing these skills. To this end, Fink, Allen, and Barak (1986) delineate an extensive, 5.5 month internship experience designed to train counselors to administer, score, and interpret ability, interest, and personality tests with clients seeking career counseling. This internship entails two components: (1) seminar sessions focused on assessment issues including the rationale for using a particular test, choosing the appropriate test for a particular client, as well as scoring and interpreting test results and the presentation and review of client cases, and (2) individual 60 minute supervision sessions with a total of three supervisors.

Elements of the internship described by Fink et al. (1986) can be used in any supervision context. Some supervision sessions could be didactic in nature, with the aim of training the supervisee in the elements of good assessment skills. The content of these sessions might include instruction on the validity and reliability of assessment tools, instruction in how to interpret the test data, and practice communicating results verbally and in writing. These didactic sessions could occur in individual supervision or could be provided in small group seminars with multiple supervisees present. Using a text that includes case material and assessment (e.g., Swanson & Fouad, 1999) can also facilitate a focus on the first component of the Fink et al. (1986) model within supervision. Another alternative is for supervisors to simply require counselors to use assessment with clients when the test is appropriate and will yield useful information. This would result in counselors having the opportunity to choose, administer, score, interpret, and present the results to clients under close supervision.

Supervisees can also practice administering assessment tools and presenting the results by role-playing with the supervisor. This method can be quite helpful to supervisees in a number of ways. Role-playing allows the supervisee to become familiar with the test, make mistakes and receive direct coaching from the supervisor, get stuck, struggle, ask questions, and eventually get unstuck without the added pressure of a real client relying upon the counselor for help. Over time, as the supervisee masters the use of assessment tools, the role-plays can focus on using tests with more difficult or intimidating clients, such as a client who complains about taking a test, a client who is argumentative about the test results, or a client who views the test result not as a tool but rather as "the definitive answer." Each counselor likely has her or his own fears about using tests with particular types of clients or in certain situations and supervisors are well advised to invite counselors to share their fears. Supervisors can also facilitate this type of discussion by disclosing some of the fears and struggles they themselves encountered with career clients as a trainee (Ladany & Lehrman-Waterman, 1999).

Resources and Information

Resources and information are inherent aspects of quality career counseling. To make planful career decisions and pursue training, education, and employment, clients must know how to utilize resources and information such as books, Internet Web sites, job trends, job descriptions, computer systems, and the like. Many clients are not familiar with such resources when they enter counseling; it is the career counselor who serves as a coach or educator, assisting the client to locate and use relevant resources. It is imperative then that counselors possess a demonstrable knowledge of and ability to use basic career resources (including books, people, and technology) that provide information about job tasks, functions, salaries, requirements, and future outlooks. Counselors also need to be skilled in evaluating the quality and accuracy of resources, especially resources and information found on the Internet, and be prepared to teach clients how to evaluate their quality and accuracy as well. Counselors must also possess basic information about the world of work such as trends in education, training, and employment, labor market information, and hiring practices. When counselors do not possess the knowledge needed to help a client, they need to be able to locate the information or resources, or refer the client to the information and resources.

Effective career counseling supervision attends to the supervisee's developing knowledge in these areas. A practical way to help a counselor become familiar with resources and information is to require the supervisee to come into contact with the materials. For example, a beginning counselor (i.e., a counselor at developmental Level 1) may be required to locate and review the *Occupational Outlook Handbook* (U.S. Department of Labor, 2008–2009), visit Web sites of recruiters and headhunters, and become familiar with current employment trends as compared to employment trends from the past. A more advanced counselor (i.e., a counselor at developmental Level 2) already possessing basic knowledge of resources and the world of work, may be required to locate, identify, and evaluate career self-help books or identify local workers willing to engage in informational interviews with interested clients. Inevitably, as the supervisee counsels clients, the need for resources and information arises. As this happens, it is natural for the supervisor and supervisee to discuss what is available and also brainstorm and investigate new options. Again, role-playing when, why, and how to introduce information and resources can be helpful to the supervisee, especially if the supervisee feels uncomfortable with these skills. And by role-playing how to help a client learn to evaluate the quality and accuracy of available resources the supervisee can also develop important skills.

The Interconnection Between Personal Issues and Career Issues

Counselors and mental health professionals tend to dichotomize clients into those seeking either career counseling or personal counseling, artificially separating the presenting problems as if a client's career life and personal life are not intertwined. Career development is impacted by clients' personal characteristics such as social contextual factors, familial, cultural and subcultural structures, decision-making style, developmental stage, identity formation and status, self-concept, psychological needs, psychopathology, and internal barriers (Blustein, 1987, 1992; Manuele-Adkins, 1992; NCDA Professional Standards Committee, 1997; Subich, 1993; NCDA/ACES Commission for Preparing Counselors for the 21st Century, 2000). Counselors who counsel the whole person assist that client in making psychologically congruent choices through a counseling process with richness and depth. To provide holistic career counseling, counselors must learn in supervision to address the overlap and interplay of personal and career concerns.

But how do we train counselors to treat the whole client and not just the career concern? Supervisors could start by never allowing themselves to dichotomize clients, client issues, or practica experiences (Swanson & O'Brien, 2002) into "career" versus "personal" domains. Supervisors then continue by exemplifying a counselor who treats a *person* presenting with career concerns and by demonstrating how to take into consideration all the factors (personal, psychological, as well as career) that impact the person as well as the career concern. For example, when a supervisee talks about her or his client Kathy, a 20-year-old, depressed, female college sophomore having difficulty choosing a major, the supervisor must attend not only to the discussion about choosing a major but also to the role that the client's depression plays in her life as well as in her college career.

If qualified, the counselor can provide counseling for the career issues as well as treatment for the psychological issues. Naturally, not all counselors possess the training and expertise to treat all of the psychological issues (including, but not limited to, depression) with which clients present. It is not necessary for the counselor who is addressing the career concerns to be able to treat all of these other concerns. It is, however, of utmost importance that the counselor be able to recognize, identify, and diagnose mental health concerns and be able to refer the client for proper treatment. The counselor can then continue to provide the career counseling while the client receives the mental health treatment with another professional. In the example of Kathy, a counselor would recognize the depression, talk with Kathy about the presence of depression, make a referral to a professional able to treat the depression (e.g., a counselor, psychologist, or psychiatrist), and continue to counsel Kathy on the process of choosing a major. Clearly, even after a referral is made, the counselor still needs to take into account how the psychological issues relate to the client's career development. A case in point, the counselor working with Kathy would still need to address how the depression impacts her process of choosing a major. For example, Kathy's depression might artificially lower her scores on the Strong Interest Inventory or cause her to inaccurately evaluate her abilities.

Bernard's discrimination model of supervision (1997) suggests numerous ways the supervisor can promote a holistic approach to working with Kathy. When using this model the supervisor can intervene from the role of teacher, counselor, or consultant, yielding the following potential interventions.

Supervisor as Teacher

1. The supervisor identifies and informs the supervisee of referral options for treating the depression.
2. The supervisor teaches the supervisee how to arrange symptoms into the diagnosis of depression.
3. The supervisor models how to conceptualize the connections between Kathy's depression, her career concerns, and all of the other personal and psychological factors that Kathy brings to counseling.

Supervisor as Counselor

1. The supervisor explores with the supervisee her or his range of feelings about working with a depressed client.
2. The supervisor explores how the supervisee's feelings about Kathy impact the counseling process.
3. The supervisor works with the counselor to remember how feelings, events, and/or psychological distress impacted her or his own career development.

Supervisor as Consultant

1. The supervisor and counselor together brainstorm how Kathy's career concerns and depression are related and how they impact each other.
2. The supervisor engages in a conversation with the counselor about her or his strengths and weaknesses to help the counselor determine her or his expertise and limitations in regards to treating the career issues and the depression.
3. The supervisor encourages the supervisee to identify as many counseling interventions as possible that would facilitate Kathy to talk about the role of depression in her life and in her career.

Promoting Supervisee Interest in Career Counseling

Promoting supervisee interest in career counseling is an important and yet often overlooked function of career counseling supervision. This involves motivating supervisees to provide quality career counseling through modeling as well as through addressing myths about career counseling. This is an important component of effective career counseling supervision for a few reasons. First, promoting supervisee interest in career counseling helps to ensure that adequate services are provided to clients. Second, interested and motivated career counselors may be less likely to overlook career concerns or attend to mental health issues to the exclusion of career issues. Also, supervisors who successfully promote a supervisee's interest in career counseling assist that counselor in developing a broader repertoire of counseling skills.

Some indications suggest that counselors are less interested in addressing career issues in counseling. In June 1999, the National Board of Certified Counselors voted to disband the National Certified Career Counselor specialization due to a lack of interest in the career speciality (Schmitt, 1999). It has been suggested that counselors and psychologists view career counseling as not prestigious, not lucrative, not intellectually challenging, not psychological, and focus primarily on preparing clients to enter the workforce (Blustein, 1992; Manuele-Adkins, 1992; Subich, 1993). For supervisees to provide quality counseling to their clients, supervisors must directly address these myths and disinterest. This is one area where empirical support exists. Research shows that clients presenting with career issues express as much psychological distress as clients presenting with personal issues (Gold & Scanlon, 1993). This same study also found that in spite of the clients' significant psychological distress, clients presenting with career concerns received fewer sessions of counseling. Apparently, clients are very interested and concerned about the career issues for which they seek counseling. And yet, counselors may not always give these clients adequate services. Supervisors can expose their supervisees to literature addressing the significance of career concerns to clients (Gold & Scanlon, 1993), as well as to literature addressing the overlap and interplay of career and personal issues (Blustein, 1987, 1992; Manuele-Adkins, 1992; NCDA Professional Standards Committee, 1997; NCDA/ACES Commission for Preparing Counselors for the 21st Century, 2000; Subich, 1993), and challenge supervisee's myths in these areas.

Given that artificially dichotomizing "career counseling" and "personal counseling" impedes supervisee interest, supervisors need to be wary of dichotomizing. Research indicates that supervisors have a powerful effect on trainees' attitudes toward career counseling, such that supervisors can either increase or decrease supervisees' interest in career counseling (Heppner et al., 1996). Heppner and colleague's study suggests that supervisees' interest in career counseling was positively influenced by supervisors who clearly communicated that career and social-emotional counseling are integrated processes rather than two separate modalities, as well as supervisors and professors who shared their enthusiasm for and creativity within career counseling. Likewise, an article by Warnke et al. (1993) describes the positive impact of a doctoral-level career counseling practicum on students' attitudes toward career services as well as their career interventions skills. Thus, it seems that supervisors foster their supervisee's interest in career counseling by respecting the seriousness of career concerns, modeling interest, sharing enthusiasm, and training supervisees that a client's career issues relate to that client's whole life and identity.

Addressing Career Issues in Developmentally and Age-Appropriate Ways

Given that the development of a person's career takes place over an entire lifetime, it is essential that counselors understand the developmental nature of a career and intervene in ways that are developmentally and age-appropriate. Ideally, supervisees would learn this directly by counseling a variety of clients who span a range of ages and developmental levels. When this is possible, so much the better. Then supervision can focus on each client's particular needs based on their age and their developmental status. For example, in a setting where counselors work with children between the ages of 6 and 18, the supervisor and supervisee can discuss the relative needs of students of different ages. They might note that elementary age children need to develop their career awareness (i.e., awareness of various life roles, awareness of occupations), but do not need to make specific occupational choices (i.e., a college major or preferred occupation). Supervision can also address how to tailor intervention strategies for this age group, in particular, given elementary children's abilities and needs. Then, as the supervisee works with clients of different ages and developmental stages—that is, middle school students or high school students—supervision can serve as a forum for exploring the similarities and differences between the clients, as well as the similarities and differences between intervention strategies used. Utilizing the counselor role in supervision, the supervisor can help the supervisee reflect on how it feels to counsel clients at various ages and stages. Questions for discussion and reflection might include: How do you feel as you work with clients of each age group? What is especially difficult for you? What is especially easy? What were your career issues at that age?

Although it is ideal for trainees to counsel clients spanning a range of ages and developmental levels, this opportunity is probably more the exception than the rule. Most supervisors supervise counselors in a setting that tends to be more age-specific, such as an elementary, middle, or high school, a college campus, or a community agency serving adult clients. When this is the case, supervision should at least acknowledge that career development need be delivered in ways that are appropriate to the clients' age and developmental stage and supervisors should discuss what this means in that particular setting. For example, while it is appropriate to help a high school senior explore several specific careers of interest, it would be premature to encourage an eighth grader to narrow her or his interests down to several specific careers. There are many possible supervision interventions that facilitate the supervisee's understanding of developmentally and age-appropriate career counseling. The supervisee might think about and talk about what is age-appropriate in various settings. The supervisee might read the NCDA policy statement about career development with respect to various life stages (NCDA Board of Directors, 2003) and could read and discuss developmental approaches to career development such as Super (1990) and Gottfredson (2002). Supervisors should ensure that their supervisee use developmentally and age-appropriate theory, assessment, and interventions in case conceptualizations. If the supervisee has had experience with clients of other ages, perhaps in another practicum or work setting, reflect with the supervisee about how the current population is similar to and different from that other population. Encourage the supervisee to alter interventions that were appropriate and effective with others to utilize those interventions with current clients.

Even within a fairly homogenous setting there are discrepancies between individuals and subgroups. For example, while high school may seem somewhat homogenous with regard to age and developmental stage, much diversity exists. The same interventions will not facilitate the developmental growth of all first year high school students. For example, both male and female first year students need assistance adjusting to high school and exploring the school, themselves, and prospective career interests. However, at this age females are at a greater risk for low self-esteem and low self-efficacy (Gilligan, 1993), ultimately putting them at greater risk for unnecessarily limiting their career goals. Thus, when counseling entry-level high school students, it is recommended to lookout for low self-esteem and low self-efficacy, especially in the girls.

Also, the needs of subgroups within high school can be quite distinct, although they are very close in age. Consider high school first year students versus seniors. Typical career tasks for first year students include identifying and evaluating interests, participating in choosing courses, and exposure to jobs and career fields, while typical career tasks for seniors include experience working, planning for what to do after graduation, and preparing for a job search or choosing an institution of higher learning. Supervision should attend to the individual differences, developmental levels, and mini-stages that occur even within a fairly homogeneous setting. Supervision should also assist the supervisee in noticing and working with these more subtle differences in age and development.

Multicultural Issues

Attention to multicultural issues in career counseling is the next component of effective career counseling supervision. For the purpose of this chapter, multicultural issues include but are not limited to issues of race and culture, gender, sexual orientation, socioeconomic status, age, religious beliefs, and ability. This component focuses on the awareness, knowledge, and skills necessary to provide multiculturally competent career counseling. Developing multicultural competence allows counselors to effectively counsel a wider range of clients and to ensure that all individuals have access to career development assistance.

To effectively train supervisees to acknowledge and work with diversity issues in career counseling, it is imperative that supervisors are multiculturally competent themselves. Supervisors must be able to acknowledge and work with diversity issues in both career counseling as well as within supervision. Supervisors need to possess the awareness, knowledge, and skills that are presented herein.

Multicultural counseling competencies have been written about, researched, and taught for some time, such that the salient attitudes, knowledge, and skills required to practice in a multiculturally competent manner have now been identified and described (Constantine, Miville, Kindaichi, 2008; Ponterotto, Casas, Suzuki, & Alexander, 2001; Sue, Arredondo, & McDavis, 1992). Briefly, multiculturally competent counselors possess attitudes and beliefs that allow them to counsel culturally diverse clients, without their own biases or values interfering with the counseling. A multiculturally competent career counselor would be willing and able to examine her or his prejudices about a client. Such a counselor might utilize supervision to sort through her or his prejudiced beliefs and how these beliefs could impact the counseling process. A multiculturally competent career counselor would be willing to learn more about how client characteristics (e.g., a client's religious beliefs) impact the client's career development as well as the career counseling process.

Multiculturally competent counselors possess knowledge about themselves; that is, about their own racial and cultural heritage and how it influences them as a person and as a counselor. For example, a multiculturally competent female career counselor knows how her gender has impacted her career development as well as the ways in which her gender impacts her professionally. Furthermore, multiculturally competent career counselors possess knowledge about the world, including knowledge of oppression, racism, discrimination and stereotyping. In the career realm this specifically includes knowledge of discrimination and limited access to jobs and careers (Betz & Fitzgerald, 1987; Thomas & Alderfer, 1989), the damaging effects of the null-environment (Betz, 1989), limitations regarding applying career theory to diverse populations (Betz & Fitzgerald, 1987; Leung, 1995; Walsh & Osipow, 1994), the nature of women's career choices, women's career adjustment, and special issues in providing career counseling to women (Betz & Fitzgerald, 1987; Walsh & Osipow, 1994), and problems associated with using assessment tools with diverse populations (Betz, 1992; Constantine et. al., 2008; Hackett & Lonborg, 1994; Leung, 1995).

Multiculturally competent counselors have developed skills and interventions that enable them to work with culturally diverse populations. They are flexible in their counseling approach and can modify their interventions to accommodate differences. For example, a multiculturally competent career counselor would be able to modify typically individualistic career theories (possibly by using an integrative theoretical approach) to work with a client who utilizes a more collectivistic decision-making approach. Also, a multiculturally competent career counselor would utilize alternative assessment methods (i.e., vocational card sorts, values clarification exercises, work samples, behavioral observation) with clients for whom standardized tests and inventories are invalid or perpetuate bias (Constantine et al., 2008; Goldman, 1990; Hackett & Lonborg, 1994).

Recent annual reviews of research and practice in career counseling and development have noted an increased focus on multiculturalism, diversity issues, multicultural competence, and social justice (Chope, 2008; Harrington & Harrington, 2006; Tien, 2007). There is movement toward making career theories useful to a more diverse population of clients and paying greater attention to the role of contextual factors in the career development process. While this suggests that the field of career counseling is becoming more multiculturally competent, there is still an absence of recommendations on how to address multicultural issues specifically in career counseling supervision. How is a supervisor to proceed?

At this point in time, it is presumed that academic courses such as career development, counseling theories, and pre-practicum address diversity issues in such a manner that the supervisee comes to supervision with an awareness of and openness to multicultural issues. When that is the case, effective supervision provides an environment in which the counselor can practice fine-tuning her or his multicultural competencies. Sadly however, it is sometimes the case that supervisees lack the basic knowledge to begin providing multiculturally competent career counseling, while possessing fears, concerns, biases, and awkwardness about diversity. Given this state of affairs, it is the supervisor's responsibility to ensure that supervisees become aware of diversity issues in career development and develop requisite skills.

Holloway's systems approach to supervision (1997) suggests places where the supervisor can intervene to facilitate the supervisee's development of multicultural competence. Holloway's model includes cultural characteristics as an important aspect of the supervision process and contends that "In SAS, cultural values are seen as salient to trainees' attitudes and actions toward their client and supervision—that is, in any interpersonal situation" (Holloway, 1995, p. 91). Thus, cross-cultural interactions may occur between the supervisor and supervisee, the supervisee and client, or both, making the supervision process ripe for multicultural learning and training regarding either of these cross-cultural relationships. For example, imagine a career counseling supervision situation involving a female supervisor, a male supervisee, and a female client. The topic of gender attitudes (i.e., Are certain professional roles more appropriate for men and less appropriate for women?) could be explored in relation to the interactions between the supervisee and supervisor as well as in relation to the supervisee and client.

For another example of how supervisors can teach supervisees to work with multicultural issues in career counseling, return to the case of Maria, the 30-year-old, Latina, married, mother of two. Maria is working in counseling with Elizabeth, a 25-year-old, single, White woman with no children. In supervision, Elizabeth and her supervisor have just listened to an audiotape of a counseling session wherein Elizabeth and Maria discuss how Maria's shyness and lack of confidence in job search situations might impact Maria's career transition. The supervisor could utilize Bernard's discrimination model of supervision (1997) to explore the role of diversity issues in this case and to ultimately facilitate the supervisee's skills in this area. Example interventions from the role of teacher, counselor, and consultant follow.

Supervisor as Teacher

1. The supervisor assigns readings on the history of Latinas' occupational attainment to educate Elizabeth.
2. The supervisor models questions that Elizabeth might ask to more fully understand Maria's experience as a Latina woman conducting a job search.
3. The supervisor presents data and information on prejudice and racial discrimination in hiring practices.
4. The supervisor initiates discussions about multicultural counseling competencies, discrimination, limited access to jobs and careers, the null-environment, assessment validity, and alternative assessment tools to use with Latinas.

Supervisor as Counselor

1. The supervisor explores Elizabeth's comfort level with multicultural issues. With which populations is she most comfortable working? What contributes to her comfort? With which populations is she most uncomfortable working? What causes her discomfort?
2. The supervisor discusses with Elizabeth her feelings about working with Maria, a client who is different from Elizabeth in terms of age, race, marital status, and parental status.

3. The supervisor explores with Elizabeth how it would feel to process the cross-cultural counseling situation with Maria.
4. The supervisor helps Elizabeth examine how her socialized biases may influence her counseling.

Supervisor as Consultant

1. The supervisor asks Elizabeth how she would like to use supervision to help develop multicultural competencies to provide effective career counseling to Maria.
2. In regard to working with a Latina woman, the supervisor and Elizabeth together discuss the supervisee's knowledge base. What does the supervisee already know? What knowledge is missing?
3. Together Elizabeth and her supervisor evaluate the relative strengths and weaknesses of various theories of career development when applied to Maria.
4. The supervisor asks Elizabeth to consider what types of supervision activities (i.e., brainstorming, case conceptualization, interpersonal process recall, role-playing) she prefers to use to develop multicultural career counseling skills.

Finally, developing multiculturally competent career counseling skills requires that supervisees see a diverse caseload of clients. Within any counseling setting, the supervisor can select clients to maximize the supervisees' exposure to diversity. Even on a predominantly white college campus it is possible for a supervisee to counsel clients from a range of ethnic, racial, and socioeconomic backgrounds, as well as women, gay, lesbian or bisexual clients, and individuals with disabilities. These counseling experiences allow the supervisee to experience both their skills in regards to diversity issues as well as their discomfort and limitations. The supervisee's experience can then be explored in supervision to help the supervisee acknowledge, but not accept, limitations.

Ethics

Ethics refers to adherence to ethical codes related to the profession of counseling as well as to the profession of career counseling (e.g., American Counseling Association [ACA], 2005; NCDA, 2003) and supervision (Association for Counselor Education and Supervision [ACES], 1995). Ethical codes and counselors' adherence to them is essential for the protection of clients as well as to ensure clients' trust. Ethical issues in supervision are addressed more completely in Chapter 16, so the focus here will be on ethical issues and dilemmas related to career development and career counseling.

Curiously, sometimes counselors believe that they do not need to adhere to ethical standards as strictly in career counseling as in other forms of counseling. Specifically, ethical standards are sometimes overlooked in regard to multiple relationship or confidentiality issues in career counseling. These are mistakes. Effective career counseling supervision ensures that the supervisee understands that ethical codes apply equally within career counseling as in any other counseling relationship.

Rules of confidentiality and rules requiring permission to disclose to a third party apply in counseling when the focus is on career issues just the same as when the focus is on other presenting problems. Conversely, the limitations to confidentiality are the same. If a client intends to harm herself or himself and discloses this to the counselor while discussing a career issue, the counselor is obligated to disclose this information in service of protecting the client from harm just as if the client had been seeking counseling for depression. These issues need to be clearly acknowledged in supervision.

Also, given that some counselors are trained primarily to address career issues with clients and do not possess the expertise to address mental health concerns in counseling, these limitations need to be clearly addressed in supervision. If and when a counselor does not possess the ability to counsel both career and mental health issues, appropriate referrals need be available and supervision needs to attend to issues of how and when to refer. It is clearly unethical to practice outside of one's expertise.

Finally, multiple relationships between a client seeking career counseling and the counselor are unethical in the same way that multiple relationships between a client seeking psychotherapy and the psychotherapist are unethical. An example of a multiple relationship would be acting as a career counselor for a member of one's own family. It is ultimately the supervisor's responsibility to ensure that the supervisee does not engage in multiple relationships with clients. To this end, the supervisor can model ethical behavior by not engaging in dual relationships with the supervisee.

Research Issues

The limited research in career counseling supervision allows for numerous interesting areas of further research. First, the 10 specific components of effective career counseling supervision, as well as the proposed supervision approaches and techniques, presented in this chapter need to be researched to determine their efficacy in relation to training career counselors. A second related research area is to examine the impact that effective career counseling supervision has on clients and the outcomes of counseling. For example, does effective career counseling supervision promote clients' understanding of their interests, strengths, and weaknesses? If so, does that ultimately lead the client to make a career choice that is more satisfying for her or him? Research could also examine if career counseling supervision is most effective when matched to trainee developmental level. That is, when considering the 10 components presented earlier, is supervision most effective when certain components are the focus early in a supervisee's training and when other components are the focus later in a supervisee's training? And last, research could also examine the ways in which supervisors can be trained to conduct effective career counseling supervision. Such studies might examine the barriers to effective career counseling supervision (e.g., lack of interest, myths about career issues, or negative attitudes toward career counseling) as well as the qualities of effective career counseling supervisors.

Concluding Comments

This chapter is a step toward providing direction for those supervising counselors engaged in career counseling. The primary goal of this chapter has been to guide current supervision practice. Hopefully, this chapter will also stimulate thought, discussion, and research that will ultimately lead to the development of clear guidelines for the supervision of career counseling. Ultimately it is hoped that the techniques and strategies presented for effective career counseling supervision will be used by supervisors to help counselors learn to provide holistic, effective career counseling.

Acknowledgment

Thank you to Jennifer Casson for her assistance with the literature search for this chapter.

References

ACT, Inc. (2008). *DISCOVER*. Iowa City: ACT.

American Counseling Association. (2005). *Code of ethics and standards of practice*. Alexandria, VA: Author.

Association for Counselor Education and Supervision. (1995). Ethical guidelines for counseling supervisors. *Counselor Education and Supervision, 34*, 270–276.

Bernard, J. M. (1997). The Discrimination Model. In C. E. Watkins, Jr. (Ed.), *Handbook of psychotherapy supervision* (pp. 310–327). New York, NY: John Wiley & Sons.

Bernard, J. M., & Goodyear, R. K. (2009). *Fundamentals of clinical supervision* (4th ed.). Boston, MA: Allyn & Bacon.

Betz, N. E. (1989). Implications of the null environment hypothesis for women's career development and for counseling psychology. *The Counseling Psychologist, 17*(1), 136–144.

Betz, N. E. (1992). Career assessment: A review of critical issues. In S. D. Brown & R. W. Lent (Eds.), *Handbook of counseling psychology* (2nd ed., pp. 453–484). New York, NY: Wiley.

Betz, N. E., & Fitzgerald, L. F. (1987). *The career psychology of women.* New York, NY: Academic Press.

Blustein, D. L. (1987). Integrating career counseling and psychotherapy: A comprehensive treatment strategy. *Psychotherapy, 38,* 790–799.

Blustein, D. L. (1992). Toward the reinvigoration of the vocational realm of counseling psychology. *The Counseling Psychologist, 20*(4), 712–723.

Bordin, E. S. (1983). A working alliance based model of supervision. *The Counseling Psychologist, 11*(1), 35–41.

Chope, R. C. (2008). Annual Review: Practice and research in career counseling and development—2007. *The Career Development Quarterly, 57,* 98–173.

Constantine, M. G., Miville, M. L., & Kindaichi, M. M. (2008). Multicultural competence in counseling psychology practice and training. In S. D. Brown & R. W. Lent (Eds.), *Handbook of Counseling Psychology* (4th ed., pp. 141–158). Hoboken, NJ: John Wiley & Sons.

CPP, Inc. (1998). *Myers Briggs type indicator.* Mountain View, CA: CPP, Inc.

CPP, Inc. (2004). *Strong interest inventory.* Mountain View, CA: CPP, Inc.

Fink, R., Allen, R., & Barak, A. (1986). Teaching and supervising career assessment interns. *Michigan Journal of Counseling and Development, 17*(2), 27–30.

Gilligan, C. (1993). *In a different voice: Psychological theory and women's development.* Cambridge, MA: Harvard University Press.

Gold, J. M., & Scanlon, C. R. (1993). Psychological distress and counseling duration of career and noncareer clients. *Career Development Quarterly, 42*(2), 186–191.

Goldman, L. (1990). Qualitative assessment. *The Counseling Psychologist, 18,* 205–213.

Gottfredson, L. S. (2002). Gottfredson's theory of circumscription, compromise, and self-creation. In D. Brown & Associates (Ed.), *Career choice and development* (4th ed., pp. 85–148). San Francisco, CA: Jossey-Bass.

Gysbers, N. C., & Henderson, P. (2006). *Developing and managing your school guidance program* (4th ed.). Alexandria, VA: American Counseling Association.

Hackett, G., & Lonborg, S. D. (1994). Career assessment and counseling for women. In W. B. Walsh & S. H. Osipow (Eds.), *Career counseling for women* (pp. 43–85). Hillsdale, NJ: Lawrence Erlbaum Associates.

Harrington, T. F., & Harrington, T. A. (2006). Annual review: Practice and research in career counseling and development—2005. *The Career Development Quarterly, 55,* 98–167.

Henderson, P., & Gysbers, N. C. (1998). *Leading and managing your school guidance program staff.* Alexandria, VA: American Counseling Association.

Heppner, M. J., O'Brien, K. M., Hinkelman, J. M., & Flores, L. Y. (1996). Training counseling psychologists in career development: Are we our own worst enemies? *The Counseling Psychologist, 24*(1), 105–125.

Hill, C. E. (2004). *Helping skills: Facilitating exploration, insight, and action* (2nd ed.). Washington, DC: American Psychological Association.

Holland, J. L. (1997). *Making vocational choices: A theory of vocational personalities and work environments* (3rd ed.). Odessa, FL: Psychological Assessment Resources.

Holloway, E. L. (1995). *Clinical supervision: A systems approach.* Thousand Oaks, CA: Sage.

Holloway, E. L. (1997). Structures for the analysis and teaching of supervision. In C. E. Watkins, Jr. (Ed.), *Handbook of psychotherapy supervision* (pp. 249–276). New York, NY: John Wiley & Sons.

Hunt, P. (1986). Supervision. *Marriage Guidance,* 15–22.

Kagan, H. K., & Kagan, N. I. (1997). Interpersonal process recall: Influencing human interaction. In C. E. Watkins, Jr. (Ed.), *Handbook of psychotherapy supervision* (pp. 296–309). New York, NY: John Wiley & Sons.

Ladany, N., & Lehrman-Waterman, D. E. (1999). The content and frequency of supervisor self-disclosures and their relationship to supervisor style and the working alliance. *Counselor Education and Supervision, 38,* 143–160.

Leung, S. A. (1995). Career development and counseling: A multicultural perspective. In J. G. Ponterotto, J. M. Casas, L. A. Suzuki, & C. M. Alexander (Eds.), *Handbook of multicultural counseling* (pp. 549–566). Thousand Oaks, CA: Sage.

Manuele-Adkins, C. (1992). Career counseling is personal counseling. *The Career Development Quarterly, 40,* 313–323.

National Career Development Association/Association for Counselor Education and Supervision Commission for Preparing Counselors for the 21st Century. (2000). *Preparing counselors for career development in the new millennium: ACES/NCDA position paper.* Alexandria, VA: National Career Development Association.

National Career Development Association Board of Directors. (2003). *Career development: A policy statement of the national career development association board of directors.* Alexandria, VA: National Career Development Association.

National Career Development Association Board of Directors. (2003). *National career development association ethical standards.* Alexandria, VA: National Career Development Association.

National Career Development Association Professional Standards Committee. (1992). Career counseling competencies. *The Career Development Quarterly, 40,* 378–386. Alexandria, VA: National Career Development Association.

National Career Development Association Professional Standards Committee. (1997). *Career counseling competencies, revised version.* Alexandria, VA: National Career Development Association.

O'Brien, K. M., & Heppner, M. J. (1996). Applying social cognitive theory to training career counselors. *The Career Development Quarterly, 44,* 367–377.

PAR, Inc. (1996). *Self-directed search.* Lutz, FL: PAR, Inc.

Ponterotto, J. G., Casas, J. M., Suzuki, L. A., & Alexander, C. M. (2001). *Handbook of multicultural counseling* (2nd ed.). Thousand Oaks, CA: Sage.

Prieto, L. R., & Betsworth, D. G. (1999). Supervision of career counseling: Current knowledge and new directions. *The Clinical Supervisor, 18*(1), 173–189.

Schmitt, S. M. (1999, August). NBCC drops career and gerontology counseling specialties. *Counseling Today,* 1, 19.

Seuss, D. (1990). *Oh, the places you'll go!* New York, NY: Random House.

Stoltenberg, C. D., & McNeill, B. W. (1997). Clinical supervision from a developmental perspective: Research and practice. In C. E. Watkins, Jr. (Ed.), *Handbook of psychotherapy supervision* (pp. 184–202). New York, NY: John Wiley & Sons.

Subich, L. M. (1993). How personal is career counseling? [Special Section] *Career Development Quarterly, 42*(2), 129–192.

Sue, D. W., Arredondo, P., & McDavis, R. J. (1992). Multicultural counseling competencies and standards. A call to the profession. *Journal of Counseling and Development, 70*(4), 477–486.

Sumerel, M. B., & Borders, L. D. (1995). Supervision of career counseling interns. *The Clinical Supervisor, 13*(1), 91–100.

Super, D. E. (1990). A life-span, life-space approach to career development. In D. Brown, L. Brooks, & Associates (Eds.), *Career choice and development: Applying contemporary theories to practice* (2nd ed., pp. 197–261). San Francisco, CA: Jossey-Bass.

Swanson, J. L., & Fouad, N. A. (1999). *Career theory and practice: Learning through case studies.* Thousand Oaks, CA: Sage.

Swanson, J. L., & O'Brien, K. M. (2002). Training career counselors: Meeting the challenges of the 21st century. In S. G. Niles (Ed.), *Adult career development: Concepts, issues and practices* (3rd ed., pp. 354–369). Columbus, OH: National Career Development Association.

Thomas, D. A., & Alderfer, C. P. (1989). The influence of race on career dynamics: Theory and research on minority career experiences. In M. A. Arthur, D. T. Hall, & B. S. Lawrence (Eds.), *Handbook of career theory* (pp. 133–158). New York, NY: Cambridge University Press.

Tien, H. S. (2007). Annual review: Practice and research in career counseling and development—2006. *The Career Development Quarterly, 56,* 98–140.

U.S. Department of Labor. (2008–2009). *Occupational outlook handbook.* Washington, DC: U.S. Government Printing Office.

Valpar International Corp. (2008). *SIGI³.* Tucson, AZ: Valpar International Corp.

Walsh, W. B., & Osipow, S. H. (1994). *Career counseling for women.* Hillsdale, NJ: Lawrence Erlbaum Associates.

Warnke, M. A., Jinsook, K, Koeltzow-Milster, D., Terrell, S., Dauser, P. J., Dial, S., … Thiel, M. J. (1993). Career counseling practicum: Transformations in conceptualizing career issues. *The Career Development Quarterly, 42,* 180–185.

Watkins, C. E., Jr. (1993). Career assessment supervision: Could what we don't know hurt us? *Counseling Psychology Quarterly, 6*(2), 151–153.

Watkins, C. E., Jr. (Ed.). (1997). *Handbook of psychotherapy supervision.* New York, NY: John Wiley & Sons.

CHAPTER 12

Family Counseling Supervision

PILAR HERNÁNDEZ-WOLFE

Counselors implementing a marriage and family counseling orientation use systems thinking in order to address and navigate the intricacies of today's health care environment and to better comprehend the process of therapeutic change within a social and cultural context (Bittner & Corey, 2001). Due to both professional interest and health care public demand, the past two decades have seen extensive growth in family counseling;* supervision has also grown as a result of this demand (Lee, Nichols, Nichols, & Odom, 2004; Morgan & Sprenkle, 2007; Todd & Storm, 1997). The family therapy field, and especially the American Association for Marriage and Family Therapy (AAMFT), has placed special emphasis on supervision training and credentialing (AAMFT, 2005), so much so that supervision itself has become a subspecialty within family therapy. In addition, marriage and family therapists have identified best practices (Storm, Todd, Sprenkle, & Morgan, 2001) and have responded to the remedial and gate-keeping challenges in supervision (Russell, DuPree, Beggs, Peterson, & Anderson, 2007). In spite of these achievements, Morgan and Sprenkle (2007) note that "there is still little agreement about how to define the scope and content of supervision" (p. 1). In their search for common factors in supervision, they observe that while there is an abundance of models, there is not enough empirical evidence to suggest greater efficaciousness of one model over another. Further, as Morgan and Sprenkle (2007) acknowledge, there is a "high degree of variation in definitions, tasks and models" (p. 1). The review presented in this chapter is based on the isomorphic nature of theory, in which the training practices of a model reflect its theoretical and therapeutic approach.

---

* For the purposes of this chapter, the terms counseling, therapy, and psychotherapy will be used interchangeably.

Although supervision and therapy are not equivalent and therapeutic approaches do not address supervision domains such as academic and evaluation standards in university contexts, with few exceptions supervision models and practices remain derivative of therapeutic models. This chapter will offer a working definition of supervision, provide illustrative descriptions of selected major family counseling supervision models based on their philosophical underpinnings, and describe supervision modalities. The contemporary training context is heterogeneous in regards to objectives, philosophical assumptions, training modalities, contexts of training, and expected outcomes. The reader is encouraged to review family counseling models' original sources inasmuch as this is an independent field in mental health with a wealth of theories, research, and applications.

Supervision

Despite the lack of robust empirical evidence in the assessment, implementation, and effectiveness of supervision models in family counseling and across the mental health disciplines, clinicians coincide about its importance for various reasons. Counseling supervision offers counselors-in-training general guidance about the counseling practice; serves to socialize them into the profession (DeRoma, Hickey, & Stanek, 2007; Paris, Linville, & Rosen, 2006; Watkins, 1997); provides them with specific feedback about their performance; exposes them to multiple ways of approaching assessment, diagnosis, and treatment (Liddle, Breunlin, & Schwartz, 1988; Ungar & Costanzo, 2007); creates opportunities for them to develop a safe relationship as supervisees experience the counseling learning process in real settings (Kaslow & Bell, 2008); and fosters an environment that nurtures curiosity and personal growth (Rudes, Shilts, & Kim Berg, 1997). Paris et al. (2006) concluded that marriage and family therapy interns experienced growth in their personal and professional lives through personal relationships, spiritual beliefs, personal therapy, and supervision and training. Furthermore, supervision practices ensure that clients are provided with satisfactory care, that counselors do no harm, and that remedial practices are set in place for those counselors in training who need to develop more adeptness (Todd & Storm, 1997; Watkins, 1997). Counseling supervision serves the profession by providing training and education, gate keeping, and consumer protection.

Definitions of counseling supervision vary depending on their scope, theoretical basis, content, and empirical support. In their review of common factors in supervision, Morgan and Sprenkle (2007) present a general definition of supervision highlighting that this activity is concerned with multiple domains. They define supervision as an activity involving "a structured relationship between a supervisor and a supervisee with the goal to help the supervisee gain the attitudes, skills, and knowledge needed to be a responsible and effective therapist" (Morgan & Sprenkle, 2007, p. 7). Although this definition attempts to establish a common ground among the multiple definitions offered in the literature, Todd and Storm (1997) offer a more comprehensive definition delineating the unique characteristics of the supervision process. They characterize it as a continuous relationship in which the development of the counselor-in-training is the focus while he or she is in the process of gaining practical experience. In their view, key elements in supervision involve: the experience and expertise of the clinician supervisor, the developmental nature of the supervisees development, the evaluative and hierarchical nature of the supervision relationship, practice in a clinical setting with a focus on safeguarding the welfare of clients, and adherence to minimal standards set forth by the profession. Still a missing component involves addressing contextual issues shaping the very nature of the supervision relationship. Storm et al. (2001) identified this gap in the supervision literature and acknowledged that although there have been advances in addressing gender issues and developing feminist models, other contextual gaps such as ethnicity, class, sexual orientation, ability, and spirituality have not been properly addressed.

It is important to note that the family therapy field's concern with addressing and integrating contextual issues in supervision and training emerged in the late 1990s and has continued to the present time. McGoldrick et al. (1999) explicated how to incorporate social justice perspectives into family therapy training within a collaborative framework. They offered a critique of traditional family counseling approaches, training, and supervision so as to move toward a more strength- and equity-based multicultural perspective. Other scholars have focused on advocating for the integration of gender and culture as organizing principles throughout the curricula (Zimmerman & Haddock, 2001); addressing gender, power, and accountability in supervision (Gridley, 2004); offering tools to work with same sex couples (Hernández & Rankin, 2008; Long & Lindsey, 2004); and addressing race in training and supervision (Hernández, Taylor, & McDowell, 2009; McDowell et al., 2002; Taylor, Hernández, Deri, Rankin, & Siegel, 2007).

The next section of this chapter will review family counseling supervision models according to their philosophical assumptions: systemic modern, systemic postmodern, postcolonial, integrative, and common factors. Because developmental supervision models emerged outside of the marriage and family therapy literature, these models will not be discussed. However, it is important to be aware of the widely accepted notion that supervisees pass through stages of growth, which, as called for by the literature, must be dealt with according to the developmental needs of clinicians, be they novice, intermediate, or experienced (Flemons, Green, & Rambo, 1996; Rigazio-DiGilio, 1997).

Systemic Modern Models of Supervision

From its inception, systems thinking in family therapy emerged as a radically different way to address the tasks of healing in the mental health field (Ackerman, 1937; Bowen, 1978; Haley, 1987; Jackson, 1957; Selvini-Palazzoli, Boscolo, Cecchin, & Prata, 1978; Watzlawick, 1976). Emerging models in the 1960s, 1970s and 1980s* offered their unique conceptual and technical contributions to family counseling and family counseling supervision. Some of the ideas that these models pioneered are as follows: diagnosing the family system as opposed to the symptoms presented by an individual, understanding and defining presented issues in context (i.e., interactional patterns), and focusing on systemic change within the family and with other members impacting the occurrence of the presenting problem (Montgomery, Hendricks, & Bradley, 2001). These models have been characterized as *modernist* insofar as the supervisor places herself or himself outside the counselor–client system. The supervisor is an observer of what goes on inside the therapeutic system. Although a supervisor may actively intervene in the therapeutic process through live supervision or phone-ins,[†] he or she does so without addressing the reciprocal influence of the relationship supervisor–supervisee family. In addition, he or she focuses on what is happening in the therapeutic process in the here and now, identifying the members of the system, their patterns of interaction and legacies, the system's rules, boundaries and hierarchy, and its ability to change. Models within this tradition include strategic, structural, transgenerational, and experiential family therapy.

Structural, strategic, and the early Milan models emphasize responsibility and purposive action on the part of the supervisor; a focus on present-time interaction, attention to small changes in interactional patterns; negotiated observable goals, positive reframing, simplicity, attention to strengths, pragmatism; and a view of change characterized by discontinuity and speed (Doerries & Foster, 2005; Minuchin, Lee, & Simon, 1996; Montgomery et al., 2001). In addition, interventions in supervision are carefully planned and deliberate.

Doerries and Foster (2005) identified essential skills in the training of structural family counselors using a modified Delphi method based on consensus from experienced therapists. They determined that relational skills constitute the foundation upon which to establish a therapeutic relationship and that facilitating structural interventions, including the ability to provide a vision of hope and establish the expectancy of change are key

---

* Other models include R. Schwartz (1995), *Internal Family Systems Therapy*, New York, NY: Guilford Press; and N. Epstein, S. Schlesinger, & D. Dryden (1988), *Cognitive Behavioral Family Therapy*, New York, NY: Taylor & Francis.

† Except in transgenerational models where coaching is the main supervisory practice and there is a focus on the relationship between past and present issues.

in the therapeutic process. Overall, supervisors train novice counselors to join with families from a position of leadership while at the same time ensuring that families understand that the counselor also works with them (Hammond & Nichols, 2008). Supervisors teach counselors how to evaluate and map a family structure: they model how to correct family hierarchies and toxic cross-generational coalitions, understand and maintain boundaries in the supervision and therapeutic relationship, enact therapy issues that have become problematic for the supervisee, and intensify issues emerging from the supervision and the therapeutic relationship. Supervisors model and teach how to use structural interventions such as unbalancing, boundary making, and reframing (Minuchin, Colapinto, & Minuchin, 1998; Minuchin et al., 1996; Todd, 1997). Live supervision and phone-ins are the most suitable to train structural clinicians, as well as videotaping and case discussion.

Like structural family therapy, strategic* models emphasize the counselor's position of leadership in the therapeutic system. Isomorphic to counseling, supervisors are also expected to lead in the training of counselors. A key element in this model involves understanding the use of directives and paradoxes. Directives in session and as assignments facilitate change keep the counselor involved with the family outside of session, offer data about family rules and boundaries (Haley, 1987; Madanes, 2006; Madanes, Keim, & Smelser, 1995; Pearson, 1987; Wetchler, 1988). Some directives involve paradoxical interventions that prescribe the problem behavior to the family. In his review of typical strategic supervisory interventions, Todd (1997) includes the use of paradoxical techniques such as restraining from change and positioning. He explains that in the former supervisees are warned of the dangers of changing too fast while in the latter supervisors "take a stance diametrically opposed to the stance typically expected of a supervisee" (p. 181). Positioning strategies are intended to create flexibility and to overcome polarization. Other techniques include rituals and pretending techniques. The use of rituals involves playful ordeals based on clinical hypotheses that supervisees are asked to design, implement, or both (Madanes, 2006). The use of pretending techniques is intended to block a problem by having the supervisor pretend to have the supervisee's problem and then requesting assistance from the supervisee by requiring supervisees to enact a problem that is already present but as yet unacknowledged. Szapocznik, Hervis, and Schwartz (2003) posit that issues presented in therapy and supervision are usually worked through in stages and with the use of multiple interventions. Training and supervision

---

* Other models include L. Boscolo, G. Cecchin, M. Selvini Palazzoli, & G. Prata (1979), *Paradox and Counterparadox: A New Model in the Therapy of the Family in Schizophrenic Transaction*, New York, NY: Aronson; P. Watzlawick, J. Weakland, & R. Fisch (1974), *Change: Principles of Problem Formation and Problem Resolution*, New York, NY: W.W. Norton.

in structural and strategic models have been sensitive to larger context factors shaping the practice of counseling as these models evolved and have been used widely and effectively with families of color, low socioeconomic status, and substance abuse related issues (Minuchin et al., 1998; Santisteban, Suarez-Morales, Robbins, & Szapocznik, 2006).

Transgenerational family therapy models in supervision value historical information, personal beliefs, and cultural inheritances and define therapeutic change beyond symptom reduction. Moreover, such models assume that past patterns of interaction and relationships affect present and future relationships. Through coaching, supervisors encourage counselors to identify transgenerational patterns in their own families so as to heighten their self-awareness within a particular context and, further, so as to assist with differentiation and triangulation issues that may hinder their work as counselors. Culture, ethnicity, gender, class, and life cycles are stressed as an integral part of the evolution of self in context (Barrett, Chin, Comas-Díaz, Espin, & Greene, 2005; Boyd-Franklin, 2003; McGoldrick, Giordano, & Garcia-Preto, 2005; Roberto, 1997). For example, developing contextual awareness through counselors' own family of origin work leads to personal agency as counselors are able to make choices free of reactivity, thereby allowing counselors to take responsibility for their own decisions. Likewise, the relationship between supervisor, counselor, and family creates a triangle wherein the counselor "first learns about psychotherapy, then learns how to do psychotherapy, and then, if all goes well, moves to the next step of becoming a psychotherapist" (Whitaker & Ryan, 1989, p. 211). Supervision techniques involve the use of experiential exercises, group supervision, genograms, coaching, and self-counseling training. Supervision modalities include live and videotaped supervision, case discussion, and supervisor–supervisee cotherapy.

Finally, feminist contributions to family counseling supervision include an emphasis on the socialization of clients, supervisees, and supervisors and an emphasis on the conceptualization of larger systems and culture, gender relationships, power dynamics, diversity (i.e., age, sexual orientation), and emotions (Prouty, Thomas, Johnson, & Long, 2001). Applications to medical settings have infused feminist ideas about the reciprocal relationships between the biological, psychological, and social contexts of illness and healing, and gender and power issues (Bischof, Lieser, Taratua, & Fox, 2003; Knudson-Martin, 2003).

Systemic Postmodern Models of Supervision

Postmodern views impacting family therapy evolved through the 1990s and continue to have a strong presence in the field today (Freedman & Combs, 1996; Monk, Winslade, Crocket, & Epston, 1997; White & Epston, 1990).

Models within this tradition assert that supervisors and counselors are an integral part of the therapeutic system. Therapeutic reality is understood to be constructed as a function of the belief systems that families, counselors, and supervisors bring to therapy and by which they operate. In other words, supervisor, counselors, and clients are cocreators of a shared therapeutic reality. Meaning is the product of social interaction over time. They believe that "theory" and "context" cannot be separated and that reality can never be known directly. They place special emphasis on issues of power, history, and context. In supervision, Anderson and Goolishian (1990) explain that the training system is a meaning generating system where supervisors and supervisees are both learners, who, through narratives and stories, create meaning. The supervisory relationship strives to be collaborative and egalitarian insofar as participants in this system share their expertise. Overall, this stance seeks to create a dialogical environment in which counselors learn to appreciate multiple perspectives, address issues in a contextual and local manner, and abstain from traditional tendencies of labeling and pathologizing clients. Furthermore, some postmodern applications assist counselors in understanding how larger dominant societal discourses negatively impact them and their clients identities, desires, and relationships. Supervisors adopt a nonexpert stance whereby they renounce to irrevocable conclusions, but at the same time maintain their knowledge and expertise as contributions in the supervisory relationship. Models within this tradition include narrative and feminist, collaborative, reflecting teams, and solution-oriented supervision.

In his application of postmodernism to supervision, Ungar (2007) advances the notion that supervisors' assumed identity constructions are experienced as "different roles in relation to those we supervise" (p. 60), and that these roles then reflect each supervisor's diversity as well as individuality. Postmodern supervisors embrace this diversity in culture, gender, ability, sexual orientation, ethnicity, and class by acknowledging both the richness and the limitations therewith and by accentuating aspects of identity for training purposes. Supervisors are responsible for examining the construction of their own supervisory identity, challenging unhelpful aspects and defining an identity that they can perform well and fits with the relationship with supervisees. He outlines six overlapping supervisory roles: as an emotional support to the supervisee to assist in exploring the experience of therapy, as a supervisor focusing on the supervisee in his or her role as therapist, as a case consultant, as a teacher who instructs supervisees on the implementation of interventions while sharing individual and collective professional expertise, as a colleague sharing clinical responsibilities, and as an advocate encouraging supervisees to take action to ensure the well-being of clients. Ungar (2007) highlights the usefulness of this approach beyond the bounds of the academic setting where flexibility is often required due to the many constraints and changes posed by funding sources, populations served, local needs, and fluctuation of professionals. Postmodern supervisors recognize the challenges of using this approach across practice settings. Philp, Guy, and Lowe (2007) discuss ethical issues that are dilemmatic to a consistent application of postmodern principles in supervision. They recommend that both supervisors and supervisees engage in conversations on modern and postmodern views and the influence of those views on actual counseling work. Thus, flexibility and collaboration among multiple perspectives and positions continues to be a hallmark of postmodern supervision. Carlson and Erickson (2001) apply narrative therapy to the supervision of new counselors by using the following ideas: privileging counselors' personal knowledge and lived experience, encouraging counselors to develop rich descriptions of their lives based on their lived experience, using stories as the primary means by which counselors make sense of their lives, discussing counselors' unique ways of thinking and being as activities both relational and moral. They outline specific supervision practices that privilege the development of rich personal stories, remembering, and creating communities of concern. Some researchers (Lee & Littlejohns, 2007) have used the practice of externalization to address supervision dynamics involving shame, discomfort, and inadequacy when exposing ideas to others in group supervision and other professional groups.

Approaches within narrative and feminist models focus on overlapping concepts in their theoretical frameworks and in their guidelines for supervision practice, to wit, constructed knowledge, deconstruction, power, and agency. In spite of the nuances between approaches, sociopolitical context remains fundamental in shaping people's lives (Weingarten, 1991; White, 1995). They both make power and agency issues central in the healing endeavor. The feminist contribution to and its integration with narrative approaches emerged as the category of gender became more and more embedded in the whole of human experience. Myers Avis (1996) argued that family therapy has to account for "an understanding of the symbolic dimensions by which patriarchy is embedded in language, culture, and experience, and is thus subtly communicated and internalized from the moment of birth" (p. 224). In supervision, it is central for feminist and narrative approaches to address issues related to oppression. It is believed that effective counselors are aware of their locations of privilege and oppression and are able to understand how these locations play out in counseling and supervision. For example, Turner and Myers Avis (2003) address tensions between oppression and hope by asking supervisors to acknowledge power hierarchies in training and supervision, clarify roles and responsibilities, consider the effects of texts and conversations about oppression on those involved, bring texts and other materials addressing resistance to oppression, localize issues and their meaning in supervision conversations, and address intersections between gender and other social locations.

Collaborative approaches (Andersen, 1987, 2007; Anderson & Goolishian, 1988; Penn, 2007), also known as collaborative language systems, share the idea that supervisors, counselors, and clients are language- meaning-generating systems. The counseling system organizes itself around the identification of problems by those who interpret and experience them directly or indirectly. Thus, counseling systems emerge and dissolve based on the views and experiences of those who create them. Through dialogue, supervisors and supervisees cocreate meaning about the relationships and issues that exist between supervisors and supervisees and counselors and clients, and how to handle them. In an ongoing process of interpretation, issues and possible solutions emerge and dissolve. Anderson and Goolishian (1988) prefer to describe this process as *problem solving* and *problem dissolving* to emphasize the dynamic nature of dialogue from a collaborative perspective. This model strives to decrease the hierarchical relationship between supervisor and supervisee by making power and positions transparent, and by valuing what supervisors and supervisees bring to this meaning-generating system. It is assumed that we are who we are in relation to others. Therefore, learning about who we are as counselors and supervisors can only occur in a relationship. Supervisors and supervisees learn with each other and from each other. The primary task of the supervisor is to facilitate dialogical conversations and introduce comments that are appropriately unusual to promote new perspectives and generate new meanings (Andersen, 1987).

Andersen's reflecting team consultation and supervision modality (Andersen & Jensen, 2007) offers an innovative way to create safety, provides a space for contemplation and multiple views, allows for attention to process and content, and paces the supervision conversations to capture the many issues emerging for the counselor in therapy and supervision. Reflecting teams have been incorporated and redefined in various other family therapy approaches (i.e., narrative and solution-oriented), but Andersen (1987) offered basic guidelines that still apply to contemporary applications of this model, for example, participating members of the team should take turns to share positive comments about the clients and comments be appropriately unusual to foster the creation of new possibilities. Reflecting teams make supervisees active participants in the group supervision process by engaging them in a way that allows them to share what is best for them and take from the process what they find most useful. Cox, Banez, Hawley, and Mostades (2003) integrated reflecting teams with microcounseling to train novice counselors as well as group counselors. They found that the reflecting teams' method offered an experiential component that facilitated emotional safety, fostered creativity, and employed strengths-based learning.

Solution-oriented therapy and supervision have enjoyed popularity in the field due to its innovative and pragmatic nature. DeShazer (1990, pp. 93–94) outlined three guiding principles of this brief therapy model: (1) If it isn't broke, don't fix it; (2) Once you know what works do more of it; and (3) If it doesn't work, don't do it again, do something different. A distinguishing characteristic, when compared with narrative and collaborative approaches, is its emphasis on the present. Like narrative approaches, there is the belief that clients have the resources and abilities to resolve their own problems. This approach emphasizes a search for solutions based on incremental change. Applications of solution-oriented approaches to supervision (Juhnke, 1996; Knight, 2004; Thomas, 1996) stress the importance of language and its construction of both problems and solutions. Solution-oriented questions are best viewed as language tools that allow for supervisors and supervisees to move from the general to the specific to identify coping strategies and past success and address presenting issues in a concrete manner. As in counseling, supervision techniques include requesting and identifying exceptions; reframing, focus, and goal development; the miracle question; negotiating achievable goals in supervision; changing patterns; and using scaling, difference, motivation, and change questions. Knight (2004) discusses the importance of training supervisors to use silence, balancing conversations about problems and solutions, and identifying if and when the time and situation requires a different approach such as in crisis intervention situations. Solution-oriented supervision is a collaborative endeavor in which both supervisor and supervisee take a stance of curiosity to learn from each other.

Cunanan and McCollum (2006) examined methods that supervisees experienced as most effective in solution-oriented therapy training. Amongst the most helpful for the participants reading and discussing materials, interacting with a nonexpert supervisor, being encouraged to build upon existing strengths, and having solution-oriented supervision on cases in which they were applying this approach. As Whitting (2007) states, a balance between teaching and practical demonstration of the model in supervision is essential in training. Finally, supervision from a postmodern perspective uses reflecting teams, case discussions, and audio and videotaping technology in supervision. These models use less live and direct supervisory intervention unless both counselor and family have agreed to a consultation or a reflecting team intervention.

Postcolonial Approaches in Supervision

Recent developments in family therapy offer an integration of feminist and social justice principles and practices to counseling and supervision (Almeida, Dolan-Del Vecchio, & Parker, 2007). Specifically, the cultural context model (CCM) offers a system of clinical theory and practice that expands the family therapy paradigm based on an analysis of the societal patterns that contribute to the social inequities that organize family and community life. The model's aim is to construct communities that support a collective consciousness of liberation, by first developing collective knowledge necessary to dismantle linkages of power, privilege, and oppression.

The CCM has been influenced by postcolonial and critical postcolonial scholars in various disciplines (Crenshaw, 1997; Spivak, 1991). This scholarship addresses the specific issues encountered by communities that have been affected by the historical phenomenon of colonialism. The term *postcolonial* is a *descriptive* concept comprising dissenting discourses that oppose colonization and subordination across the globe by focusing on a variety of histories articulated alongside larger social dimensions. It recognizes multiple points of view and realities as a contestation of domination and the legacies of colonialism (Alva, 1995). The CCM is relevant for counselors and supervisors concerned with articulating the ways in which ethnicity, class, gender, ability, and sexual orientation construct varying dimensions of social inequality in family life. In supervision, training is centered around (1) developing a critical consciousness, accountability, and empowerment; (2) valuing historical information; (3) locating supervisees' narratives within the crucible of societal power dynamics; and (4) developing collaborative, learning processes within communities. Thus, supervisees revisit their family of origin work through a critical lens of dominant discourses and learn from working with clients with diverse issues and social locations about the social norms within each ethnic group, not to mention the social and cultural critique of these norms. In addition, the use of hypotheses and different modalities of therapeutic questions is tied to the larger social context. Creativity is enhanced as supervisees learn to use tools from popular media in therapeutic work (Hernández, 2004, 2008). Training under this model involves learning to work as a team with other therapists, consultants, and sponsors, as well as live and videotaped supervision. The New Jersey Family Therapy Institute uses bug-in-the-ear supervision along with a one-way mirror. This method uses a hearing aid-like device to transmit communication from the supervision team to the counselor while in session through a one-way mirror.

Integrative Models of Supervision

In her review of integrative supervision, Rigazio-DiGilio (1997) identifies four models for synthesizing individual, familial, and larger systems factors: metaframeworks (Breunlin, Schwartz, & McKune-Karrer, 1992), systemic cognitive-developmental therapy and supervision (Rigazio-DiGilio &

Anderson, 1995), integrative problem-centered therapy (Pinsof, 1994), and mythological perspective-taking (Bagarozzi & Anderson, 1989). Integrative frameworks offer a metaperspective that guides the supervision work instead of specific definitions and techniques about supervision. This metaperspective is holistic and intends to address the supervisory and therapeutic relationships and the wider context of changing realities. According to Rigazio-DiGilio (1997) the supervision relationship seeks congruence between the supervisees' needs and the supervisory context. By identifying, validating, and encouraging the growth of supervisees' strengths, a foundation is constructed to facilitate the identification and examination of limitations and areas for further growth. An important advantage of integrative models is that they organize various therapeutic perspectives, the result of which offers multiple points of reference in the conceptualization and application of interventions in supervision. This section will offer an overview of the metaframeworks supervisory perspective as an illustration of integrative models. Metaframeworks is a systemic and holistic perspective integrating core assumptions of major family therapy schools. Breulin, Rampage, and Eovaldi (1995) applied the metaframeworks therapy approach to supervision. In this model there are five interrelated components providing a lens by which to comprehend the biological, psychological, and social aspects of systems: the family, individual, gender, culture, and complexity. There are also four interrelated processes in supervision: hypothesizing, planning, conversing, and reading feedback.

The family component addresses the development of assessment and intervention skills from the vantage point of the family system. Thus, supervision and training focus on assisting counselors to define a meaningful therapeutic system (including members not present in counseling), distinguishing between content and process, observing and identifying patterns and meanings of behavior, generating hypotheses based on observations, designing interventions, and setting treatment goals. Supervisors also attend to the meaning-making, behavioral, and emotional aspects of the supervision relationship.

The individual component deals with the unique system of the individual. It refers to the internal dynamics created by the multiple subpersonalities or parts of an individual's mind. These parts may work together or oppose each other, the latter of which creates conflict. If appropriate, supervisees are encouraged to consider this level and develop clinical hypotheses about individual family members. This level addresses the intrapsychic dynamics that may be constraining an individual and her or his family from solving a problem. Individual psychotherapy may be recommended to complement family therapy or perhaps in lieu of family therapy if deemed appropriate by both supervisor and supervisee. The gender component addresses the gender socialization that supervisees bring in their use of self and in their development as clinicians. Discussions of the feminist critique of family therapy are incorporated in training to assist in the recognition of prejudices that may privilege and oppress both genders. In addition, supervisees learn to see the levels of gender balances and imbalances through an analysis of the supervisees' family dynamics and upbringing. The model uses five positions along a continuum to describe at which stage supervisees are in their development: traditional, gender-aware, polarized, in transition, and balanced. Supervisors assist and encourage counselors to examine the impact of their own gender and gender views on treatment.

The cultural component addresses the impact of culture-based influences on the supervision relationship and in counseling. Supervisors need to be mindful of the goodness of fit between their cultural heritage and that of their supervisees, just as counselors must be attentive to this aspect in counseling. This aspect acknowledges that the supervisees' cultural lenses shape how they learn, relate to authority, develop expectations, and see themselves in social context. Supervisees are encouraged to explore their views about diversity and learn about cultures that differ from their own as it applies to their clinical work.

The complexity component avers that counselors can never fully understand a family's reality, and that counselors should strive to develop clinical hypotheses addressing the physical, intrapsychic, and interpersonal level aspects of the family. Supervisors focus on teaching and modeling how to address families' in context; they use various theoretical models and treatment interventions that best fit a particular family.

Finally, in supervision, supervisors need to ask themselves what constraints may prevent a supervisee from developing to her or his full potential and, further, how the supervisor and supervisee can collaborate to identify and work through such constraints and allow growth and expansion of strengths. There are four levels of complexity addressing supervision assessment, development, and impasses in the supervisory relationship. These levels include mastering of the basic counseling systemic skills; examining beliefs, thoughts, and feelings that could strengthen or perhaps hinder the counseling and supervisory relationships; addressing patterns of therapeutic and supervisory impasses in order to assist in the development of the self of the counselor; and exploring personal counseling as an option to complement supervision.

The Common Factors Approach to Supervision

Based on their identification of common factors in the supervision and research literature, Morgan and Sprenkle (2007) developed a model in which three specific continua were included: (1) clinical and professional competence; (2) level of specificity; and (3) directive and collaborative relationships. One side of the first continuum focuses on clinical issues, theories and interventions, and services provision; the other side focuses on professional competence, which includes ethical and legal standards and personal growth issues related to being a counselor. The second continuum identifies the level of specificity by which the counselor must be familiar with a particular population. Thus, the focus will vary between such idiosyncratic and nomothetic issues as learning to work with specific client population (e.g., Latin families in Baltimore, Maryland and learning about this population's health needs as a whole). The third continuum refers to the supervisory relationship. Though the supervisory relationship is inherently hierarchical in structure, there are many differences as to how directive and collaborative it is structured.

In addition, there are four overlapping roles characterizing the following supervision activities: coaching, teaching, mentoring, and administrating. These roles fall along the three continua described above. For example, the coach role would emphasize the development of clinical competence at an idiosyncratic level with supervisees. Activities include helping supervisees to conceptualize a case and offering feedback about their work. The teacher role would emphasize clinical practice at a more general level. Thus, the focus of supervision includes, for example, learning the principles of postmodern therapy approaches and integrating their techniques in practice. The mentoring role would focus on developing professional competence as it relates to the supervisee. As such, personal growth and contributions to both the therapeutic alliance and the profession would be areas of attention. Finally, the administrator role would focus on the learning and application of standards, ranging from ethical principles to case documentation. Morgan and Sprenkle (2007) posit that this model serves as "a template for understanding the range of responsibilities, tasks, and roles that the literature suggests a supervisor should fill" (p. 12). It allows for addressing various levels of emphasis and flexibility in regards to the overlapping nature of the dimensions and roles described.

Supervision Strategies

Contemporary training and supervision environments are flexible and adapt to the demands of changing health care settings, populations, and clinical issues. However, it is important to note that family therapy models support different types of supervisory techniques or a combination thereof. Supervisees' developmental level should be taken into account when choosing a supervision modality.

Supervision strategies include live and *ex post facto* supervision. Live supervision allows supervisors to monitor and offer interventions while counseling sessions take place and prevent clinically important super-visee nondisclosures (Ladany, Hill, Corbett, & Nutt, 1996). Supervisors have the opportunity to experience, witness, and take part in the super-visees' work with families. Conversely, *exp post facto* supervision refers to those modalities that involve reviewing counseling sessions after they have occurred.

Live Supervision

Modalities included under this strategy are cotherapy, bug-in-the-ear, tele-phone, and the reflecting team approach. Nowadays these modalities are not exclusively used in training centers but in a variety of clinical settings. Cotherapy involves the presence of the supervisor in the counseling ses-sion. Supervisors may participate by simply observing the session or by providing comments and interventions when appropriate. When a founda-tion of support and collaboration has been established between supervisor and supervisee, novice counselors' anxiety is alleviated as they do not feel solely responsible for the counseling session (Anderson, Rigazio-DiGilio, & Kunkler, 1995).

Bug-in-the-ear utilizes a hearing aid type of device to transmit commu-nication from a supervisor watching behind a one-way mirror to the coun-selor trainee. Interventions are brief and the supervisee is unable to clarify or discuss the supervisory message (Barker, 1998, as cited by Kaufman, Morgan, & Ladany, 2001). Telephone devices use a one-way mirror too. However, they allow supervisors and supervisees two-way communication. Supervisees may ask questions and discuss supervision suggestions. Its most obvious limitation is that it overtly disrupts the session. In both modali-ties, there may be either a team of supervisors and counselors behind the one-way mirror or simply a single supervisor. Mauzey, Morag, and Trusty (2000) examined the effects of delayed, phone-in, or bug-in-the-ear super-vision upon the anxiety and anger of novice counselors-in-training. They found that these supervision methods contributed to the state anxiety or state anger of the participants; while state anger declined over time, state anxiety was not significantly different over time. Another study examined the correlation between frequency, duration, and complexity of phone-in supervision interventions in counseling and the supervisees' resultant behavior (Moorhouse & Carr, 2001). Contrary to conventional wisdom, the authors found that complex phone-ins involving more than four sug-gestions were positively related to supervisees' counseling behaviors. In a subsequent study in which correlates between phone-ins and client coop-eration were examined, Moorhouse and Carr (2001) found that client cooperation was associated exclusively with the presence and quality of the collaborative behavior shown by the counselor. Supervisory behaviors were not associated with any category of client cooperation.

Another study addressed client satisfaction and live supervision (Locke & McCollum, 2001). There were 108 clients that completed the Client Satisfaction Questionnaire and a modified version of the Purdue Live Observation Satisfaction Scale at a university clinic. It was concluded that clients were satisfied with counseling, and that they, so long as they perceived the process as helpful, did not find the live supervision process intrusive. In this setting supervisors used a one-way mirror, telephones, and a consultation break with a supervision team. This study points to the need to balance training needs and responsiveness to treatment in order to fulfill the needs of clients and clinicians-in-training. Receiving client input in this process is an important element to achieve this balance.

Ex Post Facto Supervision

Supervisory modalities involving a retrospective examination of clinical material include case presentations, case notes, audiotape, and videotape review. A recent analysis of trends in family therapy supervision (Lee et al., 2004) found that the least popular modalities were audiotape reviews and verbatim reconstructions of counseling sessions. Videotape and case reviews were the most popular, followed closely by live supervision. However, supervisors use a combination of methods to address competence development in personal growth and in clinical, administrative, and professional skills.

Videotape reviews provide an objective visual and verbal examination of sessions and allow supervisors to comment on issues of process, content, and skill development. However, Huhra, Yamokoski-Maynhart, and Prieto (2008) suggest that supervisors orient supervisees as to how this modality will be used. This orientation should outline expectations for the use of videotapes in supervision, how to introduce it to clients and obtain informed consent, and how it will be used for evaluation purposes.

Audiotape review offers data limited to the voice, pace, intensity, and content solely of the verbal aspect of the therapeutic conversation. However partial these data are, they still offer an objective and fairly accurate perspective on a family counseling session. Case presentations and case note reviews are typically included in the supervision and training process of master's and doctoral level clinicians and are routine practices in clinical settings (Lee et al., 2004). These modalities work well in combination with live supervision and videotape review. However, when used as the sole supervision modality with novice clinicians, there is the potential of inaccurate reporting (West, Bubenzer, Pinsoneault, & Holeman, 1993). In addition, the reporting of issues and the observation of family dynamics is obviously filtered through the lens of the supervisee, thereby resulting in gaps in content, process, and family-counselor relationship dynamics.

Conclusion

The surfeit of supervision models in the family counseling field reflects its historical trajectory, philosophical changes, contextual adaptations, innovation and creativity, concern for social issues, and evolution as a distinct specialty in family counseling. Still, the challenge that Kaufman et al. (2001) raised regarding the importance of empirical support remains: "What kind of supervision is effective when, from whom, for whom, under what conditions, and for what type of clinical situation?" (White & Russell, 1995, p. 43, as cited by Kaufman et al., 2001). Although the literature is rich in describing applications of family counseling approaches to training and supervision, there is as yet a dearth of qualitative and quantitative studies examining the efficaciousness of these models. Morgan and Sprenkle (2007) insist that models offering a metaperspective should continue to be developed, specifically those based on factors common to all supervision.

A key issue for the field remains the systematic incorporation of diversity issues related to ethnicity, class, ability, spirituality, and sexual orientation as a part of supervision response to the diverse and complex identities and needs of consumers. The field needs to offer parameters for models that promote collaborative learning and critical thinking on the integration of contextual variables in a way that promotes human diversity instead of cultural homogeneity in supervision training.

Finally, in their analysis of family therapy supervision trends, Lee et al. (2004) identified the need to examine how supervisors integrate the various supervision strategies described in this chapter. In the contemporary arena, supervisors have access to many modalities, and clinical settings have the potential to adapt modalities to supervisees' developmental level, population served, and managed care demands.

References

Ackerman, N. W. (1937). The family as a social emotional unit. *Bulletin of the Kansas Mental Health Hygiene Society, 12.*

Almeida, R., Dolan-Del Vecchio, K., & Parker, L. (2007). *Transformational family therapy.* Boston, MA: Allyn and Bacon.

Alva, J. K. (1995). The postcolonization of the (Latin) American experience, a reconsideration of "colonialism," "postcolonialism" and "meztizaje." In G. Prakash (Ed.), *After colonialism, imperial histories and postcolonial displacements* (pp. 241–275). Princeton, NJ: Princeton University Press.

American Association for Marriage and Family Therapy (AAMFT). (2004). *Core competencies final review.* Retrieved from http://www.bbs.ca.gov/pdf/mhsa/resource/workforce/aamft_core_competencies.pdf

Andersen, T. (1987). The reflecting team: Dialogue and meta-dialogue in clinical work. *Family Process, 26*(4), 415–428.

Andersen, T. (2007). Human participating: Human "being" is the step for human "becoming" in the next step. In H. Anderson & D. Gehart (Eds.), *Collaborative therapy: Relationships and conversations that make a difference* (pp. 81–93). New York, NY: Routledge.

Andersen, T., & Jensen, P. (2007). Crossroads. In H. Andersen & P. Jensen (Eds.), *Innovations in the reflecting team process* (pp. 158–174). London, United Kingdom: Karnac.

Anderson, H., & Goolishian, H. (1988). Human systems as linguistic systems: Preliminary and evolving ideas about the implications for clinical theory. *Family Process, 27*, 371–393.

Anderson, H., & Goolishian, H. (1990). Beyond cybernetics: Comments on Atkinson and Heath's thoughts on second-order family therapy. *Family Process, 29*, 157–163.

Anderson, S. A., Rigazio-DiGilio, S., & Kunkler, K. P. (1995). Training and supervision in family therapy: Current issues and future directions. *Family Relations: Journal of Applied Family & Child Studies, 44*(4), 489–500.

Bagarozzi, D., & Anderson, S. (1989). Training and supervision marital and family therapy. In D. Bagarozzi & S. Anderson (Eds.), *Personal, marital and family myths: Theoretical formulations and clinical strategies* (pp. 274–298). New York, NY: W. W. Norton.

Barrett, S., Chin, J. L., Comas-Diaz, L., Espin, O., & Greene, B. (2005). Multicultural feminist therapy: Theory in context. *Women and Therapy, 28*(3–4), 27–61.

Bischof, G. H., Lieser, M. L., Taratua, C. G., & Fox, A. (2003). Power and gender issues from the voices of medical family therapists. *Journal of Feminist Family Therapy, 15*(2/3), 23–54.

Bittner, J. R., & Corey, G. (2001). Family systems therapy. In G. Corey (Ed.), *Theory and practice of counseling and psychotherapy* (6th ed., pp. 382–453). Pacific Grove, CA: Brooks/Cole.

Bowen, M. (1978). *Family therapy in clinical practice.* Northvale, NJ: Jason Aronson.

Boyd-Franklin, N. (2003). *Black families in therapy.* New York, NY: Guilford Press.

Breunlin, D. C., Schwartz, R. C., & Kune-Karrer, B. M. (1992). *Metaframeworks: Transcending models of family therapy.* San Francisco: Jossey-Bass.

Breulin, D. C., Rampage, C., & Eovaldi, M. L. (1995). Family therapy supervision: Toward an integrative perspective. In R. H. Mikesell, D-D. Lusterman, & S. H. McDaniel (Eds.), *Integrating family therapy: Handbook of family psychology and systems theory* (pp. 547–560). Washington, DC: American Psychological Association.

Carlson, T., & Erickson, M. (2001). Honoring and privileging personal experience and knowledge: Ideas for a narrative therapy approach to the training and supervision of new therapists. *Contemporary Family Therapy, 23*(2), 199–220.

Crenshaw, K. (1997). Intersectionality and identity politics: Learning from violence against women of color. In M. Lyndon Shanley & U. Narayan (Eds.), *Reconstructing political theory: Feminist perspectives* (pp. 111–132). University Park, PA: Pennsylvania State University Press.

Cox, J. A., Banez, L., Hawley, L., & Mostades, J. (2003). Use of the reflecting team process in the training of group workers. *Journal for Specialists in Group Work, 28*(2), 89–105.

Cunanan, E. D., & McCollum, E. E. (2006). What works when learning solution-focused brief therapy: A qualitative study of trainees' experiences. *Journal of Family Psychotherapy, 17*(1), 49–65.

DeRoma, V., Hickey, D. A., & Stanek, K. M. (2007). Methods of supervision in marriage and family therapist training: A brief report. *North American Journal of Psychology, 9*(3), 415–422.

DeShazer, S. (1990). What it is about brief therapy that works? In J. Zeig & G. Gilligan (Eds.), *Brief therapy: Myths, methods, and metaphors* (pp. 90–99). New York, NY: Brunner Mazel.

Doerries, D. B., & Foster, V. A. (2005). Essential skills for novice structural family therapists: A delphi study of experienced practitioners' perspectives. *The Family Journal, 13*(3), 259–265.

Flemons, D. G., Green, S. K., & Rambo, A. H. (1996). Evaluating therapists' practices in a postmodern world: A discussion and a scheme. *Family Process, 35*, 43–56.

Freedman, J., & Combs, G. (1996). *Narrative therapy.* New York, NY: W. W. Norton.

Gridley, H. (2004). Power, gender, and accountability in supervision. In D. Paré & G. Larner (Eds.), *Collaborative practice in psychology and therapy* (pp. 183–198). New York, NY: Haworth Press.

Haley, J. (1987). *Problem solving therapy.* San Francisco, CA: Jossey-Bass.

Hammond, R. T., & Nichols, M. P. (2008). How collaborative is structural family therapy? *The Family Journal, 16*(2), 118–124.

Hernández, P. (2004). The cultural context model in supervision: An illustration. *Journal of Feminist Family Therapy, 15*(4), 1–8.

Hernández, P. (2008). The cultural context model in clinical supervision: An illustration of critical psychology in training. *Training and Education in Professional Psychology, 2*(1), 10–17.

Hernández, P., & Rankin, P. (2008). Relational safety in supervision. *Journal of Marital & Family Therapy, 34*(2), 58–74.

Hernández, P., Taylor, B., & McDowell, T. (2009). Listening to ethnic minority AAMFT approved supervisors: Reflections on their experiences as supervisees. *Journal of Systemic Therapies, 28*(1), 88–100.

Huhra, R. L., Yamokoski-Maynhart, C. A., & Prieto, L. R. (2008). Reviewing videotape in supervision: A developmental approach. *Journal of Counseling and Development, 86*(4), 412–418.

Jackson, D. D. (1957). The question of family homeostasis. *Psychiatric Quarterly Supplement, 31*, 79–90.

Juhnke, G. (1996). Solution-focused supervision: Promoting supervisee skills and confidence through successful solutions. *Counselor Education and Supervision, 36*, 48–57.

Kaslow, N., & Bell, K. (2008). A competency-based approach to supervision. In C. A. Falender & E. P. Shafranske (Eds.), *Casebook for clinical supervision: A competency-based approach* (pp. 17–38). Washington, DC: American Psychological Association.

Kaufman, M., Morgan, K. J., & Ladany, N. (2001). Family counseling supervision. In L. Bradley & N. Ladany (Eds.), *Counselor supervision: Principles, process and practice.* (3rd ed., pp. 245–267). New York, NY: Brunner-Routledge.

Knight, C. (2004). Integrating solution-focused principles and techniques into clinical practice and supervision. *The Clinical Supervisor, 23*(2), 153–163.

Knudson-Martin, C. (2003). Gender and biology: A recursive framework for clinical practice. *Journal of Feminist Family Therapy, 15*(2/3), 1–21.

Ladany, N., Hill, C., Corbett, M., & Nutt, E. (1996). Nature, extent, and importance of what psychotherapy trainees do not disclose to their supervisors. *Journal of Counseling Psychology, 43,* 10–24.

Lee, R. E., Nichols, D. P., Nichols, W. C., & Odom, T. (2004). Trends in family therapy supervision: The past 25 years and into the future. *Journal of Marital & Family Therapy, 30*(1), 61–69.

Lee, L., & Littlejohns, S. (2007). Deconstructing Agnes: Externalization in systemic supervision. *Journal of Family Therapy, 29*(3), 238–248.

Liddle, H. A., Breunlin, D.C., & Schwartz, R. C. (1988). Family therapy training and supervision: An introduction. In H. A. Liddle., D. C. Breunlin, & R. C. Schwartz (Eds.), *Handbook of family therapy training and supervision* (pp. 3–9). New York, NY: Guilford Press.

Locke, L., & McCollum, E. (2001). Clients' views of live supervision and satisfaction with therapy. *Journal of Marital & Family Therapy, 21*(1), 129–133.

Long, J. K., & Lindsey, E. (2004). The sexual orientation matrix for supervision: A tool for training therapists to work with same-sex couples. In J. Bigner & J. L. Wetchler (Eds.), *Relationship therapy with same-sex couples* (pp. 123–135). New York, NY: Haworth Press.

Madanes, C. (2006). *The therapist as humanist, social activist, and systemic thinker and other selected papers.* Phoenix, AZ: Zeig, Tucker & Theisen.

Madanes, C., Keim, J., & Smelser, D. (1995). *The violence of men: New techniques for working with abusive families.* San Francisco, CA: Jossey-Bass.

Mauzey, E., Morag, B. C., & Trusty, J. (2000). Comparing the effects of live supervision interventions on novice trainee anxiety and anger. *The Clinical Supervisor, 19*(2), 109–122.

McDowell, T., Fang, S., Brownlee, K, Gomez Young, C., & Khanna, A. (2002). Transforming a MFT program: A model for enhancing diversity. *Journal of Marital & Family Therapy, 28*(2), 179–191.

McGoldrick, M., Almeida, R., Garcia-Preto, N., Bibb, A., Sutton, C., Hudak, J., & Moore Hines, P. (1999). Efforts to incorporate social justice perspective into a family training program. *Journal of Marital & Family Therapy, 25*(2), 191–209.

McGoldrick, M., Giordano, J., & Garcia-Preto, N. (2005). Overview: Ethnicity and family therapy. In M. McGoldrick, J. Giordano, & N. Garcia-Preto (Eds.), *Ethnicity and family therapy* (pp. 1–40). New York, NY: Guilford Press.

Minuchin, P., Colapinto, J., & Minuchin, S. (1998). *Working with families of the poor.* New York, NY: Guilford Press.

Minuchin, S., Lee, W., & Simon, G. M. (1996). *Mastering family therapy.* New York, NY: John Wiley & Sons.

Monk, G., Winslade, J., Crocket, K., & Epston, D. (1997). *Narrative therapy in practice.* San Francisco, CA: Jossey-Bass.

Montgomery, C., Hendricks, C. B., & Bradley, A. J. (2001). Using systems perspectives in supervision. *The Family Journal, 9*(3), 305–313.

Moorhouse, A., & Carr, A. (2001). A study of live supervisory phone-ins in collaborative family therapy: Correlates of client cooperation. *Journal of Marital & Family Therapy, 27*(2), 241–249.

Morgan, M., & Sprenkle, D. (2007). Toward a common-factors approach to supervision. *Journal of Marital & Family Therapy, 33*(1), 1–17.

Myers Avis, J. (1996). Deconstructing gender in family therapy. In F. Piercey & D. Sprenkle (Eds.), *Family therapy source book* (pp. 220–255). New York, NY: Guilford Press.

Paris, E., Linville, D., & Rosen, K. (2006). Marriage and family therapist interns' experiences of growth. *Journal of Marital & Family Therapy, 32*(1), 45–57.

Pearson, D. H. (1987). The strategic family therapy ritual as a framework for supervision. *Strategic and Systemic Therapies, 6*(4), 17–28.

Penn, P. (2007). Listening voices. In H. Anderson & D. Gehart (Eds.), *Collaborative therapy: Relationships and conversations that make a difference* (pp. 99–107). New York, NY: Routledge.

Philp, G., Guy, G., & Lowe, A. (2007). Social constructionist supervision or supervision as social construction? Some dilemmas. *Journal of Systemic Therapies, 26*(1), 51–62.

Pinsof, W. (1994). An overview of integrative problem-centered therapy: A synthesis of family and individual psychotherapies. *Journal of Family Therapy, 16,* 103–120.

Prouty, A. M., Thomas, V., Johnson, S., & Long, J. K. (2001). Methods of feminist family therapy supervision. *Journal of Marital & Family Therapy, 27*(1), 85–97.

Rigazio-DiGilio, S. A. (1997). Integrative supervision: Approaches to tailoring the supervisory process. In T. C. Todd & C. L. Storm (Eds.), *The complete systemic supervisor: Context, philosophy and pragmatics* (pp. 195–216). Boston, MA: Allyn and Bacon.

Rigazio-DiGilio, S. A., & Anderson, S. A. (1995). A cognitive-developmental model for marital and family therapy supervision. *The Clinical Supervisor, 12*(2), 93–118.

Roberto, L. (1997). Transgenerational models. In T. C. Todd & C. L. Storm (Eds.), *The complete systemic supervisor: Context, philosophy and pragmatics* (pp. 156–170). Boston, MA. Allyn and Bacon.

Rudes, J., Shilts, L., & Kim Berg, I. (1997). Focused supervision seen through a recursive frame analysis. *Journal of Marital & Family Therapy, 23*(2), 203–213.

Russell, C. S., DuPree, W. J., Beggs, M. A., Peterson, C. M., & Anderson, M. P. (2007). Responding to remediation and gatekeeping challenges in supervision. *Journal of Marital & Family Therapy, 33*(2), 227–244.

Santisteban, D. A., Suarez-Morales, L., Robbins, M. S., & Szapocznik, J. (2006). Brief strategic family therapy: Lessons learned in efficacy research and challenges to blending research and practice. *Family Process, 45,* 259–271.

Selvini-Palazzoli, M., Boscolo, L., Cecchin, G., & Prata, G. (1978). *Paradox and counterparadox.* New York, NY: Jason Aronson.

Spivak, G. C. (1991). Can the subaltern speak? In C. Nelson & L. Grossberg (Eds.), *Marxism and the interpretation of culture* (pp. 1–15). Urbana, IL: University of Illinois Press.

Storm, C., Todd, T., Sprenkle, D., & Morgan, M. (2001). Gaps between MFT supervision assumptions and common practice: Suggested best practices. *Journal of Marital & Family Therapy, 27*(2), 227–240.

Szapocznik, J., Hervis, O., & Schwartz, S. (2003). *Brief strategic family therapy for adolescent drug abuse* (NIH Pub. No. 03-4751, National Institute on Drug Abuse Treatment Manual Series No. 5). Rockville, MD: National Institute on Drug Abuse.

Taylor, B., Hernández, P., Deri, A., Rankin, P., & Siegel, A. (2007). Integrating diversity dimensions in supervision: Perspectives of ethnic minority supervisors. *The Clinical Supervisor, 25*(1/2), 3–22.

Thomas, F. (1996). Solution focused supervision: The coaxing of expertise. In S. S. Miller., M. Hubble, & B. Duncan (Eds.), *Handbook of solution focused therapy* (pp. 128–151). San Francisco, CA: Jossey-Bass.

Todd, T. C. (1997). Purposive systemic supervision models. In T. C. Todd & C. L. Storm (Eds.), *The complete systemic supervisor: context, philosophy and pragmatics* (pp. 173–194). Boston, MA: Allyn and Bacon.

Todd, T. C., & Storm, C. L. (1997). *The complete systemic supervisor.* Needham Heights, MA: Allyn and Bacon.

Turner, J., & Myers Avis, J. (2003). Naming injustice, engendering hope: Tensions in feminist family therapy training. In L. B. Solverstein & T. J. Goodrich (Eds.), *Feminist family therapy: Empowerment in social context* (pp. 365–378). Washington, DC: American Psychological Association.

Ungar, M. (2007). Practicing as a postmodern supervisor. *Journal of Marital & Family Therapy, 32*(1), 59–72.

Ungar, M., & Costanzo, L. (2007). Supervision challenges when supervisors are outside supervisees' agencies. *Journal of Systemic Therapies, 26*(2), 68–83.

Watkins, C. E. (1997). Defining psychotherapy supervision and understanding supervisor functioning. In C. E. Watkins (Ed.), *Handbook of psychotherapy supervision* (pp. 3–10). New York, NY: John Wiley and Sons.

Watzlawick, P. (1976). *How real is real?* New York, NY: Random House.

Weingarten, K. (1991). The discourses of intimacy: Adding a social constructionist and feminist view. *Family Process, 30*, 285–305.

West, J. D., Bubenzer, D. L., Pinsoneault, T., & Holeman, V. (1993). Three supervision modalities for training marital and family counselors. *Counselor Education & Supervision, 33*, 127–138.

Wetchler, J. L. (1988). Primary and secondary influential theories of family therapy supervisors: A research note. *Family Therapy, 51*(1), 69–74.

Whitaker, C., & Ryan, M. (1989). *Midnight musings of a family therapist.* New York, NY: W. W. Norton.

White, M. (1995). *Re-authoring lives: Interviews and essays.* Adelaide, South Australia: Dulwich Centre Publications.

White, M., & Epston, D. (1990). *Narrative means to therapeutic ends.* New York, NY: Norton & Norton.

Whitting, J. (2007). Authors, artists and social constructionism: A case study of narrative supervision. *The American Journal of Family Therapy, 35*, 139–150.

Zimmerman, T., & Haddock, S. (2001). The weave of gender and culture in the tapestry of a family therapy program: Promoting social justice in the practice of family therapy. *Journal of Feminist Family Therapy, 12*(2–3), 1–31.

CHAPTER 13

Supervision of Assessment

RAYNA D. MARKIN

In 1907, Indiana became the first state in the United States to legalize compulsory sterilization of mentally ill and mentally retarded persons. In 1924, the Racial Integrity Act followed, banning People of Color from marrying White people. Beginning with Connecticut in 1896, many states enacted marriage laws prohibiting anyone who was "imbecile" or "feebleminded" from marrying. The Immigration Act of 1924 reduced immigration from abroad, based on the threat of "inferior stock" infiltrating the American population. What do these historical policies have in common? They were all greatly influenced by the Eugenics movement of the 1900s, which used various assessment practices to identify and remove "unfit" individuals from society through institutionalization, sterilization, and immigration and marriage laws. Psychologists like Henry H. Goddard argued that research on the intelligence quotient (IQ) showed that certain racial and ethnic groups possess higher rates of mental retardation and consequently were not fit for society. What Goddard failed to see was that his bias toward persons whom he referred to as "morons," or individuals with an IQ below 51, greatly influenced his data. His research methods, and specifically his administration and interpretation of the Simon-Binet Scale to assess IQ, are extremely flawed by today's standards. However, at the time, Goddard's assessment of intelligence had significant real-world implications and serves as a current day reminder of the importance of supervision and training in ethical and competent assessment practices (see Haller, 1963; Kevles, 1985; Zenderlan, 1998).

Why is Supervision of Assessment Important?

There are four overarching rationales for devoting considerable attention to supervision of assessment, which include: the significant real-world implications of assessment practices, the central role of assessment in counseling and psychology professions, the complexity of assessment supervision, and the relationship between client assessments and counseling outcome. Looking at real-world implications first, the Eugenics movement is a daunting example of how the application and interpretation of assessments can directly influence social policies and legal reforms. On the counselor–client level, counselors' assessment interpretations could influence a client's placement in school (for example, placement of gifted children and special education programs), benefits, career decisions, diagnosis and treatment, self-esteem and self-concept, and even legal proceedings. For example, school psychologists often diagnose students demonstrating behavioral or learning difficulties in the classroom and such diagnoses can significantly alter a child's educational career (Crespi & Dube, 2005). The overall point being that assessment practices can have significant consequences. Supervision and training have the daunting task of adequately preparing trainees to conduct ethical and competent assessment practices equal to the high stakes involved.

Second, assessment has historically been a primary activity and defining feature of psychologists and plays a significant role in the field of counseling as well (Dumont & Willis, 2003; Krishnamurthy et al., 2004). Assessment is still a central activity to practicing clinicians (Butler, Retzlaff, & Vanderploeg, 1991; Guilmette, Faust, Hart, & Arkes, 1990; Lovitt, 1992; Piotrowski & Keller, 1989; Piotrowski & Keller, 1992). Application of psychological testing is typically discussed in reference to clinical psychology; for example, Maruish (1999) discussed typical uses of psychological assessment for clinical decision making. At the same time, counseling psychologists often are involved in the assessment of educational and vocational aptitudes and skills and/or factors related to personal growth and development (see Hood & Johnson, 2002). School psychologists primarily use testing to assess learning disabilities, attention-deficit/hyperactivity disorder (ADHD), emotional and behavioral disorders, and to identify gifted children (see Sattler, 2002). Across various disciplines, counselors and psychologists need to be prepared to administer, interpret, and give feedback on various assessments.

In certain respects, counseling and clinical graduate training programs echo the important role that assessment plays in clinical practice. Both the Counsel for the Accreditation of Counseling and Related Educational Programs (CACREP) and the American Psychological Association (APA) have developed training standards for assessment in graduate coursework. Specifically, CACREP states that counseling programs provide an "understanding of individual and group approaches to assessment and evaluation in a multicultural society" (CACREP 2009 Accreditation Standards, Standard 7, p. 12). Similarly, APA states that students should acquire and demonstrate substantial understanding of and competence in "diagnosing or defining problems through psychological assessment and measurement" (APA

Guidelines and Principles for Accreditation of Programs in Professional Psychology, Doctoral Graduate Program Guidelines, Guideline 3c, 2000). Although these guidelines do not directly address supervision of assessment, they do point to the professions' value on assessment training. A survey of doctoral PhD and PsyD programs in clinical psychology confirm that these training programs emphasize assessment coursework, particularly intelligence and personality measures (Piotrowski & Zalewski, 1993). Although assessment coursework is a required component of clinical and counseling programs and assessment itself is a central activity of many practitioners, the value and content of such coursework is continually questioned (see Elbert, 1984; Frohnauer, Vavak, & Hardin, 1988; Kolbe, Shemberg, & Leventhal, 1985; Moreland & Dahlstrom, 1983; Piotrowskil & Keller, 1984). Furthermore, recent graduates feel they received inadequate training in assessment on the graduate level (Dempster, 1990; Hershey, Kopplin, Cornell, 1991) and during internship (Holmes, Cook, & Rothstein, 1991). Despite the training requirements, there appears to be a disconnect between the significant role of assessment in practice and in graduate level assessment training and supervision (Krishnamurthy et al., 2004).

The third proposed rationale for devoting attention to assessment supervision is that it requires considerable expertise and specialization to execute well. Supervision in psychological assessment requires more than learning the mechanics of how to administer and score psychological tests. It also involves complex skills and processes (Fernández-Ballesteros et al., 2001; Finn, 1996; Groth-Marnat, 1999; Meyer et al., 1998; Turner, DeMers, Fox, & Reed, 2001). For example, Meyer and colleagues (1998) emphasize many different facets of the psychological assessment process, including interpreting data from multiple sources of an assessment, and placing the test data within the context of referral information, client history, and observations. Other models of assessment characterize it as a collaborative process and as a therapeutic intervention in itself (Finn, 1996). Dumont and Willis (2003) argue that counselors and psychologists of all levels of experience need to obtain assessment supervision because of the numerous complexities and challenges involved in assessment practice, such as inadequate training, attenuation of skills over time, frequency of assessment errors, attempts to acquire new competencies, and new developments in the field. In general, supervisors have the important role of maintaining professional standards (Holloway & Neufeldt, 1995), which is no simple task when it comes to the complexity of assessment practices. The final rationale for considering issues in assessment supervision is that several studies have pointed to a significant relationship between psychodiagnostic testing and psychotherapy outcome (Cerney, 1978; Keddy & Piotrowski, 1992; Phillips, 1992; Weiner & Exner, 1991). In particular, testing has been found to help validate and explain behaviors to clients in a way that they perceive as helpful (Finn &

Tonsager, 1992). What we do not know as of yet is how supervision of assessment impacts the relationship between testing and counseling outcome.

Despite the central role of assessment for counselors and psychologists, little attention in the literature has been given to supervision of assessment practices (Finkelstein & Tuckman, 1997; Krishnamurthy et al., 2004; Smith & Harty, 1987). Without empirical models for assessment supervision, such supervisory practices have been left primarily to oral tradition (Finkelstein & Tuckman, 1997). In comparison to the extensive literature on supervision in general, supervision of assessment is almost entirely ignored (Decato, 2002; Krishnamurthy et al., 2004). Looking at clinical supervision of school psychologists and school counselors as one particular example, although school counselors report wanting more clinical supervision, of which assessment is a major component (Crespi & Dube, 2005), it is largely overlooked in these specialties (Crespi, 1998; Crespi & Fischetti, 1997; McIntosh & Phelps, 2000; Page, Pietrzak, & Sutton, 2001). Research on the process and outcome of assessment supervision, along with an empirical and comprehensive model of assessment supervision is badly needed.

Assessment Competencies

To identify the qualities of effective assessment supervision, it is necessary to first identify the qualities of effective assessment practices. In general, clinical competence involves: (a) knowledge regarding a specific topic, and (b) the ability to effectively apply one's knowledge and skill in ways that benefit clients (Dumont & Willis, 2003). Competence also involves the judgment necessary to use knowledge and skills effectively. Competence can be thought of as situational; for example, a school counselor may be competent in administering vocational assessments but not personality assessments (Dumont & Willis, 2003; Overholser & Fine, 1990). In the 2002 Competencies Conference, the Psychological Assessment Work Group was assigned the task of identifying the knowledge, skills, values, and attitudes necessary for assessment competence. Eight core competencies related to psychological assessment were identified, including: (1) a background in the basics of psychometric theory; (2) knowledge of the scientific, theoretical, empirical, and contextual bases of assessment; (3) knowledge, skills, and techniques to assess cognitive, affective, behavioral, and personality dimensions; (4) the ability to assess outcomes of treatment/interventions; (5) the ability to evaluate how the multiple roles, contexts, and relationships that psychologists function in influence psychological assessment; (6) the ability to establish, maintain, and understand a collaborative relationship between assessor and client; (7) an understanding of the relationship between assessment and intervention, assessment as an intervention, and intervention planning; and (8) various technical assessment skills, such as case conceptualization, selecting appropriate assessment methods, integrating information, inference and analysis, and how to provide feedback that is understandable and useful to clients (Krishnamurthy et al., 2004). Supervisors can assess supervisee competence level in these eight areas at the start of supervision and work toward forming supervision goals that address those areas in which the supervisee needs to improve.

Counselor empathy may also be a quality of assessment competence. Despite some methodological problems in the empathy research, client-perceived counselor empathy has been found to consistently relate to counseling outcome (see Duan & Hill, 1996 for a review). Many of the knowledge, skills, and abilities pertaining to assessment competence, delineated by the Assessment Work Group, require the knowledge and ability to accurately empathize with the client and the skill necessary to communicate this empathy to the client. Empathy may assist the assessor in picking appropriate tests for the client, accurately interpreting and synthesizing the test data, and delivering feedback on the test results in a useful manner. Although there is no current research on empathy and assessment, in a related study Finn and Tonsager (1992) found that, compared to controls, clients who completed the MMPI-2 and received feedback on their test results reported a significant decline in symptomatic distress and a significant increase in self-esteem. Feedback emphasized clients' participation in the assessment and assessor–client collaboration when discussing test results. These investigators could not determine why even negative feedback from the assessments was helpful to clients, so they turned to Swann's self-verification theory for a possible explanation. This theory asserts that individuals seek feedback from others that fits their own conceptions of themselves, even if it is negative (McNulty & Swann, 1991; Swann, 1983; Swann, Stein-Seroussi, & Geisler, 1992). From a different perspective, the theory of self-psychology may see these feedback sessions as an intense experience of positive and accurate mirroring (or empathic attunement). These sessions serve to stabilize and strengthen self-structures through the therapist's accurate mirroring of the client (Kohut, 1977). The role of empathy in assessment feedback may also help explain why research has found a relationship between testing and psychotherapy outcome and cultural sensitivity in the testing of minority and nontraditional populations (see Dana, 1993 for review). These studies provide some tentative evidence that client-perceived counselor empathy is a component of assessment competence.

Components of Effective Assessment Supervision

There is a paucity of research and theory on how to provide effective supervision of assessment. Smith and Harty (1987) and Finkelstein and Tuckman (1997) provide the only models specific to assessment supervision that could be found in the literature and are described in Table 13.1. However,

Table 13.1 Existing Models of Assessment Supervision

Model	Stage 1	Stage 2	Stage 3	Stage 4	Stage 5	Stage 6	Stage 7
Smith & Harty (1987)	Test administration and scoring	Inference making	Communication of test findings				
Finkelstein & Tuckmann (1997)	Learning the basics of test administration and scoring	Generating primary inferences	From outline to written word (report writing)	Internalizing diagnostic norms	Autonomy with consultation	Striking off on one's own	Passing the torch

these models are theoretical and subject to future empirical investigations. From these two theoretical models of assessment supervision, as well as from the clinical supervision research, a tentative list is offered below, outlining specific components of effective assessment supervision. Hopefully, future research will identify whether these components are actually related to the outcome of assessment supervision, under what conditions, and for what supervisees and clients.

Specifically, it is proposed that effective assessment supervision attends to eight specific components: (1) general background in the basics of psychometric theory and appropriate administrating and scoring practices; (2) supervisee ability to synthesize and interpret the data from multiple assessments to form a holistic and empathic picture of the client; (3) supervisee ability to deliver feedback in a helpful manner (both verbally and in report writing); (4) supervision training activities and supervisor evaluation; (5) the supervisory relationship; (6) promoting supervisee interest in assessment; (7) multicultural issues; and (8) ethics. Moreover, supervision of assessment should address the technical aspects of assessment (i.e., test administration, scoring), but also the process of assessment practices and the process of assessment supervision (such as, counselor [assessor]–client relationship and the supervisory relationship).

There exist many challenges to providing effective supervision of assessment. First, there is a lack of empirically based guidelines for supervisors to draw upon in their work with supervisees on assessment (Krishnamurthy et al., 2004). Some have called for the standardization of assessment supervision for the purposes of improving these practices (Crespi & Dube, 2005). Additionally, effective assessment supervision requires considerable expertise on the part of the supervisor. Practicum and internship sites, where trainees likely receive assessment supervision, may only have one designated assessment person on staff. One person can obviously not meet the supervision needs of all trainees simultaneously. Even when the supervisor possesses expertise in assessment practices, if the assessment supervisor is also the clinical supervisor, then there may not be enough time in supervision to devote to both clinical skills and assessment skills. This is particularly problematic when supervisees do not enter supervision with a foundational understanding of psychometric theory and testing practices from graduate coursework. In fact, members of the Competency in Psychological Assessment Work Group indicated a conflict between training programs and internship sites around who should assume primary responsibility for practical training in assessment (Krishnamurthy et al., 2004).

Despite these challenges, the eight proposed components of effective assessment supervision are elaborated upon below. The first three components were derived from Smith and Harty's (1987) and Finkelstein and Tuckman's (1997) overlapping phases of assessment supervision, which include: administrating and scoring, interpreting the test data or inference making, and delivering feedback (see Table 13.1). These phases of assessment supervision parallel the stages of the assessment process. Smith and Harty's (1987) and Finkelstein and Tuckman's (1997) models are both embedded within a supervision-based developmental model of counselor supervision. The developmental perspective describes how the novice supervisee grows into an expert within a multidimensional supervisor–supervisee relationship (see Whiting, Bradley, & Planny, 2001). Developmental models purpose that the supervisee becomes increasingly independent and the supervisor less active over time. For a full description of these two existing models of assessment supervision see Finkelstein and Tuckman (1997) and Smith and Harty (1987).

The Basics of Psychometric Theory and Appropriate Administrating and Scoring Practices

In the first phase of assessment supervision, the task at hand is to develop supervisee competence in administration and scoring, practices that require knowledge of basic psychometric theory (Finkelstein & Tuckman, 1997; Smith & Harty, 1987). This phase of supervision addresses the strengths and weaknesses of each test and how to choose an appropriate test for a particular referral question. The administration and scoring phase often emphasizes macro-level scoring of tests (e.g., calculating IQs, percentiles, completing the Rorschach Structural Summary, etc.). This is mostly a mechanical process of translating raw material into a more usable form (Finkelstein & Tuckman, 1997). Some potential pitfalls that supervision can fall into during this phase include, ignoring administration and scoring issues altogether, or addressing them in a mechanistic manner. Although administering and scoring tests is not always as exciting as interpreting them, this foundational stage is crucial to successive stages of assessment. Specifically, proper administration and scoring facilitates reliable and valid results, and ultimately, meaningful inferences and conclusions about the results (Finkelstein & Tuckman, 1997; Smith & Harty, 1987). While learning the mechanics of administering and scoring is necessary and should not be ignored, the danger in doing so is in failing to go beyond this mechanical process to more creative and flexible practices. Supervisees should be familiar with the formal administration and scoring rules and then be granted the flexibility to break those rules for the benefit of the client (Smith & Harty, 1987). For example,

> Katie, a supervisee in her first practicum, was preparing to administer the WAIS-IV to a client. The client was from a different culture and experienced some language barriers. In preparing for the

test administration, Katie felt anxious about remembering all the "little rules" involved in administering the WAIS-IV and supervision focused on all these "little" procedural rules so that she felt prepared and confident to administer the test. Although Katie felt fairly confident about the mechanics of administering the WAIS-IV going into the session, once she started to administer the assessment to the client, she was taken aback by the cultural and language barriers present. For example, the client was not familiar with some of the words on the vocabulary subtest. Katie became so anxious and overwhelmed about how to remember all the administration rules while making cultural accommodations that she made "on the spot" procedural decisions that compromised the validity of the test. In their effort to cover the mechanics of test administration, Katie and her supervisor neglected to discuss how the rules of administering the WAIS-IV may need to change to accommodate the client's culture.

Both Smith and Harty's and Finkelstein and Tuckman's supervision models begin with supervisee mastery in test administration and scoring. However, in Smith and Harty's model, novices learn about administration and scoring in the classroom with a professor instead of in supervision itself. Another difference between these two models is the role of the professor–supervisor during the administration and scoring phase. Specifically, Finkelstein and Tuckman describe the professor as a "benevolent tour guide," guiding students through various test manuals that they experience as intimidating and overwhelming. On the other hand, Smith and Harty suggest that in the early phases of supervisee development, the supervisor should be more active and involved than a benevolent tour guide. Likewise, Prieto and Stoltenberg (1997) argue that research on the integrated developmental model (IDM) suggests that supervisors should be concrete, hands on, directive, and structured to help trainees understand the complex mechanisms of test administration.

These two supervision models both point to supervisee anxiety over making mistakes in the administration and scoring phase of assessment, potentially leading to more errors in administration and scoring due to anxiety. Finkelstein and Tuckman suggest that the supervisor should stress that most administration and scoring mistakes are "invisible" to reduce supervisee anxiety and consequently testing errors. While at times it can be helpful to normalize and lend perspective to supervisee anxiety over making mistakes, it seems reasonable to propose that anxiety is not a problem in itself; rather, it is how anxiety is dealt with in supervision that could be problematic. In fact, Finkelstein and Tuckman have been criticized for suggesting that supervisors ignore gaps in supervisees' knowledge and skills, rather than helping them to learn from their mistakes (Prietro & Stoltenberg, 1997). Contrary to stressing the invisibility of mistakes, Dumont and Willis (2003) argue that "there is no excuse for making errors in simply administering and scoring tests, and the consequences of such errors can be serious" (p. 165). These authors argue that supervisors should constantly check supervisee work for errors and provide feedback on these errors. They specifically suggest checking supervisee use of and attention to basals, ceilings, correct assignments of bonus points, and scoring of items. An extensive list of requirements for supervisees' administration and scoring practices may be found in Dumont and Willis (2003), which includes considering the context of the evaluation, test standardization and norms, reliability, validity, and scoring issues. It is important to note that testing errors are arguably too frequent among novices and experts alike (Alfonso & Pratt, 1997; Oakland & Zimmerman, 1986) to "emphasize the invisibility of administration errors" (Finkelstein & Tuckman, 1997, p. 93) in supervision. Rather than stressing invisibility of errors, supervisors who emphasize supervisee ability to learn from (or better yet prevent) their administration and scoring errors may be most efficacious in developing administration and scoring competencies in their supervisees.

Synthesizing and Interpreting Data From Multiple Assessments: A Holistic and Empathic Picture

Once the administration and scoring has occurred, assessment supervision then focuses on inference making, or the process of formulating hypotheses and deriving meaning from the test data (Finkelstein & Tuckman, 1997; Smith & Harty, 1987). This involves forming overall inferences from individual data points (Finkelstein & Tuckman, 1997). The supervisor's mental process for interpreting the data generally involves taking discrete responses (or individual data points) and forming conclusions at successively higher levels of abstraction (higher-order, overall, inferences; Smith & Harty, 1987). The experienced supervisor may formulate hypotheses and interpret the data without consciously thinking about how he or she arrived at such conclusions. However, it is essential that the supervisor explicitly state to the supervisee his or her chain of reasoning when reaching hypotheses and interpretations, rather than assuming such logic is obvious to the supervisee (Finkelstein & Tuckman, 1997). In essence, the supervisor thinks out loud in order to model for the supervisee how to form hypotheses from the test data. Later in supervision, the supervisee is the one generating hypotheses while the supervisor provides feedback and suggestions (Smith & Harty, 1987). A collaborative approach to interpreting assessments is suggested, along with didactic training when needed. The supervisor should model how to use the formal scores to make interpretations about the client, but also how to consider contextual and client factors when interpreting the data, including:

- Circumstances of the testing
- Client's attitude toward the examiner and toward the testing experience
- Client's expectations for testing
- Changes in the relationship between the client and counselor over time (Smith & Harty, 1987, p. 414).

For example, Brian, a psychology intern with limited assessment experience, was puzzled by the results of a WAIS-IV that he just administered to a coworker's therapy client. The client's verbal comprehension index, perceptual reasoning index, and working memory scores were all very high (ranging from the 85th to 90th percentiles). However, the processing speed index score was significantly lower (30th percentile). Brian and his supervisor collaboratively discussed different hypotheses that may explain this discrepancy in scores. Speaking out loud, Brian's supervisor wondered about the initial referral question from the referring therapist and if that may shed some light on interpreting the scores? Brian recalled that the therapist wondered if the client had ADHD? The supervisor confirmed that ADHD can be one reason why someone would score lower on processing speed and more tests to assess for ADHD were warranted.

Among the vast amount of test data, as well as client and contextual factors, the supervisee eventually needs to hone down his or her interpretations to answer the specific referral question. Dumont and Willis (2003) provide an extensive check list for supervisors to use when evaluating the quality of supervisees' interpretations. For example, they suggest that the supervisor ask, "Does the evaluator distinguish clearly between findings and implications?" and "Does the evaluator avoid interpretation beyond the limits of the test?" (Dumont & Willis, 2003, pp. 173–174). When the client is referred from an outside practitioner specifically for an assessment, then the goal of interpretation is to answer the referral question. If the supervisee is conducting an assessment as a part of ongoing counseling with his or her client, then the goal of interpretation is to integrate the assessment findings with the previous client conceptualization and treatment plan.

Interpretation of Assessment Data and the Expert–Novice Literature

When developing competency in generating hypotheses and interpreting the test data, supervisees must learn how to cluster the vast amount of test information in front of them and the related hypotheses about the test information (Finkelstein & Tuckman, 1997). Finkelstein and Tuckman suggest that early in training the supervisee looks at the test data in discrete pieces and makes discrete interpretations based on each piece of data without looking at the whole picture and without a consistent and organized system of data interpretation. With the supervisor's modeling, the supervisee learns to structure the data into related clusters (i.e., interpersonal functioning, verbal-performance IQ discrepancies, etc.). These clusters are then internalized by the supervisee and guide the supervisee's subsequent interpretation of assessment data.

Research on expert–novice development in the cognitive psychology literature supports Finkelstein and Tuckman's model of how supervisees learn to interpret test data. Cognitive psychologists have found that people mentally organize information into what they call *knowledge structures* and that experts possess more deep structures than novices who possess more surface structures (Davis & Yi, 2004). The counseling research suggests that expert counselors organize incoming client information into higher-order, general, categories, or concepts (i.e., deep structures), whereas novices organize information into client specific categories (i.e., surface structures). For example, Martin, Slemon, Hiebert, Hallberg, and Cummings (1989) found that expert counselors conceptualized their clients in relation to general counseling processes, whereas novices focused their conceptualization on client specific details. Similarly, Mayfield, Kardash, and Kivlighan (1999) asked experts and novices to categorize client statements from a transcript. Experts used similar noncase specific categories, while novices used case specific detail that differed from novice to novice. Applying this area of study to assessment practices, novice supervisees are probably more likely to interpret test data piecemeal, looking at each observation separately (i.e., surface structure), while the supervisor or expert examines the test data as a whole, according to overarching test theories and constructs (i.e., deep structure). This difference in how novices and experts approach the process of interpreting assessment data reflects the difference between surface and deep structure. Recent research shows that measures of knowledge structures (deep and surface structures) are better predictors of skill performance than are measures of knowledge and skill acquisition (Davis & Yi, 2004). Future research should examine how supervision can be used to facilitate supervisee's development of deep structure in regards to interpreting assessment data.

Delivering Feedback and Report Writing

The final phase of an assessment involves the task of communicating the test findings to the client and perhaps to the referral source (see Finkelstein & Tuckman, 1997; Smith & Harty, 1987). Feedback may be delivered verbally and/or in a written report to the client and/or referral source. Written feedback is communicated through a formal assessment report and involves supervisee report writing skills. When supervising a supervisee on report writing, an important difference between clinical supervision and assessment supervision emerges. In clinical supervision, supervisors generally do not play a direct role in the treatment of the supervisee's client. However, when supervising trainees' assessment reports, supervisors typically intervene with client treatment through editing and even sometimes writing parts of the report (Smith & Harty, 1987). Supervisors must strike a careful balance between being over and under involved in the supervisee's report writing. If a supervisor is too involved, then the supervisee is likely to become dependent and/or resentful of the supervisor. If the supervisor is not involved enough, then the quality of the report may suffer as well as the supervisee and client (Smith & Harty, 1987). Supervisors should also be careful of pushing their style of report writing onto the supervisee and instead help the supervisee to develop a personal style of report writing. To this aim, the supervisor may encourage the supervisee to try different styles of report writing (Sargent, 1951), just as a clinical supervisor may encourage a novice counselor to try out different theoretical orientations to see which one fits.

Dumont and Willis (2003) suggest a specific method for supervisors to use when providing written feedback on supervisee written reports that stresses detailed feedback. This feedback system involves typing a numbered list of extensive comments (minor corrections are made within the text) about the reasoning for a correction made in the text or a relevant and applicable testing principle. The written feedback system suggested by Dumont and Willis (2003) largely addresses the mechanics of report writing. Similarly, other models of assessment supervision also stress the importance of supervisory feedback on the clarity and overall technical quality of student report writing. Yet, they go beyond the mechanics of report writing and also stress the importance of supervisory feedback on supervisee: verbal communication of test results to the client and any referral source, effectiveness in developing a counselor–client relationship characterized by trust, empathy, and warmth in which feedback is delivered, and ability to present the assessment data within a holistic and dynamic client picture (Finkelstein & Tuckman, 1997; Smith & Harty, 1987). Creating and communicating a holistic picture of the client requires the supervisee to integrate the test data with the rest of treatment. One potential mistake is to compartmentalize the assessment experience as discrete and disconnected from the rest of treatment or the rest of the client's personhood. When delivering feedback to the client, the counselor should consider everything he or she knows about the client, integrating the assessment experience with the personal issues of the client.

The ultimate judge of supervisee competence when it comes to delivering feedback on an assessment is the client. The client needs to understand the feedback and feel understood when receiving feedback. Supervisors should work with supervisees to "tune in" to how their feedback is received and utilized by the client. Recall that certain studies have found that the process of delivering feedback on assessments is a treatment intervention in and of itself, predicting client increase in self-esteem and symptom change (e.g., Finn & Tonsager, 1992). These studies suggest feedback that "fits" or "clicks" with the client's experience, whether it is positive or negative, is a helpful ingredient to client treatment and outcome (Finn & Tonsager, 1992; Newman & Greenway, 1997).

For example, Linda was a postdoctoral psychologist with some prior assessment experience. A client of Linda's entered counseling because he was floundering and could not stick with a career. He asked Linda for career counseling with the goal of finding a permanent satisfying career. However, it soon became clear to Linda that this client had a serious alcohol addiction that needed to be dealt with first before career counseling could be effective. When Linda approached the subject of addiction with the client, however, he avoided the subject all together. Linda, with the guidance of her supervisor, administered the MMPI-2 to the client, the results of which confirmed that the client was drinking heavily and under-reporting his drinking. Although being a heavy drinker was not part of the client's self-concept, the results of the test caused the client to reflect more on his drinking behaviors. When delivering the results to the client, Linda asked him questions like, "How do these results fit with how you see yourself? How do they not fit? What would it mean if you did have an addiction to alcohol? What is it like to hear these test results?" Linda felt delivering this feedback from the MMPI-2 to the client was a break through moment in counseling that helped the client to focus on underlying issues.

Supervision Training Activities and Supervisor Evaluation

There are several supervision activities that facilitate supervisee assessment competence that are not necessarily inherent to the clinical supervision process. First, some evidence suggests that giving novice counselors access to an expert's use of deep structure facilitates novices' development from surface to deep structures (Kivlighan, Markin, Stahl, & Salahuddin, 2007). This suggests that modeling from the supervisor (or expert) should facilitate supervisee (or novice) learning and development. Following this, supervisors should arrange for supervisees to observe the supervisor administer and score assessment batteries, when the client agrees to be observed. Second, family therapy and group therapy training models have highlighted the importance of live supervision (see Kivlighan, Angelone, & Swafford, 1991; Kivlighan et al., 2007; Lewis & Rohrbaugh, 1989). Similarly, it may be helpful for assessment supervisors to observe their supervisees actually administer the assessment as the assessment is taking place, or in a videotape of the administration when live supervision is not possible. Third, when assessment supervision is separate from general clinical supervision on practicum and internship sites, then supervisees may not receive assessment supervision on a weekly basis. In this case, supervision sessions should be timed so that they occur at a minimum: before test administration to deal with administration issues, after test administration to discuss scoring issues, before the supervisee delivers feedback on the test results to discuss interpretation of results and how to deliver feedback, and during the report writing phase to give feedback on report writing skills. Fourth, supervision of assessment should be provided in individual and small group formats to provide multiple contexts for developing the vast amount of competencies involved in assessment practices (Krishnamurthy et al., 2004). Last, there is some evidence to suggest that assessment supervision focuses more on coaching supervisees on technical skills and less on emotional awareness than clinical supervision (Decato, 2002). One could argue that assessment practices require such specialized and advanced technical skills that supervision should focus more on technical skills and less on other clinical processes like emotional awareness. At the same time, one could also argue that assessments are a means to an end of developing a holistic and empathic picture of the client, and to do so successfully, supervision must also focus on how the emotions of the counselor and client impact assessment practices.

How do supervisors evaluate supervisees' level of competence across training activities? Assessment supervisors have the difficult task of striking a careful balance between didactic instruction, explaining the technical aspects and mechanics of assessment practices to the supervisee, and fostering supervisee independence. This conflict between providing structure and fostering supervisee independence was evident in the earlier discussion of supervisor feedback on supervisee written reports but exists, to some degree, in all the phases of an assessment. One way to collaboratively evaluate supervisee performance is with 360 degree surveys, where trainees obtain feedback from colleagues, clients, and supervisors (Krishnamurthy et al., 2004). In the spirit of fostering supervisee independence, Krishnamurthy et al. (2004) suggest that supervisors encourage their supervisees to engage in careful self-reflection throughout the assessment experience. In essence, supervisees must eventually learn how to be their own supervisors, relying on their ability to self-reflect on their assessment skills and practices, rather than on the ability of the supervisor.

The Supervisory Relationship

Supervisory Alliance   The quality of the supervisory relationship has been shown to be an important predictor of supervision outcome in the clinical supervision literature (see Muse-Burke, Ladany, & Deck, 2001). It is within a supervisory relationship that all supervisory interventions and supervisee learning take place (Watkins, 1997). One aspect of the supervisory relationship that has received attention is the working alliance, defined as: mutual agreement on the goals of supervision, mutual agreement on the supervision tasks, and a supervisor–supervisee emotional bond (Bordin, 1983). The goals of assessment supervision are likely to change depending on the phase of assessment. Some examples of assessment supervision goals are developing supervisee competence in scoring an IQ test, developing proficiency in interpreting the MMPI-2, or writing a formal report that integrates results from the MMPI-2 and an IQ test. The tasks of assessment supervision should be related to the goals of supervision. For example, to improve supervisee competence in administering a particular assessment (i.e., the goal), the supervisor may provide live supervision of the supervisee's administration of that assessment (i.e., the task). The working alliance theory proposes that if supervisor and supervisee agree on the goals and tasks of supervision, then an emotional bond characterized by liking, trust, and caring will emerge within the supervisory relationship. It is important to note that the quality of the supervisory alliance may impact the quality of the counselor–client alliance through parallel process (see Goodyear & Guzzardo, 2000). In assessment supervision in particular, if the supervisor adopts a purely top-down, expert-authoritarian approach, rather than a more collaborative one, then the supervisee is likely to parallel this type of relationship with the client, failing to engage the client in the assessment process in a collaborative manner. Similarly, if the supervisor and supervisee do not agree on the tasks and goals of supervision, then it is likely that the counselor and client will not agree on the goals and tasks of the assessment process. Smith and Harty (1987) suggest that to foster what they call the "learning alliance," the supervisor should act as a "loving superego," setting and upholding standards, while guiding the supervisee through the assessment process. The alliance in supervision is likely to buffer the effects of potential problems that arise over the course of supervision, such as supervisee transference to the supervisor.

Transference and Countertransference Issues

The three phases of assessment supervision may elicit different transference–countertransference themes within the supervisory relationship. The administration and scoring phase of assessment may conjure up old feelings of inadequacy within the supervisee, reflected in the supervisee's fear of making mistakes and of being punished by an authority figure for making such mistakes. Counselors-in-training must navigate feelings of inadequacy in clinical supervision as well, as they are put in the vulnerable position of being evaluated on their newly developing clinical skills, but also on their personhood as a counselor. Unlike clinical supervision, where many issues discussed are subjective, in assessment supervision, there is often a right and a wrong way of administering and scoring assessments. Consequently, administration and scoring errors may feel particularly dangerous and visible to the supervisee (see Finkelstein & Tuckman, 1997). Supervisees may experience much anxiety over making an administration or scoring error and expect the supervisor to react by punishing them with a poor evaluation, viewing them as inadequate professionally. In return, supervisors may experience countertransference feelings of wanting the supervisee to feel better. Consequently, supervisors may overlook or inappropriately deemphasize supervisee administration and scoring errors, claiming that they are invisible or inconsequential when they are not.

In the interpretation phase of assessment supervision, transference–countertransference themes around idealization may arise. Supervisees may idealize the supervisor's ability to interpret the test data, as if the supervisor possesses magical abilities to make order out of what seems like chaos to the supervisee. As the supervisee idealizes the supervisor's insight into the meaning of the test data, he or she may devalue his or her own abilities to interpret the test data (see Finkelstein & Tuckman, 1997). However, in other instances, the supervisor may not be an idealizable figure and/ or the supervisee may have had past experiences where idealizing others only led to disappointment, leading to a counteridealization or devaluing transference to the supervisor. The countertransference of the supervisor may include enjoying this idealized role. As a result, the supervisor may overemphasize his or her ability to "just know" what the test data means, rather than being explicit with the supervisee about how he or she reached certain hypotheses and conclusions about the test data.

Finally, in the feedback and report writing phase of assessment supervision, transference–countertransference issues around authority and independence may emerge. For both the supervisee and the supervisor, issues around control may surface when writing and editing the formal assessment report. As the supervisee wishes to give voice to his or her growing self-confidence, knowledge, and opinions, becoming more independent from the supervisor, the supervisor's edits may feel intrusive. At the same time, the supervisor may feel anxious about giving up control over the assessment process and may even feel some ownership of the client, leading the supervisor to become over involved in the report writing. It is important in this phase for the supervisor to encourage the supervisee's growing sense of independence and self-confidence, while guiding the supervisee when he or she steps outside of his or her area of competence (see Finkelstein & Tuckman, 1997).

Multicultural Issues in Assessment

Allen (2007) defines multicultural assessment supervision as

> Supervision of an assessment process in which the person assessed and the assessor are from different cultural backgrounds, the supervisor and the trainee are from different backgrounds, or the assessment instrument used was developed with a cultural group different from the cultural background of the person assessed. (p. 248)

Allen argues that given current demographic trends toward increasing diversity, supervision of multicultural psychological assessment will become increasingly important to maintain the competency of psychologists and counselors. Furthermore, research shows a relationship between testing and psychotherapy outcome and cultural sensitivity in the testing of minority and nontraditional populations (see Dana, 1993 for review). Despite this, similar to assessment supervision in general, there is no existing model for multicultural assessment supervision. In fact, according to Van Kley (1999), the majority of psychology trainees do not perceive current approaches to multicultural assessment supervision as useful or central to supervision.

Consequently, Allen (2007) offered a theoretical model for conceptualizing the competencies needed for multicultural assessment. To describe multicultural competence in general, Sue and colleagues (1982) and Sue, Arredondo, and McDavis (1992) use three dimensions (beliefs, attitudes, and skills) to describe three characteristics of cultural competence (awareness of values and assumptions, understanding client worldview, and development of appropriate interventions). Similarly, Allen (2007) suggests a model for training competent multicultural assessment counselors that include knowledge and skills, supervisor skills, and supervision tasks.

Multicultural Assessment Knowledge and Skills

There are many complex skills involved in facilitating a multicultural collaborative assessment experience between counselor and client, including the ability to: empower the client through the assessment experience, use the interview as a tool for collaboration, and explore clients' negative past experiences with testing. In addition, the assessor must be capable of understanding the client within his or her cultural context to appropriately conduct and interpret interviews, or any other assessment intervention with a client from a different culture. Many current clinical interviewing practices are based on Euro-American social interactions. Following this, supervisees must possess knowledge of social interactions in other cultures, along with the necessary skills to conduct an assessment interview that accounts for the client's cultural social norms. For example, Takushi and Uomoto (2001) describe an interviewing approach using the Person in Culture Interview. Supervisees should also be trained to assess acculturation status and to understand how acculturation relates to test interpretations. Similarly, it is essential for supervision to address culturally grounded test interpretations. For example, important differences on the MMPI-2 exist for Native Americans (Dana, 2005). Lastly, supervisees should possess knowledge in measurement theory and construct validity relevant to culture (see Allen, 2007).

Multicultural Assessment Supervisor Characteristics

Assessment supervisors should possess the same core multicultural counseling competencies (Sue et al., 1992) as general clinical supervisors, but also they must possess high levels of specialty knowledge and skills in the areas of multicultural assessment. These knowledge and skills include: (a) measurement theory and construct validity relevant to culture; (b) skills in multicultural collaborative assessment; (c) culturally appropriate interviewing and culturally congruent assessment practices; (d) acculturation status assessment; (e) culturally grounded tests interpretation; (f) use of local norms and tests; (g) multicultural report writing; and (h) multicultural assessment ethical decisions. Within supervision itself, supervision across cultures requires the ability to recognize cultural differences in learning styles and to adjust training modalities accordingly. Research has focused on how race is addressed between White supervisors and trainees of color. Supervisors must examine their own attitudes toward racism and prejudice when engaging in multicultural assessment supervision (see Allen, 2007).

Multicultural Assessment Supervision Tasks

Allen (2007) suggests that supervisors engage in three global task areas in multicultural assessment: culturally congruent assessment service, delivery, and practice; culture specific interpretive practices; and communicating assessment results in multicultural report writing. The goals and tasks of supervision should address these three global areas.

Ethics and Assessment Practices

Adherence to the ethical standards of professional organizations like the American Psychological Association (APA) and the American Counseling Association (ACA) is just as important for assessment practice as it is for any other clinical practice. Adherence to a professional standard of ethics is essential to protect the clients we serve. Both the APA's *Ethical Principles of Psychologists and Code of Conduct* (2002) and the ACA's *Code of Ethics* (2005) offer specific ethical guidelines for assessment practices. Competency and accountability are highlighted in these organizations' ethics codes for assessment. Competence becomes an ethical issue when psychologists and counselors are not held accountable for the work they do and mistakes they make. Assessment competence is a long-term commitment because new diagnostic techniques are continually developed that require new skills (Dumont & Willis, 2003). The goal of assessment is to help clients; however, if assessments are not done well, they may ultimately harm clients, violating an overarching ethical principle to do no harm. This is why psychologists and counselors only administer tests that benefit the client and that they are competent in or for which they are receiving supervision. These professionals are responsible for interpreting the test data based on scientific information and techniques. All assessments are completed with the client's informed consent and when test results will be shared with anyone besides the client, such as an organization, referring therapist, or school, then the client is made aware of this at the beginning. The assessor is also responsible for explaining the tests results to the client and taking reasonable steps to ensure that the client accurately understands the feedback. Since assessment practices have been used in unethical ways in the past, it is of the utmost importance for supervision to prepare competent professionals with the ability and judgment to make ethical decisions pertaining to assessment practices.

Promoting Interest in Assessment

An important but sometimes neglected component to assessment supervision is promoting supervisee interest and motivation in assessment practices. Supervisors can model for supervisees how to approach assessment with an attitude of curiosity and interest in assessment practices. The supervisor's level of motivation and interest in assessment serves as a model for the supervisee's own attitude toward assessment. It may also be helpful for the supervisor to address any myths about assessment that the supervisee may hold. To promote interest in assessment, supervision should place assessment within the broader treatment of the client, instead of being compartmentalized in a disconnected and mechanical manner. Finkelstein and Tuckman (1997, p. 95) state that supervisors must pass the "assessment supervision torch" to the supervisee to carry forward. Such a forward act requires significant motivation and interest in assessment practices.

Conclusion

Although assessment continues to be a central activity of psychologists and counselors, there is a dearth of information on supervision of assessment in the literature. Future research and theory need to offer comprehensive guidelines and specific models for supervision and training in assessment. In addition, supervisors in practicum and internship sites may themselves need further training in assessment. Specifically, increasing reliance on computerized testing and computer-based interpretations are continuing to influence testing (Tallent, 1987). Computer applications to psychological tests emphasize the practical need for cost-effective, efficient, and third-party accountability in practice (Butcher, 1987). Supervisors need to be competent in this new area of computer testing. Future models of assessment supervision should build upon existing assessment models that include three main phases of assessment supervision and practice: administration and scoring, interpreting results, and delivering feedback. In addition to building supervisee competence in these three areas, future research on effective assessment supervision should also address the specific tasks of supervision, supervisor evaluation, the supervisory relationship, multicultural issues, ethical issues, and motivation for assessment practices. Future research on effective assessment supervision and competent assessment practices is needed to ultimately develop an empirical model for assessment supervision to guide research and practice.

Acknowledgment

I would like to thank Dr. Nazish Salahuddin for her consultation on this chapter.

References

Alfonso, V. C., & Pratt, S. I. (1997). Issues and suggestions for training professionals in assessing intelligence. In D. P. Flanagan, J. L. Genshaft, & P. L. Harrison (Eds.), *Contemporary intellectual assessment: Theories, tests, and issues* (pp. 326–344). New York, NY: Guilford Press.

Allen, J. (2007). A multicultural assessment supervision model to guide research and practice. *Professional Psychology: Research and Practice, 38,* 248–258.

American Counseling Association (ACA). (2005). *The 2005 ACA code of ethics.* Retrieved from http://www.counseling.org/Resources/CodeOfEthics/TP/Home/CT2.aspx

American Psychological Association (APA). (2000). *APA guidelines and principles for accreditation of programs in professional psychology, doctoral graduate program guidelines.* Retrieved from http://www.apa.org/ed/gp2000.html

American Psychological Association (APA). (2002). *The 2002 APA ethical principles of psychologists and code of conduct.* Retrieved from http://www.apa.org/ethics/code/index.aspx/

Bordin, E. S. (1983). A working alliance model of supervision. *The Counseling Psychologist, 11,* 35–42.

Butcher, J. N. (1987). *Computerized psychological assessment: A practitioner's guide.* New York, NY: Basic Books.

Butler, M., Retzlaff, P., & Vanderploeg, R. (1991). Neuropsychological testing usage. *Professional Psychology: Research and Practice, 22,* 510–512.

Cerney, M. S. (1978). Use of the psychological test report in the course of psychotherapy. *Journal of Personality Assessment, 42,* 457–463.

Counsel for Accreditation of Counseling and Related Educational Programs (CACREP). (2009). *CACREP 2009 accreditation standards.* Retrieved from http://67.199.126.156/doc/2009%20Standards.pdf

Crespi, T. D. (1998). School counselors and clinical supervision: Perspectives to facilitate counseling services in the schools. *Special Services in the Schools, 13,* 107–114.

Crespi, T. D., & Dube, J. M. B. (2005). Clinical supervision in school psychology: Challenges, considerations, and ethical and legal issues for clinical supervisors. *The Clinical Supervisor, 24,* 115–135.

Crespi, T. D., & Fischetti, B. A. (1997). Clinical supervision for school psychologists: Bridging theory and practice. *School Psychology International, 18,* 41–48.

Dana, R. H. (1993). *Multicultural assessment perspectives for professional psychology.* Boston, MA: Allyn & Bacon.

Dana, R. H. (2005). *Multicultural assessment: Principles, applications, and examples.* Mahwah, NJ: Erlbaum.

Davis, F. D., & Yi, M. Y. (2004). Improving computer skill training: Behavior modeling, symbolic mental rehearsal, and the role of knowledge structures. *Journal of Applied Psychology, 89*(3), 509–523

Decato, C. M. (2002). A quantitative method for studying the testing supervision process. *Psychological Reports, 90,* 137–138.

Dempster, I. V. (1990). How mental health professionals view their graduate training. *Journal of Training & Practice in Professional Psychology, 4*(2), 4–19.

Duan, C., & Hill, C. E. (1996). The current state of empathy research. *Journal of Counseling Psychology, 43,* 261–274.

Dumont, R., & Willis, J. O. (2003). Issues regarding the supervision of assessment. *Clinical Supervision, 22,* 159–176.

Elbert, J. C. (1984). Training in child diagnostic assessment: A survey of clinical psychology graduate programs. *Journal of Clinical Child Psychology, 13,* 122–133.

Fernández-Ballesteros, R., De Bruyn, E. E. J., Godoy, A., Hornke, L. F., Ter Laak, J., Vizcarro, C., … Zaccagnini, J. L. (2001). Guidelines for the assessment process (GAP): A proposal for discussion. *European Journal of Psychological Assessment, 17*(3), 187–200.

Finkelstein, H., & Tuckman, A. (1997). Supervision of psychological assessment: A developmental model. *Professional Psychology: Research and Practice, 28,* 2–95.

Finn, S. E. (1996). *Manual for using the MMPI-2 as a therapeutic intervention.* Minneapolis, MN: University of Minnesota Press.

Finn, S. E., & Tonsager, M. E. (1992). Therapeutic effects of providing MMPI-2 test feedback to college students awaiting psychotherapy. *Psychological Assessment, 3,* 278–287.

Frohnauer, L. A., Vavak, C., & Hardin, K. N. (1988). Rorschach use in APA-approved clinical training programs: An update. *Journal of Training and Practice in Professional Psychology, 2*(1), 45–48.

Goodyear, R. K., & Guzzardo, C. R. (2000). Psychotherapy supervision and training. In S. D. Brown & R. W. Lent (Eds.), *Handbook of counseling psychology* (3rd ed., pp. 83–103). New York, NY: John Wiley & Sons.

Groth-Marnat, G. (1999). *Handbook of psychological assessment* (3rd ed.). New York, NY: John Wiley & Sons.

Guilmette, T. J., Faust, D., Hart, E., & Arkes, H. R. (1990). A national survey of psychologists who offer neuropsychological services. *Archives of Clinical Neuropsychology, 5,* 373–392.

Haller, M. (1963). *Eugenics: Hereditarian attitudes in American thought.* New Brunswick, NJ: Rutgers University Press.

Hershey, J. M., Kopplin, D. A., & Cornell, J. E. (1991). Doctors of Psychology: Their career experiences and attitudes toward degree and training. *Professional Psychology: Research and Practice, 22,* 351–356.

Holloway, E. L., & Neufeldt, S. A. (1995). Supervision: Its contributions to treatment efficacy. *Journal of Consulting and Clinical Psychology, 63,* 207–213.

Holmes, G. R., Cook, D., & Rothstein, W. (1991). Evaluation of a predoctoral clinical psychology internship program by intern graduates. *Journal of Clinical Psychology, 47,* 840–845.

Hood, A. B., & Johnson, R. W. (2002). *Assessment in counseling: A guide to the use of psychological assessment procedures* (3rd ed.). Alexandria, VA: American Counseling Association.

Keddy, P., & Piotrowski, C. (1992). Testing in psychotherapy practice: Literature review, survey, and commentary. *Journal of Training and Practice in Professional Psychology, 6,* 30–39.

Kevles, D. (1985). *In the name of eugenics: Genetics and the uses of human heredity.* New York, NY: Knopf.

Kivlighan, D. M., Angelone, E. O., & Swafford, K. G. (1991). Live supervision in individual psychotherapy: Effects on therapist's intention use and client's evaluation of session effect and working alliance. *Journal of Counseling Psychology, 22,* 489–495.

Kivlighan, D. M., Markin, R. D., Stahl, J., & Salahuddin, N. (2007). Expert novice differences in group psychotherapy training. *Group Dynamics: Theory, Research, and Practice, 11,* 153–164.

Kohut, H. (1977). *The restoration of the self.* New York, NY: International Universities Press.

Kolbe, K., Shemberg, K., & Leventhal, D. (1985). University training in psychodiagnostics and psychotherapy. *The Clinical Psychologist, 38,* 59–61.

Krishnamurthy, R., VandeCreek, L., Kaslow, N. J., Tazeau, Y. N., Miville, M. L., Kerns, R., … Benton, S. A. (2004). Achieving competency in psychological assessment: Directions for education and training. *Journal of Clinical Psychology, 60*(7), 725–739.

Lewis, W., & Rohrbaugh, M. (1989). Live supervision by family therapists: A Virginia survey. *Journal of Marital & Family Therapy, 15,* 323–326.

Lovitt, R. (1992). Teaching the psychology intern assessment skills in a medical setting. *Journal of Training & Practice in Professional Psychology, 6*(2), 27–34.

Martin, J. M., Slemon, A. G., Hiebert, B., Hallberg, E. T., & Cummings, A. L. (1989). Conceptualizations of novice and experienced counselors. *Journal of Counseling Psychology, 36,* 395–400.

Maruish, M. E. (Ed.). (1999). The use of psychological testing for treatment planning and outcome assessment (2nd ed.). Mahwah, NJ: Lawrence Erlbaum.

Mayfield, W. A., Kardash, C. M., & Kivlighan, D. M. (1999). Differences in experienced and novice counselors' knowledge structures about clients: Implications for case conceptualization. *Journal of Counseling Psychology, 46*(4), 504–514.

McIntosh, D. E., & Phelps, L. (2000). Supervision in school psychology: Where will the future take us? *Psychology in the Schools, 37*, 33–38.

McNulty, S. E., & Swann, W. B., Jr. (1991). Psychotherapy, self-concept change, and self-verification. In R. C. Curtis (Ed.), *The relational self: Theoretical convergence of psychoanalysis and social psychology.* New York, NY: Guildford Press.

Meyer, G. J., Finn, S. E., Eyde, L. D., Kay, G. G., Kubiszyn, T. W., Moreland, K. L., ... Dies, R. R. (1998). *Benefits and costs of psychological assessment in healthcare delivery: Report of the board of professional affairs psychological assessment work group, Part I.* Washington, DC: American Psychological Association.

Moreland, K. L., & Dahlstrom, W. G. (1983). A survey of MMPI teaching in APA-approved clinical training programs. *Journal of Personality Assessment, 47*, 115–119.

Muse-Burke, J., Ladany, N., & Deck, M. (2001). The supervisory relationship. In L. Bradley & N. Ladany (Eds.), *Counselor supervision: Principles, process, and practice* (3rd ed., pp. 28–62). New York, NY: Brunner-Routledge.

Newman, M., & Greenway, P. (1997). Therapeutic effects of providing MMPI-2 test feedback to clients at a university counseling service: A collaborative approach. *Psychological Assessment, 9*, 122–131.

Oakland, T., & Zimmerman, S. (1986). The course on individual mental assessment: A national survey of course instructors. *Professional School Psychology, 1*, 51–59.

Overholser, J. C., & Fine, M. A. (1990). Defining the boundaries of professional competence: Managing subtle cases of clinical incompetence. *Professional Psychology: Research and Practice, 21*, 462–469.

Page, B. J., Pietrzak, D. R., & Sutton, J. M. (2001). National survey of school counselor supervision. *Counselor Education and Supervision, 41*, 142–150.

Phillips, L. (1992). A commentary on the relationship between assessment and the conduct of psychotherapy. *Journal of Training and Practice in Professional Psychology, 6*(2), 46–52.

Piotrowski, C., & Keller, J. W. (1984). Psychodiagnostic testing in APA-approved clinical psychology programs. *Professional Psychology: Research and Practice, 15*, 450–456.

Piotrowski, C., & Keller, J. W. (1989). Psychological testing in outpatient mental health facilities: A national study. *Professional Psychology: Research and Practice, 20*, 423–425.

Piotrowski, C., & Keller, J. W. (1992). Psychological testing in applied settings: A literature review from 1982–1992. *Journal of Training and Practice in Professional Psychology, 6*(2), 74–82.

Piotrowski, C., & Zalewski, C. (1993). Training in psychodiagnostic testing in APA-approved PsyD and PhD clinical psychology programs. *Journal of Personality Assessment, 61*, 394–405.

Prieto, L. R., & Stoltenberg, C. D. (1997). The supervision of psychological assessment: Toward parsimony and empirical evidence for developmental supervision theory. *Professional Psychology: Research and Practice, 28*, 593–594.

Sargent, H. D. (1951). Psychological test reporting: An experiment in communication. *Bulletin of the Menninger Clinic, 15*(5), 175–186.

Sattler, J. M. (2002). *Assessment of children: Behavioral and clinical applications* (4th ed.). San Diego, CA: Author.

Smith, W. H., & Harty, M. K. (1987). Issues in the supervision of diagnostic testing. In R. H. Dana & W. T. May (Eds.), *Internship training in professional psychology* (pp. 411–418). Washington, DC: Hemisphere.

Sue, D. W., Arredondo, P., & McDavis, R. J. (1992). Multicultural counseling competencies and standards: A call to the profession. *Journal of Counseling and Development, 20,* 64–88.

Sue, D. W., Bernier, J., Durran, M., Feinberg, L., Pedersen, P., Smith, E., & Vasquez-Nuttall, E. (1982). Position paper: Multicultural counseling competencies. *The Counseling Psychologist, 10,* 45–52.

Swann, W. B., Jr. (1983). Self-verification: Bringing social reality into harmony with the self. In J. Suls & A. G. Greenwald (Eds.), *Social psychological perspectives on the self: Vol. 2.* Hillsdale, NJ: Erlbaum.

Swann, W. B., Jr., Stein-Seroussi, D., & Geisler, B. (1992). Why people self-verify. *Journal of Personality and Social Psychology, 62,* 392–401.

Takushi, R., & Uomoto, J. M. (2001). The clinical interview from a multicultural perspective. In L. A. Suzuki, J. G. Ponterotto, & P. J. Melter (Eds.), *Handbook of multicultural assessment: Clinical, psychological, and educational applications* (2nd ed., pp. 47–66). San Francisco, CA: Jossey-Bass.

Tallent, N. (1987). Computer-generated psychological reports: A look at the modern psychometric machine. *Journal of Personality Assessment, 51,* 95–108.

Turner, S. M., DeMers, S. T., Fox, H. R., & Reed, G. M. (2001). APA's guidelines for test user qualifications. *American Psychologist, 56,* 1099–1113.

Van Kley, G. R. (1999). *The assessment supervision questionnaire* (Unpublished doctoral dissertation). University of South Dakota.

Watkins, C. E., Jr. (Ed.). (1997). *Handbook of psychotherapy supervision.* New York, NY: Wiley.

Weiner, I. B., & Exner, J. E., Jr. (1991). Rorschach changes in long-term and short-term psychotherapy. *Journal of Personality Assessment, 56,* 453–465.

Whiting, P. P., Bradley, L. J., & Planny, K. J. (2001). Supervision-based developmental models of counselor supervision. In L. J. Bradley & N. Ladany (Eds.), *Counselor supervision: Principles, process, & practice* (3rd ed., pp. 125–146). Ann Arbor, MI: Braun-Brumfield.

Zenderlan, L. (1998). *Measuring minds: Henry Herbert Goddard and the origins of American intelligence testing.* Cambridge, MA: Cambridge University Press.

PART IV

Professional Issues in Counselor Supervision

CHAPTER 14

Evaluation in Supervision

LAURA E. WELFARE

Evaluation is an essential and defining component of clinical supervision. Supervisors are ethically responsible for "monitoring clinical performance and professional development of supervisees" and "evaluating and certifying current performance and potential of supervisees for academic, screening, selection, placement, employment, and credentialing purposes" (Association for Counselor Education and Supervision [ACES], 1993, p. 2). Similar statements appear in the supervisory guidelines of other helping professions (e.g., marriage and family therapy, professional psychology, social work). Despite this nearly universal declaration of importance, evaluation is often a challenge for supervisors. Indeed, evaluation has been cited as a major source of supervisee anxiety (Carroll, 1996; Robiner, Fuhrman, & Ristvedt, 1993), an area of risk for ethical and legal violations (e.g., McAdams, Foster, & Ward, 2007), a common source of supervisee grievances (Ladany, 2004), and a stimulus for negative supervisee experiences in supervision (e.g., Forrest, Elman, Gizara, & Vacha-Haase, 1999; Magnuson, Wilcoxon, & Norem, 2000). In contrast, evaluation also has the potential to be a powerful stimulus for change (Holloway, 1992), is key to supervisee satisfaction (Henderson, Cawyer, & Watkins, 1999; Kennard, Stewart, & Gluck, 1987; Lehrman-Waterman & Ladany, 2001), and may strengthen the supervisory relationship (Lehrman-Waterman & Ladany, 2001).

Why then is something so essential and potentially positive avoided, dreaded, or minimized by many counseling supervisors? Perhaps because of complexity and ambiguity of the task? When a task is complex and ambiguous, specific training and support are vital to effectiveness. As such, in this chapter we will provide specific information about how evaluation can be done accurately and effectively. We are confident that supervisors can create evaluation experiences that will be catalysts for growth rather than negative experiences for supervisees. Best practice guidelines, ethical standards, and supervision research inform the process of evaluation in supervision. The following overview will highlight valuable findings from these resources.

Preparation for Evaluation

It is clear that establishing evaluation expectations *before* supervision begins is an ethical requirement (e.g., ACES, 2003; Association of State and Provincial Psychology Boards, 2003; National Association of Social Workers, 1994) and essential best practice (e.g., American Psychological Association [APA], 2006; Ladany, 2004; Sherry, 1991) for clinical supervisors. Supervisees should be informed, verbally and in writing, of the evaluation procedures, components of evaluation, and consequences of underperformance. The evaluation plan should be included in the supervisory disclosure statement and/or contract for supervision. If supervision is occurring as part of graduate training, the course syllabus may serve as the contract for supervision and as such the evaluation plan should be included therein. However, if supervision is occurring postgraduation in preparation for licensure, the supervisor may need to develop a similarly structured contract for supervision that meets the evaluation requirements of the licensing board. A verbal explanation of the written document is helpful in ensuring supervisee comprehension (Okin & Gaughen, 1991). The evaluation plan should include the time line for evaluation (e.g., weekly verbal feedback with quarterly written evaluations), tools used for evaluation (e.g., any instruments that will be used or prompts for a narrative evaluation), a description of who will have access to the information, and the procedure for addressing performance concerns.

As part of the description of the evaluation plan, supervisees are entitled to an explanation of the consequences of underperformance. Supervisors are obligated to address underperformance early and often, as assurance that supervisees have the benefit of *due process*. In this case, due process means that the supervisee has the right to be made aware of performance requirements, receive regular evaluation and feedback including notification of underperformance, have consequences of underperformance explained to them, and have an opportunity to discuss their underperformance and the resultant consequences (Forrest et al., 1999; Lamb, Cochran, & Jackson, 1991; McAdams et al., 2007; Okin & Gaughen, 1991). The consequences of underperformance may be a structured remediation plan. Such remediation should be relevant to the area of deficit and designed to facilitate the development that is necessary for success (Okin & Gaughen, 1991).

Let's consider the example of Carole, a master's student in her first semester of practicum. Carole's supervisor notices she uses a rigid script of closed questions in her first client session. Although this is a common challenge for new counselors, it is a significant performance issue and merits attention in the first supervision session. The supervisor should (appropriately) explore the issue and Carole should be made aware of the need to work on those skills. If Carole's skills improve during the next few weeks of practicum, the intervention was a success and the supervisor has the great pleasure of highlighting Carole's progress. If Carole does not make progress with this core component of counselor performance, additional interventions are necessary. The supervisor is responsible for continuing to support Carole and attempting to facilitate her growth in this area. If Carole fails to make progress over an extended period of time, the supervisor should indicate the area of underperformance on a written evaluation (perhaps at midterm). A written remediation plan should be developed in accordance with the course syllabus that specifically delineates what Carole is required to do in order to succeed (e.g., videotape practice sessions with a peer that show evidence of open questions and reflection). The plan should include the consequences if Carole does not meet the goals of the remediation plan by the due date (e.g., repeat the practicum course). This course of action provides Carole a complete explanation of the gravity of her underperformance and ample time to make progress on her goals. The supervisor must actively monitor Carole's progress, as Carole may assume the issues have been rectified if they do not continue to be a focus in supervision. If by the end of the term, Carole has not made the necessary progress, the consequences set forth in the remediation plan and/or course syllabus can be implemented.

This process may seem straightforward in writing but, in practice, supervisors frequently face difficult decisions about how to gauge underperformance and when this type of intervention is merited. A well-meaning supervisor could be tempted to just hope Carole makes progress throughout the semester and might avoid delivering the constructive feedback because he or she is concerned Carole will get discouraged. But, if Carole's performance issues persist, the supervisor is then stuck with limited options (e.g., pass Carole even though she has not met all the practicum requirements? Inform Carole at the end of the semester that she will have additional requirements for passing the course?). Neither of these options are best for Carole's development as a counselor and neither fit within the ethical guidelines for counseling supervisors. Similarly, when supervising counselors who are working toward licensure, the supervisor should use due process when issues arise that would preclude endorsement for licensure or continued supervision.

In sum, close attention to supervisee performance, ongoing evaluation, and prompt interventions are essential to effective supervision. Even with a clear description of the evaluation process, determining what constitutes adequate performance or significant underperformance is rarely concrete and is often cited as a challenge in preparing supervisors for evaluation (Bernard & Goodyear, 2009; Goodyear & Bradley, 1983; Magnuson, 1995). Increasing supervisor competence and confidence with assessment of supervisee performance may make evaluation and addressing underperformance easier. The following section will provide some clarity as to components of counselor performance that are appropriate foci of evaluation.

Criteria for Evaluation

Perhaps the most fundamental challenge of evaluation of supervisees is the complexity of counselor performance. What are the characteristics of effective counselors? What are the essential components of counselor competency that all supervisees must be able to demonstrate? How can the evaluation take into account the differences among the many styles of counseling? Should the evaluation be individualized or standard for all supervisees?

These questions are important considerations as supervisors prepare to evaluate their supervisees. Effective evaluation plans include both standard components of competency that all counselors should achieve and individualized goals that fit the supervisee's unique style and stage of development.

Standard Areas of Competency

Although there is no single universal resource that defines counselor competence, research has informed the development of core competency areas and counselor education programs and professional organizations frequently include the following seven core competencies with slight variations (e.g., APA, 2006; Council for the Accreditation of Counseling and Related Programs, 2009; Ellis & Ladany, 1997; Frame & Stevens-Smith, 1995; Hatcher & Lassiter, 2007; Neufelt, 1999; Robiner et al., 1993).

1. Client assessment and conceptualization
2. Treatment planning
3. Helping/intervention skills
4. Therapeutic relationship development
5. Professional, legal, and ethical behavior
6. Multicultural competence
7. Interpersonal attributes

Client Assessment and Conceptualization

Effective counselors must be able to identify individual and systemic characteristics of the client in order to understand needs in counseling. A thorough and accurate client conceptualization is essential to effective treatment (e.g., Blocher, 1983; Stoltenberg, 1981). There are many ways to evaluate supervisee assessment and conceptualization competencies. For example, supervisors can look for evidence of conceptualization competency in supervisee written case reports and in verbal descriptions of clients. Supervisees may be required to use diagnostic assessments or other formal assessments in their practice. Review of supervisee documentation or recorded sessions may provide evidence of competency in client diagnosis and appraisal.

Treatment Planning

With a thorough and accurate understanding of client needs, the supervisee must then choose an effective treatment plan. Note that because of the many theories and approaches to counseling and the many settings and client needs, treatment planning may come in many forms. It is important to evaluate the supervisee's competence taking into consideration the context of his or her work (e.g., a short-term inpatient stay versus elementary school counseling). Treatment planning of some type should occur in every counseling setting, so this competency can be evaluated with all supervisees. Look for evidence of effective treatment planning in supervisee verbal descriptions and written case reports. Supervisees who are early in their development as counselors may need structured support in order to develop a treatment plan and take ownership of the counseling process (e.g., Skovholt & Rønnestad, 1992; Stoltenberg, 1981). Evaluate the supervisee's ability to develop and execute the treatment plan as well as monitor progress and revise the plan as needed.

Helping/Intervention Skills

Helping skills or intervention skills is a broad competency area (e.g., Hill, 2004). In evaluating this competency, supervisors should consider if the supervisee is able to use a combination of skills in order to help the client make progress on his or her goals. Our example of Carole above, exemplifies a skill deficit that severely limited client progress. Observing live or recorded client sessions will provide evidence of skill competence. Supervisees can also discuss their rationale for choosing particular skills or techniques in the supervision sessions. Because skills are more concrete, this competency is simpler to define and observe than some of the other core competencies.

Therapeutic Relationship Development

The supervisee's ability to develop a therapeutic relationship also is consistently included in core competencies. The ability to establish rapport is essential to counseling effectiveness as we know the therapeutic relationship consistently accounts for a significant amount of the variation in treatment outcome (Frank & Gunderson, 1990; Sexton & Whiston, 1994). Look for evidence of the therapeutic relationship in live or recorded client sessions. Does the client seem to trust the supervisee? Is the client comfortable disclosing? Does the supervisee communicate empathy and understanding? Client feedback forms (more information below) are an effective way to gather information about the client's perceptions of the counseling relationship. Note that the counselor's perception of the counseling relationship may be different than the client's perception and it is especially difficult for new counselors to self-evaluate this competency (Loganbill, Hardy, & Delworth, 1982).

Professional, Legal, and Ethical Behavior

Supervisors are responsible for monitoring and evaluating the professional, legal, and ethical behavior of their supervisees. It is of great concern that in a study of supervisees, many reported withholding clinical mistakes from their supervisors, negative reactions to clients, countertransference issues, and sexual attraction issues (Ladany, Hill, Corbett, & Nutt, 1996). As these authors suggest, a strong supervisory relationship may help supervisors create an atmosphere that encourages supervisee disclosure. Legal or ethical concerns that arise during supervision provide wonderful teachable moments. "Competence" in this area is not necessarily knowing the ethical codes verbatim or being able to determine the correct plan of action alone, rather "competence" is the ability to recognize ethical/legal dilemmas and the awareness that consultation and supervision are necessary with any ethical or legal dilemma. Supervisors can evaluate a supervisee's direct performance with ethical or legal dilemmas that arise during the course of supervision or use hypothetical situations and examples to explore a supervisee's ethical and legal judgment.

Multicultural Competence

Counselor multicultural competence has received much (and well-deserved) attention in recent years, but continues to be challenging to evaluate. The American Counseling Association recognizes age, color, disability, ethnic group, gender, race, language preference, religion, spirituality, sexual orientation, and socioeconomic status as components of culture (ACA, 2005). Given this inclusive definition it is clear that every counseling relationship is cross-cultural in some way. The Association for Multicultural Counseling and Development attempted to operationalize counselor multicultural competencies in a 1996 statement that included three areas of competency: counselor awareness of own cultural values and biases, counselor awareness of client's worldview, and culturally appropriate intervention strategies. It is unrealistic to expect any counselor to be knowledgeable about all cultures. Perhaps as important as specific knowledge, is counselor self-awareness, humility, respect, willingness to learn, and ability to broach the topic of culture (Association for Multicultural Counseling and Development, 1992). It is clear that the responsibility to broach cultural considerations lies with the counselor, not the client and that exploring multicultural issues often leads to a better therapeutic relationship (Pope-Davis, Toporek, & Ortega-Villalobos, 2002). Evidence of multicultural competence, including broaching cultural issues, can be observed through live or recorded sessions, case reports, and explored verbally with the supervisee (Worthington, Soth-McNett, & Moreno, 2007).

Interpersonal Attributes

Interpersonal attributes are frequently cited as key to counselor competence (e.g., Frame & Stevens-Smith, 1995; Seligman, 2004). Supervisors are responsible for evaluating supervisee interpersonal attributes such as ability to express emotions, personal maturity, perspective taking, ability to receive and integrate feedback, ability to manage conflict, motivation, respectfulness, and sense of responsibility. Supervisors have reported discomfort with this aspect of evaluation (Robiner et al., 1993), but it clearly fits within the realm of supervisory responsibility. Indeed, the ACES ethical code states "Supervisors, through ongoing supervisee assessment and evaluation, should be aware of any *personal* or professional limitations of supervisees which are likely to impede future professional performance." These interpersonal attributes may impact other areas of competence such as therapeutic relationship and professionalism. Evidence of interpersonal competency is observable in supervisee interactions with clients, peers, and supervisors, behaviors during and outside of the supervision session, and supervisee self-reflections. When supervisors have concerns about interpersonal attributes, it is important to seek collateral information. Do other supervisors have the same concerns? Have these concerns emerged in the past? Is the supervisee aware of this deficit? It can be difficult to evaluate and plan remediation for interpersonal deficits. Consultation with other supervisors may prove helpful in developing and executing an effective plan.

As you reflect on these multiple areas of competence, remember that supervisees develop asynchronously. That is, they may excel in some areas of competence while struggling in others. A graduated evaluation system allows the supervisor to indicate areas of ipsative strengths and weaknesses that may inform future supervisory foci. The minimum acceptable score (e.g., "minimally meets expectations") and any other requirements for passing should be stated in the contract for supervision (e.g., no areas marked "does not meet expectations").

Supervisors must learn, practice, and revise evaluation techniques just as they learned, practiced, and revised counseling techniques when they were new counselors. You will likely grow more confident in your evaluation abilities as you gain experience supervising (Inman & Soheilian, 2010).

Individualized Goals

In addition to the general areas of competence described above, supervisees benefit from setting and working toward individual developmental goals in supervision (Talen & Schindler, 1993). Lehrman-Waterman and Ladany (2001) found that goal setting may improve the supervisory relationship and supervisee satisfaction with supervision. Individualized goals can be cocreated by the supervisee and supervisor and should be based on the supervisee's strengths, weaknesses, and learning priorities. Some supervisees may find it difficult to articulate their strengths and weaknesses (Loganbill et al., 1982) and may need considerable help in developing individual goals for supervision (Borders & Brown, 2005). Other supervisees may require help making goals specific enough (e.g., "Increase use of age-appropriate language with young children" rather than "Become comfortable counseling young children"). Like client goals in counseling, it is important for the goals to be relevant, measurable, and attainable.

For example, if your supervisee, William, has demonstrated the ability to establish rapport, reflect feeling, and provide therapeutic support but has difficulty challenging clients, perhaps an appropriate goal would be to increase use of therapeutic confrontation. To monitor progress on this goal, William could describe cases where he is considering using confrontation, submit audio or videotapes of sessions that include the use of confrontation, and/or write journal reflections about his experiences using confrontation. Again, like client goals in counseling, the supervisory focus should be on progress, not perfection and active attention to goals throughout the supervision time is more effective than sporadic or a final review alone (Borders & Leddick, 1987; Bordin, 1983).

It is difficult to provide adequate attention to more than three or four goals at a time (Blocher, 1983). Goals should be reviewed and revised as needed throughout the supervision process. Inclusion of individualized goals in the evaluation plan should be stated prior to the start of supervision (as described above) and an evaluation plan for each goal should be developed. Individualized goals often fit within the scope of the general areas of competence (e.g., therapeutic confrontation as a helping/intervention skill), but will not encompass all of the core counselor competencies. Therefore, it is important that evaluation include progress on individualized goals and progress toward standard competencies.

Providing Evaluative Feedback

Ethical guideline 2.08 states

> Supervisors should provide supervisees with ongoing feedback on their performance. This feedback should take a variety of forms, both formal and informal, and should include verbal and written evaluations. It should be formative during the supervisory experience and summative at the conclusion of the experience. (ACES, 1993, p. 2)

Indeed, supervisors constantly provide feedback—verbally, nonverbally, and with silence. Your mere attention or nonattention to a particular topic is feedback on some level. Providing evaluative feedback can be difficult for supervisors (Hoffman, Hill, & Homes, 2005; Robiner, Saltzman, Hoberman, Semrud-Clikeman, & Schirvar, 1997), particularly if the feedback is corrective. Supervisors can prepare supervisees for feedback early in supervision by explaining the evaluation process, normalizing supervisee anxieties, and exploring supervisee defensiveness (Coffey, 2002).

Formative feedback occurs in every supervision session. It is crucial to include a balance of positive and corrective components in each supervision session. Frequent critical feedback may be discouraging to the supervisee and excessive positive feedback is unlikely to stimulate growth (Gross, 2005; Kadushin, 1992). Supervisors usually recognize more potential foci for feedback than the supervisee can effectively comprehend and integrate during a supervision session (Blocher, 1983). The standard areas of competency, individualized goals, and urgency of the issue may shape the few chosen foci for each session. The formative feedback given in each session informs the supervisee of his/her progress and increases awareness of areas that need attention. Formative feedback also establishes a norm for evaluation in supervision. Supervisees may be more comfortable with the summative evaluation if they have received formative feedback throughout the term.

Summative feedback is usually more formal than formative feedback and occurs at preset intervals (e.g., midterm and end of the semester or every three months). Summative feedback should include a written evaluation (Forrest et al., 1999; Lamb et al., 1991; McAdams et al., 2007). Effective summative feedback experiences include a verbal explanation of the written evaluation (Belar et al., 1993). It is important to be as accurate as possible on written evaluations, as they are a record of supervisee progress and are essential to demonstrating due process for those supervisees who are not meeting expectations. If, as ethically required, the supervisee's performance has been a focus of the ongoing supervisory sessions, scores on the summative evaluation will not come as a surprise. Note that it is important to orient the supervisee to the written evaluation for itself as well as scoring rules. For example, some supervisees may expect perfect scores (e.g., "All 5s"), and may interpret anything less as failure. Explaining the rationale for scoring may be helpful in ensuring the supervisee has an accurate understanding of the evaluation.

A complete discussion of supervisee incompetence and gate-keeping is beyond the scope of this chapter (see Forrest et al., 1999; Forrest, Miller, & Elman, 2008; Lamb et al., 1991; McAdams et al., 2007 for more information). When supervisees fail to progress in supervision, endanger clients, or it is evident that a supervisee will not be able to be successful as a counselor, supervisors are faced with many difficult decisions. Consultation with other supervisors and/or counselor educators is essential and careful attention to evaluation protocols is essential.

Evaluation Resources and Strategies

There are multiple sources of feedback that are valuable in preparing for effective evaluation. Accessing multiple sources will increase the depth of the evaluation and provide the supervisee with multiple perspectives (see Lambert & Ogles, 1997, for a review of 55 instruments with varying raters). Self-evaluation, client feedback, and peer feedback, can be incorporated with supervisor feedback into the evaluation process.

Self-reflection and self-evaluation are essential skills for counselors. Formal supervision occurs for a relatively brief time in the career of a counselor. The ability to monitor one's strengths, weaknesses, and development will be crucial in the counselor's development during and after formal supervision. Supervisees who complete a self-evaluation may be more receptive to a supervisor's feedback and more invested in continued development (Bernard & Goodyear, 2009; Borders & Brown, 2005). Supervisees can be asked to write a narrative self-evaluation of progress on individualized goals or complete a more standardized evaluation of the areas of counselor competency. It is important that the supervisee self-evaluation occurs prior to the supervisor evaluation so that the supervisee is not influenced by supervisor remarks. Discrepancies and overlap between the self-evaluation and the supervisor evaluation may lead to a productive discussion.

Client feedback is a rich and underutilized resource in supervisee evaluation. Clients of all ages and levels of clinical severity can provide feedback about their perceptions of the supervisee. It is important that the feedback form include relevant questions that the client can answer (e.g., "I think my counselor understands me" not "My counselor uses the Cognitive Therapy protocols correctly"). For example, the Working Alliance Inventory (Horvath & Greenberg, 1989) includes items such as "I am confident in [my counselor's] ability to help me" and "[My counselor] and I trust one another." The Barrett-Leonard Relationship Inventory includes items like "[My counselor] realizes what I mean even when I have difficulty in saying it" and "I feel that [my counselor] disapproves of me" (Barrett-Lennard, 1995). These items allow clients to provide feedback on how they experience the supervisee in the counseling relationship. Returning to our example above of William who is attempting to increase use of therapeutic confrontation, he may benefit from hearing directly from his clients how they perceived his confrontations. If, for example, he is concerned that he came across as too harsh, receiving reassuring feedback from the client may be even more powerful than a supervisor's encouragement.

Peer feedback is another valuable resource in supervisee evaluation and is most accessible in group or triadic supervision. Although the ultimate responsibility for evaluation lies with the supervisor, peers can provide valuable feedback about supervisee growth and areas for continued development. At times, supervisees are more receptive to feedback from peers than they are to feedback from supervisors (e.g., Hillerbrand, 1989). Peer feedback can be considered in conjunction with other evidence of progress on individualized goals and core competencies.

Gathering information from multiple sources will provide a more accurate, multifaceted picture of supervisee performance and therefore a more complete evaluation. Supervisor observations may be echoed by other sources of feedback and the supervisee may be more receptive to feedback that is consistent across multiple perspectives.

Tools for Evaluation of Supervisee Competence

Despite the importance of evaluation in supervision, there are few valid and reliable evaluation instruments. Ellis, D'Iuso, and Ladany (2008) have noted this dearth of resources and have suggested that supervision researchers use rigorous scientific practices to create and validate new instruments.

Although graduate programs frequently develop instruments for midterm and final evaluation of students in clinical internships, these instruments are rarely subjected to psychometric analysis. Such instruments usually include items that address the areas of competence described above (i.e., client assessment and conceptualization, treatment planning, helping/intervention skills, therapeutic relationship development, professional, legal, and ethical behavior, multicultural competence, and interpersonal attributes) in a format that allows the university and/or site supervisor to indicate level of performance (e.g., item "Adherence to ethical and legal practices" with response options Exceeds expectations, Meets expectations, and Does not meet expectations). This open format threatens the validity of the item, however, because the supervisor is merely indicating his or her perception of supervisee performance based on his or her interpretation of the expectations. McAdams and colleagues (2007) used descriptors of performance at each rating level to improve the consistency of supervisor ratings. For example, for the item "Willingness to accept and use feedback," supervisors are provided examples of poor performance like "Discouraged feedback from others through defensiveness and anger," moderate performance like "Showed some evidence of incorporating supervisory feedback into own views and behaviors," and high performance like "Invited feedback by direct request and gave positive acknowledgment when received." By including behavior indicators, the authors give supervisors a more specific indication of what performance at each level looks like, thus improving the consistency of ratings among supervisors. Evaluation of supervisees who are working toward licensure is often even more unspecific. For example, the Quarterly Evaluation Form for licensure as a professional counselor in Virginia simply asks the supervisor to write a brief description of the services provided and then an evaluation summary of the supervisee's performance. Until standardized instruments for evaluating counselor competence are available, supervisors must use the existing instruments with care. As described above, discussing performance expectations with the supervisee and including a description of the evaluation process in writing can help to ensure mutual understanding.

Summary

Evaluation is an essential component of effective supervision. Just as supervision is a "deliberate education process" (Borders, 2001), evaluation requires deliberate planning and careful execution. Evaluation is not a unidirectional, punitive process; rather it is a supportive, facilitative experience that is a catalyst for supervisee growth. Supervisees should be informed of evaluation procedures and consequences of underperformance before supervision begins. General counselor competencies and individualized goals shape the foci of ongoing supervision and provide structure to formative and summative evaluations. With preparation and practice, supervisors can effectively evaluate supervisee performance.

References

American Counseling Association. (2005). *Code of ethics* (rev. ed.). Alexandria, VA: Author.

American Psychological Association. (2006). *Assessment of competence in professional psychology: Final report*. Washington, DC: Author.

Association for Counselor Education and Supervision (ACES). (1993). *Ethical guidelines for counseling supervisors*. Alexandria, VA: Author.

Association for Multicultural Counseling and Development. (1992). *Multicultural counseling competencies*. Alexandria, VA: Author.

Association of State and Provincial Psychology Boards. (2003). *Supervision guidelines.* Montgomery, AL: Author.

Barrett-Lennard, G. T. (1995). Barrett-Lennard Relationship Inventory OS-40. Copyrighted Instrument.

Belar, C. D., Bieliauskas, L. A., Klepac, R. K., Larsen, K. G., Stigall, T. T., & Zimet, C. N. (1993). National conference on postdoctoral training in professional psychology. *American Psychologist, 48,* 1284–1289.

Bernard, J. M., & Goodyear, R. K. (2009). *Fundamentals of clinical supervision* (4th ed.). Boston, MA: Allyn and Bacon.

Blocher, D. (1983). Toward a cognitive developmental approach to counseling supervision. *Counseling Psychologist, 11,* 27–34.

Borders, L. D. (2001). Counseling supervision: A deliberate educational process. In D. Locke, J. Myers, & E. Herr (Eds.), *Handbook of counseling* (pp. 417–432). Thousand Oaks, CA: Sage.

Borders, L. D., & Brown, L. L. (2005). *The new handbook of counseling supervision.* Nahwah, NJ: Lawrence Erlbaum Associates.

Borders, L. D., & Leddick, G. R. (1987). *Handbook of counseling supervision.* Alexandria, VA: Association for Counselor Education and Supervision.

Bordin, E. S. (1983). A working alliance model of supervision. *Counseling Psychologist, 11,* 35–42.

Carroll, M. (1996). *Counseling supervision: Theory, skills, and practice.* London, UK: Cassell.

Coffey, D. (2002). *Receiving corrective feedback: A special set of skills.* Presentation at the Association for Counselor Education and Supervision Convention, Park City, Utah.

Council for the Accreditation of Counseling and Related Programs. (2009). *2009 standards.* Alexandria, VA: Author.

Ellis, M. V., D'Iuso, N., & Ladany, N. (2008). State of the art in the assessment, measurement, and evaluation of clinical supervision in psychotherapy supervision. In A. Hess, K. Hess, & T. Hess (Eds.), *Psychotherapy supervision: Theory, research, and practice* (pp. 473–499). Hoboken, NJ: Wiley.

Ellis, M. V., & Ladany, N. (1997). Inferences concerning supervisees and clients in clinical supervision: An integrative review. In C. E. Watkins, Jr. (Ed.), *Handbook of psychotherapy supervision* (pp. 467–507). New York, NY: Wiley.

Forrest, L., Elman, N., Gizara, S., & Vacha-Haase, T. (1999). Trainee impairment: A review of identification, remediation, dismissal, and legal issues. *Counseling Psychologist, 27*(5), 627–686.

Forrest, L., Elman, N. S., & Miller, D. S. (2008). Psychology trainees with competence problems: From individual to ecological conceptualizations. *Training and Education in Professional Psychology, 2*(4), 183–192.

Frame, M. W., & Stevens-Smith, P. (1995). Out of harm's way: Enhancing monitoring and dismissal processes in counselor education programs. *Counselor Education and Supervision, 35,* 118–129.

Frank, A., & Gunderson, J. (1990). The role of the therapeutic alliance in the treatment of schizophrenia: Relationship to course and outcome. *Archives of General Psychiatry, 47,* 228–236.

Goodyear, R. K., & Bradley, F. O. (1983). Theories of counselor supervision: Points of convergence and divergence. *The Counseling Psychologist, 11,* 59–67.

Gross, S. M. (2005). Student perspectives on clinical and counseling psychology practica. *Professional Psychology: Research and Practice, 36*, 299–306.

Hatcher, R. L., & Lassiter, K. D. (2007). Initial training in professional psychology: The practicum competencies outline. *Training and Education in Professional Psychology, 1*, 49–63.

Henderson, C. E., Cawyer, C. S., & Watkins, C. E., Jr. (1999). A comparison of student and supervisor perceptions of effective practicum supervision. *The Clinical Supervisor, 18*, 47–74.

Hill, C. E. (2004). *Helping skills: Facilitating explorations, insight, and action* (2nd ed.). Washington, DC: American Psychological Association.

Hillerbrand, E. T. (1989). Cognitive differences between experts and novices: Implications for group supervision. *Journal of Counseling and Development, 67*, 293–296.

Hoffman, M. A., Hill, C. E., & Homes, S. E. (2005). Supervisor perspective on the process and outcome of giving easy, difficult, or no feedback to supervisees. *Journal of Counseling Psychology, 52*(1), 3–13.

Holloway, E. L. (1992). Supervision: A way of teaching and learning. In S. D. Brown & R. W. Lent (Eds.), *Handbook of counseling psychology* (pp. 177–214). New York, NY: John Wiley.

Horvath, A. O., & Greenberg, L. S. (1989). Development and validation of the working alliance inventory. *Journal of Counseling Psychology, 36*, 223–233.

Inman, A. G., & Soheilian, S. S. (2010). Training supervisors: A core competency. In N. Ladany & L. Bradley (Eds.), *Counselor supervision* (4th ed.). New York, NY: Routledge.

Kadushin, A. (1992). What's wrong, what's right with social work supervision. *Clinical Supervisor, 10*(1), 3–19.

Kennard, B. D., Stewart, S. M., & Gluck, M. R. (1987). The supervision relationship: Variables contributing to positive versus negative experiences. *Professional Psychology: Research and Practice, 18*, 172–175.

Ladany, N. (2004). Psychotherapy supervision: What lies beneath. *Psychotherapy Research, 14*, 1–19.

Ladany, N., Hill, C. E., Corbett, M. M., & Nutt, E. A. (1996). Nature, extent, and importance of what psychotherapy trainees do not disclose to their supervisors. *Journal of Counseling Psychology, 43*, 10–24.

Lamb, D. H., Cochran, D. J., & Jackson, V. R. (1991). Training and organizational issues associated with identifying and responding to intern impairment. *Professional Psychology: Research and Practice, 22*, 291–296.

Lambert, M. J., & Ogles, B. M. (1997). The effectiveness of psychotherapy supervision. In C. E. Watkins, Jr. (Ed.), *Handbook of psychotherapy supervision* (pp. 421–446). New York, NY: John Wiley.

Lehrman-Waterman, D., & Ladany, N. (2001). Development and validation of the evaluation process within supervision inventory [special issue]. *Journal of Counseling Psychology, 48*(2), 168–177.

Loganbill, C., Hardy, E., & Delworth, U. (1982). Supervision: A conceptual model. *Counseling Psychologist, 10*, 3–42.

Magnuson, S. (1995). *Supervision of prelicensed counselors: A study of educators, supervisors, and supervisees* (Unpublished doctoral dissertation). Tuscaloosa: University of Alabama.

Magnuson, S., Wilcoxon, S. A., & Norem, K. (2000). A profile of lousy supervision: Experienced counselors' perspectives. *Counselor Education and Supervision, 39*, 189–202.

McAdams, C. R., Foster, V. A., & Ward, T. J. (2007). Remediation and dismissal policies in counselor education: Lessons learned from a challenge in federal court. *Counselor Education and Supervision, 46*(3), 212–229.

National Association of Social Workers. (1994). *Code of ethics* (rev. ed.). Washington, DC: Author.

Neufeldt, S. A. (1999). Training in reflective processes in supervision. In E. Holloway & M. Carroll (Eds.), *Training in counseling supervisors* (pp. 92–105). London, UK: Sage.

Okin, R., & Gaughen, S. (1991). Evaluation and dismissal of students in master's level clinical programs: Legal parameters and survey results. *Counselor Education and Supervision, 30*(4), 276–288.

Pope-Davis, D. B., Toporek, R. L., & Ortega-Villalobos, L. (2002). Client perspectives of multicultural counseling competence: A qualitative examination. *Counseling Psychologist, 30*(3), 355–393.

Robiner, W. N., Fuhrman, M., & Ristvedt, S. (1993). Evaluation difficulties in supervising psychology interns. *Clinical Psychologist, 46*, 3–13.

Robiner, W. N., Saltzman, S. R., Hoberman, H. M., Semrud-Clikeman, M., & Schirvar, J. A. (1997). Psychology supervisor's bias in evaluations and letters of recommendation. *Clinical Supervisor, 16*(2), 49–72.

Seligman, L. (2004). *Diagnosis and treatment planning in counseling* (3rd ed.). New York, NY: Kluwer Academic.

Sexton, T. L., & Whiston, S. C. (1994). The status of the counseling relationship: An empirical review, theoretical implications, and research directions. *Counseling Psychologist, 22*(1), 6–78.

Sherry, P. (1991). Ethical issues in the conduct of supervision. *Counseling Psychologist, 19*, 566–584.

Skovholt, T. M., & Rønnestad, M. H. (1992). Themes in therapist and counselor development. *Journal of Counseling and Development, 70*, 505–515.

Stoltenberg, C. (1981). Approaching supervision from a developmental perspective: The counselor-complexity model. *Journal of Counseling Psychologist, 28*, 59–65.

Talen, M. R., & Schindler, N. (1993). Goal-directed supervision plans: A model for trainee supervision and evaluation. *Clinical Supervisor, 11*(2), 77–88.

Worthington, R. L., Soth-McNett, A. M., & Moreno, M. V. (2007). Multicultural counseling competencies research: A 20-year content analysis. *Journal of Counseling Psychology, 54*(4), 351–361.

CHAPTER 15

Understanding and Conducting Supervision Research

NICHOLAS LADANY and MATTHEW A. MALOUF

The important thing is to not stop questioning.

—**Albert Einstein**

Since the publication of the first empirical supervision article in 1958 (Harkness & Poertner, 1989), nearly 300 empirical articles regarding counseling supervision have been published in journals such as *The Clinical Supervisor, The Counseling Psychologist, Counselor Education and Supervision, Journal of Consulting and Clinical Psychology, Journal of Counseling & Development, Journal of Counseling Psychology, Professional Psychology: Research and Practice*, and *Psychotherapy: Theory, Research, Practice, and Training*. This figure represents both a comparative lag in research on supervision when compared to counseling research (Goodyear, Bunch, & Claiborn, 2005) and a modest growth in interest in counseling research over the last few decades (Inman & Ladany, 2008; Ladany & Inman, in press). Indeed, nearly one third of these articles have been published during the eight years since the last update of this chapter (Ladany & Muse-Burke, 2001).

Yet despite rising interest in counselor supervision, empirical research continues to be steadily published at a rate of just under 10 articles per year (Ladany & Inman, 2008) reflecting the many challenges that still exist in conducting supervision research. Historically, counseling supervision has been limited by knowledge about counseling (Lambert & Arnold, 1987) making it difficult, if not impossible, for supervision researchers to investigate salient phenomenon occurring between supervisees and supervisors without first understanding the phenomenon occurring between supervisees and their clients. Furthermore, in contrast to client samples, samples of supervisees and/or supervisors are intrinsically smaller. However, in the last two decades, the emphasis of supervision research has shifted from simply measuring the effects on client outcome to a larger exploration of the supervision process itself (Holloway, 1984). Though this change can be celebrated as an indicator of the expansion of supervision research into a bona fide subfield of counseling psychology, it also yields a potentially overwhelming interrelated web of subjects, dyads, and variables including supervisees, their clients, their clinical supervisors, peer-supervisors and those training others to conduct supervision. Lastly, only a handful of supervision researchers are conducting programmatic research (Inman & Ladany, 2008).

It is important to note that there are also challenges faced by authors attempting to conduct reviews of the counseling supervision literature. Specifically, a wide scope of journals publish counseling-related literature, including those specific to the counseling field (e.g., *Journal of Counseling and Development, Counselor Education and Supervision*), as well as those based in similar fields (e.g., *Journal of Counseling Psychology, Addiction: Theory and Research*) and those that are interdisciplinary (e.g., *The Clinical Supervisor*; Borders, 2005). As such, just as the sheer number of potential variables involved with the supervision process make conducting a comprehensive examination of supervision a daunting task (Ladany, Walker, Pate-Carolan, & Gray, 2008) so too does the variety of journals make conducting a thorough literature review a complex undertaking. That being said a simple keyword search yields over 70 reviews of the supervision literature addressing empirical research (e.g., Bernard & Goodyear, 2004; Borders, 2005; Ellis & Ladany, 1997; Goodyear et al., 2005; Lambert, 1980; Lambert & Ogles, 1997; Neufeldt, Beutler, & Banchero, 1997; Russell, Crimmings, & Lent, 1984) and it is from these reviews that much of this chapter is drawn.

Just as the purpose of supervision research is twofold, namely to understand the process of supervision and its influence on counseling and to inform supervision practice, this chapter seeks to both describe the current state of counseling supervision research and to inform future research. To accomplish this, we will first present a model identifying and categorizing the variables of supervision research. Second, we will provide an overview of the literature pertaining to supervision research, including new trends and developments. Third, we will offer a schema of the important elements of conducting supervision research. Fourth, we will apply our knowledge about research and methodology to offer a model for assessing the adequacy of trainee evaluation approaches. It is our hope that this chapter will prove useful for students who are interested in conducting supervision research as part of theses and dissertations, for professional supervision researchers, and for consumers of supervision research.

Supervision Research Variables

The first step toward understanding supervision research is to conceptualize the primary, general research questions within which most supervision empirical work may be considered. These overarching research questions (Ladany & Lehrman-Waterman, 1999) include:

1. How does supervision influence trainee outcome?
2. How does supervision influence client outcome?
3. How does counseling influence trainee learning?
4. How do counseling and supervision processes parallel one another?
5. How does counseling influence client outcome?
6. How do external events outside of supervision influence supervision and counseling?

As can be seen, much of supervision research involves examining relationships and events outside of the trainee–supervisor interactions (e.g., counseling, external events, etc.). Presently, the "outside supervision" variables have received the least attention in the supervision literature, and the "inside supervision" question (i.e., How does supervision influence trainee outcome?) has received the most attention.

Along with Wampold and Holloway (1997), we define supervision process as activities that occur within the supervision session as well as the perceptions of these activities by supervisors, trainees, and objective observers. Similarly, counseling process concerns the events that occur in counseling sessions and the perceptions of these events by counselor trainees, clients, supervisors, and objective observers. Furthermore, we define supervision and counseling outcome as variables that change as a result of supervision or counseling, and these changes endure beyond the session proper. Notably, in some instances, it may not be clear those variables that concern supervision process or supervision outcome (e.g., trainee satisfaction can occur in session or postsession). However, we believe that the concepts of process and outcome are a useful means by which researchers can manage and conceptualize the whole supervision experience.

From these research questions, a framework for conceptualizing supervision variables can be proffered (see Figure 15.1). Similar to other models (e.g., Wampold & Holloway, 1997), it is important to recognize that there is likely to be a reciprocal relationship among most of the variables. For example, supervisor characteristics, such as supervisor style, may influence

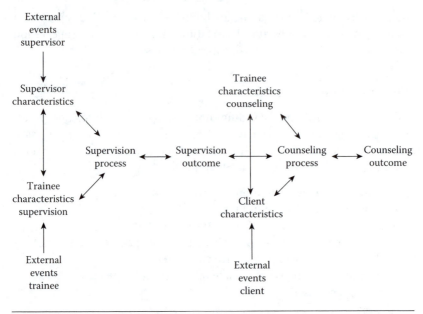

Figure 15.1 Interrelationships among supervision process and outcome and counseling process and outcome variables.

supervision process, like the development of the supervisory relationship. In turn, the supervisory relationship may influence supervisor style.

The second step toward understanding supervision research is to conceptualize the primary variables endemic to supervision that fit within the aforementioned primary research questions. Table 15.1 presents a sample of supervision variables that have been studied or that could be studied based on the theoretical propositions explicated and implied in the supervision literature. As can be seen, there are numerous variables to be considered when conducting supervision research. Hence, supervision should not be considered a unitary variable; rather, supervision should be recognized as a "heterogeneous set of conditions" (Lambert, 1980). To date, only a small percentage of these variables have been addressed in the supervision literature, and rarely have these variables been investigated in a systematic and programmatic fashion.

It is important to note that the interplay of these variables can be investigated either quantitatively (Kerlinger, 1986) or qualitatively (Creswell, 2006), with recent reviews of the literature finding that qualitative articles, though in the minority, now account for slightly more than 20% of published articles, a modest increase (Borders, 2005; Goodyear et al., 2005). Moreover, assessment of these variables can occur via self-report from the supervisor, trainee, and client, as well as through objective observer ratings. Each of

Table 15.1 Table of Supervision Variables

Variables

Supervisor characteristics

Sex
Race
Ethnicity
Sexual orientation
Age
Socioeconomic status
Religion
Gender identity
Racial identity
Ethnic identity
Sexual orientation identity
Spiritual identity
Personality (e.g., authoritativeness)
Counseling experience
Supervision experience
Counselor developmental level
Supervisor developmental level
Experience as a client
Experience as a therapist
Experience as a trainee
Supervisor self-efficacy
Counseling theoretical orientation
Supervision theoretical orientation
Expectations for supervision
Ability to tolerate ambiguity
Supervisor didactic training
Supervisor experiential training
Supervisor style

Trainee characteristics

Sex
Race
Ethnicity
Sexual orientation
Age
Socioeconomic status
Religion
Gender identity

(Continued)

Table 15.1 Table of Supervision Variables (*Continued*)

Variables

Racial identity
Ethnic identity
Sexual orientation identity
Spiritual identity
Personality (e.g., openness)
Experience as a client
Counseling experience
Supervised counseling experience
Trainee developmental level
Experience as a trainee
Experience as a supervisor
Anxiety
Counseling self-efficacy
Counseling theoretical orientation
Supervision theoretical orientation
Supervision role induction
Expectations for counseling
Expectations for supervision
Ability to tolerate ambiguity
Reflectivity
Counselor didactic training
Counselor experiential training

Client characteristics

Sex
Race
Ethnicity
Sexual orientation
Age
Socioeconomic status
Religion
Gender identity
Racial identity
Ethnic identity
Sexual orientation identity
Spiritual identity
Personality
Previous counseling experience
Expectations for counseling
Presenting issues

Table 15.1 Table of Supervision Variables (*Continued*)

Variables

Psychopathology
Social support
Ability to tolerate ambiguity

Supervision process

Supervisory relationship (e.g., supervisory working alliance)
Trainee disclosures
Supervisor disclosures
Trainee nondisclosures
Supervisor nondisclosures
Parallel process (as influenced by counseling process)
Trainee role conflict and role ambiguity
Trainee transference
Supervisor countertransference
Supervisor responsiveness
Supervisor interventions
Supervisor response modes
Supervisor intentions
Supervisor critical incidents
Trainee critical incidents

Supervision outcome

Trainee self-efficacy (change)
Trainee counseling skills (change)
Trainee conceptualization skills (change)
Trainee professional identity (change)
Trainee satisfaction
Trainee evaluation
Supervisor self-efficacy (change)
Supervisor supervision skills (change)
Supervisor conceptualization skills (change)
Supervisor professional identity (change)
Trainee regrets
Supervisor regrets
Session impact

Counseling process

Counseling relationship (e.g., counseling working alliance)
Counselor trainee disclosures
Client disclosure
Counselor trainee nondisclosures

(*Continued*)

Table 15.1 Table of Supervision Variables (*Continued*)

Variables

Client nondisclosures

Client transference

Counselor trainee countertransference

Counselor trainee responsiveness

Counselor trainee interventions

Counselor trainee response modes

Counselor trainee intentions

Counselor trainee critical incidents

Client critical incidents

Counseling outcome

Client level of distress (change)

Session impact

Client satisfaction

Client regrets

Counselor trainee regrets

Counselor trainee professional identity (change)

External events supervisor

Supervision of supervision

Environmental events (e.g., oppressive agency rules, managed care)

External events trainee

Peer feedback

Peer interactions

Environmental events (e.g., oppressive agency rules, trainee
  evaluation policies)

External events client

Environmental events (e.g., managed care, life experiences that
  influence presenting issues)

these perspectives should provide unique and relevant information about supervision (Holloway, 1984). Also, our model is most relevant to individual supervision of individual counselor trainees. Modifications could be made to accommodate group supervision of individual counseling, group supervision of group counseling, and supervision of family counseling accordingly.

What We Know From Supervision Research

As indicated previously, there have been numerous reviews of the supervision literature, which greatly vary in the extent to which they summarize and critique the research. The supervision research was examined systematically, comprehensively, and programmatically by Ellis and Ladany in 1997. Specifically, the paper reviewed every known empirical supervision article published from 1981 to 1995. From this review, a set of empirical themes or inferences that emerged from the literature were identified. Furthermore, a primary set of methodological issues was articulated.

From their review, Ellis and Ladany (1997) identified six themes or inferences regarding the state of supervision research. The first inference pertained to the supervisory relationship and contained studies related to the supervisory working alliance, client-centered conditions, Strong's social influence model, trainee role conflict and ambiguity, and the structure of the supervisory relationship. It was concluded from these studies that the supervisory relationship seems to be a key aspect of the supervision process, and it is likely to influence supervision process and outcome. However, it was also determined that the manner in which the supervisory relationship has been defined and studied has varied. These inconsistencies in definition and operationalization (i.e., measurement) have muddied the field's ability to understand how the supervisory relationship specifically influences process and outcome.

The second inference entailed trainee–supervisor matching. Specifically, this line of research examined the match between supervisor roles and supervision functions from Bernard's (1979) model, the match between supervisee needs and supervisor interventions, trainee–supervisor match in terms of individual difference (i.e., cognitive style, reactance, sex/gender, race, and theoretical orientation), and the match between trainee needs and the supervisory environment. The primary conclusion was the inference that matching trainees and supervisors on a variety of characteristics leads to positive supervision process and outcome lacked empirical validation. For example, there is little evidence to suggest that trainee–supervisor matching by race will correspond with greater satisfaction with supervision. Moreover, the authors concluded that supervision researchers may be oversimplifying their assumptions about matching and should consider using more relevant psychological variables (e.g., investigate racial identity rather than race).

The third inference concerned developmental changes that purportedly occur in trainees over time. A variety of supervision models, including ego development (Loevinger, 1976); conceptual development (Holloway & Wampold, 1986); Hogan's (1964) model; Littrell, Lee-Borden, and Lorenz's (1979) model; Loganbill, Hardy, and Delworth's (1982) model; Sansbury's (1982) model; Stoltenberg's (1981) model; Stoltenberg and Delworth's (1987) model, and general developmental issues related to trainee experience level were identified and tested. The primary conclusions that emerged from this review were: (a) the investigations had numerous and pervasive methodological shortcomings (e.g., using cross-sectional research designs to make developmental inferences) that made their interpretability suspect at best and misleading at worse, and (b) the data indicate that the developmental models are probably overly simplistic and do not attend to trainee issues adequately.

The issue of using cross-sectional designs to make developmental or longitudinal inferences seems endemic to empirical articles assessing developmental notions in supervision. To illustrate this problem, consider a researcher who examines a group of 10 beginning trainees (5 men and 5 women) and a group of 10 advanced trainees (all of whom are women). If this researcher were to make a developmental or longitudinal inference based on the variable of trainee gender, then he or she might determine that male trainees are very likely to become female trainees as they go from beginning to advanced training levels. Although this inference is clearly nonsensical, it illustrates a common mistake that developmental researchers make in their investigations and interpretations of their data. As such, one cannot make developmental or longitudinal conclusions based on data derived from the cross-sectional investigation of different cohorts.

The fourth inference pertained to the evaluation of trainees. In general, it was concluded that (a) trainees are likely to be evaluated qualitatively; (b) general supervisor perceptions may influence evaluative estimations (e.g., if the supervisor likes the trainee, the supervisor is likely to evaluate the trainee positively); and (c) evaluative measures are largely psychometrically invalid.

The fifth inference regarded client outcome and, most typically, the issue of parallel process, to which only a few studies pertained. As defined elsewhere in this book, parallel process can be generally defined as similarities that exist between supervision process and outcome and counseling process and outcome. From the studies examining parallel process, it was concluded that there may be similarities between trainee–client interactions and supervisor–trainee interactions. However, the specific mechanisms operating between these dyads have yet to be identified.

Finally, the sixth inference regarded the development of new measures to assess supervision process and outcome. Of the seven measures reviewed, only two were recommended and considered psychometrically adequate. These tools were the Role Conflict and Role Ambiguity Inventory (Olk & Friedlander, 1992) and the Barrett-Lennard Relationship Inventory (Barrett-Lennard, 1962; Dalton, 1983; Wiebe & Pearce, 1973). The general consensus was that considerable work needs to be conducted to validate existing and new measures of supervision process and outcome.

The review by Ellis and Ladany (1997) not only offered insight into the knowledge gained through supervision research but also highlighted a number of methodological shortcomings of the supervision literature. Supervision researchers are advised to consider these research limitations when planning future studies. Ellis and Ladany evaluated the literature based on the 37 potential threats to each study's validity, derived from Cook and Campbell's (1979) validity threats; Wampold, Davis, and Good's (1990) hypothesis validity threats; and eight supplemental threats described in the general methodological literature (Chen, 1990; Ellis, 1991; Kazdin, 1986; Kerlinger, 1986; Serlin, 1987; Wampold & Poulin, 1992). Across the 104 empirical studies reviewed, 14 threats emerged as the most salient methodological threats. These validity threats included: (a) inflated Type I error rate (i.e., multiple statistical comparisons without controlling for experiment-wise error; 76%); (b) unreliability or invalidity of independent or dependent measures (64%); (c) inflated Type II error rate (low statistical power or not detecting a true effect; 51%); (d) nonrandom/nonrepresentative sample (39%), (e) nonrandom assignment (38%); (f) mismatch of purpose, hypotheses, design methods, and analyses (29%); (g) violation of the assumptions of statistics (14%); (h) cohort effects such as making developmental inferences from cross-sectional data (11%); (i) confounded independent variables (e.g., single supervisor with multiple trainees; 10%); (j) uncontrolled variables (unknown third variables that moderate the effects; 8%); (k) differential attrition across groups (8%); (l) mono-method bias (7%); (m) di- or multichotomized continuously distributed independent variable or dependent variable (7%); and (n) participant heterogeneity (7%).

Clearly no one study could account for all of the potential threats to validity. Gelso (1979) referred to this inability to control for all potential threats as the "bubble hypothesis." Essentially, Gelso likened controlling for validity threats to placing a sticker on a car windshield. Inevitably, a bubble will emerge under the sticker and, when the bubble is pressed down, it creates another bubble elsewhere. In supervision research, for example, a researcher could account for the nonrandom assignment threat by randomly assigning participants to conditions in the study. However, this researcher will likely have limited generalizability, and thereby bring the external validity threat to the fore. Thus, researchers must select those validity threats that they are willing to accept for any given study with the intention of conducting future studies that will account for the threats left uncontrolled in the present study.

A closer look at the primary validity threats identified, however, reveals that most of these threats could have been easily remedied in their respective studies. For example, 76% of the studies demonstrated an inflated Type I error rate. As a result, it was likely that more than one of the findings determined to be significant were due to chance rather than actual effects in the data. A simple way to control for Type I error is to reduce the alpha rate (e.g., Bonferroni procedure) to account for the multiple statistical tests. Similar procedures could be implemented for many of the threats identified (see Ellis & Ladany, 1997, for a more thorough discussion).

Since Ellis and Ladany's article (1997), several other reviews and chapters have addressed counseling supervision research. Similar themes have emerged. Borders's (2005) review of the literature from 1999 to 2004 included 39 empirical studies, many of which focused on supervisor style and/or the supervisory relationship, something which continues to be defined in several different ways, though the majority operationalized it in terms of a tripartite model of the working alliance (Bordin, 1983), namely, mutual agreement on the goals of supervision, mutual agreement on the tasks of supervision, and an emotional bond between the supervisee and supervisor. Supervisor feedback and evaluation remained underrepresented with only two studies focusing on this topic. Similarly, though not one of Ellis and Ladany's six inferences, specific supervision interventions were also poorly researched with only two studies focusing on this topic.

Additional observations included an increase in research on group supervision, an increase in supervision surrounding issues of spirituality, a dearth of research in school and other diverse clinical settings and a lack of research ($n = 4$) on multicultural supervision, which, unlike the previously discussed emphasis on supervisor–supervisee matching based upon identity or cultural traits, specifically focuses on a discussion of multicultural variables and competencies within the context of supervision. This latter observation is echoed in an additional review (Goodyear et al., 2005), noting that this lack of emphasis is surprising given the counseling field's overall emphasis on multicultural competence. Indeed, a recent chapter (Ladany & Inman, 2008) found just five articles on the topic published in nearly a decade of scholarship. It should be noted that supervisor competence in general has also been identified as a subject area where more empirical research is needed, with only one article identified over a 5-year span (Borders, 2005), despite an increasing recognition of the potential for harmful supervision (Goodyear et al., 2005).

Finally, an emerging body of research has begun to look at supervision through an international lens. To some extent this is being driven by an increase in supervision-related publications by international authors (Bernard & Goodyear, 2004; e.g., Jen Der Pan, Deng, & Tsai, 2008). However, as counseling responds to globalization, supervision research has begun to empirically explore issues related to supervising international students (e.g., Nilsson, 2007; Nilsson & Anderson, 2004). Similarly, as interest grows in working in international settings or with international clients, Gerstein and Ægisdóttir (2007) highlight several practical and methodological challenges for conducting international research of counselor training. Specifically, gaining access to international samples and developing trust in nonnative researchers as well as the cost (both financial and time-wise) are practical challenges. Methodologically, it is recommended that researchers question the presence, relevance, and appropriateness of the constructs being investigated as well as the validity of the procedures and measures employed in conducting the study, avoid using standards or norms that are not relevant to the culture being studied when interpreting findings, and to thoroughly rule out alternative explanations for findings.

How to Create a Well-Designed Supervision Research Study

With knowledge of the methodological shortcomings found in the empirical supervision literature, Ellis, Ladany, Krengel, and Schult (1996) explicated a series of issues relevant to creating a feasible and well-designed supervision study. Although these issues are most relevant to experimental, quantitative studies, they also have generalizability to other quantitative studies (e.g., ex post facto and survey research designs) and, to a lesser extent, qualitative research. Regardless of methodology, in terms of writing the introduction, researchers should (a) explain the theoretical models on which they are relying and the theories' shortcomings; (b) create a logical argument and rationale linking the constructs of interest; (c) thoroughly define the constructs of interest; and (d) specify directional research hypotheses (i.e., make explicit what is implied).

Quantitative Designs and Supervision Research

When composing the methods section of a quantitative study, investigators are advised to (a) conduct an a priori power analysis based on the published research (Cohen, 1988; Haase, 1974; Haase, Ellis, & Ladany, 1989); (b) administer psychometrically sound instruments (i.e., valid and reliable measures used with a similar sample) and report the internal consistency for the sample studied; (c) employ random assignment whenever possible (e.g., randomly assign participants to conditions or the order of instruments); (d) collect and report comprehensive demographic information about the participants (e.g., gender, race, age, counseling experience, etc.); (e) use multiple methods (e.g., self-report and objective raters) when possible; (f) use multiple measures of the same construct when possible (e.g., trainee experience as months of counseling experience and total number of clients seen); (g) provide sufficient data regarding raters; (h) ensure that the constructs defined in the introduction are matched with the operationalizations of the constructs in the method; and (i) guarantee that hypotheses offered in the introduction are matched with the statistical analyses chosen.

Concerning the results, researchers should (a) control for Type I error; (b) control for Type II error; (c) use continuous variables when possible and not di- or multichotomize variables to avoid losing statistical power or explained variance (Cohen, 1983); (d) test for violations of the assumptions underlying the statistical procedures utilized (e.g., ceiling or floor effects, disproportional cell sizes, skewness), and make appropriate corrections to the data when assumptions are violated (e.g., data transformations); and (e) avoid violating the independence of observation assumption (e.g., each supervisor provides data for a single trainee and participants do not serve as both supervisor and trainee in a single study). In the discussion, investigators should (a) interpret the results in the context of theory; (b) stay close to the data and avoid overgeneralizing the results; (c) evaluate the study and provide relevant limitations as well as strengths; and (d) offer theoretical, empirical, and practical implications of the results.

Measuring Supervision Variables

As mentioned previously, psychometrically sound supervision measures are limited in number. However, new measures are being developed and older measures are being revised. Measures used for supervision research have varied from counseling measures revised to fit the supervision context to measures specifically designed for supervision (Bernard & Goodyear, 2004; Ellis & Ladany, 1997). In general, the most useful measures have been derived for the supervision context and have been validated (i.e., content-related, criterion-related, construct-related) and found to be reliable (e.g., internal consistency is greater than .80; Gall, Borg, & Gall, 1996). We have identified frequently used measures in the supervision literature in Table 15.2. The reader is encouraged to examine these measures and to evaluate the psychometric adequacy for her or his research purposes. Additionally, the reader may want to review the following references to determine the adequacy of these measures (Bernard & Goodyear, 2004; Ellis & Ladany, 1997; Lambert & Ogles, 1997).

Qualitative Designs and Supervision Research

As noted in a previous section, a ground swell of interest has emerged related to conducting qualitative research investigations in supervision. Supervision researchers have begun to qualitatively investigate a variety of variables including parallel process (Doehrman, 1976; Friedlander, Siegel, & Brenock, 1989), professional counselor development (Skovholt & Rønnestad, 1992), positive and negative experiences in supervision (Hutt, Scott, & King, 1983; Worthen & McNeill, 1996), trainee reflectivity (Neufeldt, Karno, & Nelson, 1996), supervisor countertransference (Ladany, Constantine, Miller, Erickson, & Muse-Burke, 2000), trainee sexual attraction and use of supervision (Ladany, O'Brien, et al., 1997), experiences of novice counselors (Williams, Judge, Hill, & Hoffman, 1997), multicultural supervision (Fukuyama, 1994), trainee nondisclosures (Hess & Hoffman, 1999; Ladany, Hill, Corbett, & Nutt, 1996), counterproductive events in supervision (Gray, Walker, Ladany, & Ancis, 1999), and harmful

Table 15.2 Frequently Used Measures to Assess Supervision Processes and Outcomes

Construct/Variable	Subconstruct/Subscale	Rater	Scale Title	Reference
Trainee cognitive complexity	1. Differentiation 2. Integration	O	Counselor Perception Questionnaire	Blocher et al. (1985)
Trainee counseling self-efficacy	1. Employing microskills 2. Attending to process 3. Dealing with difficult client behaviors 4. Behaving in a multiculturally competent manner 5. Being aware of one's values	T	Counseling Self-Estimate Inventory	Larson et al. (1992)
Trainee counseling self-efficacy	Single score	T	Self-Efficacy Inventory	Friedlander & Snyder (1983)
Trainee critical incidents in supervision	1. Most important supervision issues 2. Most important supervision interventions	T	The Critical Incidents Questionnaire	Heppner & Roehlke (1984); Rabinowitz, Heppner, & Roehlke (1986)
Trainee developmental level	1. Self- and other awareness 2. Motivation 3. Dependency/autonomy	T	Supervisee Levels Questionnaire—Revised	McNeill, Stoltenberg, & Romans (1992)
Trainee developmental level	1. Trainee 2. Supervisory needs	T	Counselor Development Questionnaire	Reising & Daniels (1983)
Trainee multicultural counseling competence	Single score	T/S	Cross-Cultural Counseling Inventory-Revised	LaFromboise, Coleman, & Hernandez (1991)

(Continued)

Table 15.2 Frequently Used Measures to Assess Supervision Processes and Outcomes (*Continued*)

Construct/Variable	Subconstruct/Subscale	Rater	Scale Title	Reference
Trainee multicultural counseling competence	1. Multicultural awareness 2. Multicultural knowledge 3. Multicultural skills	T	Multicultural Awareness, Knowledge, Skills Survey	D'Andrea, Daniels, & Heck (1991)
Trainee multicultural counseling competence	1. Multicultural awareness 2. Multicultural knowledge 3. Multicultural skills 4. Multicultural counseling relationship	T	Multicultural Counseling Inventory	Sodowsky, Taffe, Gutkin, & Wise (1994)
Trainee multicultural counseling competence	1. Multicultural awareness 2. Multicultural knowledge	T	Multicultural Counseling Knowledge and Awareness Scale	Ponterotto, Rieger, Gretchen, Utsey, & Austin (1999)
Trainee multicultural case conceptualization ability	Etiology and treatment differentiation and integration	O	Multicultural Case Conceptualization Ability Measure	Ladany, Inman, Constantine, & Hofheinz (1997)
Trainee role conflict and ambiguity	1. Role conflict 2. Role ambiguity	T	Role Conflict and Role Ambiguity Inventory	Olk & Friedlander (1992)
Trainee counseling and supervision behavior	1. Counseling 2. Supervision	S	Counselor Evaluation Rating Scale	Myrick & Kelly (1971)
Trainee counseling and supervision behavior	1. Purposeful counseling performance 2. Noncounseling behaviors 3. Supervision attitude 4. Counseling orientation	T	Counselor Evaluation Rating Scale	Benshoff & Thomas (1992)

Trainee satisfaction with supervision	Single score	T	Supervisee Satisfaction Questionnaire	Ladany et al. (1996)
Trainee and supervisor satisfaction with supervision	Trainee: 1. Evaluation of supervisor 2. Evaluation of self as trainee 3. level of comfort Supervisor: 1. Evaluation of trainee 2. Evaluation of self as supervisor 3. Level of comfort	T/S	Trainee Personal Reaction Scale & Supervisor Personal Reaction Scale	Holloway & Wampold (1983)
Supervisor behaviors	Some subconstructs include: 1. Degree of focus on therapist and client 2. Dominance of the supervisor and the therapist 3. Number of clarifying and interpretive comments 4. Intensity of confrontation 5. Empathy of the supervisor	O	Psychotherapy Supervisory Inventory	Shanfield, Mohl, Matthews, & Hetherly (1989)

(Continued)

Table 15.2 Frequently Used Measures to Assess Supervision Processes and Outcomes (*Continued*)

Construct/Variable	Subconstruct/Subscale	Rater	Scale Title	Reference
Supervisor behaviors	1–12 Factors	T/S	Supervision Questionnaire–Revised	Worthington (1984); Worthington & Roehlke (1979)
Supervisor behaviors	1. Importance of different aspects of supervision 2. Frequency of behaviors 3. Time spent on supervisory functions 4. Supervisor roles and behaviors 5. Demographic variables	S	Level of Supervision Survey	Miars et al. (1983)
Supervisor behaviors in group supervision	1. Supervisor competence ranking 2. Satisfaction ranking 3. Professional development ranking	T/S	Group Supervisory Behavior Scale	White & Rudolph (2000)
Supervisor developmental level	Single score	S	Psychotherapy Supervisor Development Scale	Watkins, Schneider, Haynes, & Nieberding (1995); Barnes & Moon (2006)
Supervisor ethical behavior	Single score	T/S	Supervisor Ethical Behavior Scale	Ladany, Lehrman-Waterman, Molinaro, & Wolgast (1999)

Construct	Dimensions	Measure	Type	Citation
Supervisory expectations	1. Role behaviors 2. Nature of relationship 3. Task focus and goals	Congruence of Supervisory Expectations Scale	T/S	Ellis et al. (1994)
Supervision evaluation	1. Goal setting 2. Feedback	Evaluation Process Within Supervision Inventory	T	Lehrman-Waterman & Ladany, 2001
Supervisor feedback	1. Positivity 2. Negativity 3. Constructiveness 4. Specificity	Supervisory Feedback Rating Scale	O	Larson, Day, Springer, Clark, & Vogel, (2003)
Supervisor feedback	1. Type 2. Specificity 3. Valence 4. Focus	Supervisory Feedback Rating System	O	Friedlander, Siegel, & Brenock (1989)
Supervisor focus	1. Process 2. Professional behavior 3. Personalization skills 4. Client conceptualization	Supervisor Emphasis Rating Form—Revised	S	Lanning & Freeman (1994); Lanning, Whiston, & Carey (1994)
Supervisor focus	1. Personality 2. Supervisory focus 3. Supervisory style	The Supervisory Focus and Style Questionnaire	S	Yager, Wilson, Brewer, & Kinnetz (1989)
Supervisor impact	1. Supervisory impact 2. Willingness to learn	The Supervision Perception Form	T/S	Heppner & Roehlke (1984)

(Continued)

Table 15.2 Frequently Used Measures to Assess Supervision Processes and Outcomes (*Continued*)

Construct/Variable	Subconstruct/Subscale	Rater	Scale Title	Reference
Supervisor self-disclosure	Single score	T/S	Supervisor Self-Disclosure Inventory	Lehrman-Waterman & Ladany (2001)
Supervisor style	1. Attractive 2. Interpersonality sensitive 3. Task oriented	T/S	Supervisory Styles Inventory	Friedlander & Ward (1984)
Supervisory relationship	1. Regard 2. Empathy 3. Unconditionality 4. Willingness to be known 5. Total score (i.e., overall of the relationship)	T	Relationship Inventory	Schact, Howe, & Berman (1988)
Supervisory working alliance	1. Agreement on goals of supervision 2. Agreement on tasks of supervision 3. Emotional bond between the supervisor and trainee	T/S	Working Alliance Inventory	Bahrick (1990)

Construct	Dimensions	Rater	Measure	Citation
Supervisory working alliance	Trainee: 1. Rapport 2. Client focus Supervisor: 1. Client focus 2. Rapport 3. Identification	T/S	Supervisory Working Alliance Inventory	Efstation, Patton, & Kardash (1990)
Supervision of international trainees	1. Multicultural discussion 2. Supervisee's cultural knowledge	T	International Student Supervision Scale	Nilsson & Dodds (2006)
Feminist supervision	1. Collaborative relationships 2. Power analysis 3. Diversity and social context 4. Feminist advocacy and activism	S	Feminist Supervision Scale	Szymanski (2003)

Note: The person doing the rating was classified as the trainee (T), the supervisor (S), the client (C), or a trained observer (O).

supervision (Nelson & Friedlander, 1999). These qualitative investigations seem to be filling important gaps in the supervision literature left untouched by quantitative researchers and, within a social justice framework, provide increased opportunities to integrate expert and stakeholder viewpoints, especially those from traditionally underrepresented groups.

The following features demonstrate ways in which qualitative research can be distinguished from quantitative research methodologies. Specifically, quantitative research frequently manipulates the research setting and utilizes instruments and measures to ascertain data. Rather than employ inductive reasoning, quantitative research entails deductive reasoning to make judgments. Further, quantitative data is collected and reported in the form of numbers (i.e., statistics), and these numbers are the product of the research. Qualitative research may at times present frequencies of certain themes either across sets of data or within one case, however, generally this is part of a larger descriptive analysis of themes and the numbers themselves are not the sole product.

Given its very different conceptual and analytical approach, a common myth about qualitative research is that it lacks the rigor of quantitative methods. However, it is becoming better understood that qualitative research is, indeed, a rigorous methodological approach and that the previous disparaging beliefs were largely unfounded. Moreover, Lincoln and Guba (1985) have suggested that traditional measures of rigor, reliability, and validity, measures that have since evolved even from a quantitative perspective (Messick, 1995; Moss, 1994, 1995), were incompatible with qualitative investigation, offering instead the concept of trustworthiness as a means for assessing qualitative research. Moreover, qualitative and quantitative methods maintain strengths and weaknesses that are complementary in nature, sometimes even combined as in the case of a mixed-methods design. Indeed, both add unique value to the supervision research enterprise.

In general, qualitative research maintains several typical characteristics (Bergsjo, 1999; Bogdan & Biklen, 1992; Eisner, 1991; Lincoln & Guba, 1985; Merriam, 1988). First, qualitative research is field focused, emphasizing the natural setting as the source of the data. Second, the researcher is the primary instrument of data collection, even in designs where preexisting data may exist, such as may be the case for content analysis. A third characteristic is that data are collected using words or pictures to ascertain a rich, thorough description. Similarly, expressive language is used in qualitative research. Fourth, the outcome of qualitative research is perceived as a process rather than a product. Lastly, the data are analyzed using inductive reasoning (i.e., conclusions are drawn directly from the information provided in the data).

Qualitative Methodologies

As with quantitative research, a variety of qualitative research methodologies have been devised, many in recent years. One way to conceptualize and manage the disparate methods is to consider qualitative methods from the context of five general traditions (Creswell, 2006). These five primary traditions of qualitative research are (1) phenomenology; (2) grounded theory; (3) narrative research; (4) ethnography; and (5) case study (Yin, 2002). To date, the primary qualitative traditions used to study supervision have been phenomenology (e.g., Worthen & McNeill, 1996) and grounded theory (e.g., Neufeldt, Karno, & Nelson, 1996).

Phenomenology research seeks to describe and understand the fundamental, underlying meaning of experiences for a few individuals with regard to a particular phenomenon. Researchers using this method collect data through in-depth interviews, typically with about 10 people. The interview questions are devised by the researcher and are directly linked to the phenomenon in question (e.g., good moments in supervision). In the end, a description of the "essence" of the experience is achieved.

Grounded theory, another tradition of qualitative research, aims to generate a theory that is based (or grounded) in the data obtained from the field. Interviews are conducted with 20–30 individuals in order to saturate the categories (i.e., ascertain new information until no more can be found). The process of data analysis is systematic and follows a standard coding format.

The purpose of a narrative research is to explore the life of a particular individual. Through interviews and historical documents, researchers gather individual stories of the person's life and group these stories according to themes of significant life moments. Next, the individual's life is placed in a historical context with consideration for the norms, issues, and ideologies of the day. In so doing, a detailed picture of one person's life is created.

An ethnography aspires to describe and interpret a cultural and social group. The researcher collects data through participant observation in which he or she is immersed in the daily lives of the people or person under investigation. Further, the researcher may engage in in-depth interviews with the individual or members of the group. Through this process, the researcher develops an understanding of the meanings of the behavior, language, interactions, and artifacts of the culture. Ultimately, a rich description of the cultural behavior of a group or individual is attained.

The last major tradition of qualitative research is the case study. This method strives to develop an in-depth analysis of a single case or multiple cases over time. Case studies require thorough data collection using numerous sources of information, such as documents and reports, interviews, and observations. Moreover, the data are collected within the natural setting of the case. Through this process, a detailed description of a case or cases evolves.

Hill, Thompson, and Williams's (1997) consensual qualitative research (CQR) is a relative newcomer to counseling and supervision research and has been enjoying quite a bit of popularity within the last decade. Stemming from the grounded theory tradition, there are nine general stages of the CQR method: (a) recruiting; (b) interviews; (c) data preparation; (d) coding into domains; (e) abstracting core ideas; (f) auditing core ideas; (g) cross-analysis; (h) auditing cross-analysis; and (i) review by the entire team. The CQR differs from many qualitative approaches in that it offers some quasiquantitative data in the form of frequencies for commonly occurring themes across cases.

In a recent update (Hill et al., 2005), the authors identified 27 articles that employed CQR and gave further recommendations for study implementation including a streamlining of the manner in which researchers reported their biases prior to beginning the investigation, charting of results and the use of "member checking" or reporting back to participants during stages of the CQR process to assess trustworthiness (Lincoln & Guba, 1985) in lieu of the stability check (i.e., holding out two cases from the initial cross-analysis), as initially proposed (Hill et al., 1997). The interested reader is directed to Hill et al. (1997, 2005) as well as to qualitative studies that have used the CQR format to study supervision (e.g., Burkard et al., 2006, De Stefano et al., 2007; Hess & Hoffman, 1999; Ladany et al., 2000; Nelson & Friedlander, 1999; Williams et al., 1997).

Certainly this is not an exhaustive list of qualitative methodologies. Indeed certain types of content analysis (Krippendorff, 2003) and discovery-oriented approaches (Mahrer & Boulet, 1999) have potential applications within supervision research. For more thorough descriptions of qualitative research the reader is directed to Creswell (2006), Denzin and Lincoln (1994), Flick (2006), Krippendorff (2003), Lincoln and Guba (1985), Mahrer and Boulet (1999), Maxwell (2004), Miles and Huberman (1994), Patton (1990), Strauss and Corbin (2007), Wolcott (1994), Yin (2002).

A Descriptive Model of Assessing Evaluation Approaches for Counselor Trainees

In the spirit of the scientist practitioner, our research skills can be used in the service of evaluating supervision practice. One supervision practice issue that seems well suited for the interface between supervision research and practice is in the context of evaluating counselor trainees. The ability to effectively evaluate counselor trainees is a primary task for supervisors of counselor trainees (Bernard & Goodyear, 2004). It is through the evaluation of trainees that supervisors are able to chart the progress of trainee growth as well as client change.

A review of the empirical literature examining the methods used to evaluate counselor trainees (Borders & Fong, 1991; Carey, Williams, & Wells, 1988; Dodenhoff, 1981; Fordham, May, Boyle, Bentall, & Slade, 1990; Lazar & Mosek, 1993; Mathews, 1986; Newman, Kopta, McGovern, Howard, & McNeilly, 1988; Norcross & Stevenson, 1984; Norcross, Stevenson, & Nash, 1986; Romans, Boswell, Carlozzi, & Ferguson, 1995; Snepp & Peterson, 1988) reveals the following: (a) trainees are evaluated primarily qualitatively (Norcross & Stevenson, 1984; Norcross et al., 1986); (b) most supervisors (90%) use trainee self-report as a method to assess trainee performance, while less than 60% rely on audiotapes and less than 40% rely on videotapes (Ladany & Lehrman-Waterman, 1999; Ladany & Melincoff, 1997); (c) general perceptions of the trainee by the supervisor may influence the evaluation (Carey et al., 1988; Dodenhoff, 1981); (d) many supervisors may not be fulfilling their evaluation responsibilities adequately or ethically (Cormier & Bernard, 1982; Keith-Spiegel & Koocher, 1985; Ladany, Lehrman-Waterman, Molinaro, & Wolgast, 1999); and (e) the measures used to assess trainee competence are largely outdated or psychometrically unsound (Ellis & Ladany, 1997). Hence, the literature concerning the trainee evaluation process seems to indicate several potential areas of concern. In particular, there is little evidence to verify that reliable, valid, and systematic methods of trainee evaluation exist. Instead, much of what is used appears to include either supervisors' subjective impressions of trainee performance or objective measures that have questionable psychometric properties.

Overall, it seems clear that the area of trainee evaluation is in need of new and innovative measures. However, along with the development of new measures, there is a need for a framework from which these methods of evaluation can be organized and assessed. The following is a summary of a model detailing how one may assess trainee evaluation approaches. This model is based in part on some previous propositions made by Ellis and Ladany (1997). It is anticipated that any given evaluation approach may be appraised based on its ability to attend to the salient components presently identified.

The fundamental components of this assessment model include: (a) mode of counseling (e.g., individual, group, family, or couples); (b) domain of trainee behaviors (e.g., counseling or supervision); (c) competence area (e.g., counseling techniques, theoretical conceptualization, professionalism, multicultural competence, clinical disorders, assessment, administration, countertransference, or supervision behaviors); (d) method (trainee self-report, case notes, audiotape, videotape, live supervision, cotherapy, role-play, experiences in supervision); (e) proportion of caseload (all clients, subgroup of clients, one client); (f) segment of experience (e.g., entire training experience, part of the entire training experience, a specific session, or a segment of a session); (g) time period (early, middle, or late in client treatment as well as early, middle, or late in training experience); (h) evaluator (e.g., supervisor, clients, peers, objective raters); (i) level of proficiency (e.g., demonstrated skill, comparison to cohort group); (j) reliability issues (e.g., trustworthiness for qualitative assessments and statistical measurement error for quantitative assessments); (k) validity issues (e.g., construct validity); and (l) format (e.g., quantitative vs. qualitative and structured vs. unstructured). It would be unreasonable to suggest that one evaluation approach could take into account all the above parameters. Nonetheless, the merit of a given evaluation approach can be assessed based on the extent to which these components are considered.

To understand how to apply this assessment model, we may examine some example items from potential measures. Although it may be the case that there are as many evaluation measures as there are training sites (Bernard & Goodyear, 2004), there are probably common criteria that are used to evaluate all trainees (e.g., competence). For example, it is likely that an evaluation scale will ask for a supervisor's assessment of a trainee's competence on a number of items. This scale may ask the supervisor to rate her or his trainee's "counseling knowledge" on a 1 (very poor) to 5 (excellent) scale. Counseling knowledge might be defined for the supervisor as "demonstrated good understanding of theories and research in psychology, counseling/psychotherapy, and psychopathology." How might a scale with this item be evaluated? First, in the context of this scale, there is no mention of the mode of therapy, method, proportion of caseload, segment of experience, or time period the supervisor is to use to make this assessment. Furthermore, the area of competence seems to cover nearly the entirety of a full graduate training program (i.e., issue of overinclusiveness). It is difficult to imagine that a supervisor could make such an assessment adequately. Hence, this evaluation instrument (assuming there are similar items to the one listed above) seems to have multiple confounding features that may limit its use.

In another example, a common type of anchor used on evaluation scales asks the supervisor to evaluate a trainee's competence while taking into consideration his or her developmental level (e.g., beginning practicum, advanced practicum, internship). In this case, the supervisor must first assess the developmental level of the trainee, then consider the level of competence associated with that particular developmental level, and finally compare the trainee's expressed competence to the associated developmental level. Given the difficulty of defining and operationalizing trainee developmental level (Ellis & Ladany, 1997; Holloway, 1987), the ability of the supervisor to fulfill this requirement in a consistent and valid fashion appears doubtful. Furthermore, given the problems with this method, it seems likely that trainee evaluation may be influenced by the supervisor's general impressions of the trainee (e.g., how much the supervisor likes the trainee; Ellis & Ladany, 1997).

In general, it seems that supervisors' ability to adequately evaluate trainees may be compromised due to deficient instrumentation and approaches. The question then becomes: How do supervision practitioners and researchers address the inadequacy of trainee evaluation? First, it would seem important to consider the strengths of the current measures from which newer measures can be built. Working from that which we do know may provide us with the foundations to discover that which we do not know. Similarly, the continued identification and investigation of the numerous factors associated with supervision process and outcome beyond client outcome seems relevant (Holloway, 1992). Second, cross-discipline collaboration via multisite supervision research centers seems necessary to create and validate new approaches to trainee evaluation. As was previously noted, currently there may be as many trainee evaluation measures as there are training sites. These multisite cross-collaborative efforts would impart some standardization to the process of evaluating trainees. Finally, the continued promotion of counselor supervision as a field related to, but separate from, the field of counseling, must occur. Along with this continued promotion would come an increased recognition of the importance of defining and operationalizing trainee performance from which reliable and valid evaluation approaches can be derived.

Conclusion

It has been proposed that the field of counseling and psychotherapy relies on a germ theory for the training of its students (Beutler, 1988). In essence, this theory suggests that if trainees are exposed to the theory and practice of counseling, they will "catch" the competence bug. Conversely, it has also been asserted that unless the systematic feedback and reflection provided by supervision accompanies counseling practice, trainees will only gain the illusion of professional competence (Bernard & Goodyear, 2004). As such, supervision is vital to the development of counselors-in-training. Despite this fact, much of the supervision realm has remained unexplored by researchers (Bernard & Goodyear, 2004) and warrants empirical investigation. In conducting it, the two primary goals of supervision research, to understand the process of supervision and its influence on counseling and to inform supervision practice, will be realized.

Consequently, the ultimate purpose of this chapter was to inform the reader of the current state of supervision research as well as to incite the reader to engage in methodologically sound supervision research. More specifically, there were four key components of this chapter. First, we described a model that identified and categorized the variables of supervision research. In particular, some primary supervision research questions were delineated, the concepts of supervision and counseling process and outcome were defined, and a listing of relevant supervision variables was suggested. Second, we provided an overview of the literature pertaining to supervision research, including current trends in research topics as well as issues related to multiculturalism and globalization. Ellis and Ladany's (1997) six inferences of supervision research were considered, as were the most common threats to validity in supervision research. Third, we offered a schema that included the salient elements of conducting supervision research. Specific guidelines for writing the introduction, methods, results, and discussion were outlined. In addition, this section included an evaluation of quantitative instruments and a description of qualitative research methods. Fourth, we applied our knowledge about research and methodology and offered a model for assessing the adequacy of trainee evaluation approaches. In addition to providing a model, suggestions for future research regarding trainee evaluation were made. After reading this chapter, we hope that trainees and supervisors will feel compelled to engage in supervision research. It is also hoped that researchers will follow the guidelines presented in this chapter and employ appropriate research methods to extend the knowledge base of the field of supervision.

References

Bahrick, A. S. (1990). Role induction for counselor trainees: Effects on the supervisory working alliance. *Dissertation Abstracts International, 51,* 1484B. (University Microfilms No. 90-14, 392).

Barnes, K. L., & Moon, S. M. (2006). Factor structure of the psychotherapy supervisor development scale. *Measurement and Evaluation in Counseling and Development, 39,* 130–140.

Barrett-Lennard, G. T. (1962). Dimensions of therapist responses as a causal factor in therapeutic changes. *Psychological Monographs, 76*(43, Whole No. 562).

Benshoff, J. M., & Thomas, W. P. (1992). A new look at the counselor evaluation rating scale. *Counselor Education and Supervision, 32,* 12–22.

Bergsjo, P. (1999). Qualitative and quantitative research: Is there a gap, or only verbal disagreement? *Acta Obstetricia et Gynecologica Scandinavica, 78,* 559–562.

Bernard, J. M. (1979). Supervisory training: A discrimination model. *Counselor Education and Supervision, 19,* 60–68.

Bernard, J. M., & Goodyear, R. K. (2004). *Fundamentals of clinical supervision* (3rd ed.). Needham Heights, MA: Allyn & Bacon.

Beutler, L. E. (1988). Introduction to the special series. *Journal of Consulting and Clinical Psychology, 56,* 651.

Blocher, D., Christensen, E. W., Hale-Fiske, R., Neren, S. H., Spencer, T., & Fowlkes, S. (1985). Development and preliminary validation of an instrument to measure cognitive growth. *Counselor Education and Supervision, 25,* 21–30.

Bogdan, R. C., & Biklen, S. K. (1992). *Qualitative research for education: An introduction to theory and methods.* Boston, MA: Allyn & Bacon.

Borders, L. D. (2005). Snapshot of clinical supervision in counseling and counselor education: A five-year review. *The Clinical Supervisor, 24,* 69–113.

Borders, L. D., & Fong, M. L. (1991). Evaluations of supervisees: Brief commentary and research report. *The Clinical Supervisor, 9,* 42–51.

Bordin, E. S. (1983). Supervision in counseling: II. Contemporary models of supervision: A working alliance based model of supervision. *Counseling Psychologist, 11,* 35–42.

Burkard, A. W., Johnson, A. J., Madson, M. B., Pruitt, N. T., Contreras-Tadych, D. A., Kozlowski, J. M., … Knox, S. (2006). Supervisor cultural responsiveness and unresponsiveness in cross-cultural supervision. *Journal of Counseling Psychology. 53,* 288–301.

Carey, J. C., Williams, K. S., & Wells, M. (1988). Relationships between dimensions of supervisors' influence and counselor trainees' performance. *Counselor Education and Supervision, 28,* 130–139.

Chen, H. T. (1990). *Theory driven evaluations.* Newbury Park, CA: Sage.

Cohen, J. (1983). The cost of dichotomization. *Applied Psychological Measurement, 7,* 249–253.

Cohen, J. (1988). *Statistical power analysis for the behavioral sciences* (3rd ed.). New York, NY: Academic Press.

Cook, T. D., & Campbell, D. T. (1979). *Quasi-experimentation: Design and analysis for field settings.* Boston, MA: Houghton Mifflin.

Cormier, L. S., & Bernard, J. M. (1982). Ethical and legal responsibilities of clinical supervisors. *The Personnel and Guidance Journal, 11,* 486–491.

Creswell, J. W. (2006). *Qualitative inquiry and research design: Choosing among five traditions* (2nd ed.). Thousand Oaks, CA: Sage.

Dalton, J. E. (1983). Sex differences in communications skills as measured by a modified relationship inventory. *Sex Roles, 9,* 195–204.

D'Andrea, M., Daniels, J., & Heck, R. (1991). Evaluating the impact of multicultural counseling training. *Journal of Counseling and Development, 70,* 143–150.

Denzin, K., & Lincoln, Y. S. (1994). Introduction: Entering the field of qualitative research. In N. K. Denizen & Y. S. Lincoln (Eds.), *Handbook of qualitative research* (pp. 1–16). Thousand Oaks, CA: Sage.

De Stefano, J., D'Iuso, N., Blake, E., Fitzpatrick, M., Drapeau, M., & Chamodraka, M. (2007). Trainees' experiences of impasses in counselling and the impact of group supervision on their resolution: A pilot study. *Counselling & Psychotherapy Research, 7,* 42–47.

Dodenhoff, J. T. (1981). Interpersonal attraction and direct-indirect supervisor influence as predictors of counselor trainee effectiveness. *Journal of Counseling Psychology, 28,* 47–52.

Doehrman, M. (1976). Parallel processes in supervision and psychotherapy. *Bulletin of the Menninger Clinic, 40,* 3–104.

Efstation, J. F., Patton, M. J., & Kardash, C. M. (1990). Measuring the working alliance in counselor supervision. *Journal of Counseling Psychology, 37,* 322–329.

Eisner, E. W. (1991). *The enlightened eye: Qualitative inquiry and the enhancement of educational practice.* New York, NY: Macmillan.

Ellis, M. V. (1991). Research in clinical supervision: Revitalizing a scientific agenda. *Counselor Education and Supervision, 30,* 238–251.

Ellis, M. V., Anderson-Hanley, C. M., Dennin, M. K., Anderson, J. J., Chapin, J. L., & Polstri, S. M. (1994, August). *Congruence of expectation in clinical supervision: Scale development and validity data.* Paper presented at the American Psychological Association, Los Angeles, CA.

Ellis, M. V., Ladany, N., Krengel, M., & Schult, D. (1996). Clinical supervision research from 1981 to 1993: A methodological critique. *Journal of Counseling Psychology, 43,* 35–50.

Ellis, M, V., & Ladany, N. (1997). Inferences concerning supervisees and clients in clinical supervision: An integrative review. In C. E. Watkins, Jr. (Ed.), *Handbook of psychotherapy supervision* (pp. 447–507). New York, NY: Wiley.

Flick, U. (2006). *An introduction to qualitative research* (2nd ed.). Thousand Oaks, CA: Sage.

Fordham, A. S., May, B., Boyle, M., Bentall, R. P., & Slade, P. D. (1990). Good and bad clinicians: Supervisors' judgments of trainees' competence. *British Journal of Clinical Psychology, 29,* 113–114.

Friedlander, M. L., Siegel, S. M., & Brenock, K. (1989). Parallel process in counseling and supervision: A case study. *Journal of Counseling Psychology, 36,* 149–157.

Friedlander, M. L., & Snyder, J. (1983). Trainees' expectations for the supervisory process: Testing a developmental model. *Counselor Education and Supervision, 22,* 342–348.

Friedlander, M. L., & Ward, L. G. (1984). Development and validation of the supervisory styles inventory. *Journal of Counseling Psychology, 31,* 541–557.

Fukuyama, M. A. (1994). Critical incidents in multicultural counseling supervision: A phenomenological approach to supervision. *Counselor Education and Supervision, 34,* 142–151.

Gall, M. D., Borg, W. R., & Gall, J. P. (1996). *Educational research: An introduction* (6th ed.). White Plains, NY: Longman Publishers.

Gelso, C. J. (1979). Research in counseling: Methodological and professional issues. *The Counseling Psychologist, 8,* 7–36.

Gerstein, L. H., & Ægisdóttir, S. (2007). Training international social change agents: Transcending a U.S. counseling paradigm. *Counselor Education and Supervision. 47,* 123–139.

Goodyear, R. K., Bunch, K., & Claiborn, C. D. (2005). Current supervision scholarship in psychology: A five year review. *The Clinical Supervisor, 24,* 137–147.

Gray, L., Walker, J. A., Ladany, N., & Ancis, J. R. (1999, August). Counterproductive events in psychotherapy supervision. In M. L. Friedlander (Chair), *Psychotherapy supervision: For better or worse.* Symposium conducted at the annual meeting of the American Psychological Association, Boston, MA.

Haase, R. F. (1974). Power analysis of research in counselor education. *Counselor Education and Supervision, 14,* 124–132.

Haase, R. F., Ellis, M. V., & Ladany, N. (1989). Multiple criteria for evaluating the magnitude of effects. *Journal of Counseling Psychology, 36,* 511–516.

Harkness, D., & Poertner, J. (1989). Research and social work supervision: A conceptual review. *Social Work, 34,* 115–119.

Heppner, P. P., & Roehlke, H. J. (1984). Differences among supervisees at different levels of training: Implications for a developmental model of supervision. *Journal of Counseling Psychology, 31,* 76–90.

Hess, S. A., & Hoffman, M. A. (1999, August). Supervisee's critical incidents of nondisclosure and disclosure in supervision. In M. A. Hoffman & N. Ladany (Chairs), *Things said and unsaid in supervision: Supervisee and supervisor perspectives.* Symposium conducted at the annual meeting of the American Psychological Association, Boston, MA.

Hill, C. E., Knox, S., Thompson, B. J., Williams, E. N., Hess, S. A., Knox, S., & Ladany, N. (2005). Consensual qualitative research: An update. *Journal of Counseling Psychology, 52,* 196–205.

Hill, C. E., Thompson, B. J., & Williams, E. N. (1997). A guide to conducting consensual qualitative research. *The Counseling Psychologist, 25,* 517–572.

Hogan, R. A. (1964). Issues and approaches in supervision. *Psychotherapy: Theory, Research, and Practice. 1,* 139–141.

Holloway, E. L. (1984). Outcome evaluation in supervision research. *The Counseling Psychologist, 12,* 167–174.

Holloway, E. L. (1987). Developmental models of supervision: Is it development? *Professional Psychology: Research and Practice, 18,* 209–216.

Holloway, E. L. (1992). Supervision: A way of teaching and learning. In S. D. Brown & R. W. Lent (Eds.), *Handbook of counseling psychology* (pp. 177–214). New York, NY: Wiley.

Holloway, E. L., & Wampold, B. E. (1983). Patterns of verbal behavior and judgments of satisfaction in the supervision interview. *Journal of Counseling Psychology, 30,* 227–234.

Holloway, E. L., & Wampold, B. E. (1986). Relation between conceptual level and counseling-related tasks: A meta-analysis. *Journal of Counseling Psychology, 33,* 310–319.

Hutt, C. H., Scott, J., & King, M. (1983). A phenomenological study of supervisee's positive and negative experiences in supervision. *Psychotherapy: Theory, Research, and Practice, 20,* 118–123.

Inman, A. G., & Ladany, N. (2008). Research: The status of the field. In A. K. Hess & T. H. Hess (Eds.), *Psychotherapy supervision: Theory, research, and practice* (2nd ed., pp. 500–517). New York, NY: John Wiley & Sons.

Jen Der Pan, P., Deng, L. Y. F., & Tsai, S. L. (2008). Evaluating the use of reflective counseling group supervision for military counselors in Taiwan. *Research on Social Work Practice, 18,* 346–355.

Kazdin, A. E. (1986). Research designs and methodology. In S. L. Garfield & A. E. Bergin (Eds.), *Handbook of psychotherapy and behavior change* (3rd ed., pp. 23–68). New York, NY: Wiley.

Keith-Spiegel, P., & Koocher, G. P. (1985). *Ethics in psychology.* New York, NY: Random House.

Kerlinger, F. N. (1986). *Foundations of behavioral research* (3rd ed.). New York, NY: Holt, Rinehart, & Winston.

Krippendorff, K. (2003). *Content analysis: An introduction to its methodology* (2nd ed.). Thousand Oaks, CA: Sage.

Ladany, N., Constantine, M. G., Miller, K., Erickson, C., & Muse-Burke, J. (2000). Supervisor countertransference: A qualitative investigation into its identification and description. *Journal of Counseling Psychology, 47,* 102–115.

Ladany, N., Hill, C. E., Corbett, M. M., & Nutt, E. A. (1996). Nature, extent, and importance of what psychotherapy trainees do not disclose to their supervisors. *Journal of Counseling Psychology, 43,* 10–24.

Ladany, N., & Inman, A. G. (in press). Training and supervision. In E. A. Altmaier & J. I. Hansen (Eds.), *Oxford handbook of counseling psychology.* New York, NY: Oxford University Press.

Ladany, N., & Inman, A. G. (2008). Developments in counseling skills training and supervision. In S. Brown & R. Lent (Eds.), *Handbook of counseling psychology* (4th ed., pp. 338–354). New York, NY: Wiley.

Ladany, N., Inman, A. G., Constantine, M. G., & Hofheinz, E. W. (1997). Supervisee multicultural case conceptualization ability and self-reported multicultural competence as functions of supervisee racial identity and supervisor focus. *Journal of Counseling Psychology, 44,* 284–293.

Ladany, N., & Lehrman-Waterman, D. E. (1999). The content and frequency of supervisor self-disclosures and their relationship to supervisor style and the supervisory working alliance. *Counselor Education and Supervision, 38,* 143–160.

Ladany, N., Lehrman-Waterman, D., Molinaro, M., & Wolgast, B. (1999). Psychotherapy supervisor ethical practices: Adherence to guidelines, the supervisory working alliance, and supervisee satisfaction. *The Counseling Psychologist, 27,* 443–475.

Ladany, N., & Melincoff, D. S. (1997, June). *The nature and extent of what psychotherapy supervisors do not disclose to their trainees.* Poster session presented at the annual meeting of the Society for Psychotherapy Research, Geilo, Norway.

Ladany, N., & Muse-Burke, J. L. (2001). Understanding and conducting supervision research. In L. J. Bradley & N. Ladany (Eds.), *Counselor supervision: Principles, process, & practice* (3rd ed., pp. 304–329). Philadelphia, PA: Brunner-Routledge.

Ladany, N., O'Brien, K., Hill, C. E., Melincoff, D. S., Knox, S., & Petersen, D. (1997). Sexual attraction toward clients, use of supervision, and prior training: A qualitative study of psychology predoctoral interns. *Journal of Counseling Psychology, 44,* 413–424.

Ladany, N., Walker, J. A., Pate-Carolan, L., & Gray, E. L. (2008). *Experiencing counseling and psychotherapy: Insights from psychotherapy trainees, their clients, and their supervisors.* New York, NY: Taylor & Francis.

LaFromboise, T. D., Coleman, H. L. K., & Hernandez, A. (1991). Development and factor structure of the cross-cultural counseling inventory-revised. *Professional Psychology: Research and Practice, 22,* 380–388.

Lambert, M. J. (1980). Research and the supervisory process. In A. K. Hess (Ed.), *Psychotherapy supervision: Theory, research, and practice* (pp. 423–450). New York, NY: Wiley.

Lambert, M. J., & Arnold, R. C. (1987). Research and the supervision process. *Professional Psychology: Research and Practice, 18,* 217–224.

Lambert, M. J., & Ogles, B. M. (1997). The effectiveness of psychotherapy supervision. In C. E. Watkins, Jr. (Ed.), *Handbook of psychotherapy supervision* (pp. 421–446). New York, NY: Wiley.

Lanning, W., & Freeman, B. (1994). The supervisor emphasis rating form. *Counselor Education & Supervision, 33,* 294–304.

Lanning, W. L., Whiston, S., & Carey, J. C. (1994). Factor structure of the supervisor emphasis rating form. *Counselor Education & Supervision, 34,* 41–51.

Larson, L. M., Day, S. X., Springer, S. H., Clark, M. P., & Vogel, D. L. (2003). Developing a supervisor feedback rating scale: A brief report. *Measurement and Evaluation in Counseling and Development, 35*(4), 230–238.

Larson, L. M., Suzuki, L. A., Gillespie, K. N., Potenza, M. T., Bechtel, M. A., & Toulouse, A. (1992). Development and validation of the counseling self-estimate inventory. *Journal of Counseling Psychology, 39,* 105–120.

Lazar, A., & Mosek, A. (1993). The influence of the field instructor-student relationship on evaluation of students' practice. *The Clinical Supervisor, 11,* 111–120.

Lehrman-Waterman, D., & Ladany, N. (2001). Development and validation of the evaluation process within supervision inventory. *Journal of Counseling Psychology, 48,* 168–177.

Lincoln, Y. S., & Guba, E. G. (1985). *Naturalistic inquiry.* Newbury Park, CA: Sage.

Littrell, J. M., Lee-Borden, N., & Lorenz, J. (1979). A developmental framework for counseling supervision. *Counselor Education and Supervision, 19,* 129–136.

Loevinger, J. (1976). *Ego development.* San Francisco, CA: Jossey-Bass.

Loganbill, C., Hardy, E., & Delworth, U. (1982). Supervision: A conceptual model. *The Counseling Psychologist, 10*(1), 3–42.

Mahrer, A. R., & Boulet, D. B. (1999). How to do discovery-oriented psychotherapy research. *Journal of Clinical Psychology. 55,* 1481–1493.

Mathews, G. (1986). Performance appraisal in the human services: A survey. *The Clinical Supervisor, 3,* 47–61.

Maxwell, J. A. (2004). *Qualitative research design: An interactive approach* (2nd ed.). Thousand Oaks, CA: Sage.

McNeill, B. W., Stoltenberg, C. D., & Romans, J. S. (1992). The integrated developmental model of supervision: Scale development and validation procedures. *Professional Psychology: Research & Practice, 23,* 504–508.

Merriam, S. (1988). *Case study research in education: A qualitative approach.* San Francisco, CA: Jossey-Bass.

Messick, S. (1995). Validity of psychological assessment: Validation of inferences from persons' responses and performance as scientific inquiry into scoring meaning. *American Psychologist, 9,* 741–749.

Miars, R. D., Tracey. T. J., Ray, P. B., Cornfeld, J. L., O'Farrell, M., & Gelso. C. J. (1983). Variation in supervision process across trainee experience levels. *Journal of Counseling Psychology, 30,* 403–412.

Miles, M. B., & Huberman, A. M. (1994). *Qualitative data analysis: An expanded sourcebook* (2nd ed.). Thousand Oaks, CA: Sage.

Moss, P. A. (1994). Can there be validity without reliability? *Educational Researcher, 23,* 5–12.

Moss, P. A. (1995). Themes and variations in validity theory. *Educational Measurement: Issues and Practice, 14,* 5–13.

Myrick, R. D., & Kelly, F. D., Jr. (1971). A scale for evaluating practicum students in counseling and supervision. *Counselor Education and Supervision, 10,* 330–336.

Nelson, M. L., & Friedlander, M. L. (1999, August). Nature of harmful supervision: A qualitative investigation. In M. L. Friedlander (Chair), *Psychotherapy supervision: For better or worse*. Symposium conducted at the annual meeting of the American Psychological Association, Boston, MA.

Neufeldt, S. A., Beutler, L. E., & Banchero, R. (1997). Research on supervisor variables in psychotherapy supervision. In C. E. Watkins, Jr. (Ed.), *Handbook of psychotherapy supervision* (pp. 508–524). New York, NY: Wiley.

Neufeldt, S. A., Karno, M. P., & Nelson, M. L. (1996). A qualitative study of experts' conceptualization of supervisee reflectivity. *Journal of Counseling Psychology, 43*, 3–9.

Newman, F. L., Kopta, S. M., McGovern, M. P., Howard, K. I., & McNeilly, C. L. (1988). Evaluating trainees relative to their supervisors during the psychology internship. *Journal of Consulting and Clinical Psychology, 56*, 659–665.

Nilsson, J. E. (2007). International students in supervision: Course self-efficacy, stress and cultural discussions in supervision. *The Clinical Supervisor, 26*, 35–47.

Nilsson, J. E., & Anderson, A. Z. (2004). Supervising international students: The role of acculturation, role ambiguity, and multicultural discussions. *Professional Psychology: Research and Practice, 35*, 306–312.

Nilsson, J. E., & Dodds, A. K. (2006). A pilot phase in the development of the international student supervision scale. *Journal of Multicultural Counseling and Development, 34*, 50–62.

Norcross, J. C., & Stevenson, J. F. (1984). How shall we judge ourselves? Training evaluation in clinical psychology programs. *Professional Psychology: Research and Practice, 15*, 497–508.

Norcross, J. C., Stevenson, J. F., & Nash, J. M. (1986). Evaluation of internship training: Practices, problems and prospects. *Professional Psychology: Research and Practice, 17*, 280–282.

Olk, M. E., & Friedlander, M. L. (1992). Trainees' experience of role conflict and role ambiguity in supervisory relationships. *Journal of Counseling Psychology, 39*, 389–397.

Patton, M. Q. (1990). *Qualitative evaluation and research methods* (2nd ed.). Thousand Oaks, CA: Sage.

Ponterotto, J. G., Rieger, B. P., Gretchen, D., Utsey, S. O., & Austin, R. (1999). *A construct validity study of the multicultural counseling awareness scale (MCAS) with suggested revisions*. Unpublished manuscript.

Rabinowitz, F. E., Heppner, P. P., & Roehlke, H. J. (1986). Descriptive study of process and outcome variables of supervision over time. *Journal of Counseling Psychology, 33*, 292–300.

Reising, G. N., & Daniels, M. H. (1983). A study of Hogan's model of counselor development and supervision. *Journal of Counseling Psychology, 30*, 235–244.

Romans, J. S. C., Boswell, D. L., Carlozzi, A. F., & Ferguson, D. B. (1995). Training and supervision practices in clinical, counseling, and school psychology programs. *Professional Psychology: Research and Practice, 26*, 407–412.

Russell, R. K., Crimmings, A. M., & Lent, R. W. (1984). Counselor training and supervision: Theory and research. In S. D. Brown & R. W. Lent (Eds.), *Handbook of counseling psychology* (pp. 625–681). New York, NY: Wiley.

Sansbury, D. L. (1982). Developmental supervision from a skills perspective. *The Counseling Psychologist, 10,* 53–57.

Schact, A. J., Howe, H. E., & Berman, J. J. (1988). A short form of the Barrett-Lennard inventory for supervisor relationships. *Psychological Reports, 63,* 699–703.

Serlin, R. C. (1987). Hypothesis testing, theory building, and the philosophy of science. *Journal of Counseling Psychology, 34,* 365–371.

Shanfield, W. B., Mohl, P. C., Matthews, K., & Hetherly, V. (1989). A reliability assessment of the psychotherapy supervisory inventory. *American Journal of Psychiatry, 146,* 1447–1450.

Skovholt, T. M., & Rønnestad, M. H. (1992). *The evolving professional self: Stages and themes in therapist and counselor development.* Chichester, United Kingdom: Wiley.

Snepp, F. P., & Peterson, D. R. (1988). Evaluative comparison of Psy.D. and Ph.D. students by clinical internship supervisors. *Professional Psychology: Research and Practice, 19,* 180–183.

Sodowsky, G. R., Taffe, R. C., Gutkin, T. B., & Wise, S. L. (1994). Development of the multicultural counseling inventory: A self-report measure of multicultural competencies. *Journal of Counseling Psychology, 41,* 137–148.

Stoltenberg, C. (1981). Approaching supervision from a developmental perspective: The counselor complexity model. *Journal of Counseling Psychology, 28,* 59–65.

Stoltenberg, C. D., & Delworth, U. (1987). *Supervising counselors and therapists: A developmental perspective.* San Francisco, CA: Jossey-Bass.

Strauss, A., & Corbin, J. (2007). *Basics of qualitative research: Techniques and procedures for developing grounded theory* (3rd ed.). Newbury Park, CA: Sage.

Szymanski, D. M. (2003). The feminist supervision scale: A rational/theoretical approach. *Psychology of Women Quarterly, 27,* 221–232.

Wampold, B. E., Davis, B., & Good, R. H., III. (1990). Hypothesis validity of clinical research. *Journal of Consulting and Clinical Psychology, 55,* 360–367.

Wampold, B. E., & Holloway, E. L. (1997). Methodology, design, and evaluation in psychotherapy supervision research. In C. E. Watkins, Jr. (Ed.), *Handbook of psychotherapy supervision* (pp. 11–27). New York, NY: Wiley.

Wampold, B. E., & Poulin, K. L. (1992). Counseling research methods: Art and artifact. In S. D. Brown & R. D. Lent (Eds.), *Handbook of counseling psychology* (2nd ed., pp. 71–109). New York, NY: Wiley.

Watkins, C. E., Schneider, L. J., Haynes, J., & Nieberding, R. (1995). Measuring psychotherapy supervisor development: An initial effort at scale development and validation. *Clinical Supervisor, 13,* 77–90.

Wiebe, B., & Pearce, W. B. (1973). An item analysis and revision of the Barrett-Lennard relationship inventory. *Journal of Clinical Psychology, 29,* 495–497.

White, J. H. D., & Rudolph, B. A. (2000). A pilot investigation of the reliability and validity of the group supervisory behavior scale (GSBS). *The Clinical Supervisor, 19,* 161–171.

Williams, E. N., Judge, A. B., Hill, C. E., & Hoffman, M. A. (1997). Experiences of novice therapists in prepracticum: Trainees', clients', and supervisors' perceptions of therapists' personal reactions and management strategies. *Journal of Counseling Psychology, 44,* 390–399.

Wolcott, H. F. (1994). *Transforming qualitative data: Description analysis and interpretation.* Thousand Oaks, CA: Sage.

Worthen, V., & McNeill, B. W. (1996). A phenomenological investigation of "good" supervision events. *Journal of Counseling Psychology, 43,* 25–34.

Worthington, E. L., Jr. (1984). Use of trait labels in counseling supervision by experienced and inexperienced supervisors. *Professional Psychology: Research and Practice, 15,* 457–461.

Worthington, E. L., Jr., & Roehlke, H. J. (1979). Effective supervision as perceived by beginning counselors-in-training. *Journal of Counseling Psychology, 26,* 64–73.

Yager, G. G., Wilson, F. R., Brewer, D., & Kinnetz, P. (1989). *The development and validation of an instrument to measure counseling supervisor focus and style.* Paper presented at the American Educational Research Association, San Francisco, CA.

Yin, R. K. (2002). *Case study research: Design and methods* (3rd ed.). Thousand Oaks, CA: Sage.

CHAPTER 16

Ethical Issues in Counselor Supervision

JENNIFER CRALL

> To care for anyone else enough to make their problems one's own, is
> ever the beginning of one's real ethical development.
>
> —**Felix Adler**

Counselors serve in a profession where ambiguity is the norm, perspectives are varied, problems are evolving, and outcomes are uncertain. This is particularly true of the counseling supervisor, who is uniquely responsible for the counseling services provided to clients, as well as the training, guidance, and support provided to supervisees. The ethical behavior of supervisors is especially important due to the multiple responsibilities supervisors assume. The importance is emphasized by the power differential that exists between supervisors and supervisees, and the potential impact on supervisees and clients. Effective supervisors maintain the ability to model ethical behavior and emphasize a focus on ethical practice throughout the process of supervision.

The ethical dilemmas that arise during the process of supervision are as diverse as the individuals involved. Ethical guidelines serve to anchor this ambiguity by providing standards to which professionals can be held accountable. They serve as a guide by which ethical decisions can be made and allow professions to govern and regulate themselves rather than risk governmental oversight. Ethical guidelines also protect the profession from internal struggles and the practitioner from malpractice suits when the practitioner adheres to the appropriate guidelines (Van Hoose & Kottler, 1985). Ultimately, ethical standards protect the public from harm. It is imperative for clinicians to fully comprehend the content and limitations of ethical guidelines so that their decisions can be well informed. The purpose of this chapter is to introduce the ethical guidelines for supervisors provided by the professional counseling organizations, provide empirical findings from the ethics literature, and stimulate critical thinking to encourage supervisors to make knowledgeable, ethical decisions.

The mental health field has recognized the importance of ethical standards for the practice of counseling and psychotherapy for over half a century (Hall, 1952). However, for many years, ethical guidelines for supervision were never directly addressed by the professional organizations. This was a result of the notion that ethical guidelines for counselors could be generalized to supervisors as well (Stoltenberg & Delworth, 1987). As the understanding of counselor supervision developed, so did the realization that unique ethical issues existed (e.g., evaluation of supervisees) in the practice of supervision. Therefore, the ethical standards for clinical supervision were cultivated by the Association for Counselor Education and Supervision (ACES, 1993) and have since been incorporated into the American Counseling Association (ACA) Code of Ethics (2005).

Principles of the ACA Ethics Code

Prior to presenting the code of ethics for supervisors, it is beneficial to recognize the overarching basis for ethical conduct in counseling. Clinical supervisors are, above all, counselors who should aspire toward the very highest ethical standards of the profession. Therefore, each ethical standard should be applied to the counseling supervisor even if the standard is not explicitly directed toward supervisors. The *ACA Code of Ethics* (ACA, 2005) contains eight main sections that address the following areas: the counseling relationship; confidentiality, privileged communication, and privacy; professional responsibility; relationships with other professionals; evaluation, assessment, and interpretation; supervision, training, and teaching; research and publication; and resolving ethical issues. Each section of the *ACA Code of Ethics* begins with an introduction that outlines counselor ethical behavior and responsibility. These introductions are aspirational and are intended to guide the counselor toward the very highest ethical ideals of the profession. Therefore, it is important to remember that, in contrast to ethical standards, these general principles do not represent requirements to which one may be held liable. However, these principles should be considered when making an ethical decision. The following paragraphs include the principles and discuss how supervisors, specifically, can aspire to apply them.

Section A: The Counseling Relationship

Counselors encourage client growth and development in ways that foster the interest and welfare of clients and promote formation of healthy relationships. Counselors actively attempt to understand the diverse cultural backgrounds of the clients they serve. Counselors also explore their own cultural identities and how these affect their values and beliefs about the counseling process. Counselors are encouraged to contribute to society by devoting a portion of their professional activity to services for which there is little or no financial return (pro bono publico). (ACA, 2005, p. 4)

Supervisors should act to protect clients by helping supervisees provide the highest quality of appropriate counseling services. Supervisors should be aware of their own cultural background and regularly work to increase multicultural awareness in an effort to minimize biases. Supervisors should address multicultural issues relevant to supervisees and clients.

Section B: Confidentiality, Privileged Communication, and Privacy

Counselors recognize that trust is a cornerstone of the counseling relationship. Counselors aspire to earn the trust of clients by creating an ongoing partnership, establishing and upholding appropriate boundaries, and maintaining confidentiality. Counselors communicate the parameters of confidentiality in a culturally competent manner. (ACA, 2005, p. 7)

Supervisors should attend to the supervisory relationship and see that supervisees work to build a strong rapport with clients. Supervisors should make certain that supervisees maintain appropriate boundaries with clients. Supervisors should communicate limitations of confidentiality with supervisees and see that supervisees do the same with clients. Supervisors should minimize countertransference issues in supervision and address the countertransference issues of their supervisees.

Section C: Professional Responsibility

Counselors aspire to open, honest, and accurate communication in dealing with the public and other professionals. They practice in a nondiscriminatory manner within the boundaries of professional and personal competence and have a responsibility to abide by the *ACA Code of Ethics*. Counselors actively participate in local, state, and national associations that foster the development and improvement of counseling. Counselors advocate to promote change at the individual, group, institutional, and societal levels that improve the quality of life for individuals and groups and

remove potential barriers to the provision or access of appropriate services being offered. Counselors have a responsibility to the
public to engage in counseling practices that are based on rigorous
research methodologies. In addition, counselors engage in self-
care activities to maintain and promote their emotional, physical,
mental, and spiritual well-being to best meet their professional
responsibilities. (ACA, 2005, p. 9)

Supervisors should model professional behavior by participating in
a variety of professional organizations and engaging in social justice
activities. Supervisors should engage in continuing education activities
to assure that they are using and teaching empirically valid interventions. Supervisors should participate in self-care activities to avoid professional burnout. Supervisors should be aware of their influence over
their supervisees and clients, be aware of conflicting interests, and be
aware of their own capacity to supervise. Supervisors should monitor
supervisees to assess levels of professional and/or personal well-being,
to help minimize affects of stress on client work and encourage self-care
activities.

Section D: Relationships With Other Professionals

Professional counselors recognize that the quality of their interactions with colleagues can influence the quality of services provided
to clients. They work to become knowledgeable about colleagues
within and outside the field of counseling. Counselors develop
positive working relationships and systems of communication
with colleagues to enhance services to clients. (ACA, 2005, p. 11)

Supervisors should maintain respectful treatment of all colleagues,
consult with other professionals when needed, and seek out their own
supervision when necessary. Supervisors should address the ethical concerns of supervisees and colleagues. Supervisors should maintain referral sources and be aware of appropriate times to refer clients to other
professionals.

Section E: Evaluation, Assessment, and Interpretation

Counselors use assessment instruments as one component of
the counseling process, taking into account the client personal and
cultural context. Counselors promote the well-being of individual
clients or groups of clients by developing and using appropriate
educational, psychological, and career assessment instruments.
(ACA, 2005, p. 11)

Supervisors should be aware of the appropriateness, relevance, strengths, and limitations of assessment tools used with clients. Supervisors should seek out training or consultation when supervisees use assessment instruments with which the supervisor is not familiar.

Section F: Supervision, Training, and Teaching

Counselors aspire to foster meaningful and respectful professional relationships and to maintain appropriate boundaries with supervisees and students. Counselors have theoretical and pedagogical foundations for their work and aim to be fair, accurate, and honest in their assessments of counselors-in-training. (ACA, 2005, p. 13)

Supervisors should receive training in the process of supervision. Supervisors should maintain respectful treatment of supervisees, respecting the dignity of supervisees, and providing accurate supervisee assessments. Supervisors should establish appropriate boundaries with supervisees, avoiding dual relationships whenever possible. Supervisors should clearly communicate financial arrangements with supervisees on the outset of supervision.

Section G: Research and Publication

Counselors who conduct research are encouraged to contribute to the knowledge base of the profession and promote a clearer understanding of the conditions that lead to a healthy and more just society. Counselors support efforts of researchers by participating fully and willingly whenever possible. Counselors minimize bias and respect diversity in designing and implementing research programs. (ACA, 2005, p. 16)

Supervisors should conduct research that is accurate, culturally relevant, and contributes to the counseling profession. Supervisors should participate in the research of others when applicable.

Section H: Resolving Ethical Issues

Counselors behave in a legal, ethical, and moral manner in the conduct of their professional work. They are aware that client protection and trust in the profession depend on a high level of professional conduct. They hold other counselors to the same standards and are willing to take appropriate action to ensure that these standards are upheld. Counselors strive to resolve ethical dilemmas with direct and open communication among all parties involved and seek consultation with colleagues and supervisors when necessary. Counselors incorporate ethical practice into their daily professional work. They engage in ongoing professional development regarding current topics in ethical and legal issues in counseling. (ACA, 2005, p. 18)

Supervisor should be aware of ethical guidelines and the process of how to address ethical dilemmas. Supervisors should integrate this knowledge into all of their professional practices. Supervisors should act to benefit and protect clients, supervisees, and coworkers, including addressing the unethical behavior of other professionals. Supervisors should receive ongoing training on issues of professional ethics.

Ethical Guidelines

Ethics codes, unlike the principles previously presented, are standards to which professionals are held accountable. Ethics are the standards of conduct governing an individual or group. Ethical behaviors are the actions and judgments made of situations based on these governing standards (Corey, Corey, & Callanan, 1998). Therefore, supervisory ethical behavior must be considered within the context of the guidelines set forth by the counseling and supervision professional organizations. The counseling professional organizations each maintain ethical guidelines intended to assist professionals by helping them (a) observe ethical and legal protection of clients' and supervisees' rights; (b) meet the training and professional needs of supervisees in ways consistent with clients' welfare and programmatic requirements; and (c) establish policies, procedures, and standards for implementing programs (ACES, 1993).

Most of the ethical guidelines of the professional organizations address training and supervision to some degree, with the *ACA ethics code* (2005) providing the most comprehensive guidelines for supervisors. However, many provide very few standards specifically for supervision. For the purposes of this chapter, a comprehensive list of ethical guidelines were generated by integrating supervision ethics research (Crall, 2010; Ladany, Lehrman-Waterman, Molinaro, & Wolgast, 1999) and the current ethical codes from the major professional organizations in major mental health disciplines. This generated a list of 16 ethical guidelines, which are presented in Table 16.1. Additionally, Table 16.1 includes working definitions, examples of ethical violations, and questions for supervisor self-examination.

Table 16.1 Supervisor Ethical Guidelines

Ethical Guideline	Definition	Examples of Violations	Questions for Self-Examination
Performance evaluation and monitoring of activities	Adequate communication between supervisor and supervisee concerning supervisee evaluation occurs. The supervisor provides ongoing, verbal, and written feedback and works with the supervisee on the identification of goals. The supervisor reviews actual counseling sessions via video or audio tapes, and reads the supervisee's case notes periodically.	Supervisor states there is no time to watch counseling tapes. Supervisor offers no critical feedback to supervisee, then provides an unfavorable evaluation.	Do I listen to or watch my supervisees' counseling tapes? Do I read case notes every couple of weeks? Do I use regular, formal written evaluations every few months? Do I provide supervisees' with access to the evaluation criteria (e.g., a blank copy of the evaluation)? Do I provide ongoing verbal feedback throughout the process of supervision?
Confidentiality issues in supervision	Confidentiality policies are communicated and implemented by supervisor (e.g., agency policy toward supervision disclosure is explained, limits of supervisory confidentiality).	Supervisor does not explain agency policy toward supervision confidentiality.	Do I review policies of confidentiality of supervision with supervisees?
Able to work with alternative perspectives	Information about theory or practice presented by the supervisor is informed by current knowledge and incorporates alternative points of view, including the supervisee's. The supervisor clearly presents her or his theoretical orientation.	Supervisor does not explain theoretical approach. Supervisor uses only one counseling theory and is critical of other approaches.	Do I communicate my own theoretical orientation to my supervisees? Am I open to learning new techniques? Am I willing to allow my supervisees to use an orientation that is different from my own?

(Continued)

Table 16.1 Supervisor Ethical Guidelines (*Continued*)

Ethical Guideline	Definition	Examples of Violations	Questions for Self-Examination
Session boundaries and respectful treatment	Adequate protection of supervision session conditions and respect for supervisee (e.g., privacy, scheduling, avoiding demeaning the supervisee) are ensured by the supervisor.	Supervisor frequently forgets supervision appointments and changes supervision time. Supervision sessions are frequently interrupted by phone calls. Supervisor speaks in a derogatory manner to supervisees.	Do I keep my full supervision appointment time? Do I let sessions run over time? Am I on time? Do I establish a private office for meetings? Do I speak respectfully to my supervisee at all times? Do I communicate respect to my supervisees even when I disagree with them?
Orientation to professional roles and monitoring of site standards	Supervisor and supervisee roles and responsibilities are clearly defined. The supervisor ensures that the supervisee is engaged in appropriate and relevant counseling activities.	Supervisor never explains the role of the supervisor or the supervisee.	Are my supervisees' counseling activities appropriate for their training? Is it clear to my supervisees what my role is as a supervisor?
Expertise/competency issues	The supervisor makes appropriate disclosure to supervisee when the supervisee or supervisor is not competent to treat a particular client or condition. The supervisor ensures adequate coordination of all professionals involved in client treatment.	Supervisor encourages supervisee treatment of clients who are at high risk for harm to themselves, in spite of the fact that neither the supervisor nor supervisee have had experience in this type of treatment.	Do I tell my supervisees if I am not trained to supervise a particular issue? Am I willing to tell my supervisee if they are not competent to perform a task? Am I always aware that client welfare is the foremost concern?

Disclosure to clients	The supervisor ensures adequate disclosure to client (e.g., conditions of counseling, supervisee's status, research participation, limits of confidentiality).	Do I review with supervisees how to communicate counseling boundaries, trainee status, informed consent and limits of confidentiality?
Modeling ethical behavior and responding to ethical concerns	The supervisor discusses and models ethical behavior, and adequately responds to ethical violations.	Supervisor encourages supervisee to withhold the fact that she or he is a student from clients. Supervisor videotapes a supervision session without informing supervisee that session is being taped.	Am I aware of ethical guidelines for both supervisors and counselors? Do I behave in an ethical manner? Do I demonstrate ethical decision making?
Crisis coverage and intervention	Adequate communication between supervisor and supervisee in the event of a crisis, as well as the provision of appropriate supervisory backup, is ensured by supervisor. Supervisor appropriately handles situations in which someone involved with client is threatened by client's behavior or when a client is as risk for hurting herself or himself.	Supervisor leaves on vacation without providing supervisory backup contact information.	Do my supervisees know how to reach me in an emergency? Do my supervisees know who to gain assistance from if I am unreachable in an emergency? Do I know the legal and ethical requirements for treatment of a client that is homicidal or suicidal?
Multicultural sensitivity toward client	Racial, ethnic, cultural, sexual orientation, and gender issues (e.g., stereotyping, lack of sensitivity) toward clients are handled appropriately by supervisor.	Supervisor makes sexist generalizations and dismisses concerns from clients who are mentally challenged.	Am I aware of my own personal biases and actively committed to challenging them? Am I able to identify clients' relevant cultural information? Do I expect my supervisees' to consider cultural information during treatment?

(Continued)

Table 16.1 Supervisor Ethical Guidelines (*Continued*)

Ethical Guideline	Definition	Examples of Violations	Questions for Self-Examination
Multicultural sensitivity toward supervisee	Racial, ethnic, cultural, sexual orientation, and gender issues are discussed appropriately and sensitively by the supervisor with the supervisee.	Supervisor avoids conversations about culture and race. Supervisor says that he or she does not see race and prefers to consider everyone a part of one human race.	Am I able and willing to consider supervisee cultural experiences in their treatment? Do I use appropriate and respectful language and attitudes through supervision?
Dual roles	The supervisor handles role-related conflicts (e.g., supervisor and supervisee have personal, advisor/advisee, or administrative work relationship) appropriately, by avoiding dual roles. When unavoidable, supervisor addresses the implication of these roles in supervision.	Supervisor and supervisee are members of the same club sports team, which brings them to several of the same social gatherings, but this relationship is never addressed in supervision.	Do I avoid dual roles with supervisees whenever possible? Do I know how to appropriately respond to invitations to social events, and so forth, with supervisees? Am I willing to discuss the boundaries of the supervisory relationship in supervision?
Termination and follow-up issues	Termination and follow-up issues are handled appropriately (e.g., supervisor assures continuity of care, prevents "abandonment" of client).	Supervisor provides no guidance to trainee in the termination process.	Do I discuss issues of termination with supervisees, including supervisees' experiences? Do I communicate agency expectation for termination and continuity of services?

Differentiating supervision from psychotherapy/ counseling	The supervisee's personal issues in supervision are treated appropriately (i.e., delineating therapy and supervision adequately, making appropriate referral of supervisee to counseling/therapy).	Do I know the difference between discussing relevant personal information in supervision and providing therapy to a supervisee? Am I willing and able to make a referral when appropriate?
Sexual issues	The supervisor treats sexual/romantic issues appropriately.	Do I refrain from social interaction that may lead to a romantic relationship with a supervisee? Am I willing to engage in my own supervision if necessary to avoid an inappropriate interaction?
	Supervisor frequently asks the trainee personal questions during supervision, without a clear purpose. Supervisor uses supervision to discuss own sexual behavior.	
Fees and financial arrangements	The supervisor specifies billing arrangements and fees on the outset of supervision. Changes to any arrangements, by either party, are clearly addressed as early as possible.	Have I clearly and legally establish all fees and billing arrangements with my supervisees and provided written documentation of these arrangements? Have I discussed what changes may occur if payments are not made?
	Supervisor never explains that phone consultations would be an additional fee.	

Current State of Ethical Behaviors in Supervision

"Modeling ethical and professional behavior along with emphasizing a focus on ethical practice through the supervisory process are essential qualities of effective supervisors" (Barnett, Cornish, Goodyear, & Lichtenberg, 2007, p. 270). Authors suggest that supervisors do agree with this statement and endorse professional ethical guidelines (Navin, Beamish, & Johanson, 1995). For example, supervisors agree with standards of ethical practice, such as refraining from a sexual relationship with a supervisee, avoiding providing personal therapy to supervisees, and the importance of addressing ethnic, racial, and cultural issues are supported by clinical supervisors (Dickey, Housley, & Guest, 1993). Additionally, the majority of supervisors report engaging in ethical behaviors such as (a) meeting regularly with supervisees; (b) establishing crisis management procedures; (c) increasing supervisee awareness of professional, ethical, and legal responsibilities; and (d) meeting standards pertaining to participation in professional organizations (Navin et al., 1995).

However, despite supervisors' adherence to some ethical practices, supervisors do not subscribe to all guidelines. Both supervisor and supervisee reports corroborate that dual relationships are a frequent occurrence (Navin et al., 1995; Siegel, 1993; Townend, Iannetta, & Freeston, 2002). Up to one third of supervisors see no ethical dilemmas with a supervisor having an undefined existing social relationship with a supervisee (Dickey et al., 1993). Additionally, the majority of supervisor feedback is based on supervisee reports while review of actual work (e.g., listening to taped sessions) rarely occurs (McCarthy, Kulakowski, & Kenfield, 1994). Approximately 50–68% of supervisees report at least one ethical violation by their supervisors (Ladany et al., 1999; Siegel, 1993). The most frequent violations include inadequate performance evaluation and monitoring of supervisee activities, problems surrounding confidentiality issues in supervision, and the inability to work with alternative perspectives (Ladany et al., 1999).

Therefore, it is not surprising that an additional study confirms the majority of supervisors have difficulty identifying the salient ethical issues in a dual relationship with a supervisee and many supervisors struggle with conceptualizing ethical issues (Erwin, 2000). This research confirms that supervisors generally agree with standards but are not always aware of how to conceptualize ethical dilemmas. Clearly, a gap exists between supervisor ideals and supervisors' application of ethical practices, pointing to the necessity of addressing ethical decision making in graduate training programs and continuing education curriculums.

Two Common Ethical Pitfalls

Dual Relationships

The literature indicates two noteworthy trends in the ethical violations of supervisors. First, dual relationships were reported by both supervisors (Dickey et al., 1993; Navin et al., 1995; Pearse, 1991) and supervisees (Ladany et al., 1999; Siegel, 1993). Difficulty managing dual relationships is evident in supervisors' ability to address ethical dilemmas in theoretical cases as well (Erwin, 2000). It is the responsibility of the supervisor to place utmost importance on client welfare, which requires that the supervisor be able to see client issues clearly and have the capacity to intervene when needed. Social or business relationships with supervisees can compromise this capacity (Welfel & Lipsitz, 1983). The ACA ethics code (i.e., code F.3.a.) strongly urges supervisors to minimize multiple roles, and clearly address the responsibilities of the supervisor in cases where dual roles are unavoidable. They (i.e., code F.3.b.) further forbid sexual contact with supervisees and require that dual relationships that might impair supervisory judgment and objectivity be avoided.

Observation of Supervisee Activities

The second trend in the supervision ethics literature indicates that direct observation of supervisee activities (i.e., audio and videotapes, or live supervision) is relatively rare (Borders, Cashwell, & Rotter, 1995; Coll, 1995; O'Connor, 2000; Townend et al., 2002). Studies conclude that supervisees place more importance than their supervisors on direct observation of their work (Gandolfo & Brown, 1987). Consistent with this conclusion, supervisees report inadequate performance evaluation and monitoring of supervisee activities as the most frequent ethical violation (Ladany et al., 1999). Pearse (1991) concludes that university counseling centers are most likely to review tapes and notes and offer feedback to trainees, while Veterans Administrations and hospitals are least likely. Observation of trainees interacting with clients is required to monitor supervisee progress and client welfare. The ACA ethics code (i.e., code F.1.a.) asserts that actual work samples, in addition to case notes, should be reviewed by the supervisor as a regular part of the ongoing supervision process. Plainly stated, quality supervision cannot occur without the objective knowledge of what is occurring within sessions.

Impact of Ethics in Supervision

Supervision as a Training Tool

Supervision is the primary teaching method used in counseling to help trainees develop the skills needed to provide effective and ethical services (Holloway, 1992). Goodyear (2007) elaborates on Holloway's description, asserting that supervision is psychology's "signature pedagogy" (p. 273). Practitioners and researchers agree that clinical supervision is an essential aspect of each counselor's training and high quality supervision is important for trainees to develop into competent professionals (Barnett et al., 2007; Corey, Corey, & Callahan, 1998). It follows that within this powerful training setting the trainee is likely to develop the roots of her or his professional identity and establish ethical beliefs surrounding the therapy relationship. Supervisors' modeling of ethical behavior is necessary to help supervisees develop ethical and competent professional identities (Barnett et al., 2007).

Effects of Unethical Supervision on Supervisees and Clients

Among the most powerful reasons to examine the ethical behaviors of supervisors is the potential of unethical behaviors to cause harm to supervisees and clients. Supervision is a hierarchical relationship in which the supervisee is in a more vulnerable position, creating a potential for harm (Goodyear, Crego, & Johnston, 1992; Olk & Friedlander, 1992; Wulf & Nelson, 2000). According to supervisees, counterproductive events in supervision, including some unethical behaviors, negatively affect client work and the supervisory relationship (Gray, Ladany, Walker, & Ancis, 2001). Unresolved conflicts in supervision can have a damaging effect on supervisees, ranging from moderate feelings of anxiety, to affecting personal lives of supervisees and finally becoming cynical about the profession (Nelson & Friedlander, 2001). Jacobs (1991) outlines the potential for supervisees to replicate the harmful supervisory interactions with their clients as well as with their own future supervisees. One preliminary study indicates that counselors who, as students during graduate training, engaged in sexual intimacies with their professors or clinical supervisors were later, as therapists, statistically more likely to engage in sexual intimacies with their clients (Pope, Levenson, & Schover, 1979). Ultimately, the need for maintaining ethical behaviors in supervision is derived from the fundamental ethical principal of nonmaleficence, the obligation of counselors to do no harm (Kitchener, 1984).

Effects on Trainee Satisfaction

Heppner and Handley (1981) argue that supervisee satisfaction is necessary for supervisees to be willing to work hard and ultimately achieve their learning goals in supervision. Supervisees who are satisfied with their supervision report greater overall job satisfaction (Schroffel, 1999), a stronger supervisory emotional bond (Ladany, Ellis, & Friedlander, 1999), and a higher likelihood that they will disclose negative reactions in supervision (Ladany, Hill, Corbett, & Nutt, 1996). In general, positive events in supervision increase supervisee satisfaction (Heppner & Roehlke, 1984; Hilton,

Russell, & Salmi, 1995), while negative supervisory events, including several supervisor unethical behaviors, can negatively affect supervisee satisfaction (Ramos-Sánchez et al., 2002). For instance, graduate students rate supervisors' failure to address ethical issues in supervision (code F.6.d.; ACA, 2005) among the most undesirable supervisor behaviors (Martino, 2001). Additionally, the ability to set appropriate goals with supervisees (code F.7.a.; ACA, 2005) is associated with increased supervisee satisfaction (Lehrman-Waterman & Ladany, 2001).

Effects on Supervisee Ethical Behaviors

The supervision literature has established a relationship between ethical supervision and effective counseling practice (Barnett et al., 2007; Bernard & Goodyear, 2008). Additionally, several researchers have identified a link between supervisor behavior and the parallel behavior of supervisees (McNeill & Worthen, 1989; Shulman, 2005). Newer models of ethics training have suggested that as counseling students develop their professional identity they experience a process of ethical acculturation where they internalize the ethical expectations of the profession (Handelsman, Gottlieb, & Knapp, 2005). A significant part of this acculturation occurs during counseling practicum supervision. Therefore it follows that supervisors play an important role in the ethical behavior displayed by supervisees in supervision. Only one study specifically addressed supervisee ethical behavior within the context of supervision. This study found that up to 85% of supervisees acknowledged engaging at least some of the moderately unethical behaviors (e.g., failing to complete client documentation within a required time frame), while 1.3% acknowledge engaging in the behavior ranked as most unethical (i.e., forging supervisor's signature on case material), and 7% acknowledge engaging in the behavior ranked second in ethicality (i.e., presenting intentionally fabricated information about a client in supervision; Worthington, Tan, & Poulin, 2002). In general, supervisees are more likely to engage in what they view are minor ethical violations. It may be inferred that unethical behaviors that are normalized may be considered less severe then those behaviors that the supervisor has not observed.

Summary of Current State

Professional ethical guidelines (i.e., *ACA Code of Ethics*) have been identified to help establish a standard of practice. This has been effective in that supervisors typically endorse ethical guidelines (Navin et al., 1995). However, supervisors and supervisees report that supervisors' behaviors do not always adhere to ethical guidelines (Dickey et al., 1993; Ladany et al., 1999; McCarthy et al., 1994; Pearse, 1991; Siegel, 1993). Specifically, dual relationships in supervision (Dickey et al., 1993; Ladany et al., 1999;

Navin et al., 1995; Pearse, 1991; Siegel, 1993) and inadequate monitoring of supervisees' counseling activities (Borders et al., 1995; Coll, 1995; O'Connor, 2000; Pearse, 1991; Townend et al., 2002) are common ethical problems in supervision. Supervisor adherence to ethical guidelines is particularly important because it contributes to supervisee learning (Barnett et al., 2007; Corey et al., 1998; Goodyear, 2007; Holloway, 1992), supervisory working alliance (Gray et al., 2001; Ladany et al., 1999; Lehrman-Waterman & Ladany, 2001; Ramos-Sánchez et al., 2002), and supervisee satisfaction (Lehrman-Waterman & Ladany, 2001; Ramos-Sánchez et al., 2002).

Critical Thinking about Ethics

Necessary but not Sufficient

Ethical guidelines are necessary for establishing a standard of professional behavior and responsibility but, as we have seen in the literature, are not sufficient for motivating ethical behavior in all supervisors. Clearly, codes and rules "are not a substitute for an active, deliberate, and creative approach to fulfilling our ethical responsibilities" (Pope & Vasquez, 1998, p. 17). Ethics is more than simply following a set of rules or abiding by some standards. Since there is rarely one correct answer in ethical dilemmas, effective ethical decision making must be tied to "a complex combination of higher level thought and deep reflection, along with the ability to choose a course of action in spite of doubt and uncertainty" (Neukrug, Lovell, & Parker, 1996, p. 101). Therefore, understanding the ethics code is simply a first step in becoming an ethical professional. To be most beneficial to clients and supervisees, supervisors should be undergoing a constant process of ethical self-evaluation.

Recommendations for Reducing Ethical Conflicts

Prevention

A strong counselor will work toward the prevention of ethical dilemmas by establishing an environment of openness and integrity. In supervision, this translates into making the supervisory relationship a priority so that conflicts and ethical concerns are addressed in a professional and supportive manner. Supervisees are more likely to openly discuss their needs and concerns in an environment where they feel safe and respected (Ladany et al., 1996). Practicing informed consent on the outset of supervision, so that formal expectations are communicated clearly, is a primary way to prevent miscommunications. Openness in supervision incorporates regularly scheduled, formal evaluations as a tool for the communication of expectations and suggestions for remediation. Additionally, the supervisory relationship includes the establishment of professional boundaries so that roles are clear and supervision remains relevant. Finally, supervisors can take an active role in the prevention of ethical transgressions by helping to create an environment of openness within the field of counseling. This may allow counselors to openly discuss ethical dilemmas without fear of judgment or exposure.

Managing Ambiguity

Ambiguity is inherent in ethical dilemmas and supervisors may be perplexed to find that ethical codes can also be ambiguous. First, ethical codes are constantly evolving toward a more comprehensive reflection of cultural values as evidenced in the ongoing process of code revisions. Though revered, ethical standards should be recognized as works in progress. Second, there are overlapping standards that exist both externally and internally. The external standards refer to the regulating boards, legal requirements, and professional codes of conduct. The internal standards refer to the supervisor's own values, culture, and life experiences. Consider, if the internal and external standards were always the same, there would be no need for the external standards. Third, ambiguity defines ethical dilemmas, where no two dilemmas will present themselves in the exact same way. An important part of the ethical decision-making process involves being able to manage the ambiguity that exists in many ethical dilemmas.

Ethical Decision Making

Knowing the ethical codes is not enough to address ethical dilemmas in supervision. Supervisors must become familiar with the process of ethical decision making. Meara, Schmidt, and Day (1996) assert that this process necessitates "practice to develop the abilities to discern the subtleties and nuances of the problem" (p. 30).

When an ethical dilemma occurs, supervisors should identify and reflect on the problem, considering the various factors and risks. Supervisors should consider the relevant ethical codes and guidelines that have been adopted by scientific and professional counseling organizations. Supervisors must also weight the direction of their own conscience (APA, 2002). A potential course of action should be generated and the consequences to all parties involved should be well measured. Consultation with other counseling professionals must be sought when necessary, to be sure all factors have been considered. One source of professional support includes the ACA, which provides free, confidential ethical/professional standards consultation to all its members (highlighting the importance of involvement in professional organizations). After considering the potential consequences of all options, one must implement a course of action. Once implemented, the ethical decision-making process should be reflected upon and evaluated by the supervisor.

There is seldom one correct response to a complex ethical dilemma. Supervisors, as all counselors, must rely on their ability to make difficult decisions. The decision must be decisively made and communicated clearly. Van Hoose and Paradise (1979) offer the assurance that a professional is probably behaving in an ethical manner if "he or she has maintained personal and professional honesty, coupled with the best interests of the client," and the supervisee, "without malice or personal gain, and can justify his or her actions as the best judgment of what should be done based upon the current state of the profession" (p. 58).

Conclusion

In any field, professionals are responsible for struggling with competing demands and multiple perspectives. Counseling supervisors, however, have the unique responsibility of helping another person help another person, which brings with it several layers of problems, situations, and stakeholders. Ethical codes exist to provide guidance in making difficult decisions and establish standards to which supervisors can be held accountable. Applying ethical behavior requires a thorough understanding of ethical standards, as well as the implementation of preventative measures and strong ethical decision-making skills. Ultimately, the ability to behave in an ethical manner is the hallmark of a true professional.

Case Example #1

Dr. G has been supervising a practicum student, Blair for six months. Blair is in her final year of earning her Master's degree in counseling at a local university. Dr. G and Blair have a strong rapport and mutual respect for each other. Blair is experiencing the usual demands of a busy graduate student in the midst of practicum and preparing for graduation. Additionally, Blair is also the mother of two adolescents and in the process of getting a divorce from a verbally abusive husband. Besides experiencing her own struggles surrounding the divorce, such as financial concerns, emotional loss, and starting to date again, her children are also in need of more attention from their mother. Blair has demonstrated some adequate beginner-level skills as a counselor. She establishes a working alliance with her clients and is able to identify appropriate treatments. In supervision, Blair addresses some client issues, but has also used it as a time to talk about her divorce and vent her frustrations toward her daughters. Dr. G feels that given Blair's personal struggles, it is appropriate to allow some venting about personal issues so that Blair can consider how her personal experiences might be affecting her role as a counselor. However, recently, Blair has begun to use supervision to talk about her personal issues more often, and even used one whole session to talk about herself. Blair has also gotten behind in her paperwork and some session notes appear to be missing altogether. Additionally, on several occasions during working hours, Dr. G has walked into the office when Blair has been talking on the phone, e-mailing, or text messaging with one of her children, lawyers, or new boyfriend. Dr. G is sure that Blair's personal life is hindering her ability to develop fully as a counselor. When Dr. G recommended that Blair seek out her own counseling, Blair acknowledged the need for it but stated that there was no time or money for such counseling. As Blair is approaching her graduation, she frequently expresses hope for her quality of life to improve, including fewer financial concerns (assuming a full-time job is secured), and more time. She has frequently stated that doing counseling is one of the few things that is rewarding in her life right now, and she does not know what she would do without the support of her coworkers at the practicum. In spite of some of Blair's professional shortcomings, Dr. G is hopeful that Blair has demonstrated enough strengths as a counselor that she will be able to do strong work in the future. However, Dr. G also recognizes that practicum is a key aspect of training and is concerned that Blair is simply not getting all that she can from the experience. Dr. G is compelled to provide an accurate evaluation of Blair, but is concerned about how some negative feedback might affect Blair.

Discussion Questions

1. Which ethical guidelines should be considered in this vignette?
2. How would you approach Blair's subpar professional behavior?
3. What recommendations would you make for Blair's future practice?

Case Example #2

Mr. O, a high school counselor, had provided supervision to a new counselor, April, for one year. Throughout that year, April frequently sought supervision for one client, Michelle, a first-year student who maintained suicidal ideations, major mood swings, and poor boundaries with others. Michelle frequently referred to April as her only friend and requested to remain in contact after April left the school for a new counseling position in a different school the following school year. In supervision, April expressed to Mr. O that it felt cruel to disconnect from Michelle completely, and felt guilty for "abandoning" her client. Mr. O firmly advised April to terminate completely with Michelle and used supervision to discuss how termination might take place. He also helped April to explore her feelings of guilt surrounding the termination. April appeared to have understood the reasons for the professional boundary and agreed to proceed as advised. However, in the following school year, after April had moved on to a position in a different school district, April e-mailed Mr. O stating that she had continued to remain in contact though e-mail with her client, Michelle. In the most recent e-mail to April, Michelle had written that she was feeling terribly alone, was having serious thoughts about hurting herself, and did not want to tell anyone at her school for fear that they would hospitalize her. April was concerned for Michelle's safety and hoped that Mr. O would meet with Michelle for counseling.

Discussion Questions

1. What is Mr. O's ethical responsibility to April? to Michelle?
2. How should Mr. O respond to Michelle?
3. Who is responsible for the boundary violations that have occurred?
4. What ethical decision-making steps should be taken?

Case Example #3

Counselor L is the only licensed counselors in a small rural town. Her practice and training has generally centered on working with adult populations. She is supervising a new counselor, Tom, who is providing therapy to a teenage girl named Ellen. Ellen struggles with anorexia, bulimia, and frequently makes superficial cuts on her arm when feeling anxious. Tom has acknowledged, to both Counselor L and to Ellen that he has had no training or experience in the treatment of eating disorders or self-injurious behaviors and would like to refer Ellen to a more experienced practitioner. Ellen only wants to work with Tom, however, and has flat-out refused to see another counselor. Additionally, the closest counselor is one hour away by car, a trip that Ellen's parents would not be able to make on a regular basis, even if Ellen was willing. Counselor L's experience with eating disorders and self-injurious behaviors is also limited, although the treatment of eating disorders was addressed in some of her graduate-level coursework and she did read a few books on the topic.

Discussion Questions

1. What are the ethical considerations of supervising Tom and treating Ellen?
2. What role does ambiguity play in this case?
3. How should Counselor L proceed?

References

American Counseling Association. (2005). *ACA code of ethics*. Alexandria, VA: Author.

American Psychological Association. (2002). *Ethical principles of psychologists and code of conduct*. Washington, DC: Author.

Association for Counselor Education and Supervision. (1993). *Ethical guidelines for counseling supervisors*. Alexandria, VA: Author.

Barnett, J. E., Cornish, J. A., Goodyear, R. K., & Lichtenberg, J. W. (2007). Commentaries on the ethical and effective practices of clinical supervision. *Professional Psychology: Research and Practice, 38*, 268–275.

Bernard, J. M., & Goodyear, R. K. (2008). *Fundamentals of clinical supervision* (4th ed.). Needham Heights, MA: Allyn & Bacon.

Borders, L. D., Cashwell, C. S., & Rotter, J. C. (1995). Supervision of counselor licensure applicants: A comparative study. *Counselor Education and Supervision, 35*, 54–69.

Coll, K. M. (1995). Clinical supervision of community college counselors: Current and preferred practices. *Counselor Education and Supervision, 35*, 111–117.

Corey, G., Corey, M. S., & Callanan, P. (1998). *Issues and ethics in the helping professions*. Belmont, CA: Thomson Brooks/Cole Publishing Co.

Crall, J. (2010). *Ethical behavior of supervisors: Effects on supervisee experiences and behavior* (Unpublished doctoral dissertation). Lehigh University, Bethlehem, PA.

Dickey, K. D., Housley, W. F., & Guest, C. (1993). Ethics in supervision of rehabilitation counselor trainees: A survey. *Rehabilitation Education, 7*, 195–201.

Erwin, W. J. (2000). Supervisor moral sensitivity. *Counselor Education and Supervision, 40*, 115–127.

Gandolfo, R. L., & Brown, R. (1987). Psychology intern ratings of actual and ideal supervision of psychotherapy. *Journal of Training & Practice in Professional Psychology, 1*, 15–28.

Goodyear, R. K. (2007). Commentaries on the ethical and effective practice of clinical supervision. *Professional Psychology: Research and Practice, 38*, 268–275.

Goodyear, R. K., Crego, C. A., & Johnston, M. W. (1992). Ethical issues in the supervision of student research: A study of critical incidents. *Professional Psychology: Research and Practice, 23*, 203–210.

Gray, L. A., Ladany, N., Walker, J. A., & Ancis, J. R. (2001). Psychotherapy trainees' experience of counterproductive events in supervision. *Journal of Counseling Psychology, 48*, 371–383.

Hall, C. S. (1952). Crooks, codes and cant. *American Psychologist, 7*, 430–431.

Handelsman, M. M., Gottlieb, M. C., & Knapp, S. (2005). Training ethical psychologists: An acculturation model. *Professional Psychology: Research and Practice, 36*, 59–65.

Heppner, P. P., & Handley, P. G. (1981). A study of the interpersonal influence process in supervision. *Journal of Counseling Psychology, 28*, 437–444.

Heppner, P. P., & Roehlke, H. J. (1984). Differences among supervisees at different levels of training: Implications for a developmental model of supervision. *Journal of Counseling Psychology, 31*, 76–90.

Hilton, D. B., Russell, R. K., & Salmi, S. W. (1995). The effects of supervisor's race and level of support on perceptions of supervision. *Journal of Counseling & Development, 73*(5), 559–563.

Holloway, E. L. (1992). Supervision: A way of teaching and learning. In S. D. Brown & R. W. Lent (Eds.), *Handbook of counseling psychology* (2nd ed., pp. 177–214). Oxford, UK: John Wiley & Sons.

Jacobs, C. (1991). Violations of the supervisory relationship: An ethical and educational blind spot. *Social Work, 36*, 130–135.

Kitchener, K. S. (1984). Intuition, critical evaluation and ethical principles: The foundation for ethical decisions in counseling psychology. *Counseling Psychologist, 12*(3), 43–55.

Ladany, N., Ellis, M., & Friedlander, M. (1999). The supervisory working alliance, trainee self-efficacy, and satisfaction. *Journal of Counseling and Development, 77*, 447–455.

Ladany, N., Hill, C., Corbett, M., & Nutt, E. (1996). Nature, extent, and importance of what psychotherapy trainees do not disclose to their supervisors. *Journal of Counseling Psychology, 43*, 10–24.

Ladany, N., Lehrman-Waterman, D., Molinaro, M., & Wolgast, B. (1999). Psychotherapy supervisor ethical practices: Adherence to guidelines, the supervisory working alliance, and supervisee satisfaction. *Counseling Psychologist, 27*, 443–475.

Lehrman-Waterman, D., & Ladany, N. (2001). Development and validation of the evaluation process within supervision inventory. *Journal of Counseling Psychology, 48*, 168–177.

Martino, C. (2001). Supervision as a self object experience. In S. Gill (Ed.), *The supervisory alliance: Facilitating the psychotherapist's learning experience* (pp. 107–122). Lanham, MD: Jason Aronson.

McCarthy, P., Kulakowski, D., & Kenfield, J. A. (1994). Clinical supervision practices of licensed psychologists. *Professional Psychology: Research and Practice, 25*, 177–181.

McNeill, B., & Worthen, V. (1989). The parallel process in psychotherapy supervision. *Professional Psychology: Research and Practice, 20*, 329–333.

Meara, N. M., Schmidt, L. D., & Day, J. D. (1996). Principles and virtues: A foundation for ethical decisions, policies, and character. *Counseling Psychologist, 24*, 4–77.

Navin, S., Beamish, P., & Johanson, G. (1995). Ethical practices of field-based mental health counselor supervisors. *Journal of Mental Health Counseling, 17*, 243–253.

Nelson, M. L., & Friedlander, M. L. (2001). A close look at conflictual supervisory relationships: The trainee's perspective. *Journal of Counseling Psychology, 48*, 384–395.

Neukrug, E., Lovell, C., & Parker, R. J. (1996). Employing ethical codes and decision-making models: A developmental process. *Counseling and Values, 40*, 98–106.

O'Connor, B. P. (2000). Reasons for less than ideal psychotherapy supervision. *Clinical Supervisor, 19*, 173–183.

Olk, M. E., & Friedlander, M. L. (1992). Trainees' experiences of role conflict and role ambiguity in supervisory relationships. *Journal of Counseling Psychology, 39,* 389–397.

Pearse, R. D. (1991). Ethical practices in the supervision of predoctoral psychology interns (Doctoral dissertation, West Virginia University, 1990). *Dissertation Abstracts International, 52,* 1734.

Pope, K. S., Levenson, H., & Schover, L. R. (1979). Sexual intimacy in psychology training: Results and implications of a national survey. *American Psychologist, 34,* 682–689.

Pope, K. S., & Vasquez, M. J. (1998). *Ethics in psychotherapy and counseling: A practical guide* (2nd ed.). San Francisco, CA: Jossey-Bass.

Ramos-Sánchez, L., Esnil, E., Goodwin, A., Riggs, S., Touster, L. O., Wright, L. K., … Rodolfa, E. (2002). Negative supervisory events: Effects on supervision and supervisory alliance. *Professional Psychology: Research and Practice, 33,* 197–202.

Schroffel, A. (1999). How does clinical supervision affect job satisfaction? *Clinical Supervisor, 18,* 91–105.

Shulman, L. (2005). The clinical supervisor-practitioner working alliance: A parallel process. *Clinical Supervisor, 24,* 23–47.

Siegel, J. L. (1993). Ethical issues in the supervisory relationship: A review with a proposal for change. *Dissertation Abstracts International, 54*(2-B), 1113.

Stoltenberg, C. D., & Delworth, U. (1987). *Supervising counselors and therapists: A developmental approach.* San Francisco, CA: Jossey-Bass.

Townend, M., Iannetta, L., & Freeston, M. (2002). Clinical supervision in practice: A survey of UK cognitive behavioural psychotherapists accredited by the BABCP. *Behavioural and Cognitive Psychotherapy, 30,* 485–500.

Van Hoose, W. H., & Kottler, J. A. (1985). *Ethical and legal issues in counseling and psychotherapy* (2nd ed.). San Francisco, CA: Jossey-Bass.

Van Hoose, W. H., & Paradise, L. V. (1979). *Ethics in counseling and psychotherapy: Perspectives in issues and decision-making.* Cranston, RI: Carroll Press.

Welfel, E. R., & Lipsitz, N. E. (1983). Ethical orientation of counselors: Its relationship to moral reasoning and level of training. *Counselor Education and Supervision, 23,* 35–45.

Worthington, R., Tan, J., & Poulin, K. (2002). Ethically questionable behaviors among supervisees: An exploratory investigation. *Ethics & Behavior, 12,* 323–351.

Wulf, J., & Nelson, M. L. (2000). Experienced psychologists' recollections of internship supervision and its contributions to their development. *Clinical Supervisor, 19,* 123–145.

CHAPTER 17

Training Supervisors

A Core Competency

ARPANA G. INMAN and SEPIDEH S. SOHEILIAN

Supervisors play a key role in the clinical and professional development of a counselor, and as such, supervision has been identified as a core functional competency (Rodolfa et al., 2005). Relatedly, since the 1990s a greater focus has been placed on approaches to supervision training along with a movement toward credentialing of supervision as part of licensure and accreditation (Freeman & McHenry, 1996). For instance, in 1997, the National Board of Certified Counselors established the Approved Clinical Supervisor credentials and minimal competencies, recognizing the integral role of supervisors as gatekeepers of the profession (Getz, 2001). In addition, the Association for Counselor Education and Supervision (1990) developed a task force to establish ethical standards for credentialing counselor supervisors. These standards not only highlighted the range of responsibilities that supervisors have in their different roles (i.e., administrative, clinical) but also the type of training supervisors need to maintain legal and ethical protection of client and supervisee welfare. An important premise underlying these guidelines is that supervision should occur throughout one's counseling career and not stop because a counselor has achieved a particular level of education, certification, experience, or membership in an organization.

Many states now require formal training of supervisors (Getz & Schnurman-Crook, n.d.) with the Council for Accreditation of Counseling and Related Educational Programs (CACREP, 2001) stipulating specific supervisor training in counselor preparation programs (Granello, Kindsvatter, Granello, Underfer-Babalis, & Hartwig Moorhead, 2008). For instance, the CACREP standards not only require that counselor education doctoral programs prepare students to work as counselor educators, practitioners, and supervisors in advanced clinical and academic settings, but also require that supervising faculty have appropriate training and supervision experiences, including supervision of supervision (Bernard & Goodyear, 2009). These strides are important in asserting the key role that supervision and supervisors play in the clinical field.

As supervision becomes a mainstay in training programs, there is an increased need to attend to the multiple facets inherent in supervisor development (e.g., supervisor identity, supervisor roles, and supervisory relationships). Subsumed within a didactic and experiential curriculum, supervisor training needs to highlight the distinctive role of supervision and supervisors, and the core professional competencies needed to engage in effective supervisory practice. In this chapter, we highlight the differences between supervision and counseling, specific functions and roles of supervisors, and recommend a conceptual model for training supervisors.

On Becoming a Supervisor: Supervisor Identity and Development

It has been typically assumed that the experience as a counselor and a supervisee is sufficient to become a supervisor (Baker, Exum, & Tyler, 2002). A basic assumption underlying this belief is the notion that counseling and supervision are similar with little formal training required to assume the role of a supervisor. Multiple studies (e.g., Stevens, Goodyear, & Robertson, 1997; Vidlak, 2002) however have revealed that supervisor development is not solely influenced by experience, but that formal, didactic, and experiential training in supervision is essential to the development of a supervisor. Furthermore, training in supervision has been associated with reduced anxiety, increased confidence in the use of supervisory interventions, and more supportive, less critical, and less dogmatic thoughts toward supervisees. Consistent with these differences, researchers have argued that supervisor roles and skills are distinct from those of counselor roles and skills.

Specifically, while a counselor's focus is on the welfare of the client and a dyadic experience, the supervisor's focus and influence occurs at two levels—the welfare of the client and the professional development of the counselor resulting in a triadic supervision experience. Such an experience requires supervisors to manage multiple cognitive complexities (e.g., vicarious client-related liability issues and supervisee development) as they monitor and respond to two people, respectively, the client and the supervisee (Hein & Lawson, 2008). Inherent in this role is a second important distinction: legitimate power (Jenkins, 2006). Unlike clinical relationships, supervisory relationships are involuntary, evaluative, and didactic (Bernard & Goodyear, 2009). For instance, in supervisory relationships, supervisors not only assess and provide feedback on skills but also take on an instructive role in imparting knowledge and skills to supervisees (Hess, Hess, & Hess, 2008). In essence, Borders (1989) states that supervisors need to think of their supervisees "as learners and of themselves as educators who create a learning environment" (p. 6).

However, taking on this educative and evaluative role requires a shift in one's thinking. Specifically, authors (Baker et al., 2002; Borders, 1989; Stevens et al., 1997; Vidlak, 2002) have noted that new supervisors need to develop a perceptual shift from thinking like a counselor (e.g., focusing on client dynamics) to thinking like a supervisor (e.g., focusing on the supervisee's training needs). In essence, taking on a supervisory role requires one to relinquish the direct clinical role and focus on the intersection of the various contextual factors (e.g., client, supervisee, supervisor, and the institution) wherein supervision occurs (Holloway, 1995). Beyond assessing a supervisee's clinical abilities, supervisors also help the supervisee develop a professional identity and navigate the institution within which supervision occurs.

Holloway (1995) highlights some important supervisory functions (e.g., advising/instructing, supporting/sharing, consulting, modeling, monitoring/evaluating) that can be performed with the specific supervision tasks (counseling skills, case conceptualization, emotional awareness, professional role, and evaluation) that are part of the supervisory role. In effect, through supervisory functions (e.g., advising, sharing, and modeling), supervisors are responsible for facilitating supervisee growth by managing two interlocking systems in supervision: the therapy system (e.g., increasing supervisee self-awareness and understanding of the client, deepen his/her knowledge of theories and concepts) and the supervision system (e.g., awareness of supervisee's professional role, developing organizational competency, being open to feedback and evaluations) that exist within a larger institutional context (Holloway, 2005). In assuming the supervisory role and developing role identification, it becomes important for supervisors to internalize behaviors that are specific to a supervisor (Mordock, 1990). Attaining competence involves both a dynamic interaction of internal qualities (e.g., developing self-efficacy) and external factors (e.g., training, organizational support) that result in the use of interventions and skills at multiple levels beyond simply applying specific counseling techniques (Bernard & Goodyear, 2009).

Frequently, when discussing skills, supervisor developmental models have typically focused on how supervisors can facilitate a supervisee's cognitive (Granello, 2000) or skill development (Chapter 4 of this book). As such, there is a tendency for supervisors to use a problem-focused supervision format wherein the emphasis is on tasks involved in working with the client (i.e., teaching the supervisee specific interventions that may be helpful in solving client problems). Within this context, supervision often focuses on the supervisor role and competence as it relates to the client rather than supervision as a whole (Emilsson & Johnsson, 2007). While being focused on tasks and clients is important, literature (e.g., Bernard & Goodyear, 2009) suggests that the relational dynamics between the supervisor and supervisee are instrumental in hindering or facilitating any type of task in supervision. Yet, little attention has been paid to explicit strategies that increase supervisor confidence and improve the development of a productive supervisory process that leads to effective outcomes (e.g., satisfaction with supervision; effective clinical practice). A process-oriented supervision wherein supervision is conceptualized from an interpersonal perspective, the supervisory relationship is at the center and supervisors-in-training learn the craft of supervision by actively participating in the process, becomes an important approach to training supervisors (Emilsson & Johnsson, 2007). We believe that engaging in process-oriented supervision will automatically allow for task-oriented issues to be addressed in an effective manner. As such, we present a model for training supervisors that highlights what the supervisors-in-training need to know about supervision and the supervisory process and how they translate this knowledge to specific strategies that can be used in training supervisees.

What Supervisors Need to Know

A key aspect of effective supervisory process and outcome is the supervisor's ability to establish a productive supervisory relationship (Ladany, Friedlander, & Nelson, 2005). Thus, taking into consideration the relational variables that influence the supervisory relationship is important for good supervision preparation and practice (Bernard & Goodyear, 2009). In this section, we highlight some specific overt (setting the environment, attending to counseling skills, evaluation; Ladany, Walker, Pate-Carolan, & Evans, 2008) and covert relational processes (parallel process, nondisclosure, countertransference, corrective relational experience) that supervisors-in-training need to attend to in order to create an effective supervisory relationship. Much of this can be addressed through didactic coursework and active discussion of issues.

Overt Processes

Setting the Environment

Since supervision can both facilitate and hinder a supervisee's growth, the first step in supervision is to create a supervisory environment that will be conducive to effective supervisory process and outcome (Hess et al., 2008).

Irrespective of the modality (individual or group), an environment that is deliberate and purposeful can go a long way in building a good supervisory relationship (Bernard, 2005). As such, we identify some key issues to consider in creating an affirming supervisory environment:

1. *Understand Organizational Support for Supervision.* Supervision while time-consuming is integral to delivering effective mental health services with institutions playing an important role in facilitating this activity (Hess et al., 2008). However, institutional factors can sometimes derail the most sincere supervisory efforts. As a supervisor, supervisors-in-training need to assess the institutional culture as it pertains to support and commitment for supervision, to its clientele, to professional ethics, and to resources (Bernard & Goodyear, 2009).

2. *Supervisory Style.* More than interventions, it is the delivery style of the supervisor that has been noted to moderate the supervisory process. Specifically, being warm and supportive without being therapeutic, being instructive without being blaming, and being evaluative without being disrespectful are important in building trust and an emotional bond in the supervisory relationship (Gray, Ladany, Walker, & Ancis, 2001; Nelson & Friedlander, 2001). These factors often trump the particular intervention or style (authoritarian, participatory, cooperative, or consultative) that may be used in supervision (Bernard & Goodyear, 2009).

3. *Aware of Role Relationships.* Recognize that the supervisory relationship is not an equal relationship. Acknowledge the hierarchy and power inherent in the supervisory role but actively work at diffusing this hierarchy through empathizing and balancing critical feedback with acknowledgment of supervisee strengths. Keep in mind the vulnerabilities that supervisees experience and the potential shame and humiliation they may experience as they share their ideas and thoughts (Yourman, 2003).

4. *Role Induction.* An important role of the supervisor is that of role induction. Supervision is not a onetime relationship or a set curriculum (Hess et al., 2008). Socializing the supervisee into their therapeutic role, educating them about the institution and the intersection of the different systems are key to a supervisees' evolving personal and professional development.

5. *Clarity in Communication.* Supervisees need clarity with regard to the expectations in supervision. They need to know how supervision proceeds and what is expected of them (Nelson & Friedlander, 2001). When supervision is reactive rather than organized and deliberate, supervisees are likely to experience

greater dissatisfaction and decreased self-efficacy (Gray et al., 2001). Thus, providing standards of accountability (e.g., evaluations), adequately preparing for supervision based on supervisee needs, and being clear with regard to role expectations can reduce the ambiguity experienced by supervisees (Nelson & Friedlander, 2001).

6. *Supervisee Needs.* Addressing supervisee needs requires supervisors to be invested and interested in supervisee growth and aware of supervisee needs. As such, taking the pulse of each supervision session, identifying short (e.g., attending to countertransference) and long-term (e.g., case conceptualization) goals, and identifying specific tasks (e.g., use of audiotapes) that will be used to achieve the goals on a regular basis becomes important (Hess et al., 2008).

7. *Accessibility and Structure.* Being accessible and available, providing structure and reliability through regular and frequent meetings can bring about predictability to an otherwise changing system (Ramos-Sanchez et al., 2002).

8. *Multicultural Competence.* Given that supervisors are ultimately responsible for facilitating supervisee cultural competence (Inman, 2006), it is important for supervisors to create a space for explicit discussion of culture-specific issues. This involves showing their vulnerability in sharing their own struggles, being sensitive to supervisee nonverbal cues, addressing cultural issues in supervisor–supervisee personal development, case conceptualization, interventions, supervisory process, and outcome/evaluations (Chapter 4 of this book; Dressel, Consoli, Kim, & Atkinson, 2007; Killian, 2001). Supervision that encourages the exploration of culturally specific issues in these different areas tends to promote growth in trainees' multicultural competence (Inman, 2006; Killian, 2001) and is consistent with ethical practices identified in the literature.

9. *Methods of Supervising.* It is important to address methods by which clinical work will be supervised. For example, the use of self-report, process notes, audiotapes, videotapes, and live supervision have been effectively used in supervision (Bernard & Goodyear, 2009). However, discussing the advantages and disadvantages of each of these methods is important. For example, videotapes while time-consuming create the ability to view process and interpersonal dynamics. Self-report gives the supervisee an opportunity to evaluate him or herself, but only provides the supervisor one perspective. Live supervision gives the supervisee immediate attention in the moment, but is time-consuming and utilizes too

many resources (i.e., takes the supervisor away from other clinical work).

Attending to Clinical Skills

Attending to clinical skills is an important role of the supervisor. However, supervisors need to attend to a range of clinical skills—from basic helping skills to higher level conceptual skills. Frequently, supervisors and supervisees tend to focus on developing a theoretical-conceptual framework at the risk of minimizing the specific moment-to-moment therapeutic processes. While developing a theoretical foundation is pertinent, understanding the moment-to-moment interactions (e.g., nonverbal response modes) becomes even more important as it allows trainees to understand why and how something may transpire in the therapeutic process.

Evaluation

Evaluation processes should be discussed early in the supervisory relationship with clear learning objectives and specific behavioral illustrations. However, the evaluative role of a supervisor is perhaps the most challenging of all skills that needs to be developed. Based in a position of authority and power, supervisors must gain comfort in being able to develop distinct goals but also provide clear feedback to their supervisees (Lehrman-Waterman & Ladany, 2001). Goals need to be clear, specific, measurable, and achievable in relation to resources, opportunity, and capacity, flexible and modifiable over time, related to tasks, and mutually agreed upon. In assessing these goals, these authors have identified two types of feedback that need to be provided to supervisees. First, formative evaluations are those that are ongoing and occur throughout supervision. The focus typically is on skill acquisition and professional growth (Bernard & Goodyear, 2009). A second type of evaluation is summative in nature. This involves a more formal review, is based on specific criteria (e.g., multicultural competence, professionalism), and typically occurs at the middle and end of an academic semester. However, irrespective of the type of evaluation, feedback should be balanced, descriptive, and evolve out of a shared partnership.

Covert Processes

Nondisclosure

Frequently, what is not said may have more valence than what is overt and verbalized in a relationship. For example, authors (Ladany, Hill, Corbett, & Nutt, 1996; Yourman, 2003) have found that supervisees tend to withhold information when they experience shame in supervision (Yourman, 2003), or when supervisees feel negatively judged for their clinical mistakes

(Ladany et al., 1996) with nondisclosures occurring more frequently in group supervision than individual supervision (Webb & Wheeler, 1998). Supervisor self-disclosure particularly with regard to counseling struggles can potentially create shifts in the supervisory working alliance, supervisee disclosure, and supervisee learning ability (Ladany & Lehrman-Waterman, 1999).

Countertransference

Another variable that can influence the supervisory relationship is supervisor countertransference. Countertransference occurs in the form of positive (e.g., identification with supervisee, provision of support, commitment to rapport building) or negative (e.g., being bored in supervision, distraction by external events, less engagement) feelings, thoughts, or behaviors as a function of interactions between the supervisor and the supervisee (Ladany et al., 2008). Whether based in supervisee's interpersonal style, supervisor's own personal issues, environmental factors, problematic therapeutic interactions between the client and the supervisee, countertransference can influence supervision outcome (Ladany et al., 2008).

Parallel Process

In speaking about the reflection process (Searles, 1955) or the isomorphic (Haley, 1976) replication between counseling and supervision, authors (Ekstein & Wallerstein, 1972) have identified parallel process to play an important role in supervision. Parallel process can be bottom up (therapy to supervision) or top down (i.e., supervision to therapy; Doehrman, 1976). Bottom up parallel process occurs when a certain dynamic, interaction, or behavior that occurs in therapy is replicated in supervision. Top down parallel process on the other hand is the unconscious replication of the supervisory relationship in the therapy relationship. In other words, because of identification with their supervisors, supervisees recreate the feelings that they experience with their supervisors with their clients in therapy.

Corrective Relational Experience

A corrective relational experience occurs when a negative experience (e.g., conflict, rupture) in supervision is corrected or fixed through the efforts of the supervisor and/or the supervisee. Given the intimate nature of a supervisory relationship, ruptures and conflicts can significantly influence the supervisory process. Therefore, how a supervisor handles or corrects these mishaps or ruptures (e.g., corrective relational experience) can be instrumental in maintaining a productive supervisory climate.

Skills and Strategies in Training Supervisors

The transition from counselor to supervisor is critical to the development of a supervisory identity. Authors (Ellis & Douce, 1994; Ladany et al., 2005) have found that beginning supervisors who have difficulty with this transition report strong feelings of anger, anxiety, and self-doubt. When these feelings are not addressed, supervisors experience doubts about their supervisory interventions. Thus, a clear training module that addresses these issues while providing the needed knowledge (identified in the previous section) is essential to training supervisors. Specifically, in addition to the foundational knowledge base achieved through didactic coursework, engaging in an experiential process that allows supervisors-in-training to experience their role as supervisors is key to developing competency as a supervisor. In developing a training module, we strongly encourage supervisors-in-training have several opportunities to not only supervise but also receive supervision of supervision. In this section, we highlight some specific steps involved in training supervisors within a group format.

Self-Reflection

An important first step in becoming a supervisor is a focus on self (Hawkins & Shohet, 2000), with a critical self-assessment of one's beliefs, values, and behaviors that may influence one's future work. Watkins (1995) believes that being self-critical is a crucial factor in supervisor effectiveness over time. Self-critical supervisors are able to consider and integrate multiple perspectives and maintain flexibility in their thinking through careful listening, asking questions, admitting uncertainty, tolerating ambiguity, and suspending judgment (Granello et al., 2008; Watkins, 1995).

Self-reflections are important as supervisors assume a new role. An important activity may involve reflecting on both past and current experiences that have brought on feelings of doubt or inefficacy. For example, supervisors-in-training can be encouraged to explore similarities between the feelings associated with being a new supervisor and those associated with their first clinical experience (Bonney, 1994). Taking on a new role typically brings about anxieties for trainees—anxieties that lead to dualistic thinking, rigid and mechanistic interactions, and doubts about their abilities to function in their new roles (Stoltenberg, McNeill, & Delworth, 1998). These issues can significantly affect their confidence levels. Helping supervisors-in-training reflect on the similarities in these new experiences and drawing their attention to their abilities to move beyond these fears can help alleviate the anxieties they may experience.

A second step in becoming a supervisor is appreciating the difference between counseling and supervision. An excellent reflective activity that can be used to initiate this process is to ask supervisors-in-training to review their past counseling and supervision experiences as a trainee or supervisee. What differentiates supervision from counseling? What responsibilities and tasks did you see your supervisors perform in your supervisory relationship? What thoughts and behaviors differentiate a counselor from a supervisor? Does a skilled counselor make for a skilled supervisor? What factors made for a positive and effective supervisory experience? What factors made for a negative and ineffective supervisory experience? These are questions that can allow supervisees to distinguish not only between counseling and supervision but also identify specific roles that supervisors take and factors and behaviors that influence the supervision process.

Relatedly, authors have proposed different approaches to engage in this exercise. For instance, Aten, Madson, and Kruse (2008) propose the use of a supervision genogram that can provide a visual depiction of these positive and negative experiences. Similar to other genograms, a supervision genogram can symbolically represent or reflect beginning supervisors' past supervision experiences and relationships. In particular, it can promote self-awareness by helping supervisors-in-training gain a deeper understanding of how their previous experiences and relationships may influence their current roles and relationships. Within this context, supervisors can speak to issues they wish to emulate in their own supervisory roles. Similarly, Hoffman (1990) proposes having supervisors-in-training complete a supervision life line (SLL). Drawing a vertical line, they arrange their previous supervised experience in a chronological order that highlights the year and duration of supervision received, the demographic characteristics of a supervisor, and characteristics of supervision such as a supervisor's approach to supervision, salient learning's from the supervisory experience, the manner in which conflicts were handled, and barriers in learning to name a few.

The need to examine multiple perspectives and be a critical supervisor becomes even more salient when considering cultural issues, with supervisor multicultural competence having received much attention in recent years (Chapter 4 of this book; Inman, 2006). Therefore, a third area of self-reflection is based on supervisors demonstrating appropriate cultural awareness, knowledge, and skills. A supervisor should actively explore his or her multiple cultural identities (e.g., racial identity, social class, sexual orientation, gender, religion, ethnic identity) and the oppression and privilege associated with each of these identities (Chapter 4 of this book). One way to engage in this self-exploration is to have supervisors-in-training reflect on how frequently (e.g., never, sometimes, frequently) they are aware of their different social identities (e.g., ethnicity, class, race, gender). Typically supervisors-in-training may speak of their awareness being contextualized (e.g., awareness of race is heightened in a majority–minority context). Having supervisors explore the implications of this contextualized awareness (e.g., How effective are my interventions when

I am only aware of racial issues when I am with a supervisee of a visible racial minority?) can increase awareness of the potential blind spots (e.g., privilege of not having to think of one's race as a member of the dominant group) of supervisors. Relatedly, a second activity can involve supervisors-in-training reflect on a particular dominant identity and highlight at least five advantages (privileges) they experience as a function of this identity and highlight five disadvantages (oppression) they experience as a function of a nondominant identity. Such activities help bring the self of the supervisor into focus.

Shift From Counselor to Supervisor Role

In taking on the supervisory role, supervisors-in-training need to relinquish their direct counselor role. Supervisors who think like supervisors ask themselves, "What supervisory intervention will help this counselor perform differently with the client?" (Borders, 1989, p. 5). Specifically, this can entail asking "What did I do in that supervisory hour? Why did I do that? How did I help my supervisee? How did I hinder my supervisee? Are my supervisory interventions becoming more effective? If so, how and why? If not, why?" (Watkins, 1995, p. 116). An important avenue in which this processing occurs is when supervisors-in-training get supervision of supervision. Being engaged in supervision of supervision, allows supervisors-in-training to engage in a learning environment that is conducive to taking risks, asking some difficult questions, and trying out different approaches that help develop their supervisor identity.

One activity that has been identified by Borders (1989) seems to tap well into creating this shift. Supervisors can be shown a segment of a session and asked to review the tape and make notes that they would discuss with the counselor. After about 10–15 minutes, the tape is stopped and supervisors are asked to review their notes and count the number of statements they make about the client and the number of statements they make about the counselor. An activity such as this allows one to process the potential shift that needs to occur by focusing on the counselor. In engaging in this process, supervisors-in-training can be asked such questions as "What might be the most challenging aspect in this process? What strength do you bring to this process?" A contrasting yet similar activity that can be used involves showing supervisors-in-training a segment of a supervisory session and having them evaluate the session by identifying their thoughts and feelings about the session, highlighting strengths and weaknesses of the supervisory approach, and noting aspects/techniques that they might use in their own work.

Another activity that can be used is the task analysis model developed by Ladany et al. (2005). The primary focus of the three step model (i.e., Marker—Task Environment—Resolution) is to help supervisors focus on supervisee development by attending to supervisee clinical competencies and supervisee development. This allows the supervisor-in-training to attend to both the therapy system and the supervision system. The first step involves identifying a Marker that signifies the task to be addressed. Thus, within the supervisory context, this can occur when the supervisor-in-training indicates (either by a statement or behavioral signal) that he or she needs a specific kind of help (e.g., supervisee is continuously late to supervision, misses supervision, and fails to give recordings of therapy sessions). After the Marker is understood (e.g., supervisee's noncompliance or unprofessionalism and supervisor's difficulty asserting authority in supervision), step two involves moving into the Task Environment that entails interaction sequences comprised of supervisor interventions (e.g., exploring feelings, focusing on countertransference, etc.). Thus, in addressing this Marker, the trainer can focus on the supervisory alliance by coming to a mutual agreement of discussing the supervisor-in-training's concerns with taking on his/her authoritative role in supervision. This can be followed by exploring how the supervisor-in-training feels about the supervisees' behavior, address any countertransference that may be experienced in relation to this situation, as well as focus on the supervisor-in-training's self-efficacy as a supervisor (i.e., confidence in supervisory skills, and ability to function in various roles as a supervisor). Finally, the trainer can model for the supervisor-in-training the importance of owning authority and the evaluation process by discussing the supervisor-in-training's performance as a supervisor, and his/her professionalism in general. This interactional sequence of the Task Environment is followed by the final stage—Resolution—which refers to the outcome of a specific supervisory intervention. Resolutions can occur in four broad categories: self-awareness, knowledge, skills, or the supervisory alliance. The Resolution of the particular Task Environment noted above can entail the supervisor-in-training having a raised awareness of his/her discomfort with exerting authority, and the knowledge and skills to help him/her assert authority. Such an experience can strengthen the supervisory alliance due to the parallels that are drawn through modeling in supervision of supervision.

Initiating Supervision Planning for the first supervision session is an important first step. Given the anxieties with taking on a new role, engaging in a role-play that outlines the first supervision session typically allows supervisors-in-training to get a firsthand experience of being in a supervisory role. The trainer can first engage in this role-play with a supervisor-in-training and then have the supervisor-in-training practice this role-play with his/her peer supervisors. It is often helpful to provide an outline of issues to consider in the role-play. For instance, the first author has used the following outline to help supervisors-in-training prepare for the first supervision session: (1) introduce self (background experiences); (2) have supervisee give an introduction; (3) ask supervisee about thoughts and feelings when starting practicum (e.g., be empathic); (4) role induction (e.g., provide information about supervisory process as distinct from counseling process, clarify supervisor–supervisee roles, address evaluative component of supervision); (5) discuss confidentiality; (6) discuss multicultural issues; (7) process potential multiple roles (e.g., when supervisors-in-training are students in the same program as supervisees); (8) ask about supervisee's goals for supervision and obtain specifics of what they would look like; (9) review supervisee's goals; (10) discuss supervisee's feelings pertaining to first supervision session; and (11) plan for the next session. Such role-plays highlight the need for supervisors to be prepared, planful, and deliberate in session. A similar process can be modeled in supervision of supervision. Specifically, trainers can create learning goals for supervision of supervision, state clear objectives, and create an agenda based on supervisor-in-training needs in each session.

Beyond the first session, it is important to prepare for each subsequent session. Thus, similar to a counseling session, writing case notes after each supervision session is a key component of developing a plan and goals for each subsequent session. In the case notes, supervisors should include: a brief summary of the session, strengths and areas for improvement of the supervisee, assessment of skill and developmental level of supervisee, and evaluation of own performance including internal thoughts and feelings as a supervisor. Referring to these notes just prior to a session is also helpful to discuss any issues that remained unresolved from previous sessions. These notes can also help highlight whether the supervisor is focusing on the supervisee or the client.

Engaging in supervision of supervision is a salient ingredient that helps supervisors plan for upcoming supervision sessions. In supervision of supervision, supervisors-in-training consult with their supervisor as well as their peer supervisors-in-training. Considering multiple perspectives help supervisors-in-training discuss supervisor goals and provide concrete examples of how to work through that goal in supervision through modeling and role-plays with peers and/or a supervisor. Furthermore, supervisee feedback through evaluations of supervisor's performance in supervision is another perspective that will aid the supervisor in preparing to attend to supervisee needs in supervision.

Supervisory Role and the Appraisal of Skills

Taking on the supervisory role involves addressing skills at two systems—the therapy system and the supervision system. Thus, this involves assessing both supervisee skills and supervisory skills. We highlight several approaches that we have used to address these two skills.

Assessing Supervisee Skills

An important role of the supervisor is to evaluate a supervisee's counseling skills. Assessment is an ongoing process and should occur not only throughout the duration of supervision but also highlighted in a midterm and final formal evaluation of the supervisee. Assessment of skills can be carried out through listening or viewing recordings of sessions, and evaluating recordings via writing transcripts of sessions.

Listening or viewing recorded sessions can occur through the use of audiotapes, videotapes, or digital recordings. Supervisors-in-training can be encouraged to review sessions both during and outside of supervision. These types of evaluations can be focused on specific skill development (e.g., using silence in session) or highlighting counselor intentions (e.g., instilling hope) with a particular response (e.g., paraphrasing), assessing a therapeutic intervention (e.g., behavioral rehearsal) or getting a sense of the flow of an entire session. Through thoughtful feedback, supervisors can provide some positive encouragement and constructive criticism of counseling skills. To balance feedback and foster a safe learning environment, supervisors-in-training should list at least three strengths and three growth areas in which the supervisee can further develop and grow.

A second approach to evaluating supervisee skills is reviewing recordings by examining written transcripts of the session. The first author has typically used a format (see Table 17.1) that has been found to be beneficial in examining the moment-to-moment interactions in session. In assessing the transcript, the supervisor can comment on (1) overt or covert response modes; (2) client response; and (3) therapeutic strategies and interventions. Overt response modes pertain to the content of the interview, *what* was said (e.g., gather information, give information, direct guidance, and deal with relationship). Covert responses pertain to *how* things were said, the *type of exchange* (e.g., challenge, attending, listening, reflection, interpretation, self-disclosure, immediacy, silence, set limits, focus, and identify feelings). Client responses involve what the client said (*content*) and how the client said it (*type of exchange*). These include if the client wants guidance, emotional exploration, insight, education, or a new perspective. The client may come across as resistant, agreeable, display emotions, or exhibit nondisclosures. The congruency of client response modes can also be highlighted in the transcript (e.g., emotionally related question and response). Moreover, the supervisor comments column can comment on and suggest therapeutic strategies for supervisee such as open or closed questions, restatements, or highlight a specific intervention such

Table 17.1 Evaluating Supervisee Audiotapes

Client Comment	Counselor Comment	Supervisor Comment
I felt better after I left here last time.	Did you?	Covert response: challenges client. Follow up with open-ended question: What made you feel better?
Yeah	Do you feel that this is in any way … related to counseling?	Covert: assessing client's feelings about counseling. Ask open-ended question: What does feeling better look like for you?
Yeah it is. It's helpful.	Good. I would like to keep meeting with you every week. How does that sound?	Clarify meeting times, setting routine. Overt response: direct guidance for client.
Yeah, I just don't see what there is to talk about, so whenever I come here I'm just like, "Okay, what are we going to talk about today?"	We can really talk about anything you want to talk about.	Establishing structure of therapy. Overt response: information about therapy, also empowering client to take responsibility for therapy.
I just don't know where to start. They're just regular problems that everyone has.	Well, everyone has problems, that's true, but everyone has their own problems, and it doesn't always have to be a problem, or what you've defined as a problem, it can be anything.	Validation of client: should empathize or provide covert response of interpretation here, "It sounds like you feel a little lost or overwhelmed in feeling like you don't know where to start. I can imagine this might be difficult for you."
Yeah	Maybe this can become another outlet for you … a more productive one than the ones you've found so far.	Reframing perception of counseling for her, providing support.

(Continued)

Table 17.1 Evaluating Supervisee Audiotapes *(Continued)*

Client Comment	Counselor Comment	Supervisor Comment
Yeah	Last week we were talking about your writing, do you think that I could read some of it?	Overt response: direct guidance of session … closed-ended question, showing interest in client.
Sure, actually I write more poetry than stories.	I'd like to read anything you've written. Have you written anything recently?	Overt response: information gathering, showing interest in client, building relationship. Ask open-ended question here to gather more information, for example, "Tell me about something you have written recently."

Note: Client and counselor columns contain brief summaries of what is being said during the interview. The supervisor column highlights counselor skills and processes observed.

as challenging distortions using CBT. Finally, at the end of the transcript, supervisor should include a summary paragraph noting three primary areas on which to attend (highlighting strengths and growth edges). Also, the supervisor should meet with the supervisee to review and discuss the feedback.

Assessing Supervisor Skills

A useful skill for training supervisors in developing supervisory skills can involve creating a supervisee case conceptualization (see Table 17.2). The supervisee case conceptualization aids the supervisor-in-training in effectively linking supervisee issues to a supervision plan that provides the basis for addressing supervisee needs. Specifically, it helps highlight a supervisee's progress on goals, tasks of supervision, as well as a supervisee's strengths and growth edges. Another advantage of the case conceptualization is its ability to help link theory to practice. As such, it can assist supervisors-in-training develop a theoretical framework that includes supervisory interventions as well as relationship dynamics between supervisee and supervisor.

A second approach to evaluating supervisor skills is having supervisors-in-training videotape their supervision sessions. This serves as

---

Table 17.2 Supervisee Case Conceptualization Outline

I. Supervisee summary (note: use a false set of initials)
   A. Demographic description of supervisee (gender, race, age, experience)
   B. Mutually agreed upon goals

II. Supervisor impressions
   A. Supervisory relationship
   B. Description of supervisee (strengths and weaknesses)
      a. Supervision (interpersonal interactions)
      b. Counseling (skills, conceptualization ability)
   C. Supervisee–supervisor match
      a. Dynamics related to gender, race, sexual orientation, age, racial identity, and so forth.
      b. Conflicts: current or potential
      c. Supervisor countertransference issues

III. Supervisory intervention
   A. Supervisee's progress to date (include number of supervision sessions, summary of sessions up to the present, interventions that were effective/ineffective, her or his work with clients, assessment of client progress, etc.) (integrate theory)
   B. Progress on supervisory goals
   C. Proposed future intervention strategies (integrate theory)
   D. Unanswered questions (rank order most salient first)

an excellent teaching and training tool. Video recordings allow one to observe the supervision process and highlight the interpersonal dynamics (e.g., nonverbal and metacommunication) that is typically missed in audio recordings. Furthermore, within the context of class, having other supervisors-in-training observe the recordings allows not only for active feedback on potential growth edges, but also normalizes and validates any challenges observed in the supervision session.

A third approach involves engaging in the evaluation process. There are multiple supervisory evaluation forms that have been developed (see Bernard & Goodyear, 2009) that can be used for this purpose. Evaluations should focus on three important components: knowledge gained, the ability to translate this knowledge to practice, and finally how this may influence the internalization of a supervisory identity. It is most helpful to have the supervisor-in-training evaluate themselves and see how it matches up with the trainer's evaluation of the supervisor-in-training.

Monitoring Processes in Supervision

Given the complex nature of the supervisory process and the importance of the relational component in supervision, modeling what supervision looks and feels like becomes very important. It allows supervisors-in-training to develop self-efficacy through internalizing roles (e.g., counselor, teacher, consultant) along with the functions (e.g., supporting, instructing, sharing) of a supervisor. An important aspect of the supervisory role is to monitor processes that occur in the supervisory relationship (e.g., supervisee resistance, parallel processes, countertransference, etc.) that help with managing ambiguity and owning authority. Within the context of supervision of supervision, the trainer can help supervisors-in-training identify these issues through parallel processes (e.g., how supervisor-in-training resistance to authority may be similarly played out by supervisees in their own sessions with supervisors), countertransferential issues (e.g., feelings surrounding loss of authority that evolve at both levels), self-disclosing one's own struggles as a trainer and providing a corrective/educative experience (e.g., being thoughtful rather than reactive in dealing with difficult situations) can help supervisors-in-training get a firsthand experience of the supervisory processes.

In order to provide a glimpse into this training model, the second author reflects on her own development as a supervisor-in-training.

> As I reflect on my experiences as a new supervisor, initially, I recall feeling extremely anxious about my supervisory role. I doubted my skills and capabilities as a new supervisor. I feared not being able to effectively supervise counselors who worked in settings in which I lacked experience. I also found it challenging to manage my multiple

roles as a student, peer, and supervisor when working with supervisees with whom I had classes, or even with whom I worked as a practicum counselor in the same clinical setting. I noticed that my self-efficacy was in question as I attempted to own my role as a supervisor. Paralleling this, I found myself struggling to build a relationship with supervisees who were resistant to the idea of supervision. Nonetheless, I worked toward building a strong supervisory alliance with my supervisees. Specifically, I supported and encouraged them, while also attending to their individual supervisee needs to create a safe environment in which effective supervision can take place—issues that were paralleled in my supervision of supervision.

Throughout this journey I was faced with the barrier of learning how to trust in the process of supervision and sit with the ambiguity of the process. I remember an experience in which one supervisee constantly challenged both my supervisory interventions and my authority as a supervisor. He was resistant to attending supervision sessions and when he did, was defensive in reaction to any constructive criticism of his counseling. I struggled in my work with this supervisee, especially when I had to evaluate him. I presented this supervisee in a case for my supervision of supervision course to receive feedback on how to approach my work with him. Having been able to videotape the supervision session allowed my colleagues and instructor to view the interpersonal dynamics as well as the moment-to-moment interactions on the video segment of the session. As part of the feedback, we role-played different scenarios of how to effectively challenge and evaluate this supervisee in a corrective and supportive manner. I was encouraged to reflect on my experience with this supervisee and discuss my feelings of countertransference (e.g., feelings of frustration, defensiveness, anger, and disappointment) in relation to him. Nonetheless, the evaluation session with this supervisee was challenging as I had to discuss his lack of professionalism and commitment to supervision with him (e.g., challenge of owning my authority). It was uncomfortable to confront him about these issues as he was not just a supervisee, but a fellow student in my program (e.g., challenge of multiple roles). This supervisee was guarded for most of this session. Practicing this scenario during one of the role-plays in my supervision of supervision increased my confidence and helped me to not only challenge my supervisee, but also disclose some of my own feelings. Specifically, I was able to empathize and validate his feelings, while at the same time, self-disclose my feelings of being challenged by him in supervision. This process allowed the supervisee to become receptive to supervision.

Eventually toward the end of my work with this supervisee our relationship grew stronger. Together, we repaired the rupture in our relationship. Having been able to experience validation in my own supervision of supervision, I was able to appreciate the struggles and parallel this experience in my work with my supervisee. Engaging in this corrective relational experience allowed us to better communicate with one another. The ruptures in our relationship were needed in order for us to both change and grow in our roles as supervisor and supervisee.

I had the privilege of experiencing the process of supervision from beginning to end. Becoming a new supervisor was difficult at first. However, being in a supervision of supervision course with other beginning supervisors who shared a similar experience, helped validate my experience and feelings during this process. It challenged me to balance my multiple roles as supervisor, student, and colleague, while at the same time helping me own my authority as a supervisor in an evaluative role. Although I had my doubts in the process, after having been through it I finally realized that there is some truth to "trusting in the process."

Conclusion

As a core competency, "it would be no more ethical to improvise supervision if one lacked education, training, and supervised experience than if one were to 'improvise' hypnotherapy, systematic desensitization, or administration of a Hallstead-Retan Neuropsychological Test Battery without adequate preparation" (Pope & Vasquez, 2007, pp. 282–283). Taking on a supervisory role is complex and multifaceted. Understanding and negotiating the interplay of multiple levels (therapy and supervision) requires a certain level of self-awareness, knowledge, and skills on the part of the supervisor. As such, receiving adequate training, preparation, and supervision of supervision is a cornerstone of engaging in effective and ethical supervisory practice.

References

Association for Counselor Education and Supervision. (1990). *Standards for counseling supervisors*. Retrieved from http://www.acesonline.net/ethical_guidelines.asp

Aten, J. D., Madson, M. B., & Kruse, S. J. (2008). The supervision genogram: A tool for preparing supervisors-in-training. *Psychotherapy: Theory, Research, Practice, Training, 45*, 111–116.

Baker, S. B., Exum, H. A., & Tyler, R. E. (2002). The developmental process of clinical supervisors in training: An investigation of the supervisor complexity model. *Counselor Education and Supervision, 42*, 15–30.

Bernard, J. M. (2005). Tracing the development of clinical supervision. *The Clinical Supervisor, 24,* 3–21.

Bernard, J. M., & Goodyear, R. K. (2009). *Fundamentals of clinical supervision* (4th ed.). Upper Saddle River, NJ: Pearson.

Bonney, W. (1994). Teaching supervision: Some practical issues for beginning supervisors. *The Psychotherapy Bulletin, 29,* 31–36.

Borders, D. L. (1989, August). Learning to think like a supervisor. Paper presented at the 97th Annual Convention of the American Psychological Association, Louisiana.

Council for Accreditation of Counseling and Related Educational Programs. (2001). *2001 standards.* Retrieved from http://www.cacrep.org/doc/2001%20Standards.pdf

Doehrman, M. (1976). Parallel process in supervision. *Bulletin of the Menninger Clinic, 40,* 3–104.

Dressel, J. L., Consoli, A. J., Kim, B. S. K., & Atkinson, D. R. (2007). Successful and unsuccessful multicultural supervisory behaviors: A Delphi poll. *Journal of Multicultural Counseling and Development, 35,* 51–64.

Ekstein, R., & Wallerstein, R. S. (1972). *The teaching and learning of psychotherapy* (2nd ed.). New York, NY: International Universities Press.

Ellis, M. V., & Douce, L. A. (1994). Group supervision of novice clinical supervisors: Eight recurring issues. *Journal of Counseling and Development, 72,* 520–525.

Emilsson, U. M., & Johnsson, E. (2007). Supervision of supervisors: On developing supervision in post graduate education. *Higher Education Research & Development, 26,* 163–179.

Freeman, B., & McHenry, S. (1996). Clinical supervision of counselors-in-training: A nationwide survey of ideal delivery, goals, and theoretical influences. *Counselor Education and Supervision, 36,* 144–158.

Getz, H. G. (2001). Assessment of clinical supervisor competencies. *Journal of Counseling & Development, 77,* 491–497.

Getz, H. G., & Schnurman-Crook, A. (n.d.). Utilization of online training for on site clinical supervisors: One university's approach. *Journal of Technology in Counseling, 2.1.* Retrieved from http://jtc.colstate.edu/vol2_1/Supervisors.htm

Granello, D. H. (2000). Encouraging the cognitive development of supervisees: Using Bloom's taxonomy in supervision. *Counselor Education and Supervision, 40,* 31–46.

Granello, D. H., Kindsvatter, A., Granello, P. F., Underfer-Babalis, J., & Hartwig Moorhead, H. J. (2008). Multicultural perspectives in supervision: Using a peer consultation model to enhance supervisor development. *Counselor Education and Supervision, 48,* 32–47.

Gray, L. A., Ladany, N., Walker, J. A., & Ancis, J. R. (2001). Psychotherapy trainees' experience of counterproductive events in supervision. *Journal of Counseling Psychology, 48,* 371–383.

Haley. J. (1976). *Problem solving therapy.* San Francisco, CA: Jossey-Bass.

Hawkins, P., & Shohet, R. (2000). *Supervision in the helping professions: An individual, group, and organizational approach* (2nd ed.). Philadelphia, PA: Open University Press.

Hein, S., & Lawson, G. (2008). Triadic supervision and its impact on the role of the supervisor: A qualitative examination of supervisors' perspectives. *Counselor Education and Supervision, 48,* 16–31.

Hess, A. K., Hess, K. D., & Hess, T. H. (2008). *Psychotherapy supervision: Theory, research, and practice.* Hoboken, NJ: Wiley.

Hoffman, L. W. (1990). *Old scapes, new maps: A training program for psychotherapy supervisors.* Cambridge, MA: Milusik Press.

Holloway, E. L. (1995). *Clinical supervision: A systems approach.* Thousand Oaks, CA: Sage.

Inman, A. G. (2006). Supervisor multicultural competence and its relation to supervisory process and outcome. *Journal of Marital and Family Therapy, 32,* 73–85.

Jenkins, P. (2006). Supervisor accountability and risk management in healthcare settings. *Healthcare Counseling and Psychotherapy Journal, 6,* 6–8.

Killian, K. D. (2001). Differences making a difference: Cross-cultural interactions in supervisory relationships. *Journal of Feminist Family Therapy, 12,* 61–103.

Ladany, N., Friedlander, M. L., & Nelson, M. L. (2005). *Working through critical events in psychotherapy supervision: An interpersonal approach.* Washington, DC: American Psychological Association.

Ladany, N., Hill, C. E., Corbett, M. M., & Nutt, E. A. (1996). Nature, extent, and importance of what psychotherapy trainees do not disclose to their supervisors. *Journal of Counseling Psychology, 43,* 10–24.

Ladany, N., & Lehrman-Waterman, D. (1999). The content and frequency of supervisor self-disclosures and their relationship to supervisor style and the supervisory working alliance. *Counselor Education and Supervision, 38,* 143–160.

Ladany, N., Walker, J. A., Pate-Carolan, L., & Evans, L. G. (2008). *Experiencing counseling and psychotherapy: Insights from psychotherapy trainees, supervisors, and clients.* New York, NY: Taylor & Francis.

Lehrman-Waterman, D., & Ladany, N. (2001). Development and validation of the evaluation process within supervision inventory. *Journal of Counseling Psychology, 48,* 168–177.

Mordock, J. B. (1990). The new supervisor: Awareness of problems experienced and some suggestions for problem resolution through supervisory training. *Clinical Supervisor, 8,* 81–92.

Nelson, M. L., & Friedlander, M. L. (2001). A close look at conflictual supervisory relationships: The trainee's perspective. *Journal of Counseling Psychology, 48,* 384–395.

Pope, K. S., & Vasquez, M. J. T. (2007). *Ethics in psychotherapy and counseling: A practical guide* (3rd ed.). San Francisco, CA: Jossey-Bass.

Ramos-Sanchez, L., Esniel, E., Goodwin, A., Riggs, S., Touster, L. O., Wright, L. K., … Rodolfa, E. (2002). Negative supervisory events: Effects on supervision and supervisory alliance. *Professional Psychology: Research and Practice, 33,* 197–202.

Rodolfa, E., Brent, R., Eisman, E., Nelson, P., Rehm, L., & Ritchie, P. (2005). A cube model for competency development: Implications for psychology educators and regulators. *Professional Psychology: Research and Practice, 36,* 347–354.

Searles, H. (1955). The informational value of the supervisor's emotional experiences. *Psychiatry, 18*, 135–146.

Stevens, D. T., Goodyear, R. K., & Robertson, P. (1997). Supervisor development: An exploratory study in changes in stance and emphasis. *The Clinical Supervisor, 16*, 73–88.

Stoltenberg, C. D., McNeill, B., & Delworth, U. (1998). *IDM supervision: An integrated developmental model for supervising counselors and therapists.* San Francisco, CA: Jossey-Bass.

Vidlak, N. W. (2002). Identifying important factors in supervisor development: An examination of supervisor experience, training, and attributes. *Dissertation Abstracts International, 63*(06), 3029B.

Watkins, C. E., Jr. (1995). Researching psychotherapy supervisor development: Four key considerations. *The Clinical Supervisor, 13*, 111–118.

Webb, A., & Wheeler, S. (1998). How honest do counselors dare to be in the supervisory relationship? An exploratory study. *British Journal of Guidance and Counseling, 26*, 509–524.

Yourman, D. B. (2003). Trainee disclosure in psychotherapy supervision: The impact of shame. *Journal of Clinical Psychology, 59*, 601–609.

Index